The Groveland Four

The Sad Saga of a Legal Lynching

by

Gary Corsair

ISBN: 1-4140-7244-9 (e-book)
ISBN: 1-4140-7243-0 (Paperback)

Library of Congress Control Number: 2004090689

This book is printed on acid free paper.

Printed in the United States of America
Bloomington, IN

1st Books - rev. 02/23/04

Dedicated to
Gwendolyn Nani Corsair,
Who never said, "Why?"
Who seldom said, "When?"
Who always said, "You must."

iii

Acknowledgments

Obviously, an undertaking of this magnitude would not have been possible without the aid of many. I owe a debt of gratitude to:

Nani, Stuart, Cassandra, Caleb, Garrett and Angela for your understanding, support and patience. Taking time from you to research, write and edit this book ate at me from the first day to the last. I love you all.

My parents, David and Adrienne Corsair, for raising me to be color-blind and for allowing me to follow the career path I did.

Those who granted me access to their memories and hearts: Most especially Henrietta "Big Momma" Irvin. Also: James Shepherd; Harold Shepherd; Fannie (Shepherd) Bell; Beatrice and Jimmie; Jackie Perkins; Paul Perkins Jr.; Jack Greenberg, Horace Hill, Lawrence Burtoft; Ethel Retha Jackson; Irene Akerman; Lucy Akerman Taft; Tom Hurlburt Jr.; Noel "Evy" Griffin; Johnny Griffin, and last, but certainly not least, **Charles Greenlee.**

For those who believed: Brian Corsair; Michael LaBarr; Tommy Barstow; Theresa, Ralph, Anthony and Joey Rao; Dottie Richards; Mark Giblin; Brenda, Tony & Nikki Shepherd; Dwayne & Kim; Robert Mann.

To proofreaders Toni Phillips and Chopper Rao.

To **Norman Bunin** for courageously seeking the truth 50 years before I did.

Special thanks to four very special people who will keep the story alive: Robert Thompson, Aaron Hose, Ryan Retherford, and Kristi Bartlett.

Front & back cover design by Ryan Retherford

www.grovelandfourbook.com
Contact author at Garyplus5@aol.com

Groveland Four
P.O. Box 922
Lady Lake, FL 32158-0922

"Someday, God willing, the true facts of the Groveland case will be unearthed and brought to light. It is my firm belief that when this occasion does arise that even your editorial writers will no longer condemn but will respect me for my activities in this case."

-- **Alex Akerman** in a letter to the editor of the
Orlando Morning Sentinel, mid-1950s.

"I can't really see the need of bringing something up 40 years afterwards... You talk about the people interested in it and wanting it, I don't think you can find a half dozen people all over the county that say you should put it in the press and have them people have to read that and bring it up and keep stirring it up. And another thing, when you stir this stuff up, you talk about somebody being a racist, to me, that's being racist, to keep stirring it up and stirring it up and cause tension between the races. That's the way I look at it."
– **Willis McCall**, 1989 interview with Jim Clark.

Introduction

The old man debated answering the door. He knew who was knocking, even though there was no peephole to peer through, no window to look out of.

Behind the door, Charles Greenlee was safe, shielded from the stranger who had traveled hundreds of miles to find him in this nondescript block building with no driveway, no address, and no mailbox. Greenlee hadn't answered the man's letters or phone calls, but the stranger had come anyway. Somehow he had found the overgrown lot and weatherworn building Greenlee used as an office for the heating and cooling business.

For years, Greenlee had expected someone to come knocking, someone seeking answers he never had, and never would. There had been so many questions during "the trouble." Thankfully, the feeling of dread gradually faded as years passed. Greenlee had long ago stopped looking over his shoulder. It had been probably 30 years since anyone had asked him what *really* happened that summer night. He had been certain he had been forgotten. And then – a year ago -- the first letter arrived. And then another. And then the phone messages. Greenlee wondered how the man had found the address. Not that it mattered how his hiding place of 40 years had been discovered. Not now.

Greenlee had worked hard to put the past behind him. In fact, few people in his second life knew about his past. His mother-in-law didn't even know. And those who knew, knew enough not to talk about it around him.

In his heart, Greenlee knew he must face the man. If not today, then someday. His refuge had served him well, but it had finally been discovered. And he was too old, too tired and too settled to move again.

As he slowly moved toward the knocking, Greenlee remembered being front-page news 51 years ago. As if he could ever forget. That was why the man had come: to see what had become of the wide-eyed kid in T-shirt and dungarees standing in front of a jail cell. In the photo he had been the tall one, or the young one. To thousands of newspaper readers, he was the one with hope etched into his features while the men flanking him showed resignation and defeat.

But that was another lifetime. A closed book -- or at least it should have been. Greenlee had earned his solitude. He had triumphed over lynch mobs, beatings, prejudice and lies hatched to ruin him. He had persevered and achieved a good life. Not the life he had wished for five decades ago, but a better life than most attained -- even better than many of the people who put him behind bars; people who figured he was long dead.

In a sense, the 16-year-old in the photo *was* dead. He died in prison. The Charles Greenlee who entered prison in 1949 was naïve and trusting; the 28-year-old man who emerged in 1961 was guarded and cautious. He was also mentally, morally and emotionally strong.

Those traits served him well after he gained his freedom. Greenlee had done well. He owned a business and had been happily married for years. He had put his children through college. He was a grandfather. He traveled whenever, and wherever, he wanted. And here, in the grime and decay of the city, he had taught himself to paint lush landscapes of young trees, brilliant flowers and sparkling lakes and rivers. Paintings of places untarnished by racism, hatred and intolerance. The kind of places people dream of.

He really was lucky. The other men in the newspaper pictures didn't live to have wives and children and grandchildren. They were long dead. Charles didn't think about them much anymore. There was no reason to: he had barely known them, although their names would be forever linked with his. He no longer woke up in the middle of the night hearing their cries of pain or seeing their blood-stained clothes. It had taken years to bury the memories. And now the writer outside had come to take him back.

As he opened the door, Greenlee knew there was no turning back. Standing on the stoop was a middle-age man with eyes shining with recognition and face filled with emotion. A white man. Behind him was a kind-looking woman bearing a bag of oranges as a gift. There was no use pretending to be someone else. The stranger knew. Greenlee may have been 67 years old, but he still bore the physique and bright eyes of his youth. A moustache and glasses did little to obscure the face seen in newspapers throughout the world 51 years ago.

"I know who you are. I was going to write back, but I've been busy," Greenlee told the man. "I know why you are here, but I really don't like to think back to that time. I haven't decided whether or not I'm going to talk to you about it." Still, he invited the man and his wife inside. They had traveled a long way. It would be rude to turn them away. After an awkward silence in the dark hallway, Greenlee showed them into a dingy, cluttered office. Motioned to a well-worn chair, he sat on the edge of the desk and said what had to be said. "I really don't see any benefit that can come to me from what you want to do. I don't need money. Maybe 25 or 30 years ago, but not now. When I left Florida, in my world, that whole chapter was over." There, he had said it. Surely, the man would understand.

The writer had expected reluctance. Greenlee would have returned the calls or answered the letters if he had wanted to talk. The stranger had come because a face-to-face plea was his only resort. He had come too far -- literally, as well as emotionally -- to be disappointed. "The world needs to hear your story, how you beat the bigots and those filled with hate who tried to put you in the ground. They killed Sammie and Ernest and Walter, but they couldn't kill you," the writer reasoned. Greenlee sat silent, head bowed, looking at the floor. He knew that telling his story to the man, this stranger, could only bring unwanted attention. Nothing he could say would bring back the other three men in the picture or give him back the 10-and-a-half years that had been stolen from him.

The silence between the men lingered. Both were out of words. And then the man's wife spoke for the first time. In a quiet, but firm voice she said, "My kids had never heard of

x

Groveland. They would have never known about it. All kids should know so it doesn't happen again." As Charles Greenlee slowly raised his head, he marveled at the tears in the woman's eyes. A woman he had never met. A woman who couldn't possibly know what he had gone through, how he had cheated death and the price he had paid. She couldn't know, yet somehow she had been moved by his ordeal, an ordeal that took place before she was even born. He uttered a slow, deep sigh. "What do you want to know?" he quietly asked. In that moment Charles knew he was going back to Groveland, Florida. Back to July 16, 1949. Back to hell.

Table Of Contents

Chapter 1 -- Alone

Charles Greenlee was alone and afraid.

He was in a strange place, sitting in the darkness of a railroad depot shed amid the sound of chirping crickets and the faint smell of citrus. His meager "dinner" of cookies, peanuts and a bottle of soda water were long gone. Tired and dirty after hitchhiking 100 miles in the hot summer sun, Charles had tried to sleep, but the mosquitoes wouldn't let him. He wondered why his friend, Ernest hadn't come back for him. As midnight arrived Charles resigned himself to spending the night in a place he never knew existed. A place called Groveland.

Charles and Ernest Thomas had left Gainesville at 9:30 that morning, Friday, July 15, 1949. They were an unlikely pair. The son of a turpentine man, 16-year-old Charles was working as a delivery boy at a drug store during the day and packing beans and produce at a packing house at night. Thomas, 25, was a flashy dresser who developed a taste for sin hanging around his mother's Groveland juke joint, a place where one could indulge in the illicit pleasures of whiskey, women and gambling. They had met just four months earlier at the Humpty Dumpty drive-in, where Charles had worked as a dishwasher and Ernest as a short-order cook.

They appeared to have little in common, although both were country boys who had moved to the big city -- Ernest to get away from the orange groves of Lake County; Charles to escape a small house filled with six brothers, a sister, and his grieving parents, Tom and Emma. It was a home filled with misery since May, when an Atlantic Coastline train struck and killed his 4-year-old sister. The misery was compounded three weeks later

1

when Charles' 2-year-old sister died on the same train tracks. Charles couldn't endure his mother's incessant crying, so he set out on his own to become a man. "He wanted to go on his own. My daddy and momma didn't try to stop him -- I think Daddy had left home at 17 himself. Charles thought he could do it, so Daddy said 'go ahead and try,'" recalled Charles' sister Ethel Retha.

The hardest part of leaving was saying "goodbye" to his father. "My dad would take measurements to fit people for suits. He tailored suits, and even though I was only 15 or 16, I was tall. I was about 6 feet tall and I figured I was a man and it was time I had a suit. I asked him, 'Why won't you make a suit for me?' and I will always remember his answer. He told me, 'Size don't make you a man, and age won't have nothing to do with it. It's when you can look in the mirror and be at peace with yourself, that's when you will know you are a man," said Charles. "He was the biggest man in my life. I wondered how a man with a third- or fourth- grade education could know so much about life."

Charles was often mistaken for a man. Most adults outside of his hometown of Santa Fe assumed Charles, who was 6' 0" and still growing, was at least 18. The perception helped him land jobs when he moved 21 miles south to the nearest big city, Gainesville, where he had no trouble securing work as a truck driver, dishwasher and delivery boy.

In Thomas, Charles found an older, worldlier mentor. Ernest was married, or at least he was living with a woman. He knew how to dress. He knew how to make money. And he owned a gun. Ernest had obviously been around. When Ernest suggested hitchhiking to Groveland where work was plentiful, Charles didn't hesitate. Besides, he didn't have many options. Charles had just lost his delivery job to his boss' son. "I owed Ernest Thomas some money, 'cause I had been eating around there (the Humpty Dumpty). Ernest told me the orange picking season was opening up in Groveland and that I could probably come down there and get a job. Ernest left his job to come there with me," Charles said.

But Ernest had no intention of going into the orange groves himself. Not when there was easy money to be made in a bolita, a gambling lottery popular in Negro quarters throughout Florida. The game was all the rage in south Lake County, where Henry Singleton controlled the action.

People were crazy about bolita, a game in which 100 ivory balls with bold black numbers were placed in a sack, which was then tightly tied and passed from person to person. Eventually, the bag landed in the hands of a designated catcher, who isolated one ball in his fist. The game operator then tied a string around the imprisoned ball, which was revealed when the operator cut the bag above the string and the ball dropped out. Winners collected directly from the bolita house, or from their agents. Floridians first caught bolita fever in the early 1900s. By 1920, bolita was a nightly occurrence in smaller communities -- particularly Negro communities. In fact, Lake County Sheriff Willis McCall was fond of saying that whenever a group of blacks got together there would be "booze, sex and bolita."

How big was bolita? In Lake County, bolita was estimated to be a $1 million a year business, generating 10 times as much money as the annual citrus crop and twice the revenue of watermelons harvested. "Lake does, of course, have bolita, as does every other county in Florida... It is as hard to eliminate as the common cold, as easy to get as a drink of water, as attractive to some people as a T-bone steak," wrote *Orlando Morning Sentinel* reporter Ormund Powers. Bolita was big money, not only for operators like Singleton, but for policemen and public officials who lined their pockets with payoffs to ignore the games. Thomas figured he could earn a few bucks working for Singleton -- but Greenlee didn't need to know about that.

At the railroad depot, Charles awoke around 2 a.m. It had been nine hours since he had last seen Ernest, who had promised to return with clean clothes because Charles wanted to make a good impression on Thomas' parents. Thomas had left on foot around 4:30 p.m., returning a half hour later in a 1941 Pontiac, but without fresh clothes. He explained that he couldn't go to his parents' house until his mother closed the juke joint at "10:30, maybe 11 o'clock." Charles, dirty from riding in the back of trucks and worn out from hitchhiking, decided to wait at the depot. He really wanted to be presentable when he met his friend's family. "I had walked enough. I was ready to sit down." After making his decision, Charles asked Ernest to loan him his .45 Colt revolver. "In the seat of the car, I saw a revolver and I asked him if I was going to stay up there that long during the night, would he let me keep that... I told him I had never been there and had not been around there much. I don't know what kind of a place it was, whether it's a swamp or not." Ernest handed over his pistol. He wouldn't need it.

Charles instinctively reached for the gun when thirst woke him in the blackness and still of the pre-dawn morning. "I took the gun out of my bag and stuck it in my belt. I walked around to the gas station to get more water and saw the two night watchmen sitting down the road apiece. As I straightened up they shined the light on me." As the surprised youth turned toward the approaching men, the beam of a flashlight held by Harry McDonald, night watchman for Edge Mercantile, hit him in the face. Panning down, the light fell on the .45 stuck in the teen's belt. Charles tried to hide the gun, but it was too late. "Hold still a minute, boy," McDonald barked as he withdrew his own gun and trained it on the young Negro. Charles stopped and raised his hands over his head. "I knew I had no business with the gun," he would later say.

Charles thought fast, explaining that the gun was not his and it was not loaded. He also explained that he had arrived in Groveland the night before with a group of Negroes and was waiting for a friend to return to pick him up. Naturally, McDonald was suspicious, but at least the stranger was carrying identification. After studying Greenlee's Social Security card and driver's license, the watchman was leaning toward releasing the kid. Then one of the men from the filling station ambled over.

The second man gruffly asked what road camp he had escaped from. After Charles again told his story, the man turned to McDonald and said, "You don't know what that boy done done. You better hold him till morning." McDonald studied the boy's face for any sign of guilt. The boy certainly wasn't acting like a criminal. "I knew I hadn't done nothing and the gun wasn't nothing. So I figured if he put me in jail I wouldn't stay there long," Greenlee recalled.

"Better safe than sorry," McDonald thought as he left to phone the law. When Groveland's lone policeman arrived, Charles again related his story. Like McDonald, the officer also thought the teen looked harmless. Still, "the kid" was a stranger and he was armed, if you could call an old pistol with a taped handle a firearm. The policeman reasoned, "I'd better hold him until I see if there were any break-ins or armed robberies reported." The officer told the boy, "You come on around to the jailhouse and if we don't find nothing on you after morning, we'll take your gun and let you go."

Charles was certain he would be released when the friendly watchman visited him in jail and brought him a plate of food his boss had told him to deliver. After eating, Charles finally lay down to sleep. As he stretched out on the cot to spend his first night in a jail, he figured things could be worse. At least there weren't mosquitoes in his cell.

Chapter 2 -- Trouble

Sammie Shepherd and Walter Lee Irvin were thinking of sleep as they returned to Groveland after a night of "juking" -- drinking beer, flirting with women and listening to music in Eatonville, a Negro community more than an hour from Groveland. Sammie, who was driving, would have kept his friend out all night, but Walter had to get home; his father needed him in the groves later that morning.

Walter figured a few hours sleep would be enough to get him through the day. He'd roll out of bed alright. He wasn't about to give his father another reason to dislike Sammie. "I understand the night Walter Lee went out with Sammie that Daddy begged him not to go out with him. Sammie was one of those bad red boys," said Walter's sister, Henrietta. Walter respected "Cleve" Irvin, but he wouldn't be dissuaded. He had been home from the military less than a month and he wanted to have as much fun as possible before returning to California and getting married to the girl he had met in the Philippines.

The evening had provided plenty of fun, although it had started on a sour note. The men had set out in Henry Shepherd's 1937 Ford, but the car began acting up about seven miles past Clermont, the first town east of Groveland. Sammie was angry, but wouldn't be denied. He would simply swap his father's car for his brother's Mercury. Determined to unwind after a long day helping his father install a ceiling, Sammie headed back toward his parents' home in Bay Lake, a rural community of poor farmers southwest of Groveland.

The home Henry Shepherd built in 1943 was one of the nicer dwellings in the sparsely-populated community, especially considering what Shepherd had to work with after moving his family from Georgia to Lake County, Florida. The 30 acres Shepherd bought for $255 was overgrown with trees, shrubs and bushes. And what wasn't overgrown, was swampy lowlands. But Shepherd tamed it. Henry and his wife, Charlie Mae hoped Florida would provide a better life for their 12 children. "He was an honest and hard-working man. He grew up on a farm and only had a second-grade education, but with the skills he had learned on the side, you would think he was a highly-educated man. He could do a variety of things you wouldn't believe by just looking at him, such as mechanic, building houses, carpentry, wood or concrete, listen to a car run and tell what's needed to be done. He could take a motor out of a car and take it apart and put it back together and make it run like new. Also, build furniture: chairs, rockers or straight chairs. And when he couldn't get other work, some people would hire him to do little repair jobs. He was just an all-around handyman," said Henry's daughter, Fannie.

Henry worked hard, but rheumatism in his knees limited what he could accomplish. Thankfully, his 10 children pitched in. Sammie, especially, had been a big help since coming home from the Army. A chip off the old block, he wasn't afraid of hard work and was a quick learner. "He was smart in school, but he and my other brother had to quit school to work. They were working every day," recalled Fannie.

The Shepherds' hard work didn't go unnoticed by their white neighbors who had laughed when the Negro farmer paid good money for useless swampland. Now, six years later, some thought the Shepherds were doing a little too well. And they didn't bother masking their hostility. It was an atmosphere that made Sammie bristle. He knew those Bay Lake Crackers hated his black skin. No matter. He didn't care much for them either. Sammie was his own man. He worked hard, and Lord knows, he played hard. He had no intention of staying home and wasting a perfectly good Friday evening. There was still plenty of night left.

By the time Sammie arrived home, his brother, James and his wife of 10 days, Henrietta were already in bed. "And then my brother-in-law came in about 9:30. And he asked to borrow the car. And it took James an awful long time to say 'yes.' An awful long time. Finally, I said, 'Why don't you let him have the car?' So he did," Henrietta recalled. James, who had to be at his job at Dan Fields' Chevrolet by 7 a.m. the following morning, only agreed after Sammie promised to return the car by 6 a.m. Good jobs – jobs outside the citrus groves -- were hard to come by for Negroes and James wasn't about to get fired for being late.

Now the only thing standing between Sammie and a night of fun was a fuel gauge showing "E." But that wouldn't be a problem, even though the service stations were already closed. Sammie knew that Clermont patrolman Sam Doto would gas cars after hours. It took 30 minutes, but he finally found the officer. Things were finally looking up.

An hour later, the men arrived in Orlando. First stop: Church Street, where Walter and Sammie chatted with girls, but failed to talk them into coming along for a night on the town. No big loss: Sammie and Walter were sure they would find female companionship at the always-crowded clubs in nearby Eatonville. It was a far cry from south Lake County, where you could count the number of establishments that catered to Negroes on one hand. Sure enough, Club Eaton was bustling. After consuming French fries and soft drinks, Sammie and Walter headed to Club 436 in nearby Altamonte Springs. At the second club, they stayed well past midnight, playing the jukebox and sharing a quart of beer. By 2 a.m., they were on their way home. Walter was asleep in the passenger seat when Sammie drove through Leesburg and turned south toward Groveland. The night was quiet, but theirs wasn't the only car on the dark country road.

Just ahead, Willie Padgett's '40 Ford was stalled with a dead battery in the middle of nowhere, at least a 15-minute drive from Clermont, where he and his wife had attended a dance until 1 a.m. As Willie cursed his car, his estranged wife, 17-year-old Norma, sat and stewed. The night had turned out far differently than either husband or wife had anticipated. Willie had hoped the date would lead to reconciliation. Norma just wanted a fun night out. Being tired, hungry and stranded on a lonely road with her drunken husband wasn't what she had envisioned when she agreed to go to the square dance. But it was typical: her life since marrying Willie hadn't been what she expected when she said, "I, do."

Born into poverty, the fair-haired farm girl had little going for her -- until she caught the eye of an older man, Willie Padgett, in the fall of 1948. It was a whirlwind romance that ended in a marriage with little chance of success. Norma was naïve of the ways of the world, while 22-year-old Willie had already been hardened by a life of back-breaking work cultivating stubborn soil. Theirs was a life of second-hand cars, a cheaply-furnished home and little time for diversion. Not that there was much to do besides work in Bay Lake. Recreation consisted of fishing, eating out, an occasional dance or movie, or a shared bottle of cheap booze. There always seemed to be money for a bottle.

The honeymoon didn't last long. There was never enough money, and Willie got mean when he drank. The last time he got soused she took the beating but resolved it would be the last time. She was welcomed back home by her parents, who made sure Willie understood he wouldn't get another chance to slap their daughter around. Since then Willie had repeatedly begged for another chance. Finally, she gave in. Coy Tyson and his wife weren't happy when Norma told them she was going to a dance with husband.

The dance had promised something better than another boring evening at home. Instead, Willie bought a bottle of whiskey on the way to dance and spent most of the evening drinking. Once he realized she wouldn't come back to him, he figured he might at least talk her into parking and playing around in the back seat. But Norma's mind was on her stomach, not sex, as they left the dance. There were few restaurants open at that time of the morning, just a few joints between Clermont and Leesburg. Their best bet was Burtoft's, nearly 20 miles north in Okahumpka, a one-horse community that wasn't even on most maps. Reluctantly, Willie agreed to take her there. Maybe they would both get what they wanted.

Gary Corsair

But Willie's car wouldn't start. Norma waited 15 minutes while her husband tried to find someone willing to push start the Ford. He finally succeeded. As the car sputtered to life, Norma thought she might get a sandwich after all. But she soon changed her mind. Willie was plenty drunk and he was all over the road. The couple argued as they drove, until Willie angrily agreed to head back to Bay Lake. In turning around, the car stalled. When Willie tried to restart it, his spent battery wouldn't even trigger the starter. Now, Norma was really upset. So was Willie, who was fed up with Norma's complaining.

As the couple fought, the headlights of a car appeared on the horizon. Sammie Shepherd drove past, but a few hundred yards down the road, he turned around and drove back to offer help. As Norma peered through the windshield, she thought she recognized the niggers. As they climbed out of their car she tried to study them. Yes, she was certain one of the men was Sammie Shepherd, whom she'd known for years. The other man, the little one, looked like one of the Irvin boys she had worked with in the fields when she was growing up. Norma gave no sign of recognition. She hated niggers. But tonight she would put her hatred aside. She didn't care who helped get the car started.

After a brief discussion with the men, Willie slid behind the wheel and the Negroes moved to the back of the car. Willie depressed the clutch pedal and directed his helpers to "get to pushin'." The men pushed and pushed, but the car failed to start each time Willie let out the clutch. Finally, they stopped to rest.

Willie and Norma got out of the car, Willie to see if they would try pushing with their car, Norma to extend the bottle her husband had been drinking from. She really wanted to get home. The men accepted the whiskey, took swigs and passed it back to Norma, who handed the bottle to Willie. "I ain't gonna drink after no nigger," he stammered. In a moment Sammie had Willie by the shirt. He wasn't about to let this ignorant, drunk Cracker insult him. "The fight" was over in a moment. They left the poor Cracker's wife standing alongside her battered husband. They felt no pity. He got what he had coming. For all they cared, the man and his wife could walk home. Sammie had pride. No man, white or black, could talk to him that way. "In my book, Sam was quick on the draw. Didn't nobody bother him. He was the image of his dad," said his sister-in-law, Henrietta.

Before the Negroes stopped their car, Norma was certain the evening couldn't get any worse. Now, as they sped away, she realized it could. And it still wasn't over.

8

Chapter 3 -- Law And Order

At Dean's Service Station in Leesburg, Curtis Howard awoke with a start to the sound of squealing tires. As the 17-year-old attendant turned to look at the clock, a man jumped out of an old Ford and ran to the door.

Willie Padgett had pulled into the all-night station as a last resort. He had crisscrossed the back roads of Lake County without finding his wife and he wasn't about to return to Bay Lake without her. He simply had to find Norma. He'd really be in a spot if she hitchhiked home and told her pa about how he got liquored up and tried to force himself on her.

Willie breathlessly told Howard that four Negroes in a "black or dark-colored Mercury sedan" had assaulted him and kidnapped his wife. Howard promptly called the Lake County Sheriff's Office, where Deputy James L. Yates was in charge until Sheriff Willis V. McCall returned from Ohio. Yates promptly notified the Florida Highway Patrol that a couple of black men had assaulted a white man and possibly kidnapped his wife. Officers were told to be on the lookout for a "dark, or green, Mercury," possibly headed north toward the state line. The suspects were described as "possibly armed and dangerous." Yates also tried to radio the sheriff on his radio, but his attempts were met with static. The calls made, Yates and Deputy LeRoy Campbell hurried to the gas station to interview the man who had been assaulted.

At Dean's, a thin, young white male with bloodshot eyes and a small cut on his forehead told deputies he had been attacked by four Negroes who abducted his wife in a Mercury, probably a "'41 or '46." Willie Padgett then took the deputies to the scene of the attack, where Yates studied the dirt where a car had backed into a lane. Yep, there was more than one pair of footprints. Something had happened, but what? Yates told Padgett to go home and see if his wife was there. "No sense turning the county upside down if she wasn't in danger," Yates figured. Howard closed the service station and volunteered to help search. There was no telling the peril she might be in.

But Norma Padgett wasn't in danger. She was dirty, tired and worried as she walked along the Center Hill-Okahumpka road. Morning had broken. She had to find Willie, and find him fast.

The sun had just come up when 19-year-old Lawrence Burtoft looked out the window and saw a young, slight, blonde woman outside his father's Okahumpka restaurant. "She was standing out on the corner of the road going to Center Hill in Okahumpka. I had gotten up and fixed some coffee. I don't know how long she was out there. I just thought maybe she was waiting for a ride or something." As Burtoft thought how odd it was to see a woman along the roadside so early in the day, he realized he had seen her before. "I knew her ahead of time; they'd been in the restaurant from time to time. I didn't know her name, but I'd seen her in the restaurant. She didn't say anything, and I wondered why she was out there. It was probably 7 or 8 a.m. When I opened the door just to look out, she was there. I recognized her. I just said 'good morning' and asked her if she'd like a cup of coffee."

Inside, he poured coffee and sat down across from her. "She told me what had happened, that their car broke down when they were headed home toward Groveland and the black fellas came along and asked if they needed any help. She said they had hit her husband over the head and then carried her away in the car. She said they drove towards Center Hill, but after a while they let her out." Burtoft instinctively eyed her for evidence of assault, but saw none. "I said, 'Did they hurt you?' and she said, 'no.'" He didn't know whether to believe her or not. He didn't doubt that she had been out all night with someone, but she sure didn't act like she had been kidnapped. He was trying to figure out what he should do when Norma asked him to help find her husband. Burtoft wasn't sure if he should get involved, but what if she was telling the truth? Her husband might be laying alongside the road, bleeding to death. The arrival of the restaurant's cook made up his mind; Burtoft could leave. "She was probably in there with me about 15 minutes and then I went across the road to my parents' and got their car and went to see if we could find him," Burtoft recalled.

After driving just a few minutes, Norma told Burtoft to pull over. Heart pounding, the young man followed her into a field, all the while fearing he would find the woman's husband badly injured, or worse, dead. But there was no sign of Willie Padgett. Burtoft wondered if the man had ever been there. And then a car pulled up. Two white men climbed out, and one walked toward Norma. As he watched the reunion of husband and wife, he marveled that they didn't seem overly excited, or relieved, to see each other. "When he pulled up, he didn't say anything. He got out, they talked and then they drove off toward Leesburg."

Sheriff Willis McCall's radio crackled to life as he neared Lake County. McCall wasn't happy when he learned a girl had been kidnapped and her husband assaulted. Heck, he couldn't even go away for a few days without all hell breaking loose. "Why couldn't the darkies stick to their own kind?" It was a question McCall had asked himself, and others, many times since he was elected sheriff in 1944. You'd be hard pressed to find a Negro in the county who was unaware of McCall's views on mixing races. Everyone knew McCall considered Negroes "the inferior race." And the sheriff made no effort to hide his feelings. "I don't think there is any question about it that the white race is superior to the black race. I believe that's a proven fact. In their native country, they're still eating each other. We don't do that," said McCall.

The sheriff's reputation for using violence and intimidation to "keep nigras in their place" was also common knowledge. McCall made no apologies for his heavy-handed tactics. The 6-foot-1, 225-pound lawman knew first-hand that a punch, slap or kick was often the only ways to get a nigger's attention. "Hell, you had to let them know who was boss," was his way of thinking. It was a philosophy he had practically been weaned on. It was the way his daddy believed, and his daddy before him.

McCall had worked hard to become the most powerful man in the county. It was a job he planned on keeping. McCall had come a long way in a short time, and he never forgot that he was just one election away from being sent back to the life he had worked hard to rise above. Willis was born on July 21, 1909 in northeast Lake County on rolling, citrus-filled hills. His father, Walter, and mother, Pearl had homesteaded the land, which his grandfather settled before the freeze of 1895.

As a child, Willis was a Rockwellian portrait of Americana -- a simple Cracker boy who hunted, fished and toiled in the family fields and stuck his feet in cow manure to warm them on cold mornings. Willis learned the value of hard work early on. He also learned to deal with pain at a young age when his little brother drowned in a pond on the family property. But Willis rose above adversity and humble beginnings, parlaying ambition, strong work ethic and an intense loathe of poverty into a better life. "I got my education mostly in the university of hard knocks," he was fond of saying.

After graduating from high school in 1927, McCall embarked on a yearlong tour of the United States before returning to Umatilla and the family farm. By 1930, Willis was not only farming, he was milking his uncle's cows and selling the excess milk. When word reached the State Board of Health, an inspector was dispatched to Umatilla. "Look, if you're going to run a dairy, then you'd better abide by the rules," the inspector told the young dairyman. McCall agreed to comply. Beginning with just two heifers, he soon built a profitable dairy, complete with cement floors, pasteurizing plant and pre-cooling plant. The Board of Health man was impressed. McCall had not only met the board's guidelines, he had constructed Lake County's first modern dairy. By the time his business had grown to 50 cows, he was well-known throughout Lake as a no-nonsense young man who got things done. In 1935, McCall sold his business for a handsome profit and took a government job

11

as a state fruit and vegetable inspector. It was a career choice that would prepare him for the job that would define him.

McCall was inspecting citrus at the Mount Dora Growers Co-op packing house when he decided to try his hand at politics. "He was a fruit inspector and went to my granddaddy and told "Crip" he wanted to run for sheriff of Lake County. Granddaddy made a contribution to his campaign… My granddad loaned him some money, along with some other people to run for sheriff," recalled Tom Hurlburt, grandson of co-op president, G.B. "Crip" Hurlburt. To "Crip," and the growers who depended on Negro labor to work their groves, McCall would be the ideal sheriff. If anyone understood the importance of keeping Negroes in line – and working in the fields -- it was McCall.

McCall, ever a good listener and shrewd enough to recognize those who could help him advance, used relationships with bankers and citrus growers as a springboard for his campaign. There may have been dirty money behind him as well. The *Leesburg Daily Commercial* boldly proclaimed that McCall was financed by "the biggest gambler in the county." Of course, the story could have been planted by one of his opponents. McCall faced five hopefuls in the primary, including incumbent, Clarence W. Cooper. McCall also had a "name" candidate to worry about, former Pittsburgh Pirates pitcher Emil Yde. It was a tight race, but McCall won the Democratic Primary by 105 votes. In November, in the general election, he was unopposed and garnered an impressive 4,809 votes.

Stung by accusations his campaign was financed by gamblers, McCall went to great pains to prove he was his own man. Early in his first term, he cleaned up a slot machine racket and drove punchboard operators out of the county. He would later brag that he turned down a $2,000-a-week bribe and trapped the would-be bolita bribers into an indictment. And it didn't take long for McCall to reward his financial backers for their faith and support. Once in power, he quickly became a strong arm for the men who harvested Lake's abundant citrus crop. "People in Lake County paid for law and order and if that meant keeping black folks scared to keep the reputation going, that's what people paid for," Tom Hurlburt said.

In the mid-1940s, when labor organizers concentrated on unionizing the South, McCall chased a number of "troublemakers" and "agitators" from his county and used anti-vagrancy laws to imprison "uppity" and "lazy" workers. In April 1945, six black fruit pickers charged the young sheriff with brutality after he arrested them for vagrancy. Two of the men, Nathan Bailey and Mark Fryar, were bold enough to submit affidavits accusing McCall of forcing them to work in the fields. When McCall learned of the charges, McCall angrily accused Bailey and Fryer of telling "damn lies." When they denied they had lied, McCall struck them with his revolver. The reluctant fruit pickers got the message: by the time United States Justice Department investigators arrived in Florida to see if workers' civil rights had been violated Bailey and Fryar were long gone. McCall reported that the men had moved out of Florida. The other four workers weren't about to speak up. They had to continue living in Lake County after the Federal men left. McCall had survived his first controversy as sheriff.

Not only did McCall relish rounding up Negroes and delivering them to the groves, he also enjoyed intimidating union organizers who dared try to improve working conditions for poor, black laborers. Most of McCall's antics went unreported, but the young sheriff made headlines when he not only arrested union leader Alex Axelrod in 1946, but heaped indignity upon injustice by parading him through the orange groves, telling workers, "Look at his wrists," -- a reference to marks left by McCall's handcuffs.

Word quickly spread that McCall not only *was* "the law," he was *above* the law. "In Lake County, where citrus is king and the word 'nigger' still part of the local lexicon, blacks often refer to McCall as 'The High Sheriff... most of the cases that have made his name a symbol in Florida political circles have involved black defendants," a newspaper reporter wrote decades after McCall came to power. "He was unpredictable, and in those days law enforcement could do what they wanted," recalled David Connelly; who grew up to become mayor of Leesburg in the county McCall ruled with an iron fist. "I remember him as being a man black people feared... It was instilled in most of the black children that when you saw Willis V. McCall, that was a man you didn't want to tangle with," said John Griffin, a lifetime resident of Groveland.

McCall was cunning as well as tough. The Lake County power brokers -- and in Lake, citrus was power -- clearly had their boy. McCall wasn't polished, but that was all right, the citrus men didn't need a politician, they needed a bully. As long as Willis administered their brand of "law and order," he could shoot his mouth off as much as he wanted. Not that anyone could stop him. The sheriff wasn't shy about sharing his views. From day one, he was brash, opinionated and outspoken. His supporters didn't always appreciate his candor, but at least they always knew where McCall stood on an issue. "He was a man who stood up and said what was on his mind. Right or wrong. If you didn't want his opinion, you didn't ask for it," said Willis' oldest son, Malcolm.

Chapter 4 -- The Tale

In Groveland, Deputy James Yates radioed the sheriff that the missing woman had been located, and was being taken to a diner in Groveland where officers could question her. And there was something else the sheriff needed to know: Norma Padgett claimed she had been raped.

In Groveland, the sheriff commandeered a back room to interview the young couple. Both appeared tense and nervous. Willie Padgett recounted how their car had stalled about four miles north of Groveland at approximately 1:45 a.m. He said that a few cars passed, but none would stop until a car carrying four Negroes came along after about 10 minutes. Willie claimed that the Negroes pushed the car a short while, then stopped and began whispering among themselves. After "some time," Willie went behind the car to see why they weren't pushing. After talking with them for "about 15 minutes," a fight broke out when Willie picked up "a heavy stick" and approached the Negroes. A scuffle ensued, and Willie was knocked down. Stunned, he recalled the Negroes picking him up and throwing him over a fence into a field. The Negroes then forced Norma into their car and drove off. Willie estimated the time was about 2:30 a.m.

McCall asked for details about the men and the "dark Mercury" used in the abduction, but the couple could only provide fuzzy descriptions. When pressed for specifics, Willie offered few particulars. McCall was skeptical. Plus, the boy didn't look like he'd been in a 15-minute fight with four men. The sheriff wanted the truth, and he wasn't sure Padgett was telling the whole story. Maybe the wife would have better recall. He turned to Norma.

Norma told essentially the same story about the car breaking down and them waiting for help. As for the kidnapping, Norma said that the four Negro men drove across the Sumter County line, then turned around and went down a dead-end, abandoned road. She guessed they had driven about 25 minutes. She said one of the men threatened her with a gun and her captors took turns raping her until about 3:20 a.m., and then changed the license plate on the car. After arguing a minute or two about what to do with her, they gave Norma a choice: stay with them and be killed, or get out of the car. Naturally, she left, running into the woods when the men drove off toward Center Hill.

McCall weighed her words carefully. She had obviously been through something unpleasant, but gang rape?!! A girl that young and slight wouldn't be so composed and calm if four Negroes, that's right *four*, had ravished her five hours earlier. Hell, she'd probably be unable to walk. But Norma wouldn't alter her story. She insisted it had been four men that had forced her to have intercourse. And, no, she didn't know them. McCall wondered what had really happened. Perhaps the sex had been consensual. It wouldn't be the first time a white girl hatched a story when she got caught with a black buck. To McCall it didn't matter either way -- niggers had no business with white women. Period. Didn't matter who sought out whom.

True story or not, Norma Padgett had handed the sheriff a reason to show everyone what happened to niggers who forgot their place. Uppity niggers like that Shepherd boy, who had been parading around Groveland in his Army uniform since being thrown out of the service. McCall knew where to look. He told Yates and the highway patrol officers who had since arrived to take Willie to the Negro quarters of Groveland. Norma was escorted to her parents' home in Bay Lake.

Sammie Shepherd was the kind of black McCall most loathed – one who had tasted life free of Jim Crow and was emboldened by his wartime experiences. "They didn't like no veteran's attitudes," Sammie's father Henry claimed. Translation: McCall and the Crackers he served didn't like no *"Negro"* veteran's attitudes. McCall had no use for stubborn Negroes like Henry Shepherd and his mouthy son. McCall knew all about the Shepherds. Old man Shepherd was a troublemaker. There was no denying Sammie's dad knew how to work, but he sure as hell didn't know how to get along with his white neighbors, particularly Oscar Johns, whose cows had the annoying habit of escaping from their pen.

"After eating my first crop and my second crop, the next year when they eat up my crop, my wife tried to tell Mr. Oscar Johns about it -- he lives below us -- and he wanted to beat my wife up," Henry Shepherd said. "He cussed her out -- picked up a stick and threatened her. Later when the cows came back a man said it was Mr. Storey's cow. Mr. Storey said it wasn't his cow -- but would tell Oscar Johns, whose cow it was, about it. The next morning Oscar Johns came over and again cussed my wife out -- it was his cow."

Shepherd finally erected a fence to keep his neighbor's cows out, but he awoke one morning to find the fence torn down and Johns' cows again grazing on his land. An angry Shepherd noted that the fence hadn't fallen down, and it hadn't been knocked down by the cows. Someone had deliberately wrecked the fence. According to Sammie, the fences had been torn down by "white boys." Henry decided it was time to involve the law. "I went to Tavares to see McCall the high sheriff to get some protection. He told me, 'Boy, is you got the cows shut up? You shut up the cows and I'll come out and make 'em pay for it or sell the cows.' So I went back and built a pen and run eight cows in there, then went and called McCall. He didn't come but sent a deputy. I called him at 3 in the afternoon and a deputy came Saturday afternoon. Deputy saw cows and field. The cows broke out next morning except one, him I turned out. Later Mr. McCall came out and brought up Oscar Johns -- who said 'I want to do what's right.' They asked me what damage they done. I asked for $150 -- he cussed me then! Sheriff took Johns away then came back... Next morning McCall came out with a bunch of men. I was talking to (neighbor George) Valree. I told him I turned cows out. He got mad and left," recalled Henry Shepherd. Relations between Shepherd and his neighbors had been strained ever since. Now, McCall had an excuse to shut Shepherd and his boy up for good.

News that the Padgett girl had been attacked by Negroes was already spreading beyond Groveland, but word hadn't yet reached the Shepherd home, where Henrietta and her husband James were up at the crack on dawn on Saturday only to find that Sammie and James' car were not there. "So my father-in-law, Henry, he brought me into my mother's house and James on to Clermont, cause James was working in Clermont at (the Chevrolet dealer) Dan Fields," said Henrietta.

At the Irvins, Walter had overslept and his father had left for work without him. Walter was getting dressed to join his father in Mr. Edge's grove when a Lake County sheriff patrol car and a Florida Highway Patrol unit pulled into the yard. Deputy James Yates met Dellia Irvin in the front yard and demanded to talk to her son. Inside, Walter calmly told his mother, "Don't worry, Mama, I haven't done anything." Outside, Yates roughly grabbed Walter and led him to the patrol car. Walter's pleas of innocence went unanswered; Yates only glared as he shoved Irvin into the back seat, where Sammie was huddled in the corner. "The fight on the roadside," Walter thought as he looked at his friend. It was then he noticed Sammie's swollen features. Now, Walter was really frightened.

As the car pulled away, Walter's attempts to learn why they had been arrested were met with glares and silence. After a short time, the car pulled off the asphalt onto a clay road. Sammie and Walter realized they weren't being taken to jail. McCall's deputies stopped at a secluded spot, pulled the prisoners out of the car and began demanding confessions. "Hadn't they attacked a white man and taken his wife?" "Didn't they rape the girl?" So that was it: the boy they had roughed up had told a story on them -- a story that could cost them their lives. They had to think, and talk, fast. The lawmen were in a foul mood. Both men denied committing any crime, saying they had gone to Orlando to take in a movie, then visited a cafe and a club. Convinced the men were lying, deputies began beating Sammie and Walter with fists and billy clubs, then worked them over with blackjacks. The Negroes were bloody and bruised by the time the lawmen paused to rest, but Sammie and Walter continued to profess their innocence, swearing they were nowhere near Okahumpka or Center Hill in the wee hours of the morning. Their tormentors weren't convinced. These niggers were more stubborn than most, but they would get the truth out of them. The deputies and highway patrolmen would really get down to business now. Walter and Sammie were jerked to their feet, but the redoubled fury of their attackers soon left them panting and heaving on the ground. They tried to protect their heads and groins, but there were too many fists, too many clubs, too many boots. Soon their bodies were awash with pain and warm blood.

As the torture increased, the frightened suspects feared they would die there, just two more unfortunate niggers who "disappeared" or ended up swinging from a tree. After 30 minutes of savagery the friends were still holding firm, but both men wondered how much more abuse he could take. Finally, the lawmen paused to huddle. A new tactic was agreed upon: the battered prisoners would be tied to a tree and threatened with being burned alive. Sammie and Walter were handcuffed together, one on each side of the trunk. While the deputies gathered kindling, they were surprised by a young girl on horseback. Realizing there were probably adults nearby, the startled officers quickly decided to continue the "interrogation" at the jail. The exhausted prisoners were handcuffed and thrown in the backseat of the squad car for the trip to Tavares. Along the way, their tormentors said little, other than warning Walter and Sammie not to bleed on the seats. At the jail, the prisoners were thrown and kicked into cells. Perhaps the worst was over.

Too soon the angry white men returned. Irvin, the meeker of the two, was dragged from the cell and taken to the basement. His wounds stinging and his thoughts clouded by pain, Walter realized he was in for more torment when he saw the faces of the sullen men and the rubber hoses they held. As a man in plain clothes watched, two deputies roughly dragged Irvin to the center of the room, jerked his arms above his head, and handcuffed him to an overhead water pipe. Then they pulled down his pants and began beating his body with a hose and a billy club. Walter may have been the quieter of the two prisoners, but deputies had underestimated his resolve. He stubbornly denied every accusation they threw at him, regardless of how violently they beat him. No, he hadn't kidnapped anyone. No, he hadn't raped a woman. The white men marveled at his defiance, which only made them step up their torture. They took turns kicking Walter in the groin, and then someone hit him in the face so violently that he nearly blacked out. Through the pain, Walter was sure his jaw was broken. Death couldn't be far off. Still, he wouldn't confess to a crime he didn't commit. If he died, he died. He had never harmed a woman, and he'd die before he said he did. After what seemed like an eternity, the men finally unlocked the handcuffs. Irvin's limp body crumbled to the floor. The deputies, panting and sweating, had finally given up. So they failed to get a confession. This nigger was bound for the electric chair whether he fessed up or not.

Sammie knew what was happening in the basement, but he was still shocked by the sight of deputies dragging his bloody friend back to the cell. Walter's eyes were closed and he wasn't moving. Sammie feared he was dead. And then, suddenly, a new fear overwhelmed him. A deputy was ordering him out of the cell. It was his turn. In the basement, deputies handcuffed Sammie to the overhead pipe, jerked down his pants and beat him with fists, rubber hose and club. This time, the brutality had the desired effect: when the pain became unbearable, Sammie confessed. He knew it was the only way to stay alive. There was no reasoning with these men; they would just as soon kill him as look at him. Sure enough, the torture ended the moment he told them what they wanted to hear. Back in his cell, Sammie took stock of his injuries: three broken teeth, a split lip, bruises, welts and "excruciating pain" from being kicked in the testicles. As Shepherd used his shirt sleeve to soak up blood dripping from his mouth, he realized there was moaning coming from the back of the dark cell. The noise was coming from Walter, still crumpled in the corner. He was alive. Thank God he was alive. Maybe they would get out of this jam yet.

Chapter 5 -- The Way It Was

Two behind bars, two at large.

Sheriff Willis McCall told reporters he had two culprits locked up and hinted that the other perpetrators might be hiding "not far from this section," although he conceded they had possibly fled the state. McCall assured reporters that his department's investigation had produced promising leads and that Florida Highway Patrolmen were conducting an extensive search for the other members of the "gang."

McCall was partially right: one of the suspects was nearby. But young Charles Greenlee wasn't hiding. He was behind bars in the tiny Groveland jail, being held for possession of a firearm. The sheriff didn't tell the press that one of his deputies and the "victims" were on their way to Groveland at that very moment to eyeball the prisoner. McCall chose to hold his tongue since neither Shepherd nor Irvin had mentioned the Greenlee boy, so there was a chance he wasn't involved. Plus, McCall wasn't about to give any credit to the Groveland police. That colored kid had practically walked into the jail and locked himself up.

Charles awoke to sunlight pouring through the window of Groveland's only cell. He had slept fitfully. Friday had been a long, long day, but Charles was certain everything would be straightened out in the morning. But the mood was different Saturday. "The next morning a deputy came down there and said, 'stand up boy.' Then he started asking me where was the boys I was with the night before; then he asked me where was the car we was in. I told him I was in no car the night before. I did not tell him about Ernest. He kept asking me questions -- asking me if it was a new Buick or an old Buick," Charles recalled. The deputy left without explaining his line of questioning.

Charles was confused. "What boys was the man referring to? Had Ernest been in trouble? It must have been someone else -- Ernest had a Pontiac. Why was he being questioned about a Buick?" Charles was jolted from his musings by the arrival of a young white couple. As the whispering whites peered into his cell, he heard the man say, "That's not one of the boys," to which the woman replied, "He looks like one of them." "No," the man corrected. "Not him. He wasn't there." Charles was more confused than ever as the couple walked away.

A moment later, the man returned, alone, and approached the cell. In a voice just above a whisper, he asked Charles if he had been with the boys. Charles was puzzled. "I asked him what boys he's talking about, and he said the boys what took me out of the ditch last night. I said, 'no sir, I wasn't one of them.'" Without another word the man left, but others soon followed. "A lot more mens came around and kept questioning me about boys and cars and the same thing. They never would come to the point about what they wanted me for. Then the man what put me in jail came around and told me that, 'Boy, if you don't know it you in trouble. Some boys raped a white woman last night and robbed the man.' He said, 'If I don't hurry up and get you away from here they gonna take you out and kill you.'" Charles felt sick to his stomach. "I always thought rape was a vicious crime. Not a sex crime, but a violent crime. I thought that was the worst thing for a man to hit a woman." Charles was just a kid, but he was old enough to know there was nothing worse a black man could be charged with. Men had been hanged for a lot less.

Outside the jail, Willie Padgett remained quiet while his wife told a deputy the boy in the cell was one of her attackers. Officers didn't ask Willie, and he didn't volunteer his conviction that the boy hadn't been involved in the events of the previous evening. After instructing Deputy Leroy Campbell to take Norma to the Leesburg hospital for an examination, Deputy James Yates and highway patrol troopers headed for the Negro communities in the south end of the county. Charles had given them the name of his "accomplice," although he insisted he hadn't seen Ernest Thomas since early Friday evening. The boy was obviously lying. The Padgett girl had implicated him. She had also said there were four attackers. Thomas had to be the fourth. As the frightened teen was escorted from his cell, he was struck by the change in demeanor of the men who had previously held out hope. There were no smiling faces, only glares, as Charles was led to the squad car. He felt hatred follow him out of the jail and into the car.

At the county jail in Tavares, McCall got his first look at the third suspect, a slight, gangly, wide-eyed boy. The sheriff watched intently for signs of recognition as deputies put the boy in with Shepherd and Irvin. There were none. Either the two were damn good actors or they really didn't know the boy. No matter. All three had been identified. It was an open and shut case. As for Charles, he definitely reacted at seeing the blood-stained clothes and swollen features of the two Negroes. One was alert, but the smaller man was lifeless. "Irvin wasn't speaking to nobody because he had a big hole knocked in the back of his head," Charles recalled.

As he studied the spindly youth, McCall tried to picture the teen with Irvin and Shepherd. The sheriff was convinced the older prisoners were lying about their trip to Orlando, and figured this kid had made up a story as well. The circumstantial evidence against the Greenlee was overwhelming. He was new in town. He was carrying a gun. And the night watchman had said the young Negro, "looked suspicious and told a funny story of hiding in a shed waiting for the next train." McCall was certain Greenlee was a member of "the gang." Well, the sheriff would have the answer soon enough. He'd get confessions -- he always did. He already had Shepherd's, and he had thought that stubborn S.O.B. would be the hardest to break. McCall figured it wouldn't be too hard to loosen the tongue of the new prisoner, who was obviously scared. As for Irvin, well, it was just a matter of time.

Alone in his cell, Charles tried to make sense of his predicament. He couldn't stop thinking about the deputy who had told him he would have been killed if he hadn't been taken to the county jail for safekeeping. If only Ernest would come and vouch for him, maybe this thing could be straightened out. Charles knew he hadn't done anything wrong, but he had no idea how to convince the deputies. He cursed his bad luck. "I was so close to being released. They were going to release me, then they decided to hold me for questioning. When I was in that jail the deputy told me it looked like I would be getting out soon and he said when I did I should get out of the county. And that's just what I was going to do."

That morning, McCall briefed State Attorney Jesse Hunter, who quickly realized there appeared to be a woeful lack of physical evidence supporting Norma Padgett's claim. Hunter told the sheriff in no uncertain terms that he wouldn't try a death penalty case on accusation and speculation. The sheriff and his boys sure as hell better have something more than the word of a girl, a girl who could have been a willing participant in back road shenanigans with darkies. McCall told Hunter not to worry; there'd be plenty of evidence. Immediately after meeting, the sheriff dispatched his deputies to find it. The last thing he needed was Hunter on his back.

McCall liked Hunter well enough, even though he was a character. Hunter was in his 24th year as State Attorney, and he had done his job so long and so well that no one ever ran against him in an election. Hunter's wisdom was matched only by his wit, which he displayed without pause in and out of the courtroom. His gift of gab had served him well; in fact, it was one of his most endearing traits. He never tired of regaling anyone who would listen with tales of his hard-scramble rise to prominence. One of his favorite stories concerned his interview before the Florida Supreme Court when he passed the bar exam on June 14, 1913. According to an article in the *Mount Dora Topic*, "When Jesse Hunter stood before the justice of the supreme court to begin his examination to pass the bar, and he heard the several other candidates name their colleges -- 'University of Florida,' 'Virginia,' etc., his sparkling sense of humor came to the front. So when he was called to name his college, he said, in a low voice, 'The University of Scuffletown.'" Hunter never apologized for his lack of formal education. Like McCall, he was proud of the lessons he had learned from the "school of hard knocks."

Born in Naylor, Georgia, in 1879 to a Umatilla farm wife, Hunter completed only two years of formal schooling. But what Jesse lacked in "book smarts," he more than made up for with determination and effort. At age 16, Hunter decided to become a school teacher. After six weeks of preparation, Hunter took, and passed, the teaching exam. He began his career in Mascotte, a small south Lake County town where residents expressed pride that their community was 100 percent white, unlike nearby Clermont and Groveland, which had Negro neighborhoods. His first salary: $19 a month.

After just six years in the classroom, the ever-ambitious Hunter was named principal of a small school in the little town of Anthony in northern Marion County. Still not satisfied, Hunter set his sights on becoming a lawyer, and begged and borrowed books that would help him reach his goal. Shortly thereafter, Hunter took a $100-per-month job as a railroad mail clerk, not for the money, but because the "two days on, three days off" schedule would give him plenty of time to study law. Hunter toiled for five years before he felt ready to tackle the bar exam, which he passed in the summer of 1913. He arrived in Tavares that September, borrowed $200, and rented a tin building around the corner from the courthouse for $10 a month. He furnished the humble law office with a secondhand typewriter, an old desk and a chair. There was also a box in the corner, which Jesse sat on when he had a caller. He earned $7.50 his first month, but things improved from there. By 1923, Hunter was the county attorney, and two years later, he was appointed State Attorney by Gov. John W. Martin. In the 24 years since, Hunter had become a household name among the well-to-do, as well as the poor and ignorant. He moved comfortably among Lake County's Crackers. Hell, he was one of them. But while Hunter could act like a rube, he was no dummy. He was rustic and folksy, but cunning and clever.

In newspaper parlance, Jess was "good copy." Reporters assigned to cover Lake County loved the folksy attorney. "Jess Hunter is a man of medium height who quite often wears a single-breasted hard-finished wool suit, belt and suspenders, a white shirt and black shoes which are often untied because they are more comfortable that way. His hair is thin and gray, and he wears horn-rimmed glasses, often eats peanuts in public, smokes cigarets chain-fashion and throws the burning butts over his shoulder. He likes to put his feet on a desk when he sits down. He likes people, coffee, good food, tough problems, legal tangles, the church, driving a car, newspapers, old friends, America, the Democratic party, conversation... Jess Hunter has sometimes been accused of being a shrew man masquerading in the guise of a county bumpkin. The only thing wrong with this statement is that Hunter has never pretended to look or act like a Wall St. lawyer, although his intellect meets the test," wrote *Orlando Morning Sentinel* reporter Ormund Powers.

Deputy Yates' first stop was the Irvin home, where concerned family members were trying to figure out what to do about Walter's arrest. Seeing Dellia and "Cleve" on the porch talking with Henry Shepherd, Yates yelled, "I came for the little black nigger's clothes." With that Yates yanked open the door and strode into the house. Walter's frightened mother followed him into Walter's bedroom. After giving Yates the clothes her son had worn the night before, Dellia boldly asked when the trial would be held. Yates curtly replied, "There may not be no damn trial," and walked out of the house. His next stop: Bay Lake, where he impounded James Shepherd's car. If what the Padgett girl said was true, the back seat of the Mercury should have all kinds of evidence. The sheriff would be pleased. The clothes would tie Irvin to the crime and the car would implicate Shepherd. Plus, they already had the gun the night watchman took from the Greenlee boy. They had more than enough evidence.

By noon, all sorts of rumors were circulating, especially in Mascotte, where dozens of enraged citizens took up arms after a woman on her way to church reported seeing Negroes carrying guns. By late afternoon, bands of white men armed with rifles, pistols and shotguns were roaming the county, hell bent on avenging and protecting the honor of their women. Some of the would-be vigilantes were pillars of the community, as a maid to a Groveland city commissioner could attest. "And it was unusual for him to come home in the middle of the day on Saturday. Because Saturday was a business day at the store. So he came home and he got his shotgun, and he got his sheet. And his little son, who was maybe 4 years old at the time said, 'Daddy, where are you going?' So (he) said to him, 'Son, Daddy's going hunting.'"

Soon, dozens of angry white men in cars bearing out-of-county plates began arriving in Groveland. A resident counted 20 cars with Orange County license plates roaring up and down the streets. Another 15 cars from Polk County were parked just outside city limits. Ku Klux Klan members were pouring into Lake County in response to a message from Eustis Klansman, I.B. Hall that "something was going to happen" in Groveland.

As the Klan mobilized, bands of sullen white men were already gathered in clusters throughout town. Something was obviously brewing, but it would wait till the sun set. One man was overheard to say, "We gonna kill us all these young niggers. The old ones is all right, but we gotta git the young ones." Another white, seen driving his Negro maid home in the early evening, would be part of the angry mob after sundown. Negroes returning from work Saturday afternoon were warned trouble might erupt if they went into Groveland to do their shopping. At Edge's General Store, whites were buying guns at an alarming rate. In fact, the entire stock would be exhausted by nightfall.

Family friend George Wright warned the Shepherds that they had better get out of town before the sun went down. "I was upset and didn't understand," Henry said. "I walked into town to see Mr. Anderson. I got as far as Wilcox house -- he was coming in a truck -- he said he would drive me to town. On way we passed Bauknight's house. He waved us down. I walked out to meet him. I said, 'Howdy' -- and I asked him for protection. He said your 'friends' told you to leave, 'you better take heed,' and he rolled up his fist..." Shepherd didn't know Bauknight was in the Klan. Perhaps Wilcox was too -- he changed his mind about driving his neighbor to town after the meeting with Bauknight. Henry walked the rest of the way. In Groveland, Anderson also refused to help, but arranged for two patrolmen to escort the Shepherds out of town.

As the sun set, a group of trigger-happy men began stopping cars traveling the Mascotte-to-Center Hill road in hopes of finding armed Negroes. Thankfully, they were unsuccessful. "You would have seen what we would have done to them," a mob member told a *Tampa Tribune* reporter who said a bullet was fired over his car as he drove by. Gunshots were also heard in Mascotte. For many Negroes, the threat of violence was enough to prompt them to pack up and leave. But not everyone fled the Negro communities in and around Groveland. Some refused to be intimidated by threats. Others felt the "hothead" talk would die out.

After meeting with a committee of concerned community leaders, McCall reluctantly agreed to request National Guard companies from nearby Leesburg and Eustis to help maintain law and order. It was a decision some felt should have been made hours earlier, at the first sign of trouble. As the troops readied themselves 20 miles north of Groveland, a caravan of 20 cars and trucks poured into the Negro quarters. One press report estimated the "heavily armed" mob at 100 men, who "drove through their sections of town shouting threats and firing guns." The sheriff and his men kept wary eyes on the hell-raisers to make sure they didn't go too far. McCall told deputies they best let the riled-up Crackers get it out of their systems. Hell, they had a right to be angry. Besides, McCall figured one night of joy-riding would go a long way toward reminding niggers where they belonged. The way he saw it, things would pretty much return to normal in the morning.

"Concerning the allegation that he had requested Klansmen from Orange County to go to Groveland, (I.B.) Hall stated that the Law had called the Klan in to protect the alleged rapists from Lake County citizens. When questioned specifically regarding the persons responsible for the 'calling of the law' Hall declined to elaborate or give any information as to the identity of such persons." -- Report of FBI Special Agents Frank F. Meech and James P. Shannon, April 22, 1952

While the sheriff and his deputies cruised the south end of the county in separate cars, trouble was brewing in Okahumpka, not far from the diner Norma had wandered into earlier that morning. Around midnight, a call came in that the café where the shooting occurred Friday night was on fire. By the time officers arrived, the building had been reduced to charred rubble. The long night finally came to an end when the nightriders finally dispersed around 4 a.m. McCall hoped they had had their fill of mischief.

The rape was Sunday-morning talk throughout the county. In many homes, God-fearing men grimly changed from their "Sunday-go-to-meeting clothes" into more casual attire: lynching attire. Already, people were calling the attack on the farm girl, "the worst crime ever in Lake County history."

Throughout the state, sensational press accounts fueled an already white-hot blaze of racial passion. According to UPI, AP and *New York Times* reports, the victim claimed, "she had been raped by each of the four Negroes as they held a gun in her face" as she pleaded with them not to kill her. The *Leesburg Commercial* reported, "She said she was threatened with death if she did not give them time to get away… She was taken about 15 miles along the old Okahumpka-Center Hill road and attacked by all four of the Negroes with a large gun pointed at her head, the girl told authorities... Frightened, the girl hid along the roadside for each car that passed." A later edition reported that Norma was, "kicked out of the car," and was found later that morning "crouched along the roadside." *The Clermont and South Lake Press* also reported, "Later the girl was found wandering by the roadside in an almost senseless condition. She said her kidnapper had warned her not to call for help until three cars had passed." Another account described Norma as, "found walking in a dazed condition along the Okahumpka road."

The Sunday morning newspapers also carried sensational stories of the arrests and confessions of three Negroes. One wire story claimed that the men in custody "admitted they beat and robbed Willie Padgett of Groveland, then kidnapped and raped his wife early last Saturday." McCall failed to tell reporters that the suspects repeatedly professed innocence; Irvin never admitted guilt, and Shepherd only confessed after brutal beatings.

In Mims, Florida NAACP Executive Secretary Harry T. Moore read the news accounts with alarm. Moore, a former school teacher and principal who lived about two hours east of Groveland, immediately contacted J.P. Ellis, president of the Orlando chapter. There was no one to call in Lake County, where the NAACP was virtually unknown. In fact, the NAACP had just two dues-paying members in all of Lake. Moore had never been to Groveland, but he had seen a hundred Grovelands. In fact, Moore had been looking for Grovelands since 1934, when he learned an organization devoted to the advancement of colored people existed. He found out about the NAACP through a cousin, who passed along literature he had received. The cousin was terrified by what he read, but Moore immediately embraced it. "This is what I've been looking for," he said.

Moore was especially heartened by the NAACP's push for anti-lynching legislation. The South of Moore's youth was a dangerous place for Negroes, particularly men, who comprised the majority of the 3,693 people lynched between 1889 and 1929. The 10-year period from 1918 to 1927 marked the peak of violence: 47 black Floridians met their demise at the end of a rope -- nearly 10 percent of the 416 lynchings of blacks in the nation during that time period.

Violence against Negroes became more frequent as Florida's population exploded (by 28 percent or more each decade from the turn of the century until 1940). A large percentage of the newcomers were black, which didn't sit well with white Floridians, many who shared the views of Gov. Napoleon Broward (1905-1909), who actually proposed that Congress purchase territory -- either foreign or domestic -- and transport blacks to regions where they could live separate lives and govern themselves. His successor, Gov. Park Trammell was no better: during his term, he ignored lynchings of 21 blacks.

Much of the violence against Negroes was orchestrated by the Ku Klux Klan, which had fallen into disarray during the late 1800s, but was revived in Georgia in 1915 when the release of the motion picture "Birth of a Nation" rekindled interest. The movie, which portrayed the Klan in heroic and romantic terms, ran for 47 weeks in New York. Wherever the movie was shown, race relations deteriorated and acts of racial violence usually occurred. Most white Southerners strongly identified with the part of film where Klansmen ride to save the South from a cowardly black militia.

While the Klan reorganized, a young organization with opposing ideals, the National Association for the Advancement of Colored People, was trying to get the attention of U.S. lawmakers. The NAACP was born from the ashes of the Springfield, Illinois race riot of 1908, which began when Mabel Hallam accused a black man of rape. She later told authorities she made up the story to cover up an affair she was having. After days of rioting, the official death total stood at seven (two blacks and five whites). Property damage exceeded $200,000. Forty homes were destroyed, dozens damaged, and 24 businesses were forced to close. City officials expressed deep regret for the incident and called for swift justice. A special grand jury handed down 107 indictments, but incredibly issued just one conviction -- against a man who stole a saber from a guard.

Springfield was only one of many cities where blacks were terrorized by their white neighbors. Each week brought new reports of violence, but limited resources forced the NAACP staff to consider only the most disturbing cases. If a preliminary investigation indicated a Negro committed the crime he or she was accused of, the NAACP usually declined to get involved. The only exceptions: when police brutality clearly existed, basic human rights were denied, or mob action was a definite possibility.

In 1916, the NAACP formed an anti-lynching committee to determine the scope of brutality. Committee members soon learned the horrifying truth: lynching was a small epidemic, one that could break out at any time, anywhere. As the numbers were compiled, and horror stories mounted, NAACP officials appealed to the highest reaches of government for relief. For the most part, the cries fell on deaf ears. That is until 1918, when President Woodrow Wilson listened and publicly denounced lynching. Unfortunately, Wilson's statement turned out to be lip service. Lynchings of black Americans continued with alarming frequency. For instance, during the first 14 months of U.S. participation in World War II, 259 Negroes were lynched in America.

Presidential condemnation or not, Florida blacks harbored no illusions that things would be any better under Gov. Sidney Catts, who replaced Trammell. Catts campaigned on an anti-Negro platform, and he more than lived up to his racist image after being elected, publicly labeling black residents as part of "an inferior race," and refusing to criticize two lynchings in 1919. When the NAACP denounced Catts for his silence, the governor callously declared, "Your race is always harping on the disgrace it brings to the state by a concourse of white people taking revenge for the dishonoring of a white woman, when if you would.... [teach] your people not to kill our white officers and disgrace our white women, you would keep down a thousand times greater disgrace."

The NAACP leadership finally persuaded Missouri representative L.C. Dyer to introduce an anti-lynching bill in 1921, but the Dixiecrats weren't about to let the legislation become law. The bill passed the House, but was killed in the Senate when Southern Democrats organized a filibuster. Southern representatives spoke around the clock to keep civil rights legislation from being voted upon, in fact, some urinated into hot water bottles so they wouldn't have to yield the floor.

In Florida, the violence continued unchecked. In January of 1923, the greatest blight on the state's already inglorious record occurred when angry whites destroyed the black township of Rosewood in Levy County. At least eight lives were lost during the days of violence sparked by a white woman's accusation of rape against an unnamed black assailant. The trouble started on New Year's Day when Fannie Taylor reported an attack by an unidentified Negro at her house. By Jan. 8, every black home in Rosewood had been burned to the ground and three Negroes – Aaron Carrier, Mingo Williams and a black man from Newberry -- had been murdered. When the smoke cleared, Rosewood had been obliterated from the map, never to be rebuilt.

Sadly, Rosewood was hardly an isolated incident. It was, however, the most violent demonstration of the reality all Southern blacks lived with: when whites turned violent against them, the law usually looked the other way. In fact, many officers exchanged their badges for white hoods when the sun went down. Political and economic leaders in most Florida communities belonged to the Klan, and the members often conducted publicly-advertised parades in southern communities.

In the early days of the NAACP, exposing Negro-hating lawmen took a back seat to challenging blatantly biased verdicts rendered by all-white juries. Preventing lynching would always be a high priority, but if the judicial system didn't change, "guilty" would continue to be the only verdict for the black defendants. One of the earliest challenges came in 1923, when the NAACP made headlines by trying to overturn a conviction by a mob-influenced jury in Arkansas. The case, Moore v. Dempsey, was the first to address a defendant's constitutional right to be tried in an atmosphere free of prejudice. The challenge didn't change a badly flawed judicial system, but it did serve notice that the NAACP was willing to use every legal means available to protect the rights of Negroes on trial. That commitment would be fully tested eight years later in Scottsboro, Alabama.

The events that led to more trials, convictions, reversals and retrials than any race case in American history began on March 25, 1931 in Chattanooga, Tennessee with a stone-throwing fight between white youths and a larger group of blacks on a south-bound train. The confrontation culminated with the blacks forcing some of the whites off the train as it passed Stevenson, Ala., where the banished boys reported that a gang of blacks had assaulted them. The stationmaster wired ahead, and the train was stopped by an angry posse in Paint Rock, where dozens of armed men rounded up every black youth they could find on the train. Things went from bad to worse for the blacks when a woman traveling with the white boys claimed she and her friend had been raped by a gang of blacks armed with knives and guns.

News of the "crime" resulted in angry mobs forming, cries for lynching, the prisoners being transferred out of the Paint Rock jail to a safer facility, and finally, shameful trials.

Gary Corsair

They came to be known as the Scottsboro Boys, named after the Alabama town where they were tried and convicted. Williams and Roy Wright were the youngest, at 13. Also arrested: Ozzie Powell (16); Andy Wright (17); Willie Roberson (17); Haywood Patterson (17); Olin Montgomery (17); Charles Weems (21) and Clarence Norris (21). Tried in three groups, an all-white jury convicted eight of the boys, despite an expose' charging a frame-up by the communist newspaper the *Daily Worker* just days after their arrest. Local attorney Milo Moody was assigned to the case, but he didn't bother preparing a defense. The accused pleaded not guilty to all 20 indictments before an all-white jury while 10,000 whites surrounded the courthouse and a band played "There'll be a hot time in the old town tonight." The eight oldest were sentenced to death. A mistrial was declared in the case of Wright.

Appeals, retrials, a recantation by one of the "victims," and even a jail escape would keep the Scottsboro Boys in the headlines for years to come. Scottsboro was the first high-profile case the NAACP embraced. Not only did the organization help with appeals and provide financial assistance to the defendants and their families, it made good use of the notoriety of the Scottsboro Boys. In interviews, published pamphlets and speaking tours, NAACP representatives pointed to the case as a graphic reminder that black Americans remained second-class citizens.

NAACP leaders hoped the 1933 election of Franklin D. Roosevelt would usher in an era of long-needed reforms. As expected, the new president came out swinging on the issue of race after his election, taking a courageous stand against lynching during a Federal Council of Churches of Christ in America radio broadcast. "We do not excuse those in high places or low who condone lynch law. We know that it is murder, and a deliberate and definite disobedience of the commandment, 'Thou shalt not kill.'" Like Wilson, Roosevelt appeared committed to reform, but nothing happened after his rousing speech. In a private meeting, FDR told Walter White of the NAACP that he had to sacrifice the rights of black Americans for the economic needs of the country as a whole. Roosevelt reasoned that if he pushed for an anti-lynching bill, lawmakers would retaliate "by blocking every bill I ask Congress to pass to keep America from collapsing."

In Florida, Harry T. Moore was becoming more and more convinced that blacks would continue to suffer unless they made their presence felt at the ballot box. By the end of 1934, Moore had organized the first Brevard County branch of the NAACP. Soon he was spending evenings and weekends trying to establish new chapters throughout the state. The next year, he led a group of Negro teachers who sued for equal pay. Clearly, Moore wasn't afraid to demand his due.

Moore's activism led him to organize Florida's first NAACP State Conference in 1941. His goal: spreading the gospel of equal rights and encouraging members of his race to exercise their long-denied right to vote. He would spend most of his waking hours during the next four years distributing literature and asking ministers to let him to bring the NAACP message to their congregations. Moore literally traveled thousands of miles. No town was too small to be considered for an NAACP chapter. It was tiring, tedious work, and not

28

without danger. The white bosses didn't like their field hands talking to outsiders with big-city ideals. Moore lost count of how many threats he received, how many times he was followed to the city limits. But it was necessary work. In town after town, he found the two most oppressive masters were ignorance and fear. Too few Florida Negroes believed they could rise above their lot in life. Others felt that relations with whites had improved and would get even better with the passage of time. They preached patience. Moore disagreed, stressing that registering and voting was the only way to bring about change.

Buoyed by a 1945 Supreme Court ruling abolishing the white primary (which excluded Negro voters from Democratic primaries), Moore formed the Progressive Voters League of Florida and stepped up his efforts to register blacks. The campaign slogan: "A Voteless Citizen is a Voiceless Citizen." The crusade was a success; by the end of November, 37 percent of blacks were registered, a phenomenal 22 percent increase. It was an increase whites couldn't ignore.

By the summer of 1946, the Brevard County school board had had enough of Moore's outspoken ways. In June, the board fired Harry and wife Harriette from their teaching jobs. It was a devastating financial setback, but Moore soon realized the termination was a blessing in disguise. Now he could devote more time to building up Florida's largely unorganized NAACP chapters.

In 1947, Moore became executive director of the Florida Conference. His immediate focus: increasing Florida's lagging membership. His efforts soon bore fruit: Florida's membership swelled to 6,000 as the number of branches grew from 61 in 1946 to 78 by October 1947. But Moore wasn't satisfied; he had set a goal of 25,000 new members by Dec. 31. Moore designated November as NAACP Month and asked ministers across the state asking them to devote a portion of each service to tell parishioners about the good work the NAACP was accomplishing. "What he was doing was extremely suicidal. At that time, what they would say is 'the nigger is getting too big for his britches,'" said former Broward County NAACP chapter president Clarence Rowe.

Moore was still focused on increasing membership when news of racial trouble in Groveland made headlines. In Groveland, Moore would find a cause worthy of his time and energy, a cause worth risking his life for. Franklin Williams was the only member of the NAACP's Legal Defense Fund staff in the office when Moore called for help. The Groveland case sounded like a typical Southern frame-up, but Williams couldn't promise the national office would get involved. That decision would be made by his superiors Thurgood Marshall and Bob Carter, and both were out of town. Moore stressed that time was of the essence. The three black men charged with the crime couldn't wait, they were in danger now. Williams promised to immediately discuss the Groveland matter with Walter White.

Chapter 6 -- The Pot Boils Over

In Bay Lake, Sunday morning dawned with both Willie Padgett and Norma's father Curtis Tyson in an ugly mood. Bone-tired, and feeling the effects of alcohol consumed Saturday night, they were tired of talking and ready for action. The handful of men who gathered at Tyson's farmhouse just after sunup agreed. Sheriff Willis McCall wouldn't be at the jail on a Sunday, and they were certain the deputy on duty would see things their way and let them have the prisoners. And if the sheriff *did* happen to be there? "So what? He's one of us," they reasoned. All McCall had to do was look the other way. They'd do the rest.

"He claimed he was present when Willis McCall, Sheriff of Lake County, was initiated into the Association of Georgia Klans Apopka Klavern by Phillip Huggins, probably in 1947. I.B. Hall of Eustis, Florida, recruited Willis McCall into the Klan. McCall was an active member all the time T-2 was in the Klan and has been seen at the Apopka Klavern many times by T-2." -- FBI report summarizing interview with confidential informant (T-2), April 22, 1952

Late Sunday afternoon, a caravan of cars and trucks carrying angry men armed with clubs, pitchforks and shotguns was on the move. By the time Padgett and his father-in-law hit the Tavares city limits, at least 70 vehicles trailed behind them. Cars were still roaring down Main Street when the sheriff came out of the courthouse to survey the swarm of irate men. McCall couldn't help but be impressed. "By God, there were at least 200 of them." Tyson was dismayed to see the sheriff, but he wasn't about to turn around and go back home. He had his courage up. Willis would just have to step aside because they meant business. But so did McCall. The sheriff wasn't about to be upstaged by the mob. He was ready. "Upon learning that the crowd was headed for the jail, I got Deputy J.L. Yates and Bill Young to take the two men charged and hide them out in an orange grove," McCall recalled. There would be no lynching this day.

McCall stood at the top of granite steps, stopping the advancing mob not with a shotgun, but with a smile. On the road in front of the courthouse: six carloads of highway patrolmen anxiously waited to see if McCall could appease the mob without force. Conspicuous among the FHP officers was Capt. Olin Hill, who grew up in Groveland, but settled in Lakeland after the war. Hill found himself in the uncomfortable position of confronting men he had known in high school. "He went up and these guys were ready to lynch those guys. One of his former friends stuck a shotgun in his stomach and dad said, 'You're not going to make a mistake,'" recalled Hill's son Olin Jr. The man wisely withdrew the shotgun, but he and his friends weren't happy. "They called him every name in the book," Hill said.

McCall knew he couldn't show even a trace of indecision. He knew he was sitting on a powder keg that only he could diffuse. "I met them at the door unarmed so as not to agitate them. They demanded that I turn the prisoners over to them. The men were armed to the gills, but I knew them all and they were sober, reasonable fellows. I sat on the steps in front of them and talked fast." The sheriff told the would-be lynch mob that he understood their anger, "But we have got to handle these things in a legal manner. These Negroes are going to be held and tried in court."

The promise that the accused would receive punishment from a jury instead of at the end of a rope caused redoubled demands that McCall hand the prisoners over. The sheriff's conciliatory tone took on a harder edge as he again addressed the mob, which one bystander estimated was 100-400 strong. After telling the assembly to, "let justice be done," McCall said, "Folks, you elected me sheriff and my job is to uphold the laws of Florida and the United States and to protect my prisoners. This is a crucial moment that could cause a crisis here and throughout the state. Let's let the law handle this calmly." Jeers and catcalls greeted his words. Finally, McCall told the crowd that the prisoners had been transferred to another county for safekeeping. The ringleaders remained unconvinced, reasoning that if that was the case, he would have said so right up front. McCall had to be bluffing. The sheriff was running out of options – and patience. He certainly couldn't arrest the entire mob for unlawful assembly. McCall realized he had just one play: to open his jail to inspection. Convinced there was no other way to disperse the crowd, McCall offered to let Willie Padgett and his father-in-law search the jail. The men readily accepted the offer.

In the fourth floor jail, most of the 27 Negroes incarcerated cowered at the sound of footsteps coming up the stairs. They had spent an anxious half hour since the cars and trucks carrying hundreds of incensed white men shattered the tranquility of the sleepy city. They had heard the angry voices and the cries for blood. All wondered what the bloodthirsty men below would do when they learned that the prisoners they sought had been removed from the jail. Some feared that any old nigger would satisfy the mob's craving for vengeance. Charles Greenlee was especially anxious. While some of his cellmates wondered what the fuss was about, Charles knew exactly what had sparked the hatred. For a moment, as the prisoners were ushered out of their cells and ordered to line up for inspection, Charles recognized the skinny, brown-haired man who had come to the Groveland jail and told the woman with him that Charles wasn't one of the men who jumped him. Charles hoped the man remembered. Sure enough, Padgett recognized Greenlee, but didn't so much as pause to question the worried youth. "The mob came to the jail that Sunday night and the members of the mob saw me and said, 'he is not the one. That's the boy they picked up in Groveland for carrying a gun,'" Greenlee recalled. Willie was looking for Shepherd and Irvin, and they weren't in this group.

Still suspicious, the men insisted on searching the floors below, including the basement. Outside, the crowd was growing restless. What was taking so long? Finally, the courthouse door swung open and Padgett and his father-in-law emerged shaking their heads. The sheriff had spoken the truth. The niggers weren't there. With that, the mob reluctantly began to disperse. One man was overheard to say, "We can't fight the law." Another reportedly said, "If we continue this tonight, somebody's going to get hurt." According to the *Orlando Sentinel Star,* the prevailing attitude of the enraged citizenry was: "We will wait and see what the law does, and if the law doesn't do right then we will do it." As the cars and trucks began pulling away, Charles relaxed. For the first time since being told men were out to kill him the day before, he felt optimistic. "After that I thought, 'I'll be getting out of here soon.' All the fellows there with me thought I would get out of there anytime."

Crisis averted, the sheriff radioed his deputies, telling them to take Shepherd and Irvin to McCall's home in Eustis. The sheriff knew he wasn't out of the woods yet. He fully expected the Bay Lake boys to turn the county upside down trying to find the prisoners. There simply wasn't a safe place to keep the prisoners in Lake County, but his home would do for a temporary solution. The lynch mob wouldn't dare set foot on his property. Or maybe they would. McCall had to get Shepherd and Irvin as far away as he reasonably could.

On the drive home, McCall basked in the glow of outsmarting the rabble. The last thing he needed on his record was some boys busting prisoners out of his jail and killing 'em. No siree, these Groveland boys would get what they had coming soon enough: a quick trial, followed by justice in the electric chair. McCall's musings were interrupted by a message over his radio that the warden at the state prison in Raiford had agreed to take the prisoners for safekeeping until the unrest died down in Lake County.

Meanwhile, Irvin and Shepherd were huddled in the back seat of a patrol car. Were they being returned to the woods for more torture? Were they about to be handed over to the lynch mob they had heard discussed on the car's two-way radio? The uniformed, grim-faced deputies weren't saying. Walter and Sammie fully expected the car to stop at any moment. Sure enough, the car soon slowed and pulled off the road. An angry white man jerked open the rear door. "And white men came up and stomped them in the car. He said, 'These are the niggers that raped her.'... the boys told me that he stopped at least twice, maybe three times, and men came out and beat them in the car. Stomped them with their foot and their heads were cut and their faces were cut," NAACP attorney Franklin Williams recalled.

Battered, bruised and bloodied from blows inflicted by men they didn't recognize, Shepherd and Irvin wondered what awaited them at the end of their journey. After a while, they realized that the car hadn't stopped for a long time. Still, they tried to be as quiet as possible. They didn't want to give the deputies any reason to pull over. As the miles slowly passed, they felt a faint glimmer of hope. Perhaps they would live through this day of horrors, after all.

In Leesburg, Norma Padgett had just left the Theresa Holland Hospital, where Dr. Geoffrey Barneveld had examined her. She was tired of the endless questions, and the doctor's poking and prodding. She never dreamed it would be like this when she told the deputy she had been kidnapped and raped. All she wanted to do was sleep.

By evening, most Negroes had heard about the mob that stormed the courthouse, as well as new rumors of impending violence. Those who recalled the racial violence that swept through Clermont in the late 1930s advised those who had since moved to the area to barricade their homes, or better yet, get out of town. Dozens of families, many warned by white employers or acquaintances, spent Sunday afternoon packing meager belongings and preparing to relocate until order was restored. "Just about everybody left but the old people. They decided to stay. They didn't leave. It was a ghost town. I was scared. I was sad. I wanted to be with my mom and dad. I knew right then that I wanted to go back to being that little girl," said Walter Irvin's sister, Henrietta.

Henrietta was at her mother-in-law's home when word came that trouble was brewing. The Irvin and Shepherd families had spent an anxious day discussing the fate of Sammie and Walter. They had considered driving to Tavares to see if they could visit the boys, but now talk turned to their own safety. Word on the street was that the Bay Lake Crackers were planning on doing a little night riding. For Henrietta and her husband, James their dilemma was solved by the arrival of his boss, Dan Fields, who couldn't afford to let one of his best mechanics get chased out of town. Fields offered to put the couple up in a trailer he owned in Clermont, where things were more peaceful. Fields was fairly certain the impending trouble would be confined to the southwest end of the county. Clermont Negroes didn't have anything to worry about, as long as they stayed in Clermont, that is.

Walter's father refused to budge. "Cleve" had heard the talk too, but he wasn't convinced it would become anything more than talk. Henry Shepherd also decided to stay and ride out the trouble.

Late Sunday night, Sheriff Willis McCall returned to the jail. It was time to have a private chat with the young Negro arrested in Groveland for carrying a gun. Even though Willie Padgett had said Charles Greenlee wasn't one of his attackers, McCall wasn't so sure. It had been dark and things had happened quickly. Maybe Padgett didn't get a good look at all four men. Not only did Greenlee have a gun, but he had come to town with Ernest Thomas, who had fled the county. Why would Thomas scoot if he hadn't been involved in the attack against the Padgetts? And if Thomas was involved, it stood to reason that Greenlee was too. Maybe he just wasn't smart enough to run. One look at the sheriff told Charles that McCall and Deputy Leroy Campbell weren't making a social call. "Sunday night the same man that told me to stand up in Groveland jail came and took me out of the cell and carried me down in the basement. He said, 'Boy, I boy, I believe you lying, that gun what you got came from Groveland.' I said, 'No.'"

In the bowels of the building, Charles was shoved to the middle of the room and ordered to raise his hands. The frightened teen knew enough to obey. The deputy roughly handcuffed Charles to an overhead pipe while another broke a Coca-Cola bottle on the floor around his feet. As pain shot from his wrists through his biceps, the prisoner braced for a beating. "My feet were just barely touching the floor. The two men began whipping me with a rubber hose. They kept asking me, 'wasn't I with the boys?'" As he bounced up and down, twisting from the force of the blows, his feet were repeatedly sliced by the glass. "I first told him 'no' and then the other one started helping him to whip me -- both at the same time." Finally, Charles could bear no more. "Everything they say then, I say 'yeah.' They hit me across my back and legs and face. I was bleeding all over, my arms, face and all was bloody." As promised, his tormentors ceased their savagery the moment Charles confessed. He wasn't sure how long he had been handcuffed to the overhead pipe, but he was certain he couldn't have lasted much longer. The pain was so great he could barely think straight. The lawmen, sweating profusely, shoved Charles toward the elevator. "As I was fixing to get in the elevator, the tall man, he kicked me. I got in the elevator and turned around and faced him and he kicked me again and it hurt so bad I kneeled down on the floor. They put me in my cell," Charles recalled.

McCall was dog-tired, but content as he headed home. He had stared down a lynch mob and found the third rapist. In the morning he would tell the press that he had arrested the third assailant and obtained a confession. There was only one loose end: the fourth suspect, Thomas was still at large. McCall was certain that the man who had given Greenlee the gun was miles away by now. Word on the street was he had hopped a Greyhound out of town after hearing that his friend had been arrested. The sheriff doubted Thomas had gone far, probably back to Gainesville. McCall would phone the law up that way in the morning. He'd get Thomas too.

But locating the fourth man wasn't the sheriff's only problem. Reports of new trouble drew McCall back to the south end of the county. Some said the Klan was planning to march right down Groveland's Main Street. The talk was so widespread that concerned citizens in Clermont were making arrangements to transport blacks out of town. As the sheriff drove through Groveland and Mascotte, he observed several small knots of grim-faced men talking in whispered tones. Something was definitely in the works, and it wouldn't be good. McCall was optimistic his men and the state troopers could control whatever was being planned. The extra show of force by the National Guard would certainly help.

"Leland George also admitted that he was among the 500 or 600 Klansmen who gathered together at Groveland at the time of the Groveland race riots. He further admitted the purpose for going to Groveland at that time was to find the Negroes who allegedly were involved in the rape and that they were 'going to string them up.'" -- FBI report of interview with Leland George, 1952

It didn't take the Klan long to organize. By early evening, a convoy of approximately 25 automobiles, the majority bearing license plates from nearby Orange County, rolled into Groveland. Most vehicles contained four men each, "all unhooded." Occupants of the cars distributed an eight-page leaflet entitled, "Ideals of the Ku Klux Klan." Those who took the time to read the pamphlet -- and dozens did -- were greeted with the message, "THIS IS A WHITE MAN'S ORGANIZATION exalting the Caucasian race and teaching the doctrine of white supremacy. This does not mean that we are enemies of the colored and mongrel races. But it does mean that we are organized to establish the solidarity and to realize the mission of the white race." The locals already knew what the Klan stood for. "The Klan ruled this county with an iron fist," said Tom Hurlburt Jr., whose father served as special deputy for McCall. "I believe the only thing more powerful than Willis McCall was the Ku Klux Klan in those days... My daddy once told me, 'Hell son, in Lake County just about everybody who's white was in the Klan, and those who weren't thought they were.'"

Groveland's small klavern was soon bolstered by brethren from as far south as Miami and as far north as Georgia. Regardless of where they came from, the Klansmen were united, not only in their hatred and penchant for violence, but by their operating methods. Nearly all of the cars that came to Lake County had illegally darkened license plates. McCall wasn't surprised, he knew they would come -- they had to -- but he didn't expect them to stay long.

"When questioned about the possible connection of Sheriff Willis V. McCall of Lake County with the Groveland riots Bogar insisted that McCall had passed the word to the Klan that he did not want to have anything against his record, that he wanted the Negroes to have a fair trial." -- FBI report of interview with Klansman William Jackson Bogar, April 22, 1952

Klan members and armed locals lined Groveland's streets by the time 50 Lake County National Guardsmen under the direction of Lt. Jimmy Herlong arrived. The show of force didn't faze the mob ringleaders. They already knew what Herlong quickly determined: that the guardsmen were easily outnumbered. After dispatching his soldiers and meeting with McCall, Herlong phoned the governor with his initial assessment: his force was too small to control the situation, but his men would do their best.

At 9:30 p.m., Gov. Warren placed a call to The Florida National Guard in Tampa, ordering troops mobilized to "protect persons and property and to maintain order" in Groveland. "They said it was a racist situation, that there had been a rape over there and that the Ku Klux Klan had practically declared war on the black community and they were shooting up homes. And if there was anybody there that really had a real strong feeling about that, they should speak up. Nobody said anything," recalled 18-year-old guardsman Don Garlits.

After conferring with Herlong and the Florida Highway Patrol commander, McCall directed the small band of guardsmen to encircle the Negro quarters of Groveland. Lake County deputies and highway patrolmen were ordered to roam back roads and patrol the smaller communities outside Groveland. By spreading out the manpower, McCall hoped to create the impression that the peacekeepers were everywhere. McCall could only hope the Tampa guard, stationed 80 miles away, would arrive before violence erupted.

The reinforcements from the west coast arrived at approximately 11 p.m., finding relative peace and quiet, and the two small Lake County units patrolling Groveland's "colored quarters." The Klan and local Crackers bent on retribution were lying low, hoping the law would pull out, and take the guardsmen with them.

By midnight, the "entire colored quarters," had been canvassed. Guardsmen reported, "no indication of any brewing disturbance or rioting, nor was there any groups collecting around town indicating that they may be intending to start something." Guardsmen noted, "many, many people" in town, on benches, curbstones or in their cars sightseeing. Some jeered at the soldiers setting up camp in vacant lots. "This big sedan came down the highway where we had the .50-caliber machine gun set up. They called us 'nigger lovers' and all that kind of stuff. Hollered out the windows at us. And this guy made a smart aleck remark about we were a bunch of tin soldiers and we didn't even have ammunition," Garlits recalled. "And my master sergeant was carrying what they call a grease gun, which was what they called a .45-caliber submachine gun. It was just kind of on a sling. And he just aimed it up in the sky and burst off about 20 rounds and just looked at them, as if to say, 'Do you want a little of this?' And they didn't."

Of course, none of the riled up Crackers were foolhardy enough to challenge armed guardsmen. While the locals held whispered conferences, the troops prepared for a long night. They could only hope the vigilantes would tire and return home. As Sunday became Monday, the weary sheriff was sure Klansmen and locals alike understood he meant business. A weary McCall dismissed the 50 local guardsmen at 1:30 a.m. By sunrise, most of the men who had gathered to take out their frustration and anger on the Negro neighbors had returned home.

Monday morning began with the National Guard troops from Tampa extending their patrols beyond Groveland. Some guardsmen went door-to-door in the Negro quarters to allay fears. "They even came to Clermont. I suppose that's why James was afraid to branch out too far. He didn't go outside of that trailer. He didn't leave that trailer," Henrietta (Irvin) Shepherd recalled. The presence of guardsmen in Clermont confirmed the young couple's fears that trouble could spread from Groveland. For Henrietta and her new husband, Monday was a day filled with uncertainty, worry and hunger. James wasn't about to go in to town to get food. "We drank water. I think we had some cookies. We'd save a cookie to eat tonight, and drink some water. We'd wash our clothes out and we'd put 'em on and stand in the sun in the mirror, in the glass where the sun was coming through and dry. It was something," Henrietta recalled. But seeing guardsmen patrolling their quarters also gave many local Negroes hope. They were safe as long as the National Guard stayed. Unlike the sheriff and his deputies, these protectors really were protectors, of whites *and* blacks.

That morning, McCall patrolled the hot spots of the previous evening. He still felt tension, but was confident each passing day would lessen the likelihood of violence. Hopefully, the new week would bring both whites and Negroes to their senses. The grove owners and packing houses certainly couldn't survive without their laborers, and the workers sure as hell couldn't afford to stay away from paying jobs. Still, the sheriff would spend another night in Groveland, grabbing sleep whenever he could. He wasn't about to let his guard down. He would stay until he was satisfied the threat of aggression fully passed. But he also needed to be in Tavares. After a quick breakfast, the sheriff headed to his office. He knew it was safe to leave since the mob wouldn't act in broad daylight. Besides, most of them were probably sleeping off their drunk from the night before. He would be in his office and finished with his business long before the newspaper reporters came calling, as he knew they would. The sheriff needed to get Charles Greenlee out of town before telling the press he had arrested another one of the Groveland rapists. Reporters couldn't interview a man who was 110 miles away.

Charles awoke to pain. "When I woke up the next day, I was swollen and covered with bruises." His feet throbbed from being cut by broken glass. His wrists were puffy. He felt dried blood on his right cheek, arms and chest. His privates were sore and swollen. In short, every inch of his body ached. As his mind cleared, he tried to make sense of the events of the previous 24 hours. He couldn't understand why he had been forced to confess when the brown-haired man had twice cleared him. Charles could only think of one explanation: "Based on what I could piece together and figure out, I think I was involved because he needed a fourth guy to fit their story."

For a moment he fixed bloodshot eyes on his captors drinking coffee and talking down the hall from his cell. Without moving a muscle, he listened closely, determined to learn the names of the men who had tormented him the night before. "The main man that was hitting me was named Leroy. He's heavyset; about 185 pounds; about 5-feet-11 inches. I could recognize every one of the men I saw; even the one that put me in jail. I would point them out at any time. I will never forget them." Campbell may have led the brutal assault, but he had plenty of help. "I was beat by three deputies. Deputy Yates, and there was another deputy who kind of had a fat face, but I can't remember his name. There were three of them. The two deputies and the sheriff was there. He (McCall) was the one directing the traffic, so to speak."

The deputies sprang into action with the arrival of the sheriff, who immediately called his men into his office, where he outlined a plan. The nigger boy had to go, and he had to go now. At McCall's direction, deputies dressed Charles in a prison work outfit, gave him a scythe and directed him to cut tall grass from the courthouse to an unmarked patrol car nearby. The deputies told the prisoner that he better do as told because a mob was coming after him. Charles was glad to be out of his bloody clothes, but he could barely walk, let alone swing a scythe. Still, he moved as quickly as his aching muscles allowed. The ruse worked, and soon Greenlee was crouched behind the driver's seat of a patrol car speeding through Tavares toward the state prison at Raiford.

With Greenlee out of town, McCall began preparing for reporters. He'd be ready; in fact, he would give them more than enough to write about. By the time local scribes arrived, the sheriff was flanked by Clermont Police Chief George Mays, the night watchman who apprehended Greenlee, and State Attorney Jesse Hunter. McCall was in an expansive mood as he welcomed the press. Asked about reports of violence in and around Groveland, McCall told reporters, "everything is orderly" and "there'll be no lynching of Negroes in Lake County as long as I am sheriff." Mays parroted Lake's top lawman -- for the most part: "There may be demonstrations for another night or two, but I don't expect any violence." The sheriff then announced his big news: the third member of "the gang" had been arrested at approximately 3 a.m. Saturday morning. McCall told reporters that 20-year-old Charles Greenlee of Santa Fe was taken into custody by a night watchman at the Edge Mercantile Co. outside Groveland. "He looked suspicious and told a funny story," Harry McDonald told reporters. "I held my gun on him, and my flashlight between my legs while I disarmed him. He had a .45 revolver stuck in his belt. He told me at first it was not his gun and that it was not loaded. He told me a story of having caught a ride to Groveland with some Negroes, and of sleeping in a shed at the depot until the train came in. I thought it sounded funny, so I locked him up."

The reporters accepted the news at face value. No one zeroed in on the fact that Greenlee hadn't initially been arrested as a suspect in the Groveland case. No one asked how long the teen sat in jail before lawmen connected him to Shepherd and Irvin. No one wondered if Greenlee might have just been in the wrong place at the wrong time. The reporters didn't even think to request an interview with Greenlee. Hunter told reporters he would travel to Raiford to question all three prisoners and arrange counsel. "We will make sure they get a fair trial. We're not going to run anything over on them. They will get a fair, square deal from the beginning." McCall was his usual colorful self, saying, "If I could have been free to act Saturday night, we would have had them all by now." He then told of receiving a call from a woman representing the NAACP who had the nerve to ask what he was doing to protect the rights of Negro citizens in Groveland. "I told her we were looking after them all right, and I said we'd take care of half of those in Harlem if they wanted us to. Then I hung up." The anecdote produced the desired guffaws.

Despite McCall's bravado, he didn't have things under control. Still, the reporters were impressed. McCall told them Shepherd and Irvin had recently served time in prison, "for assault in a northwestern state," although the sheriff couldn't remember which state. Clearly, he had captured two desperate, dangerous men.

Chapter 7 -- Stuckey Burns

Tension, fear and rumor blanketed Lake County as the work week began. Sheriff Willis McCall, who had spent day and night in and around Groveland over the past two days, finally caught a few much-needed winks at his Eustis home.

While McCall slept, Henrietta (Irvin) Shepherd spent an anxious – and lonely – Monday waiting for news from Groveland. James, who never cared much for conversation, wasn't talking. As the silence between husband and wife grew, Henrietta realized she was seeing a side of her husband she had previously overlooked. "James was like a child person. He was really backwards." Henrietta missed her mother and father more than ever.

"Momma" was the backbone of the Irvin family, which settled in Groveland in 1940. "Cleve" moved from Gainesville in hopes of improving life for his wife and seven children. "It had just gotten so bad farming. My father was farming and each year he was sharecropping, working for nothing… that's what it was called, you know. And each year it was we didn't come out (ahead), we came out even, and said we would do better next year," Henrietta recalled. "We worked hard. We didn't go to school. We didn't go to school, maybe two days a week. We were a very, very poor family… You had to work. You had to go in the orange groves, the grapefruit field and we had to work, work, work."

It seemed like every Negro in Groveland was in the same boat as the Irvins. None of the families working in the groves were getting rich; most earned just enough to put food on the table and clothes on the backs of their children. An experienced picker could make $35 a week, but that didn't go far when there was more than one mouth to feed. Few pickers owned their homes. "Cleve" was determined to be different. He wanted to be independent like Henry Shepherd.

"My dad and mom met James and Samuel Shepherd's father. He was a builder. He built the (Irvin) house in Groveland. And that's how we came to know about him," said Henrietta. Henry would often be accompanied by one or more of his children when he worked on the Irvin home, and friendships soon developed, including one between Walter Irvin and Sammie Shepherd. It wasn't long before Sammie's older brother James was also looking for reasons to visit the Irvins. He had his eye on 16-year-old Henrietta. "From one to the other, by seeing the father and coming up with the kids and all we got to know each other. Walter and Samuel were the same age. My brother Joshua and one brother were the same age, his name was Henry Jr. My sister was the same age as one of the Shepherd girls," Henrietta recalled. While Henrietta eyed the handsome Navy veteran, James, her younger sister, Louise was noticing James' fiery little brother, Sammie. The head of the Irvin household made no secret of the fact that he liked James a whole lot better than he liked Sam. "My dad one time had it out with Samuel over Louise. Sam was drinking and cursing and Daddy told him, 'Out here you can't do that,'" Henrietta said. "Sam was a terrible person, he was a fighter. She (Louise) was scared of him."

Cleve worked for L.D. Edge, a citrus baron whose Edge Mercantile Company was one of the oldest businesses in Lake County. It wasn't an understatement to say that Groveland's economy depended on L.D. Edge, who had a reputation for treating his workers fairly. "Mr. Edge treated my father good. Mr. Edge was a nice guy… He never had any problem with him. He did the best he could for him. He could always go to Mr. Edge when he couldn't go to anybody else. I know this. And I think he went to him a lot," Henrietta recalled.

Cleve noticed the Shepherds were doing better than most colored folks, but there were still 10 people crammed into Henry's three-bedroom dwelling. And there was no indoor plumbing. The Irvin house was nearly as crowded, which meant keeping the family fed was an on-going challenge. Everyone did their part to help, especially the oldest son, Walter. But Walter, like his mother Dellia, longed for a different life. He didn't enjoy farming, and he didn't like picking citrus. Walter had a thirst for education, which he cultivated while living with his older sister in nearby Palatka. But after the family moved to Groveland -- and the workload Cleve was expected to perform increased -- Walter spent more time working and less time in school.

"All he wanted to do was go to school… that was all I ever heard him ask for is to, 'please, let me go to school.' But when you got a boss, and he controls you, he got more land, Walter had to come back to the farm. But as he grew older, my father started listening and started looking. Expression tells all. And he decided one day, finally, I think Walter was about 14, he said, 'ok, you can go back and you can go to school and finish. Do the best you can, and make something out of yourself.' And there was something Walter Lee always wanted better. His sights was always on betterness. He wanted to be a teacher… He always wanted to teach… He used to always have us lining up and he would teach us, even when we was on the farm. He would teach us. But, ah, he never had the chance to do it,"

Henrietta recalled. The return to school in Palatka was everything Walter thought it would be, but he soon became homesick. "So he came back home, and he started going to school at Edgewood High in Groveland. And he worked a little to help out around the house. But then when he finished school he decided, 'well now, there's not enough work around here, I want to do something else.' Like maybe work in a restaurant... maybe, anything else but picking oranges. That was a big thing there. So he decided to go," Henrietta remembered.

Walter found work in a restaurant an hour and half away in St. Petersburg. Washing dishes and clearing tables was far from glamorous, but he enjoyed living in a "big city" and having spending money of his own. And then the patriotism bug bit him. "And when he became 18 he came home and said 'I want to go into the service, I decided that I want to serve my country.' So that's what he did," Henrietta recalled. "We was excited about that because, we thought that, you know, he had signed up for three years and we knew for three years he would be stable and could get something going for him..."

While Walter saw the world as a serviceman, the family struggled to get by. Demanding work in the groves was one thing, the attitude of the whites was another. "I recall walking 'side (State Road) 50 and bottles being throwed at us and words being yelled at us. It was just bad. We wasn't allowed to go into places, in the front of places. We weren't allowed to do anything," Henrietta said. Henrietta was beginning to understand why her big brother needed to get away.

Walter's letters from the Philippines, where he was stationed, left no doubt that he had made the right decision. It was clear he wouldn't be coming back to Groveland. "He decided it was going to be in California. He made this decision when he was discharged from the Army," Henrietta said. "He didn't come home. So, we kept writing him and we kept saying, 'We want to see you. Please come home. Why don't you come home? Why don't you come home?' And he would always say 'no.' My mother sent him a ticket, he sent it back. So one day I decided, 'Ok, you won't come home so I'm fixing to tell you something.' So I wrote him a little letter. And it wasn't a nice letter. It was always 'so and so, goddamn it, come home, your mother want to see you.' You know. And this and that, and so on and so on. It was a dirty little letter. So when he got the letter, he came home. And his words to me was, 'I'm only here because of you and I'm going to put my belt on you for using those kind of words.' And that's why he was home," said Henrietta, who soon realized her brother was a different person than the man who had left nearly three years earlier. He was happier.

"He must of just grew up in that time. He went to Manila, the Philippines. And he told me that he had met a girl over there and he wanted to marry her. He also told me he had a kid over there. But you know, we never got a chance to pursue that. But he grew up in the time that he left and the time he came back. And when Walter Lee came back for 29 days, Walter Lee was very, very happy. I never seen him angry. Only thing he was angry about, you know what it was? When I told him I was getting married. Forgive me! He got so angry with me. He said, 'What did you say? Who do you think you are?' You know, he was tellin' me, 'you're too young to get married. You don't know what you're doing. What you talkin' about?' He was so angry. I can see these little things on the side of his head up there just running, and I knew he was angry. He called me stupid. He said 'you're stupid. You don't even know life.' He was so right. He was so right. God knows. I thought about what he said a lot of times," said Henrietta.

Walter *had* grown up in the service. Everyone noticed. He was happier, but he was also a bit hardened. He had been behind prison bars. "…from what he told me, from what he said to us, there was a fight. The Filipinos and the Americans. There was some kind of fight that they got into. And, I guess, it was just like, whatever it was, you know, was causing them to be disciplined through the Army… I know he was dishonorably discharged. But other than that I don't know. He didn't say very much just about it. Other than there was just a fight," said Henrietta.

Walter had seen enough of the white man's world to know how the game was played, and to know he wanted something better than his father had achieved. He had no desire to grow old in the groves, making money for white men who viewed him as little better than a plow mule. He had discovered there was a whole world beyond Groveland. He had found respect, and love. "I think that was why he wanted to stay in California. That he was going to go back, or she was going to come to him. One of the two." Now, it appeared his decision to return home for a visit had cost him his freedom.

James wondered what Sammie and Walter had done, if anything. He didn't know what to do. And he didn't know what to say. "James cried for two days and two nights when the trouble happened. He just cried and cried," said his young bride. James was plenty worried. His boss, Dan Fields had told James things were too hot for him to return to work, and that Negroes and whites alike sensed more trouble on the horizon. Fields told James to be ready to leave town at a moment's notice.

The fear and uncertainty felt by members of the Negro community intensified with the withdrawal of National Guard troops. Evidently, some Crackers who had retreated to their homes when guardsmen arrived were promising to resume their night riding when the sun fell. With the Guard gone, few Negroes were willing to stick around and see what the evening would bring. Many hastily packed and went to stay with friends and relatives in other parts of the state. And they prepared to stay away as long as the threat of violence existed. Others repeated their exodus of Saturday and Sunday, when they left for the night, then returned to work in the morning. Those brave souls realized that the white men who donned sheets at night would grudgingly pay them for field work in the daylight.

Several families escaped to the safety of Orlando 40 miles east, where strangers went to great lengths to feed and shelter the refugees. According to McCall, the frightened Negroes were taken away in trucks by "responsible white citizens" who wanted to avoid violence. In Orlando, the Salvation Army provided shelter and cots, while the American Legion Auxiliary served meals. The Red Cross joined black and white churches in providing rooms for the displaced. "Civic-minded residents went into action immediately," reported Ramona Lowe in the *Chicago Defender*. "Their first step was to organize an Emergency Committee." That committee of unsung heroes even covered the expenses of a baby born to a Groveland woman who had been moved to Orlando when things got hot. Orlando residents opened their hearts and purses as well. The Orlando Planning Board contributed $50 and promised to double the amount if refugees had to stay longer than three days. The white Methodist and Presbyterian churches also each contributed $50. Other groups, white and black, also provided aid.

In Groveland, a small number of Negroes who naively believed promises that they would be given protection by law officers remained. Among whites, most seemed to believe the sheriff's promise that things would soon return to normal, but there were clearly two other camps: those who feared further violence; and those who were planning to participate in terrorizing the Negroes. Some whites were bold enough to implore their neighbors to stay home and let the law handle things. Local game official H.A. Buckner, confident that reason would prevail, met with the ringleaders of the mob and beseeched them to end their intimidation and violence and to spare public property.

As tension escalated, rumors of a full-blown race war were rampant. In Mascotte, talk that Negroes in Stuckey Still had, "armed themselves and were coming to town," had whites discussing how to deal with the threat. Reasonable whites no doubt dismissed the story as just more wild talk. No Negro would be foolish enough to organize such an action, which surely would result in wholesale bloodshed since whites easily outnumbered blacks. Even the most defiant Negro realized rising up against the whites would be foolhardy and likely result in obliteration of the Negro community, just as it had in Rosewood in '23 and Ocoee '20. Unfortunately, the number of unreasonable whites far outnumbered the rational. The rumor continued to spread. In fact, many of the Negroes in Stuckey Still *had* armed themselves, but not to attack whites; those who had taken up arms did so to protect themselves and their loved ones in case the mob returned.

In Mascotte, McCall soon realized that the rumor that, "a whole mob of Negroes are armed and ready to march in on us tonight," had traveled from one end of the tiny community to the other. It took awhile, but McCall finally found the source of tittle-tattle. When confronted, the woman admitted that she "had just heard that someone saw two Negroes with guns." The sheriff was annoyed, but not surprised. People were jumpy to the point of panic. As he climbed into his car, the sheriff was struck by the grim realization that the rumor had taken on a life of its own. At one home, an eggplant farmer reacted to McCall's claim that the rumor was unfounded by saying, "I've got my gun ready. Iffen it's the truth that those colored folks are coming in with guns, I'll shoot. But, sheriff, I ain't goin' out after a one of 'em... and that gal's a kin of mine. I jest don't see how that will help matters." The farmer may have been staying put, but other white men were moving. The pot was simmering and McCall could only guess when, and where, it would boil over. A betting man would have wagered on the southwest side of the county, where a group of good ole' boys were planning to "wipe out Stuckey Still," a settlement of approximately two dozen Negroes.

McCall, who had hurried to the scene, was determined to ruin their party. From a distance, he sat watching with his 17-year-old son Malcolm, sometime deputy Tom Hurlburt and Deputy Leroy Campbell. As the angry men drove off, McCall radioed for all available

Florida Highway patrolmen to lend assistance. He also made an emergency call to the National Guard headquarters in Eustis, asking for the return of local troops that had patrolled on Sunday night. McCall, doubtful the reinforcements would arrive soon enough, quickly rounded up "a score of men," whom he deputized in hopes of forestalling a riot. His choice of men left something to be desired.

Things were moving rapidly. "Dad said that all those rednecks from Groveland, Stuckey Still and Bay Lake were trying to find those colored boys. They were going to hang 'em. The crowd had pitchforks and there were men holding shotguns in the back of their pickup trucks. They were looking to kill them," said Tom Hurlburt Jr. Evidently, the vigilantes wouldn't wait for nightfall, which meant McCall and his men were on their own. The sheriff was being forced to make a stand. "Before the National Guard arrived, there was a group of fellows bent on cleaning out the Stuckey Still colored settlement west of Mascotte. As several cars of armed men turned into Stuckey Still, I turned in behind them. A short distance down the road the truck stopped and the men started firing. A few bullets struck the house, but most went wild," McCall recalled. "Fortunately, no one was hurt."

The locals were in a nasty mood, and clearly wouldn't be dissuaded by another dose of the sheriff's cracker-barrel psychology. McCall, realizing they wouldn't listen to reason, grabbed a shotgun and tear gas grenade and stepped out of his car. He knew full well that whatever action he took in the next few minutes would determine whether he remained in charge of the county or waived that right. And he wasn't about to let a bunch of rowdy clay-eaters cost him his badge. He had fought too hard to become high sheriff to let some liquored-up rednecks get an upper hand. "I threw a tear gas bomb into the crowd," McCall recalled. "They loaded up and moved about one hundred yards down the road and stopped again. This time I loaded a tear gas gun I had with me with a non-piercing load and fired it at the pickup truck. It landed right under the pickup load of men. This time they got in their cars, wiping their eyes and drove across Highway 50 down a clay road to get their eyes cleared up." The tear gas dispersed the mob, which included many of the men McCall had confronted at the jail 24 hours earlier. The sheriff knew that he had to make it clear that he meant business. While the hacking men wiped their eyes, the sheriff moved in and made his play. He was direct and to the point, telling the men to cease their hell raising at once or risk spending the night in jail. According to McCall, "I convinced them to go home and they all agreed and were loading up the cars, approximately 100 men, give or take a few." Still, the men lingered. Perhaps McCall was bluffing. Perhaps it was time to find out.

The uneasy truce was interrupted by the arrival of 17 guardsmen from the Lake County battalion H Company, 124th Infantry in Eustis under the direction of Lt. Paul Hudson. A few men fled into the woods at the sight of the armed guardsmen, but most mob members remained defiant. They were intent on shooting up Stuckey Still, and by God, that's what they were going to do. The band of angry men weren't backing down this time. They had gained boldness since their previous retreat after National Guard intervention Sunday. The arrival of reinforcements didn't have the effect McCall had hoped for. "This got the crowd all stirred up and I was told the deal was off unless the Boy Scouts left first," McCall recalled. "Someone went up to Jim Livingstone in the National Guard and told him to take his peashooter and go home. Another remarked, 'The damn thing is not loaded, they are just bluffing.' At this point Livingstone fired several shots into the ground and asked the man if that sounded like a Boy Scout with a BB gun. This got their respect. Still they refused to go home. At this point Jim Herlong, the captain in charge of the National Guard, and I went into a huddle and both agreed that the best way to cool the hot potato was for the National Guard to go home if the troublesome group would go home."

Herlong ordered the guardsmen to pull back and give McCall a chance to reason with the troublemakers. The sheriff knew arresting any of the men was out of the question. That would only pour gasoline on the fire. Besides, he was one of them, and they knew it. He may have been sworn to uphold the peace, but most men in the mob knew "Ole Willis" would be right alongside them if he wasn't wearing a badge. Guardsmen reluctantly retreated down the road, leaving McCall to face down the mob. "I told them I could sympathize with their emotions, but that I had to uphold the law," McCall remembered. "They agreed to go home after they saw I meant business." Some of the men promised there would be no more trouble. It had almost been too easy, the sheriff thought as he watched the men disperse. He should have known better. The vigilante ringleaders were determined to teach the coloreds a lesson. They would bide their time. McCall and the guardsmen couldn't be everywhere at once. At the very least, the mob was going to drive the "five or six undesirables" out for good, if it was the last thing they did. The men drove off, but few returned to their homes.

As night fell, Negro residents who had foolishly refused to leave braced for the worst. Many boarded up windows and doors. Most extinguished lights, crawled behind furniture and hoped the nightriders would pass them by.

In Bay Lake, just eight miles south, Charlie Mae Shepherd was becoming more concerned with each new rumor. Her worst fears were confirmed when a family friend warned her that a gang of angry whites was planning to pay a visit. Sammie Shepherd's mother needed a plan to protect her children, but leaving wasn't an option; she didn't have a car. Her husband had driven to their daughter's house in Orlando after dropping James at work that morning. "My family had to hide away out in the woods. Somebody warned them they were coming out, that's how they got away, by hiding in the woods," Fannie (Shepherd) Bell recalled. Charlie Mae and her children hid just in time.

"The Negroes were hardly settled before they were warned by friendly whites that they had walked into a trap and that a wholesale slaughter was planned Monday night," Ramona Lowe reported. "Most of the evacuees frantically retraced their steps to the refuges they had originally sought. But there were those who stayed. And when they heard the cars of the night riders they flattened themselves on the floors of their home. Bullets peppered the frame houses, shattering the windows and peppering the beds." The first documented violence occurred at the Blue Flame Café, the Groveland juke joint owned by Ernest Thomas' mother. Angry whites poured shotgun pellets and rifle balls through the windows of the establishment. Just 75 feet away, 90-year-old Warren Moore cowered in his bed, but the mob moved on without stopping at his home. He was lucky. Some homes were looted. At others, gasoline bombs were thrown. At the Shepherd home, men fired buckshot through the front door. By now dozens of frightened Negroes had joined Charlie Mae and her children in the woods.

The violence was especially fierce in Stuckey Still. Joe Maxwell, who had recently returned home from the war to his wife and three small children, was in the thick of it. "Screaming, you know rough riding. Screaming and going on," Maxwell recalled. "Well, I told them all to get into bed. To get under the bed. And I took mattresses and piled them up, and you know, tried to keep them safe. Told 'em to stay away from windows, everything. Yeah, they were shooting. I heard a window break. And that's when they shot into the house. About 30 or 40 cars." "That's what made it so scary. Hearing all that glass breaking, and these cars all lined up, and saying all kinds of things," said Josephine Maxwell, who was 6 years old at the time. "And when you'd look out you'd see long guns hanging out the windows. I remember Daddy shooting his gun too."

Nearby, Isaiah Hodges watched in fear from his darkened bedroom as the convoy passed through the neighborhood. Cary and Joe Lucas were among the homeowners who found bullets in their walls the next morning. "The community was considered ideal before the riots. Refugees here feel certain many former residents will never call it home again," Lowe reported. The bloodthirsty mob had grown to 200 inflamed whites by the time the mobsters headed south to terrorize the few Negro residents in Bay Lake.

"As I was there in Groveland I overheard I.B. Hall who was driving in his black 1941 Ford say that he was going after five gallons of gasoline... Several weeks after this incident I heard that I.B. Hall burned the Negro houses in the Groveland area." -- William Jackson Bogar, former Exalted Cyclops of Apopka Klavern of the Association of Georgia Klans, interview with FBI agents, April 22, 1952

Soon the Shepherd home was engulfed in flames. Moments later the arsonists torched the home of well-known voodooist George Valerie, who had grown rich through telling the fortunes of local Negroes and anxious whites who came from hundreds of miles away to have their fortunes told. While the law turned a blind eye, at least 100 whites gathered to watch the homes burn. Most were still present when McCall arrived, but there would be no arrests. As the flames died, most spectators finally returned to their homes.

Three homes had been reduced to smoking embers by the time Guardsmen returned. It could have been a lot worse. At least no one was injured or killed. After touring Stuckey Still and Bay Lake, Lt. Herlong called the National Guard commander in Tampa to discuss the situation. The two agreed that the worst was over, that the local troops could handle the situation, and reinforcements would arrive Tuesday to relieve the locals. At 1:30 a.m., all was quiet as a weary McCall released the Lake County troops. Nine Florida Highway Patrol cars would crisscross the Groveland area until daybreak to make sure things stayed quiet.

The next day, McCall would give the impression he had rushed to the scene, but arrived too late to prevent the acts of destruction. "Later on, we saw a big fire in the Groveland area.

By the time we got there, two houses had burned to the ground and were just smoldering." McCall didn't explain how he was close enough to see the light cast by a big fire, but too far away to reach the scene before the buildings were reduced to ashes. Those acquainted with the sheriff knew better. Heck, he gave himself away when he told reporters, "…soon as the fire lit up people began to swarm there from every direction." How could he know that if he wasn't there? So where was McCall during the pandemonium? Two schools of thought prevailed: either the sheriff had underestimated the determination of the mob and had left the area, or he had turned a blind eye, thinking peace wouldn't come until they had made their statement. The prevailing opinion: the sheriff had agreed to allow the mob one night of violence if they would return to their peaceable ways the following day.

The night of unrest was front-page news Tuesday. UPI reported, "A crowd of 150 to 200 men congregated at Mascott (sic), between Groveland and Stuckey's Still, following the shooting there but they caused no trouble. They told officers there would be no violence if the officers left." According to The Associated Press, "Nearly 300 fully armed National Guard troops moved in tonight as new outbreaks threatened from a white mob which has terrorized Negroes by home burnings and shooting forays." The *Miami Herald* reported, "Mobs of angry White men roamed the pine woods of Lake County early Tuesday, burning rural Negro houses as law enforcement officers, and Florida National guardsmen threw up barricades to save larger Negro communities." McCall had done it again. All three reporters focused on the valiant peace-keeping efforts of law enforcement personnel and the National Guard. Not one questioned how a mob could inflict so much damage right under the noses of Lake County's sheriff, deputies, special deputies, highway patrolmen and dozens of soldiers. None asked how many members of the mob had been arrested for their lawless activity. Incredibly, newspaper editor Mabel Norris-Reese implied the acts of violence were justified. "We learned too that the mobs didn't just wantonly burn Negro homes in wild vengeance for the crime. No -- it was a cunning mob… it burned the house of a bearded, fantastic Negro, who had amassed a fortune in voodooism, and the house of another -- which was known to be the headquarters for bolita in south Lake County."

McCall brashly laid blame for the night of terror on the doorstep of the Negro community, not frenzied whites. "A lot of good Mascotte people were mixed up in that thing. They believed the stories they heard and they weren't gong to let those Negroes come into town carrying guns. They believed they were in danger." It was the kind of brazen, twisted logic McCall would become famous for. "Good" people were merely protecting themselves and their belongings. When asked what precautions he would be taking from now on, McCall told reporters that he didn't expect further unrest, but Guardsmen would rope off the main roads and side streets leading to the Negro section of Groveland to discourage further trouble.

In Bay Lake, a handful of Negroes who survived Monday's reign of terror picked through the rubble of the torched homes searching for a 7-year-old girl who had been missing since the previous night. The frightened girl finally appeared, telling family and neighbors she spent the night in the woods after being scared out of her home. The events of the previous evening had also scared Joe Maxwell and his family. He wasn't about to go through a

47

second harrowing evening. He resolutely boarded up the windows the mob had shot out, packed a few bags and loaded his family onto a train bound for Fort Lauderdale, where he had relatives. But not everyone had kin to run to. The few Negro families without a place to go spent Tuesday preparing for another tumultuous night. As reporters toured the south end of the county, one noted, "The faces of a few frightened Negro children could be seen peering from behind the doors before their parents nailed and barricaded the openings." The fear of the unknown was compounded by the realization they would again be on their own. They had waited in vain for the law to step in and protect them Monday evening, only to be disappointed. They wouldn't be that gullible again.

Community leaders awoke to a public relations nightmare. Reporters from all corners of the state, and even some from northern newspapers, had descended upon Groveland. And the reports they were filing were anything but favorable. But there was a larger concern. Many long-time residents feared that the incidents of Monday night were a precursor of greater aggression ahead. So far, the Negro quarters of Clermont had been undisturbed. But who was to say that now that the Negroes of Bay Lake, Stuckey Still and Groveland had been put in their place, that Clermont's Negroes weren't the next targets?

Few people shared the sheriff's optimism that the troublemakers were finished. Groveland city councilmen hurriedly instituted a curfew prohibiting loitering on town streets after 10 p.m. With the arrival of 300 National Guard troops, councilmen had no doubt the curfew would be enforced. Perhaps widespread violence would be averted through the threat of martial law. Dan Fields wasn't taking any chances. Early Tuesday, he and his wife picked up James and Henrietta Shepherd to take them to Jacksonville. It was a car ride Henrietta would never forget. Before long, the news of the mob action of the night before came over the car radio. "I heard on the news… I will never forget what Mrs. Fields said to James and myself as we were on our way to Jacksonville. As she was talking you would have thought she was judge and jury, that as far as she was concerned both Sam -- James' brother, and Walter -- my brother, were guilty. Her words to us was, 'James and Henrietta, they should kill them. They had no right to be with a white woman.' When she was talking she was looking into our faces."

Henry Shepherd also learned about his home being destroyed from a radio news report. "The time it happened, I was here (Orlando) trying to get a home started. My father came over to help us. The house wasn't even finished yet. We heard it on the radio and it was all we could do to keep him," recalled Fannie (Shepherd) Bell, who begged her father not to return to Bay Lake. She had already "lost" a brother; she couldn't let her father risk his life by returning to Lake County.

While radio broadcasts were mostly free of editorializing, the *Orlando Morning Sentinel* displayed it bias on Tuesday, July 19, 1949 by running a large, front-page editorial cartoon depicting four electric chairs above the caption: "The Lake County Tragedy…No Compromise -- The Supreme Penalty." The editorial inside was nearly as offensive. Laced with anti-NAACP sentiment, it also contained a veiled threat. "A few smart lawyers who are agents of different organizations, seek to hamper justice through the employment of legal technicalities. They may bring suffering to many innocent Negroes." Apparently, McCall had told a *Sentinel* reporter about the phone call he received from the NAACP.

Each day seemed to bring another reporter to Florida's hot spot. The *Miami Herald* even chartered a plane to fly staff writer Jack E. Anderson and photographer William Kuenzel to Groveland. Their assignment: to record how the community "of approximately 600-800 whites and 400 Negroes living nearby" was dealing with the unrest, and unwanted attention of the world. The journalists were greeted by a town of weary, tense whites and nearly-deserted Negro quarters patrolled by helmeted National Guardsmen. Anderson found that most residents shared three views: they were uneasy about the presence of gun-toting soldiers; that the troops had infuriated, "the mobsters into further rioting;" and that Sheriff McCall had things under control. But what most bothered those interviewed was the black eye Groveland was receiving. "It all happened west and south of here. We folks here in Groveland don't approve of it a bit. Nobody living here has had anything to do with that rioting," said "prominent businessman" L.D. Edge. Anderson concluded that, "Groveland misses its Negroes, not only because of a loss of their business, but because most of them work in the town. Their exodus has left it with a labor shortage... I drove through the Negro section Tuesday night and only one out of every four or five houses showed light. Perhaps less than a hundred Negroes remain here. The central Florida town of Groveland has a civic black eye -- and its white residents contend it is undeserved... They want to make clear to the outside world that it was not the Grovelanders who attempted to take three Negro rape suspects from the sheriff or who set fire to and shot at Negro homes."

So much was being written that Groveland residents didn't know who – or what to believe. One story that caused considerable consternation intimated that Willie Padgett and his father-in-law knew both Shepherd and Irvin. Other accounts were accepted without question, like an *Orlando Morning Sentinel* report that the Negroes had "bludgeoned Padgett," and that, "all three men have confessed, and have been positively identified by Mrs. Padgett." The truth was far different. Norma *hadn't* identified Irvin or Shepherd – both men had been transported to the State Prison in Raiford before anyone thought to have Norma identify them. The same story had McCall saying Shepherd had recently returned to Groveland after serving, "a three-year term for assault in a penitentiary where he was sent from Army." Naturally, the misinformation further inflamed already edgy whites. And distortions weren't limited to members of the Fourth Estate. In Leesburg, Curtis Howard was telling everyone that *he* had found Norma wandering in the woods on the morning of July 16.

By Tuesday morning, McCall was tired of three things: newspaper reporters; chasing vigilantes; and a growing sentiment that he couldn't quell the violence without "outside" help. When told that groups of men were still loitering around Groveland, McCall remarked, "I'm going to break that up down there. I'm getting tired of it. I've played around with them long enough."

Later that morning, 5th Judicial Circuit Judge Truman G. Futch announced his intention to call a grand jury in the Groveland case. Like Jess Hunter, Futch had been raised on a farm, didn't finish school, became a teacher, and studied law at home. Futch had passed the bar at age 21 with Hunter, who had practically worked by his side since 1915, when Futch arrived in Lake County and joined the practice of Leesburg lawyer J.G. Gaines. Like Hunter, Futch was also something of a character. A stern man who favored loose shirt collars and brown suits, Judge Futch was known for whittling aged cedar sticks -- preferably from old fence posts -- during trials. Futch, who had spent 35 years as an attorney, claimed that whittling helped him stay focused on what was being said.

While Hunter drafted the indictment, the 116th Field Artillery's 221 soldiers were on their way from Tampa to protect what remained of Groveland's Negro community. McCall, still smarting from the rioting that broke out when he prematurely released the Guard, announced the soldiers would remain the entire week. "I may want them to stay longer than that. I'm going to keep them here until I'm satisfied this thing is quiet." McCall had reason to be concerned. One only had to drive through Groveland to see that things were still far from normal. Associated Press reporter James Fowler summed up the situation when he wrote, "Cowboy booted townsmen glared sullenly Tuesday night at ghostly National Guardsmen patrolling silently through rain-spattered streets." More than one soldier was taunted or teased. One local was overheard saying that there would be no trouble while the guard remained, "but you wait until they leave." Mob members had unfinished business to conduct. They hadn't got to the Irvin house yet.

This time Guardsmen were prepared to stay for the long haul. A large citrus packing house was converted into a command post and communications center for the detail of 202 enlisted men, 18 officers and a warrant officer. By Tuesday night, the Guard had set up its own field kitchens and stationed detachments at four possible points of friction: Clermont's Negro section; Mascotte; Stuckey Still and Groveland. Commander Col. Harry Baya Jr. set up headquarters at Groveland High School, transforming the football field into a motor pool. He also stationed two observer planes at the Leesburg Airport. It was an impressive display. "At Highway 50 and 33, I remember seeing sand bags and a 50-milimeter machine gun. And at the time, people that lived on one side of town, the black people, per se, if they wanted to come over to the other side of town, there would be a National Guardsman, he would get on the hood of the car and ride with them to the other side, I guess for their own personal protection," recalled lifelong Groveland resident John Griffin. Community leaders breathed a collective sigh of relief. Perhaps law and order would soon return.

Northern Negro newspapers expressed doubts. Many echoed the NAACP in asking when the sheriff was going to arrest the men responsible for the burning, shooting and looting. When reporters came calling, McCall admitted being present when the homes were torched, but pitifully claimed the crowds were too great for him to get tire tracks or footprints. And he claimed not to recognize any of the men in the crowd. As usual, no reporter challenged the sheriff. Of course, McCall had known who torched the homes. So did Hunter, who later told the *Mount Dora Topic*, "...that he had been the school teacher of some of those men who had plunged into the havoc of destruction."

By sundown, a disturbing rumor was circulating: that the Negro section of Clermont would razed by a "new mob," not the vigilantes who had terrorized Stuckey Still. In Clermont, McCall found nothing amiss, but news that men with weapons were roaming the area soon came over his radio. Evidentially, the boys over Mascotte way were still restless. At 10 p.m., Capt. James Baldwin, commander of Battery C of the 116th, radioed an emergency message for an additional detail to be immediately dispatched. McCall and Guardsmen rushed to his aid, where they found three armed men. After questioning, the sheriff told them to go home and stay there. Moments later, McCall's radio crackled again. Two gunshots had just been reported in Stuckey Still. Again, McCall sped to the scene. He wasn't amused by what he found: a Battery C private had fired two shots to prove that his weapon was indeed loaded. McCall was fit to be tied. He didn't know which was worse: the damn fools who wouldn't let this thing die, or the damn fool Guardsmen who didn't know which end of the gun to point away from themselves. It would be after midnight before McCall finally returned home and wearily climbed into bed.

As Wednesday morning dawned, many Negroes quietly returned to their jobs in the orange and grapefruit groves. A strained tranquility had finally arrived. With 300 Guardsmen joining McCall's deputies -- sworn and enlisted -- and Florida Highway Patrolmen, the Negroes of south Lake County were finally the best protected people in the state.

But at least one Cracker remained undaunted by the army of law enforcers patrolling the county. A Guardsman reported firing shots at a vehicle that sped through Groveland at an estimated 80 miles per hour early Wednesday morning. The car was driven by a "masked figure." It was an isolated incident, to be sure. The few remaining Klansmen from outside Lake County had finally left. Unable to continue terror in Groveland, several Klansmen took their night riding to Polk City in an adjacent county. On Wednesday, random shooting and cross-burnings were reported there.

In Jacksonville, Henrietta and James were trying to understand the events that had driven them from their home. They could only hope and pray that their family members had been fortunate enough to find safe havens as they had. "Me and James went to Jacksonville to his uncle and aunt, who was out-of-sight people. If it wasn't for them I don't know what we would have done. And this family had seven or eight kids of their own. And here was two people comin' in. And you're eating once a day. It was hard. It was very hard. But we never saw that we wasn't welcome. We never saw that," Henrietta recalled. Each day, Henrietta scoured the newspapers in search of news about her brother and brother-in-law. She usually found an article about developments in Groveland, but no mention of the whereabouts of the men who had been arrested. She hoped they were still alive. Henrietta couldn't have known, but Walter and Sammie weren't far away. They weren't far from death, either.

At the state penitentiary in Raiford, prison officials had been so shocked at the condition of their new prisoners that they photographed the injuries Irvin, Shepherd and Greenlee had suffered while in McCall's custody. The warden wanted proof the mistreatment occurred before they arrived at "The Rock" in the event the men died.

Chapter 8 -- Moore & Mr. Civil Rights

In Mims, Florida, NAACP Executive Secretary Harry T. Moore had dropped everything to devote all his energies to the Groveland situation. He desperately needed to make a report to the national office, but couldn't until he located the men who had been arrested and charged with rape. Unfortunately, Lake County officials weren't saying what had become of the suspects. For a fleeting moment, Moore thought of traveling to Tavares and demanding access to the prisoners, but his good sense prevailed. The NAACP didn't carry any weight in Lake County. There, he would be just another uppity nigger who didn't know his place. A trip to that county could very well be his last trip.

Instead, Moore appealed to Gov. Fuller Warren and demanded McCall be held accountable for the violence that had engulfed south Lake County. Moore's hope: that the state's highest executive would force the sheriff to grant access to the prisoners. Moore figured it was time to find out where the Governor stood, time to find out if the newspaper story was true. A few months after the November of 1948 election, a report had surfaced that Warren was a member of the Ku Klux Klan. The governor addressed the rumor in a press release on March 15, 1949: "Many years ago, after repeated requests by a friend who said he received a commission on each new membership procured by him, I paid $8 for membership in the Ku Klux Klan," said Warren, who then pointed out that he quit after attending several meetings. Moore had heard the, "I belonged a long, long time ago, but I quit," line before. Moore had watched the governor closely since that statement. Gov. Warren would never be mistaken for a civil rights crusader, but there was talk that Warren was considering backing an anti-Klan bill during an upcoming legislative session.

The letter wasn't the first Moore had written to a Florida governor. He had repeatedly petitioned for an end to police brutality and the epidemic of Negroes being railroaded through the courts, or worse yet, convicted at the end of a rope. Protection from those charged with upholding the law had been an on-going theme for Moore, not only in letters and telegrams to elected officials, but also to NAACP members he hoped would join their voices to his. In a Jan. 13, 1947, call to action to Florida's 63 NAACP chapters, Moore had written, "Unfortunately, there are many peace officers who seem to think that their most sacred duty is to beat and intimidate Negro citizens." And Moore knew why that was the case: many "lawmen" were card-carrying members of the Ku Klux Klan.

"He claimed he was present when Willis McCall, Sheriff of Lake County, was initiated into the Association of Georgia Klans Apopka Klavern by Phillip Huggins, probably in 1947... In addition to McCall, I.B. Hall recruited the following persons in Lake County: Wilbur Law, Chief of Police, Tavares; James Dickson, Chief of Police, Eustis..." -- FBI report of interview with confidential informant, April 22, 1952

By 1948, atrocities against Negroes were so commonplace that Moore demanded a state investigation into police violence against blacks. For Moore, the final straw may have been the brutality of a New Smyrna Beach deputy who roughed up a Negro woman so badly that she miscarried. Florida Negroes desperately needed the NAACP, although many didn't even know an organization dedicated to their protection and empowerment existed.

As the NAACP grew and extended its influence, it became clear a separate division was needed to handle the growing number of legal cases. In 1939, a young Baltimore attorney named Thurgood Marshall was given the task of drafting the charter for the organization's Legal Defense and Educational Fund (LDF). The intent: to develop a charitable organization to perform the NAACP's non-lobbying activities. The primary goal: "To render legal aid gratuitously to such Negroes as may appear to be worthy thereof, who are suffering legal injustices by reason of race or color..." Poor and uneducated blacks faced with racial injustice would finally have hope. The formation of a legal division wouldn't halt the disturbing flood of frame-ups and convictions by all-white, racist juries, but it would certainly save more than a few lives and free more than a few wrongly-accused blacks.

Marshall's ascension was hard-fought and fraught with battles and barbs. Respect was hard to come by for Negro attorneys in the 1930s, especially down South, where some poor whites had never seen a black man wearing a suit and tie. Marshall endured more insults and threats than he could count. One confrontation that occurred in the South of the late 1930s would stay with him forever. "Well I was changing trains and I had about a two- or three- hour stopover and while I was waiting I got hungry and I saw a restaurant over there so I decided that if I got hungry enough I'd go over there and put my civil rights in my back pocket and go to the back door of the kitchen and see if I could buy a sandwich," Marshall recalled. "And while I was kibitzing myself to do that, this white man came up beside me in plain clothes, with a great big pistol in a case on his hip, and he said, 'Nigger boy,' or something, 'what are you doing here?' And I said, 'Well, I'm waiting.' And he said, 'What did you say?' I said, 'Sir, I'm waiting for the train to Louisiana. Shreveport.' And he said,

'Well, there's only one more train comes through here and that's four o'clock and you'd better be on it because the sun is never going down on a live nigger in this town.' And you know what? I wasn't hungry anymore."

In 1940, Marshall scored his first Supreme Court victory in Chambers v. Florida when he appealed the conviction of five black farmers arrested for murdering an elderly white farmer. After interviewing the men, it was clear their "confessions" had been obtained through mental and physical torture. For days they had proclaimed their innocence. The men, described as "young, ignorant, black tenant farmers" were tried in a highly-charged atmosphere of racial tension. Not surprisingly, they were convicted and sentenced to death. Before the high court, Marshall argued that the men had been coerced into confessing. The justices agreed.

In the beginning, Marshall *was* the LDF. With a budget of just $13,910, there was barely enough cash to cover his salary, let alone pay for travel and assistants. But the staff gradually grew. By the summer of 1949, when Groveland exploded, five attorneys and a secretary were on the payroll. Marshall doled out the casework as it came in. Often, two or more equally important cases were juggled simultaneously. Everyone pitched in where needed, realizing that priorities, and their duties, could change from day to day. It was an exciting, challenging time. "The Legal Defense Fund was not a highly structured place and everything was kind of free form and intuitive and subject to change," LDF attorney Jack Greenberg recalled.

Like Moore, Marshall was tired of cops looking the other way when whites oppressed blacks. And Marshall had something else in common with Moore: he couldn't hold his tongue when he learned of such atrocities. In the early 1940s, Marshall began speaking out. One of the first incidents he examined led him to lambaste the FBI for failing to prosecute anyone in a 1940 Brownsville, Texas, case where one Negro was killed and several others run out of town. On the morning of June 23, 1940, Albert Williams' body was found floating in a river near Brownsville shortly after a group of local Negroes approached election officials to inquire about voting in the 1940 elections. When Marshall investigated, he found a witness the FBI had been unable to locate. Still, no one was brought to justice for the murder. Fed up with inaction by federal investigators, Marshall wrote a strongly-worded report demanding vigorous prosecution of state officials for their failure to act in lynching cases and for denying Negro voting rights. The report was adopted by the National Executive Board of the National Lawyers' Guild.

Marshall's reputation was seemingly born overnight. He appeared to have everything going for him: a sharp legal mind, a persuasive manner, determination, and the ability to smooth-talk his way out of tight jams. But more than anything, it was Marshall's single-mindedness and unwavering commitment to the ideals he embraced that made him truly special. He didn't want special treatment; he just wanted the same rights white men were accorded. "The doctrine of 'separate but equal' was created by the court and can be removed by the court... We are only asking for what the Supreme Court said we are entitled to," Marshall was fond of saying.

In 1944, Marshall convinced the U.S. Supreme Court to strike down the South's "white primary" in Smith v. Allwright, opening the voting rolls to thousands of excluded blacks. The good ole' boy, lily-white conservative Cracker congressman was an institution and until the ruling Negro voters weren't going to unseat him. Case in point: in 1940, less than 1 percent of eligible blacks in Mississippi, Louisiana and Alabama were registered to vote. The Democratic Party, which typically represented the interests of large landowners and their business supporters, was, for all intents and purposes, the *only* political party. Democrats were the ones making the laws and policies that ensured Negroes would remain second-class citizens.

In the summer of 1946 at the NAACP's annual conference, Marshall received the organization's highest award, the Spingarn Medal. But he never lost sight of the fact that he was just another nigger when he stepped off a train or plane in places like Columbia, Tennessee, where Marshall gained acquittal for Lloyd Kennedy and William Pillow, who were accused of shooting a police officer. Following that trial, on Nov. 18, 1946, Marshall, local lawyer Z. Alexander Looby and two associates were stopped by a constable and two deputy sheriffs. Tipped off by a Negro informant that Marshall was transporting liquor through dry Maury County, officers searched his car. According to Thurgood, a few miles later, he was stopped again. This time officers wanted to inspect his operator's license. Fearing further trouble, Marshall asked Looby to drive, since it was his car and Thurgood did not have a Tennessee license. Sure enough, barely 100 yards later, the cops pulled the car over again. This time Marshall was arrested. The charge: driving while intoxicated. "That's when they tried to lynch me," Marshall recalled.

After putting Marshall in the police car, an officer told Looby to get lost. "He said he told Looby to go to Nashville and don't follow them and then they drove toward Duck River. We didn't know until afterwards that's where the mob was waiting," Marshall recalled. After a few minutes, Looby boldly disregarded the order, turned around, and followed the police car to the bank of the river, where a hanging rope dangled from a tree. The rope was around Marshall's neck when the black men who had been riding with him appeared. The lawmen quickly adopted another plan. They weren't prepared to hang four black men. "So eventually they got a little meeting together and they said hell with it, we'll take him back to town," said Marshall, who was hauled before the magistrate and questioned about being drunk behind the wheel. Fortunately, the informant had a change of heart, revealing that the sheriff had put him up to it because he wanted "one last crack" at the NAACP attorney. The magistrate concluded Marshall had not been drinking and ordered him released. Expecting further trouble, Marshall and Looby concocted a plan to outwit the men who had planned the lynching party at the river. Marshall was given a different car, while another black drove Looby's car in the opposite direction. The ruse worked. Perhaps it worked too well. "...sure enough the mob was coming around when we left. So they followed Looby's car which we'd hoped they would do. And incidentally, when they found out I wasn't in it, they beat that driver bad enough that he was in the hospital for a week. That's how bad they beat him," Marshall recalled.

By the summer of '49, Marshall was on a roll. His latest Supreme Court triumph: Shelley v. Kraemer, in which the justices held that restrictive covenants excluding Negroes and other minorities from renting or buying real estate were unenforceable in the courts. No attorney, white or black, was having more success in front of the highest court in the land.

In Lake County, the wheels of justice began grinding on Wednesday, July 20. State Attorney Jesse Hunter spent the morning putting the finishing touches on an indictment charging Samuel Shepherd, Walter Irvin and Charles Greenlee with "criminal assault" against one Norma Padgett. Sheriff Willis McCall felt the charge fell short. He wanted the prosecutor to include kidnapping, theft and inflicting bodily harm. But Hunter held fast, insisting it was best to focus only on the most serious charge: rape. His thinking: keep it simple. Rape carried the death penalty, so why worry about lesser offenses?

After meeting with Hunter and McCall, Judge Truman G. Futch drew the names of 36 men, from which 12 would be selected to consider the indictments that evening. The three most powerful men in Lake County agreed that speedy expedition of the matter was essential to maintaining peace in the county. McCall had promised the leaders of the mob there would be a swift trial, and he was bound and determined to make sure that's exactly what happened. He knew too well that even a semblance of delay could cause the pot of racial hatred to again boil over. Another benefit to a quick trial: nothing would quiet the Northern press and shift the spotlight away from Lake County better than three guilty verdicts.

Hunter and McCall had to be careful now that the NAACP was sniffing around. Well aware that the NAACP had raised holy hell because the juries that convicted the Scottsboro Boys were entirely white, Hunter arranged for Negro truck driver March DeBose to sit on the grand jury in the Groveland case. Anticipating that someone might ask why *only one* Negro was on the panel, Mabel Norris-Reese explained that, "…a proportionate number of Negroes are chosen -- but the trouble has been to get the Negro to serve after they have been summoned…" From Hunter's standpoint, DeBose, a soft-spoken man who knew his place, was the perfect choice, although he was none-too-enthusiastic about being the first of his race called to serve. When McCall learned of DeBose's reluctance to appear, the lawman barked, "He'll come or I'll go get him." Of course, DeBose was present when the hastily-called grand jury met at the courthouse at 5 p.m., Wednesday. The inclusion of a Negro shocked his fellow jurors. Still, DeBose quietly entered Judge Futch's courtroom, and dutifully took his place in the jury box when called.

With the grand jury empanelled, Hunter read the indictment. Norris-Reese, the only reporter present, noted it was nearly 7 p.m. as testimony began. DeBose, seated in the back row, was trying to look inconspicuous, wishing he was somewhere else, anywhere else. The *Topic* reported that the history-making Negro, "was a mild-mannered, short and poorly dressed man. He sat in the top left corner of the jury box, his eyes wide as he glued his attention to the judge." He didn't dare look at the white men beside him.

Norma Padgett and her husband Willie were first to testify. They told of their car stalling and a carload of niggers stopping, then jumping Willie and taking Norma in their car.

The homely, plainly-dressed brunette said all four men assaulted her. Willie testified that after coming to, he repaired the car and got it started, then headed to Leesburg for help. Supposedly, while Willie was headed back to Leesburg, his young bride was being repeatedly raped in a car parked in a grove of moss-laden trees near the Sumter County line.

Sheriff McCall was next. He detailed the arrests of Samuel Shepherd and Walter Irvin, then summarized the considerable physical evidence his deputies found in James Shepherd's car and at the scene of the scuffle. And yes, all three men had confessed to the crime. Deputies Leroy Campbell and James Yates and State Patrolmen Bill Norris and C.S. Carroll provided details of their involvement. Jurors also heard from: Curtis Howard, who said he overheard Norma tell her husband that she had been raped by the niggers; Harry McDonald, the night watchman who had apprehended Charles Greenlee; and Dr. Geoffrey Binnevald, who said his examination of Norma revealed she had *appeared* to have been sexually violated.

Testimony extended well into the evening. Futch recessed the grand jury at 9 p.m., but not so jurors could get a good night's sleep before deliberating. Instead, they were taken to the scene of the crime in west Lake County, more than 30 minutes away, even though it had long been dark. It may have seemed like an imprudent thing to do, but Hunter knew exactly what he was doing. He wanted the jurors to see just how dark and desolate it was where the kidnappers ravaged the helpless young white woman. The barren, tree-lined dead end where the men had supposedly taken Norma was certainly secluded. It looked every bit like a place where four men could rape a woman without fear of discovery.

It was nearly 11 p.m. when the jury reconvened at the courthouse to discuss what they had seen and the testimony they had heard. There was little discussion. Each man agreed that the evidence warranted an indictment. As for DeBose, he didn't have much to say. He wisely kept his mouth shut, choosing not to challenge any "evidence" jurors examined. At 11:55 p.m., Futch accepted the jury's recommendation to indict Shepherd, Irvin and Greenlee for criminal assault. The trial would begin at 10 a.m., Monday, Aug. 29. The judge then pointed out that the fourth suspect was still at large, which meant jurors could be "called back for further investigation at the pleasure of the court," presumably when the last suspect was arrested.

The haste of the indictment wasn't surprising. According to the Thursday, July 21, *Mount Dora Topic*, "The trial, State's Attorney Jesse Hunter indicated, will be held as speedily as possible to bring to a close the mass demonstrations in Groveland." In addition, the *Topic* article claimed that the grand jury would also investigate the mob violence that had driven Negroes from their homes. "There is more to this special session that can be told," Hunter cryptically told Norris-Reese. Inside, a *Topic* editorial, "Honor Will Be Avenged," all but deified McCall and Hunter. "The hasty calling of the special grand jury to start the wheels of justice in Lake County's eye-blackening rape case bespeaks of the calibre of the county's law enforcement officials," Norris-Reese wrote. "It is the belief of many that had irate tempers held back, the law would have apprehended the suspects even more rapidly than they did. As it developed, however, Sheriff Willis McCall earned a badge of honor for the manner in which he prevented more harm than was dealt to property owners in South Lake. Now… justice is going to act speedily. But also, it will act fairly. Sage and trail-trained Jesse Hunter, state's attorney, will see to it that the accused will have an honest and fair hearing before the bar of justice." Norris-Reese also used the editorial to take a few swipes at the Yankee press, criticism spoon-fed by McCall and Hunter, who deeply resented their sanctuary being invaded by outsiders with typewriters. "The action should bring to a definite close the turbulent affairs down at Groveland -- the unhappy target of sorry publicity. It should satisfy concerned questioners in some sections of the country that Lake County is a law-abiding place -- determined to have trial by jury, not mobs."

By Thursday morning, McCall was convinced he wouldn't have any more trouble from night-riders. His Klan friends had promised him as much. He could finally begin searching for the fourth suspect: Ernest Thomas, the man who had left young Charles Greenlee at the railway depot. McCall had information that Thomas left Groveland on a Greyhound bus the previous Saturday morning. Another rumor had Thomas on his way to New Jersey. The sheriff immediately notified the FBI, which issued a warrant for unlawful flight to avoid prosecution. But that was just a precaution. McCall didn't believe Thomas had left the state. Not after bolita dealer Henry Singleton told the sheriff that Thomas had a woman in Gainesville.

In Groveland, the 116th Field Artillery Battalion continued to patrol. Things remained quiet Friday, but there was enough tavern talk about more violence to concern McCall. Outwardly, the sheriff expressed confidence that the tension was easing, but privately, he wasn't about to relax. Those south Lake boys were too unpredictable. It would only take one liquored up good ole' boy to rekindle the fire. And then McCall hit upon a way to kill two birds with one stone: he'd invite some of the rabble-rousers to join the posse he was forming to hunt Thomas. That way, they'd get what they wanted and he wouldn't have to worry about them tearing up Groveland because they'd be right under his nose.

The citizenry, both black and white, were ready for the unrest to end. Days filled with tension, followed by nights of terror and uncertainty had finally been replaced by a quiet, idyllic atmosphere. "Business is going on as usual in Groveland today, but the people don't seem to be satisfied yet," remarked a local official who asked to remain anonymous. Things had quieted considerably, but another weekend was beginning. And there were still isolated incidents -- some ignored by the local press -- that prompted concern. For instance, three unruly youths were arrested in Clermont after one attempted to take a Guardsman's rifle. The boys were turned over to McCall, who released them after questioning. There were also reports from the Bay Lake area that white men bent on retribution were on the move in cars with darkened license plates. As a precautionary measure, the Groveland City Council issued a "no-sale order" on liquor for the weekend. As for moonshine, now that was another matter. Wasn't no way to control that.

South Lake County may have been calm, but the courthouse in Tavares was bustling with scores of reporters assigned to cover the "race conflict" trial. McCall had never dealt with such intense media scrutiny, and soon tired of answering the same questions over and over.

"Do you know who the fourth suspect is? When will you bring him in? Where are the prisoners? Now that things have quieted down, will they be brought back to Tavares? Who will defend them? Have the suspects been in trouble with the law before? Do you fear more rioting?" McCall didn't have time, nor patience, for such nonsense. When a reporter asked if the trial would be moved out of Lake, Hunter roared, "That trial is going to be held here. And if anyone opens his mouth in that courtroom who shouldn't, he will go to jail."

In the rush to keep readers abreast of the latest developments, many newspapers published inaccuracies and/or half-truths about the events of July 16. In one version of the story, Willie was pushing the car when the men attacked. In another, Willie said he was inspecting his engine when he was struck from behind and robbed. In yet another version, the men hit Willie with a club, left him in a ditch, and kidnapped his wife. And it wasn't just local reporters taking liberties in an effort to top the competition. According to UPI, AP and *New York Times* reports, Norma said, "she had been raped by each of the four Negroes as they held a gun in her face," as she pleaded with them not to kill her. "She said she was threatened with death if she did not give them time to get away," the *Leesburg Commercial* reported.

News of Lake County's impending trial was front-page news from the Florida Panhandle to the Everglades. In Jacksonville, Henrietta and James Shepherd needed only to step onto the street to see that racial passion had spread well beyond Groveland. "We went downtown… we went down and picked up a few things to put on. And when we got downtown, ah, my stomach fell in. First of all, the cars was coming through Jacksonville just like a parade. The cars was coming through Jacksonville going to Groveland. Klanspeople. And the paperboy was hollering out, yelling it, hollering out, 'The Ku Klux Klan is going to Groveland, read all about it,'" Henrietta said.

Chapter 9 -- The Hunted

With the homefront still quiet on Saturday, McCall gathered a posse and set out for Gainesville to get Ernest Thomas. Dead or alive. Didn't matter one way or t 'other to McCall and the men who jumped at the opportunity to join the manhunt, most who had been "deputized" when things had heated up in Stuckey Still the week before. McCall didn't have to worry about cooperation from other law enforcement agencies. Every officer in Florida was aware of the Groveland rape case and anxious to assist.

At the Gainesville Police Department, a lieutenant confirmed he knew the girl McCall asked about; in fact he had seen Thomas hanging around her home a few times. McCall and his men immediately went to the woman's house. With any luck at all, they would have Thomas in custody within the hour. "We proceeded to her house and questioned her about Thomas, when she last saw him, etc. She replied that she had not seen him for a week or 10 days. It was obvious she was lying," McCall remembered.

McCall, certain the woman would contact Thomas to warn him that the law was hot on his trail, decided to keep his eye on her. But, patience was never his long suit. When local officers decided to canvass the Negro quarters to locate anyone who knew Thomas or his kin, McCall returned to the woman's house. He was in no mood to play games. This time she'd tell what she knew or wish that she had. The woman wasn't home, but the mailman had been there. Inside the mailbox, McCall discovered a letter addressed to the girl. "It happened it was not sealed very well and came open with very little effort," the sheriff said with a sly smile. "It was a letter from Ernest Thomas telling her where he would be until things cooled off. He stated that he would be using an assumed name of Willy Green and gave her an RFD and box number at Shady Grove."

McCall and his men would have plenty of help when they traveled to Shady Grove on Sunday morning. You'd think John Dillinger was on the loose. In addition to Madison County Sheriff Simmie Moore, there was Sheriff Bill Towles from Perry, Mayo Sheriff Sue Pridgeon and a patrolman, Sheriff Wilson from Perry, Patrolman Carlan from Perry, sheriffs from Lafayette and Taylor counties, and a few Florida Highway patrolmen. Approximately 15 officers would accompany McCall.

Early Sunday morning, sheriffs Pridgeon and Towles located a Negro woman who knew Thomas' aunt and agreed to take the lawmen to her home near a colored section called Moseley Hall. After parking three-quarters of a mile away, Moore, Towles and Pridgeon surrounded the shack, and then charged in. But Thomas wasn't there. "We didn't find the Negro there, but after seeing this Negro woman there I knew that she had some more kin-people further down the road... I knew she was kin to Retha Jones. She lived down the road about two miles farther. We decided to go down there and ask them about the Negro, and we drove up and he was not there. However a Negro there, John Wright I believe is his name, I asked John -- I told him that Ernest Thomas was down there Friday and I wanted to know where he was going," Moore said. Wright was too scared to lie to the law. "He said, 'Mr. Simmie, he was here Thursday. I talked to him. I don't know where he was going, but he talked to Henry Huston out in the tobacco patch Thursday afternoon.'" The trail was finally growing warmer. Huston was home, but feigned ignorance when asked if he had talked with Thomas. "At first Huston said he didn't know about him, and hadn't seen him, and didn't know him or anything about him. But I told him that John Wright had told me he was there talking with him Thursday afternoon, and he told me he wanted to talk to me privately. I went out in the back to talk with him and he told me to hurry up to this house about a hundred yards from there; that the Negro was there then and he had been staying there," Moore recalled.

Moore reported back to McCall, who decided the lawmen should surround the house and make their move when Thomas was asleep. "Around three o'clock in the morning, we moved in. There were three tenant houses on this farm and as it was night and we had not cased the place as well as we would have liked, we went to the place where the mailbox was located," McCall said. The house was occupied, but no one admitted knowing Thomas. A quick search proved they were lying. "We found his clothing; his trousers with his money in it, and no shoes," Moore said. The posse couldn't know just how close Thomas was. "It so happened that Thomas was in the next house and heard us and gave us the slip through a back window and hit the woods," McCall said. Moore immediately placed a call to the state road camp at Perry. It was time to bring in the bloodhounds. Even though it was now nearly 3:30 a.m., the prison camp supervisor promised to rouse his dog man and send him over. An hour passed before a truck carrying a bloodhound and the dog's handler, prisoner W.B. Andrews, arrived from the prison. The dog immediately picked up Thomas' scent.

As the sun came up, two things were clear: Thomas obviously knew the backwoods of Madison County, and additional bloodhounds were needed. The dog was all but worn out after hours of following Thomas' scent through heavy woods. Moore contacted the road camp at Perry and another at Live Oak to request additional dogs, and then paid a visit to Wash Johnson to ask the local man to saddle his horse and join the search. Moore also invited another civilian, Henry Cruce, to get his mule and join the posse. Both men were told to bring guns since the prisoner was armed. By now, Towles was also on horseback.

As morning turned to afternoon, then afternoon to evening, the elusive suspect was still at large even though armed men had been arriving throughout the day. McCall had seriously underestimated Thomas. By late evening, Moore estimated "at least a thousand men" were combing the woods. It was just a matter of time before the kidnapper/rapist was captured. By now, seven bloodhounds were scouring the area, following Thomas' scent through a cotton patch, hog pen, swamp and woods. Thomas was proving to be elusive, resourceful and indefatigable. Members of the posse resigned themselves to tracking the fugitive through the night.

When the sun rose on Tuesday, July 26 many of the weary locals quit and returned home to families and jobs. No one had anticipated one man would be so hard to catch. McCall didn't mind seeing them go. Hell, they had practically been tripping over each other. It's a wonder somebody didn't accidentally get shot. Thomas couldn't run forever; he had to be exhausted. The dogs had covered approximately 25 miles of south Madison County since being put on his trail early Monday morning. Thomas couldn't be far away. McCall expected to get his man any moment now.

Just before 11 a.m., Andrews' dog came across the wanted man sitting under a tree near a swamp. "I figure the boy was half asleep or maybe asleep... when this dog seen him he tried to make a dash for this Negro, and in the meantime this Negro tried to get up or was getting up with his left hand, and he got up, I believe, on one knee trying to get up, and in the meantime he reached in his pants or his shirt and come out with an object I taken to be a gun. I think he got up with the intention of shooting, from what I could see. He had his gun in his right hand," Andrews said. Fellow prisoners Leonard Morin and D. H. Milligan and their dogs were close behind. "When we caught up on him he was kind of laying down and he raised up and the man said, 'Don't move, stay where you are.' And he kind of raised up and drew his right hand from his belt and I saw an object in his hand," Morin recalled. Startled, Thomas shouted, "'Don't shoot, white man, don't shoot,' and he grabbed for his gun," Morin said. But Thomas never had time to squeeze off a shot, his pursuers peppered his body with bullets as he raised his gun. It didn't take long for the rest of the posse to arrive. More than a hundred men had been resting, eating and talking on a dirt road about 100 yards away. More shots were fired even though Thomas had already taken his final breath. He was 23.

Sheriff Moore instructed two locals to stand guard over the bullet-riddled body, which Moore covered with newspaper and a cloth because, "it was a little bloody." Thomas had been shot at least four times in the head alone: once in the back of the head, twice in the right temple and at least once in the forehead. There were also numerous bullet holes in his body. Thomas came to rest face down, his right hand clutching a .32 Harrington and Richardson revolver with four cartridges in it. In Thomas' pockets, lawmen found a three-blade knife, a pack of Camel cigarettes and a handkerchief. On his hand, a gold ring with the initials "E.T." inside.

Reporters arrived on the scene before McCall and his men made their way out of the woods about five miles east of Shady Grove and 10 miles south of Greenville. McCall was more than happy to reveal how Thomas had met his end. "About midmorning on the third day the posse caught up with him. We had enough men by then. We were working in relays, giving us a break now and then. However, Thomas had no relief," McCall explained. "We had all avenues of escape blocked. When he tried to cross a road, finding it was guarded, he would turn back. Thomas was tired and sat down and leaned up against a tree and dosed off to sleep. The swamp was very dense at this point." McCall was emphatic that Thomas had only been fired upon because he drew his gun on the law officers. According to McCall, Thomas was, "belligerent as the devil. He had a loaded pistol in his hand and he had his finger around the trigger."

Conflicting stories soon began circulating. One story quoted Towles as saying Thomas was shot as he fled. Amazingly, all three sheriffs claimed they weren't present when the fugitive was shot. While some questioned how Thomas met his end, others wondered if the posse even got the right man. McCall assured his critics that they had, while Towles pointed out that the body had been identified by Thomas' wife Ruby Lee. But McCall needed a different identification.

Arrangements were made for Norma Padgett to identify the deceased. And she did. Beggs Funeral Home employee A.A. Truelove was present when McCall and prosecutor Jesse Hunter ushered Norma and her husband Willie into a back room. On the table lay the bullet-riddled body of a 5-foot-3, 135-pound Negro male with a "Ginger cake" complexion. The body was clothed in tan slippers, dungarees and white flannel shirt. According to Truelove, Norma said, "He is the one. I would know that face anywhere I saw him. He is the one that had the gun and the one that drove the car." Hunter wanted Norma to take another, longer, look. "I want you to look at him good. Are you positive that that is the man?" Hunter asked. This time she did more than glance. "I am," Norma said. And what about Willie Padgett? According to Truelove, "He never said a word."

By the time Norma confirmed that Thomas was one of the men who had ravaged her, concerned Negroes were asking why Thomas had been killed instead of apprehended. Sheriff Moore, responding to cries of protest from the NAACP, refused to be intimidated. "I am not trying to hide anything, but the case is being completely investigated by a coroner's jury," he professed. When pressed for details, the sheriff told reporters he believed Thomas was killed by, "four or five shots," but refused to elaborate.

The nation wouldn't have long to wait to find out the particulars. The coroner's jury convened before Madison County Judge Curtis D. Earp on July 26. Surprisingly, even though McCall and more than a dozen officers participated in the hunt, Simmie Moore was the only lawman called to testify. But his testimony was significant. Moore said that McCall was one of two sheriffs (along with Taylor County's Bill Towles) in the immediate vicinity when Thomas was killed, which seemed to contradict McCall's claim that he wasn't present. Moore also testified that "Sheriff McCall's deputy" was also present. Unfortunately, Moore couldn't shed light on who fired the fatal bullet(s) because *he* wasn't on the scene. So who pulled the trigger? No one seemed to know. McCall wasn't certain, but told reporters, "it was a good bunch of fellows." Even the men who admitted seeing Thomas before he was killed had amnesia when it came to naming who did the shooting. Andrews came closest to solving the mystery when he testified that Cruce, Morin, Johnson and "a boy from Camp 7" were with him when shots were fired, but he stopped short of saying which man, if any, killed Thomas. Morin confirmed he was present, but didn't actually say who had fired their weapons. As for Milligan, he claimed he didn't know who did the shooting. Johnson didn't admit to killing Thomas, either. When asked if he was present when Thomas was killed, Johnson replied, "I was nearby." Cruce was even more evasive. He claimed to be "30 or 40 feet" away when the shots were fired, and when asked who else was present, Cruce said, "I don't know that I know." The so-called "witnesses" had clearly agreed to "dummy up."

The judge and jurors were noticeably unconcerned about *who* killed Thomas. Witnesses were only asked if they knew who fired the fatal bullets -- none were asked if they had done the shooting. The testimony seemed to indicate that the local men, Johnson and Cruce, had fired the fatal bullet(s), but to accept that conclusion is to believe that the men would have done so when several law officers were no more than 100 yards away. The men handling the dogs certainly hadn't done the shooting, since prisoners wouldn't have been carrying weapons. The most plausible explanation is that the bloodhounds led the posse to Thomas, the other searchers were then called to the area and then several men -- perhaps dozens -- opened fire.

After a short hearing, the jury found that, "the said Ernest R. Thomas was then and there attempting to shoot and murder public officers... Thomas, was lawfully killed." But no one outside Earp's court would learn how the jury reached its verdict: the group refused to release a transcript of testimony. The silence only led to further speculation. Rumors abounded that Thomas had been massacred, a claim bolstered when the *Baltimore Afro-American* printed a disturbing, albeit unsubstantiated, claim that "nearly 400 slugs were found in the dead man's body."

On Wednesday, the day after Thomas was killed, Futch told reporters that the trial would begin as soon as McCall returned from Madison County and lined up witnesses. Only then would he appoint an attorney to defend the Groveland Three. Groveland and the surrounding area had been quiet for days. That morning, as National Guard units pulled out, white locals quietly, but forcefully passed the word to a dozen of the most successful Negro farmers: "leave everything and get out now and stay out." As soon as the Guardsmen left, six Florida Highway Patrol cars returned to the area as a precaution, concentrating primarily on a 12-mile stretch of State Road 50 from Clermont west through Groveland to Stuckey Still.

With peace apparently restored, reporters moved in to question locals about the week of unrest. The few citizens who spoke to the press were quick to blame the violence on outsiders. One "prominent farmer" said he personally knew of two carloads of angry whites from Alabama, another from Georgia and, "at least 10 from Orange and Polk counties" that had come to Lake County to terrorize its Negroes. "The people of Groveland don't believe in mob violence. We have had good relations with Negroes. Except for one incident all of the terrorism has taken place outside of Groveland." The farmer speculated that 30-35 Negroes who fled would never return. Another grower worried that further unrest would completely deplete the workforce. "If there is any more shooting or house burning the entire Negro population may move away -- and never come back." That sentiment, more than any other, explained why a strained peace had returned to the area. McCall didn't restore order. Neither did the National Guard. The reality: fear of permanently losing their labor pool prompted white citrus men to prevail upon the vigilantes. The Crackers needed the coloreds to pick, wash and pack their fruit.

White grove owners had been depending on black labor since Groveland was established in 1910. During the citrus boom of the early 1900s, white bosses wrestled with a dilemma. They needed more and more Negro workers, but they didn't want Negroes as neighbors. Blacks were encouraged to live in Groveland and Stuckey Still, but weren't allowed to make their homes in Mascotte. The arrangement worked just fine for the white citrus men, who were the only ones getting ahead. Workers had to pay for their picking equipment, in addition to room and board. Wages of 15 to 17 cents an hour didn't go far. In most camps the average worker was fortunate to bring home $40 a week. The white grove owners couldn't find cheaper labor. They literally couldn't afford further rioting.

On July 28, Harry T. Moore wrote a letter asking Hunter to investigate the mob violence against Groveland citizens, pointing out that it should be easy to identify the culprits who burned down three homes since McCall had admitted to knowing many of the men. "Not only did these Negroes suffer serious property damages. Their very lives were jeopardized by the fury of the mob... Surely those responsible for this disturbance should be punished to the fullest extent of the law. We therefore ask that a special grand jury be called to investigate this unfortunate affair and to indict the guilty parties. Inasmuch as Sheriff McCall talked with members of the mob on at least two occasions, it should be easy to identify them. In fact, when Sheriff McCall talked with the mob at the jail, he said he 'knew them all.' We note also that you and the Sheriff held a conference with the leaders of the mob at Mascotte. Undoubtedly, members of the mob can be charged with arson. We also wonder if they cannot be charged with carrying weapons without permits, as Sheriff McCall said that many of those who visited the jail were armed."

Moore also detailed his concerns to Gov. Fuller Warren in a July 30 letter. After commending the governor for sending the National Guard into the troubled area, and McCall for removing the prisoners to another jail before the mob arrived, Moore launched a stinging criticism of McCall's "lenient attitude toward the mob." Moore wrote, "Was it necessary for him to invite members of the mob to search the jail to satisfy them that the accused Negroes were not there? These men were not deputies. So what right did they have to search a jail? Sheriff McCall also said that many of the men were armed. Did any of them have permits to carry weapons? If not, will charges be brought against them for this violation of the law? We feel that local officers made a serious mistake when they tried to 'compromise' with the mob. This conciliatory attitude no doubt was a direct cause of the subsequent outbreaks that resulted in the complete loss of three homes owned by innocent Negroes. Instead of trying to 'persuade' the mob to disband, officers should have disarmed them and put their leaders in jail as a precautionary measure. Mob violence cannot be curbed by compromise. Mobsters must be made to realize that the law is supreme in our democratic society."

For more than a week the local and state press had served as a mouthpiece for McCall, printing his version of events as the gospel truth, and doing little, if any, investigating to verify the lawman's claims. But the tone of news coming out of Lake County was about to change. So was the shade of those doing the reporting. Ted Poston, the lone Negro reporter at a major white metropolitan paper, had talked his editors at the *New York Post* into sending him to Groveland.

At the NAACP Legal Defense Fund offices in New York, attorney Franklin H. Williams rejoiced at the prospect of Lake County being overrun with Northern reporters. He figured that the more press Groveland received, the safer he would be when he returned to Florida. Perhaps now the racist Crackers would think twice before taking him for a ride or arranging a mysterious accident. The presence of a *New York Post* reporter was practically an insurance policy. He was especially pleased because Poston was an old friend who had championed NAACP causes in the past. Their friendship began when Poston worked as a columnist at the Negro paper the *Pittsburgh Courier* in the 1930s. Six years later, Poston became the first African-American to work as a reporter at a major white newspaper when he convinced *Post* city editor Walter Lister to give him a chance. Poston got his foot in the door when Lister agreed to pay him 30 cents an inch if he could produce a front-page exclusive. Poston immediately delivered a story about a process server who had been accosted by a group of whites after giving a summons on self-proclaimed "Negro messiah" Father Divine. Beginner's luck? Not hardly. He then broke the story of Gov. Thomas E. Dewey raiding the Harlem numbers game. And the exclusives kept coming. Poston was soon making so much money as a stringer that Lister realized it would be cheaper for the paper to hire him as a full-time reporter. So he did. Before long, rewrites of Poston exclusives were regularly appearing in most major Negro weeklies.

By the time the Groveland story broke, Poston was 43 years old and had established a reputation as a man of principle that refused to back down in the face of injustice. Few, if any, reporters assigned to cover Groveland were as qualified. And there was another, unpublicized, reason why Poston was uniquely qualified to report on the Groveland controversy. While most white reporters unquestioningly bought the story that Norma Padgett had been kidnapped and raped by four Negroes, Poston knew the reality may have been far different. Poston had no trouble believing the rumor that Samuel Shepherd had been having consensual sex with his accuser. It was a scenario he had lived. According to one of Poston's longtime friends, a teenage Ted had regularly been coerced into bed by a "grown young lady" at the home where he worked tending fireplaces. When Poston finally told the lady he was going to quit his job she threatened to tell a doctor that he had raped her. He continued to comply when she demanded sex.

Poston would also be without peer in covering a racially-charged trial, which promised to be full of the kind of courtroom shenanigans he had witnessed while covering the most notorious race case to date. Poston's courage, imagination and resourcefulness had been tested to the limit when the *Amsterdam News* sent him to Decatur, Alabama, to cover the retrial of the Scottsboro Boys. Poston attended the trial, not as a newspaper reporter, but as a spectator who would, "sit up there in the Negro gallery in ragged overalls pretending to be a country boy, looking, and I would make notes under the overcoat on my lap." During breaks, Poston would go to the colored restroom, where he would put his news copy on top of the partition separating the colored and white facilities. Tom Cassidy of the *New York Daily News* would then take Poston's copy and wire it with his story. At other times, Poston would sneak to the railroad depot at night and put his stories in the mail car of the midnight special bound for New York. Once, a group of whites caught him at the train and accused him of being a reporter, but Poston avoided trouble, perhaps saving his life, by presenting identification that showed he was the Rev. A. Parke Williams of the African Methodist Episcopal Church.

Poston brought impressive credentials to his latest assignment, even though he was just another darkie to Willis McCall. The sheriff knew nothing of Poston's background, and wouldn't have been impressed if he did. Although far from imposing, Poston he projected an air of determination and boldness that served him well. Poston rubbed some people the wrong way. When asked by a southern sheriff whether he worked for a "white paper or one of them nigger papers," Poston replied, "I understand that here in the south if you got one drop of Negro blood then you're a Negro. Well, I'm one drop of Negro blood on the *Post*, so I guess it's a Negro paper." Poston was not easily ignored.

The *Post* wasn't the only big-city publication willing to put a reporter in the midst of Lake County's racial maelstrom. In Miami, *Chicago Defender* correspondent Ramona Lowe was preparing to spend a few days in the Negro quarters of Groveland. Lowe didn't have Poston's experience, but she did have a distinct advantage over the *Post* reporter, and other writers who would follow him to Florida. Lowe had lived in the Sunshine State for years, which gave her contacts from Tallahassee to Miami. Another advantage: she had less homework to do since she was already combing the large Florida daily newspapers for leads she could turn into stories for The Associated Negro Press (ANP), which provided news releases to Negro newspapers. Lowe had been filing stories for the ANP since the mid-1930s, but her primary source of income came from working clerical jobs. A versatile reporter who could produce investigative pieces as well as features, Lowe was willing and able to travel at a moment's notice to obtain a story. She had been stringing for the *Chicago Defender* since January, when the paper offered her a "temporary part-time job" covering the state.

Thanks to Lowe, the *Chicago Defender* on Saturday, July 30 became the first newspaper to put Groveland under the magnifying glass. An editorial headlined, "A Reign Of Terror," detailed the exodus of hundreds of Negroes threatened by angry whites: "The mad whites could not wait on the law. Hundreds of innocent Negroes have been made to suffer for a crime that no Negro may have committed. Here is the threat to our democracy that the Federal government cannot ignore. This reign of terror uncovers the cesspool where democratic ideals are being buried."

Lowe and Poston were the first out-of-state reporters to converge on Groveland, but they wouldn't be the last. Editors at the *Christian Science Monitor, The New Leader, Time* and *Life* were also preparing to send representatives to Lake County, Florida. Much to McCall's dismay, Groveland had become a national story. While the sheriff tried to keep an eye on the newly-arrived colored reporters Poston and Lowe, he didn't feel at all threatened by the arrival of *Life* magazine photographer Wallace W. Kirkland, who asked for a tour of the significant sites of the "Groveland Story." McCall arranged a sightseeing venture like no other, and Norris-Reese spared no hyperbole in describing it. At Stuckey Still, "the Negroes' own little community they had built up from their gains in laboring for the white man," she wrote, "There, we saw the half-finished house of one of them, going up on a lot he had bought from his savings. When wildness broke out that night, the Negro laid down his hammer and saw, and fled... leaving his dreams behind him." Norris-Reese also attempted to capture the fear that lingered in the Negro quarters. She quoted a storekeeper as saying, "We'uns don't know what to do.... Yes, suh, the majority of thems pulling out and leavin'. They's scared." A school teacher told Hunter, "I've just signed my contract, but now I don't think I should stay."

The group also stopped at Burtoft's café. McCall must have felt comfortable with Kirkland and Norris-Reese, since he hadn't taken any other reporters to the Okahumpka restaurant, let alone directed anyone to the boy who "found" Norma Padgett a few hours after she had been raped by the savages. Inside, Burtoft related his encounter with the young woman he saw standing against a road sign at 6:30 a.m. Burtoft was quoted as saying, "Yes, she was sort of sobbin'. Her eyes were all red... I guess she's 'bout cried herself out... And she asked me if someone could carry her to find her husband... she said she was afraid he was lying dead down the road..." It was here that Norris-Reese strayed from the "narrative" and engaged in a display of her trademark editorializing. She wrote that Norma's assailants "committed the act that will surely send them to the electric chair as quickly as would have their discarded plan to kill the frail, fear-ridden blonde who submitted to them... Of course, we cannot -- not *Life* magazine -- picture the tortuous horror that girl suffered after the Negroes threw her out of the car and threatened to come back and shoot her if she didn't wait until the third car passed on the highway before she tried to get help... of her crouching in the road, sorely abused, and of her four-mile walk back to the café... dodging into the weeds like a hunted rabbit when she heard a car -- a car that might be the Negroes coming back... Of her inability to tell young Lawrence of being raped as they went to the spot where it had started... and found nothing there..."

Kirkland left town a happy man. Not only had he gained access to Lake County's powerbrokers, he had captured all the images he came to Florida for. He had even met Norma Padgett, her husband and father. But his favorite part of his guided tour may have been the burned-out home of a bolita dealer where McCall posed with a long-barreled gun and blackened slot machines he found in the rubble.

Chapter 10 -- Raiford

At the NAACP offices in New York, Franklin H. Williams was sifting through newspaper clippings about the violence that had sullied the reputation of Groveland, Florida. Williams' gut feeling: "Groveland" was a case the Legal Defense Fund staff should accept. Of course, a decision couldn't be made until someone traveled to Florida to interview the prisoners. Unfortunately, no one seemed to know where Samuel Shepherd, Walter Irvin and Charles Greenlee were being held. Associated Press reports out of Florida said only that the suspects were being held at an "undisclosed location."

With Thurgood Marshall out of town, it fell upon NAACP Secretary Walter White to decide whether Williams should go to Florida to investigate. White was agreeable, but he wasn't about to dispatch one of the NAACP's best young lawyers into such a dangerous situation on scant information. White told Williams to find a Florida attorney to locate the prisoners and interview them. Williams chose one of the senior Negro attorneys in the state, L.C. Thomas, of Miami.

As Williams waited to hear back from Thomas, he realized he had heard of Lake County before. For a while, he couldn't make the connection. Then finally, it came to him. "Long before the Groveland case broke, we had received a complaint from St. Louis or Texas or both places in the National Office from Negro workers who had to flee Lake County who had been working in the orange groves as pickers and who had not reported as consistently or worked as many hours and as many days as this particular grove owner wanted them to work... And we had heard therefore, of the fact that down in Lake County there had been this pattern of beating and abusing and the rumors were even killing blacks who had worked in orange groves and who did not work the way the local sheriff and the grove owners thought they should. So, we had heard of Willis McCall. He was supposed to be the sheriff that did this."

A day passed without Thomas learning where the prisoners were being held. White was unwilling to wait any longer. He knew all too well the seriousness of the case, after all, he had personally investigated 41 lynchings and 12 race riots since *he* joined the NAACP. White decided to send Williams to Florida. But first, calls were made to the press. "One of the things that gave me great comfort was in the NAACP, when you went off on a case like the Columbia, Tennessee, case or something like that, you got a lot of publicity in the Negro press. The theory was, if the world knew you were there, you were safe. So, we would send out press releases in New York, 'and the NAACP Special Counsel, Franklin Williams is leaving Thursday morning, 8 o'clock plane for, expected in Orlando around 11:00.' You know, that kind of thing. So, the theory was, if the public knew and the people knew that everyone knew you were there, you were safe," Williams said. At least, that's the way it was *supposed* to work.

Florida NAACP Secretary Harry T. Moore had also heard of Sheriff Willis McCall. That's why he wasn't waiting on the national office to act. Moore enlisted the help of a young Negro lawyer in Tampa, William A. Fordham, who had graduated from law school just three months earlier. Moore was pretty sure the Groveland Three were being held in the state prison in Raiford, and Fordham agreed to make the three-hour drive to obtain their statements. Moore was pleased. Fordham may have been inexperienced, but the price was right. The young lawyer wasn't worried about money. That would come if he agreed to represent the Groveland boys.

On Friday morning, July 29, Williams flew into Orlando. It wasn't his first visit to the South, nor his first rape case, but he was still nervous about being in the land of Jim Crow. He was met at the Orlando airport by J.F. Ellis, a young Negro doctor who was president of the local NAACP branch. The first order of business: finding the prisoners. "We did not know where the boys were. We could not find them. There were rumors that Ernest Thomas had been killed and that came out. All of this is bam, bam, bam, bam, bam, you know. You get on the plane, you come down and things are happening and you are calling back," Williams recalled. Time was of the essence. The Groveland boys had already been behind bars for a week-and-a-half, and the trial was less than two weeks away.

But first Williams needed to find lodging. He soon realized that in Lake County, no hotel would have him, no restaurant would serve him, and many blacks were afraid to take him in, even for a night. "Tavares we could not stay. It was very clear. Negroes there told us not to stay after dark. And we would not," said Williams, who ended up lodging with a Negro family in Orlando who opened their home to visiting Negro entertainers and athletes. "There were no hotels you could stay in. No decent hotels. You could not stay in any white hotel. We ate in restaurants in the Main Street in the black area," Williams said. A bed secured, Williams began searching for an attorney who could help him track down leads and interview potential witnesses. The task would be more difficult than his search for a place to sleep. There were no Negro attorneys in Lake County, and none in adjacent Marion, Sumter and Orange counties. There were probably fewer than 20 Negro lawyers in the entire state. Enlisting the help of a white attorney wasn't even considered since Williams didn't have much money to offer, even if by some miracle he could persuade a white lawyer to defend three colored boys accused of raping a white woman.

The nearest Negro attorney was Horace E. Hill, who was born and raised in Clearwater, had graduated from Bethune-Cookman College and served in the Army before joining the Florida bar in 1948. Hill was just starting out, but Williams was willing to consider the young Daytona Beach lawyer who had set up practice next door to his alma mater, where he taught business courses. Williams met the 24-year-old attorney at an NAACP meeting in Sanford where Hill spoke out against lawless whites who had displaced Groveland's Negro community. Williams was impressed enough to ask Hill to help. Hill was flattered, but hesitant to get involved. Talking about the case was one thing, jumping into the middle of it was quite another. He had read about the rioting in south Lake County, as well as the stories about Thomas being hunted and killed by an angry mob that called itself a posse. "I was kind of intimidated because of what had happened. You have a sheriff that has men out trying to track down a person they considered a criminal and escaping justice. It's not a comforting scene to be involved in or atmosphere, or condition. I didn't relish it at all," Hill recalled. In the end, the young lawyer was no match for the persuasive Williams, who wouldn't take "no" for an answer. When Williams learned that the prisoners had been transferred to Raiford for safekeeping, he asked Hill to drive him there. With some trepidation, Hill agreed. "My aunt wanted to know if I had lost my mind," Hill said. "…I even called my parents, and they wanted to know whether or not I was crazy, and they said how dangerous it was."

Interviewing the prisoners was Williams' top priority, but he also desperately wanted to visit Groveland to see what people were saying. Unfortunately, Williams wouldn't have time to visit Groveland since he was expected back in New York before the end of the week. Not that he needed to visit Lake County to get a snapshot of the racial climate: Negroes in Orlando provided a pretty clear picture of race relations in the adjacent county. "Blacks were very humble and subservient and obsequious and that was the only way they could survive. They owned land that they had worked hard, like Henry Shepherd, to clear, but it was subject to abuses of white neighbors any time they want to abuse it, such as letting their cattle roam on it. They had nobody to turn to to complain," Williams said. Besides, Groveland Negroes were afraid to talk. They feared retribution from McCall. In Tavares, some blacks begged Williams to leave town. They not only feared for Williams' safety, they feared for anyone who might be seen talking with him.

"There are all kinds of stories that I got about Willis McCall when I first went in there to the effect that he had actually murdered people. Murdered Blacks," Williams said. "One woman whose husband had been a bolita dealer and he had died. She allegedly had collected some insurance. He went to her and demanded the insurance claiming that he had owed him some money, the husband had owed him some money and she would not turn it over, arrested her and a few days later she was found outside of the Tavares County Courthouse, where the jail is up on the top floor, had fallen out of the window. And they got stories like that all the time about McCall."

In New York, Marshall denounced the "official" version of what happened to Thomas in the woods of Madison County as fiction and wired his feelings to U.S. Attorney General Tom Clark and Florida Gov. Fuller Warren. "This wanton killing by a deputized mob is worse than a lynching," Marshall charged. Marshall feared for Shepherd, Irvin and Greenlee. He could only hope that McCall wouldn't be bold enough to turn them loose and shoot them down, saying they had tried to escape.

McCall steadfastly supported the ruling of the coroner's jury. He also told reporters that a Negro attorney from Tampa, William A. Fordham had been retained by the NAACP to represent the accused. With all four suspects accounted for, the bombastic lawman had turned his attention to ensuring convictions for the three men in Raiford. After conferring with Hunter, McCall quietly arrested Thomas' parents Luther and Ethel and transported them to Tavares where he could keep an eye on them. They would spend the days leading up to the trial behind bars. McCall needed to make sure that their testimony about their late son supported state charges that he had participated in the crimes against the Padgetts.

Unbeknownst to Williams, Fordham set out to interview the accused on July 29. During the long drive he wondered if he would be able to tell if the men were telling the truth. His doubts vanished as soon as he reached the cell, and saw the deplorable condition of the men who had been arrested 13 days earlier. As Fordham met with each, he was shocked to find them still badly bruised, swollen, tender, scarred and showing discoloration, even though the beatings had occurred two weeks prior. He was amazed they hadn't perished at the hands of the sadistic lawmen. The prisoners, who hadn't seen members of their families since being arrested, were glad to see a friendly face, even though it belonged to a stranger. None of the men had heard of the NAACP, but they took heart in Fordham's assurances that the organization would help them. They literally had no one else to turn to. The last two weeks had been a nightmare filled with fear, doubt and pain. They had to trust this NAACP and the quiet young man who came to see them. Of course, Fordham couldn't promise legal representation, but before leaving he pledged that he would report their beatings and claims of innocence to the national office.

Late Friday, Williams learned that the prisoners were being held at the state prison, and that an attorney named Fordham had already visited them at the bequest of Moore. Williams was relieved that the Groveland Three had been located and interviewed, but was dismayed to learn Fordham hadn't obtained sworn statements. No matter, Williams needed to hear their stories for himself. After considering Fordham's grim report, Williams asked the young attorney to return with him to Raiford on July 31 to obtain affidavits. Williams also asked Hill and his wife, Dorothy who would serve as stenographer, to accompany them.

During the 110-mile drive, Fordham tried to prepare his associates for the ghastly condition of the men, but Williams and the Hills were still shocked by the appearance of the prisoners. "Mr. Williams said they smelt like hogs. He said the blood on their shirts in back was stuck to them, dry... So he said they just smelled like hogs. Said when you walk around the corner. And they had them away from other prisoners. He said when he got close to their cell they smelled like bloody hogs, they was beat up so bad," Walter's sister, Henrietta recalled.

"The thing that stands out in my mind is the fact that they had scabs you could feel as you would run your hands through their hair. That was indicative to me that they had been beaten, mistreated," Hill said. "One of the men, Greenlee, said that he had been put with handcuffs to a pipe that ran through the basement of the jail and that they had put glass under his feet. When they would hit him and they reacted, they moved their feet across this glass and it would cut the soles of their foot. It was a very moving experience. For that kind of mistreatment to have existed, if what he was telling me was the truth, and I had every reason to believe it was." Williams, who had many times seen the scars of white-on-black hatred, was also shocked: "Their heads were a mess. Their hair was a mess. It was shocking to me that in a state prison, they had not even been able to wash their hair. Because the blood, encrusted, dry blood was still in their hair."

One by one, the men told the lawyers their heart-rending stories. Irvin, still wearing pants caked with blood, told of being picked up by Shepherd around 9 p.m., driving to Orlando, talking to some girls, and drinking beer before returning home. The next morning, he was getting dressed for work when, "three or four carloads of policemans" pulled up in front of the Irvin home. Walter then recounted a tale of shocking brutality that occurred immediately following his arrest. "They drove out in the woods with me and Sammie, all the cars came along. We were both in the same car... They drove out and parked along the woods on a clay road, told us to 'get out of the car boy.' I didn't see who grabbed Sammie, but one short guy in plain clothes who had a pistol belt grabbed me and hit me with his billy a lot of times across the head. He held me, and a lot of the others started to hitting me with billies and fist, and knocking me down and kicking me and picking me up and knocking me down again. This went on for about 20 minutes. When they were beating me, they said to me: 'Nigger, you the one that picked up this white girl last night.' I said to them what white girl? They said, 'Well you might as well tell us, you're the one did it 'cause we gonna beat the hell out of you until you tell us you did do it.' I still told them I was not the one. As far as I remember I always told them I was not the one. When they beat me up they pushed me into the car like that (gesture). I was bleeding pretty bad mostly from my head. They had me handcuffed all this time and made (me) sit up on the edge of the seat of the car to keep from getting blood on the seat." But the torture wasn't over. Irvin and Shepherd were then taken to the county jail and put in a large cell with other prisoners.

"They let us stay in the cell a while and then they came back and taken us down in the hole of a jail. They taken me down first. Three went down with me. There wasn't anyone else down there. They handcuffed me, over a pipe, so that my feet could not touch the floor, then they started beating me again with a rubber hose. I was bleeding all the time around my head. They kept saying that I was the one that picked the girl up last night and said they would beat me until I told them I was the one. I don't (know) how long this went on, but in my estimation it was more than five minutes. I don't remember very well because

I was very dizzy. They hit me in my nose with their fist and beat me across my back and chest and they beat me all over, but I had my pants on." Walter was then returned to his cell, but he didn't stay there long. "They taken me back down in the hole the second time and beat me again. I was bleeding pretty bad. One of then (sic) kicked me in my balls and after the second time, I don't know what time it was, they taken me and put me into the car and they put Sammic in there too, then they taken us out into the woods again. They didn't beat us that time. They handcuffed us around a tree, I'm on one side, Sammie on the other side. They told us they were getting us away from there -- we were lucky that we didn't get killed cause they said a mob were after us." After a short time, a call came over the radio and the prisoners were uncuffed and put back into the car, where they were told to lie down. "They taken us out. We stopped by a sheriff's house -- somebody said he was a sheriff. I think the next town after this stop was Eustis or some place. This guy came out of the house and he said, "Where are those niggers at?' He had a big flashlight. We were lying down in the car and he hit Sammie with his flashlight and stomped him with his foot. Then he came around on the other side of the car and beat me across my arms and legs. The next time I remember I was here."

After Irvin signed his statement, Williams noted Walter's injuries: numerous healing scars -- one in particular about an inch long -- on his head; wide bruises on his chest and stomach; "lash marks" on his shoulders; "slugs" behind each ear; scars and lash marks across his back; healed scars encircling his right wrist; distinct bruises on his jaw and forehead. As the interview drew to a close, Williams asked Irvin if he, Shepherd and Thomas had encountered the Padgetts in the wee hours of July 16. Walter told the attorney that Thomas wasn't with them, and that he and Sammie had gone to Orlando and Eatonville, where they went drinking. Quietly, he told Williams that upon returning to Lake County in the early morning they had in fact encountered Willie Padgett and his disabled car. According to Irvin, the men helped push the stalled car, but left the couple there. They most certainly did not assault Norma.

Shepherd confirmed that he and Irvin had been at bars in Orlando and Eatonville after midnight on July 16. As for the abuse suffered after being arrested, Sammie told essentially the same story as Walter. "Then they drove us about four or five miles in the country on a clay road. They took Ervin (sic) out of the car and started to beating and asking him about this man's wife, then they took me out of the car and whipped me up too. They whipped me with their fist and billies. They must have beat us about a half hour. After this, they put us into the car and took us to the place where this is suppose to have happened, then they took (us) to Tavares… Late that afternoon after they had taken Ervin out of the cell, they called me and took me downstairs. They handcuffed me to a water pipe heating system, which ran across the ceiling, my (feet) barely touching the floor. They pulled off my clothes, dropped my pants around my feet and started whipping me. They beat me with a rubber hose and with a billy; hit me a few licks in the face and across the head with it. My mouth was bleeding where a front tooth went through my lip. I have three teeth broken in the back of my mouth… They tried to make me say that I had been with the group of fellows that raped a white woman the night before and beat her husband. I told them I had been in Orlando. Then they kept beating me. They told me everything that was supposed to have happened…

Gary Corsair

then they started beating me again. It was terrible the way I was whipped, there was just knots all over me. They said they were not going to stop whipping me until I said that I was the one. "I kept telling them I was in Orlando where I was. Finally, when I couldn't take it anymore, I said 'yes.' While they were beating me, a white man from Groveland who was not a officer or a deputy came down there and whipped me also... I would recognize him if I saw him. They put me back in the cell and we stayed there till about six o'clock. When they came for us about six o'clock they said a mob was on its way so they put us in the car. They drove us out in the country, where they handcuffed the two of us around the tree with one pair of handcuffs. They had their radios going. They were talking about how they had beaten colored people up, they also mentioned how they had killed some colored people in that vicinity. We stayed there about 45 minutes, then they made us get down in the car. They took us to somebody's house -- where I don't know. A fellow came out with a five cell flashlight and a billy and he whipped the two of us with his flashlight, billy and fist and he stomped me. After they left and stopped and picked up another man, then they drove us to Raiford." Williams noted Shepherd's visible injuries: broken rear tooth on each side; scar on upper lip ("obviously caused by tooth puncture"); lash scars across back and chest; small scars on wrist; small scar on top of head.

Greenlee, who had only known Shepherd and Irvin for the few hours they had shared a jail cell in Tavares, also professed innocence. He didn't need to confirm that he had been brutally beaten, the attorneys could see the evidence of the savagery. The wide-eyed teen told of hitchhiking to Lake County with his friend Ernest Thomas, who left him at the packing shed for the night. According to Charles, a handful of people saw him there: a crippled man; a man driving a new Lincoln, "a little boy" who "rode by delivering papers" and the night watchman. Williams made a mental note to find those people. Charles next related his experience in the Groveland jail, particularly his visit from the "deputy" (Williams wondered if it was actually McCall). "He kept asking me questions -- asking me if it was a new Buick or an old Buick. He didn't say anything to me about a rape... He left me and then a woman and a man came down here. The man said, 'That's not one of the boys.' The woman said, 'He looks like one of them.' The man said again, 'No, he's not one of them.' Then they turned and went on off. Then the man came back by hisself (sic) and asked me was I with the boys. I asked him what boys he's talking about, and he said the boys what took me out of the ditch last night. I said, 'No sir, I wasn't with them.' He went on off then." Williams sat up with a start as Charles quietly related his horrifying experience in the basement of the county courthouse where three men worked him over. "He handcuffed my hands up over my head to a pipe. My feet were just barely touching the floor. The two men began whipping me with rubber hose. They kept asking me wasn't I with the boys. I first told him 'no'; and then the other one started helping him to whip me -- both at the same time. Everything they say then I say 'yeah.' They hit me across my back and legs and face. I was bleeding all over -- my arms, face and all was bloody."

The story rang true. Any doubt Williams may have had about his innocence dissipated when the teen told him about his night in the rickety Groveland jail, where his keepers left the door unlocked. According to Williams, Charles told him, "Jesus, if I, if I thought a white woman had been raped within a hundred miles of here and Negroes were being

76

suspected, I would have opened the door and left." Williams' examination of Greenlee revealed: "double scar across right cheekbone. Left eye red and bruised. Scars all around his neck. Lash marks across back, arms and chest. Scars that look like cuts and lash marks across and about chest and arms. Marks and lash scars across right knee and upper thigh. Sole of left foot is cut with glass. All around his privates, front and back, are short scars and across his penis. His testicles are swollen. Sore scars all around wrists." Williams marveled at the brutality the men had endured. They were lucky to be alive.

Before leaving, Williams asked Shepherd and Greenlee if they had signed the coerced confessions. Neither had been asked to sign anything. As the attorneys prepared to leave, the men remained quiet and sullen. Hill realized the depth of their despair and fear when Shepherd offered him a warning. "The prisoners said to us that we need not be walking around in that air of glory because of the fact that they would put us right there where they were," Hill recalled. "The prisoners said that one of the deputies had said that to him." Evidently, the suspects had been optimistic after Fordham's first visit, but prison guards quickly brought them back to reality.

The attorneys were quiet as they left. It was a day none of the lawyers would forget. All agreed that the stories rang true and seemed to jibe on nearly every significant point. For example, Irvin said that when he was handcuffed to the overhead pipe that his feet, "could not touch the floor." Shepherd said when he was handcuffed to that pipe that his feet were, "barely touching the floor." Greenlee had said his feet were cut by glass when he was handcuffed to the pipe. The statements added up: Greenlee was taller than Shepherd, who stood 3 or 4 inches taller than Irvin.

There were few discrepancies between the stories told by Irvin and Shepherd. The only contradiction seemed to be the time Shepherd picked Irvin up: Sammie said "between 10 and 10:30," but Walter remembered it being "9 p.m." Of course, Shepherd had added details Irvin didn't mention. Only Sammie mentioned encountering a friend who asked them to take a drunk home; named the two clubs they visited; said that he arrived home between 2:30 and 3 a.m.; recalled the prisoners being taken to the crime scene for a brief time and the officers telling them a mob was after them.

Williams was convinced the LDF should get involved, although he doubted the men could get a fair trial in Lake County. Hill and Fordham concurred. But who would lead the defense? Williams couldn't since he wasn't licensed to practice law in Florida, and neither Hill nor Fordham were experienced enough to spearhead a defense. The young attorneys knew they didn't have the know-how to head such a high-stakes case, but both promised to help in any way they could. Hill was especially adamant about lending his time and energy: "After I saw this situation where somebody had beaten them in the head and the scabs were there and the sole of his foot was cut because of glass and being strapped with handcuffs to an iron or galvanized pipe in the basement, it didn't matter much anymore. I was just willing to give whatever I could to see that justice was done."

Williams phoned Marshall that night, detailing the injuries and explaining why he believed the suspects were innocent. For instance, Greenlee had told Williams that the woman had said he was one of her attackers. A guilty man would have just repeated the husband's statement that Greenlee *wasn't* one of the assailants. Then there were the accounts of hanging from the overhead pipe in the basement, and how the shorter men had said their feet didn't touch the ground, but Greenlee's feet dragged on the floor. They were little things to be sure, but Williams felt strongly that a lot of little things led to one unmistakable conclusion: the prisoners were telling the truth. And if they were telling the truth about jailhouse conversations and beatings in a basement, they were probably telling the truth about not kidnapping and raping Norma Padgett.

Williams told Marshall that when the Padgett girl cried rape, McCall saw a golden opportunity to put Irvin and Shepherd in their place. Why? Because they had been hanging around in their Army uniforms when they should have been working in the orange groves. Williams reasoned that once McCall learned the men had been with Thomas on the night of the 15th, the latter became the third suspect. As for Greenlee, Williams told Marshall, "And they needed a fourth, because she had said she had been raped by four guys and the sheriff heard they had this fellow down there and charged him. And according to Irvin and Shepherd, they had never met Greenlee in their life, and Greenlee insisted he had never met them. But that rounded out the four."

Marshall agreed that the NAACP law staff should get involved, not only by providing legal assistance, but also by raising funds to hire a capable -- preferably Negro -- attorney. They needed someone who could go head-to-head with a state attorney who had been practicing for decades, was in cahoots with the local sheriff, and had gone to school with the judge who would try the case. "The resources of the association will be thrown behind the defense of these boys, and at the same time, we will insist upon protection of other Negroes in the area," Marshall told reporters. The NAACP was in.

The next day, Ramona Lowe's front-page article in the *Chicago Defender* carried the startling claim that Samuel Shepherd and Norma Padgett had known each other for years. "Mrs. Willie Padgett, the purported victim, is reported as declaring that if anything happens to Sam Shepherd, one of the accused: 'I will leave this place, (Groveland). I have known Sam all of my life.'" Lowe also claimed that the "week-long reign of terror in Groveland," was caused by, "seething jealousy of poor whites over prosperity of Negro farmers." The reporter maintained that the rioting in Groveland was the result of long-festering resentment of "prosperous Negroes" like Matthew Maxwell, who employed "a large number of poor whites" on his citrus plantation; Joseph Maxwell, who owned one of the most successful "Negro farms;" Moses Siplin, a well-to-do citrus contractor who was driven from the polls when he tried to vote in all-white Mascotte in 1940 and 1944; and Johnson Hodges, who made his money trucking fruit and working more than 100 acres of watermelons. Will Brunson and Franklin Hodges also felt they were targeted by jealous and resentful whites. Lowe claimed whites were upset that Matthew Maxwell held a "white man's job," and first threatened his life in 1948. Siplin also had his life threatened. The sensational account continued, "It is reported that the trio stopped in passing because they recognized the

Padgetts. The husband admitted himself, he knew the men. It was also revealed that Padgett had been drinking heavily." It was a sensational scoop, one that she owed to being able to move among members of the black community because she was a Negro woman first, and a reporter, second. Soon other Yankee newspapers were picking up on the questions Lowe had raised, even though she hadn't named her sources. Florida reporters, who had been content to publish one-sided accounts spoon-fed to them by McCall and Hunter, continued to look the other way.

Williams' brief investigation supported *most* of Lowe's assertions. He too had uncovered evidence of racial tension and claims that poor whites resented prosperous Negro farmers. The NAACP attorney was convinced that the, "alleged attack cry was merely an excuse for terrorizing the community because colored persons refused to work for starvation wages." While Lowe's article cast an onus that the Padgetts were part of a conspiracy to ruin the Shepherd family, the claim that Greenlee *was* with Irvin and Shepherd contradicted the defendants' claims. Lowe's assertion that Greenlee had been with Shepherd and Irvin was troubling, and could derail the defense Williams envisioned. Williams needed to find out who had given that information to Lowe. He also needed to pay another visit to Raiford. He had to make sure the prisoners had told him the truth about not being together on July 15 and 16.

Chapter 11 -- The Godsend

State Attorney Jesse Hunter assumed that William Fordham, whom he had never met, would be the attorney of record. Intent on a speedy trial, Hunter called Fordham on Monday, Aug. 1. "I told him it was my policy in all cases, and it would be especially so in this case, to lay my cards on the table and give him any information which my office had, including the names of the witnesses, or any other information I could give him." Hunter then volunteered to call the superintendent at Raiford and arrange an interview with the prisoners for the defense. Fordham didn't bother telling Hunter he had already seen the accused. When Hunter tried to pinpoint a date for arraignment, Fordham replied that he couldn't give an answer until he talked to the NAACP's national office.

That afternoon, Fordham called Williams. It was a phone call that put the NAACP practically back at square one, and all but ended Fordham's involvement in the case. "He did not want to follow through. I do not know whether he backed off because it was too big a case or too difficult for him or whether the obviously oppressive atmosphere of Lake County frightened him off," recalled Williams, who had just returned to New York armed with statements from the accused, along with affidavits from "persons who had some information concerning the circumstances surrounding their detention." After examining the documents, Marshall agreed that the case had merits, although he didn't view Groveland as a historic case. It wasn't another Scottsboro. Williams disagreed. "Surprising as it may seem, there was not a lot of interest in New York in the Groveland case. I was the one involved in it. I was the one down here aware of -- suddenly aware of -- the oppressiveness of it and the extreme brutality that had been involved, but communicating this to the National Office was not easy," Williams said. Finding an attorney wouldn't be easy, either. With Fordham out, and

Hill too inexperienced, Marshall told Williams to return to Lake County as soon as possible to find representation.

After dispatching Williams to Florida, Marshall went to Washington to demand an FBI investigation into Thomas' death. "There is serious doubt that the man killed was in any manner connected with the alleged rape," Marshall told reporters. During the tense meeting, FBI officials wouldn't commit to looking into the death, but they confirmed that Assistant Attorney General Alexander Campbell had ordered an investigation into reports that the Groveland Three had been "brutally beaten, kicked in the groin, strung up by ropes and have suffered other brutalities."

FBI agents had been ordered to conduct a preliminary investigation, but two days later, FBI Director J. Edgar Hoover called for a "full and exhaustive investigation into the entire matter of the arrest and mistreatment by the authorities of all the victims." New York City agents were promptly dispatched to interview Williams, while Miami agents were directed to obtain statements and take photographs at the Florida State Prison. Agents were instructed, "If it appears the prisoners did not commit the alleged crime, the investigation should be extended as far as necessary." The assistant attorney general also directed agents "to ascertain whether violations (of) civil rights statutes may have been committed." The bureau appeared ready and willing to go all the way.

While FBI agents searched for answers, the national Negro press kept the story on the front page with updates and exclusives from Florida. Unfortunately, the reports were often a two-edged sword. NAACP officials welcomed the articles from Groveland, but shuddered when unsubstantiated rumors appeared as facts. The *Chicago Defender's* Ramona Lowe continued to scoop the competition with details others missed, but Marshall and his staff wondered how accurate her stories were since her sources remained anonymous. At least one story caused considerable consternation at the NAACP and LDF offices; an article in which Lowe wrote, "There are those here who question that any criminal act was performed by the accused quartet on the Padgett woman and have said that she entered the boys' car of her own free will." The statement was obviously a reflection of local sentiment from the Negro community, but the NAACP lawyers blanched at the very insinuation that: a) Greenlee and Thomas had been with the other two suspects; b) the accused had shared an automobile ride with Norma Padgett.

FBI agents interviewed Williams the day Lowe's story hit the streets. Williams willingly provided copies of the statements the prisoners had made on July 31, although he privately doubted the agency would collar McCall and his men. Williams told agents that his preliminary investigation revealed, "...there has been a continually increasing bad feeling between whites and Negroes in Bay Lake area near Groveland and (the) alleged rape of Norma Padgett furnished an excuse for whites to give vent to their emotions against Negroes." But under questioning, Williams admitted he had, "conducted very little investigation at Groveland or Tavares." Evidently, much of the information Williams received was provided by *New Leader* reporter Terrence McCarthy. Williams also admitted that he, "had not talked to any of the law enforcement officials in Tavares." The interview concluded with Williams telling agents that, "he had some doubt that the rape actually occurred."

During the flight to Florida, Williams considered the numerous tasks ahead of him. Finding competent counsel was his first concern, but he also needed to visit the families of the accused, track down rumors and witnesses, and arrange for medical examinations of the prisoners. In effect, he was being asked to do two months worth of work in two weeks -- and to do it in a hostile, dangerous environment. Where to begin? Marshall and Williams agreed that their case could hinge on a physician confirming the men had been tortured and that confessions were coerced. Before leaving New York, Williams had arranged for Dr. Nelson Spaulding and dentist Jean C. Downing, both of Jacksonville, Florida, to accompany him to Raiford on Sunday, Aug. 7. Based on what he had seen a week earlier, Williams had no doubt the men would still bear evidence of the beatings they had endured three weeks earlier.

Finding a lawyer was a more pressing concern. There were only a handful of black lawyers, and the few Negroes who were practicing weren't exactly embraced by the legal community -- in fact, they weren't even allowed to join the American Bar Association. "There were no black lawyers," LDF attorney Jack Greenberg recalled. "Florida was not the worst state for finding a black lawyer, but it was almost the worst state. There were some states like Alabama and Louisiana and Delaware that had only one black lawyer in the whole state. Florida had about four."

The situation was grim, but not totally hopeless. Horace Hill was too inexperienced to lead, but Williams could see that he would be a tremendous help. Hill knew about bucking the odds in the Jim Crow South. Since no Florida law school would accept him, Hill went to Pennsylvania to earn his degree, and then petitioned the Supreme Court to allow him to join his white peers in the Florida bar. And Hill had energy and enthusiasm. The opportunity to work with Marshall and Williams held great appeal to Hill, who was just establishing his practice. Fordham could also assist, but Fordham's failure to secure written statements from Shepherd, Irvin and Greenlee didn't sit well with Williams. It was a beginner's mistake, and there wasn't much room for error when three lives were at stake. Williams had been banking on Thomas in Miami, but when veteran lawyer waffled, Williams realized it was time to search for a white lawyer who would risk damaging his reputation by defending three Negro rapists. The prospects for finding such a man were about as slim as the odds of finding an experienced Negro attorney.

In Florida, Williams was soon reminded he was no longer in the enlightened North as he rode to Raiford in Dr. Spaulding's yellow Cadillac convertible. As the morning sun and temperature rose, Williams expected the physician to pull over and lower the top, but Spaulding explained he couldn't. "Did not have air conditioning in cars in that day and he said we have to keep the top up because driving to Raiford from Jacksonville we go through a lot of small towns, and if the police see Negroes in a yellow convertible Cadillac then they would be in trouble. We had the top up then, they will not notice us," Williams said.

At the prison, Spaulding grimly noted graphic evidence of beatings the defendants described. By the time he had examined all three men, the doctor was marveling that the prisoners had survived. He could only imagine their condition immediately after the beatings 22 days earlier. "It is a fact, that those boys were subjected to tortures capable only by Nazis," Spaulding wrote in his report.

The youngest, Greenlee, appeared to have come closest to death. Spaulding had no trouble believing Charles' claim that he had been "handcuffed and flogged with a rubber hose." The teen's injuries included: a blackened, bloodshot and swollen left eye; bruised and scarred right cheek; three large scars on the back of his neck; 14-20 bruised and scarred places on his chest and back; a large (1 ½-inch wide by 2-inch long) scar on his back; swollen, inflamed and bruised genitals; circular scars on both wrists; numerous scars and bruises along his arm; numerous scars and bruises on his legs; scars "due to laceration on glass" on three of his toes. Spaulding's conclusion: the injuries were the result of a "severe beating and flogging."

Irvin's injuries also spoke volumes. The prisoner quietly told the doctor and dentist, "I got beat up." When pressed, he stated that his injuries were caused by clubs and blackjacks. He also said he lost consciousness during one beating. Irvin's face was unmarked, but like Greenlee, his body testified to horrific mistreatment. Spaulding noted: numerous bruises on his chest and back; "whelps and swollen ridges" under the skin covering his abdomen; a scalp laceration and a swollen scrotum. Irvin also complained of tenderness and pain when opening and closing his mouth, which Spaulding attributed to dead bone in his right jaw, which was possibly infected. In examining Shepherd, Spaulding found: a scar on the right side of the scalp; numerous bruises, scars and lacerations on his chest and back; dense scar tissue over the abdomen; and tender genitalia. Downing noted loose teeth and a fractured left molar.

After the examinations, Williams explained to the prisoners that the NAACP was willing to represent them if they gave their consent. He also explained why he couldn't lead the case, but promised to stay involved, and find a respectable lawyer. They unanimously agreed to authorize Williams to "take every legal step necessary." Not that they had other options: none of them even knew an attorney, and even if they did, their families couldn't afford one. Williams didn't tell them just how hard it would be to find someone willing to take the case, a case the attorney would certainly lose.

The FBI also chose Sunday to examine and interview the prisoners. Agents also shot two rolls of photos to document, "bruises, welts, marks and scars," the prisoners claimed were inflicted by Lake County lawmen. Agents noted that Irvin had 19 large bruises on his stomach and chest, 12 bruises on his back and shoulders and scars on his wrists from being handcuffed. The first thing agents noticed about Shepherd was his mouth: his upper lip bore a half-inch scar. Two teeth were chipped. Closer inspection revealed Shepherd's chest, back, hips and shoulders bore bruises or were discolored. It wasn't difficult for investigators to imagine the police brutality the prisoners claimed. That evening, Special

Agent C. H. Carson filed his report: "Taken on outskirts of town where they state they were beaten with blackjacks by number of individuals who were not known to them... then taken to county jail at Tavares, Fla., county seat of Lake County, where they were again beaten in basement of building while handcuffed to a ceiling pipe... both denied participating robbery and rape... and disclaimed knowing Thomas." Upon hearing the agent's report, J. Edgar Hoover personally authorized further investigation into the alleged rape, as well as the rioting.

Before returning to New York, Williams contacted a handful of attorneys, but no one wanted anything to do with the rape case. Things were looking bleak. Then Williams learned of Alex Akerman Jr., an Orlando attorney who had earned his law degree from the University of Florida in 1933 and began practicing law in Tampa shortly thereafter. He moved to Orlando in 1940, went into the Navy in '42, and then returned to his law practice in '45. Williams didn't know the man personally, but he made inquiries and found out Akerman wasn't a typical Southern lawyer. In 1947 and 1948, Akerman was the lone Republican in the Florida Legislature.

Harry T. Moore could have pointed Williams toward Akerman if Franklin had asked, but Williams had not. Moore met Akerman back in 1945 when he was searching for a conscientious attorney to represent a Negro war veteran who had disarmed a deputy and supposedly beaten the law officer. Akerman had taken the case without hesitation. "He truly was a remarkable man. His dedication to not being prejudiced and giving everybody justice really was remarkable. He was ahead of his time. He was a southerner, but he recognized the situation. He really had a true sense of justice," his daughter Lucy remarked.

When Williams came calling, Akerman listened politely, and then explained that he had his hands full. Besides, entering the Groveland case could only bring trouble. Williams was disappointed, but told Akerman he would leave the door open in case Alex changed his mind. Before leaving, Williams asked Akerman if he would at least contact Hunter on behalf of the NAACP to find out when the arraignment would be held. Akerman agreed to make the phone call. The following day, he kept his promise. Akerman explained that he was not employed as defense counsel, but had been repeatedly asked to take the case. He also told Hunter that he would only enter the case if no other attorney would take it. Hunter was shaking his head as he hung up the phone: he doubted the NAACP could find anyone who would take the case. Not that he was surprised, hell; he wouldn't have touched it with a 10-foot pole himself.

Before leaving Florida, Williams told reporters that he had made an, "on-the-spot investigation of violence and race rioting at Groveland," and determined the defendants were *entirely innocent*. Williams figured the more pretrial publicity he could create, the better. He wanted the eyes of the nation focused on the Tavares courtroom when the trial opened.

Now that the NAACP's national office was heading the search to secure competent counsel for the Groveland Three, Harry T. Moore devoted himself to getting Willis McCall. The former school teacher intensified his criticism of Lake County and state officials for failing to protect not only the defendants, but the Negro residents living in south Lake County. Moore was a whirlwind, dispatching pointed letters and telegrams to the governor, making bold public statements and constantly admonishing NAACP chapter chairmen to rally support in their communities. In one telegram to Gov. Fuller Warren, Moore boldly charged McCall and his deputies with beating the Groveland prisoners and implored Warren to appoint a "special guard" to ensure the prisoners' safety during transport from Raiford to the trial in Tavares. Pressure also came from an unexpected source. *The Christian Science Monitor* asked Warren to personally look into the case. Several days later, the governor wired the magazine his answer: no investigation had been ordered.

While the State of Florida dragged its feet, FBI agents were substantiating many of Moore's claims, although the agency's official position remained, "an investigation is continuing." McCall's didn't like the attention one little bit. The last thing he needed was the Justice Department or FBI uncovering misconduct within his department. McCall conferred with State Attorney Jesse Hunter, who suggested the best way to keep the feds out of the county was by taking the offensive. Hunter agreed to go to bat for the embattled sheriff, and hastily booked a flight to Washington to meet with Attorney General Howard McGrath in hopes to getting the spotlight off McCall and deputies Yates, Young and Campbell.

By the time Hunter left, the FBI probe was in high gear. On Aug. 10, FBI Special Agent Carson dispatched an urgent teletype to Washington. The contents were explosive: Irvin claimed Sheriff McCall and Deputy Yates, "at different times from arrest until removal to Florida State Prison, Raiford, Florida, participated actively or otherwise in beating of him together with other unidentified white men." Irvin also said he and Shepherd had requested medical attention, "shortly after being admitted to Florida State Prison but did not receive any." On Aug. 11, agents met with U.S. Attorney Herbert S. Phillips in Tampa to compare notes. Phillips suggested agents interview the National Guard commanders who had responded to the violence in Lake County, also directing them to interview, "prominent citizens in that section who were considered reliable and who had some knowledge of the happenings." And that should about do it, Phillips thought. He told the agents that after completing the interviews, the matter should be discontinued so that it could be considered and studied further. He didn't explain how a matter could be studied further if the investigation was discontinued. And another thing, how could Phillips table the matter before he even knew what the agents would learn? Phillips acted as if he wanted the whole mess to quietly go away.

FBI agents crisscrossed Lake County over the next few days, interviewing Willie Padgett and dozens of witnesses. Even prisoners who had been in the county jail at the time of the beatings were queried, although none were about to implicate McCall and his men. They knew better. And they weren't the only ones abiding by a "see-no evil, hear-no evil" creed; most of those interviewed were less than forthcoming. The G-men were learning what Williams already understood: the locals still had to live in Willis McCall's county long after the "outsiders" left.

Hunter returned home confident he had stalled an investigation into McCall's handling of the Groveland case by explaining how the sheriff had protected the prisoners from the lynch mob. He also stressed that a suspension or indictment for denying the prisoners' rights would surely touch off a firestorm that would make the July trouble look like a church social. What was done, was done. Nothing would be gained by validating the NAACP's accusations against one of Florida's most respected law officers.

Hunter had barely settled into his office after his whirlwind trip when he learned that Fordham had dropped out of the case and a Miami attorney named L.C. Thomas had called to say he was considering representing the Groveland boys. Hunter immediately called Thomas. When Hunter explained that he wished to arraign the Groveland Three that week, Thomas explained that the NAACP had only retained him to make a preliminary investigation, *not represent* the defendants. He had only agreed to touch base with Hunter and then contact the NAACP with information about the indictment and date and time of arraignment. Thomas fully expected the NAACP to appoint an attorney any day now, and promised to call Hunter before Friday, Aug. 12.

Williams was vigorously courting Thomas, one of the few Negro attorneys in the state with significant courtroom experience. Thomas had proved his mettle in August 1947 when the Daytona Beach branch of the NAACP hired him to represent 19-year-old Aaron Quince, a Negro charged with murdering a white woman near Holly Hill. Thomas tackled the assignment with zeal after replacing a court-appointed lawyer who was named just hours before the arraignment and hadn't even bothered to interview his client. Thomas immediately filed a motion for delay, and then attacked the all-white grand jury and Volusia County's record of excluding Negro jurors with such passion that Judge Jackson postponed the trial "indefinitely." On Sept. 30, the judge upheld the defense plea that, "Negroes were unlawfully, arbitrarily and systematically excluded from the grand jury." He then quashed the murder indictment and ordered county commissioners to "purge the entire 1947 jury box and refill it." Yes, Thomas could handle Groveland, but he had serious reservations about getting involved. As he debated taking the case, it became clear there were many more cons than pros. There could only be two pros: the notoriety of such a high-profile case would solidify his standing among the Negro community at large, and (hopefully) a healthy payday. But once Thomas learned the NAACP coffers were bare, he could see little reason to sign on. He didn't relish the thought of driving 250 miles one way to represent the accused. Besides, his health wasn't the best... perhaps if he were younger and healthier.

Thomas called Hunter on Thursday, Aug. 11, explaining that he would not be representing the defendants, but was authorized to request the arraignment be postponed, "a week or 10 days in order to enable persons interested to complete their plans for employing defense counsel." Hunter flatly refused. He was tired of the NAACP's stalling. They had dumped Fordham and now Thomas was opting out. Hunter curtly told Thomas that he would request arraignment no later than the following day, and that the court could, and would, appoint counsel. Thomas immediately telegrammed Williams: "Personal health will not permit my engagement in rigorous trial unless other counsel unavailable (stop) Prosecutor declines arraignment delay but will thereafter waive right against motions on indictment (stop) Court in session counsel will be appointed temporarily trial date 7 to 10 days away. Prosecutor awaiting information on counsel." Time was running out for Williams. Sure enough, Hunter scheduled arraignment for that very afternoon. Judge Futch, citing the threat of violence, postponed the hearing a day.

A steady rain fell as McCall hauled the prisoners into the Lake County Courthouse on Friday, Aug. 12. McCall had to admit postponing arraignment for a day had been a good idea -- Thursday had been clear, but the lousy weather on Friday would keep spectators away. Only a handful of onlookers joined newspaper editor Mabel Norris-Reese in the courtroom. Most of the spectators were there for another case, which Judge Truman G. Futch recessed so he could conduct the arraignment of the prisoners from Raiford the moment McCall arrived.

Norris-Reese intently studied the criminals she had heard so much about, but not yet seen. Well aware of their claims of mistreatment three weeks earlier, she searched for telltale signs of abuse. She saw none. "In our mind, they had not been beaten. At least there was not a sign of the effects of it in the faces of the trio. They walked easily -- there were no broken limbs. We looked at them closely, because we were studying their types -- and the horrible fear that was in the eyes of them." Evidently, she didn't look close enough. Hunter admitted in the same newspaper article that the men bore bruises. "The husband of the young bride who says she was raped by all four is claiming "credit" for what bruises the Negroes have," Hunter said. Of course, that "horrible fear" Norris-Reese noted -- if it existed at all -- was fear of the unknown. The accused men scanned the courtroom for a friendly, familiar face, but saw none of the attorneys who had visited them at Raiford. No Franklin Williams, no Horace Hill and no William Fordham. Why weren't they there? Instead, they were met at the defense table by an unfamiliar white man. Only Charles Greenlee had family present: Hunter had told his father Tom to appear because his son was a minor.

Futch began the proceedings by naming local attorney Harry E. Gaylord to defend the accused. The judge then asked the defendants to state their ages. After Charles told the judge that he was 16, Hunter called the boy's father Tom to the bench. A weary "old Negro shuffled" forward. The prosecutor told the elder Greenlee that Gaylord had been appointed to represent Charles and asked if that was satisfactory. "I got a letter from a lawyer saying he was going to defend the boy," Tom Greenlee replied. Hunter responded, "Let the record show that William A. Fordham of Tampa has made it known to the state attorney that he will not represent Charles Greenlee; or any of the defendants; that he is not in the case at present, and that the court appointed Mr. Gaylord, is that satisfactory to you? You can hire anybody else later if you want to." A surprised Greenlee weakly replied, "I haven't made any arrangements for a lawyer for the boy. I don't know any."

Next, the indictment was read. The trio quietly stood before Futch, heads held high. All three men entered pleas of "not guilty." Futch set the trial for 10 a.m., Monday, Aug. 29, after Hunter and Gaylord agreed to the date. Hunter then volunteered to summon any witnesses the defense planned to call. The judge told the clerk to, "Give the list of witnesses to Mr. Gaylord so he can present it to the state attorney." Gaylord then informed the judge that the defendants wanted to be examined by a physician. Futch granted the request, appointing physicians C.M. Tyre and S.C. Colley to perform the examinations and supply the court with their findings in writing. Hunter smiled to himself: they wouldn't find anything. Hunter assured Norris-Reese that the examinations would prove that the prisoners' claims of being beaten were "ridiculous." With that the defendants were quickly whisked out of the courthouse. But this time they weren't taken to Raiford for safekeeping, they were taken upstairs to the jail where they would spend the next two weeks until the trial began.

Williams' statement from the state prison hit newspapers outside Florida on Aug. 13. *The Pittsburgh Courier* reported that the NAACP investigation had convinced Williams that the "trumped up rape charge, the burning of Negro property, the open participation of the Ku Klux Klan, and the continued intimidation of Negroes in the area is all part of one great plot to intimidate the Negroes in the community, to force them to work for little or no wages and to stop them from being so uppity." The *New Leader* published an in-depth look at the Groveland controversy, reporting that "Sworn affidavits prove beyond a doubt that, although Willis McCall was supposedly elected to serve and protect Lake County citizens in observance of the law, one of his main functions for years appears to have been to dragoon the color pickers used in the county's citrus fields and packing plants."

The following day, Aug. 14, the *Orlando Sentinel* finally printed the charge of police brutality that had been whispered in Lake County bars and backrooms. The article, which was based on a press release supplied by Harry T. Moore, carried the sensational claim that the Groveland Three were, "brutally beaten by local officers in an attempt to force confessions from them." Moore also boldly called for swift identification and suspension of the officers involved in brutalizing the prisoners and asked for "swift and determined action" from Gov. Warren. When reporters called at the sheriff's office, McCall called the charges, "a damn lie." According to the sheriff, "They might have got in a fight somewhere in prison or somewhere and had a mark or two on them, but they didn't get that in Lake County." Off the record, McCall told everyone who would listen that the NAACP was behind the story, and that the organization for coloreds was hell bent on stirring up hatred against the whites. And the damn FBI men were playing right into their hands, swallowing every lie the NAACP fed them and sticking their noses into all sorts of places they didn't belong.

The rumor that the FBI was acting as an arm of the NAACP soon extended beyond Tavares. And it spread quickly. In less than 48 hours after the *Sentinel* article appeared, the FBI investigation went from progressing steadily to stopped dead in its tracks. Suddenly, agents who had been making inroads among the white citizens experienced changes in attitude as immediate and devastating as an unexpected frost in July. C.H. Carson was processing a signed statement in which Willie Padgett admitted to being, "leader and spokesman for mob of around 100 men" that confronted McCall in front of the jail on the evening of July 16 when agents reported that their sources had suddenly clammed up. The sentiment was across the board: talking to white investigators who promised anonymity was one thing, but helping them aid the nigras was quite another. Carson's agents soon learned there was no combating the rumor. Anonymity or not, no one with knowledge of what went on during the week of violence had anything more to say, and anyone who talked to outsiders best be ready to accept the consequences if McCall found out. By Aug. 16, the flow of information coming into the FBI was hardly a trickle. Carson told his superiors that, "Citizens in Lake County as well as officials have shown obvious resentment to such publicity." Carson doubted his men could accomplish much more. Phillips agreed, telling agents in the Miami field office to suspend the investigation. Moore's publicity push had backfired.

The *Sentinel* editors soon felt the wrath of Hunter, McCall and other prominent Lake Countians, who lambasted the newspaper for printing NAACP lies. Stung by the charges, *Sentinel* editors did an about-face and returned to trying the Groveland Three in the press, primarily by reinforcing the notion that the evidence was overwhelming and convictions were foregone conclusions. Printing Moore's accusation that confessions had been beaten out of the prisoners was one thing, but no Florida newspaper -- especially not the *Sentinel* -- was about to investigate the possibility that the accused were innocent. With the trial less than two weeks away, reporters in Lake and adjacent Orange County returned to basing their stories entirely on dogmatic statements made by McCall.

Unaware that the FBI investigation had ground to a halt, Marshall, Williams and Moore continued feeding information to investigators and reporters. On Aug. 17, Marshall dropped the biggest salvo yet, telling the Justice Department that the NAACP had learned that the physician who had examined Norma Padgett the morning of the "rape" had contradicted her charges. That got the FBI's attention. If Dr. Geoffrey Binneveld didn't initially realize the importance of the information he held, he did by the time FBI agents showed up at his Leesburg, Fla. office. This time, he chose his words more cautiously. "He could not say that she had been raped, and he could not say that she had not been raped, but there were signs of irritation at the entrance and inside," FBI agents reported. Carson immediately realized the significance of the physician's statement. Medical evidence *didn't support* the girl's claim that she had been repeatedly raped, a conclusion even the most prejudiced juror would have to reach.

Williams flew back to Orlando on Aug. 17 to renew his search for counsel. He wasn't optimistic. Few attorneys, white or black, would be willing to take a capital case they had less than two weeks to prepare for. Secondly, it would be nearly impossible to find an attorney willing to take a case couldn't win. Plus, few white attorneys could afford to have their reputation jeopardized by being linked to the National Association for the Advancement of Colored People. Finally, Williams didn't have big money to throw around, just $1,500 the NAACP had raised for the defense. After securing a room in Orlando, Williams immediately called Hill. The young attorney agreed to serve as Williams' driver, and the two headed out that day in Hill's 1948 Chevrolet. Meanwhile, Marshall's staff and Florida NAACP officials were working to find something that would spare the lives of Greenlee, Shepherd and Irvin.

While Marshall and his aides discussed how to get Dr. Binneveld to testify or provide a copy of his examination report, prosecutor Jess Hunter was trying to figure out how to keep Lawrence Burtoft off the stand. The prosecutor had initially hoped to call Burtoft as a state witness after Norma revealed the young restaurant worker was the first person she spoke with the morning after the rape. But the young man told Hunter that Norma hadn't been distraught, frightened, or battered on the morning of July 16. And her clothing wasn't torn. "I don't think I gave them what they were hoping to hear... It wasn't what they wanted to hear, but the truth is the truth. When you tell the truth you don't have to worry about it."

Nearly everything Burtoft remembered would damage the prosecution and aid the defense. Burtoft told Hunter that Norma said she didn't know her assailants and couldn't identify them. Burtoft also insisted Norma was calm, not hysterical, and didn't mention being raped. And Burtoft saw no evidence of assault. Hunter left the interview knowing it would be a disaster to put the teen on the stand. Before leaving, Hunter elicited one other important piece of information: Burtoft hadn't been contacted by NAACP attorneys or other northern "do-gooders" sniffing around Lake County. Of course, Hunter wasn't about to reveal that there was a white boy who could cast doubt on Norma's tale of rape. Hunter needn't have worried. Williams was too busy searching for a lawyer to worry about interviewing prospective witnesses.

After five days of searching, Williams was still at square one, having been turned down by 11 attorneys. All echoed the view of the lawyer who told Williams that taking the case "would be harmful." Most dismissed Williams promptly, although some were courteous enough to examine the defendants' statements before saying "no." Only a few considered taking the case, but their fees were out of this world. "One requested a retainer of $10,000, and another a retainer of $25,000. I informed these men that the defendants and their families were paupers and could not pay such a retainer; that they were entirely dependent upon charity to obtain funds to pay defense counsel," Williams recalled. The $25,000 request came from a prominent Miami criminal attorney who was approached by a liberal white Southerner on behalf of the NAACP. Williams was shocked by attorney's request, which was only to "study" the case, not to represent the Groveland Three. The $10,000 demand came from an attorney practicing in the small town of Inverness, but the man telephoned to withdraw his offer before it could be accepted. The attorney's reason for his about-face: his wife would not let him act in a rape case involving a white woman and Negro men.

A lawyer who had done work for the CIO also expressed interest, but would only get involved if his partner also received a fee. He too wanted $10,000. "Well, we obviously did not have that kind of money. Any money we would have for a trial or a case, we would raise in connection with the case, through our branch meetings and so forth," Williams said. And the rejections kept coming. One of the most enlightening meetings occurred in the office of a "very distinguished criminal lawyer." According to Williams, "We talked to this lawyer and I will never forget his saying that he would not even consider it. And I recall his saying that, 'You know, Franklin, those clay-eating Crackers,' I will never forget that phrase -- 'down there in Lake County would just as soon stand off and shoot me with a high-power rifle as they would you.'" Daytona Beach lawyer, Billy Judge said he would consider taking the case for $4,500.

Williams hoped to have better luck in Vero Beach at the law office of Spessard Holland Jr., son of liberal U.S. Senator Spessard Holland. "I had heard of him because we had heard that he had represented some black migrant workers who had been kept against their will in confinement in some orange grove by some growers and he had filed the charges with the Department of Justice and so his name had come to the NAACP's attention," Williams recalled. Perhaps the search was finally about to end. "We got there about quarter 'til six. He said he would wait for us and I went into his office and no one was in his office except himself. I talked at great length about the case and the perception I had of it and things that I had found," Williams said. The NAACP attorney concluded his pitch by detailing the injuries he had seen at Raiford and telling Holland that the national Negro press was keeping the story on page one. "Holland was impressed and he impressed me as a rather brave young man. He said, 'Well, come back tomorrow morning and let me think about it.' Horace and I went back the next morning about nine o'clock and again, I will never forget this…he sat down at his desk and began to weep. He said, 'I can't do this, Frank. 'I said, 'Why not?' He said, 'You may not understand this, but my wife is a typical flower of Southern womanhood and this is a rape case and I can't take it.' Just like that. Nothing more, nothing less," Williams said. As Williams and Hill prepared to leave, Holland told remarked, "Although I disagree with many of my father's political beliefs and actions, I just can't take a step which would undoubtedly bring about his defeat in the next election." Holland did agree to assist as an undercover investigator and volunteered to try to locate potential witnesses. He also offered to assist in drawing up a petition for change of venue.

Miami attorney Burnett Roth also expressed regret that he couldn't take the case. "At that time I was requested to assume responsibility as chief counsel, but felt that because of my familiarity with the central portion of the state, having been raised just a few miles from Groveland, that it would not be to the interest of the defendants themselves, for me to represent them. The prejudices existing in that community against persons of certain races and religions would have made my representation harmful to my client's interests." Roth knew all too well that many Lake Countians despised Jews nearly as much as they did Negroes. To his credit, Roth did agree to help with fund-raising.

With Florida newspapers finally reporting NAACP claims that confessions had been beaten out of the Groveland Three, Hunter needed McCall to reiterate that the suspects' admissions of guilt were *voluntary*. Once again, the sheriff called on the local press to give him a platform. On Aug. 18, the *Leesburg Commercial* provided the soapbox. "McCall said he had no written confessions from the suspects but that two of them had taken officers to the scene of the crime and recounted the event in detail. All admitted verbally to the crime, the Sheriff said." To Williams' dismay, the court-appointed lawyer seemed to believe such press accounts. Gaylord had told Williams he was willing to take the case, but made it clear he didn't want, or need NAACP assistance. Gaylord also revealed that he had no intention of filing either a motion to quash indictment or a motion for change of venue. To Williams, that was the final confirmation that Gaylord's defense would be lacking. Gaylord had to be replaced.

As the clock ticked toward the Aug. 29 trial, Williams despaired of finding a white lawyer brave enough to get involved, and give the Groveland Three a wholehearted defense. He couldn't stop thinking how three lives depended on locating such a man -- if one existed in central Florida. As the third week of August neared its end, Williams and Marshall knew there wouldn't be time to prepare any kind of case. The search for an attorney was consuming precious days needed for crafting a defense. Precious time and energy that should have been devoted to preparing for trial was also hampered by the NAACP's need to organize fund-raising drives. As was so often the case in the late 1940s, the NAACP was taking a case without adequate funds to see it through. In late August, a statewide appeal for financial support brought in a trickle of much-needed cash. A miracle was needed, but the only phenomenon that could save the Groveland Three wasn't going to happen; there was no way in heaven or hell Norma Padgett would recant. The charges weren't going to be dropped. There would be a trial.

McCall got hot under the collar when he learned the NAACP wanted to replace Gaylord. The sheriff wished the outsiders would go back to wherever the hell they came from. In his mind, the crime happened in Lake County, the guilty men were in custody, and the upcoming trial was a mere formality. And the NAACP lawyers weren't the only interlopers. Members of the communist Civil Rights Congress and a labor group, the Workers Defense League were also busy gathering information and conducting interviews. McCall made it clear to his deputies that they were not to cooperate with the "outside agitators." They weren't needed, and they certainly weren't welcome. "When the remaining three were brought to trial, a whole battery of outsiders came in. Several lawyers from out-of-state, Civil Liberties Union, NAACP, you name it," McCall recalled. "This complicated things greatly. They were here for what they called, 'To see that justice was done.' Instead, with their meddling, they created more unrest than they did good." To McCall, it seemed he was being attacked from every direction. All the attention only strengthened the sheriff's resolve. He had never let anyone shove him around, and he wasn't about to start now. Anybody who pushed him could expect to be pushed back, only harder.

The NAACP attorneys definitely felt the heat, and they wanted protection. But they weren't in an enlightened city like New York anymore. "Naturally, being in a strange place they were in fear of danger coming their way," McCall remembered. "They demanded that I furnish police protection, in fact, bodyguards around the clock. I explained to them that with my limited manpower, I had my hands full with proper law enforcement and protection as was my sworn duty to do. I informed them that no one had invited them to Florida. They were not needed here and were only making things more complicated. I did not have sufficient personnel to furnish bodyguards for do-gooder curiosity seekers and meddlers from out-of-state. I suggested they return home or where they could feel safe, that we could handle things here in a orderly and legal manner without the interference and confusion they were causing."

Williams and McCall never exchanged words, but the New York attorney knew exactly where he stood. "Willis McCall was just another thing altogether... Willis McCall always intimidated me. I never felt comfortable around him. He never spoke to me. He never said anything to me. But rumors came to us that he was going to get that nigger lawyer from New York and that did not make me feel comfortable," Williams recalled.

And Lake County was about to become more crowded, as reporters from the North made plans to cover the trial. *New York Post* reporter Ted Poston was especially anxious to return. "I had to go. I'd become complacent about the status of the Negro after so many years in New York," said Poston. Poston's editor Jimmy Graham finally agreed to send him back into the South, but with a condition: Poston was required to immediately give the defense lawyers and "other persons" Graham's telephone number, "just in case anything happens." The NAACP volunteered to put the reporter up in a Negro hotel in Orlando, and then secretly secured rooms with local Negro sympathizers. According to Poston, he and Williams, "went through the hotel's front door every evening, later sneaked through the back to one of the private homes." In Poston, the NAACP now had a mouthpiece to rival McCall's shills at the *Mount Dora Topic, Orlando Sentinel* and *Leesburg Commercial.*

With time running out, Williams paid another visit to Akerman, who had since discussed the offer with his wife of 16 years. Just as he expected, she adamantly opposed him getting involved. "My mom was not as open-minded as Dad. She grew up in Eufaula, Alabama. I'm sure it was hard for her, but if it was what Dad wanted, that was what they did," Akerman's daughter, Lucy stated.

When Williams visited Akerman, the attorney and his nephew were well on their way to building a successful practice. In fact, they had just expanded, taking on a partner, Joseph E. Price, Jr., who had graduated from law school in June. "I was right out of law school, in three months he made me a partner... When I went in to talk to him, he told me, 'trial lawyers aren't made, they're born. I plan to throw you right in the pond -- if you swim I'll make you a partner. If you don't, you'll be gone.' So almost immediately he had me working on robbery cases, criminal cases, civil cases," Price said. Akerman again told Williams he couldn't take the case, but also left the door open to further discussion. According to Price, "Alex told them, 'I won't leave you in the lurch, if you can't get adequate counsel then we'll try it.'

A few days later, with the trial now just a week away, Williams revisited Akerman in desperation. "On the evening of August 22, 1949, at approximately 5 p.m., I went to the office of Alex Akerman, Jr. and from five until approximately 8:30 I explained to him in great detail the effort I had expended in trying to obtain defense counsel, and I pleaded with him to act in such capacity for these boys," Williams stated. Akerman listened closely and made notes, then again declined, saying, "A lawyer's first responsibility is to his existing clients, and I have six clients whose interests might be prejudiced if I took this case." Akerman explained that his clients were Negroes seeking to break the color barrier at all-white University of Florida. The leader of the group, Virgil Hawkins had applied for admission in April 1949, but the university's board of control, citing the school's constitution, denied admission. Since then, five other Negro students had joined Hawkins. It was the kind of groundbreaking case Akerman had been looking for. Since the University of Florida was the only tax-supported law school in the state, denying admission to the six Negroes was clearly a violation of the 14th Amendment.

Williams was now thoroughly convinced Akerman was the man to head the defense for the Groveland Three, and he wasn't leaving until Akerman realized it as well. He finally won out. "With great reluctance Mr. Akerman agreed to do so and did act in this capacity," Williams recalled. In the end, Akerman's conscience wouldn't let him refuse. Williams obviously had nowhere else to turn. In his mind, Akerman had to say "yes." It was simply the right thing to do. He might not save Shepherd, Irvin and Greenlee, but he had to try; the defendants had absolutely no chance of avoiding the electric chair without him. "The defense of the Groveland accused was the performance of a duty not sought by me. I knew that I would be criticized by the ignorant, the prejudiced and the bigoted, but I believed that in the main the good citizenry of Central Florida would not condemn one who had the courage of his conviction and performed this duty regardless of choice," Akerman said. "I didn't see how in good conscience I could turn it down although I realized what the consequences would be." There was definitely a sense of, "if I don't, who will?" Akerman told his daughter, Lucy that "he didn't know at first if they were actually innocent. He just knew that they needed representation."

If filing suit to integrate the University of Florida didn't soil his reputation, he figured the Groveland case surely would. Akerman knew from the start that his decision would forever change his life. "I had just started my political life. Being the only Republican in the Florida Legislature in 1947 and 1948, I knew that this would be an end to that. In weighing the balances I didn't see how I could turn it down. So I took the case." It was a decision that friends, family and associates would question for years to come. In the days to come Akerman would find many of his friends agreed the accused deserved competent representation, they just couldn't figure out why Akerman had to be the one to provide it. "Well, different people said, 'What in the world are you doing in that thing?' and so forth and so on," Akerman recalled.

Akerman agreed to defend the Groveland Three for $2,500, more than the LDF had to spend, but Williams was in no position to negotiate. It was fair money, but a pittance for such a formidable challenge. Williams was pleased. Anyone bold enough to try to integrate a Southern university was sure to give three accused rapists his best effort. Yes, Akerman would do. Akerman may have been born in the South (Georgia), but as the *Chicago Defender* noted, he was "a southerner with a conscience." Open-mindedness ran in the family: his grandfather, Amos T. Akerman, Georgia District Attorney had prosecuted the original Ku Klux Klan, supervising federal grand juries that returned more than 3,000 indictments in 1871. Six hundred Klansmen were convicted, and 65 ringleaders imprisoned for up to five years at the United States penitentiary in Albany.

Akerman was the right choice, but the time-consuming search for an attorney proved costly. By the time Gaylord was released and replacement counsel employed, the defendants had languished for 26 days without representation. Twenty-six days of lost preparation.

Akerman took the case knowing that the lapse would likely prove fatal for Greenlee, Irvin and Shepherd.

After meeting with Gaylord, Akerman knew he had made the right decision. "I conferred with him and he said he would neither move for a change of venue, nor would he attack the jury panel, which were the only two things that had any possibility of success... he said that in his opinion, the jury panel was properly selected and that there was no need for a change of venue." Akerman was shocked. Considering the inflammatory press coverage and Lake County's history of all-white juries, a change of venue request and challenge to the jury pool were automatic actions any lawyer worth his salt would pursue.

Gaylord was happy to be off the hook. It was a case he couldn't win. Besides, even if by some miracle he did prevail, everyone agreed representing the Groveland rapists would ruin his career.

Chapter 12 -- Mission Impossible

The newly-formed defense team of Alex Akerman, Jr., Franklin H. Williams, Horace Hill and Joseph E. Price Jr. immediately began working to disprove Norma Padgett's allegations. To a man, they knew they were between the proverbial rock and hard place. The task would have been formidable even if the team had two or three months to prepare; instead they had less than two weeks. Not only was time against them, but their efforts to learn the truth were met with a veil of countywide silence. Most Negroes were afraid to talk, and Lake County's whites had no desire to get involved and invite the wrath of their God-fearing neighbors.

Akerman hoped to make the most of the weekend preparing for the trial, but as Friday afternoon wore on, radio reports detailing an impending storm became more urgent. A hurricane that had been hovering off the coast was heading inland. When the storm made landfall late in the day, it swamped the central part of the state, knocking out power lines from Orlando to Tampa and dumping nearly 2 inches of rain. By the time the winds eased just before 11 a.m. on Sunday, trains were running two hours behind schedule, phone lines were down and some roads were closed. The storm not only impeded trial preparations, it also torpedoed NAACP fund-raising efforts, which had only brought in $700, a sum that "would not pay preliminary costs." The freak storm would cost Akerman and his assistants dearly. They were stuck in Orlando, unable to travel to Lake County, make phone calls or send telegrams. As they waited for the weather to break, Williams and Akerman discussed strategy. Neither man had ever gone into court with the deck so clearly stacked against him.

Mabel Norris-Reese (editor of the *Mount Dora Topic*), her articles were vicious," Williams said.

Meanwhile, the prosecution's case looked solid. Hunter had witnesses, both white and black, who would impugn Shepherd and Irvin. He also had physical evidence Deputy James Yates had gathered. Plus, his practice sessions with the Padgetts were going well: especially with Norma, whose poise and confidence improved with each meeting. He had no doubt the jury would find her convincing. The prosecutor was ready to go to trial. Well, almost ready. Hunter decided to call Lawrence Burtoft in for another round of questioning. Perhaps his story would be more favorable to the state now that he had time to think things over. In Hunter's office, Burtoft didn't remember anything differently. The woman hadn't been upset, her clothes weren't torn, she said she didn't know the men who had kidnapped her and she didn't say anything about being raped. Yes, he was sure on all four points. Obviously, Burtoft's testimony would be of no use. Hunter was disappointed, but far from distraught. He still had more than enough ammunition. He knew that when all was said and done, all the state needed was Norma and Willie Padgett. The jury would do the rest.

Hunter was confident the defense would continue to overlook Burtoft, but Jess decided to subpoena Burtoft just to be safe. Hunter figured that even if Akerman saw the list of state witnesses, he would assume everyone the prosecution intended to call would corroborate Norma's story. Of course, Hunter would never call Burtoft, and the defense would be none the wiser.

With Burtoft "hidden," Hunter turned his attention to finding someone who could bolster the case, an ace in the hole in case the Padgetts faltered on the stand. Hunter discussed his quandary with McCall, who suggested that Groveland bolita dealer Henry Singleton could be counted on to testify against the defendants. He would say whatever the sheriff told him to, or wind up in jail for gambling or bootlegging. "Henry Singleton? He was a bootlegger. He was everything McCall wanted him to be. He sold liquor, he wrote numbers, he was in McCall's pocket," Walter's sister, Henrietta recalled. It was common knowledge among the Negroes in south Lake County that Singleton was a stoolie, and it was rumored that he gave McCall a cut of his action to keep the lawman from closing down his racket. "I've heard everything. The bolita thing (that McCall received payoffs to look the other way) was investigated. I heard he was in whiskey and gambling and everything else," said Tom Hurlburt Jr., whose father worked for McCall.

Singleton readily agreed to implicate the accused, and the news was immediately leaked to the local press. Mabel Norris-Reese swallowed the bait, hook, line and sinker. In an Aug. 18 article, Norris-Reese reported that "Surprise Witness," Henry "Singletary" would testify that Shepherd and three other men had tried to rob him on the evening of July 15. To bolster the incredible story, Hunter claimed that Shepherd had confessed to the attempted robbery. Norris-Reese wrote, "Their plot was foiled, Shepherd told Hunter, when Singletary appeared at his door with a gun, and they all fled. It was then, Hunter said Shepherd told him, that they set forth for Leesburg and found the young couple stranded on the road." Once again, Norris-Reese had allowed herself to be used by the McCall-Hunter tandem. The *Topic's* editor had been wearing rose-colored glasses from the get-go, painting McCall and Hunter as white-hatted heroes. Some of her hyperbole bordered on nauseating. To wit, her two-part "Lake County Personalities" feature on Hunter, which read in part: "Consider the Groveland story. Jesse was plunged into the thick of it when he pitched in to aid Sheriff Willis McCall in quelling the aroused feelings of white against Negro. Jesse's understanding of and method of dealing with the race problem is one that could be taken up as a course in a university. He could probably talk with some of the most hard-bitten Klansmen in the South, and have them doff their sheets and adopt his form of reasoning -- if he could meet with them... so even as the affair still bristled with its potentialities of death, Jesse Hunter stepped in with McCall and used his personality on those men. He was severe -- "when circumstances demand it, I can be as tough as the next fellow" -- but he was reason in the blackness of mob unreasoning. He won. Between him and the soft voice of Sheriff McCall, the sullenness disappeared and the men indicated their willingness to wait for law to take its course."

The *Topic* continued to publish propaganda right up to the start of the trial. In reporting Judge Truman Futch's announcement of special rules for the trial, Norris-Reese reported that, "The judge indicated that he is less fearful of Ku Klux Klan action at the trial than he is of 'agitators or agents being sent in to purposely start trouble to the end that the critics of the south might have something to base criticism upon.' He mentioned possible action by the National Association of (sic) the Advancement of Colored People, which has published accusations in the north that the defendants were beaten by sheriff deputies in an effort to obtain confessions from them." Such sensational accounts ensured that the trial remained the number one topic of conversation throughout the area. Many whites spoke of the approaching trial as if it was a county fair, or carnival. And it wasn't just the men. An Aug. 18 article in the *Topic* headlined, "Women Beg For 'Reserved Seats' At Trial; Conduct Laws Cited," stated that aides to court officials were kept busy answering requests from, "a multitude of women wanting to observe the trial of the three Negroes accused of raping a young Lake county (sic) bride." Many of the women asked for "reserved seats."

For central Florida, the Groveland case would be the trial of the century, but Judge Futch wasn't about to allow his courtroom to be turned into a circus. He spent the days leading up to Aug. 29 drafting a lengthy list of stringent rules. Visitors in the courtroom would be limited to those who could be seated, and no standing or loitering in the hallways, stairways or other parts of the courthouse would be allowed for 30 minutes before court convened and after it recessed. Also, the elevators were to be closed, except to officers of the court or individuals to whom the sheriff gave special permits. Futch also mandated that anyone bringing a, "valise, satchel, bag, basket, bottle, jar, jug, bucket, package, bundle, or other such item," would be searched. Crutches, canes and walking sticks would only be allowed after they were searched and determined to be, "necessary aids." Cameras and packages were prohibited.

Once again, Norris-Reese was happy to get the word out, reporting that, "'Agitators' and critics of the south will have little opportunity of stirring the boiling pot of Lake County's notorious rape case... Judge Futch's precautions were aimed at preventing the necessity of a change of venue in the trial as occurred in its parallel in Gadsden County about seven years ago. In that case, three Negroes took a white woman and carried her to a field where they raped her. She was shot, covered with leaves and branches and left for dead. However, she regained consciousness, made her way to county officials and turned in the alarm. The three were arrested, and readily confessed. But the feelings that had been aroused over the crime prevented it from coming to trial at Quincy near where it happened. The trial was transferred to Gainesville to escape angry mobs, and there the trio was sentenced to the electric chair." On the surface, the article appeared to be an example of good old-fashioned newsgathering. But Norris-Reese wasn't even living in Florida in the early 1940s when the "parallel" case occurred. She obviously was reporting an account related to her by McCall or Hunter, probably the latter. Not that a true parallel existed; the men in Gadsden County raped and attempted to murder a woman. Not even McCall had accused the Groveland Three of attempting murder. Once again, the *Topic* had printed as fact, hearsay that would surely further inflame the public.

With pre-trial motions taking shape and the trial still a few days away, Williams turned his attention to completing the investigation he had begun a month earlier before being called away by the search for an attorney. With one eye out for "the law," Williams set out to learn the truth about what happened in the wee hours of July 16. Few people were willing to talk, but he eventually picked up bits and pieces of information from, "almost 40 to 50 people, different kinds of people from all around the place." The interviews, some no more than brief conversations, convinced Williams that Norma and Willie Padgett were, "very low class people" and that Norma had returned to her parents because Willie used to beat her. After the interviews Williams theorized what took place on July 16.

"Now what happened thereafter, this in my judgment, I pieced together. He drives Norma down the road, drives off the road and assaults his wife. She gets hysterical and she jumps out of the car and runs away. He tries to start the car and cannot. Along comes a car with these three Black guys in it. Shepherd, Irvin and Ernest Thomas, who had apparently had been in Orlando, at a bar, drinking and they stopped to give him a push and they pushed him and took off. And went home, because they were in bed. He is scared to death that Norma is going to go home and tell the Cracker parents and brothers of hers that he had attempted to rape her, that is the end of him. He frantically tries to find his wife. He goes into the nearest town... stops at a gas station, gets the gas station attendant and says that four niggers had stopped him and accosted him and kidnapped his wife and had left him by the side of the road. They get back in his car to go look for Norma. They are driving down the road, this night man at the gas station had said that he had come down the road and he thought he had seen a woman walking along the side of the road. If a woman had been raped by four Negroes, she would have flagged down the car. So, they, coming along and they see her and Padgett jumps out and he runs up to Norma out of the hearing distance of this night guy and he says to her, 'You know, baby, you just been raped by four niggers. Don't say anything else. This is what I have told him.' Now, what had happened, Norma, and now this is pure conjecture, but just a month before in a local magazine, a Mount Dora girl had been picked as Miss Lake County or something and her picture was on the cover of this magazine... She pictures herself a heroine, either at that moment or subsequently and when they come back to the car with this night gas station attendant, he says, 'She was raped by four niggers, weren't you?' And she say, 'Yes.' The die is cast and from there on she became the center of all kinds of attention. And she went along with the game," Williams concluded.

Williams' memory of a local girl making the cover of a magazine is accurate, but it wasn't just any magazine. Lake County's Lois Driver graced the August 1949 cover of *Ladies Home Journal*, which had a circulation of 4,500,000. The issue with Driver on the cover didn't reach Florida until July 29, nearly two weeks *after* Norma Padgett cried "rape," but Driver had been in the headlines prior to July 16. In fact, in the months leading up to July, no woman appeared in local newspapers more frequently than the daughter of Mr. and Mrs. J.E. Driver. The *Topic* ran her photo when: Lois won a beauty contest at the Wildwood Labor Day celebration in 1948; won the beauty contest at the Miss Merry Christmas contest in Orlando the following month; and again when she was crowned Tangerine Queen in Winter Haven one week later. Next came a photo of Lois boarding a school bus after being named Tangerine Queen. She was back on the front page in the spring when she was crowned Agriculture Queen at the University of Florida. And, finally, "Lois Driver, Cover Girl," was on the front page in the spring of '49 when she was named Miss Mount Dora. Yes, it's safe to assume that Norma Padgett -- and every other young woman in Lake County -- was aware of Lois Driver prior to July 16, 1949.

When Williams and Hill weren't running the back roads of Lake County, they were usually in Orlando conferring with Akerman or members of Samuel Shepherd's family, who had moved in with Sammie's sister. "Fannie. She was the, what you call it, the Rock of Gibraltar. And she had all the family, me, everybody, with one person, two people working. She and her husband," Walter's sister, Henrietta recalled. Actually, Fannie's husband was the only one working, for a while, that is. While he got along well with his wife's family, the strain of having them live with them, compounded by frequent visits from attorneys and reporters and rumors that the violence would follow the Shepherds to Orlando, soon overtook him. "He was a good man, but used his lack of education as a crutch most times. So when his mother heard of our troubles, she sent the other two sons down to get my husband and took him back up there (to Georgia). And he was the only one here working and he went that next day after they arrived and I had no money or job and no food in the house. Yes, I knew that he was afraid too, but to leave like that with me and six of my family members who had just lost their home and everything, that didn't seem real to me. And what money he had made that week, he took that too," said Sammie's sister, Fannie. After a few days, Fannie realized her husband wasn't coming back, and everyone agreed to find jobs. Fortunately, help was on the way for the nearly-destitute family. The NAACP's Orlando chapter organized a special committee to provide food and clothing for the families of the prisoners.

Having the family so close to Akerman's law office was one of the few breaks the lawyer had. As the attorneys worked to establish alibis and learn more about the men they were charged with saving, members of the legal staff frequently visited Fannie's home. Family members were also called to Akerman's office. The meetings were especially helpful for

Williams, who had the unenviable task of determining the veracity of dozens of rumors he had heard. For instance: Shepherd and Irvin had incurred McCall's wrath by refusing to return to the orange groves. The rumor may, or may not, have been true regarding Shepherd, but Henrietta Irvin said it certainly didn't apply to her brother. "He did go to work in the fields. He went to work with my father. I don't know what Sammie said, but I know Walter never say that. Walter was working in the fields. Mr. Edge's fields. He was on his way to work that morning. So he was working. He was working for his pay for his own convenience. He didn't lay around on my father."

Chapter 13 -- Beginning To Fight

On Aug. 24, Harry Gaylord officially withdrew from the case, a request Judge Truman Futch quickly granted. Alex Akerman Jr. then stepped forward and became attorney of record. He was accompanied by Franklin Williams, making history as the first Negro attorney to set foot in a Lake County courtroom. Sheriff Willis McCall studied the defendants' new attorney with a wary eye. He was young, probably about 35, and far from imposing. And he seemed a little stiff. He was nowhere near as folksy as Hunter. No way the jury was going to warm up to Akerman. Not in a coon's age. Sure, he'd play better than Williams, but McCall was sure jurors would immediately see that the Orlando lawyer was no better than the NAACP "agitators" that were paying him. Most would say Akerman was nothing but a nigger-lover.

The change of attorneys wasn't exactly front-page news. In most stories it was a sentence, or a paragraph, at most. Some reporters who had been following the case didn't mention it at all. But that's not to say the local press was taking a hiatus until the trial started. Mabel Norris-Reese remained foremost in fanning the flames of righteous indignation. Her editorial, "When The Truth Will Out" called Lake County "a Garden of Eden," and stated "…it will be a relief when Aug. 29 rolls around and the truth is out… That is when the court of law will bring reason into the turbulence that the case has caused; when the true story of what happened to that young Bay Lake couple will be told, probably in unpretty details so that a jury can be convinced. However, it must be told so that the jury can get at the actual crime, too long submerged by the Northern press because a Negro bolito king's home and a Negro fortune teller's home were burned in reprisal by angry white men. That jury must be reminded that a young woman was violated, horribly, and that justice is due her." Norris-

Reese's editorial all but ensured the courtroom would be packed. To high-minded whites like Norris-Reese, the trial was part justice, part entertainment. An "undelivered letter" to Judge Truman G. Futch published on the editorial page, spoke volumes: "Dear Judge: We overheard someone say: 'Of course, I hope there's no trouble in this trial, but it sure would be fun to see all those women scamper.'" Three men facing the electric chair, and Norris-Reese was making jokes.

As the trial approached, Henrietta (Irvin) Shepherd continued to have moments of despair and uncertainty. Instead of enjoying the glow of being a newlywed, she spent most of her waking hours worrying about her brother, Walter, and her brother-in-law, Sammie. Henrietta was sure things could only get better. But they didn't. "So the trial was getting ready to start, so James, we all would go downtown every night to the lawyers' office... We all had to assemble there for some reason. Downtown Orlando. And so James was told he had to go to court for some reason. I don't know. If I had been older I would have been thinking, 'Hey, what do you have to go to court for? You haven't done nothing.' But anyway, he left, that morning, going to court," Henrietta recalled. James didn't come home that night, or the next.

In Tavares, a deputy arrested James Shepherd without explanation on the afternoon of Aug. 24. Henrietta and her family had no idea that James was behind bars. There had been no phone call, leaving his young bride to wonder if perhaps James was with his boss, Mr. Fields, or God forbid, had run off. James was a timid man, and Henrietta knew all too well the toll the arrests and racial uprising had taken on him. Henrietta spent a sleepless night, but finally dozed off. Nothing had changed when she awoke: James hadn't come home.

The much-anticipated courtroom drama began on Aug. 25 with defense motions to withdraw pleas of not guilty and set aside arraignment. The hearing started with both sides moving to bolster their legal teams. Hunter sought to have his son Walton sworn in as assistant state attorney, while Akerman asked that Williams be allowed to join the defense. Futch loathed allowing Williams inside the rail, but couldn't very well say "yes" to the state and "no" to the defense. And he was definitely not going to say "no" to Jess. The judge quietly granted both requests.

Akerman opened the proceedings by explaining that he didn't enter the case until Aug. 22, just three days prior, and hadn't had time to "inquire into the summoning, empanelling and qualification or disqualification of the grand jury." Translation: the defense team wasn't in place when the indictments were handed down and Akerman wanted time to investigate the charges. Hunter replied that Akerman had agreed the trial could be scheduled any time after the 22nd. Akerman denied agreeing to anything. To support his contention, Akerman called Williams, who detailed being sent to Florida by Thurgood Marshall because, "we had made numerous efforts by telephone to obtain a report from some competent person in the State of Florida as to the true facts of this case." Williams also said that the defendants had asked him to continue his investigation when he visited them in prison on July 31.

Hunter was determined to dash defense claims that there wasn't time to prepare. The prosecutor cited the Aug. 13 *Pittsburgh Courier* article that quoted Williams as saying the NAACP had been retained to handle the defense. Surprised that Hunter had a copy of the Negro newspaper, Williams lamely answered that he had not spoken "to any one connected with that paper." Hunter scoffed, asking Williams if he had told the newspaper he was convinced the accused were innocent. Williams admitted that he had. Hunter then asked, "At the time you are alleged to have given this interview you had completed your investigation hadn't you?" But Williams wasn't about to fall into the trap. There was no way he was going to support the absurd insinuation that the defense had concluded its investigation (and therefore must have been ready for trial) by Aug. 13. "The purpose of my investigation was to obtain information to enable me to decide whether they were innocent or guilty, not information for the defense. I had no way of knowing whether we could assist them or not," Williams curtly stated. Hunter also took exception to the quote in the *Courier* that the rape charge was "trumped up" to keep Negro workers in line. Hunter asked, "Did you know when you made that statement that the vast majority of the law-abiding colored men in that community, fruit pickers, made from $15 to $25 per day every day they wished to work?" Williams replied, "I did not," to which Hunter asked, "You jumped to conclusions?" Akerman objected as Williams answered, "I didn't jump at conclusions." Futch overruled. Hunter again pounced. "You still affirm that is a fact?" Williams tersely answered, "I affirm that is my opinion."

Before Williams could step down, Hunter forced the NAACP attorney to admit that the defense couldn't even find a Lake County resident willing to testify that the trial should be moved. Williams explained that the two parties he had contacted were, "both frightened and afraid to sign such affidavits." Rather than allow Williams to elaborate on the racial tension that permeated the county, Hunter adeptly shifted gears and chided the NAACP attorney for bypassing his office during his "investigation." The prosecutor hit a home run when he forced Williams to admit that NAACP investigators hadn't attempted to contact the sheriff's office nor State Attorney's Office after coming to Florida on July 31. Hunter's line of attack was clear: Williams would have gone through "official channels" if he was *really* interested in learning the truth.

If Williams didn't realize Hunter was a wily opponent before taking the stand, he knew by the time he stepped down. As Williams returned to the defense table, Hunter passionately addressed the court, declaring that he expected to try the case on its merits and present a fair case, but the NAACP was, "publishing scandalous and slanderous lies… in an effort to create, not good feeling among the races, but to create hatred and disharmony among the people in this county." Of course, the defense took exception. Akerman charged that Hunter had been so intent on a speedy trial that he had completely disregarded the defendants' rights to be represented by counsel at the indictment. Moments later, Futch denied both the Motion to Withdraw Pleas and Set Aside Arraignment.

Akerman countered by arguing the Motion to Quash Indictment, which contended, "that unless sufficient and reasonable time for such investigation and consideration is granted to the said defense counsel by this Court your defendants will be denied rights guaranteed them by the Fourteenth Amendment to the U.S. Constitution..." Akerman then submitted a strongly-worded, 12-part Motion for Continuance. It was an impressive piece of lawyering, especially considering that the motion was based entirely on extensive newspaper reports, Williams' interviews, and good old-fashioned common sense. Two points were at the heart of the motion: that Akerman hadn't had time to sufficiently prepare, and that an atmosphere of violence threatened not only the Groveland Three, but their lawyers' attempts to establish their innocence. The motion contended that:

- The prisoners were, "transported to the State Prison at Raiford, because of the general state of excitement, prejudice, mob violence and lawlessness... caused and created by an attitude of prejudice directed at and towards your defendants and because of the fear that your defendants would be subject to physical harm and violence by lawless persons."

- "Lawless mobs were roaming throughout the County of Lake determined to seek and find your defendants and to then inflict grievous bodily injury upon them... a state of hysteria, prejudice and ill-feeling was rampant throughout the County and among a large body of citizens... that local and county law enforcement officials were unable to cope with the situation."

- The media had fanned the flames of racial passion. The *Orlando Sentinel* cartoon of the four electric chairs was singled out for, "calling for and demanding that the extreme penalty of death be leveled against your defendants thereby creating in the minds of the readers of such publications prejudiced, biased and pre-conceived notions of the innocence or guilt of your defendants of the crime for which they were subsequently indicted..."

- "No member of your defendants race, namely, the Colored or Negro race has ever served upon a grand jury of such County with the exception of one Negro, a County employee, who served on the grand jury which returned the indictment herein... that your defendants' counsel desires and needs a sufficient and reasonable time to investigate and ascertain whether there has been a systematic exclusion of Negroes from grand jury service in such County..."

- "That your defendants' counsel has not as yet been furnished with a copy of the indictment herein and has not had the opportunity to investigate the summoning, impaneling, qualifications or disqualifications of said grand jurors and thus does not know whether the indictment herein is valid and unless given a reasonable opportunity to investigate..."

- "A change of venue is necessary if they are to receive a fair and impartial trial... but their defense counsel has not had sufficient time to properly investigate the facts and prepare a motion for change of venue and obtain the necessary affidavits..."

- "That your defendants are held in custody in the State Prison at Raiford and that their only opportunity to contact parties who may be material witnesses for their defense is through their counsel and that because of the mob violence herein above set out many of these parties have been driven out of their homes in Groveland in the County of Lake to distant points in Florida and have been warned not to return to Groveland which makes it extremely difficult for your defense counsel to confer with these parties and to ascertain whether they are material witnesses, and if so, to procure their attendance at the trial..."

- That Raiford was, "a distance of more than one hundred miles from Lake County, Florida, and more than one hundred miles from the office of their defense counsel which makes it extremely inconvenient and impractical for your defendants to confer with their counsel..."

- "That shortly after their arrest, a mob of several hundred persons gathered around the jail in Tavares... said mob did seek its vengeance by destroying and damaging the property of other members of your defendants race and generally intimidating and terrorizing all of the citizens of the Negro race in and around the town of Groveland... that the great public indignation and hostility was aroused not only against your defendants, but against many members of their race, which indignation continues up to the date of this Motion; that widespread newspaper publicity has been given and your defendants have been warned through the editorial column of at least one of the newspapers, which is widely read throughout Lake County, that if their attorneys attempt to diligently defend them, that mob violence may occur... it was practically impossible for your defendants to obtain counsel... a situation now exists in the County of Lake which makes it practically and psychologically impossible to secure a fair and impartial trial..."

- "That your defendants are charged with the crime of rape, a capital offense under the laws of the State of Florida; that due to the serious and heinous nature of this charge a proper defense demands unusual diligence and the careful exploration of every avenue and byways of law and facts..."

Futch promised a timely ruling on the motion and brought the hearing to a close. The judge was definitely a tough, no-nonsense customer, who had already shot down two well-written motions. Naturally, the defense team was frustrated, even though Akerman had held his own in arguing the motions. Sure, Hunter had scored points with the *Pittsburgh Courier* (who had given him that clipping?), but Akerman had proved himself a worthy opponent by presenting statistics breaking down the racial composition of the county, which showed the absurdity of only one Negro being called for grand jury duty.

By the evening of the 25th, Henrietta (Irvin) Shepherd still hadn't heard from her husband. That night, family members finally brought their concerns to Akerman, who immediately contacted Hunter. The state attorney denied an arrest had been made, but Akerman wasn't convinced. He then called the sheriff's office, where a deputy revealed that Futch had ordered James Shepherd be held as a material witness. When Akerman reached the judge at his home at 7:30 the next morning, Futch brashly confirmed he had issued an order to hold Samuel Shepherd's brother as a suspect. When asked what bail had been set at, Futch said he would fix bail at 10 a.m. that morning. Akerman contacted McCall's office at approximately 10:12 a.m., but was told bail hadn't been set and probably wouldn't be.

Akerman tried again around noon, but was again informed that no bail had been set. James Shepherd was staying in jail.

Akerman was fuming. James wasn't a suspect or a material witness, as McCall claimed. "The NAACP charges the action was taken to prevent its attorney, Franklin H. Williams, from interviewing James. Williams stated there is no legal authority for the arrest," wrote Ramona Lowe in the *Chicago Defender.* "They told him (James) he was there for his protection," Henrietta remarked. "I said he was not there for his protection. I said he was there because they knew that the NAACP had gotten involved, and I think that they didn't want James talking. But James wasn't going to do much talking anyway. He was a soft guy. He was a very soft and humble person."

And James wasn't the only relative of the defendants' to end up behind bars just before the trial. Officers also paid a visit to the Greenlee home in Santa Fe. "The police arrested my daddy and my brother Tom Jr., who was home on leave from the Air Force. I'm not sure who it was; I think it was the Alachua County Sheriff. They weren't in jail very long. It wasn't no seven or eight days," Charles Greenlee's sister, Ethel Retha said.

With the testimony phase of the trial just around the corner, the state was working overtime to frustrate the defense and ensure the convictions McCall had guaranteed. "I think there was a feeling that Lake County was on trial, and that this crime had been committed in Lake County; there had been an attempt to break into the jail; there'd been a burning of these homes. I think the whole idea was, 'let's try this case and get it over with,'" Akerman recalled. The state's maneuvering was understandably frustrating, but Akerman couldn't continue fighting the shenanigans; he had a defense to prepare, and precious little time left to do so. Convinced there was no way to free James, Akerman devoted himself to writing additional pretrial motions worded to buy the defense an extension, while his assistants searched for witnesses who could help their case. Unfortunately, the good people of Lake County still weren't talking. Barely any information trickled in, and what little that did was second- or third-hand. Significantly, more than one person swore that Norma hadn't been raped, but no one was willing to testify in a court of law about what was being whispered throughout the county. "Everybody was frightened... There were people who were afraid to give affidavits saying that they couldn't get a fair trial -- the motion for change of venue has to be supported by affidavits," Horace Hill recalled. Williams, Akerman and Price agreed they had to get the indictment thrown out. But to do that, they first had to file a motion to withdraw the not guilty pleas. It was a long shot, but if the judge upheld the motion, another arraignment would be necessary, which would pave the way for the defense to make a motion for change of venue.

As Akerman pieced together scant pieces of information, he became convinced his clients were innocent. He still wasn't sure exactly what *had* happened, but the rumor that Norma and Willie got into an argument and she left him made sense. Some said Norma had been with another white man. Had Norma concocted the "rape" story to make her husband jealous? Or did Willie persuade his wife to make up the story to cover her indiscretion? Or perhaps Willie made up the story after Norma ran away because he tried to force himself on her, as Franklin Williams believed. Akerman thought all four scenarios were possible. Marshall's assistant, Jack Greenberg was also convinced the Padgetts had concocted a story. "Having said it maybe impulsively in the excitement of maybe having an altercation with her husband or what, then she was stuck with the story and then didn't want to back away from it," Greenberg said. "I've heard a lot of theories. One is that she and her husband had a fight and she went off and just made up this story. Another is somebody raped her but not these people. I think it's pretty clear it was not these." Norma may have been with someone other than her husband, someone of her choosing, but the defense held little hope of learning the man's identity. A blanket of fear still enveloped the county: fear of the sheriff and fear of the Klan. No one dared risk drawing the ire of either by running their mouth.

Back against the wall, Williams again visited the Shepherd and Irvin families in hopes of finding a way to save the Groveland Three. After interviewing Henry Shepherd and his wife, Williams had a clearer understanding of the forces at work in Lake County. The trouble didn't begin on July 16; it had existed for years just under the surface of everyday life, just one match strike away from blowing sky high. Henry told the attorney of the back-breaking work he had done to drain a swamp and build a home, only to have his white neighbors tear down his fence and let their cows eat his crops. Henry also told Williams that the Sheriff McCall was of no help. "...according to Henry Shepherd, he called him and sheriff came out and did not back him up. He said, 'No white, no black man, no nigger has any right to file a claim against a white man.' The man who led the mob that burned and shot the blacks in Stuckey Still was Shepherd's neighbor," Williams said.

From talking with the Shepherds, and a number of local Negroes, Williams learned the story behind the story. He, like the *Chicago Defender's* Lowe, became convinced that McCall bore a grudge against Shepherd and wanted to humble him. More than one person told Williams that local whites resented Irvin and Shepherd wearing their Army uniforms around town after they returned from the service. "There was some real resentment, I heard, against them walking around in their uniforms. Resentment that had been communicated to them from the sheriff incidentally, from Willis McCall. They were both, at least, Walter Irvin was a picker and I believe Shepherd had been a picker before he went into the Army and Shepherd had not gone back to picking. I think Irvin had, but the antagonism towards them was that they were hanging around, not working when there was a shortage of pickers in the orange groves, especially in view of the Korean War. It had taken so many young people away and the story was that the sheriff was gonna get them unless they went back to work. So that, the way that it was reconstructed, both in my head and from the bits of talk that I picked up, was that when Norma Lee Padgett and her husband claimed she had been raped, McCall knew exactly who he wanted to get. He wanted to get Shepherd and Irvin. He wanted to get them. And he went right away to Irvin's house," Williams recalled.

Williams was becoming more and more convinced the Groveland trouble was about citrus, not race or sex. It's a conclusion he shared with the national office, which in turn convinced a reporter from the *Christian Science Monitor* to air the NAACP's findings. The article quoted Roy Wilkins as saying, "Groveland's economy is based almost entirely on citrus culture... According to local sources, law enforcement officers in the county have made a practice of arresting Negro workers who failed to report to the citrus groves, even if engaged in some other gainful occupation. They would be charged with vagrancy before the local police officers and fined." Wilkins firmly believed that the acts of violence against the Negro community, "grew out of a long-festering rancor on the part of sections of the white community against prosperous Negroes. The fact that the three homes burned were miles from Groveland, and were the homes of more prosperous Negroes indicates this strongly." The article quoted Sammie's father as saying, "I had no trouble for a while until I got my house all fixed up and painted -- and then I began to have trouble. I was trying to farm there -- the white folks let their cows into my stuff every time I plant it."

Williams and Hill found corroboration of Henry Shepherd's claims as they quietly moved through Lake's Negro quarters. "We just did not tell anybody we were in town. We would go and somebody would say, 'Go see Mrs. Jones down the street,' and away we went," Williams recalled. Crossing into Lake was always accompanied by anxiety. "Well, we had heard a lot of stories about Lake County. Obviously, I was not completely at ease. Horace and I went in by ourselves and we talked to a number of people," Williams said. "Everybody we could find that knew anything about Shepherd and Irvin." Not everyone knew the accused, but it seemed that everyone had a Willis McCall story.

"Everybody I met was afraid of Willis McCall and of what he might do and of what he could get away with and you would hear all kinds of things. You would hear that you would talk to someone and they would tell you about a sister that had been arrested and that they would try to bring food in to the courthouse and they would hear her screaming at night and they would go down there and McCall would not let them see her. You know, these disjointed stories," Williams said. Most stories were third-person accounts, but not every story was hearsay, as Williams learned after being directed to interview a local woman. "This was the woman that said that her sister was in jail and she could hear her screaming at night and the sheriff will not let her see her. She had gone up to see her two or three times and allegedly, subsequently, the woman was found dead outside of her window."

While the defense scrambled to find someone to contradict Norma, the prosecution team was putting the finishing touches on an already strong case. And Jess Hunter didn't have to worry about members of the Shepherd, Thomas, Greenlee and Irvin families running to the press or providing alibis for the defense. James Shepherd was safely under lock and key, and his parents would soon be joining him. Ernest Thomas' parents were also behind bars, and Mrs. Thomas seemed willing to testify against her slain son in exchange for keeping her juke joint. What choice did she have? Greenlee's kin were also in jail. When McCall learned that Henry and Charlie Mae Shepherd were staying in Jacksonville with relatives, he set out to bring them back as well.

Williams didn't know the parents of the accused were in jail, but he still felt strongly that the Irvins and Shepherds should forget about attending the trial. "We were advised not to try to see them (Walter and Sammie). They didn't know what would be done. For our benefit. And I think Walter told them to tell us to stay away, you know. But there would be times you know, I remember we drove over to Tavares just to look up to see if we could see them up there, you know, somewhere way up there waving their hands or something. But we didn't never see them until after the trial," Henrietta recalled.

Chapter 14 -- Into The Lions Den

Defense attorney Alex Akerman was working on additional pretrial motions when his assistant, Horace Hill, delivered the good news that he had secured four affidavits speaking to the impossibility for the accused to receive a fair trial in Lake. The Negro residents who boldly agreed to lend their names to the cause were: John Dingle, a 41-year resident; Willie Odum, a 28-year resident; M. A. Peterson, who had lived in Lake nine years, and Henry C. Dean, a 25-year resident. All signed a prepared statement that began, "That because of ill-feeling and prejudice on the part of a great number of citizens of Lake County, Florida towards Charles Greenlee, Walter Irvin and Samuel Shepherd and because of undue excitement and prejudice among the people of Lake County, Florida, he does not believe that the said Charles Greenlee, Walter Irvin and Samuel Shepherd can receive a fair and impartial trial..."

Akerman, Joseph Price and Franklin Williams spent the eve of the Aug. 29 pre-trial hearing racking their brains trying to think of anything that would buy them time. They fully expected the judge to deny the motions they already submitted, but they would counter by bombarding Judge Truman Futch with additional motions in the morning. A conversation with Clerk of the Court George Dykes provided the basis for the defense's strongest pretrial motion, an attack on Lake County's whites-only jury selection process. Dykes told Akerman that he couldn't remember the last time a Negro served on a jury, but he'd heard tell of some that had served back in the '20s. Intrigued, Akerman asked just how jurors were selected. The clerk was happy to explain. "The whole panel of jurors in Lake County was selected from names that were put into the jury panel by the county commissioners, each one naming so many in direct proportion to the population. They were selected from white and colored registered voters, and of course, that was a farce. It appeared to be a very fair system, but when you consider at that time the great number of Negroes that were not registered, it was a nice way to exclude them," Akerman said.

Dykes gladly supplied a breakdown of the voting rolls by race, not realizing he was providing ammunition the defense would use against his employer, Lake County. Dykes' numbers showed that 13,380 of the county's 14,182 registered voters were white. Akerman and Williams did the math: whites outnumbered Negroes by a ratio of more than 16-to-1. No wonder Negroes didn't serve on juries. The information, coupled with comments Dykes volunteered, led to a motion charging that officials, "have systematically excluded colored people from Grand Juries for 25 years." The claim wasn't quite accurate; three of the 150 members of the present jury panel were Negroes. Still, three out of 150 was a far cry from adequate representation. Akerman found it ludicrous that even though Negroes comprised a fourth of Lake's population (13,500), only one Negro had been called, and he was a county employee with a reputation for Uncle Tomism. To Akerman, it was clear that the lone Negro juror was included, "for the sole purpose of creating the impression of compliance with the 14th Amendment." That man, March DeBose, may as well have been mute, because he didn't dare vote to return a "no bill." The motion further stated, "that the presence of one Negro upon the grand jury which returned the indictment against your defendants herein did not result from a fair, impartial or lawful summoning..." The motion also charged there were "a great many" who met all of "the statutory qualifications for grand jury service" among Lake County's 4,500 Negroes over 21 years of age. The Orlando lawyer wasn't pulling any punches. He even pointed out that the exclusion of Negroes, "was a systematic and deliberate plan" by the "state officers charged with the responsibility of impaneling grand jurors."

Of course, Dykes told prosecutor Jesse Hunter about his conversation with the defense counsel. Akerman didn't care that Hunter knew. Unlike Harry Gaylord, the court-appointed attorney he replaced, Akerman wasn't afraid to challenge the status quo. He intended to subpoena jury rolls for the past 30 years to prove his contention that Negroes had been excluded. Tipped off that the defense would focus on the lack of Negro representation among potential jurors, Hunter laid the groundwork to undermine Akerman with a story in the local press. In the Aug. 29 edition of the *Mount Dora Topic*, Mabel Norris-Reese duly reported, "As far as he (Hunter) is concerned, there will be little difficulty in selecting the jury. He'll allow the attorneys hired by the National Association of Colored People to make the extended challenges. Jesse's questions will be perfunctory -- he'll ask questions mostly because he is expected to do so. The main thing he'll be hoping for in that jury selection today is that he is able to seat at least one -- and perhaps two -- Negroes. He'd like them there so that he can further convince the N.A.A.C.P. of the sincerity of Lake County in giving a fair trial." Akerman and Williams weren't fooled by Norris-Reese's latest attempt to color the proceedings. They expected Hunter to be anything but contrite when things got under way that morning. They only hoped the judge would be in an agreeable mood.

Futch entered the courtroom promptly at 10 a.m. to hear arguments on the defense motions. Akerman began by asking for a ruling on the Motion to Quash Indictment presented to the

Court on the 25th. Before the judge could answer, Hunter said, "My understanding was that the motion was considered and denied." Akerman shot back that the motion hadn't been argued, to which Hunter replied, "Well it is untimely filed for one thing, and testimony taken here on the motion as made and was denied by the Court is my recollection of it." Futch thought for a moment, then told Akerman that the motion had been filed too late, would not be considered, and was being stricken from the record. Akerman was dumbfounded: it was as if Hunter was pulling a string that made the judge talk.

Akerman recovered quickly, asking the court to set bail for James Shepherd. Futch immediately denied the request. Disgusted, but unruffled, Akerman forged ahead to the amended Motion for Continuance. After reading the motion, Akerman further amended the motion to reflect that Raiford was, "more than 100 miles from the offices of their defense counsel and that it is extremely inconvenient and impractical" for the defendants and their attorneys to confer. Picking up steam, Akerman then submitted a 14-point Application for Removal of Cause, which thoroughly detailed the obstacles the defense had encountered, and outlined the prevailing hostility directed toward the accused. Attached to the application: 20 press clippings, 17 of which were published between July 17 and July 23, and most from the *Orlando Evening Sentinel*. The Application for Removal of Cause stated:

- The prisoners were moved to the State Prison "because of the general state of excitement, prejudice, mob violence and lawlessness;"

- On July 31, the prisoners requested Franklin Williams to obtain for them competent counsel;

- That Williams made "a constant and diligent effort" to obtain qualified counsel, but was unable to until Aug. 22 when Akerman agreed to take the case;

- Since being retained, Akerman, "had to appear before this Court in numerous hearings and has had to prepare numerous pleadings... and that this is the earliest opportunity the defense had to file this Motion for removal of the Cause;"

- The defense was unable to obtain affidavits "because of the feeling of ill will and prejudice"... and citizens feared "for their own safety if they made such affidavits;"

- Because of mob violence and "inflammatory newspaper articles... a situation now exists in the County of Lake which makes it practically and psychologically impossible to secure a fair and impartial trial;"

- "That your defendants believe that if they are brought to trial in Lake County, Florida, lawless and threatening mobs will be in and around the court house evincing a hostile and threatening attitude... and that the jury will not be able to calmly and deliberately consider their case;"

- "That rumor is prevalent.... That unless your defendants are found guilty at their trial, mobs will take the law into their own hands and lynch your defendants;"

- "That the prejudice and ill-feeling... is so great that it has been necessary for this Court to adopt and post rules for the intended trial;"

- That the defendants feared "grievous bodily harm may be inflicted upon them or they may be lynched" if they testify in their own behalf;

- That the defendants were "brutally beaten and abused by persons purporting to be law enforcement officials.... They are in great fear of said law enforcement officials;"

- The Shepherd and Irvin families had been forced to flee and were told they would be lynched if they returned... "the mere return to Lake County, Florida will so terrify them that they will not have control of their mental faculties and be able to testify in this cause;"

- The defendants would "be deprived of life or liberty without due process of law," if compelled to stand trial in Lake County.

To further solidify the motion, Akerman submitted the four affidavits Hill had secured from longtime Negro residents bold enough to swear that Irvin, Shepherd and Greenlee couldn't receive a fair trial in Lake. Akerman also filed an amendment to the Motion for Continuance he had presented on the 25th. Two additional paragraphs had been added: first, that, "many purported facts, which, if introduced as evidence in the trial, would prove their innocence" had been found since the filing of the original motion, and the defense needed "considerable time" to investigate and obtain witnesses; secondly, the hurricane that swept through Lake and Orange counties made it, "impossible for your defendants to utilize two nights and one day in the preparation of their defense."

After Akerman sat down, Hunter presented his replies to the Motion For Continuance, the amended Motion for Continuance, and the Application for Removal of Said Cause: His reply to all three: "The State of Florida... denies each and every allegation... and demands strict proof of each allegation." Hunter wasn't as brief, or direct, in replying to the Motion to Withdraw Pleas of Not Guilty and Set Aside Arraignment filed four days earlier. Hunter charged that the NAACP had been involved in the case since July 26 when William Fordham telegrammed the prison superintendent that he had been retained by the NAACP, and also later when Williams announced he had made "an intensive investigation" and shared the results with Akerman. The hearing ended with Hunter suggesting that the defense make one all-encompassing argument since many of the defense claims were repeated in more than one motion. Akerman agreed. So did Futch, who closed the hearing by stating he would hear arguments at 10 a.m. the following day.

Hunter wasn't as contrite when court reconvened. He opened the hearing by saying he didn't appreciate the flurry of pretrial motions. Hunter was especially peeved by the Motion for Change of Venue, saying it was a serious reflection on the courts of Lake County and the courts of Florida. "There are a lot of absolutely false things going into these pleadings that are being sworn to here. I presume now that Mr. Akerman will want to prove," Hunter thundered. According to Hunter, Akerman and his cohorts were most definitely stalling, in fact, the prosecutor told the judge he had reliable information that the defense intended to "dillydally along and delay the trial." Akerman testily responded, "I move that that remark of the state attorney be stricken from the record. There is a proper method of determining whether these will be true or not by the giving of testimony before the court, today." Hunter countered, "Then I will amend and say that since it is a libel upon the people of Lake County, that we demand strict proof to each one of these allegations." A bemused Futch held his tongue. As the two combatants glared at each other, Futch allowed the amendment to be filed, and then told Akerman to proceed with arguing his motions.

Hunter was back on his feet moments later when Akerman asked the Court to issue subpoenas to: the managing editor of the *Lakeland Ledger*, name unknown; and the two FBI agents who had interviewed the prisoners at the state prison on Aug. 7, names also unknown. Hunter was beside himself: the defense was still trying to construct its case and the trial was already under way. Akerman not only didn't know the names of the FBI agents, he didn't know if their testimony would even help the defense. "Your honor, I object to that. It is entirely beyond any request that should be made of this Court. If the defendants want these witnesses here let it be not by a special order of this Court but by a regular method of filing a praecipe with the clerk of this Court for the issuance of those subpoenas," Hunter barked. Without hesitation, Futch said, "The Court will not issue any order requiring the subpoenaing of the witnesses mentioned." Akerman should have known better. He wisely asked for a recess so the praecipes could be written. Futch wasn't amused. He ordered the hearing to continue. Akerman had no choice but to move on.

Akerman began the tedious task of introducing the newspaper articles into evidence by calling *Orlando Daily Sentinel's* Business Manager Charles Medlin to the stand. After establishing the *Sentinel's* circulation figures, Akerman moved onto Exhibit A, the article headlined, "Lake County Bride Kidnapped." Hunter didn't like where the defense was heading. Rising from his seat, he requested permission to question Medlin. Given the go-ahead, Hunter asked if the newspaper in question had come from Medlin's private files. When Medlin replied in the affirmative, Hunter asked, "Do you object to using them in a proceeding of this kind under a subpoena of this kind?" Medlin promptly played along. "Well, we like to continue to hold our files intact." Akerman had heard enough. "In reply to the objection of Mr. Hunter, I think the lives of three persons are possibly more important than the private files of a newspaper," Akerman boomed. Thankfully, the judge agreed.

Hunter had barely settled into his chair when Akerman handed Medlin the July 17 issue of the *Sunday Sentinel Star* and asked him to read the article headlined, "Lake County Bride Kidnapped." Hunter reacted immediately. "Object to that. First, the article is irrelevant and immaterial to any issue in this case. Second, the article has been introduced, itself. Now I want to make this statement. I may be mistaken but I have been informed -- those gentlemen can correct me if I'm not correct -- that it is their purpose to read newspaper articles and other things for the balance of this week so that the Court cannot function here in the trial of this case on Thursday. Now that's my information," Hunter roared. Akerman wore a wry smile as he replied, "The gentleman is entirely incorrect. We do not intend to put into this record every newspaper article that disseminated throughout Lake County, Florida. It is definitely material to our motion for a removal of cause and for continuance in the case." This time Futch sided with Hunter, telling the defense that the newspapers would be admitted into evidence and the articles didn't need to be read aloud. "The Court is able to read," Futch tersely told Akerman.

Undaunted, Akerman introduced the July 19 issue with the front-page editorial cartoon of the four electric chairs and headline, "No Compromise. The Supreme Penalty." Hunter cringed. He would have to try and undo the damage under cross examination:

Hunter: "Does this cartoon referred to by Mr. Akerman bear any names? Mention any names?"
Medlin: "No sir. There is not any names on it except the cartoonist."
Hunter: "Is that cartoon intended to express a principle behind which this paper stands?"
Medlin: "I couldn't say on that."
Hunter: "Well, don't you think it expressed very strongly the idea that whoever was guilty of viciously raping a woman on the public highways of this county should pay the supreme penalty for it?
Medlin: "I do."

Akerman would have been amused if he wasn't so perturbed. When Hunter finished with his dog-and-pony show, Akerman returned to his pile of press clippings, introducing article after article with headlines like "Night Riders Burn Negroes Homes" and "Flames From Negro Homes Light Night Sky in Lake County." Finally, he reached the bottom of the stack: the Aug. 14 edition containing the article, "McCall says beating charge damn lie." Once again Medlin confirmed that the article appeared in a *Sentinel* edition circulated in Lake County. It was Exhibit O. Medlin had been on the stand for more than an hour.

Akerman next detailed the NAACP's frustrating efforts to find counsel, a prolonged search that ate up precious time that should have been used for trial preparation. Gaylord, the Eustis attorney who had been appointed on Aug. 12, was called to the stand. The deposed lawyer explained how he had been willing to defend the Groveland Three ("to the best of his ability") but had refused to assist the NAACP. "Williams asked me if I would be employed by the NAACP, or the defendants, to try the case. I told him no, under no circumstances, for no amount of money..." Gaylord, who had been present when Akerman initially refused to take the case, also related his first-hand knowledge of Williams' futile attempts to find an attorney. Gaylord said he had repeatedly contacted Hill to find out if a lawyer had been retained, and also recalled visiting a Daytona Beach attorney who agreed to get involved, then changed his mind. Gaylord's testimony clearly showed that the NAACP had spent three to four weeks searching for counsel. But putting Gaylord on the stand was about to backfire. Hunter would point Gaylord in a different direction during cross-examination.

Hunter: "You say you told Mr. Akerman you didn't think any change of venue was necessary in this case?"
Gaylord: "That is true."
Hunter: "You live in this county?"
Gaylord: "Yes, sir."
Hunter: "Knowing what you do, you thought these men could get a fair and impartial trial here?"
Gaylord: "Yes, sir. I told Mr. Akerman that I knew of my own knowledge there had been a colored man on the grand jury, and of my own knowledge knew that for several years colored men had been in the box, and I didn't feel that the disturbance that had occurred at Groveland would affect the trial; that we have always had good jurors in Lake County."
Hunter: "Where do you live?"
Gaylord: "Eustis."
Hunter: "Did the people there know of this disturbance that was going on down at Groveland?"
Gaylord: "I knew of it."
Hunter: "Was there any rioting or burning of buildings in Eustis?"
Gaylord: "No, sir."
Hunter: "Did you hear of any widespread prejudice against the colored race there which would prevent them from getting a fair trial?"
Gaylord: "No, sir."
Hunter: "It is your opinion now that they can get a fair trial -- in this county?"
Gaylord: "Yes, sir."

Hunter couldn't be more pleased. Gaylord not only confirmed the state's claims, but also painted Akerman as uninformed and ignorant of how things were done in Lake County. Akerman hoped to salvage the witness during re-direct. He asked Gaylord if jurors could be expected to erase the newspaper reports that the men had confessed from their minds. "That will depend on the individual juror," Gaylord matter-of-factly replied. On re-cross, Hunter asked if it would be impossible to get a jury. Gaylord answered, "I felt I could get a proper jury if I had tried the case, or get a better jury in Lake County than in any other county." Akerman couldn't let that pass. "Didn't you tell me it might take two weeks to get a jury?" Gaylord was trapped. "I did tell you that, to get one that you felt would fairly and impartially try it," Gaylord stammered.

As Gaylord stepped down, Akerman yielded to Williams. The Negro attorney called Jacksonville physician W.V. Spaulding, who had examined the prisoners at Raiford. It was time to play the trump card: evidence that could get the indictment thrown out -- evidence that the prisoners had been beaten, treated inhumanely and denied their rights after being arrested. After establishing Spaulding's education and experience (a nine-month internship in Kansas City and nine months at Jacksonville's Brewster Hospital), Williams moved to the heart of the issue: his examination of the Groveland Three on Aug. 7. Hunter objected before Spaulding could detail his findings. "I object to that as being totally irrelevant and immaterial. It has no connection whatever with this case." Futch immediately sustained the objection, leaving Akerman utterly flabbergasted. "At this time, may it please the Court, the defendants make a proffer of proof by this witness," Akerman interposed. "It is the intention of the defendants to prove by this witness that he in his capacity…" He never finished the sentence. The judge interrupted, "That has all been gone over. There is no use to encumber the record with it any further." Akerman stubbornly asked, "Is it the ruling of the Court that we cannot make a proffer of the proof?" Futch's terse answer: "You have already proffered the proof." With that, Dr. Spaulding was forced to leave the stand. The ruling was a devastating setback. His star witness silenced, Akerman reluctantly returned to question and answer with newspaper reporters and editors he had been subpoenaed.

The defense didn't have many options remaining. Obviously, Akerman's best line of attack was to prove that racial unrest made a fair trial an impossibility. Akerman called Capt. James Herlong of the Leesburg company of the Florida National Guard to support the contention. Incredibly, under cross-examination, Herlong testified that there was *no* violence when his troops were sent to Groveland on July 17 and 18. He failed to mention that all hell broke loose shortly thereafter. He also failed to mention that his family had huge citrus holdings in the county and that the family business depended on subservient Negro labor.

W.V. Morrow, editor of the Clermont and Groveland newspapers, was next. Since the trouble happened under Morrow's nose, Akerman figured he was the one journalist who couldn't pretend nothing out of order had taken place. But Morrow tried. When questioned about an article which reported that the men had confessed, Morrow explained, "(the) information is based on articles in the various daily papers, and personal conversations I had with people generally… (If) articles appear in those papers that have stood the test two or three days without denial or correction, based on my previous experience as an editor, I assume them to be true. The article you called my attention to appeared to the best of my recollection in a number of daily papers and was not denied for a period of three days. I don't think they were ever denied." Akerman was dumbfounded by the response. According to Morrow, any statement published anywhere must be true if not immediately refuted. Ok, so Morrow got his information secondhand that the sheriff had talked down a lynch mob. That didn't mean he wasn't aware of the unrest in the community he was *supposed* to cover. Akerman wasn't about to let Morrow off so easily. "At the time you printed this article you believed that to be a correct representation of the conditions existing in regard to this particular matter at that time -- in other words you believed these statements about Sheriff McCall having to spirit the Negroes away to prevent serious harm being done to their persons?" Hunter quickly objected. "I object to the question on the ground that the article speaks for itself, and in rather plain language." Again, Futch sustained.

Akerman was dismayed as he turned the witness over to Hunter. In a moment he would be livid.
Hunter: "You were the editor when this thing happened?"
Morrow: "Yes, sir."
Hunter: "Was there any rioting in Clermont, or any colored people's houses burned there?"
Morrow: "I didn't see any or hear of any in Clermont."
Hunter: "How far are you from Groveland?"

120

Morrow: "I think six and half or seven miles."
Hunter: "Everything was peaceful there?"
Morrow: "Yes, sir. Mrs. Morrow and I drove through there that Sunday night, coming from Cypress Gardens. We cut around there someplace."

Price had been listening intently. He would handle the re-direct examination while Akerman and Williams quietly discussed their options.

Price: "Did you go over to Groveland at any time during this period?"
Morrow: "Yes, sir. I was in Groveland quite a number of times."
Price: "Were you there any time around from the 16th to the 19th of July?"
Morrow: "I was there yes, sir."
Price: "Do you recall seeing any Negroes there at that time?"
Morrow: "No, I didn't see any there."
Price: "Just from your own personal feeling, do you think if you had been a Negro yourself, do you think you would have gone over there?"

As Hunter started to object, Morrow answered, "I am not able to put myself in a Negro's mental process. I don't know just offhand." It was perhaps the most telling comment of the entire hearing. *No white* could put himself in a "Negro's mental process." That was the whole problem. Price sat down. He had failed to get a concession that fear and the threat of violence had permeated south Lake County after the arrests. Perhaps Akerman would have fared better, but he had used the time to prepare for the next witness, Willie Padgett.

Akerman knew he had to tread lightly. And that's what he did. Padgett was on the stand less than 15 minutes, and spent most of the time naming his many relatives living in the Groveland area. It was a productive exercise for the defense, which sought to prove that south Lake County was filled with members of the Padgett and Tyson families. At the defense table, Williams counted 18 family members. How could the defendants receive a fair trial when practically everyone in the county was kin or acquainted with Norma and Willie's families? As Padgett returned to his seat, the judge ordered a short recess.

McCall used the break to call the FBI office in Miami, where Special Agent Carson expressed surprise that the defense planned to subpoena his agents. The sheriff figured that little tidbit would shake the G-man up. Carson thanked McCall, hung up, and immediately consulted his superiors. Naturally, he wanted to stay out of the spotlight as badly as McCall wanted him to. After lengthy discussion, Carson decided agents could refuse to testify under Departmental Order 3229, citing the confidential nature of the FBI investigation. But Carson wanted to be sure. He refused to commit either way until discussing the matter with U.S. Attorney Herbert Phillips. When Carson finally contacted Phillips just before 6 p.m., he learned that Departmental Order 3229 would not apply if subpoenas were issued under the agents' true names. Since Akerman didn't know the agents' names, Phillips believed that the men could not be summoned.

After the break, it was back to the press clippings. After a dozen more newspaper articles had been introduced, Akerman had exhausted his line of attack. The time was 5:40 p.m. Akerman was relieved; he was more than ready to drive back to Orlando, lick his wounds and come up with a plan for the next day. But Futch and Hunter had other ideas: they were ready to get on with the trial. Akerman resolutely moved for adjournment, reminding Futch that the defense team had to drive 30 miles to and from the court; was "working night and day" and spending evenings discussing the case with potential witnesses; and that it was the usual custom of the Court to adjourn at a reasonable hour. Futch was unmoved, saying simply, "Proceed with the next witnesses."

But there weren't any other witnesses. After a hasty conference with Williams, Akerman decided to again try to get the coerced confessions in front of the court. Walter Lee Irvin was called to the stand. Akerman quietly led Walter through his arrest, and then asked the $64,000 question: "After you were arrested, were you at any time beaten or abused?" Walter answered, "I was." Hunter immediately objected, calling the line of questioning, "irrelevant and immaterial." Futch upheld, to which Williams boldly asked for an opportunity to prove that the defendants had been beaten. The judge said he would not permit it. Undaunted, Williams called Sammie Shepherd to the stand. He was also asked if he had been abused. The judge didn't appreciate the question. "Just a minute. I ruled on that same thing in the other witness. I don't want you to attempt it any more," Futch scolded. The defense was shut down.

It was now nearly 6 p.m. Akerman was spent. "That's all the witnesses we have at the present time. We have subpoenas out on some others," Akerman said. Hunter piped up, "You have Luther Thomas there." Akerman fired back, "I haven't had even an opportunity to talk to him, Your Honor." Hunter's response: "You have other witnesses that you're going to use." For the umpteenth time that day, Akerman wondered who was conducting the hearing, the judge, or the prosecutor. "We have subpoenas out. If they get here, we're going to use them. I don't even know what subpoenas we have out at the present moment. We have so many. I intend to use the Clerk of the Court," Akerman remarked as he looked to the judge for help. Futch just stared back. "He's right here. You don't have to subpoena him," Hunter commented. He knew what Akerman wanted from Dykes: a list of grand jurors for the past 30 years. Hunter approached the bench. "I am going to ask the Court to intervene and not require the Clerk of this Court to furnish a list of grand jurors up to 30 years at this time, unless it can be shown that it is material to this case," Hunter said. Again, the judge went along, telling Akerman, "I think the request is entirely unreasonable from the present viewpoint." Akerman wearily sat down, his ammunition spent. But Hunter had plenty, and he was ready to get down to business.

When asked how long his witnesses' testimony would take, Hunter replied, "two or three hours." To Akerman's dismay, Futch remarked, "Well, it's just 6 o'clock. Let's go ahead for a while." Akerman inwardly groaned. Even though he knew Futch wouldn't be swayed, he had to object. "If the Court please, at this time the defense counsel respectfully objects to holding of a night session in the hearing of this case upon the grounds that defense counsel has been working night and day in the preparation of this case, with arrangements already made for the meeting of a great number of prospective witnesses for the trial in chief, in Orlando, tonight; that, if the defense counsel is unable to meet the witnesses tonight, we do not know when we will be able to get them again. The trial is set for Thursday morning, which necessitates the issuance of praecipe for witnesses' subpoenas, which will take considerable time on the part of defense counsel. Further, it necessitates the preparation of a great deal of law. We hoped that sometime during the night or the early hours of the morning, we would be able to work some on the law in this case." The silence that followed was interrupted by Hunter. "I would like to call to the attention of the Court, again, the statement which I made this morning. A member of counsel for the defense has stated that he intends to dilly dally this case along." As Hunter glared at Joseph Price, Akerman stepped forward to confront the prosecutor.

Akerman: "I'll ask Mr. Hunter, is that statement made to him?"
Hunter: "To me?"
Akerman: "Was it made to you?"
Hunter: "No. It wasn't made to me."
Akerman: "I object to Mr. Hunter testifying."
Hunter: "I am not testifying. I am telling that the statement was not made to me."
Akerman: "I made no such statement, and I am chief defense counsel in this case."
Williams: "I made no such statement."
Price: "I made no such statement."
Hunter: "To me?"
Price: "To you or to anyone else."
Hunter: "That's the information that I have and it is borne out by the acts of the counsel here, today."
Judge Futch: "I don't think you can discuss that part of it, Mr. Hunter, unless you heard the statement yourself."
Hunter: "Well I can prove it. I don't believe this gentleman will deny it under oath."
Price: "Would you like to put me on the witness stand?"
Hunter: "No."

Akerman knew Hunter had the goods on Price. The defense *was* trying to stall to give Williams and Hill more time to find witnesses. "...we toyed around with reading in the newspaper clippings into the record in order to give the other team the chance to go around and obtain statements of witnesses, since the continuance wasn't granted," Horace Hill later admitted. Akerman tried to save face by retreating, and playing innocent: "...it is a known fact that defense counsel have not had the many, many years experience that the State Attorney has had and we may be inept and inapt in our handling of this case and also it may be that some of the evidence we put in is not necessary, but as an officer of this Court, charged with defense of these defendants, I am going to endeavor to put in every bit of lawful evidence that I can in this case. And if, through ignorance, lack of experience, inability, I do make some mistakes, I would appreciate the advice of counsel of both the Court and the State's Attorney." Hunter wasn't appeased. He remarked, "I am not employed by anyone defending the defendants in this case. Therefore, I decline to give advice," and curtly asked to call his first witness.

The prosecution had prepared a number of community leaders to enthusiastically extol the racial harmony of Lake County. George G. Ware, president of First National Bank in Mount Dora said that racial problems were unknown in his community, and that, "many people in our city try to help the Negroes get ahead." Mount Dora Mayor J.E. Fortner agreed, saying that Negroes were encouraged to buy homes. Not only had he helped them become homeowners, he also hired "colored help" at his place of business, Citrus Culture Corp., where, "there had never been any trouble." At the defense table, Williams felt loathe. If Fortner and White were to be believed, Mount Dora was a Mecca for Negroes. Leesburg Mayor Luther Miller swore that he could, "bring you 50 colored people who will testify to the good relations between white people and Negroes in Lake County." Of course, the 50 happy Negroes weren't presented. After stating that he had denied the KKK permission to hold a parade, Miller proudly told the court, "We refused the Ku Klux Klan permission to go down and intimidate any Negroes. And I would do the same thing over again." Curiously, he then added, "The Ku Klux Klan have their place. If they want to have it there, it is perfectly all right. I might even join it myself, sometime." A banker from Mount Dora also attested to Lake's racial harmony, saying there were hundreds of men in the county who would consider the evidence with an open mind. By the time the banker stepped down, it was after 8 p.m. Futch was finally ready to call it a day. The marathon session had effectively killed any defense hopes to interview potential witnesses. The hearing would resume in 13 hours.

Tavares Mayor E.I. Burleigh was Hunter's first witness the following day. Like those who preceded him, Burleigh testified to the peace, love and understanding that existed between the races. According to the mayor, the racial climate was "very satisfactory." He then said that colored people "are protected and given encouragement." Williams had heard enough, but Hunter wasn't finished painting his portrait of Lake County as a place where Negroes prospered alongside, even because of, their benefactors. County Agent R.E. Norris told the court that the "colored farm population" in Lake County increased from 50 percent from 1940 to 1945, and that 75 percent of all colored farmers owned their own farms. Negro insurance agent F.L. Hampton of Leesburg delivered the coups de grace, characterizing relations between white and colored people in Leesburg as, "the best in Florida."

But not every state witness wore rose-colored glasses. Asked about the mob violence that scattered and scarred Groveland's black community after the arrests, a bank president testified, "You could not expect any other situation." The vice president of the bank shared the sentiment, saying that if a defendant were acquitted and walked out of the courtroom that "it might be a good idea to keep on walking."

After the last state witness, Akerman was told to call the remainder of his witnesses. Unfortunately, his cupboard was bare. Akerman had been counting on the appearance of the two FBI agents who interviewed the defendants at Raiford since he had given subpoenas to the sheriff and advised McCall that the men worked out of the Miami bureau. McCall explained that when he had contacted the FBI during the previous day's noon recess, Chief Investigator Carson had told him that the agents in question did not work for him. Another dead-end for the defense. Akerman and Williams were not surprised. G-men weren't in the habit of revealing the results of their investigations in a court of law. And who knew if McCall even attempted to serve the subpoenas?

The members of the defense team were grim during their lunch break. No one expected Futch to grant the pending motions. A shaken Akerman considered the fruits of two weeks of painstaking preparation: the pretrial motions and subsequent hearings had consumed two days, but produced no gains. All the pretrial legal wrangling had accomplished was to irritate Futch and anger Hunter. The only defense victory had been a minor one: when the judge agreed to push the trial back a day after acknowledging that the hurricane had practically brought central Florida to a standstill for a day or two. Jury selection would begin the next day, Sept. 1.

When court resumed in the afternoon, Akerman again called the unnamed agents. No one stepped forward. The defense was finished. Futch promised to rule after a recess of an hour and a half. While waiting, Akerman hoped against hope the FBI agents would appear. Ninety minutes came and went. Court was reconvened. Futch began with the Application for Removal, which he denied, saying, "the motion for such removal does not comply with what I understand to be the requirements for such a motion. A great deal of time has been spent in the introduction in evidence of certain newspaper articles. Very little evidence of any other nature has been introduced and nothing has been introduced to show the slightest necessity for the removal of this cause to another county. So far as the defendants are concerned, no evidence has been introduced to support their allegations of prejudice, of violence, or threatened violence." Akerman could hardly believe his ears. Perhaps if he had been able to present dozens of frightened Negroes, the judge might have ruled differently. But then again, probably not.

The judge also ruled against the Motion for Continuance, saying, "One of the attorneys of record in this case has been connected with it in one capacity or another, according to his statements, since the 31st day of July. And, according to his statements made a sufficient investigation to convince him of the absolute innocence of the defendants. And I can't imagine a lawyer coming to that conclusion without making a pretty thorough investigation." The logic was doubly flawed: Williams hadn't been the attorney of record, and even if he had been, he was so busy trying to find an attorney that he had little time to locate witnesses, or prepare a defense. But Futch didn't see it that way. He reasoned that Williams had been investigating the case for more than a month, and had evidently given, "Akerman the benefit of his thorough investigation." The hearing was over. Jury selection would begin in the morning.

The *Chicago Defender* harshly criticized the preliminary hearing, calling it "a farce -- rushed through to get the jump on the FBI, which is investigating the conduct of officers who beat the prisoners so brutally that bruises still showed three weeks later." Despite the article, McCall continued to wear the "hero" label in the local press. *Orlando Sentinel* reporter Ormund Powers reminded readers that the sheriff had, "suppressed two riots and quelled three mobs during the tension which followed the attack of the slim, blonde Bay

Lake bride by four Negroes one Friday night…" To Akerman and the NAACP attorneys, Powers and the other local reporters had yet to display even a hint of objectivity. They continued to buy into McCall's claims that outsiders had come to Lake County to sully its fair name.

That evening, Akerman and his cohorts took stock of their plight. Akerman hadn't even had time to check the alibis of Irvin and Shepherd, and there hadn't been time to pick apart the story the Padgetts told. The defense would literally be playing it by ear, placed in the unenviable position of waiting to see how people testified and then responding. Akerman hadn't even had time to get to know his clients, spending just enough time with them to convince him none of the three would sway an all-white jury.

While Akerman had spent every waking moment preparing for the trial, Williams carved out a little time to meet with the defendants to go over their stories, explain what they could expect in the courtroom and coach them on how they should answer accusatory questions by Hunter. But Williams didn't get much time. He had been repeatedly rebuffed when he demanded access to the Groveland Three. Finally, McCall grudgingly allowed a visit. It was a visit that shocked Williams' already ravaged sensibilities. "As late as when the trial occurred, I visited the boys in their cells. The very cells that they had been put in the first night they were arrested and the blood-stained sheets were still on the bed. You would have thought that at least they would have done was to change the sheets. So, they had either been bleeding profusely recently having come back from Raiford or those were still the sheets that they had been on in the first instance."

Efforts to bolster the defendants' spirits and prepare them for the trial were hampered by the presence of McCall's deputies, who menacingly stood outside the cell during Williams' interview. The stench of the cells, the air of hostility and the briefness of the sessions ensured little was accomplished, but Williams was thankful he was permitted even a brief visit. "I never really got to know them well as human beings, as young men. I do not know whether they were good, bad or indifferent men. I had a sense of them from my interviews with them," Williams said. His impressions:

- Greenlee "was just this side of illiterate… Tall, gangly, overgrown country kid… Greenlee was in many ways just a big, gangly country kid who did not know what the hell was happening to him."

- "Shepherd was a less impressive fellow to me. I could see Shepherd not wanting them to go back to work, you know, and maybe, maybe wearing his uniform around, just wanting to hang around the hell with it."

- "I thought Irvin was a very fine man. He seemed to be a very quiet, hard working, at least the appearance of a kid who wants to go back to work. He was part of a family that loved him… I think Irvin was, of the three of them, the most intelligent, the most sensitive…"

Williams didn't have nearly enough time with the accused; just enough to tell him the men were nowhere near ready to testify. No doubt about it, Hunter would chew them up and spit them out.

Jury selection began Thursday at 10 a.m. The hallway outside the courtroom was crowded and noisy, as most of the 100 men waiting to be called laughed and joked about the justice they would administer if they were lucky enough to get on the lynch jury. Others stood quietly by themselves hoping they wouldn't be accepted. The men had been picked from a pool of 500 prospective jurors whose names had been picked by county commissioners, put on slips of paper and placed in a box, which was then sealed until a criminal case was placed on the docket. Only three of the names belonged to Negroes, and only one was summoned to appear.

The session began with Futch excusing a handful of prospective jurors, including a Negro handyman, who the clerk of the court called, "one of the best niggers in Lake County." The man was excused to attend his father-in-law's funeral. As the first group of men was led to the jury box, most stole glances at the sullen young Negroes dressed in white T-shirts and new dungarees. Others looked right past the defendants to the defense table where two colored men in their Sunday clothes were sitting. None of the white men called for jury duty had ever seen a Negro lawyer. Few had seen a Negro businessman. The defendants sat quietly, trying to avoid the stares of their accusers sitting 20 feet away. Willie Padgett was clad in striped shirt and blue gabardine pants. His slender, fair-haired wife wore a neat print dress -- and a faint smile. "This Bay Lake Cracker who said that she was raped, she was just basking in the sunlight of this whole thing, of what had happened to her," recalled Horace Hill. "I remember commenting on the fact that she hadn't gotten this much attention before in her life, and this really catapulted her to a level she had never experienced, in which she got great comfort… I don't know what it is, but it just didn't strike me that she would have been promenading around as she did if she had actually been raped -- as provoking as she would make it appear, by a black person -- she would be shamed, from what she was saying, rather than the kind of public notoriety she was getting."

As Hunter questioned the men in the jury box, the defense attorneys began to get an inkling of how difficult it would be to seat an impartial jury. It didn't take long to realize that only a handful of the men appeared to be professional, lettered men. Almost everyone was a blue-collar sort, men who made their living off the sweat of the land, toiling at jobs where brawn was valued over brain. Williams doubted that few, if any, had college educations. If there had been time to study the situation, a look at the May 19, 1949, *Mount Dora Topic* would have explained things. In an article headlined, "Let's Overhaul Our Jury System, Adopt Jury Commission,' Says Hunter," the outspoken state attorney said Lake County's current system for selecting jurors needed "modernization." Hunter said the problem with commissioners picking names was that, "those men (prominent businessmen) call on the commissioners beforehand and ask that their names not be put on the list." It was an age-old practice, and one Hunter hadn't been able to get changed in the year since the article appeared.

The first man questioned, B.B. Green, was exactly what the defense didn't want. Not only was he a long-time resident (35 years), he was also a citrus grower. Based on what Williams and Hill had learned about animosity between grove owners and their colored workers, citrus growers would only be considered as a last resort. There was no sympathy for the defendants among area citrus men, many who felt verdicts of "not guilty" would trigger a revolt among Negro citrus workers. The second man, Reed Hollinger, was also a citrus grower and farmer. A grocer and two farmers followed.

Akerman was looking for educated men, preferably single, but if married, without children. Obviously, the defense didn't want a panel of fathers with teenage girls. The attorneys were also looking for men from the north end of the county (as far away from Groveland as possible) who had previously served on juries, weren't born and raised in Lake and didn't read the *Orlando Morning Sentinel*, the paper that published the front-page editorial cartoon calling for "The Supreme Penalty." Akerman wasn't about to seat any juror who had lived in the south end of the county his entire life.

The defense attorneys entered the trial knowing full well that inflammatory press accounts had saturated the county, but none dreamed how extensive that blanket had extended until jury selection began. Twelve of the first 13 men questioned admitted reading newspaper accounts of the case or hearing radio reports. The other man probably had as well, but he was excused before the question was asked when he admitted he lived in Bay Lake and was related to the Padgetts. This was going to be tougher than Akerman realized.

After asking the first 13 prospective jurors if they were opposed to capital punishment (all 13 said "no"), Hunter yielded to Akerman. The very first man the defense questioned, Clermont resident B.K. Fergeson admitted he had already formed an opinion and could not go into the jury box with a "mind free and open." Naturally, the judge excused him. Moments later, grocer Roy Beasley, a 20-year resident of Mount Dora, also admitted he felt the accused were guilty. He too was excused. Akerman wondered if he would find anyone who hadn't already formed an opinion. It seemed everyone had either read that the men had confessed, or heard a rumor that they had admitted guilt.

On a positive note, nearly every man swore they would be open-minded if chosen, even though they had read or heard news reports regarding the case. Akerman was understandably skeptical. Each man also claimed he could accept a Negro attorney participating in the trial. The defense wasn't buying that either. Most of the men said they had no objection to Negro counsel cross examining state witnesses, but few elaborated. Andrew Postella, however, said a mouthful when Akerman asked, "How do you feel about the two of the defense counsel being Negroes?" Postella replied, "I am glad to see them trying to make something out of themselves." The operative words: "trying" and "something." Translation: Postella didn't mind Negroes trying to raise themselves up to a white person's station.

Clearly, most prospective jurors were already convinced the defendants had kidnapped and attacked Norma Padgett. It was repeated over and over among the men waiting in the hallway. To them it wasn't a question of whether the Negroes had done it, it was only a question of how, and when they would die for their crimes. One of the better educated men, a young white minister, verbally doubted an impartial panel could be seated. When asked if he had been influenced in the case, he answered, "How can anyone in this section who read the papers be free of some prejudice in this case?" While waiting to be called the minister had overheard another prospective juror say, "What they ought to have done is take those niggers out, tie them to a stake and burn them." The minister was later dismissed, but he insisted that the other man was accepted to serve on the jury.

By the time court recessed for lunch at 1:15 p.m., it was obvious the odds of finding a Lake County resident unfamiliar with the case were slim. As the defense attorneys headed to lunch, they realized *none* of the 15 men they had questioned would be sympathetic. Not one. Mechanic Ernest B. Green, a 26-year Mount Dora resident, was a "maybe," but far from ideal. On the plus side, he was experienced, having served "three or four times" on juries in criminal cases. On the downside, Green's family consisted of a daughter and a stepdaughter.

Moments after the afternoon session began, the state excused its first potential jurors: Edward Wineman, who said he didn't know anyone in the south part of the county, didn't know any of the witnesses and only believes, "a third of what I read in the papers." The defense hated to see Wineman go. Anyone who didn't trust the press was all right with Akerman. The state also used an exemption to dismiss Bernard Griffis, a resident of eight years who worked for the state road department.

After just 18 men had been interviewed, the state tendered the jury. Williams would have laughed if the situation wasn't so ludicrous. Imagine choosing a 12-person jury after questioning just 18 men. It was far from the jury Akerman wanted. He was prepared to use all 30 pre-emptory challenges (10 for each defendant) if need be. As the afternoon wore on, it looked like he might very well do just that. As his pre-emptory challenges evaporated, Akerman tried to be picky, but knew he would have to make some concessions. For example, James Bevis was attractive because he was one of the few white-collar men to appear, but on the down side, Bevis also admitted to knowing two deputies and a member of the highway patrol. As the day wore on, Akerman's only hard and fast rule became that he simply couldn't accept someone who outwardly appeared to be prejudiced. By the time Futch adjourned the day's proceedings, another 35 men had been questioned. It had been a tedious, exhausting afternoon of questions and answers, but Akerman had replaced every juror Hunter had accepted hours earlier. Of course, Akerman burned 25 of his 30 challenges in doing so.

That night, the defense team met to review their notes and to determine which five jurors to replace. It wouldn't be an easy decision: Williams didn't think any of the men chosen so far would vote for acquittal. And with just five challenges left, at least a few biased jurors would be in the group that determined the fate of the Groveland Three. The best prospect to acquit may have been Charles Blaze, a carpenter and 30-year resident of Fruitland Park, a tiny community on the north edge of Leesburg, about 25 miles from Groveland. The 20th man called, Blaze, was the first to say he hadn't heard about the case, telling Akerman, "I looked at the headlines, that's all." Akerman doubted that was true, but there were other pluses: Blaze had served on juries in criminal cases and he did not have a wife or children. And Akerman liked the man's straightforward answer to the "Negro attorneys" question. When Akerman asked, "Two of the defense counsel here are Negroes. How do you feel about that?" Blaze responded, "Go to it." Two other men, citrus growers William F. Austin and J.B. Norris, also looked like keepers. Both had a wife and three sons, no daughters. And that was it. The rest of the panel would vote "guilty" in a heartbeat. Williams was certain of that.

The second day of jury selection began on an auspicious note. Five of the first seven men questioned were excused, two because they admitted they had already formed an opinion regarding the defendants, two by the state, and one because the man lived in Groveland. The other two were soon excused at the request of the defense, which was now down to three challenges. The defense attorneys held little hope of finding three open-minded white men.

The 61st man called, John W. Jones, was a possibility. A five-year resident of Paisley in the northeast corner of the county, Jones said he had only read the (weekly) Eustis newspapers. Accepting Jones allowed the defense to jettison Pearl Gentry, a 26-year resident of Okahumpka. After four of the next six men were excused by Futch because they had formed an opinion regarding the defendants' guilt, Akerman accepted the 70th and 71st men called. Henry G. Gatch, a 15-year Eustis resident with a wife and four sons, was appealing because he was on vacation when the incidents occurred. Leesburg citrus and watermelon grower R. M. Holloway had also been out of town: he was in Minnesota when the "crime" occurred. Akerman could also live with R.N. Dillard, a carpenter who was in the hospital on July 16 and who had read about the case in the *Tampa Tribune* and *St. Petersburg Independent.*

Finally, after questioning 78 men, Akerman had a jury he could live with, albeit with reservation. It wasn't the most enlightened group, but it was a far cry stronger than the panel had been 24 hours ago. But then the state used exemptions to excuse Leesburg banker Gilbert Ault, retiree Simon Bair and 35-year Leesburg resident George Rast. By waiting until the defense exhausted its challenges, Hunter had ensured the defense would be stuck with the next three men called (unless the judge excused them for living in the Groveland area or having an opinion regarding the defendants). Akerman was about to be saddled with three men he probably wouldn't have picked.

The three vacant seats would be filled by: T. Grady Simpson, a 25-year resident of Lake County who read the *Orlando Morning Sentinel,* had a wife and three children and worked in tourism and citrus; Wilbur T. Adams, a Lady Lake citrus and real estate man in his early 40s who had a wife and son and was a daily subscriber to the *Orlando Morning Sentinel,* and Alto M. Royal, a farmer from Cassia, who also read the Orlando newspapers. Adams most certainly would have been excused if the defense had any challenges left. Not only was he a *Sentinel* reader, he stated that it seemed "rather odd" that two Negro men were serving as defense counsel. When asked to elaborate, Adams replied, "Well, we are used to white people mostly, as lawyers, especially. And it does seem rather strange to sit with colored lawyers." Still, Adams said it made no difference to him. Royal would have been gone as well after admitting he had been represented by Hunter in a case three years ago.

Most of the jurors were clearly working men. The all-white jury was an accurate representation of Lake County's agricultural and blue collar personality. Citrus men J.B. Norris, R.M. Holloway, Henry G. Gatch, P. Grady Simpson, William F. Austin Jr. were joined by farmers John W. Jones and Alto N. Royal, mechanic Ernest B. Green and carpenter R.N. Dillard. Akerman figured his best hope for a fair judgment rested on the "educated" jurors on the panel: Bevis, a Lake County Board of Education supervisor, real estate agent Wilbur T. Adams, and retired businessman Charles Blaze.

The testimony phase of the trial would begin the next day. It was an event the entire county had anticipated, redneck or well-to-do having been titillated for weeks by relentless newspaper accounts. Ramona Lowe hit the nail on the head when she wrote, "Through sentiment whipped-up by Florida daily newspapers, the trial has become a side-show for thrill-seeking, sadistic country-bred whites." It was a given that the courtroom would be standing-room only, and white faces would outnumber black. Akerman was far from ready. A man who prided himself on preparation and attention to detail, he wasn't often caught unprepared. But he hadn't had any choice. His back had been up against the wall from day one, and then the judge tied his hands with his late-night hearings. By the time the Groveland Boys went to trial, "Florida's Little Scottsboro" was being watched throughout the nation. Akerman could only hope The Groveland Three would fare better than the Scottsboro Boys had. At least they would be better represented.

Chapter 15 -- Stacked Deck

Prosecutor Jesse Hunter had never been more certain of an outcome before testimony even began. This was literally a case he couldn't lose. Besides having an all-white jury, he had the "home field" advantage, a judge he had been friends with since college, and jurors who saw the defense attorneys as pawns of uppity Yankee niggers. Plus, Hunter had subpoenaed more than a dozen potential witnesses, including a number of Negroes.

And Hunter had an ace in the hole: a sheriff telling reporters that the defendants had confessed. It was a lawyer's dream. Newspaper accounts of confessions were far better than McCall detailing the declarations of guilt from the stand. Alex Akerman couldn't cross examine a newspaper. Not that Hunter needed the confessions. In the final analysis, Hunter knew he would need only two witnesses: Norma and Willie Padgett. Even a layman could see the case boiled down to a white woman's word against a colored man's denial. "Guilty" was the only possible verdict. The trial wouldn't be about guilt or innocence; it would be about life in prison or death in the electric chair. Akerman's challenge was to raise sufficient doubt so the jury would choose life instead of the chair.

The scene inside the courthouse as Akerman, Joseph Price, Horace Hill and Franklin Williams entered was unlike any the men had witnessed. "They had deputies who stood every 10 stairs coming up the staircase into the courtroom. They were all big characters with guns on. It was a very intimidating scene," Williams remembered. But the guards weren't law enforcement officers. McCall had deputized a number of local rednecks for the trial. "They had all of these Bay Lake Crackers with snuff in their mustache and all, supposed to be bodyguards and all. Hell, I was scareder of them than I was the people who they said was the perpetrators," Hill said.

The threat of violence didn't dampen the enthusiasm of hundreds of spectators who came from all ends of the county to fill the gallery. Every seat in the room was occupied, but only 50 Negroes were among the estimated 480 persons who packed the courtroom, and they were relegated to the balcony. Williams was struck by how subdued the Negro spectators were. "They were quiet. I guess, resigned to the fact that these boys are going to be found guilty. Some of them were afraid. They were all afraid of McCall. They showed no signs of pleasure or joy or anything else. Just, they were just there watching."

The hum of excitement dropped an octave as deputies closed the heavy wooden courtroom doors. A moment later, all eyes followed the noise of a metal jail door opening in the hallway behind the judge's bench. As the door clanged shut, three shackled prisoners appeared. The expressionless men, dressed in dungarees and white T-shirts, kept their eyes on the floor as they were led to the table where their attorneys nervously waited. Williams would later describe the atmosphere as "fairly tension-filled." After recognizing counsel and warning spectators that he would not tolerate any disruption, Judge Truman G. Futch directed Hunter to begin. Newspaper reporters who wondered why wood sticks were piled on the judge's desk understood when Futch picked up a stick and began to whittle.

The courtroom was quiet as Hunter called Willie Padgett. While his young wife appeared to be basking in the spotlight as she sat in the front row, Willie seemed less comfortable as he walked to the stand. Despite advance preparation by Hunter and his assistant Sam Buie, the young farmer was clearly nervous. Hunter would go slow and hope Padgett's nerves steadied.

Willie haltingly told of taking Norma to a square dance and staying till 1 a.m. "We started home and decided we would go to Okahumpka for a sandwich, and about four miles north of Mascotte we decided we were too far up there and we would return home. So when I was turning around my car choked down and the battery wasn't strong enough to crank it again." Padgett then testified that a car heading the other direction went about 50 yards past his car, stopped, turned around and pulled alongside the disabled vehicle. A "Negro" got out, crossed in front of the headlights and asked him what was wrong. "I told him I needed some help, I had a dead battery. And three more got out and came over to the car." Padgett said the men agreed to push his car, but after pushing it partially onto the roadway they stopped and began talking among themselves. "And I got out and they stood up there, I guess for 10 or 15 minutes. And I asked them to push and they just kept hesitating, wouldn't push. So I saw they was up to something and I saw a stick laying behind me, my car, and I walked behind my car and got that stick and when I did, two of them came towards me. And I started beating on them."

Willie's initial nervousness had passed; bravado was creeping in. "Several licks passed. And I knocked one of them down. And when I knocked one of them down, another come up behind me and grabbed a hold of me and I hit him several times, and when I did, one of these other two overpowered me. Throwed me on the ground. Addled me. And skinned my forehead and nose. They carried me on across the road and throwed me through a gate." Padgett said that when he got up, his wife was missing and he saw the Negroes' car heading north. He waited 30 minutes until a car came along and, "a fellow pushed me off," then drove to Leesburg, where he reported the attack and abduction to the attendant at an all-night service station. "He called the deputy sheriff and he came in about three minutes and he and I got in his car and I took him back out there to the place and showed him where it was and he looked and shined the light on it and saw that there was some trouble there so we went back to Leesburg and got another deputy and then we headed back toward Groveland."

When Hunter asked Willie to describe the vehicle the men were driving, Padgett stumbled, badly. He replied, "I didn't know what kind of a car it was. But I thought it was a '46 Mercury or a '48." He also told the deputy that he saw the number 12 (the Lake County prefix) on the license plate, which was partially covered by a "greasy cloth."

Willie said he accompanied the deputy to Groveland, then to Clermont, "inquiring around there and some fellow told them who had a car of that make." That information led Padgett and the deputies to "a Negro house on this side of Groveland, right at the railroad between Groveland and Clermont." A Negro man was in the car in front of the house. "The deputy sheriff called, he asked that fellow that was in the car was he driving that car that night and he told him, 'No,' but the two fellows driving his car was inside. And he called them out. Those two Negroes."

Hunter: "Did you observe them as they came out?"
Padgett: "Yes sir. I knew them."
Hunter: "How did you know them?"
Padgett: "Because I saw them that night. That morning."

Knowing his case depended on positive identification, Hunter pressed the point.

Hunter: "What opportunity did you have to observe those two men out at the car?"
Padgett: "You mean, seeing them?"
Hunter: "Yes."
Padgett: "Well, they kept the lights on all the time and they was right there at me. Just as close as I am to you, and the moon was shining bright. There wasn't nothing to keep me from not seeing them."

Padgett then rose and pointed out Shepherd and Irvin. It was the first dramatic moment of the trial. But the state's first blunder was soon to follow.

Hunter: "Now do you have -- sit down -- opportunity, you say, there were four of these men?"
Padgett: "Yes sir."

Hunter: "Did you have opportunity there to observe the other two men sufficiently to identify them again?
Padgett: "Well, no sir. Not as good as I have those two."
Hunter: "You didn't know the other two men?"
Padgett: "No sir."

Hunter quickly abandoned the subject, disappointed Padgett had missed the chance to finger all four defendants. He made a mental note to repair the gaffe when Norma took the stand. According to Padgett, he then went home because he thought his wife might be there. There he showed the gas station attendant, Curtis Howard a photo of Norma, and to his surprise, Howard said he had seen the woman alongside the road that morning when he was driving from Leesburg to Groveland. The men headed toward the spot, and found her riding in a car with a white man at approximately 7:30 a.m.

Akerman voiced his first objection when Hunter asked Willie what his wife told him when they were reunited. "Objected to, if the Court please, as hearsay. The witness is here. She can tell what happened." Akerman was hoping to show that the rape charge wasn't a "fresh complaint," but was based on hearsay because Willie Padgett wasn't present at the time of the alleged rape. Hunter anticipated the objection. "This was the first time that she had met any person that she knew and the Supreme Court has held that she might at that time state whether or not she had been raped and that it would be competent evidence." Judge Futch agreed. The word "raped" produced the second dramatic moment of the trial. Padgett took the cue, telling Hunter that his wife told him four men had raped her. He said his wife's knees were bruised, but she was "not then" bleeding. He also observed cotton lint on her dress similar to the cotton he later saw in the Shepherd automobile.

The courtroom was quiet as Hunter adroitly moved from rape to theft. Padgett told the court the men had taken his wallet, driver's license and $20. Assault, kidnapping, rape, and now, theft. Hunter had stacked the deck expertly with his first witness. But he had also left plenty of openings. How did Padgett see a stick behind his car and then walk past the men to get it without them intervening? Did he really get "several" licks in when he was outnumbered four to one? Why did Padgett take the lawmen to Groveland and Clermont to look for the car when he last saw it heading north, away from those communities? How did Padgett see a number 12 at night on a license plate that was not only partially covered by a greasy cloth, but "didn't have any tag light." Willie needed to explain why he could identify two men, but not the other two. After all, all four had been pushing his car under the light of the moon. Also, who was this man Willie found his wife with early Saturday morning? Why hadn't Willie questioned the man? Had the man been subpoenaed? Would he testify? Surely, Akerman would take advantage of the holes in Padgett's testimony.

Williams whispered suggestions from behind the rail as Akerman slowly stood to cross examine. The reporters from the Northern papers waited for Akerman to pick Padgett apart, but the attorney seemed tentative and unsure as he began questioning Norma's husband. The pretrial hearings had taught the attorney to tread lightly, lest he incur the judge's wrath. Akerman went slowly; spending considerable time questioning Padgett on how and where the car stalled, even having the witness sketch how he pulled into a side road, "backed off the hard road on the shoulder" and "started pulling back up on the hard road," when the car died. It wasn't clear what Akerman hoped to prove.

Akerman fared better when challenging Padgett's recollection of events he had described. Willie said he and his wife left the dance at 1 a.m., then needed a car to push-start his Ford, although he couldn't recall who assisted him, or what kind of car they drove. Finally, Akerman brought Padgett to the encounter with the Negroes who stopped to push his stalled car on the road to Okahumpka.

Akerman: "Then did you have any conversation with them at all?"
Padgett: "Well, yes, but I don't remember what was said or nothing."
Akerman: "You don't recall what the topic of conversation was? What the discussion was about at all?"
Padgett: "No. No, I don't."

Akerman hoped the witness would remain vague as he recalled the "attack." Padgett told essentially the same story about his fight with the men, adding that the wood stick he defended himself with "was round. About two inches thick and about 2 ½ foot long... felt like a shovel handle or hoe handle." Padgett then testified that "about 15 minutes" had passed from the time the car full of Negroes stopped till they drove off with his wife. Padgett's recall was improving. But that was about to change.

Akerman: "What did you do then?"
Padgett: "Well I got all right, where I could get up and got back across the fence. I went to my car and found my wife was gone so I tried to push the car then myself and I couldn't. And I guess, about 30 minutes a car came by and they stopped and offered assistance to give me a shove."
Akerman: "What kind of automobile was that?"
Padgett: "I don't know. I didn't notice it."
Akerman: "How many people were in it?"
Padgett: "I'll say three or four."

Surprisingly, Akerman didn't press Padgett about his cloudy memory. He also failed to jump on Padgett's assertion that no car passed on that road for 45 minutes from the time the Negroes stopped to help to when Padgett finally flagged down a car. True, it was between 1 and 2 a.m., but dozens of cars must have left the dance around the time the Padgetts did. Not everyone would have headed south. Padgett's memory of the Negroes' car was a bit better, although he told Akerman he thought it was either a '46 or '48 Mercury. He also admitted that he had told the deputies the car was black, "but I later learned that it wasn't." The most significant "point" Akerman scored was when Padgett testified he had purchased a half pint of whiskey and drank it at the dance. The line of questioning made Padgett squirm, but Willie recovered nicely when the defense sought to portray the young farmer as a drunk.

Akerman: "Did you have anything else to drink other than this half pint? Did any of your friends give you a drink?"

Padgett: "No."

Akerman: "This was all of the intoxicants that you had to drink?"

Padgett: "That's right. And I didn't drink all that by myself, either."

Akerman concluded by establishing that the stick Padgett used to defend himself hadn't been found by McCall's deputies, and that the young farmer didn't know the name of the restaurant he was taking his wife too. Unclear on how many people were in the car that "jumped him off," unclear about the year of the attackers' car, and unclear about what he and the Negroes talked about, Padgett's testimony was far from the tour de force Hunter had hoped for. By the time Akerman finished with Padgett, the farm boy's bluster had vanished. There was no bounce in Willie's step as he left the stand.

Akerman had scored points, but he had failed to ask the tough questions. Was it lack of time to prepare the case? The pressure of trying a case in such a hostile environment? Probably both. He had certainly been handicapped by not being able to interview the Padgetts beforehand, or at least peruse statements they made to the prosecution. Akerman hadn't thrown a knockout punch.

Padgett's admission he had been drinking hadn't caused a ripple in the courtroom, but the appearance of the state's second witness certainly did. Head held high, Norma strode to the stand. Whites and blacks alike moved to the edge of their seats as the 17-year-old farm wife calmly began telling *essentially* the same story as her husband. She didn't contradict him, but there were discrepancies. For instance, Willie had painted a picture of breaking down on a deserted road, but Norma remembered it differently. "Well, there was a quite a lot of cars that came along and the car that stopped, well, it pulled on ahead of us and turned around and come back and stopped and we asked them -- they asked us did we need any help and we told them, 'yes' and they got out of the car then, and pushed the car up."

Norma also confirmed that her husband had a lengthy conversation with the men before they began pushing the car. "And I was setting in the car waiting on him to come on and I told him two or three times to come and get in if they were going to push, and he said, 'OK, in a minute,' and I looked back and I seen him and then I turned my head and looked towards the road and by that time I heard some scuffling in the back and then one of them said, 'Grab the lady.'" A hush hung over the courtroom as Norma recounted how the men, "drove up toward Okahumpka and one of them, he tried to put his arms around me and I shoved him." She then described the seating arrangements: in the backseat on her right was "the darkest one... He was short. And kind of chunky. And later, I learned his name and it was Irvin." On her left was, "the light-skinned, bushy-headed one, and I later learned his name and he was Shepherd." Norma said Ernest Thomas was driving and Charles Greenlee was also in front. The car turned west on "the Center Hill road," and drove to the Lake/Sumter County line.

Hunter: "Where did you go then?"

Norma: "We went out just this side of the Center Hill line. I mean, the county line. Lake County."

Hunter: "Did they stop at any place before they got to the edge of Lake County?"

Norma: "Well, they pulled in to the side road and one of them said, 'there's a house.' And one of them said, 'Well, that's what we want.' And they pulled out and went on down the road just a little piece further and they stopped and that Thomas nigger, he got in the back with me. And that Shepherd nigger, he drove then."

Norma remained calm as Hunter brought her to the scene of the attack: "a little pavement road" that dead-ended near the county line. Finally, the lurid details that had fueled so much speculation, gossip and rumor were about to be revealed. "Well, on the way out there, after they pulled in and backed out from that road, well, this Thomas nigger -- later, I learned his name -- well he forced me to pull -- jerked up my dress and I pulled it back down and he jerked it up again and he told me to leave it alone," Norma said in a clear voice. "He was pointing a gun at me. And so he made me pull off my pants and he still had the gun on me and when we got out to that place, well, he raped me first." While jurors weighed her words, Hunter moved in for the kill.

Hunter: "Go ahead and tell them what happened. Don't tell them that they raped you. What did happen? What did he do to you?"

Norma: "Well, he shoved me down on the seat and he pulled my legs apart and he got on me and he kissed me and then he put his thing into my privates."

Hunter: "Did he have intercourse with you?"

Norma: "Yes sir."

Norma matter-of-factly told Hunter that Irvin remained in the back seat while Thomas raped her.

Hunter: "Then what happened?"

Norma: "Then the Thomas nigger, he got out and then Irvin, he raped me."

Hunter: "The same way?"

Norma: "No sir. The Thomas nigger, he got out and got in the front and then Irvin, he taken me and done me the same way. Only he didn't kiss me."

Norma said the other two men also raped her, but she didn't know which went first.

Hunter: "Then what happened?"

Norma: "And then one of them told them to go change the tag."

Hunter: "Do what?"

Norma: "To change the tag. And one of them went back there and changed the tag. And then they was kind of standing. One of them asked them to turn me loose and the other one said, "I'm not." And so they kind of stepped to the side of the car and they were talking and they come back and asked me which I would rather do, ride on and be killed or get out and walk. And I told them I rather to get out and walk."

Hunter knew Akerman would ask Norma if she had fought the men. He knew he had to ask first.

Hunter: "Did you fight them or resist?"
Norma: "No sir."
Hunter: "Why didn't you?"
Norma: "Because I was scared to. Scared they might kill me."
Hunter: "You were afraid to resist?"
Norma: "Yes…No. I didn't want to do it but I had to or be killed, one."

Hunter also knew Norma's identification of the men would be challenged. He had to address it before the defense did.

Hunter: "Now, while you were on that drive, could you see those men?"
Norma: "I could see the front ones better than I could the back ones."
Hunter: "Why?"
Norma: "Because of the headlights and the light on the dashboard of the car."
Hunter: "What were the lights on the dashboard?"
Norma: "Well, the clock and the speedometer and where the, and where it tell the temperature and how much gas and how much oil and stuff."
Hunter: "What kind of a night was it as to visibility?"
Norma: "It was a moonlight night."

After being released, Norma said she squatted down by some bushes and watched as the men backed out and drove west toward Center Hill (away from Groveland).

Hunter: "Now tell this jury what you did from then on until you found your husband?"
Norma: "Well, after they turned me loose and I seen they stopped, I run into the woods and I stayed out in the woods, well, I don't know how long it was. When I come out, though, I could see the sun coming up. It wasn't quite daylight. And so I walked to Okahumpka and I was standing on the side road waiting on some people to open up so I could tell them to take me down where Hazen (Willie) was at."

Norma then recounted how a man in the restaurant borrowed his dad's car and took her to look for her husband. She said she found Willie and "another boy" whose name she couldn't remember. "And we seen that it was him, and so we stopped and I got out of the car and I met him about halfway and then we got in the car and turned around and went back to Groveland to the city hall and they told me that they had a nigger in there and wanted me to go in there and identify him. And so I told them I didn't want to go and they told me I was all right, to go on in and see if I could identify him. I went in, into the city hall and identified him." Norma then pointed out Greenlee as the man she had seen in the jail. She later identified Irvin and Shepherd at Raiford before being taken to Madison County to identify a dead man, Ernest Thomas as the fourth rapist.

139

The trial might as well have ended right then and there. "Probably the most dramatic moment in that trial was late in the afternoon when Norma Padgett was testifying and Jess Hunter asked her if she sees the men in the courtroom who raped her and she stood up and she pointed at Greenlee and Shepherd and Irvin, not necessarily in that order, and she said, "Yes, the nigger Shepherd, the nigger Irvin, the nigger Greenlee." Christ, she could have cut, you could have cut that air with a knife," Williams recalled. "The defendants sat slouched in their chairs and none except Greenlee showed the slightest emotion or hardly even interest when Norma and Willie Padgett pointed an accusing finger directly at them," the *Leesburg Commercial* reported. "Irvin and Shepherd stared back unblinkingly."

With all four suspects identified by the victim, Hunter decided to fill in some blanks.
Hunter: "Now, did you tell your husband immediately upon reaching him that you had been raped by these four men?"
Norma: "Yes sir.'
Hunter: "In whose presence did you tell him?"
Norma: "I told him and this boy that lived at Leesburg that was with him when I first seen Hazen."
Hunter: "Did those men notice any condition of your clothing, the outside of it that was mentioned there?"
Incredibly, Akerman didn't object to the hearsay testimony about to go into the record.
Norma: "Well, they didn't mention it to me. This other boy didn't, but Hazen did. My husband."
Hunter: "What did he say about it?"
Norma: "He just told me that my dress was dirty in the back and I told him I already knew it."
Hunter: "Did it have any particles of anything on it? Your dress?"
Norma: "Yes sir."
Hunter: "What was it?"
Norma: "Well it was that linen on the back of it."
Hunter: "Lint, you mean?"
Norma: "Yes sir."

Next, Norma told of identifying the car, which she recalled had cracked windows on both the left and right sides. She also testified that she saw "a bright piece of metal laying on the floorboard of the car," then related how she took officers to the scene of the attack, which was near, "two little Australian pines and a tall one." There she pointed out the tire tracks made when her attackers drove into the dirt lane. With that, Hunter handed his star witness to Akerman, who was well aware that his cross examination would likely determine the outcome of the trial. Willie had been a warm-up, an opening act. Norma was the reason the courtroom was filled to capacity. Her attention to detail was impressive, to say the least.

Akerman and his associates had debated long and hard about how to handle Norma. Of course, they had discussed attacking her character, after all, it was rumored that her reputation was less than wholesome. That strategy was discarded when Hill and Williams failed to find anyone willing to testify under oath that Norma was anything less than a society lady. Akerman decided his only option was to proceed carefully, mindful not to accuse or assign motives. "Unless you really knew what you were going after, you'd been a damn fool to attack that gal; that would have really foretold it," Akerman said. "Unless you had something, it had to be treated with kid gloves."

As he approached the witness, Akerman reminded himself that his task was to attack her story, not her character. And he would have to proceed cautiously in doing that. In a different place, perhaps a different time, he could have cast doubt on her identification of her attackers. But this jury would never cotton to Akerman calling one of their own a bold-faced liar, even though that's what he believed her to be. "I still say that it would have been impossible for her to identify those Negroes. It was a semi-moonlight night; it wasn't bright daylight. If taken at full face value, according to what she said, she must have been extremely frightened, and I don't see how in the world she could have identified them. I say until you get to know them, it's awfully hard for a white man to identify a Negro, and I guess the reverse is true," Akerman reasoned.

Akerman began by seizing on the fact that Norma and Willie were separated, an area Hunter had wisely skimmed over.
Akerman: "Did you stay at your daddy's house or just what did you do?"
Norma: "Well I was there at my daddy's house but I don't know what I was doing."
Akerman: "What had your husband been doing?"
Norma: "I don't know."
Akerman: "Was he working?"
Norma: "No, he wasn't staying over there then."
Akerman: "He wasn't staying at your daddy's?"
Norma: "He was staying with his mother, then."

Akerman paused to let the implication set in: Norma and Willie were having marriage troubles and weren't even living together. A point scored, Akerman moved on. He doubted the young woman would admit to an on-going spat anyway. As for the night in question, Norma stuck to the story she and Willie had told Hunter: they had picked up a pint of whiskey, left the dance at 1 a.m., headed toward Okahumpka for a bite to eat, and then decided to return home instead. Akerman marveled at how composed Norma remained. He might have shaken Willie, but the young farm wife was clearly up to the challenge of his interrogation.

Akerman: "Now how long would you estimate it took you from the time you left the dance until you drove down the road there, backed it around and stopped and waited until this car came up with the four people in it?"
Norma: "Well, I don't know. I didn't have no watch. It was just a little while."

It was almost as if Hunter had explained how crucial the time factor was to the defense, that the defense case depended on simple math. Akerman had a two-hour hole to fill. He desperately needed time estimates of events that took place from when the couple left the dance (1 a.m.) to when Greenlee was arrested (just after 3 a.m.). He needed to know how

141

long Norma and Willie were stranded before the men came along, how much time passed before the fight, how long the fight lasted, how long the men drove before pulling over to rape her, and how long the sexual assault lasted. Akerman was confident the numbers would add up to more than two hours. He needed tangible time estimates to wreck the state's case, but Norma wasn't cooperating.

Akerman: "Was he in a hurry that night?"
Norma: "Nope."
Akerman: "That after you tried to -- you can't give us any estimate of the time, then?"
Norma: "Nope."

Moments later, he tried again.

Akerman: "And could you estimate about how long it took you to put that automobile -- took that automobile to ride from the place where they left your husband out to the Center Hill road where they stopped?"
Norma: "Well, just as I told you a while ago, I didn't have no watch and I don't know."

Norma repeated the account of the men stopping and offering to help, pushing the car onto the road, and scuffling with Willie. Then Akerman made a terrible blunder. He put a loaded gun in his clients' hands.

Akerman: "Now when did they first draw this gun on you?"
Norma: "After they all got in the car."
Akerman: "Just as you were leaving the place?"
Norma: "Yes."

Behind the defense table, Williams cringed. Incredibly, Akerman continued to strengthen the state's contention that the men were armed and dangerous.

Akerman: "They point their gun at you?"
Norma: "Yes."
Akerman: "Say they were going to kill you?"
Norma: "No. They told me they weren't going to hurt me."

And with that, Akerman should have abandoned the subject. But he didn't.

Akerman: "But they had that gun there?"
Norma: "Yes."

And instead of leaving bad enough alone, Akerman made things worse.

Akerman: "They didn't ever threaten to kill you with the gun?"
Norma: "Well they had it on me and told me if I didn't hush they would?"
Akerman: "They held that gun on you all the way on this road?"

Norma: "Yes."

And once more, for additional emphasis.

Akerman: "They had the gun there all the time?"
Norma: "Yes."

Hunter couldn't have scripted it better. Thanks to Akerman, every juror was now certain the accused were cold-blooded killers. The botched cross-examination concluded with Norma testifying about seeing Greenlee in the Groveland jail, accompanying deputies to identify the car, identifying Shepherd and Irvin, and explaining which way the men's car faced when they stopped to help. Norma had every reason to be proud as she returned to her seat. Norma had proven her dad wrong. She didn't screw up. Jurors couldn't help believing her straightforward testimony, attention to detail and unwavering identification of the defendants. Some were ready to cast their "guilty" vote right then and there. Hunter was understandably pleased. For the most part, Norma's story jibed with the one her estranged husband told. In fact, reporter Ramona Lowe thought it was almost too perfect. "The rehearsed note in the testimony was as clear as the tinkling of a cow bell on a quiet evening," she declared in the *Chicago Defender*.

Perhaps using the "kid gloves" approach had been a mistake. Such a passive cross-examination was devoid of questions that needed to be asked. The most glaring omissions: failing to ask how a woman could be raped in the back seat of a car occupied by two men -- one "chunky;" and her claim that she saw the men in the front of the car better than the ones sitting beside her in the back seat. Evidently the jury also had difficulty envisioning how the four defendants took turns raping the young girl, but when the foreman asked Futch if they could examine the car, the judge denied the request, saying it was, "a little out of line, and can't be permitted."

His case all but sewed up, Hunter called Walter Irvin's mother, Dellia. It was sound strategy because he knew Akerman would probably try to prove the seizure of Irvin's clothes was illegal. Unfortunately for Walter and his attorneys, Dellia Irvin was a God-fearing woman. She would not, could not, lie to save her son's life. Within minutes of taking the oath, Mrs. Irvin admitted that she went to bed early and didn't know what time her son came home on the night in question. It was another blow to the precious timeline Akerman needed to establish. Hunter could hardly believe his good fortune. He wanted to make sure the jury caught the significance of Dellia Irvin's statement.

Hunter: "Do you know what time he came in?"
Mrs. Irvin: "No sir, I don't."

Either Walter's mother naively believed the truth would set her son free, or she was too proud or too honest to help her son by lying. And it didn't get better for the defense. Mrs. Irvin testified that she *willingly* gave Deputy James Yates "the pants and the shoes" her son had been wearing the night before.

Hunter: "Now, did they search your house?"
Mrs. Irvin: "No sir."
Hunter: "They just asked you for them?"
Mrs. Irvin: "They said they wanted these shoes and shirt, Walter Lee's, and shirt and trousers."
Hunter: "And you went and got them?"
Mrs. Irvin: "I expect my husband got them for him, I think."
Hunter: "But, you gave them to them?"
Mrs. Irvin: "Yes."

Hunter had handled Mrs. Irvin masterfully. The prosecutor had deftly extracted exactly what he needed, portraying Walter's momma as perfectly willing to cooperate with the investigation. Hunter had derailed Akerman's illegal search and seizure argument before that train even left the station. But Akerman wasn't about to concede defeat. As he strode toward the witness, he was determined to regain lost ground. He too had done his homework. Williams had thoroughly discussed the "search and seizure" of Walter's clothes with the Irvins.

Akerman: "Now, did they come to your house, they come up to the door and asked you for this, or, what did they do? Did they come into your house?"
Mrs. Irvin: "They come in on the inside. Gone in the bedroom."
Akerman: "They came right into the bedroom?"
Mrs. Irvin: "Yes."

After Mrs. Irvin identified Yates as one of the men who came into the bedroom to get Walter's things, Akerman boldly played his hand.

Akerman: "And you knew he was some kind of law enforcement officer, did you not?"
Mrs. Irvin: "Yes sir. I knew it was the law."
Akerman: "You knew it was the law, didn't you?"
Mrs. Irvin: "Yes sir."
Akerman: "You don't ever argue with the law, do you?"
Mrs. Irvin: "No sir."
Akerman: "When the law tells you to give them something, you give it to them, don't you?"
Mrs. Irvin: "Yes sir. I don't argue with nobody."
Akerman: "You are not going to stand up there and say, 'This violates my constitutional rights and I ain't going to give it to you, are you?'"
Mrs. Irvin: "No sir."

Amazingly, Hunter didn't object. Akerman had the momentum for the first time in the trial. And he had no intention of easing up.

Akerman: "You wouldn't say that to any law enforcement officer, would you?"

Mrs. Irvin: "No sir."
Akerman: "When the law tell you to do something, you think you have got to do it?"
Mrs. Irvin: "Yes sir."
Akerman: "And with no argument?"
Mrs. Irvin: "Yes sir."
Akerman: "And no back talk?"
Mrs. Irvin: "No. I don't do it."
Akerman: "You think when the law tells you to do something, you know you're going to do that?"
Mrs. Irvin: "Yes sir."

Akerman should have left well enough alone, but he couldn't resist revisiting the bedroom search. That decision would cost him a bit of his hard-earned momentum.

Akerman: "And they came busting into the bedroom in your home, didn't they?"
Mrs. Irvin: "They never busted in. They walked in."

Perhaps, for just a moment, the attorney forgot that Dellia was incapable of embellishing, or even exaggerating the truth, even if doing so could benefit her son. Akerman quickly concluded his questioning. Both the state and defense had scored points with Dellia Irvin. Unfortunately for the Groveland Three, the state was already miles ahead before she took the stand.

A 15-minute recess allowed the defense a brief opportunity to access the damage from the testimony of Willie and Norma. The consensus: it was considerable. To balance the scales, Akerman would have to destroy the state's scant physical evidence. And that would be a challenge: he didn't even know what exhibits Hunter had.

When court reconvened, Hunter called Yates, who began by recalling meeting Willie in Leesburg. "We drove up to -- they drove up to where I was. And Mr. Padgett's head was bleeding from up here, somewhere, run down on his nose." Yates then recounted visiting the scene of the fight and the rape. Hunter then led him to finding James Shepherd's car. "We went from Groveland into Clermont. There, we obtained information that the car that was described, the same description as Padgett had given us, had bought some gasoline. They bought a dollar and 5 cents worth of gasoline there and we got the information as to who owned the car." That information led Yates to the Shepherds' home, where he found James Shepherd behind the wheel of the car. According to Yates, the driver volunteered that his brother and a friend had borrowed it the night before. Next: Padgett's immediate identification when Sammy Shepherd and Walter Irvin came out of the house. Hunter was pleased. The deputy was doing fine. Time to move on to the physical evidence Yates uncovered at the scene of the attack.

Hunter: "What did you do?"
Yates: "Compared the tracks on the ground with the tracks of the two boys we had in the car, Irvin and Shepherd."

Hunter: "Did they compare?"
Yates: "No sir."
Hunter: "Why?"
Yates: "Irvin had on a pair of rubbers over his shoes. Had changed his shoes."
Hunter: "That morning?"
Yates: "Yes sir."

Akerman failed to object to what was obviously speculation, since Yates had neither been with Irvin the evening before, nor witnessed him changing shoes. But the attorney sat silent. However, Akerman didn't stay silent for long.

Hunter: "Then where did you go?"
Yates: "Mr. Padgett and Mr. Campbell and myself got in my car and went back to Groveland. Put Mr. Padgett out in Groveland. We went up to the Irvin house and I asked her for the...."
Hunter: "Who?"

With that, Akerman was on his feet, objecting, "to anything he asked at the Irvin house" as being "pure hearsay." Hunter requested the jury be excused, and Futch so moved. With jurors out of earshot, Hunter implored the judge to rule on the relevancy of the conversation between Yates and Walter's mother. Despite Akerman's objections, the judge ruled that Yates' testimony was both relevant and proper. The jury was ushered back in.

Hunter: "Now, Mr. Yates, you went back up to the house of Irvin?"
Yates: "Yes sir."
Hunter: "And what did you say to Irvin's mother where he was living at his home?"
Yates: "I asked her would she give me the pants and shoes that Irvin wore the night before."
Hunter: "What did she say and do?"
Yates: "She said, 'Yes,' and give them to me."
Hunter, turning to the judge: "Now I don't know any other way that you can do."
Akerman: "Did you have a search warrant?"
Yates: "No. She told me to come in."
Akerman: "In Walter Irvin's home?"
Yates: "That's right. Her home. The mother's home."
Akerman: "Objected to, if the Court please, because the evidence received is based upon an unreasonable search and seizure, not incident to a lawful arrest."

The attorneys again approached the bench to argue their positions. Both knew this was a crucial moment. Akerman, citing Florida law, claimed articles from Irvin's home were obtained unlawfully because a search warrant wasn't served. Hunter was sure he could find precedent supporting the legality of the "seizure" and asked the judge to "just leave that question pending until tomorrow morning," so he could research the point. Futch granted the request and recalled the jury.

After Yates established that the crime occurred in Lake County, he introduced the first piece of physical evidence: a dirty handkerchief with a "little piece of cotton" hanging on it he found "laying up on the bushes." The significance of the cotton became evident moments later when Yates revealed that the "floorboards and the seat" of James Shepherd's '46 Mercury were full of "lint or cotton." Of course, Yates didn't produce photos, or samples from the car. Akerman could barely believe what he was hearing. He couldn't allow the handkerchief to be entered as evidence. "Objected to as irrelevant and immaterial; has nothing to do with the issues of this case. Proper predicate has not been laid." But Futch overruled. With the handkerchief received, Hunter moved onto the place where Norma was raped, "just a common little old sand road." A sand road with "fresh tire marks."

Hunter: "Will you describe to the jury the character of those tire marks, sir?"
Yates: "The right front tire was, left a slick impression in the ground. The left front tire left a slick impression in the ground. The rear left wheel left a slick impression. The right rear wheel left a Firestone track. That is, a zigzag track, which the Firestone company puts out."
Hunter: "It had tread on it?"
Yates: "Yes sir. Only the right rear was the only tire on the car that had any tread on it."

Akerman was on his feet again when Hunter asked if the deputy had gone to the garage housing the Shepherd automobile to compare tracks. "We are going to object to this line of testimony, if the Court please. The Court will take judicial notice of the number of automobiles and the numbers of tires. This could have been made by hundreds of cars in Lake County or from other cars having the same thing. It doesn't tend to prove a thing," Akerman said. Again, the judge overruled the objection.

Yates explained the tires on the car were "identical" to the tracks and explained that he had made plaster casts of the tracks. Hunter then reached into a cardboard box and pulled out plaster casts of footprints and tire tracks. Akerman sat bolt upright. "We didn't even know that they were going to put in alleged tire tracks," Akerman recalled. The plaster casts were lightning bolts out of the blue. The defense couldn't possibly counter. Again, Akerman found himself in the impossible position of trying a case by reaction instead of preparation. Thinking quickly, he objected to the casts on "the ground that it is irrelevant and immaterial." Judge Futch overruled him on both the left and right footprint casts. The casts were admissible.

Akerman immediately tried another tack. "Now if the Court please, the defendants object to this question upon the ground that the witness is not qualified as an expert." Hunter agreed to withdraw the question, but he wasn't about to abandon the subject. He needed to establish that his witness was experienced in methods of detection. Yates testified that he had "been at the work" for four years, learning how to make casts from books and experience.

Hunter: "Do you feel that you can qualify for that sort of work as an expert?"
Yates: "I don't know sir. The sheriff has kept me for four years."

The jurors smiled, but Akerman failed to see the humor. Yates had left him an opening, and he wasn't going to wait until his turn to exploit it. "I think we should be given the opportunity to inquire into his qualifications by way of cross examination," Akerman said. Surprisingly, Hunter agreed and Futch followed suit. Akerman was clearly ready.

Akerman: "You say this technical procedure you are talking about was a plaster cast?"
Yates: "Just pouring a cast of a track."
Akerman: "What's this method known as? Has it got a name?"
Yates: "Comes under identification."
Akerman: "You say you have read a book on it?"
Yates: "Yes. Read the FBI books."
Akerman: "You went to one of the FBI schools?"
Yates: "No sir."
Akerman: "You didn't attend the schools?"
Yates: "No sir."
Akerman: "It came by way of correspondence. Is that right?"
Yates: "No sir."
Akerman: "What do you do? What does the method consist of?"
Yates: "By pouring plaster paris into the track and letting it harden and then lift it out of the ground."
Akerman: "And then how do you compare that with the tire?"
Yates: "It just looks like the tire."
Akerman: "Is it round like a tire?"
Yates: "No. It looks like the tread on the tire. It looks like the part which touches the ground of the tire when you are driving an automobile."

Akerman soon turned to the sand road where the deputy found the impression.

Akerman: "You don't know whether or not any other automobiles had been in there?"
Yates: "No. I don't know that. There was only one track."
Akerman: "There was only one track, you don't know whether any other automobile had gone in there after that?"
Yates: "No. There hadn't been another automobile in there."
Akerman: "There had been just one automobile in there and backed out. Are you stating that of your own knowledge or because of the tracks?"
Yates: "Because of the tracks."
Akerman: "I'm asking you, though, then you saw one track there but you don't know how many automobiles other than the one you detected from the tracks?'
Yates: "No more than one automobile went in there. If it did, it didn't touch the ground."

As the ripple of laughter dissipated, Akerman tried to regain the offensive by again challenging Yates' "expertise."
Akerman: "How many of these track impressions have you made during your experience as a law enforcement officer?"

Yates: "I don't know. I couldn't even guess. I have noticed hundreds of them."

If the defense caught the word "noticed" it didn't let on. It was a poor choice of words, to be sure. Experts don't "notice" footprints and tire tracks. They examine them.

Akerman: "How many of them have you compared and identified with others?"
Yates: "Well, I caught two little boys in Umatilla the other day with them. And that had broken in two packing houses out there, one was barefooted and one with shoes on."
Akerman: "Do you make the same kind of thing for a footprint as you do for a car print, do you?"
Yates: "No sir."
Akerman: "Don't make fingerprints that way, do you?"
Yates: "No sir."
Akerman: "I'm asking you how many of these impressions you made with cars that you subsequently identified."
Yates: "I don't know. I have made a lot of them."

Akerman was back in control, but instead of pressing the point and pinning Yates to the wall, he abandoned the line of questioning to establish that the car had been in the possession of the sheriff's office since the arrest. It had been a productive cross-examination, but once Akerman finished the grilling and renewed his objection, Futch again overruled him. Four objections by the defense, zero sustained.

Hunter wasted little time getting back to the evidence, establishing that on the front floor of the car Yates had found a "dirty handkerchief" allegedly used to cover the license plate, and that the plaster casts "compared, identical as far as I could tell," with the tires. Of course, Akerman objected to casts of all four tires being introduced as exhibits, and of course, the judge overruled. The defense was now 0-for-8. Curiously, the "dirty handkerchief" wasn't introduced. Yates then detailed finding lint on the handkerchief that covered the license plate, "a little fuzz" hanging off the end of the bolt that held the license plate, and grease on a rag found in the car. With that, Hunter finished with Yates and the first day of testimony in the most sensational case in Lake County history ended. Day two would begin with Yates back on the stand for Akerman's cross-examination.

As Akerman watched armed guards escort the defendants from the courtroom, the attorney couldn't help feeling uneasy that the very man who beat his clients was also the man charged with guarding them. As the attorneys for the Groveland Three left the courtroom, Williams was approached by jovial court clerk George Dykes. "Well, Mr. Williams, how do you like the way the trial is going?" Williams shot back, "It's the worst framed-up case I have ever seen in my years of practice!" The trial wasn't even over and the Crackers were gloating as if they already knew the outcome. Despite being physically tired and mentally drained, the defense attorneys met at Akerman's Orlando office to fine-tune the case they would present the next day. They had sustained heavy losses. Hopefully, they could regroup.

One of the most pressing questions: Would Yates testify that the accused had confessed? Members of the defense team hoped so. If Hunter introduced confessions, the door would swing open for the defense to prove the "confessions" had been coerced through cruel beatings. It was doubtful that Hunter would pursue that tack, considering that Futch had already ruled against hearing from the physician who had examined the prisoners. But perhaps Yates would falter and mention the confessions. Akerman would have to be at his shrewdest during cross-examination.

Chapter 16 -- The Verdicts

The air was thick with tension in the packed Tavares courtroom as the prisoners entered. Once seated, Sammie Shepherd turned to Franklin Williams, the NAACP lawyer from New York. "Mr. Williams, when the trial is over, be careful," Sammie whispered. "They told me that the sheriff had told them that when this trial is over, 'I'm going to get that nigger lawyer,'" Williams recalled. Nearby, *New York Post* reporter Ted Poston was sure the warning included him. "Ted Poston was equally as concerned and upset. He had had some personal experiences in calling in his stories on the telephone, from Tavares which caused him some concern. He had had his glasses allegedly accidentally knocked off and stepped on on the staircase," Williams said.

The second day of testimony began with State Attorney Jesse Hunter moving to introduce into evidence the trousers and shoes taken from the Irvin home. Akerman, determined to prevent jurors from seeing the items, promptly asked Judge Futch to remove the jury. Before Futch could reply, Hunter charged, "He is in conflict with the Supreme Court because they said the jury should hear it." The judge agreed. Akerman doggedly objected to the testimony as hearsay, but again the judge overruled him, not once, but twice. The defense had now raised 11 objections, and all 11 had been overruled.

Hunter called Deputy James Yates to the stand to recount how he obtained Walter's pants and shoes. "I asked Dellia Irvin for the pants and shoes that Walter wore the night before and asked her could I get them and she said 'yes,' to come in," Yates said. "And I went in and she got the pants and shoes and laid them on the bed in front of me. And I took them and went back out to the gate and compared the shoes with the footprints..." Akerman bolted out of his chair, saying, "Now if the Court please, I am going to object to that. I think we have now reached the state where the...." Hunter knew Yates had overstepped, and quickly brought the deputy back into the house.

Hunter: "Don't talk about that. You took the shoes and the pants?"
Yates: "Yes sir."
Hunter: "Did you make any search of the house?"
Yates: "No sir."
Hunter: "She just gave them to you?"
Yates: "Yes sir."

When Hunter offered the shoes and pants into evidence, Akerman objected the "evidence" was "irrelevant and immaterial" and "neither tends to prove or disprove any of the issues in this case." Futch again overruled. The introduction of the pants was clearly a blow to the defense, but it wasn't a surprise. Williams wasn't even surprised the trousers had gained a mysterious stain since Walter shed them on the morning of July 16.

As the pants passed before the jury box, Akerman continued to protest. He wanted his opposition to be part of the official record for the Supreme Court appeal he was already planning. After Futch excused the jury, Hunter cited two cases where an officer had obtained evidence without a warrant after being invited into the house by the homeowner. Ironically, in one case, a pair of shoes was removed. Hunter had prepared well. Akerman responded by pointing out that Walter paid rent to his parents and the door to his room was padlocked. Akerman contended that Dellia Irvin was acting as landlord, and not a mother, when she illegally allowed Yates into her tenant's room. The judge listened patiently, then again ruled for the state. It was a crucial decision. Yates could now recount taking Irvin's shoes to the scene of the assault and matching them to the footprints. The ruling also meant jurors could see anything and everything McCall's men had found at the Irvin home, in James Shepherd's car, or at the scene of the scuffle. The judge had thrown open the door. Hunter didn't waste any time rushing through it.

If anyone felt the defense had any chance for acquittal, it had to be fading fast. The prosecutor was obviously pleased, and with good reason: everything was going his way. Hunter knew his opponent only had two avenues to pursue: attack the character of state witnesses, or try to discredit the evidence. Hunter had done his best to block both. By now Akerman just wanted Yates off the stand. During cross-examination, which lasted just five minutes, the deputy refused to admit he had searched for a 1946 dark *green* Mercury as newspaper accounts had reported, instead insisting he had always sought a "1946 dark colored Mercury." The deputy more than held his own during the 13-question interrogation, but Akerman finally scored a point when Yates couldn't recall what size Irvin's shoes were. It was a small victory, but a triumph nevertheless. Akerman concluded by leading Yates through a short course in tire identification, which initially caught the lawman off guard. The deputy hadn't expected the approach, but he recovered quickly.

Akerman: "What kind of impression does a Kelly tire make in the sand?"

Yates: "I have no idea."
Akerman: "What kind does a Goodyear make?"
Yates: "Make a diamond tread."
Akerman: "What kind does a Goodrich make?"
Yates: "I believe it is a zigzag tread."
Akerman: "No further questions."

Yates obviously wasn't exactly an expert on tire tracks, but jurors didn't seem concerned. Like Norma Padgett, Yates' testimony had been nearly flawless. Any gains Akerman made during his questioning of Willie Padgett were completely overshadowed by Yates' plaster casts, shoes and the pants handed to the jurors.

James Shepherd, who had spent the past 10 days in jail, was the state's next witness. He confirmed that the car he loaned to his brother was a "dark blue '42 Mercury 4-door sedan." When questioned about the car being returned, Sammie's older brother also missed an opportunity to make Akerman's timeline work. James testified, "I really don't know when he got back. I was asleep when he got back." Again, Hunter kept his questioning short. And again, he got exactly what he wanted. The defense was taking a beating because there hadn't been time to interview the defendants' family members. Of course, the jury couldn't know that. As Hunter sat down and Akerman approached the witness, the defense attorney was determined to show that Sammie acted like anything but a guilty man on the morning of July 16.

Akerman: "But the car was right out there in the open?"
Shepherd: "That's right."
Akerman: "Sam didn't tell you to hide that car anywhere during the day?"
Shepherd: "No sir. He never said a thing. Nothing like that."

According to his older brother, Sammie's demeanor stayed unchanged Saturday morning as he accompanied James and his wife to the Irvins.

Akerman: "Do you remember coming to town?"
Shepherd: "Yes sir. We was talking and funning along, when we was coming to town."
Akerman: "He didn't appear nervous, did he?"
Shepherd: "No sir. No sir."

Before allowing Sammie's brother to step down, Akerman established that James had spent the last week in jail. On cross-examination, Hunter addressed the insinuation that James was imprisoned so the defense couldn't question him.

Hunter: "Did these defense attorneys talk to you up there?"
Shepherd: "Well, I don't know exactly the names. Two that questioned me Sunday."
Hunter: "They talked to you, privately?"
Shepherd: "Yes sir."
Hunter: "They talked to you all they wanted to, didn't they?"

Shepherd: "Yes sir."
Hunter: "Wasn't anybody hiding you there?"
Shepherd: "No sir."
Hunter: "Everybody told you to talk to them every time they came there?"
Shepherd: "That's right."

As Hunter returned to the prosecution table, Akerman rose and addressed Futch. "If the Court please, we are through with this witness. We ask at this time that he be discharged from custody. He has given the testimony in the case, now. Been incarcerated over a week, now." For once, Hunter didn't interfere. "I have no objection. He is under the rule of the Court, here, and I want to see that he has a square deal and everything else." It was a strange choice of words. Had Hunter promised James Shepherd a "deal?" As in, "say the right things and you can go home?" As a weary, but relieved James headed toward the courtroom door and his first taste of freedom in more than a week, Futch granted a recess.

Williams was also drained and needed some fresh air. As he angrily left the courtroom, he nearly ran into Mabel Norris-Reese in the hallway. The outspoken attorney had been anxious to confront her, and now he had his chance. Williams berated the newspaper editor for an article that portrayed the life of Southern Negroes as peaceful and harmonious. Norris-Reese fired back that Williams should live in the South for a while if he wanted the "true picture." Williams saw red. He thundered, "I... would... not.... live....in..... the...SOUTH!" Williams was in no mood to be baited. "Mrs. Reese, I have learned one thing out of this case -- one thing I'll always remember. I have learned that what is wrong with the South is not the southerners....it's the Northerners -- like you -- who come down here and try to out-Southern the Southerners," Williams railed.

"She did not like me, but then a lot of people do not. She thought I was arrogant. I guess, she and others expected all blacks to show them a certain amount of respect beyond that which they by virtue of their character or position deserve. I had no reason to do that. You know, there was nothing about me or my background or personality that led me to believe that I was anything but what I was: an attorney, a well qualified attorney from New York who had come down to represent these young men, but she did not like me and she took out after me." -- Franklin H. Williams, Feb. 11, 1985

When court resumed, the state called Curtis Howard, a Department of Agriculture inspector and part-time service station attendant who was working at his father-in-law's gas station on the outskirts of Leesburg on the evening of July 15. The defense attorneys listened intently as Howard told an unbelievable tale that produced more questions than it answered: Among the more incredible claims Howard made: that around 7 a.m. Saturday he "started down the road... from Leesburg headed for Groveland" and saw "Mrs. Padgett" in Okahumpka sitting in the grass alongside the road. Curiously, he didn't stop, even though four hours earlier Willie had told him his wife had been abducted in that area.

Hunter: "Did you tell him what you had seen?"

Howard: "No sir. Not then. They wanted me to take him out to the house so he could change clothes."

Howard didn't explain why he didn't tell Padgett about seeing a young woman along the roadside. According to Howard, he finally put two and two together at the Padgett home when he asked the farmer if he had a picture of his wife. Willie's sister produced one, and Howard recognized the girl in the photo as the woman he had seen and immediately agreed to take Willie to the spot. She wasn't there, but they found Norma "in a car with another boy" two miles from the spot. Howard recalled that husband and wife kissed upon being reunited, then walked over and got into Howard's car. "I asked her if she was hurt anyway (sic), and she said, her leg. I could see that the legs were all scratched up and feet was swollen real bad, and I asked her if the Negroes did anything to her and she told me that all four of them had attacked her," Howard testified. After establishing that Norma had told *both* Willie and Curtis that she had been attacked, Hunter handed the witness to Akerman.

Akerman got right to the point. He wanted to know why Howard didn't stop when he passed a young woman on the side of the road hours after a man told him his wife was missing.

Akerman: "Just where were they?"
Howard: "That's a fork, there, just as you turn off to go to Center Hill. She was sitting in the grass, there."
Akerman: "Any stores around there?"
Howard: "There's a, I don't know if it is a dining place or a juke or what it is, on the right side of the road, there."
Akerman: "She was by herself at that time?"
Howard: "That's right."
Akerman: "You didn't stop and talk with her then?"
Howard: "No."
Akerman: "And you just saw her seated there and went on down the road?"
Howard: "Well, she got up and went over to that other place when I started slowing down."
Akerman: "She went?"
Howard: "Ran over to the other place."

Under re-direct, Hunter led Howard through the identification of Charles Greenlee when Curtis accompanied the Padgetts to the Groveland jail. "She just said, 'That's one of them,'" Howard recalled.

After Hunter questioned Harry McDonald, the night watchman who found Greenlee with a loaded gun "between 3:15 and 3:30 a.m." on July 16, the state called Henry Singleton, owner of a Groveland "beer garden." Akerman sat up with a start as the Negro began relating an incredible tale of Greenlee walking into Singleton's home on the evening of July 15 and asking for change for a dollar, which Singleton refused. Why? He "suspicioned" the stranger, who then asked "where he could get some Cuba (bolita) tickets." The time:

155

about 9 p.m. "I asked him what would he play if he were playing. He said, '13 and 10.' He wanted one piece of each. And he turned and walked away after I refused on either thing he asked me about. Because I had done suspicioned him and he was nervous. Had one hand in his right-hand pocket and his left hand out and I walked to the door and I called him and I asked him, I says, 'Who do you work for?' He said, 'I work for the Revenue men.' And he walked on in the direction toward the asphalt road and I came out the door and got in my car and went on over on the other part of Groveland and when I came back several ones run up there and told me, says, 'We chased off someone knocking at your back door.' Said that they were trying to bust the door down," Singleton testified.

During his short time on the stand, the old Negro implied Greenlee was a gambler, armed, a liar and a would-be thief. Rape was about the only thing Singleton didn't accuse Greenlee of. Akerman knew the witness was lying, and he didn't waste any time attacking Singleton's testimony.

Akerman: "Now do you have to wear your glasses all the time?"
Singleton: "By no means. No sir."
Akerman: "Do you wear them most of the time?"
Singleton: "Well sometimes I usually wear them just to hold my eyes up."
Akerman: "Do you have any trouble with your eyesight?"
Singleton: "Well, they are not too good. They're not the best."

After casting doubt on Singleton's ability to identify the man who wanted to buy bolita numbers, Akerman launched an all-out attack on the character of the witness.

Akerman: "When does Cuba throw?"
Singleton: "Well it throws, throws today and tomorrow. Sometimes throw today and sometimes throws next Saturday."
Akerman: "Did he have any reason to ask you for any Cuba tickets?"
Singleton: "No reason that he had far as my knowing."
Akerman: "Have you ever been in the business of selling Cuba or bolita?"
Singleton: "I have. But I wasn't at the time when he came in there."
Akerman: "How long were you in the business of selling bolita and Cuba and other lottery tickets?"

Akerman clearly had the witness on the defensive. Hunter could stand no more.

Hunter: "Wait a minute. Now that's irrelevant and immaterial."
Akerman: "I think it goes to the character of the witness, if the Court please."
Hunter: "Not in cross-examination, anyway."
Judge Futch: "I don't think it is material. Sustain the objection." Akerman and the other members of the defense team were incredulous. The defense hadn't had a single objection sustained in 16 tries. Unruffled, Akerman immediately returned to issue of Singleton's character.

Akerman: "Have you ever been convicted of crime?"
Singleton: "Yes sir."
Akerman: "How many times?"
Singleton: "I disremember."
Akerman: "What crimes?'
Singleton: "I was convicted...."
Hunter: "Just a minute. Hold on.
Singleton: "I was convicted of impersonating an officer once."
Akerman: "Convicted of any other crimes?"
Singleton: "I don't remember."

Akerman had made his point. Hunter hoped for a better showing from his next witnesses, Luther and Ethel Thomas, parents of the late Ernest Thomas. Hunter wasn't worried; the couple had had plenty of time to think about their testimony after McCall jailed them a week earlier. Sure enough, the Thomases followed the state's script. Luther identified the gun, which Hunter then introduced into evidence. Ethel remembered her son arriving from Gainesville "between 4 and 5 p.m.," on July 15 and said she last saw him around 8 p.m. Ethel said that she invited Ernest to come home with her, but he wouldn't. Akerman vigorously objected when Hunter asked what her son told her.

Hunter: "What did he tell you?"
Akerman: "Objected if the Court please, as hearsay testimony."
Thomas: "They told me...."
Akerman: "I objected to it. Don't answer it."

After Futch overruled Akerman, Thomas told the court that her son was going to "a ball" or "party" friends were giving for him. Akerman declined to cross-examine. The defense team hadn't had time to look into Ernest Thomas' background, or interview members of his family. Besides, they couldn't do him any good now. The defense goal was to make sure Shepherd, Irvin and Greenlee didn't join him in the grave.

Akerman was jolted from his musing by the announcement that the prosecution rested, even though several subpoenaed witnesses hadn't been called. The case was brilliant in its simplicity: Hunter wanted the jurors to understand the trial was about the horror Norma Padgett endured at the hands of four black demons. No subplots, no need for a parade of witnesses to corroborate her claims. Willie Padgett's testimony and Yates' plaster casts were more than enough to "prove" Norma was telling the truth. Without medical evidence that she had been raped, no torn or stained clothing, and no scratches or bruises to show the jury, the casts became *the* critical pieces of physical evidence. And by keeping their existence a secret until presented, the impact was like a thunderclap on a clear day. The defense had been left naked, with no way to counter.

It was 11:40 a.m. when Akerman asked for a recess. Futch granted the request, giving Akerman, Price, Williams and Hill two hours to digest the strengths and weaknesses of the state's case and finalize their plan of attack. While Akerman gathered his notes, Williams headed for the judge's chambers. He had a few things on his mind about the way Futch was pandering to the prosecution and figured he had nothing to lose by speaking out. The NAACP attorney was waiting for the judge when the door opened, but in walked Mabel Norris-Reese, not Futch. Still stinging from their earlier argument, she had followed Williams so she could give him both barrels. "You appear to be a Negro who has intelligence and education -- tell me, why did you mix yourself into this case and attempt to fan racial hatred?" Williams bristled. His eyes were afire as he answered, "Do you mean it was wrong for me to come down here and defend these boys?" Norris-Reese replied, "Not at all. It was the right thing to do. But through your representation of the NAACP in such a case as this, and with your attitude, you are fanning racial hatred. Why should an educated Negro as yourself get mixed up in it?" If the newspaperwoman had meant to pay Williams a compliment, it was lost on him. Williams explained that he had joined the NAACP because it was a noble and necessary cause and that he willingly sacrificed a prosperous career to advance Negro rights. He boomed, "Do you realize the good NAACP has done?' Norris-Reese replied, "Yes, but we know what it has not done. We know, from being assigned to investigate, what it has not done about red light districts. Why doesn't it take up that problem?" Williams failed to see what red light districts had to do with Groveland, and wondered if he could ever make this white woman understand -- understand that Thomas wasn't just killed by a sheriff's posse in Madison County. "He'd been dead long before that, Mrs. Reese," Franklin remarked. Disgusted at Williams' single-mindedness, Norris-Reese angrily left.

Meanwhile, Akerman was understandably grim as he considered his limited options. No one knew better than Akerman that the defense didn't have a case. How could it with the judge overruling every defense objection and sustaining every ploy by the state? Outside of the defendants, Akerman didn't have a single witness to refute Norma Padgett's rape charge. Plus, there was no way to combat the lies and trickery the state had used.

"They had so much manufactured evidence… it was like a story. Like a Hollywood story. They had it down pat," Williams said. "They had Irvin's shoe prints. Imagine making a cast at the scene of the crime. That only happens in movies. You know, of course they could make a cast. They had taken his shoes when they arrested him. They had the handkerchief that belonged to either Irvin or Shepherd which they claimed they had tied over their license plate to hide their license plate. Come on. That is too pat. They had the tire mark. Of course, they had the tire mark. They had the car. They made the tire mark and they made it so you have this country jury impressed by all of this high falutin' FBI-type evidence clearly in my judgment as an attorney, manufactured evidence. We could not prove that. How could we prove, you know, how could you prove it?"

The case was over before it began. As court resumed, Akerman knew full well he had no chance of winning an acquittal, but maybe, just maybe, he could keep the defendants out of the electric chair. Samuel Shepherd, the eldest and most outspoken of the defendants, would take the stand first. To Akerman, Shepherd was least likely to be intimidated or trapped by Hunter, The defense was banking on a confident, clear accounting of what really happened, and Sammie was the best bet to deliver. Young Charlie Greenlee would go last.

But Shepherd was nervous. Akerman's hope that Shepherd would come off as honest and credible evaporated quickly. Sammie seemed anything but forthcoming; in fact he appeared secretive about the trip he and Walter took to Orlando. "I went around through the quarters with my girlfriend and I come back to his house, which was the second time. I asked his mother if he was there and she said, 'No.' My girlfriend, I asked her to get out. She asked me why couldn't she go with me. I said, 'Well,' it started misting and raining and the right front glass in my father's car was broken out and I told her, I said, 'For fear you might get wet.' I said, 'You better stay home.'... She got out. Well, before she went in the house, she said, 'Where are you going after you find him?' I said, 'Well, I'm yet undecided.' I said, 'We might go over to the club.' And she said to me, 'Well, can I go?' And I said, 'Well, I don't figure you should.'" The testimony sounded like the story of a man who didn't want his girlfriend around while he and his buddy chased some tail and raised a little hell. It was an auspicious beginning to the defense: Sammie Shepherd, who just related how he lied to his girlfriend, was asking a jury to believe his story of what happened on July 15 and 16. Akerman obviously hadn't had time to coach his witness.

Sammie also told of encountering Thomas "after 10 o'clock" at the Blue Flame. An argument broke out when Ernest accused Sammie of seeing his girl. Shepherd denied the accusation, saying, "I have a girlfriend. In fact, I am expecting to get married soon." Thomas warned Sammie not to see her again, or he "might have to do something about it." If the point of the story was to show Sammie wouldn't be playing around with any white women because he was nearly engaged, it missed the mark. Or maybe the intent was to portray Thomas as violent and Sammie as a peacemaker. At the very least, Akerman hoped the story showed there was no love lost between Thomas and Shepherd. If the confrontation at the Blue Flame did in fact happen, it proves the two men wouldn't have been running the back roads of Lake County together on a Friday night. On the down side, it also showed that the men knew each other.

After picking Walter up, Sammie said he drove to Clermont for gas, but his father's car began to "spit, pop and backfire." Shepherd told night patrolman Sam Doto, who would sell him gas, that he was "going out of town," and would return with his brother's car. He also told of encountering Henry Singleton, who was trying to find Ernest Thomas. The claim that a known gambler was looking for one of the men who would be accused of kidnap and rape was startling, but the defense never developed the connection. Was Thomas part of Singleton's bolita operation? Apparently it didn't occur to Akerman that by painting the now-deceased Thomas as a villain, he might have been able to shift some of the spotlight off the three men he defended. After all, dead men tell no tales.

Shepherd told of awakening his brother James, and asking to borrow his car, then going back to Clermont to find Doto to sell him gas. But instead of finding the patrolman, Shepherd and Irvin ran into a drunk with a man named Odum, who asked the men to take the drunk home. They tried to oblige, but the wino wouldn't get out of the car, so the men took him back to the park and put him out there. Sammie and Walter then found Doto and bought gas. Finally, they were off to Orlando. To the jury, the rambling tale of sputtering car engine, searching for the town policeman, switching cars, buying gas and a drunk who wouldn't get out of the car smacked of a story concocted by someone trying to pad an alibi. Shepherd was hanging himself. Fortunately, his testimony would improve.

Shepherd said he drove Irvin to Orlando, then Eatonville, where they had supper at Club Eaton. Next, they headed to Club 436 to drink beer and play records. Finally, well after midnight, they headed home -- straight home. The next morning, after breakfast, Sammie and James went to the Irvins. Moments later, a highway patrolman arrived. "And he asked me, he said, 'Where is the guy that was with you last night?' I said, 'He's in the house.' He said, 'Call him out.' I then called Irvin and he come out of the house. After he had come out of the house, some man got out of one of these cars... This man got out of one of those cars, one of the first two, and he come around the back of my brother's car and he attempted to jump, to fight with me. He didn't fight Irvin. He didn't hit Irvin. He only started towards him and he was cursing and threatening." Again, Shepherd had inadvertently put himself in a bad light. The men on the jury understood that the man who got out of the car (Willie Padgett) obviously recognized Sammie and had a score to settle with him. Shepherd was obviously telling the truth, a liar would have said the man in the car hadn't recognized him. Or perhaps he was providing details McCall had warned him not to omit. Shepherd's testimony ended with him denying he was in the Okahumpka-Mascotte area in the early morning hours of the 16th and that the first time he saw Greenlee was in the county jail. It had been far from a command performance.

Hunter declined to cross examine, an announcement that caused a murmur of surprise from the spectators. Hunter didn't bat an eye. He knew what he was doing. He had considered grilling Shepherd, particularly about his dishonorable discharge from the Army for theft, but opted to create the impression the state's case was so strong that cross-examination wasn't necessary. As Hunter glanced at the jurors, he knew he had made the right decision. Their faces confirmed his gut: they knew the niggers were guilty. Mabel Norris-Reese saw a different reason behind the unorthodox strategy: "He knew, too, that the defense attorneys wanted him to question the defendants -- that they wanted to be able to include some remark of his to the defendants as part of their hue and cry to the Supreme Court."

Walter Irvin, the quiet one, the one who wouldn't confess no matter how much torture was inflicted upon him, followed Sammie to the stand. Akerman wasn't about to let Walter ramble like Sammie did. He began by dispelling the notion that Irvin and Thomas were together on the night in question.

Akerman: "Are you a friend of Ernest Thomas and did you and he run around any?"
Irvin: "No sir. Fact, I hadn't been long got back home. I wasn't running around with anyone but this Samuel."

The rest of Irvin's testimony wasn't spectacular, but his matter-of-fact, deliberate answers easily made him a more credible witness than Shepherd. Again, Akerman finished by leading his witness to the scene of the alleged crime.

Akerman: "Now, did you at any time on the night of July 15, or the early morning hours of July 16th, go up to the Okahumpka area and have anything to do with this white lady who has testified in this case?"
Irvin: "I did not."

Again, Hunter declined to cross-examine. When Futch ordered a 10-minute recess, the defense attorneys wisely used the brief respite to prepare Greenlee. Akerman grimly realized that Shepherd was doomed, and Irvin too, if nothing else because he admitted being with Sammie. Greenlee, however, was different. Charles had a clear-cut alibi for his whereabouts for 3 a.m. on July 16. No juror, no matter how bigoted, could rationalize that Greenlee could be in two places at the same time. If Akerman could make the rest of the timeline work, the kid might just escape the electric chair. The wide-eyed teen was a good choice to finish with: perhaps jurors would feel some pity for the naïve, semi-literate kid.

Greenlee explained that he had met Ernest Thomas at a café in Gainesville, and that the two had hitchhiked to Groveland. They arrived "about 4:30 or maybe 5 o'clock," then parted ways.

Akerman: "What did you do then, Charles?"
Greenlee: "Well, I had on dirty clothes and so he told me he would go down to his mother's house and get me some clean clothes and would bring them back and give them to me and then he said I could come on down to his mother's place."
Akerman: "Where did you stay?"
Greenlee: "He told me to go over there at the packing shed which was (at) the back of the depot."

And that's where Charlie stayed until Thomas returned in a '41 Pontiac just before nightfall. But Ernest didn't bring clothes, just a bottle of soda water, two boxes of cookies and a package of peanuts.

Akerman: "What did he say about the clothes?"
Greenlee: "He told me that his mother wouldn't close up her place until about 10:30 maybe 11 o'clock, that he would go then to his mother's home. He talked as though it was a long ways from Groveland and he would go then and get his, get the clothes and bring (them) back to the depot where I was waiting."

So far, so good, Akerman thought. Now the hard part: the gun Thomas had given him. "Well, in the seat of the car, I saw a revolver and I asked him if I was going to stay up there that long during the night, would he let me keep that. Though in a joking way... I told him I had never been there and been around there much. I don't know what kind of a place it was, whether it's a swamp or not. Still I was joking with him about getting the gun." Akerman was pleased. It was a believable explanation.

Charles said he slept off and on, then woke up with a thirst. "So I went around to the packing shed...I mean, to the filling station and got, to get me some water. But just before I went around there, I thought about the gun which I had in my suitcase what Ernest Thomas gave me. Well, I then opened my suitcase and I said, 'If I'm going around there tonight,' to myself, 'I believe I'll be a big man. I'll put the gun on there.' Those are the words I said in my mind. And I taken the gun and stick up in my belt and walked around the shed. I wasn't thinking about the gun that I had on me because I didn't try to hide it and whenever I leaned over the faucet, the fountain, that was, that was there to get a drink of water, I heard footsteps coming toward me but I made no preparation to leave because I know it wasn't no harm to get water. And then I wasn't thinking about the gun that I had in my belt. And I then raised up. Well the man was close enough on me to shine the light on me. So he shined the light on me and whenever he shined the light on me, I, he saw the gun. Well, I then thought about the gun I had. Well I turned, slightly, trying to shield the gun to keep him for seeing it but he did see it. He say, 'Hold still a minute, boy.' And so I stopped. And raised my hands because I knew I had no business with the gun," Greenlee testified.

Charles remembered being scared, but explained how he came to be in Groveland and produced a Social Security card and driver's license. Then another man arrived and suggested that they call the law. "I knew I hadn't done nothing and the gun wasn't nothing. So I figured if he put me in jail I wouldn't stay there long. So I just sit there because if I had wanted to I could have run… So I was sitting there, waiting in suspense till the cops come and so whenever he came, he looked at me and he said, he asked me where I came from. Well, before I told him anything, this here night watchman showed him my identification what I had showed him. So after he had showed him that, he told me, say, 'You come on around to the jailhouse and if we don't find nothing on you after morning, we'll take your gun and let you go.'"

Charles then told of spending the night in Groveland's rickety jail. "The door wasn't even closed. It was a big enough hole in the door I could get out on the night I was in there. But I knowed I hadn't done nothing and me running would only press more charges on me so I even took my foot and pushed the door out far enough for me to get out if I wanted to. But unaware of what was going on, I stayed in till morning, depending on what these mens had said." According to Charles, the night watchman brought him dinner and told him, "You seem to be a right nice boy and if we don't find nothing on you until morning, we'll let you go. So, well, I felt good then because I know I was going the next morning… And so I laid back down on the bed and went to sleep." When he awoke a "big fat man" was standing outside his cell. "Say, 'stand up nigger.' So I stood up. Well, he kind of scared me because I didn't know what was coming off. He say, 'Where's that boy that was with you last night?' I say, 'There wasn't no boys with me last night except these two night watchmen.' Say, 'I ain't talking about them.' Say, 'Where's that new Buick, or old Buick, you was in?' I say, 'I wasn't in no car last night. Came here yesterday evening on a gasoline truck or oil truck. It had a drum on it, on the back. I don't know nothing about what was in it.' And he say, 'You lying.' Well, he turned and walked off."

The room adjacent to the cell then got very busy, with men "going in and coming out." Charles was beginning to sense something was very wrong. "Directly an old fellow came in there. I don't know who he was. He about the size of Mr. Hunter, and looked like him but

I don't think it was. I don't think he was as old as Mr. Hunter. He say, 'Nigger, you sitting up here and telling a lie like that,' say, 'I ought to go get my shotgun and put you through this hole and shoot you.' I say, 'What about mister?' He say, 'You know what I'm talking about.' Well, he walked on off. Because, I said to myself, 'Something must be wrong around here, somewhere.' I know I hadn't done nothing." Then a man brought in a young white couple. "Man, he walks up to the cell first. Say, 'Stand up.' I stood up. He looked at me a while. He say, 'No.' Say, 'This ain't one of the boys.' Well, then his wife looked at me. She say, 'Look like one of them.' Well, he said again, say, 'No.' Said, 'This ain't none of the boys.'" With that the couple left. But Charles wasn't in the clear yet.

"Well, the cell commenced to clearing out. Wasn't nobody left there but me and the man who put me in jail. I didn't know what was happening. So he come around there. He say, 'Boy,' Say, 'If you don't know it, you in a bad spot.' I say, 'Yes sir? What about?' He said, 'Some niggers raped a white woman last night.' Say 'And if I don't hurry up and get you away from here, these people going to kill you.' So I begged him to hurry up and take me away from here somewhere, I don't care where. So he said he done already sent for the officers and they ought to be here any minute." Moments later a car full of angry men pulled up. "One fellow say, 'If you'll lay the keys down, I'll go in there and get him.' Another fellow say, 'If you'll just tell me that I can have him if I get him.' And people kept talking, questioning and telling what they would do if they had me." One man even brandished a knife and told 'the black so-and-so' to 'stand up to the door.'

Akerman gently encouraged Charles to continue. "Well, as he was unlocking the door, one of these here patrolmans, I don't know which one it was, say, 'We got this man,' say, to this effect, 'We don't know what he done or what he haven't done. So we are going to hold him until we find out more about it.' Say, 'Ain't no use in killing the man now.' Say, 'We'll take him on to Tavares.' Well, whenever the man handcuffed me and all the people standing around there, I run and jumped in the car. And so I got in the back seat and set down and looking at the people what wanted to kill me," Greenlee recalled. For the first time since the trial began, Akerman was pleased with a witness. Greenlee was exuding wide-eyed innocence. The newspaper reporters were hanging on his every word.

Akerman: "All right. Now, Charlie, were you in the jail at the time the people came up and surrounded the jail here that night?"
Greenlee: "Yes sir. Some people did come up here."
Akerman: "Yes. And what happened at that time?"
Greenlee: "Well, the little man what was on the stairs…"
Hunter: "Now your honor, I object to that class of testimony. It is a far way now, from the offense, itself and has no bearing on this case. Irrelevant and immaterial."

Of course, Futch sustained the objection. But Akerman wouldn't be dissuaded. "We want to show by this witness that at the time the group was at the jail that the husband of the prosecutrix came up to the jail; he was brought out and shown to him and he said, 'No. That's not one of them.' That he was the boy down in the Groveland jail. That is what we would like to prove by this witness." Hunter replied, "Go ahead and prove that. Because it's already been testified by the husband, himself. That he didn't have an opportunity to see this man before that night. Still irrelevant and immaterial. But then let him go ahead and make that statement." Futch, as usual, followed Hunter's direction.

Akerman: "When you were up there in the jail and the people came around the jail, did some of the officers bring somebody up there to your cell?"
Greenlee: "Well, I don't know whether they was officers or not, but one guy come up, I did see him have a gun. Say, 'All of your boys come out the cell.'"
Akerman: "Did you come out and stand under the light?"
Greenlee: "Well, the light was up above there. Well, we came out and stood in front of the light."
Akerman: "Did you see Mr. Padgett in the courtroom, testifying?"
Greenlee: "I sure did."
Akerman: "Did that man come up there?"
Greenlee: "Yes sir."
Akerman: "What did he say about you?"
Greenlee: "They say, 'Ain't that one of the niggers?' And he said, 'No, that's not one of the boys. That's the boy that we had over to Groveland for carrying a gun.'"

Akerman was clearly pleased as he concluded the questioning. Considering the lucid, clear testimony Charles had offered, the defense fully expected Hunter to pounce, but the prosecutor again waived cross-examination. Akerman was surprised, but relieved. Greenlee's account had advanced his case considerably. Charles had taken the stand as a rapist and returned to his seat a victim of bloodthirsty racists. And Akerman was willing to gamble the young defendant could take it a little further. Charles had barely sat down when Akerman recalled him. If Hunter wasn't going to challenge the teen, perhaps Akerman could further reinforce the defense case.

Akerman: "Now did you go up around the Okahumpka area to commit this crime against this white lady?"
Greenlee: "I went nowhere after I got to Groveland. I went nowhere but to that shed and because I had nowhere to go. I stayed on that shed waiting on Ernest Thomas to come back with some clothes."
Akerman: "Did you commit this crime against that white lady?"
Greenlee: "I did not commit it."
Akerman: "Would you have been hanging around down there in Groveland if you had done something like that, Charlie?"
Greenlee: "Me? If I'd even thought something like that had happened, I would have been on my way back to Santa Fe or somewhere."

It was a powerful conclusion to the defense's case. As Akerman sat down, Hunter recalled McDonald. The watchman testified that he didn't see any suitcase around the depot when he made his inspection between 9 and 10 p.m., but that the satchel was there after Greenlee was arrested around 3:30 a.m. Akerman wasn't concerned. The implication that Greenlee hadn't been there all night carried little weight after the teen's impressive testimony.

Akerman announced that the defense rested. All that remained were closing arguments. And, of course, the decision of "12 good men."

Naturally, Hunter was ready. He knew exactly how to ice the prosecution's cake and wasted little time getting to the heart of the matter: character -- particularly the character of cold and calculating criminals and the innocent, but brave young women they prey upon. Hunter dismissed Akerman's claim that Greenlee couldn't have been in two places at the same time with the statement that, "a lot can happen with a good fast car and vicious men." It was a memorable line, one that would be often repeated in the days to come. No matter that it wasn't supported by fact. Wisely, Hunter didn't elaborate on the "criminal masterminds" approach. Reinforcing the positive identification by husband and wife was much easier for jurors to grasp. After all, who could forget that moment yesterday when the young housewife pointed out the men who had ravished her.

Leaning toward the jury box, Hunter passionately asked, "Do you, sir, after you had seen a man with features as distinctive as those of Irvin, and after he had knocked you down and robbed you and attacked your wife, think you'd ever forget him? Do you think you'd ever forget his face? If the husband had wanted to lie, don't you think he'd have said he saw them all there? Gentlemen, I ask anyone of you -- if four men had robbed you and taken your wife to rape her, could their faces ever be erased from YOUR memory?" Turning toward Norma, he sealed his case. "This woman is a remarkable person. She realized from the first she was in the power of four evil men, who carried with them a pistol. So she made up her mind not to resist them and be killed. She knew that if she were to come out of it alive, she was going to have to submit to them. So she began to fix in her mind the things that would help her turn them over to the law. The only hope she had was to save her own life. She adopted the course she did to save her life. You will recall that she remembered two trees when they first stopped. They're there. You'll recall she remembered the cracks in the glass of the car windows. They're there. That she remembered other marks and the lights on the dashboard. They're there. Gentlemen, probably no human being ever went through such a terrible night as this girl did. Do you think the memory of the faces of those men could ever be wiped away?"

Hunter then deftly parlayed the arrests of Shepherd and Irvin while in the military into a convincing portrait of hardened criminals, calling them "...men of large experience, who probably knew if they did a thing like this, the thing to do was to go quietly back to Groveland and pretend nothing happened. These men with their dishonorable discharges from the United States Army were very shrewd -- too shrewd to leave in the car, knowing that they would be caught within a few minutes. They knew they had to go back to Groveland and pretend. It was the reasonable thing for the criminal mind to do." The argument didn't make much sense, but Hunter was on a roll. "The defense says Irvin was in Orlando. Yet the testimony has proven that his tracks were in the dirt at the scene of the crime," Hunter thundered. "You saw the shoes that he wore that night, and you saw the cast of the track and that they matched perfectly. Irvin was there. Shepherd was there. Yet the defense would have you believe that they were taking this trip around central Florida -- always in the opposite direction of the scene of the crime -- and they have not brought in a single witness to substantiate it. No, they brought in no witnesses because those two men were not in Orlando that terrible night -- they were out on the road to Center Hill raping this woman!"

With Shepherd and Irvin placed securely in the electric chair, Hunter turned his attention to Greenlee. "They would have you believe Greenlee came to Groveland with Ernest Thomas that night, and went to a packing shed to spend the night. Yet Henry Singleton told you that it was Greenlee who came to his home that night. He was not in the packing shed because he was at Henry Singleton's place, casing it with the view of robbing him. He told him, gentlemen, that he was working for the revenue agents. The night watchman at Groveland has told you that he went to the packing shed that night and that Greenlee was not there," Hunter concluded as he finally came up for air. After a pregnant pause, he offered, "Gentlemen I have been talking to you about 10 minutes. You probably thought it was a lot longer than that. Now -- don't you think you could have pushed a car off the road and held quite a conversation in that time?" Mabel Norris-Reese would later capture the moment for posterity in the *Mount Dora Topic*. "Involuntarily, the jurymen turned to look at the clock on the wall, and almost to the man an amused smile crossed their faces. They liked that trick Jesse Hunter had just pulled. They liked the way he had impressed in their minds his claim that the defense attorney had been adding minutes and then hours to his story of the crime in an effort to prove his clients could not have been on that road out of Mascotte that night, because the state's evidence had said so.

Hunter continued to work his "good ole boy magic" on his -- make no mistake about it, he owned it -- jury. "Gentlemen, Sam Shepherd, when he told his story of that night, made a better speech than I ever could. I'm not an orator, gentlemen. I do not have Darrow's or Webster's ability to make a great speech before a jury. But even if I did have, I would not make such an appeal to you in this case. Even though the circumstances would permit it, I am not going to appeal to your sympathies. I want you only to take the facts as they have been shown to you and use them to reach your verdict." Hunter then reminded jurors of the lint on Norma's dress that matched lint found in the car and how Deputy Yates' plaster casts matched the tires on the Shepherd automobile. "If the Shepherd story is true, not one single witness has been brought to court to substantiate a thing he has said," Hunter boomed. "That defendant Shepherd made a better speech than I could make if I had the facts. I ask you to take the facts, not speculation, and bring in without prejudice a righteous verdict." As Hunter returned to his seat, even his opponents had to admit his presentation had been masterful.

Akerman feared the worst as he began final summation. The old prosecutor was a tough act to follow, to be sure. Akerman knew cold logic was the only thing he had left to derail the runaway emotion that had saturated the trial, but he held no delusions that anything he could say would save the defendants. The death sentence was passed the moment Norma told the deputies she had been raped. Akerman knew his hands were tied. Attacking the testimony of Norma and Willie would be akin to signing death warrants for the accused. Questioning their credibility -- or even insinuating the "rape story" sprang from marital discord – could only backfire. Akerman's only hope was to reason with the jury on the merits of the evidence.

Realizing that the power, sincerity and credibility of Greenlee's testimony were the strongest aspects of the defense, Akerman wisely started with the "time element." It was the only line of defense the state hadn't been able to adequately counter. The jurors may have been "clay-eating Crackers," but even the most ignorant couldn't dispute three facts: 1) Norma Padgett wasn't abducted before 1:30 a.m.; 2) considerable time passed while the men drove and then took turns raping the woman; 3) Greenlee was apprehended just after 3 a.m. some 19 miles away from where Norma claimed she was attacked. Akerman wanted the jurors to realize that there was no way Greenlee could be in McDonald's custody and raping Norma Padgett at the same time. And if Greenlee wasn't with Norma, the gun she swore was pointed at her wasn't there either.

Akerman hoped to match Hunter's indignation as he began. "This is a very serious case. This case depends largely upon identification, and the time element is important. Mathematically, it does not add up that Greenlee could have been arrested when he was if he had attacked this woman." Direct and to the point. Now to touch on the most glaring inconsistency in the Padgetts' combined testimony. "It could well have been a dark green Mercury, but not a dark blue one belonging to James Shepherd that went on to Center Hill and other places. The time factor that night conclusively establishes their innocence. It is mathematically impossible for the auto Samuel Shepherd was in to have been involved. The time factor that night conclusively establishes their innocence." And there were other claims that didn't make sense. "If Shepherd and Irvin were intelligent, trained criminals, do you think they would have left the woman out there? Positive identification is a dangerous thing," Akerman reasoned. It was a persuasive point. After all, the men were armed and Norma admitted to seeing their faces. Why didn't they kill Willie and then Norma? Akerman then asked why the prosecutor hadn't cross-examined the defendants. He paused to let the question sink in. And now for what Akerman hoped would be the knockout punch. "Are you willing to send Greenlee to the electric chair after this testimony? The fact that these men came back to their homes shows the absence of guilt. Gentlemen, in all the cases I have ever heard of, it has been shown that flight proved guilt... This is the first time I have ever heard that when a defendant remained in his home that it proved his guilt as the state's attorney had just told you." It was a strong conclusion. Akerman had saved his best for last.

The courtroom remained full as the 12 white men shuffled out to begin deliberation at 7:25 p.m. Four hundred whites and 75 Negroes sat, wondered and waited. Few believed the jury would be out long. As jurors filed out, Futch left the bench and strode over to Hunter. As Akerman and his associates watched in astonishment, the judge pumped Hunter's hand and said, "Jesse, I have never heard a better argument in all my life."

Williams had yet another encounter with Norris-Reese while waiting for the jury to return. "She charged that I had coached the boys after Greenlee testified, for example, she said to me, "When are you going to put him on Broadway, Mr."....no, "When are you going to put him on Broadway, Franklin?" Never called me Mr. Williams. 'You know, he is obviously a good actor,'" Williams recalled. "She was vicious in her presence, the things she would say to me and to Ted Poston, her manner as well as the material that she wrote." Angry and disgusted, Williams turned away and re-entered the courtroom.

The jurors weren't the only ones deliberating. A group of Klansmen was meeting to plan some post-trial excitement for the lawyers who defended the Groveland boys. "On the days when three Negroes tried for rape at Tavares were convicted I witnessed the following incident: Sheriff Willis McCall of Lake County told some Klansmen whose identity I do not know that he needed help. Edward Hayes and Lawrence Smith who were present at the trial in Tavares telephoned this information to Melvin White... Phillip Huggins came by and I told him White had said they were going to run the Negroes' lawyers," former Exalted Cyclops, Southern Knights of the Ku Klux Klan, William Jackson Bogar, told FBI agents.

While Klansmen prepared their post-trial "party," jurors returned to a tense and hushed courtroom at 9:26 p.m. At the press table, Poston sat on pins and needles. He figured the only conceivable danger was if the defendants were let off, but that was "one chance in a million." Back in Hoboken, *New York Post* Editor Jimmy Graham was nervously pacing the floor of his home, "like an expectant father," after unsuccessfully trying to reach Florida Gov. Fuller Warren to arrange protection for his star reporter.

As jurors filed in, Futch measured the tension-filled air. "...Judge Futch called Alex and me up to the bench, and said 'I assume if there's a verdict against your client -- which we assumed there would be -- you'll want a little extra time for motion for a new trial, etc. and I'll grant that motion. But get your valises all packed and as soon as jury verdict is returned -- and he pointed to a little door behind the bench, which is usually reserved for access by the judge -- you all go on out this door by the bench, and I'll hold everyone here for half an hour to give you a chance to leave,'" attorney Joseph Price recalled.

As foreman Charles Blaze stood to deliver the verdict, Futch warned against, "hand clapping or other demonstrations" and told spectators to remain seated until the defendants left the courtroom. In a firm, even voice Blaze read the verdicts: "Samuel Shepherd, guilty. Walter Irvin, guilty." Just as their defenders had feared. And then, a surprise: "Charles Greenlee, guilty, with recommendation of mercy." Irvin and Shepherd received the sentences without emotion. Greenlee felt as if the air had knocked out of him. "I was scared on the stand, but after I gave my testimony I still thought I would be released. I didn't know what was going on, not until they put shackles on me. Then I was terrified."

Akerman immediately asked that sentencing be deferred for three days to give him time to file a motion for a new trial. Futch agreed. The "whittlin' judge" had finally granted a defense request. Williams and Hill were so stunned they didn't immediately realize the white half of the defense team was escaping through the judge's chambers. The Negro attorneys were watching Hunter, who was imploring the crowd to remain orderly. "This is the verdict of the people of Lake County. I ask you to accept it and to retire quietly to your homes," Hunter boomed. As Hunter finished, Williams realized Akerman and Price had left, and urged Hill to hurry and get the car.

Samuel Shepherd, U.S. Army, 1947 (Author's collection)

The NAACP hastily published this 8-page brochure to call attention to the Groveland rape case and to solicit contributions to fund the defense in August 1949. The brochure detailed the "hate-inspired hoodlumism" that engulfed Groveland and the surrounding area. (Author's collection)

Norma Padgett, 1949 (Ryan Retherford collection)

The suspects, flanked by jailer Reuben Hatcher (left) and Sheriff Willis McCall, after being returned to Tavares from Raiford for the Aug. 29 trial From left to right: Charles Greenlee, Samuel Shepherd and Walter Irvin. (Ryan Retherford collection)

VOL. XLV, No. 22   CHICAGO, ILL., SATURDAY, SEPTEMBER 10, 1949   PART ONE

3 RAILROADED FOR RAPE IN FLORIDA PLAN APPEAL

HERMAN MARNETT, 23, former army pilot and honor graduate of Samuel Huston college, will be the first Negro to enter the University of Texas when he is enrolled in the university's medical school late this month. He's a native of Lockhart, Texas.

Five Lynch Well-To-Do Ga. Farmer

BAINBRIDGE, Ga. — A wealthy Negro farmer, owner of a 200-acre tract in Northeast Decatur county, was shot to death Friday by four or five white men whom he ordered from his fish pond.

Sheriff A. S. White reported Saturday that the body of Hollis Riles, age 52, was found riddled with buckshot. He had been hit 15 times apparently from that gun blasts.

The only witness to the shooting was Jesse Gordon, 52, who told the sheriff he had gone with Riles to the pond to fish late Friday.

Soon after they arrived four or five white men appeared on Riles' property and attempted to fish in the pond.

Riles objected to their trespassing on his land and ordered them off. The white men, angered at the order, drew guns and fired while he and Riles fled for their...

Force Defendants' Kin To Testify At Hearing

By RAMONA LOWE
(Defender Florida Bureau)

TAVARES, Fla. — A motion for a new trial for three young men convicted last Saturday of a rape that later fanned into race demonstrations in this central Florida area, will be filed this week by defense counsel.

The three were charged with raping a 17-year-old white farm wife last July. The all-white jury found the three guilty, but recommended mercy for Charlie Greenlee, 16, one of the defendants.

Because the jury did not recommend mercy for Samuel Shepard and Walter Irvin, both 22, death sentence is mandatory under Florida laws. Greenlee will be sentenced to life imprisonment by Judge Truman G. Futch.

Immediately following the announced verdict of the jury, defense counsel petitioned the court to delay sentence three days until a motion could be filed for a new trial.

Ernest Thomas, the fourth suspect in the alleged criminal assault, was killed by a posse a few weeks ago. His body was taken to Madison...

...sleep but awoke some time later and went to a filling station for a drink of water.

The terror-stricken mother of Thomas, Mrs. Ethel Thomas, was raised to testify against her son and the three defendants. Mrs. Thomas and her husband, Luther, had been held in jail above the court room following their arrest after their son was lynched.

The trial got underway Thurs-

See **FLA. TRIAL**, Page 2, Col. 8

Bias Housing Bill Killed

Baptists In Houston Get Boyd Report

HOUSTON, Texas — A report showing that the National Baptist Publishing board donated more than $20,000 to support mission work was one of the first made at the 69th annual session of the National Baptist Convention, of America in session here this week.

The report was made by Dr. Henry Allen Boyd, secretary of the board. He was introduced by Rev. J. B. Ridley, pastor of Mt. Olive Baptist church, Nashville.

Gathered here for the convention scheduled from September 7 to 11 are hundreds of delegates representing 38 state conventions and general associations.

Program Mapped

During the five days of the confab, they will be executing a program worked out months in advance by the executive committee. Every board and every arm of the convention will submit reports.

Chicago Defender, Sept. 10, 1949

The picture seen around the world. Marie Bolles' photo shows Sheriff Willis McCall, hair mussed, glasses cracked and shirt pulled out, standing in front of the car he was driving while transporting Shepherd and Irvin back to Lake County for their retrial. McCall said he shot the prisoners because they jumped him. Shepherd (farthest from car) died from a gunshot to the head. Irvin survived three bullets and told the world that McCall fired without provocation. (Florida State Archives)

Sheriff McCall said he shot Sammie Shepherd (left) and Walter Irvin because they tried to escape. The discovery, 50 years later, of a letter Shepherd wrote to his mother just before the incident reveals Sammie and Walter were optimistic about being exonerated at their retrial. From his hospital bed, Irvin said there was no escape attempt. (Florida State Archives)

Orlando attorney Paul Perkins (left) welcomes Thurgood Marshall, head of the NAACP's Legal Defense Fund Inc. to Florida. Marshall got the headlines for leading the fight to save Walter Irvin's life at the retrial in 1952, but it was Perkins, working behind the scenes, who located crucial alibi witnesses vital to the defense. (Author's collection)

The Marion County Courthouse was packed for the February 1952 retrial of Walter Irvin. Blacks, including Irvin's mother and sisters, were relegated to the balcony. (Photo by Marion W. Mann, Jr.)

The grim expressions on the faces of Walter Irvin (center) and his defenders speaks volumes about the defense's frustration with Judge Truman Futch. From left to right: Alex Akerman, Jr., Thurgood Marshall, Irvin, Paul Perkins, Jack Greenberg. (Photo Marion W. Mann, Jr.)

This jury deliberated just an hour and a half before finding Walter Irvin guilty of rape. One bystander said the only reason jurors took that long was because they had cigars to smoke. (Photo by Marion W. Mann, Jr.)

Walter Irvin during a recess in his February 1952 retrial. (Photo by Marion W. Mann, Jr.)

Walter Irvin is led from the courthouse moments after being found guilty of rape for the second time. Deputy Dane Atkinson leads Irvin, who is escorted by Marion County Sheriff Don McLeod. (Photo by Marion W. Mann, Jr.)

Walter Irvin in a Miami nightclub after being released from prison in 1968. His sister, who took him in after he spent 19-plus years in prison, said her brother was bitter and angry during his year of freedom. He died of a heart attack a short time later. (Author's collection)

The Shepherd family, Miami, Florida, May 2003. In the middle, in striped shirt is Henrietta Irvin, sister of Walter Lee Irvin and sister-in-law of Samuel Shepherd. Far left is James Shepherd, nephew of Walter and Sammie. (Photo by Cassie Corsair)

Chapter 17 -- The Chase

The jury's recommendation of mercy for Charles Greenlee came as a shock to many of the angry whites who felt the slick Yankee lawyers had fooled the jurors. As spectators and participants filed out of the courtroom, Ted Poston, the maverick reporter who had outsmarted the Alabama rednecks during the Scottsboro trial, was clearly frightened. Realizing Sheriff Willis McCall's deputies were nowhere in sight for the first time in two days, Poston approached the bench. Judge Truman Futch reassured him that there was no danger. State Attorney Jesse Hunter overheard the conversation and offered to drive Poston and Negro attorneys Horace Hill and Franklin Williams back to Orlando. Poston declined, saying he and *Chicago Defender* reporter Ramona Lowe were riding with Williams in Hill's car.

Hill and Williams had quickly gathered their note pads and files and hastily left the courtroom. In the corridor outside the courtroom, the attorneys breathed a sigh of relief when they saw a familiar, friendly, face. "The lieutenant of the Highway Patrol took me and Horace Hill and we went down the stairs and out the back door... As we came out into the back alley, I said to the State Highway Patrol officer... his patrol car was to the right and our car was way down the alley and across the lawn and out into the street. He turned towards his car and I said, 'Aren't you going to escort us to our car?' He said, 'No, my job is over. The trial is finished.' That was the first time I was afraid because the alley was dark," Williams said.

The attorneys anxiously hurried into the night, all the while wondering what danger might be lurking in the shadows. Then Williams spotted highway patrolman W.D. Floyd standing near Hill's car. Relieved, Williams asked if *he* was there to escort them. "I said, 'no,' thought the sheriff was going to do that," Floyd recalled. But McCall and his deputies weren't in sight. Floyd continued, "I said 'no,' but that I was going out that way, so get in your car and I will follow you to the main road." As the patrolman drove away, the lawyers nervously climbed into the car. As Hill cranked the starter, both men wondered what was keeping Poston and Lowe. "As we were getting into the car, people were coming out of the courtroom and, out of the courthouse rather, and Horace and I were sitting up front and I saw smoke coming out of his cigarette lighter and I grabbed it and burned this finger right there. Grabbed it and as I pulled it out, flame jumped out at me and I dropped it on the floor. Somebody had jammed that cigarette lighter in just a few minutes before we got to it. It was only to short circuit the car. I guess that is what would happen, if the thing stayed stuck in that way," Williams recalled. Now the men were sure their lives were in jeopardy. And still no sign of their passengers. Inside the courthouse, the reporters had lingered to record Hunter's remarks, then, in the corridor, Lowe had stopped to answer a question.

"We were really nervous. People were coming by. I remember one guy came over with his wife and daughter and looked in the car and said to his wife, "Boy, nigger boy." And then they continued on and I said, 'Now where the hell is Poston and Lowe?' Lowe was a big fat woman, so we finally saw them coming along and Ted is carrying his coat over his shoulder and walking along to get to the car. I said, 'For Christ's sake. Hurry up and get in.' He said, 'Jesus Christ, I am scared stiff.' He says, 'Let's get the hell out of here,'" Williams remembered.

Hill was out of Tavares in less than 10 minutes, finding open road when most of the cars in front of him turned off to the north, headed toward Eustis. Moments later, as he drove toward Orlando 35 miles away, Hill realized they were being followed. "'Jesus Christ,' I said. 'There is somebody behind us,'" Williams recalled. Hill and his frightened passengers feared an ambush was imminent. "As we were approaching the Mount Dora (just east of Tavares) area, someone was standing in the road shaking a white cloth requesting stoppage. Instead of stopping, I speeded up," Hill said.

As the man in the road jumped aside, Williams saw a car on each side of the road. As the Negroes sped past, the lights of a parked car blinked on. "The lawyer (Hill) who was driving doused his lights, and stepped the sedan up to 90 miles an hour. At several points they passed between dark and parked cars pointing toward Orlando, which joined in the chase as they raced," Poston recalled.

"Alex Schmitt said someone would chase the car and when they came by we would chase them and run them out of the county. It was dark at the time when the cars came by. Walter Goding was driving Emmett Hart's car extremely fast chasing the other car. The Hart car lights were blinked and Alex Schmitt pulled onto the road right behind them. Alex Schmitt pulled away from me chasing this car and I never saw him any more that day." -- FBI report of interview with confidential informant, 1952

As the gap between the cars decreased, Hill began to zigzag. "Straighten up, Horace," Williams shouted. "Getting closer. Might shoot at the tires," Hill nervously replied. According to Poston, as the car approached Apopka, two more cars joined the chase. After Hill ran a red light, a pickup truck pulled in front of his car. "He just swung around a truck that was moving in and I turned around and looked. And not 50 yards behind us was the first of these three cars and it come through the red light. I said, 'Oh shit. This is it,'" Williams recalled. "All we could see now, when we got back out on the road were the silhouette of three men in this first car. They were silhouetted in this car behind us. One of them had sort of a cowboy hat on, the kind that Willis McCall wore. He was in the middle."

"I thought the police might have held up the chase in Apopka but when I got there I did not see anyone and went home. Later I found (sic) from general talk in Apopka that Sheriff Willis McCall had escorted the car carrying the Negro defense attorneys through Mount Dora and to the Lake-Orange county line where he turned back. Near there was Walter Goding driving Emmett Hart's car. Hart being a passenger. They took up the chase of the Negro defense attorneys in the car and blinked the headlights of the car on approaching the point where we were parked near Lake Ola in order to signal to our cars to stop the attorney's car. Alex Schmitt was supposed to stop them but could not because they were going too fast. I also heard through general conversation that the constable, Fred Reisner, and the Chief of Police, Bill Dunnaway, were upstairs in a building in the business district of Apopka to be out of sight and to watch the chase as it went through Apopka." -- FBI report of interview with confidential informant, 1952

"I was going at the top -- you couldn't get no more -- 90 to 95 miles an hour," Hill recalled. As the city limits of Orlando finally came into view, Lowe looked out the back window and shouted, "They're not back there anymore." Williams would never forget the moment: "As you come to Orlando down that road, the first thing that you see is a motel built like Indian wigwams and you know then that you are in the city. And you swing left, and right into the Main Street of the black section of town and we literally raced this car and swung into this. I never have been so happy to see so many black folks in my life. They were all over the place. We tore down the street, pulled up in front of this little hotel, looked back up, I do not know what happened to those cars." After steadying their nerves with a few drinks, Williams, Hill and Poston headed to Akerman's office. "He and Joe (Price) were there and we told them this story. He said, 'Aw, you have got to be kidding.' I said, 'For Christ's sake, we weren't kidding,'" Williams recalled.

The day after the trial saw the reunion of Henrietta Shepherd and her husband. Once alone, James shocked his wife by telling her that her parents had also been jailed. He said, 'Henrietta, saw your mommy and daddy was in jail.' I said, 'What?' He said, 'Yeah, they went all the way to Gainesville and got them and brought them back to Tavares. And put 'em in jail.' They stayed there for 11 days also. My mom and dad didn't know anything. Why lock them up? So he said that's all they told him. We going to take you home. They brought him home. They didn't abuse him. Just him in the same clothes and everything. Just had him in a cell," Henrietta said. The young couple received another surprise a few days later when James' parents, Henry and Charlie Mae Shepherd revealed *they* had also been jailed by McCall. The news came when Henry and his wife moved in with their daughter, Fannie who welcomed them with open arms even though there was barely enough food for her brothers and sisters. The small house, which was cozy for two, was now home to seven.

On Tuesday, Sept. 6, the defense filed a motion for a new trial. Akerman claimed that the court erred in denying the request to withdraw the "not guilty" pleas, that the defendants hadn't been allowed to testify at the preliminary hearings, and that they had been beaten by law enforcement officers. In all, the motion cited 19 errors by the court. While he held no hope that the "Whittlin' Judge" would grant the motion for a new trial, Akerman knew the motion would pave the way for a Supreme Court appeal. Futch promised to rule on the motion at the sentencing two days later.

Akerman clearly had a solid base for an appeal. First and foremost: the jury never heard from the physician who examined Norma after she cried "rape." Surely, the Florida Supreme Court would recognize that medical evidence existed that could have proved or disproved the victim's claim, yet the judge refused to allow it. The attorneys were anxious to get copies of the trial transcript to pinpoint improprieties the judge had committed. "I think in his own mind that Judge Futch thought he was doing everything possible right, but there was no doubt about it -- the pressures were on," Akerman said. "I do not think Judge Futch was knowingly influenced, but I think there was extreme pressure on him, and I do not think there was enough to have him challenged or to remove him. If there had been, I would have. But there is no doubt about it; it came through in all of his rulings." And what about prosecutor Jesse Hunter? He had also taken liberties. "Jess was a very capable attorney," Akerman said, adding, "He was too hard with them and went too far."

As for Akerman, he had done a respectable job. When one considers the factors working against him: having just a few days to prepare a defense for not one, but three defendants; a hurricane that restricted travel for two days; the resistance of the sheriff and prosecutor; working with attorneys he had never met; and the hostile atmosphere that permeated the county, his performance was more than credible, it was closer to exceptional.

On Thursday afternoon, the Tavares courtroom was again full for the sentencing, but the drama wouldn't unfold until Futch replied to the defense motion for a new trial, an acerbic motion that all but accused him of criminal acts. Not surprisingly, Futch saw the challenges to the trial proceedings as a personal affront. After accusing the defense of "…injecting the racial question into the record," Futch thundered, "... the defendants were accorded a fair and impartial trial throughout the proceedings… The record will show that when there was any possible room to question the qualification of a juror to sit in this case he was excused. The record will further show that the State's Attorney was particularly careful to be fair and honest with the defendants in presenting the state's case. The record shows that the defendants were given ample opportunity to prepare their defense, and there is a total lack of so much as a suggestion on the part of the attorneys for the defendants that they were unable to procure the attendance of any witness which they desired. There appears to this court not the slightest reason for granting the motion on either, any or all of the grounds set forth herein."

After delivering the rebuke, Futch moved on to the orders that would send Irvin and Shepherd to the electric chair. One glance at the stoic judge's face told Akerman what he already knew, that this court would not spare Walter and Sammie. As expected, Futch sentenced both to death with a recommendation of "no mercy." The sentence for Greenlee: life imprisonment at hard labor. At least Charles would live.

The Groveland Three received their sentences "without a flicker of emotion," maintaining "the stoical calm which characterized them throughout the week of hearings and the trial." Williams wasn't surprised by the sentences. There could be no other outcome. A new era of Southern justice had begun. "Well, at that particular time, there was beginning to become a strong feeling against lynchings, not only outside of the South, but within the whole South," Akerman recalled. "So what we ended up doing was to substitute mob violence for judicial lynchings. That's what the trials were, just judicial lynchings. That's all there was to it." Akerman promptly announced he would file an appeal to the state Supreme Court within three days.

As usual, the local press was quick to provide analysis. "Greenlee's testimony and the evidence offered in his behalf, left some doubt as the proof of his guilt," the *Leesburg Commercial* reported. "The evidence confirming the guilt of the other two defendants was overwhelmingly conclusive and left no doubt as to their guilt in the robbery, kidnapping and rape of the Bay Lake wife, Norma Padgett... States Attorney J.W. Hunter, in his address to the jury declared, that the defense dealt entirely in the realm of speculation." Not surprisingly, Hunter's quote that "a lot can happen with a good, fast car and vicious men," was repeated in the article.

Mabel Norris-Reese also weighed in with a few thousands words, but she wasn't nearly as objective as her Leesburg counterparts. She likened the defense presentation to a play, and Greenlee to an actor. Her article in the *Mount Dora Topic*, "At Long Last, The Groveland Story Is Put Into Production" was laden with sarcasm and bile. Among the most memorable passages: "That boy, then, became the star in the play. His wide eyes, his speech inflection, his play with his hands would have made a Broadway critic cut the rope of racial prejudice to give him a rave notice in his column. The story from the boy who would have made a great actor held together in tight sequence as he continued -- even to the point of peanuts making him thirsty so that he hunted up a drinking fountain in the Groveland service station... He brought in the finale as would Negro singer Paul Robeson emphasize the crescendo of a song. He told of his bewilderment over his arrest; of his fear again in the county jail, and of the white man who said he did not think he was 'one of them.'" Norris-Reese concluded her account by recounting the moment Circuit Court Clerk George Dykes announced the jury's recommendation of mercy for Greenlee: "There was a moment of tense silence then. Shepherd and Irvin remained impassive, completely unchanged. Almost, Greenlee did. But he looked down to see a hand slipped to him... another dark hand as Franklin Williams reached behind his chair to grip the hand of Charles Greenlee. Then a smile -- a smile of boyish triumph over the face of the Negro boy. The play was done. Charles Greenlee had no reason to be acting then. He was accepting the plaudits due anyone who kept an audience spellbound."

Norris-Reese also had plenty to say about Williams. The Sept. 8 article, which included a photo of a glaring Williams, completed the picture of an unreasonable, bigoted Negro attorney who had come to Lake County to stir up trouble. The front page also included a photo of Deputy Yates with the plaster casts of the footprints under a gleefully preposterous headline "Scotland Yard, Please Don't Take Our Yates." The accompanying article was a sappy puff piece that began with the maudlin lead, "Should Scotland Yard hear of Deputy Sheriff James L. Yates and his work on 'The Groveland Story,' then Lake county (sic) might be out a deputy." On the same page, a "pseudo letter" from "Lady Dora" addressed to Alfred Hitchcock, Hollywood, Cal. under the heading "Undelivered Mail," read, "Deal Al: Too bad you didn't have a scenario writer in Lake county last week. His imagination would have been stirred by the local production of 'The Groveland Story.'" The Crackers were having their day, shouting their vindication from the rooftops. Of course, McCall loved the articles. The days immediately after the trial were heady ones for the sheriff. "The evidence was overwhelming, all three confessed," McCall said. "The two older ones later claimed they had been beaten into confession. However, the younger one stuck by his story that the older ones had influenced him, against his better judgment, to take part in the crime. In fact, it was due to his pleas that they spared the victim's life. Greenlee helped us close the case."

McCall had one final order of business to take care of before transporting the condemned men back to the state prison. Without informing Akerman, the sheriff privately interviewed the men one by one, asking them to make a statement, "to get right with their Lord." Shepherd and Irvin both declined, instead restating their innocence. But Greenlee buckled. Shepherd and Irvin later told a reporter, "that after Greenlee's session with the Sheriff, the boy returned to his cell crying and told them he had been afraid not to make the false statement demanded of him." Greenlee said he confessed after asking the sheriff if he would be beaten if he didn't say what the sheriff wanted to hear. In reply, McCall yelled that he would not beat Greenlee, but kill him. The threat had the desired effect. "He didn't actually hold a gun to my head, but he was going to hand me over to the mob if I didn't confess... I guess you could say the sheriff intimidated me," Greenlee recalled. In the "confession" McCall captured on a wire recorder, Greenlee admitted he had lied on the witness stand and that he was one of four men who had committed the rape. Later, Greenlee would swear that McCall turned the recorder off several times to tell him what to say.

To McCall, the Groveland matter was all but wrapped up, even though the case was still a high priority for federal agents who had obtained proof that the prisoners' civil rights had been horribly violated. On Sept. 13, U.S. Assistant Attorney General Alexander Campbell asked U.S. Attorney Herbert Phillips in Tampa to advise the Justice Department whether action should be taken against McCall since there was "substantial evidence... the victims had been and tortured as charged..." Phillips balked at the suggestion, which he had already privately considered and dismissed. "There are certain matters connected with this case that should be carefully considered before prosecuting the parties for beating the alleged victims," Phillips replied. "A strict interpretation of the law, it is true, protected them from being beaten in order to procure a confession from them, but, the beating, standing alone, is a small matter as compared to what would have happened if the sheriff had not handled the matter as he did." Incredibly, Phillips' position was that McCall and his men were entitled to brutalize the prisoners since the lawmen had protected the prisoners from a mob that would have certainly killed them. Campbell wasn't satisfied with Phillips' answer that the beatings were "a small matter." He had heard too many reports about misdeeds by Lake County law officers. Campbell wanted action.

In mid-September, the car chase story finally hit the Northern papers. Reporter Ted Poston detailed the harrowing car chase in a story headlined "By the Light of the Moon" in the *New York Post*. Poston's description of being chased after the trial also appeared in the Sept. 24 edition of the newspaper industry magazine *Editor and Publisher* in an article "N.Y. Negro Reporter Has Some Advantages" by Doris Willens. Poston told Willens that, "things went along smoothly enough," until "it was discovered he was working for a white newspaper. Then there was some jostling in the corridors, and someone stepped on his eyeglasses when they fell, he said." Naturally, the article caused a sensation in Florida, where McCall angrily charged that Poston's articles were graphic evidence that liberal newspaper reporters from the North were hell-bent on sullying Lake County's fine reputation.

"Bogar denied emphatically that he was involved in the chase and insisted he only went to the rendezvous at Lake Ola because Willis McCall needed help... Bogar admitted it was probably the intention of the Klan to get the two Negro attorneys and run them out of the county. It was his opinion the Negroes were causing Sheriff McCall too much trouble and he wanted them run them out of the state so they would not come back. McCall himself did not attend any of the Apopka Klan meetings during the period of the Groveland Rape Trial for fear of an unfavorable public reaction." -- FBI report of April 17, 1952 interview with Klansman William Bogar

On Sept. 24, *The Nation* carried Ted Poston's article, "The Story of Florida's Legal Lynching," accompanied by a photo of the three suspects outside a jail cell, and another of Henry Shepherd's house engulfed in flames. The NAACP braintrust was pleased. In fact, the story was so well written that it would be reproduced as part of a flier that was being prepared for mass mailing to solicit funds. In the article, Poston revealed several items not previously reported, including:

- "After the rioting was quelled by the National Guard, word was sent to at least a dozen fairly successful Negro farmers to 'leave everything and get out now and stay out.'"

- That the "liberal son of a prominent Florida politician reluctantly decided that he could not take the case," but did act as an undercover investigator for the defense."

- That Akerman had shown, "such fervor in the Tavares defense that another young white Florida lawyer, Joseph E. Price, Jr., volunteered his services without a fee."

With things returning to normal in Lake County -- or as normal as could be expected after a race riot and weeks of racial tension -- the Shepherd and Irvin families finally made the three-hour drive to Raiford to see Sammie and Walter. "We went to Raiford the first weekend after the trial, the whole family, both families was together and we both went to Raiford to see them," Walter's sister, Henrietta said. "And that's when I saw a whole lot of things that wasn't there when he left momma's house. He (Walter) had knots on his head, he had his tooth knocked out. His stomach was like jelly. You could just touch it like that and it would roll like it was nothing but water." The family members were shocked, but Walter and Sammie were in surprisingly good spirits. Especially Sammie. "He said he wasn't going to die in that chair. Sam went right to the chair and sat in the chair and started laughing. He said, 'I'm not going to die in this,'" Henrietta recalled.

The prisoners may have been upbeat, but their stories would horrify, anger and sadden their loved ones. It was an emotional day for all concerned, especially the mothers who hadn't seen their sons for more than a month. Sammie told Charlie Mae that after he and Walter had been beaten in the woods, Deputy Yates had told him, "I wish you all would run so I could shoot the damn hell out of you."

After telling his family about the beatings he had endured, Walter quietly related what happened in the early morning hours of July 16, 1949. "Well, he said that they stopped that night, he and Sam to help Norma and Willie 'cause they was broke down. Sam was a mechanic also. So when they stopped to help, they fixed what was wrong. And Walter Lee said that the woman, he didn't know who she was. He said the woman had a bottle, and she was showing her appreciation. So she gave him the bottle. And she give him the bottle and her husband said, 'Do you think I'm going to drink behind a nigger?' So... there were a confrontation. There was something that was said, and someone was hit... You could tell that Willie had been in a fight because he was bloody like. But rape...?" Henrietta Irvin shook her head, "no." Walter didn't elaborate about the fight, but his sister felt strongly there had been a physical altercation. "Walter Lee didn't never say they had a fight. He didn't never say they had a fight... So what happened had to happen after... why couldn't it have been four other boys?... I don't think it was anybody. I don't think she was raped."

The Greenlee family, which lived much closer to the state penitentiary than the Irvins and Shepherds, visited Raiford frequently. More often than not, they found Charles feeling optimistic. He had resigned himself to quietly doing his time. For the active 16-year-old, boredom was his biggest problem. "He was cheerful. He asked momma to buy him a radio and she did. They would let him have little electrical things to work on, to put together or fix. That's probably where he learned electric work. He put a radio together while he was in there," Charles' sister Ethel Retha said.

In New York, the LDF attorneys wondered how they would fund an appeal to the Florida Supreme Court. NAACP officials were banking the brochure being prepared by the Committee of 100, a group dedicated to supporting the ideals of the NAACP, to generate much needed funds. The soon-to-be-released pamphlet was direct and to the point: "These boys are innocent. They did not receive a fair trial in the hate-ridden atmosphere of the

Lake County Courthouse in Tavares, Florida. Walter Irvin, Samuel Shepherd and Charles Greenlee were not convicted for a crime they committed. They were victims of the racial distrust and fears of a rural Southern community."

Additional funds would be raised during a speaking tour featuring Williams speaking about Groveland. The sharp-tongued attorney was the natural choice. "Frank Williams was really very eloquent. I would refer to him as silver tongued and other people did too," Greenberg recalled. "To some extent his stories were so fantastic that you wondered whether you should believe them. Some people thought Frank was exaggerating that a 100-mile per hour chase and that he was in danger of his life being lost and so forth and so on, but it was probably true. I guess I'm sure it was true. It was something that was extreme." Williams' discourses were moving, to say the least. "I recall Frank at meetings talking about not only having seen the boys being beaten and they were strung up and they were really badly injured," Greenberg said. There was also talk of sending Sammie's father on a speaking tour, although that idea was soon abandoned. Henry Shepherd had a commanding presence to be sure, but he was a farmer, not a public speaker, and he still had a large family to attend to. Plus, his drinking had increased since his son's conviction.

Ever helpful Harry T. Moore encouraged NAACP branch presidents to increase their efforts to solicit memberships. Moore's appeal stated, "Greenlee's parents could not get into Raiford to see about their son, but the NAACP could get in there. NAACP lawyers went in and found that these 3 Negroes had been beaten and tortured in the Lake County jail; that Irvin's jawbone had been fractured; that several of his teeth had been knocked out, and that somebody had kicked his sex organs. NAACP lawyers carried those men clean clothes and medical assistance." After quoting from a letter of appreciation from Greenlee's father, Moore pleaded, "At least 25,000 Florida Negroes should join the NAACP this year and thus let the world know that we don't like the way our people were treated in Groveland. Talk alone won't do it. It takes money to carry on this fight for justice. Isn't it worth at least $2.00 per year to you? (Youth memberships, for persons under 21 years, are only 50 cents per year.) It happened in Groveland this time. The next time it might happen in your community -- it might even happen to you... "

Despite Moore making approximately 90 speaking engagements and visiting more than 40 branches throughout the state, Florida's NAACP chapter remained strapped for cash. "We are still handicapped by financial difficulties. Our present deficit in operating expenses is approximately $1,450," wrote Moore, who saw a direct correlation between declining membership and the national office raising annual dues from $1 to $2. In a Nov. 25 letter to branches, Moore expressed his frustration, saying, "We must try to get our people to understand that this increase was necessary to meet the increased cost of carrying on the work of the NAACP. It takes more to run every organization now -- from the church on down. In these times of high prices how can we expect the NAACP to operate on dues of $1.00 per year as it did 10 years ago? Yes, the cost of everything is up now. Even coffee is up. But people will not stop drinking coffee. Then, shall we stop buying our freedom just because the price is up? 'Freedom is not free.' If we want to continue this fight for our complete emancipation, we must keep the NAACP strong and active. We must sell the NAACP to our people -- even at the increased price of $2.00 per year."

Moore could see the fight would be both lengthy and costly. In a Sept. 30 letter, he had chided chapter officers that, "Florida branches are far behind with memberships for 1949. Our entire state had sent in only 2,100 memberships through Aug. 15th. The total for the 5th District at that time was only 492. Ten branches in this district had made no membership reports at all from 1949. The 5th District led the state with a total of 3,144 memberships in 1948. We cannot afford to lag behind this year. Let us not forget that Lake County is in the 5th District. Yes, the Groveland disturbance occurred right here in our midst. Do we intend to take it 'lying down?' Are we doing our share in the defense of the Groveland boys when we produce only 492 memberships for the NAACP during the first 8 months of this year? Surely we are not satisfied with our present standing. The Groveland affair is a 'slap in our face.'"

Moore also continued to stress the need for Negroes to register and vote. "We must urge our Senators and Representatives to support the Civil Rights Program in this session of Congress. And if some fail to do this, we must consolidate our voting strength in future elections in an effort to replace these Congressmen with men who are more favorable to our cause... Last year only 22% of the eligible Negroes in Florida were registered for voting," Moore wrote.

Chapter 18 -- Poston Tells All

The LDF attorneys would certainly appeal to the Florida Supreme Court, but they faced a dilemma: what to do with Charles Greenlee, the only defendant to be sentenced to life imprisonment instead of death? After much discussion, Thurgood Marshall made the final decision: Greenlee's conviction would not be appealed because he might be sentenced to death if again convicted. "On the other hand, if we managed to put together a sufficiently convincing case and could find Irvin and Shepherd innocent, we could probably get the governor or someone to commute Greenlee's conviction and sentence," Williams reasoned. "But if we took Greenlee up and then came back down a year or two later, he would then be 18 or 19 and the only reason Greenlee, in my judgment, had a recommendation of mercy, was his age. Because if there was any other reason in the whole theory of these four kids being together is shot, goes right out the window. There is really no reason to differentiate among them. If all four of them were… supposed to have raped this girl."

Greenlee didn't object. The decisions being made by his attorneys were far beyond his experience. "So I talked to his family and I advised them not to. I told them that I would go ahead and appeal it, but under the circumstances, I thought it was far better not to," Akerman said. Charles was asked to sign an affidavit stating that he had made his own decision, to deflect possible criticism that the NAACP had abandoned their client, or hadn't acted in his best interests. On Sept. 9, Greenlee put his decision in writing. "I, Charles Greenlee, a defendant of the crime of rape. I have been tried and found guilty, thoe (sic) I am not guilty but they have found me guilty and I am afraid that there is a chance that I will be found guilty again and they don't have mercy on me and give me the chair. So if the other boys repail (sic) go through, I will be represented by them to a certain extend (sic).

So if God be with me I'll pray that he do I will get a pardon if the other boys go free. But if they don't I am afraid that I will be found guilty again and no one will have merch (sic) on me: Not that I am guilty is the reason that I don't want a repail (sic) but I am afraid. And I don't want to go through it again, for that reason. I do no (sic) not want to take the risk that I this (sic) is involed (sic). I have talked it over with the lawer (sic) and they said that it is a good reason. This is not thir (sic) Idear (sic), but mine I only ask thir (sic) opinion about it."

The decision made, Charles settled into prison life to do his time. "I didn't see much of Irvin and Shepherd. They were kept in a different part of the prison. I didn't really follow their case." As the spotlight faded from Charles, he focused on being a model prisoner. "I just decided to make the best of my situation in prison. I turned my energy toward something positive." Greenlee was initially on the road gang, but his good behavior soon earned him a better job. "I was in the tractor squad. I operated the bulldozer as a free trustee... I ended up being a trustee. I could come and go as I please," he said.

Sheriff Willis McCall hit the roof when he received a copy of the NAACP's Committee of 100 Oct. 17 fund-raising letter. He wasn't about to sit by idly while checks poured in from all over the country. State Attorney Jesse Hunter was just as worked up. He immediately called his friends in the press, and as always, they provided a newsprint soapbox. Under the guise of "setting the record straight," Hunter issued a statement saying the defendants didn't need funds because Lake County was bearing the cost of the appeal. "The record will be very long and will cost the taxpayers of Lake County a large sum," Hunter told reporters. "There is, therefore, no reason whatever for the NAACP to raise any funds to perfect this appeal except to pay their lawyers. There is no place for this money to go except in the pockets of the defense attorneys."

Of course, no one connected with the defense was swimming in money. In Orlando, Fannie (Shepherd) Bell was still struggling to get by. Her husband's income was sorely missed, and he hadn't sent a dime since he moved back to his family in Georgia. "He stayed about two months I believe, and after not hearing a word from him, I decided to write and ask where was he or if he was coming home and then knowing that he couldn't write or read his self. Finally, my mother told me to write him again and tell him that she was sorry she had come in on him with all her troubles and chased him away from out of his own home. That letter brought him back home. In a few days he was knocking on the door, apologizing to my mom and everybody for his actions and told us, that was the only letter he had gotten out of all the others I had written. He said his mother hid them and finally one sister that could read got a hold of the last one and read it to him. So I guess that woke him up to what his family was trying to do to him," Fannie recalled.

By October, copies of Ted Poston's articles about the chase after the trial had made the rounds of every office in the Tavares courthouse, where righteous indignation was the common reaction. With McCall's blessing, Hunter and Futch began implementing a plan to discredit Poston and his "commie" newspaper. On Oct. 31, Futch wrote to Horace Hill to ask for his version of what happened when he drove the reporters and Williams to Orlando the evening the trial concluded. The query surprised Hill. Surely, Futch wasn't sincerely interested in bringing to justice the men who had chased his car. There had to be another motive. In the end, after seeking advice from the NAACP, Hill decided to co-operate. Silence would be construed negatively.

Hill wrote back: "Immediately following our request of you to have the audience take their seats until the defendants had left the Court room, we contacted an officer of the State Highway Patrol who agreed to furnish us escorts to the adjoining County line. Upon the return of the verdict, and the signal given by you, we left escorted through the corridor and down the stairs by members of the State Highway Patrol until we reached the back of the Courthouse. Then and there two of State Highway Patrolmen on the outside proceeded to get into one of their cars. There was a request made by Attorney Franklin H. Williams that one of them escort us to my car. Then and there, the officers replied stating they would drive around and meet us on the next street, saying at the same time, the Sheriff was supposed to furnish us with protection out of the County. We reached the car safely, driving back along the side entrance waiting on our other occupants, Ramona Lowe and Ted Poston. After they arrived at the car, we proceeded to drive off and continued to drive past the stop light out of town until about two and a half miles therefrom. I noticed a car light through my rear window blinked its lights twice, what then seemed to be a signal. Two cars parked at my right, as I passed, drove out into the highway and proceeded behind the car trailing me. At this time, I was driving at an accelerated rate of speed coming on and upon two other cars parked on each side of the road and individuals crossing to and fro thereon. One individual having a piece of white cloth in his hand, motioned it up and down. As to whether they joined the chase, I don't know. With the above mentioned cars behind us, we raced until reaching the County line adjoining Lake County and they then and there turned around. This succinctly gives you in brief my version absent the drama and fright accompanied therewith."

Futch noted with satisfaction that Hill's account differed from Poston's on two significant points: Hill said the chase ended at the Lake County line, but Poston said the pursuers traveled well into Orange County, where Hill ran a red light and a truck pulled in front of the chase car to end the ordeal; plus there was no mention of the cigarette lighter that Poston claimed had been tampered with to start a fire.

While Futch maneuvered to discredit Poston, the NAACP kept pressure on Florida Gov. Fuller Warren through telegrams and letters charging McCall, Hunter and Futch with denying due process to the Groveland Three. On Nov. 17, the governor sent his investigator Jefferson J. Elliott to interview Irvin to ascertain the validity of the prisoners' claims of police brutality. The interview was telling. Irvin confirmed he had been beaten so severely that he "had a hole in my head," but he insisted most of the mistreatment was administered by Sheriff McCall's deputies and highway patrolmen. Elliott gave Irvin plenty of opportunities to implicate McCall, but Walter insisted the sheriff wasn't present when the prisoners were beaten in the woods or the basement:

Q: Did you see them when they beat Shepherd?

195

A: "I was there the first time, in the country."

Q: "In the woods?"

A: "Yes, sir."

Q: "What did the sheriff do? Was he present, Sheriff McCall, at the time you were beat?"

A: "No sir. I didn't see him."

Q: "Either the first time or the second time?"

A: "No, sir. Neither time."

Q: "Has he ever beat you?"

A: "No sir. But he kicked me up the stairs, but he never beat us with no black-jack or hose."

Q: "Did you see Sammie Shepherd at the time of the beating?"

A: "Yes, sir. Out in the woods."

Q: "How bad did they beat him?"

A: "They beat him pretty bad. They messed him up, me too, in my jaw. It feels better now."

Q: "Did they bloody him up?"

A: "He was bloody."

Q: "Was he as bloody as you?"

A: "Well, I don't know if he was bloody as I was. I was pretty bloody."

Even though the sheriff wasn't present during the torture, Irvin made it clear that McCall wasn't exactly the prisoners' benefactor:

Q: "He kicked you at the time of the trial?"

A: "Yes, sir."

Q: "Did he kick the other boys too?"

A: "Sammie -- he hit Sammie with his fist."

Q: "But Sheriff McCall kicked you on the stairway going back to the jail?"

A: "Yes, sir."

Q: "Was this during the trial, as you were coming out of the courtroom?"

A: "Yes, sir. He kicked me then, and kicked me before the trial also."

Q: "During this time, every time you come out of the courtroom he kicked you?"

A: "Yes, sir, when we started back up to the cell."

Irvin also told about being taken to the basement of the jail and being beaten. Again, he said McCall wasn't present. According to Irvin, he was beaten by deputies Yates and Campbell and a "Mr. Evans." Later, he and Shepherd were taken "out in the country" and beaten again.

The families of Walter and Sammie continued to visit Raiford at least once a month, usually on Sunday. The visits were always emotional for both prisoner and loved ones, and often informative. For instance, according to James Shepherd, his younger brother told him that one day McCall had shown up at his cell and loudly remarked to the guard, "You all haven't electrocuted those niggers yet? When you do, I want to watch them flinch." McCall wasn't about to let 150 miles keep him from intimidating the Groveland Three, especially Shepherd and Irvin.

On Dec. 29, Hunter convened a hearing in Tavares to officially debunk Poston's chase story. Ten members of the Florida Highway Patrol were called to testify, along with Apopka Police Chief W.J. Dunaway, Mount Dora Police Chief R.G. Shipes Sr. and Lake County Deputy James L. Yates. Significantly, none of the occupants who rode in Horace Hill's car were summoned. One by one, the lawmen testified to peaceful proceedings and denied knowledge of any car chase after the trial. L.R. Marchington, the patrolman stationed between Tavares and Mount Dora testified that there was, "very little traffic that night, and no cars were parked at the side of the road." He did not see any cars traveling at excessive speeds. Neither did Shipes, but some of his answers were curiously worded.

Q: "Was there any driving through red lights at high speed through Mount Dora that night?"
Shipes: "We didn't catch anyone."
Q: "Was there any car passing through there being pursued by other cars?"
Shipes: "Didn't see anything."
Q: "If a thing like that had occurred, wouldn't it have been reported to you?"
Shipes: "Well, I couldn't say about that -- sometimes people report such things, sometimes not."
Q: "Don't you think you would have heard of it if a mob had chased through town that night?"
Shipes: "If a mob, I would have heard of it."

C.E. Bullock, who had been stationed between Eustis and Tavares, didn't see a speeding car either. He did, however, confirm that the road was blocked for a short time, but by a semi-truck, not a pickup. According to Bullock, a "semi-car carrier" went into a ditch when it attempted to turn around. The officer said the road was blocked about five minutes and that, "another truck pulled him out almost immediately." He didn't explain how "another truck" could arrive, attach a chain and pull the first truck out of a ditch in five minutes.

Hunter recalled Capt. Hill to ask why he didn't authorize a police escort for the lawyers and reporters. "In view of the quiet manner and normal procedure that was observed during the course of the trial -- no violence, the Negro attorneys and reporters were extended every courtesy and I saw no friction at any time," Hill said. The chase story thoroughly contradicted, Hunter moved on to Poston's claim that someone had stepped on his glasses. Florida Highway Patrolman Clyde Carlan told Hunter that he was stationed in the courtroom, "adjacent to the jury box, immediately by the colored lawyers," but neither saw, nor heard of such a thing happening. "It didn't happen in my presence and I was there all the three days. He did wear glasses but I didn't notice him dropping them," Carlan said. The patrolman also testified that Poston never mentioned such an incident, nor did he complain of "any discourtesies."

The hearing was terribly one-sided, in fact, more one-sided than the actual trial. After reading press accounts of the hearing, attorney Horace Hill understood why Futch requested his version of events: to help Hunter script the hearing that would discredit Poston. Marshall and Williams didn't even know of the hearing until it had passed. Not that they would have attended anyway. For the time being, Groveland was on the back burner. The LDF staff was busy plotting strategy for school integration suits against the University of Maryland; University of Texas Law School; University of North Carolina; and University of Oklahoma Graduate School of Education.

Even though the LDF's focus had narrowed, Marshall was committed to seeing the Groveland case all the way to the U.S. Supreme Court, if necessary. But that couldn't happen until Akerman and Price exhausted appeals in Florida. The Groveland Three's defenders weren't optimistic for a reversal in the Sunshine State, and it wasn't because they didn't have a strong case. They did. "The Florida Supreme Court was a terrible court on race in those days," Greenberg remarked. "I was not too hopeful of the state supreme court," Akerman recalled.

Akerman, who had moved to Virginia after being decommissioned by the Navy, wanted to stay as involved as his busy practice would permit but was willing to allow Marshall and his staff to take the lead. Thurgood would oversee the defense, but wouldn't head the attack. "So Thurgood essentially turned the case over to me and I had to use judgment when to ask him what to do," Jack Greenberg recalled. "(Robert) Carter was not involved in it at all because he was beginning school segregation cases. Williams sometime during this process left to become secretary or administrator who ran the NAACP in California so I was the only one there and I did it with Akerman and (Orlando attorney Paul) Perkins, and when something had to be done that called for a grown-up I got a hold of Marshall." Greenberg was young, but had already been involved in a handful of important cases since joining the LDF staff in October 1948.

On Sunday, Feb. 26, McCall sounded off when he learned Poston's coverage of the Groveland Three trial had won a $500 award from the CIO American Newspaper Guild in New York. Poston had got under Willis' skin, and stayed there. McCall told the *Orlando Sentinel-Star* that the Newspaper Guild, "is a damn bunch of Communists," adding that the award was the Guild's way of, "paying off one of their henchmen who did a good job for them. That's all that prize could be." The front-page story also quoted McCall as saying, "This is the damndest bunch of lies ever written. Those three were guilty and a fair impartial trial proved them to be. Poston is just part of a Communistic element trying to tear down racial relations; trying to separate the races instead of bringing them together. He did a good job for the Communists." Greenberg had heard it all before. "Southern leaders and the Southern press called us Communists so often that many Americans came to believe that where there was smoke there must be fire," Greenberg said.

McCall particularly took exception to Poston's claim that he was chased out of the county after the trial. "He asked me for a police escort mainly to be able to say he had to have a police escort to get out of the county safely. I told him this was not necessary, that no one would bother him, and no one did. I also told him that he came to Lake County unescorted and without an invitation, and that he could get back the same way. He came and went at will in Lake County and mingled freely with people in the board room and during the trial and was not molested at all. He said that when he dropped his glasses in a crowded hallway, someone stepped on them deliberately, but I don't believe this is true." It was bad enough that Poston had given Lake County another black eye. But to win an award for it?!! That was more than McCall could stomach.

Chapter 19 -- Unexpected Help

Sheriff Willis McCall wasn't surprised when Florida's Little Scottsboro was back in the news nine months after the trial. But he was surprised who put it there. It wasn't a seasoned reporter who broke the biggest story of the Groveland case, and it wasn't Ted Poston, Mabel Norris-Reese, Ramona Lowe or any of the pundits who had been involved since the pretrial rioting of the previous summer. It was a man McCall had never met, Norman Bunin, a young copy editor at the *St. Petersburg Times* who would rock Lake County with his investigative skills. "Actually, it was a personal thing. It was not an assignment; I did it on my own with a friend. I was mostly on the copy desk, but I wrote an occasional feature. My friend was a retired New York lawyer. He subscribed to the *New York Post* and in reading Ted Poston's articles, we realized that here in Florida we weren't hearing anything like that," Bunin said.

Bunin was so intrigued he obtained a copy of the trial transcript and began picking it apart. Sure enough, several inconsistencies and unanswered questions jumped out at him from the hundreds of pages. By the time he finished reading, he was convinced the entire story hadn't been told at the trial. And it certainly hadn't been told in the months since -- not in Florida anyway -- and probably not in entirety, anywhere. Bunin was determined to challenge "the official version."

The Groveland saga soon consumed most of Bunin's free time. "It was mostly weekends over a period of a couple of months. I just kept driving over to Lake County and kept on snooping." Pouring through court records, Bunin came across the list of witnesses that had been subpoenaed by the state. He realized that many of the people on the list were never put on the stand. Bunin decided to find as many of the "uncalled" as he could to learn what they knew and why they didn't testify. He hit paydirt when he called Lawrence Burtoft.

The young man confirmed he was the one who "found" Norma in the wee hours of July 16, but his story was drastically different than the account Norma and Willie told at the trial. According to Burtoft, the young woman appeared "extremely calm" and only asked if he could give her a ride to Groveland. Only after Burtoft finished his coffee did she tell him she had been abducted by four Negroes who assaulted her husband. Norma said the Negroes hadn't harmed her and that she had not seen her captors clearly enough to identify them. Naturally, Bunin wondered why Burtoft hadn't come forward with his story back in the summer of 1949. The young man's reply: he had. Burtoft explained that he twice told his story to prosecutor Jesse Hunter.

The meeting with Burtoft was a turning point for Bunin. "I looked and looked and the more I found out, talking to Larry Burtoft and reading the trial transcript, I realized something was there. As far as their guilt or innocence I thought the most telling thing was Burtoft. He said she wasn't hurt or hadn't said anything about being raped." Now, Bunin wondered what else, or who else, had been hidden. Returning to the trial transcript, Bunin began to challenge every piece of testimony. He would also try to follow up on the growing number of rumors he was hearing as he questioned Lake County residents. But first, he had to interview the Groveland Three. After carefully reviewing the testimony of the defendants, Bunin set out for the state prison to see if he could poke holes in the stories they had told. It wouldn't be a normal interview by any means. Bunin had prepared trick questions designed to trap the prisoners.

At Raiford, all three prisoners came through with flying colors, repeating the accounts they had told at the trial, with little or no variation. But words were only part of the story. After telling Bunin about the mistreatment he had suffered, Shepherd showed the reporter the thick welts that remained on his back and stomach nine months after the beatings. It was a sobering visit, one Bunin would never forget. "They were scared but humble. Their stories pretty much were what they had said before," said Bunin, who was now certain the case was a frame-up. But could he prove it? After all, four attorneys had tried and failed. It was time to take a trip to Bay Lake to interview Norma Padgett.

Bunin surprised Norma and her family, who lived in the middle of nowhere in "a farmhouse in poor shape, threadbare, but relatively neat." For a moment, Bunin wondered if his unannounced visit was a good idea. In Bay Lake, visitors weren't expected and strangers weren't welcome. After Bunin assured Norma and her dad, Coy Tyson that he hadn't been sent by the NAACP Norma agreed to answer a few questions. The woman Bunin had heard so much about was a, "plain girl, slim figure, unkempt blonde hair, blue eyes, slightly flattened nose, heavy lips with very slight scar left above upper lip." She greeted him in, "a baggy green house dress, unbuttoned at top revealing much of brassiere." Her legs and feet were bare, "and very dirty." Norma "readily" repeated the story she told at the trial, but Bunin was quick to catch significant discrepancies. For instance, Norma couldn't identify the weapon the men had brandished. "She could tell only that it had a short barrel.

About 4 inches. Was not able to identify gun found on Greenlee at arrest as one used to threaten her," Bunin noted. Her comment jumped out at the reporter, who knew that the gun found on Greenlee *was* distinctive, in that it had a homemade, taped handle. Also, Norma revealed for the first time that the car she and Willie had been riding in had stalled near a house, although they didn't realize at the time they could have asked people there to help them push start their car. If true, perhaps the people living in that house witnessed the confrontation, if one took place at all.

Initially, Norma's tale closely paralleled her testimony, but as she talked, Bunin noted more and more discrepancies. For instance, she recalled that one of the men had told another to change, "to the *Florida* tag." The intimation that the kidnappers/rapists had at least one out-of-state license plate was a revelation Bunin hadn't heard before. She also said that during the ride she had pretended she couldn't remove her wedding band when the men demanded her jewelry, but that they "forced it off." She also said that she had given the dress she wore that night to Hunter. Bunin wondered why the prosecutor hadn't introduced it into evidence during the trial. Another deviation: Norma said she didn't remember their car stalling and needing to be pushed when they tried to leave the dance. Norma estimated that she stayed in the woods about an hour and a half after her attackers left, and that, "the sun was just going up when she started to walk, and was fully up when she got to Burtoft's." Bunin made a mental note to plug Norma's estimates into the timeline the state had presented at the trial.

When questioned about her encounter with Burtoft, Norma related a much stronger story than she did on the stand, telling the *Times* reporter that she had been crying profusely when she told Burtoft that she had been raped by four Negroes who had beaten her husband. She said that she feared her husband was dead, and urged Burtoft to help her find him. She didn't say much else about meeting Burtoft, but said that she did tell him that she had been raped, and that she was "crying and twisting" all the time.

Another contradiction surfaced when Norma was asked about her identification of her assailants. Norma said she wasn't taken to identify Shepherd and Irvin until sometime in August after they had been moved to Raiford. Bunin could barely contain his surprise that Shepherd and Irvin had been arrested and charged with criminal attack *without* being identified by the victim until weeks had passed. Without Norma's identification, the men should have only been charged with assaulting Willie, not rape. She then claimed that she had, "never seen any of them before the incident," which contradicted reporter Ramona Lowe, who wrote that Norma and Shepherd knew each other. Norma was, however, sure of the identity of her attackers. She identified Thomas from a photo, and then was taken to view the body. Norma said she felt no remorse at viewing the corpse, but worried that the families of the other men might seek revenge.

The interview also provided valuable insight into Norma's character. She stated that she, "Never have liked a nigger and don't guess I ever will." Also, that the "nigger lawyer" made her mad. Norma tried to impress upon Bunin that she still bore emotional scars from the incident, saying she, "doesn't like to go out now," and is, "scared of car." She also said she went to Leesburg for treatment every day from, "July 16 to August 26...then again (a) week later for blood test." She didn't explain what kind of treatment she underwent. Bunin gleaned more gems when questioning Norma about pretrial preparations. The girl said she, "went once or twice a week to Tavares, talks to FBI." She also revealed that her "daddy" had told her that she would "mess up" her testimony. In fact, he even bet another man that she would.

The meeting convinced Bunin it was imperative he interview Dr. G.H. Binneveld about his examination of Norma after the alleged rape. Bunin was especially interested in proving or disproving a rumor he had heard: "The original story was that Norma had been bit on the breast and buttocks," Bunin recalled. If true, why hadn't such graphic evidence been presented to the grand jury? Perhaps because the teeth marks wouldn't match any of the defendants? If the teeth marks did exist and did match, what better evidence of savagery could the state hope for? At Teresa Holland Hospital in Leesburg, Bunin earnestly tried to persuade Dr. Binneveld to share his report, but the doctor refused. The physician would only confirm that Norma had been to the hospital, and a report had been sent to the sheriff's office. "He just wouldn't say anything," Bunin said.

Bunin had better luck doing what Akerman hadn't had time to: locate alibi witnesses. It was a time-consuming task, but the copy editor-turned reporter found employees at the Eatonville nightclub who remembered Shepherd and Irvin. "They specifically said they saw the two guys at a specific time," Bunin said. And another thing, the people Bunin questioned were certain no one else was with the two Lake County Negroes. The interview not only supported Greenlee's claim that he didn't know Sammie and Walter until he met them in the jail; it also confirmed that Ernest Thomas was not with them. Bunin then found witnesses at a second Negro establishment, Club 436 in Altamonte Springs. According to two witnesses there, Shepherd and Irvin played the jukebox and drank beer.

Bunin also tried to track down as many rumors as possible. One rumor had Norma having sex with her estranged husband and then getting into a fight. Another had Norma refusing Willie's advances and getting out of the car to walk home. "There was something about her and her husband making out even though they hadn't been getting along." Bunin heard several disconcerting things that weren't brought out in the trial. "A person at the dance in Clermont said they (Norma and Willie) were roaring drunk when they left the dance," Bunin said. He was also told that Norma and Sammie knew each other before July 16. Perhaps the most disturbing rumor concerned Thomas' wife, who said she had seen Ernest Thomas' corpse and that his throat was cut so badly that he was nearly decapitated. She told a different story at the trial, where she appeared in a new dress, a dress the prosecution allegedly bought for her. Another rumor circulating throughout the Negro quarters of Groveland was that the murdered man wasn't Thomas at all, and that Ernest had escaped to the North and was living somewhere in New York.

His interviews concluded, Bunin decided to run the roads of Lake County to test the accuracy of the timeline Akerman outlined at the trial. He also timed a trip to Orlando and

Eatonville. His "roadwork" confirmed his gut feeling that the suspects couldn't have been with Norma near the Lake-Sumter line when she claimed they were.

As weeks of research turned into long hours of drafting and rewriting articles, Bunin sought a confidant to review his work before he gave it to his editors. Since he hadn't attended the trial and wasn't directly involved in the case, Bunin turned to *Tampa Morning Tribune* reporter Emmett Peter, who had followed the Groveland case from the beginning. Bunin quietly submitted his stories to the reporter at the *Times'* chief competitor. It was an unorthodox move, but Bunin wanted to make sure his articles accurately reflected what had transpired at the trial. The thoroughness of Bunin's research surprised and impressed Peter. "Although I can't agree with all your conclusions, the series is certainly an exhaustive, well done and accurate study of the case," Peter wrote Bunin in an April 5 letter. "I am not completely convinced that Shepherd, Irvin and Greenlee are innocent -- but this I do know: there's an awful lot in the case which hasn't ever come to the surface."

Peter offered only a few "very minor corrections." Most significantly, he addressed the conversation Norma and Willie had at the Groveland jail when Deputy Yates took the couple there to identify Greenlee. "I talked at some length with both Mrs. Padgett and her husband, Deputy Yates and night watchman MacDonald shortly after the Padgetts went to the Groveland jail to see Greenlee. According to reports from all of them, Mrs. Padgett expressed some doubt that Greenlee was one of the attackers. She said, according to these sources, "I <u>think</u> that's one of them." Her husband countered by saying: "No, that one wasn't there." Peter also wondered how Willie Padgett could have talked with the four Negroes for 15 minutes before they attacked him and not be able to recall the conversation. "That appeared to me to be a weak link in the state's case. If you spent 15 minutes talking with four Negroes beside your stalled car, wouldn't you remember something of the conversation?" Peter also cited "two other extremely weak links." First, that medical testimony wasn't introduced even though Dr. Barneveld examined Norma, and secondly, Judge Futch's refusal to allow jurors to look at the car Shepherd drove July 16, even though "in countless thousands of other criminal cases, jurors have been permitted to view bulky evidence which couldn't be introduced in the Courtroom."

Satisfied his articles were accurate, Bunin met with his editors, who marveled he had uncovered so much previously unreported information. The *Times* editors decided to publish Bunin's series over three consecutive days as soon as a staff artist could complete maps to accompany the copy.

The Times dropped Bunin's initial bombshell, "Did Groveland Negroes Get A Fair Trial? Supreme Court To Decide," on April 7. The powerhouse story began, "Sometime during the next few weeks Florida's Supreme Court must determine whether the State of Florida has proved its right to kill Samuel Shepherd and Walter Irvin." The first installment primarily dealt with a point-by-point dissection of the appeal filed with Florida's high court. It was a meticulous, unemotional piece of reporting that filled four newspaper columns. The story was accompanied by the editorial "Rape, Justice and Florida's Reputation."

The second installment, "Did State Get Right Men in Rape Case? Story Of Three Raises Doubt!" focused on the defendants' whereabouts in the wee hours of July 16, 1949. Bunin revealed that he found personnel at Club Eaton and Club 436 who remembered the men, and were certain no one else was with Shepherd and Irvin. Some confirmed that Sammie and Walter had left the second club just after midnight. In the final paragraphs, Bunin related that he had recently interviewed the Groveland Three at Raiford, and that, "despite questions designed to trap them, they said nothing to indicate that their stories might be false." Bunin then detailed the prisoners' accounts of being beaten, and of McCall's attempts to elicit confessions after the trial. Bunin wrote, "Lake County Sheriff Willis McCall eagerly plays for interested visitors a wire recording which he says was made after the trial in which the three men were convicted. It reproduces the voice of Charles Greenlee. Although incoherent in part, it can be heard to say that the story told by Greenlee on the witness stand (as outlined here) is false and that Greenlee, Shepherd, Irvin and Thomas did commit the rape for which they were charged." Bunin continued, "Interviewed recently at the Road Department camp where he is a prisoner, Greenlee said that McCall took him into his office alone and, with a gun, forced him to make the statement. Greenlee said he asked if he would be beaten if he did not say what the Sheriff wanted him to, and that the Sheriff yelled in reply that he would not beat him, but kill him. The prisoner said the Sheriff turned the recording machine off at several points during the statement to tell him what to say."

The first article hadn't caused much of stir -- probably because it contained little new information -- but Bunin's second installment did. No other Florida paper had dared accuse one of the state's best known lawmen with threatening a prisoner's life and condoning -- perhaps even participating in -- torture in the basement of his jail. Readers could hardly wait for the third and final article.

Bunin didn't disappoint. "Time Table, Based On State Testimony, Raises Grave Doubts in Lake Rape Case" spanned six columns and punched several holes in the prosecution's case, in addition to criticizing Judge Futch's conduct. Bunin wrote, "No excuse was offered by the state for the failure to produce medical testimony. The doctor who examined Mrs. A (the Padgetts' names were withheld) refused to tell *The Times* whether there was evidence that she had been criminally attacked." As for Norma's testimony about the four men taking turns raping her, Bunin wrote, "Apparently uncertain as to how this grim game of 'Musical Chairs' could take place in the narrow confines of a small car's rear seat, the foreman of the jury which tried the case asked if the jury could see the car. Judge Truman G. Futch said the request was, 'a little out of line, and can't be permitted.' Yet, in countless thousands of other criminal cases, jurors have been taken to view the bulky evidence which couldn't be introduced in the courtroom."

Then Bunin threw the knockout punch: he had located a young restaurant worker who had spoken with Norma after her abduction and before she was reunited with her husband. Bunin revealed that the man told a story vastly different from the account Norma "glossed over" during her testimony at the trial. Bunin also made it clear that the defense didn't know of Burtoft's existence during the trial but that Jesse Hunter. Burtoft told the reporter that Norma not only appeared "extremely calm" when he met her, at first she only asked for a ride to Groveland. Also, she didn't immediately tell Burtoft she had been abducted by four Negroes who assaulted her husband. There was absolutely no sense of urgency. Norma said the Negroes hadn't harmed her and that she had not seen her captors clearly enough to identify them.

Next, Bunin attacked the inconsistencies in the stories the Padgetts told: Willie couldn't identify the men who helped him restart his car after the attack; he went home to change his shirt before looking for his wife, "even though it meant traveling 12 miles South on some of the worst roads in Florida;" Norma's initial description of the Shepherd car tallied "in make only;" Willie disagreed that Greenlee was one of the attackers when he and Norma visited Greenlee at the Groveland jail.

Finally, Bunin picked apart the state's case, beginning with the casts of the tire tracks. Bunin inferred that the casts could have been made at any time since the sheriff held the Shepherd car from the time of the arrest until the trial. "There was no attempt made to support Yates' word that the mold was made at the scene," wrote Bunin, who also wondered why Judge Futch didn't "disqualify Yates as an expert witness on tire tracks." Bunin also gave little credence to the cast of Irvin's footprint since the sheriff had the accused's shoes in his possession from after the arrest to the trial. Bunin capped his analysis of the physical evidence by making it clear he didn't share Mabel Norris-Reese's view that Lake County was in any danger of losing Yates to Scotland Yard. "Although he indulged in these bits of fancy detective work, Yates apparently failed to look for fingerprints on the back of Mr. A's car, which the defendants were supposed to have pushed. His superior, Sheriff Willis McCall, explained months later that the finish of the car was too old and weather-beaten to show prints. However, upon examining the car, I had no difficulty making visible prints without the aid of any powder." Bunin obviously didn't believe the lawmen hadn't checked the car for fingerprints. After all, the fact that McCall examined the car closely enough to determine it was too weather-beaten to show prints seemed to indicate attempts were made to lift prints. Bunin was certain fingerprints had been found, but they didn't belong to the arrested men. "If Yates did find the defendants' prints on the car, he would have had far more conclusive evidence for the State than the automobile tire and shoe tracks. If, on the other hand, he searched and did not find their prints -- and there was no testimony offered to indicate that this did not happen -- Mr. And Mrs. A's testimony must be discounted."

Bunin was even less impressed with the state's witnesses. He pointed out that both Luther Thomas and Henry Singleton owned establishments where liquor was sold and therefore needed to stay on the "right side of the law." Even more serious was Futch allowing hearsay testimony of Thomas' mother concerning her son's whereabouts on the evening Norma was attacked. "Mrs. Thomas was permitted to repeat for the jury a statement which could never be proved true or false -- the alleged words of a man now dead. By this normally impermissible method, the State was allowed to second the previously unsupported contention of Mr. and Mrs. A that Thomas was with the defendants on the night of July 15."

Perhaps the most powerful portion of the third article, indeed the entire series, was a painstakingly reconstructed timeline, which was primarily based on testimony from the trial and undisputed events:

- 1 a.m. - Dance ends. Norma and Willie try to leave, but car won't start.
- 1:15 a.m. - Padgetts leave dance to go eat.
- 1:45 a.m. - Padgetts drive 12.6 miles before stalling.
- 1:55 a.m. - A car stops. Padgett explains problem, accepts offer of help.
- 2 a.m. - Negroes stop pushing, talk among themselves and Willie for 15 minutes.
- 2:15 a.m. - Fight breaks out. Willie subdued after 15 minutes.
- 2:30 a.m. - Men take Norma 13 miles, stopping enroute to change drivers.
- 2:55 a.m. - One at a time, the four men rape Norma.
- 3:15 a.m. - Men change license plate on car.
- 3:20 a.m. - Men argue with Norma for "a minute or two," then drive away
- 3:15-3:30 a.m. - Greenlee arrested 19 miles from scene of rape

Bunin's conclusion: Irvin and Shepherd were probably not involved, and Greenlee *couldn't* have raped Norma Padgett. And since Greenlee carried Ernest Thomas' pistol, it couldn't have been the weapon Norma was pointed at her. The implication was clear: the state's case was groundless. The defendants had told the truth.

It was a remarkable piece of reporting. But did anyone read it? "Actually it really did create quite a bit of reaction," Bunin recalls. "We received some adverse criticism. Of course, a lot of it had to do with Senator Claude Pepper, who was running for re-election. The *Times* was endorsing him and the conservatives were out to get him." Hunter spearheaded the attack. "On behalf of the decent people of Lake County, I request you to publicly repudiate these documents, forbidding the *St. Petersburg Times* from connecting your campaign with these libelous articles," Hunter implored Pepper in a letter Jess gladly shared with the press.

A few days after the *Times* shook things up, Hunter officially and emphatically slammed shut the door on the "chase" story Ted Poston had reported in the *New York Post* and two national magazines. In a letter to Judge Truman Futch, Hunter wrote, "It will be observed from the testimony of these men who are highly regarded in this part of Florida, that Poston's story was entirely false and without any basis whatever in fact. Of all the fantastic stories that I have read, the Poston story has the least basis of fact of them all." While Hunter branded Poston a bold-faced liar, he brazenly declared that attorney Horace Hill's version of the "chase" contradicted Poston, when in fact Hill merely differed on a few details. Hunter wrote, "...while Hill did not go far in disputing the Poston story, his letter indicates very strongly that the Poston story is without foundation." The truth was that Hill never said Poston's account was groundless.

Like Sheriff Willis McCall, Hunter was perturbed that Poston won the prestigious Heywood Broun Award for his coverage of the Groveland trial. Hunter was so upset, he persuaded Mabel Norris-Reese to write a protest letter to the chairman of the awards committee, Wade R. Franklin. Not that it did any good. The committee stood behind its selection 100 percent.

Franklin wrote, "As to the accuracy of Mr. Poston's coverage of the events in Tavares the Justice Department in Washington has testified. This testimony was in possession of the Brown (sic) Award judges when they were considering the entries. The Justice Department said that Mr. Poston's stories were accurate in every detail." After reading the letter, Hunter immediately dispatched a letter to U.S. Attorney General Howard McGrath asking for a copy of the Justice Department file on the Groveland trial. The reply from Assistant Attorney General Peyton Ford came on April 17. According to Hunter, the letter refuted Franklin's claim, although Hunter didn't produce the letter so reporters could see for themselves.

While McCall and Hunter worked to shame Poston, Florida Supreme Court justices were considering the Brief of Appellants from the Groveland rape case defendants. In addition to detailing the factors that made seating an unbiased jury impossible in the summer of '49, the appeal for a new trial expanded on the theme of Akerman's closing argument: the timeline that proved the accused couldn't have raped Norma Padgett. Attorneys Alex Akerman and Joseph Price noted that any reasonable estimate of events would place the Padgetts at the scene of the alleged crime time at 2:50-3 a.m. The brief stated that, "If the story of the prosecutrix is to be believed and these defendants are the parties involved it would mean that after approximately three a.m. a woman could be ravished four times, the tag on the automobile changed, the car driven down the road several hundred yards, stopped, then turned around and driven back to Groveland, a distance of nineteen miles, in a period of time not exceeding thirty minutes because the State's own witness, Harry McDonald, testified he arrested the defendant, Greenlee, in Groveland, between three fifteen a.m. and three thirty a.m. It is submitted that the testimony of the State, rather than pointing to the guilt of these defendants, conclusively proves that they were not the persons involved in this crime."

It was a persuasive argument, but Akerman wasn't putting all his eggs in one basket. The appeal would focus on five points, any one of them grounds for reversal: 1) The trial should have been moved to another county because excessive prejudice against the defendants made a fair trial impossible; 2) The trial should have been postponed to allow the defense time to prepare an adequate case; 3) Lake County's jury selection system discriminates against Negroes; 4) The beatings deputies administered to obtain confessions were clear violations of the prisoners' Constitutional rights and the indictments should have been dropped; 5) The State failed to prove beyond a reasonable doubt that the defendants were guilty.

Akerman and Franklin Williams presented the oral arguments before Florida's Supreme Court justices. Akerman told of the violent mob action and what he called "newspaper hostility," most notably the *Orlando Sentinel Star* editorial cartoon that demanded the death penalty. Akerman stressed that the trial should have been transferred to another county. Finally, he pointed to Greenlee's sentence of life imprisonment with a recommendation of mercy as an "indication of reasonable doubt" by the Tavares jury as to the guilt of *all* the defendants. Akerman also declared he hadn't had time to prepare an adequate defense, saying he was forced to go to trial just seven days after being retained. And then there was the matter of the all-white jury. Williams told the court Lake County was violating the United States Constitution by systematically excluding Negroes from jury service.

Florida Assistant Attorney General Reeves Bowen countered, "...the Negroes obtained a fair trial and there was no racial prejudice against them existing at the time of the trial." According to Bowen: county commissioners didn't abuse their discretion in selecting jurors from voter registration lists; and the jury was properly examined. In addressing Akerman's claim that there wasn't sufficient time to prepare, Bowen noted that the court appointed a competent attorney, but Akerman dismissed Harry Gaylord. Besides, Williams was in Florida for a month investigating before the trial began. Bowen also told the court that the mob action following the crime was brief and limited to a small area, and that there was *no threat of violence* at the trial itself.

While the justices reviewed the appeal, a grand jury called by U.S. District Judge Dozier A. Devane was quietly investigating the alleged beatings of Shepherd, Irvin and Greenlee. U.S. Attorney Herbert Phillips, pressured into acting by the Justice Department, half-heartedly called 15 witnesses, including the defendants and McCall's deputies James Yates and Leroy Campbell. Significantly, the two people most qualified to document the injuries of the Groveland defendants never testified: by the time Dr. Jean Downing and Dr. Nelson Spaulding arrived, the hearing was already finished. The prison officials who had photographed the prisoners at Raiford weren't even called. Neither were the FBI agents who had interviewed and photographed the defendants.

The outcome of the hearing was never in question. The grand jury found no evidence of beatings and refused to return an indictment against McCall and his deputies. On the contrary, Foreman Jesse C. Lanier praised the sheriff for "... protecting and saving the said Walter Lee Irvin, Charles L. Greenlee and Samuel Shepherd from great violence at the hands of an infuriated citizenry and aiding them in having a trial by a jury of the offense charged against them." The jury's conclusion sounded hauntingly like the words Phillips had told his superiors while trying to beg off from investigating McCall the previous September.

It was a bitter decision -- or non-decision -- that prompted NAACP officials to boldly charge that Phillips had failed to subpoena key witnesses. U.S. Assistant Attorney General James McInerney also found fault with the ruling. McInerney wrote Phillips on May 12 to inform him that the Justice Department was "... disturbed and disappointed in the inaction of the grand jury, for we are convinced that the victims were beaten and mistreated as charged." Phillips had been handed the perfect case to test new federal Civil Rights statutes and he had bungled it.

Another setback was around the corner. The Florida Supreme Court lived up to its woeful reputation on race issues by upholding the convictions of Shepherd and Irvin in a unanimous decision announced May 16, 1950. The justices gave no weight to charges of prejudice or incompetence by Judge Futch. "As we study testimony, the only question presented here is which set of witnesses would the jury believe, that is, the State's witnesses or the testimony as given by the defendant-appellants. Disputes and conflicts in the testimony are for the jury." The court also discounted the defense claim that there had been a rush to judgment: "Placing defendants on trial approximately 45 days after commission of alleged crime did not deprive defendants of sufficient time in which to prepare case for trial." And the court disagreed that a change of venue should have been ordered, finding that "harmony, goodwill and friendly relations... continuously existed between white and Negroes races." Finally, the justices disagreed that mob violence had any bearing on the trial, ruling that "inflamed public sentiment was against the crime," not the defendants' race: "It is true that the newspapers carried reports of the alleged crime, but the impression of prejudice, if any made, yielded to the sworn testimony."

In all, the justices found the evidence convincing, and cited "detailed corroborative testimony" by Norma Padgett. Like the 12 good men who filled the jury box in September of '49, Florida's highest court ultimately based its verdict on one thing: the word of a young white woman. To members of Florida's highest court, the decision of the Lake County jury was as clear as black and white.

The LDF attorneys immediately asked the court to rehear the case. As expected, on July 5, 1950, the justices refused to review the case, leaving the U.S. Supreme Court as the only remaining avenue of appeal. The Florida justices granted a 90-day stay of execution for Shepherd and Irvin to allow the defense to prepare and file a petition to the higher court.

Akerman and the LDF staff were confident they would fare better in front of the U.S. Supreme Court, which had recently decided the question of the racial composition of juries in Cassell v. Texas. The justices determined that "...Jury men should be selected as individuals, on the basis of individual qualifications, and not as members of a race... An accused is entitled to have charges against him considered by a jury in the selection of which there has been neither inclusion nor exclusion because of race."

LDF attorney Jack Greenberg welcomed the challenge of drafting the formal request for the high court to hear the case. Naturally, he would focus on the jury selection, which was performed "contrary to principles announced by this court in Cassell v. Texas." The writ charged that "the long and continued absence of any Negro from a grand or petit jury in Lake County" was by "design" and "obvious discriminatory intent" clearly existed. The petition also charged that, "The only apparent reason for setting an early trial date and opposing its change was... to bring to an end mass demonstration in Groveland. Editor and owner of three newspapers which circulate in Lake County, she testified that the State's Attorney, Hunter, stated to her that the trial would be held as speedily as possible in order to accomplish this end."

While the LDF staff prepared, Moore was canvassing Florida to make sure funds were available to complete the fight. Moore also found time to write a two-page letter to *Mount Dora Topic* editor Mabel Norris-Reese, who had irked him by criticizing the NAACP during the trial and now, a year later, was still blasting the organization. When the newspaperwoman questioned why the NAACP had been so quick to come to the aid of the

Groveland defendants, but had sat idly by while a Negro named Lee Cossett was tried for murdering two men, Moore could no longer hold his tongue. In the Aug. 18 letter, Moore castigated Norris-Reese for her attempts, "to smear the record of the NAACP and laud the unquestionable justice of Lake County courts," then explained that one of the objectives of the NAACP was to fight injustice in courts when based on race prejudice. Since the two men Cossett killed were Negroes, there was no need for NAACP intervention.

Moore was especially disturbed by Norris-Reese's characterization of Futch and Hunter as "pillars of justice in Lake County." Moore wrote, "If Lake County justice is so ideal, how do you account for the fact that your State Attorney was so anxious to have the Groveland Boys tried and convicted that he called a special grand jury for them, while he has failed to bring any of the mob leaders before a grand jury? If the 'pillars of justice in Lake County' are so 'solidly constructed with the ingredient of truth,' who is going to pay for the homes of those innocent Negroes that were destroyed by the mob of Whites? And in view of the fact that Lake County 'justice' apparently is clamoring for the execution of two Negroes charged with a capital offense against a white person, can you find in the records any case where a white person in Lake County was given the supreme penalty for a capital offense against a Negro? In fact, in cases involving Negroes and Whites, we hold that the 'justice' meted out in Florida and in many other states is usually very one-sided." To illustrate his point, Moore pointed to the NAACP's efforts to save the lives of seven Negro men in Virginia charged with raping a white woman. "These men were 'railroaded' through court, and there is serious doubt as to their guilt. However, in that same state, just a few months earlier, two white policemen were convicted for raping a Negro woman. Although those seven Negro men have been given death sentences, these two white policemen received only seven years for the same charge. In response to an inquiry from NAACP attorneys working on this rape case, the superintendent of the Virginia State Penitentiary recently issued the following statement: 'A search of our records reveals that no white person has ever been electrocuted in Virginia for rape.' In the face of this, it is estimated that at least 30 Negroes in Virginia have been electrocuted for rape. Would it not be interesting to make a similar search of the records at Raiford?"

By the time LDF lawyers filed the petition with the high court, Akerman had been back on active duty in the Navy for nearly a month. Not that his absence would affect the hearing. Marshall would do the talking. The writ, which was filed Sept. 30, 1950, included 21 legal cases and a hefty packet of newspaper clippings from July 17 to Aug.14, 1949: 22 stories, at least six photos with captions, an editorial and the infamous editorial cartoon of the four electric chairs ("No compromise -- the Supreme Penalty"). Stories included, "Mob Violence Flared After Kidnapping," "Mob Violence Flares in Lake," "Negro Houses Burned," "New Violence in the Groveland Kidnapping," "Sheriff Promises to Halt Violence," and "Groveland Under Virtual Martial Law." On Nov. 27, Marshall was informed the Supreme Court would hear the appeal. He was more than ready to take center stage.

Chapter 20 -- Supreme Court

Thurgood Marshall was riding a wave of success as 1950 came to a close. The NAACP's attack to end segregation in schools was picking up steam and Marshall was optimistic about appealing Groveland.

Jack Greenberg had done a superb job of writing the brief, which was filed with guarded optimism on Feb. 12, 1951. Thurgood would present the oral argument, much to the chagrin of Franklin Williams, who felt strongly he should have the honor since he had been involved in the Groveland case from the start. He had seen the welts and bruises on the bodies of the defendants, he had crisscrossed the state searching for an attorney, he had felt Sheriff Willis McCall's icy glare. He had even been chased out of town after the trial. Even though he had been transferred to the NAACP's San Francisco office, Williams made it known that he would gladly fly back to handle the oral presentation.

Marshall finally, albeit reluctantly, yielded to Williams, but not because Frank was better suited. He wasn't. Marshall stepped aside because the school segregation cases needed his undivided attention. Marshall was swamped, but he would make time to oversee the appeal. The NAACP had invested too much time and money defending the Groveland Two for Marshall to totally step away at such a crucial time.

The basis for appeal was fairly cut and dried. "There were two issues. There was the jury issue and there was the change of venue issue," Williams recalled. Marshall decided that Williams would fly back from San Francisco to argue the change of venue issue, while Bob Carter, who was hired in 1944 and named assistant special counsel the following year, would handle the jury issue. The delegation of duties irritated Williams, who went along with the plan rather than risk being replaced. "...(It) irritated me a little bit that Thurgood gave him that assignment because that was the issue on which I was probably at the time, according to Thurgood, the nation's leading authority. But Thurgood and I did not get along anyhow, not too well."

Williams was confident when he appeared before the Supreme Court on March 9, 1951. It soon became apparent Carter wasn't. Williams recalled that Carter, "Botched it up and started presenting his case, his argument, when he was cut off by Justice Frankfurter, who said, 'You know, isn't this just like...' and he cited five or six other systematic exclusion of jury cases and Bob said, 'Yes.' So, he said, 'Well, what is the point of arguing for them,' and he sat down." So much for the jury issue. It was Williams' turn. "I rose to argue the change of venue. The way you do that, see, they have the record before them. They have your brief before them. First of all, you have to know your record backwards and forwards. You have to know on what page everything is said and you paint a picture. You try to summarize your case, and I attempted to do that by painting the, verbally painting the atmosphere. Describing the atmosphere within which these young men were being tried and how that atmosphere had been made constitutionally unacceptable by virtue of the press coverage and the atmosphere that surrounded the trial," Williams said.

Assistant Attorney General of Florida Reeves Bowen drew the unenviable task of arguing for the respondent. Akerman, who helped prepare the brief and attended the session, felt his opponent's discomfort. "I knew him very well. When we went to Washington, I said, 'Reeves, what are you doing up here?' He said, 'Well, I wasn't going to send anybody else up to be slaughtered.' He knew he was going to get reversed."

Bowen found himself in the uncomfortable position of trying to explain Dixie's racial attitudes. He reasoned that it was the "historical background of the South" that kept Negroes off juries, not biased men with ill intentions. According to Bowen, Lake County commissioners "...just don't think about Negroes as jurors," just as they would not "think of having Negroes on a list for a social function."

The few thousand dollars spent on the Groveland appeal finally dividends on April 9, 1951 when the U.S. Supreme Court ordered a new trial for Samuel Shepherd and Walter Lee Irvin. The ruling touched off a celebration at the NAACP offices, even though the Court's opinion was limited to the issue of racial proportional representation in jury selection. "It was a slam dunk because the prosecution thought that they would show they were really fair on the basis of blacks on the jury. Well, the Supreme Court said, 'You can't do that. You just have to pick people without regard to race,'" Greenberg recalled. Jess Hunter had outsmarted himself by making sure a Negro, March DeBose, served on the grand jury that indicted Shepherd, Irvin and Greenlee. The Supreme Court held that no one, white or black, should be chosen solely because of race. Arraignment was set for Aug. 15, 1951.

The attorneys were disappointed the ruling didn't address the climate of mob violence, intimidation and slanted press coverage, but a strongly worded opinion of Justice Robert

Jackson indicated that those factors had been discussed at length. Jackson wrote, "But prejudicial influences outside the courtroom, becoming all too typical of a highly publicized trial, were brought to bear on this jury with such force that the conclusion is inescapable that these defendants were prejudged as guilty and the trial was but a legal gesture to register a verdict already dictated by the press and public opinion generated... Most damning for the Groveland Three were newspaper reports that the men had confessed." Jackson was bothered that Sheriff McCall was the source of news reports that the accused had confessed. "No one, including the sheriff, repudiated the story. Witnesses and persons called as jurors said they had read or heard of this statement. However, no confession was offered at the trial. The only rational explanations for its nonproduction in court are that the story was false or that the confession was obtained under circumstances which made it inadmissible or its use inexpedient. If the prosecutor in the courtroom had told the jury that the accused had confessed but did not offer to prove the confession, the court would undoubtedly have declared a mistrial and cited the attorney for contempt. If a confession had been offered in court, the defendant would have had the right to be confronted by the persons who claimed to have witnessed it, to cross-examine them, and to contradict their testimony. If the court had allowed an involuntary confession to be placed before the jury, we would not hesitate to consider it a denial of due process of law and reverse. When such events take place in the courtroom, defendant's counsel can meet them with evidence, arguments, and requests for instructions, and can at least preserve his objections on the record. But neither counsel nor court can control the admission of evidence if unproven, and probably unprovable 'confessions' are put before the jury by newspapers and radio... It is hard to imagine a more prejudicial influence than a press release by the officer of the court charged with defendants' custody stating that they had confessed, and here just such a statement, unsworn to, unseen, uncross-examined and uncontradicted, was conveyed by the press to the jury."

Jackson refused to accept Florida's argument that the rioting was against the crime, and not members of the Negro race. "Such an estimate seems more charitable than realistic, and I cannot agree that the prejudice had subsided at the time of the trial," wrote Jackson, who then addressed Judge Futch's extensive list of rules to ensure an orderly trial. "The trial judge, anxious to assure as fair a trial as possible under the circumstances, was evidently concerned about violence at the trial... such precautions, however commendable, show the reaction that the atmosphere which permeated the trial created in the mind of the trial judge." Jackson didn't mince words in his overall assessment of the Groveland case, writing, "I do not see, as a practical matter, how any Negro on the jury would have dared to cause a disagreement or acquittal. The only chance these Negroes had of acquittal would have been in the courage and decency of some sturdy and forthright white person of sufficient standing to face and live down the odium among his white neighbors that such a vote, if required, would have brought... The case presents one of the best examples of one of the worst menaces to American justice."

In Lake County, the reversal hit McCall like a punch in the stomach. Naturally, the sheriff was anything but tongue-tied when reporters tracked him down. "The fact is that our U.S. Supreme Court let a few minority groups such as the NAACP and their eloquent and sensational lies and the receiving of awards from the CIO Newspaper Guild, such as received by Ted Poston, Negro writer for the *New York Post*, influence them to such a prejudiced extent that they saw fit to reverse one of the fairest and most impartial trials I have ever witnessed. It is shocking to think that our Supreme Court would bow to such subversive influences," McCall declared.

For the first time since being arrested, Walter Irvin was all smiles when his family visited him at Raiford. His sister Henrietta, who was pregnant with her first child – Sammie Shepherd's nephew -- was thrilled to see her brother and brother-in-law in such good spirits. "They were hopeful that they were going to come out. They were really hopeful. It looked hopeful that they were going to be freed. It had… a lot of evidence had pointed that they did not rape this woman. So they were hoping, they were saying, 'we're going to get out of this,' and Walter Lee had said, 'When I get out of I'm just gonna go on back to California.'"

Thurgood Marshall appointed Jack Greenberg to lay the groundwork for the court-ordered retrial. Alex Akerman, now living in Virginia, would again be the attorney of record, but his involvement would be limited by his naval duties. Marshall and Greenberg agreed there was little chance of reversal if the case was retried in Lake County in front of Judge Truman G. Futch. They simply had to get the trial transferred to another county. But how? Both the circuit court and Florida Supreme Court had previously dismissed overwhelming proof that racial unrest had permeated the area during the first trial. The defense needed something more than a parade of witnesses saying the defendants couldn't get a fair shake. The prosecution would have no trouble finding dozens of upstanding citizens to testify to the open mindedness and fairness of Lake Countians.

While Marshall wrestled with the change of venue issue, Greenberg made his official foray into the case by formally refiling most of the original motions. The motion to Withdraw Plea of Not Guilty was based on Shepherd and Irvin being "ignorant in matters of law and criminal procedure." The defense contended their clients had only pleaded "not guilty" because their court-appointed lawyer never told them that by entering such a plea, "they would waive the right to file pre-arraignment pleas or motions." Further, it was contended that once counsel was obtained on Aug. 25, 1949, that the "defendants and their counsel had grave and serious doubts as to the legality of the indictment and did request a reasonable time to investigate the legality of said indictment."

The improper impaneling of the grand jury was the foundation of a motion to throw out the indictment. The defense also cited "systematic exclusion" of Negroes from jury duty for "over 25 years" as being "discriminatory and purposeful;" the inclusion of one Negro on the grand jury was, "for the sole purpose of creating an appearance of compliance with the requirements of the equal protection clause of the 14th Amendment.

Marshall expected the motions to be denied, which would put the defense back at square one. They simply had to find another way to get the trial moved out of Lake. And then Greenberg hit upon a solution. It would be a long shot, but the defense team had already exhausted traditional arguments for a change of venue. "I got the idea of taking a public opinion poll, which nobody had ever done in American jurisprudence," Greenberg recalled. Marshall gave Greenberg the green light to pursue the unorthodox strategy. "I got a hold of some young pollster called Lew Harris. He was sort of a junior on the staff of the Elmer Roper Company. Harris got a hold of some esteemed member of the public opinion polling profession," Greenberg said.

The defense also began developing a motion built on the charges Akerman made to the Florida Supreme Court that prosecutor Jess Hunter had repeatedly overstepped the bounds of proper courtroom decorum during his charge to the jury. The idea was fueled not only by Hunter's leading questions and sensational comments during his summation, but also because Hunter hid a witness from the defense. Nearly two years after the trial, Akerman was still steaming over Hunter keeping mum about his interviews with Lawrence Burtoft, interviews in which the young restaurant worker cast doubt on Norma Padgett's story of abduction and gang rape. Soon, a motion to disqualify J.W. Hunter began taking shape. Williams would have been proud of the final draft, which was by far the defense's strongest attack yet on the Lake County Crackers. Marshall wanted Hunter to know that this time, in round two, the NAACP was going all out.

The acidic motion charged Hunter with: "bias and prejudice," and said that as prosecuting attorney he, "has not conducted the prosecution in this case in a fair and impartial manner and has gone far beyond the conduct required of the State Attorney in his endeavor to insure that your defendants pay the extreme penalty." The motion then detailed the improper actions, saying Hunter had:

• "...given interviews to newspapers and assisted in the dissemination of stories of confessions of other crimes alleged to have been made by your defendants, well knowing said purported confessions to be inadmissible as evidence in this case."

• Called Lawrence Burtoft to his office, where he learned that Norma Padgett did not say she had been raped, and that she told Burtoft that she "would not be able to identify any of the four Negroes" that had abducted her. Hunter also "did fail to advise your defendants or their counsel of the testimony that would be given by the said Lawrence Burtoft..."

• Made a trip to Washington, D.C. to ask the attorney general to drop the Justice Department's investigation into allegations that McCall and his deputies had beaten the defendants.

• "...on every occasion in which your defendant sought to obtain the protections guaranteed them by the Constitution of the United States and the Constitution and Laws of the State of Florida, the said J.W. Hunter would immediately reply and argue that such action on the part of your defendants was 'An attack upon the fair name of Lake County, Florida,' well knowing by his statement and argument he would increase the indignation and hostility of the inhabitants of Lake County, Florida toward your defendants."

- …attempted to impede NAACP fund-raising efforts by issuing "a statement to the press to the effect that no funds were needed by your defendants in their appeal and endeavored to create the impression that all of the expenses incident to the appeal were being paid by the County of Lake."

" …issued numerous statements to the press stating that the articles published by the St. Petersburg newspaper were 'an attack upon the fair name' of Lake County, Florida."

As for the nuts and bolts of the defense, this time the attorneys would be able to challenge material evidence they hadn't known about during the first trial. And the attorneys now had a "star witness" in Lawrence Burtoft. The most pressing question facing the defenders of the Groveland Two was whether to use Charles Greenlee, who chose not to appeal the original conviction in fear he would get a death sentence in a retrial. Obviously, he wouldn't be able to testify to Irvin's whereabouts prior to arrest since they weren't together, but he could detail the beatings and torture McCall and his deputies inflicted to obtain confessions – *in the unlikely event* the judge would allow such testimony. "We would have had to weigh his independence of spirit against pressure on him while in prison. We wouldn't have wanted to take a chance," Greenberg recalled. "Legally, we could have called him. He'd have no self incrimination defense because he'd already been convicted."

Chapter 21 -- Alibis Found

As the case took shape, it became clear that it couldn't be adequately developed from the LDF offices in New York, nor Akerman's office in Virginia. A Florida attorney, preferably one in or near Lake County, was needed to file motions, secure affidavits, run down tips, confer with the defendants, monitor the local press, etc. Marshall contacted the Orlando NAACP for guidance -- he knew he wouldn't find a Negro attorney in Lake -- and was given the name of Paul Perkins, a bright young Negro lawyer who had recently moved to town from Jacksonville, where he had been intent on following in the footsteps of his uncle Daniel Webster Perkins, one of the first Negro attorneys in Florida.

Like Marshall, Perkins had earned his law degree from Howard University Law School in Washington, D.C., which he attended on the GI Bill after serving in the Army. After an honorable discharge, Perkins cut his legal teeth at his uncle's practice, but soon tired of the "Colonel's" dogmatic ways. Young Perkins couldn't stop trying to "modernize" the office, and the Colonel finally sent him packing. Perkins headed to Orlando, where the elder Perkins had friends who would keep an eye on him.

When contacted by the NAACP, Paul was struggling to establish his practice with partner James Collier. "He was the second black attorney in town. He came at Collier's invitation when he saw he couldn't run his own practice by himself," Paul's wife, Jackie recalled. Naturally, Perkins jumped at the opportunity to work with Marshall. "That was the biggest thrill for him, to be aligned with Thurgood Marshall and Walter White. Thurgood was probably the top appellate lawyer in the country at that time," said Paul Perkins Jr. Besides, Perkins couldn't be choosy; work was hard to come by. Poor blacks couldn't afford representation, and more affluent Negroes often hired white lawyers because they knew Jim Crow courts wouldn't be fair to a black attorney. "There wasn't any specialization; you just took whatever came through the door. Most cases never exceeded $45 an hour. Paul would probably just say, 'I'll take $200 to take the case.' He often accepted ham or oranges to represent someone who couldn't pay him," Jackie Perkins said.

Perkins stood just 5-foot-5, but what he lacked in size, he made up for with swagger. In the Army he had risen to the rank of captain in a segregated unit. He was even less imposing then, weighing about 120 pounds and standing 5-foot-4, but he established a reputation as a man who commanded respect. "He had a booming voice. He was like Napoleon. He felt like he really had to stand tall, and he would stand tall in any kind of case," Paul Perkins Jr. recalled. The addition of Perkins completed an already impressive defense team, but one that would be an oddity in any Southern court: Akerman, whose grandfather had boldly unmasked the KKK; Marshall, a colored attorney who was at the forefront of a national civil rights initiative; Greenberg, a white Jewish lawyer working for an organization founded to advance the position of Negroes; and Perkins, a black attorney in a state where Negro lawyers were few and far between. Although the egos and personalities were diverse, Akerman welcomed the additional legal firepower; it was help he desperately needed back in the summer of 1949.

Perkins was assigned to finding potential witnesses and checking and rechecking the testimony from the 1949 trial. "He was going to Groveland looking for anyone who could tell him about what happened," said Paul Perkins Jr. "They had little house gatherings," said Jackie Perkins, who was his fiancée at the time. "I wasn't ever sure what they were for. I think the only reason he took me, I went along as a decoy so it wouldn't seem like he was an attorney from Orlando. I went with him twice, at different places both times. Lake County was pretty conservative back then. In those small towns in Lake County you didn't walk through them at night." And Jackie wasn't the only decoy. A young boy, Donald Everett, was occasionally sent. "Donald used to go to Lake County with Dad. He'd ride down with him because they thought there was some strange code of ethics that the Klan wouldn't mess with you if you had children with you," Perkins' son, Paul said.

Perkins' proximity to Lake County meant he had to do the dirty work, like running down rumors that filtered into the NAACP offices. At the top of his list was a wild card: to find confirmation that Norma Padgett and Samuel Shepherd had known each other, perhaps romantically, and that the "rape" story was concocted because Norma feared her husband was about to discover her dirty little secret. "The story was that she was seeing one of the guys and was close to being caught. That was one of the stories," Paul Perkins Jr. said. "He was going to Groveland looking for anyone who could tell him about that."

Marshall was pulled into the case through a rambling two-and-a-half page letter sent to the NAACP office in New York from John Dingle, a Negro man living in Clermont. According to Dingle, juke joint operator Henry Singleton claimed Charles Greenlee attempted to rob him on the evening of July 15. Also, Singleton told Walter Irvin's father the sheriff was looking for his son. "Now I don't think that Singleton knew about the rape charge he just knew about the so call robbery attempt so he warned Irvin that his boy had better look out." Marshall, who had to read and re-read several of the poorly-constructed sentences, practically needed a scorecard to keep track of who said what. The letter continued, "Singleton either came to Clermont leading the sheriff or behind them for I John Dingle saw him about 7:30 AM July 16, 1949 and I wondered what had him over here so early I knew it could not be anything good for I have known him for more than 25 years and I don't know that of Henry Singleton. He has been chased from Clermont he will not work but has a Bolita office runs a juke joint and what I call a stool pigeon… Henry Singleton is mixed deeply in these boys arrest and conviction." Dingle closed by suggesting Marshall, "contact with Smith Willson who saw and talk with the boys 12:30 p.m. July 16, 1949."

Obviously, Dingle wasn't someone Marshall could put on the witness stand. Besides, Thurgood wasn't sure there was anything in the letter he could use. Still, Marshall directed Perkins to interview Dingle, who claimed to be on a first-name basis with Walter Irvin's father and appeared to be well acquainted with Singleton. Dingle's assertions, especially that "bolita operator/stool pigeon" Henry Singleton led the sheriff to Irvin's house on the morning of July 16, needed to be verified.

Perkins had little trouble finding the 67-year-old man, who had become one of the pillars of Clermont's Negro community since arriving from South Carolina in 1908. Perkins dutifully took notes and pressed Dingle on unclear and contradictory points, but didn't come away with any new leads. Still, the man was happy to sign an affidavit saying the defendants couldn't receive a fair trial in Lake County. Before leaving, Perkins asked Dingle if he knew of anyone else who would sign an affidavit and was directed to John R. Jones, another leader in Clermont's Negro community.

John R. "Doc" Jones was born just south of Lake Louisa in Clermont in 1902 at a turpentine camp that employed his father. One of 13 children, "Doc" had lived and worked in Clermont his entire life, and had done well for himself selling wood from a lot he bought on the corner of Fifth Street and Highway 50. Now 46, "Doc" had run the business since he was 19. A hard-working, affable man, Jones was pleased to sign the document Perkins presented. Perkins also secured affidavits from Benjamin Willis, a 17-year resident of Lake County, Ernest Smith (14 years) and M.A. Peterson (10 years). The affidavits stated that, "ill feeling and prejudice on the part of a great number of citizens... and because of undue excitement and prejudice that Irvin and Shepherd cannot receive a fair trial."

The visit to Peterson produced an unexpected bonus. Perkins learned that the man's son, Charles, had been in the Lake County jail with the Groveland Three. Perkins immediately arranged to obtain an affidavit. "I was arrested on Thursday night the 14th of July by Deputy Sheriff Yates of Lake County, Florida and taken to the county jail at Tavares," the younger Peterson told Perkins. He continued, "I was in the county jail on Saturday morning July 16th, 1949 and early that morning saw Samuel Shepherd whom I knew and another boy whom I later learned was Walter Irvin taken up to a cell in the jail. I was on the first floor of the jail and saw these two boys as well as another who I later learned was Charles Greenlee, taken by my cell, which was at the foot of the stairs on up to a cell on the floor above me. I recognized Shepherd as they brought them by and he saw me and asked me what I was doing in there but Sheriff Yates told him to shut up that they weren't to talk to anybody in there. A little while later that morning Sheriff McCall and Deputy Sheriff Yates went up to the floor above and then came back down by my cell with Shepherd, Irvin and Greenlee and took them somewhere apparently below the jail, some hour or so later McCall and Yates returned bringing Shepherd, Irvin and Greenlee, returning them to their cell as they passed I could see that they had been severally and brutally beaten. I know that it was Sheriff McCall and deputy Sheriff Yates who brought them by my cell at these times because I knew who Sheriff McCall and Sheriff Yates were before this happened." As an afterthought, Peterson added, "I was beaten by Deputy Sheriff Yates when he arrested me but I haven't thought too much about it because that is more or less the usual procedure with the Sheriff's office here. I have made this statement without fear or compulsion or hope for award." It was a sensational statement, but Perkins doubted Peterson's account could be used. After all, what were the odds that an all-white jury would accept the word of a Negro prisoner? Besides, Peterson claimed that the three defendants were beaten at the same time, but Perkins knew that Greenlee wasn't abused until *after* Walter and Sammie had been sent to the state prison in Raiford.

Perkins had better luck when he met with members of the Irvin family in mid-June. Walter's sister Louise revealed that her cousin Daisy Lee Graham claimed she was with Sammie and Walter at Club Eaton on the night in question. Upon returning to his office, Perkins immediately sent Graham a letter asking her to pinpoint the time she saw the men at the club. The young attorney then went to Raiford to visit the Groveland Two in hopes of developing alibis. Perkins met with Irvin first:

Q: "Who were you with before you met Sammie and went to Orlando?" A: "Eugene Sally."
Q: "Did you know that Ernest Thomas was involved with Singleton's bolita business?" A: "No."
Q: "Did you have a conversation with Daisy Lee Graham at Club Eaton?" A: "If I talked to her, I did not talk to her knowingly. I wouldn't know her if I saw her."

The interview with Shepherd was also fruitful:

Q: "When was the last time you had dealings with Henry Singleton?"
A: "I worked for him hauling watermelons about two weeks," before the alleged crime.
Q: "Did you know that Ernest Thomas was involved with Singleton's bolita business?" A: "No."
Q: "Did you see a man named Smith Willson of Clermont who was with Bud Odum on the night of the 15th?"
A: "If Smith Willson was with Bud Odum, I saw him. Otherwise, I didn't."

Next, Perkins met with Mike Thomas, who had volunteered to help the defense. Thomas had uncovered startling information: that Hunter's assistant A.P. Buie had stated that "the Padgett girl was in the doctor's office only 20 minutes, and did not lie down but was very active during the examination, and did not appear excited or frustrated." Even though the information was third-hand, Perkins was excited that a member of the enemy camp had confirmed that a medical exam had taken place, and that it had been a superficial one.

While waiting for permission to conduct a private interview with Charles Greenlee, Perkins traveled to Clearwater to interview Graham, who had allegedly encountered Shepherd and Irvin at Club 436 after midnight on July 16. Sure enough, she confirmed that she had a glass of beer with Sammie and Walter around 2 a.m. Perkins was ecstatic, but the more he thought about Graham, the more he realized the defense probably couldn't call her because she was Walter's cousin. While that relationship would explain how she remembered the accused men two years after the encounter, a skilled prosecutor like Jess Hunter would certainly say she invented the story to save her kin.

Tracking down Graham was just one example of how Perkins proved to be a tremendous asset to the defense. The young attorney not only displayed a keen legal mind, but also a penchant for attention to detail. Perkins' most significant contribution was finding Carol Alexander, "the young lady who served the men at Club Eaton on the night of the alleged crime." Alexander told Perkins that she served the men two quarts of beer around 12:30 a.m. and that Sammie and Walter remained at the club "until around 2 or 3 o'clock the following morning." Perkins had located her just in time -- Alexander was leaving her job in a few days to begin classes at Clark College in Atlanta. When Perkins promised to send her a check for her expenses if she would testify, the waitress agreed to appear.

Perkins took extra care in recording Alexander's statement, which provided the unshakable alibi the defense had so diligently searched for. Alexander recalled, "I worked at Club Eaton on the night of July 16, 1949. I remember seeing Walter L. Irvin and James (sic) Sheppard (sic) entering Club Eaton on or about 12:30 a.m., anyway it was between 12 and 1 o'clock in the morning of July 17, 1949. I was a waitress and the above two boys were sitting at one of the tables I was serving. The boys above stated bought two or more quart bottles of Ballantine beer. The said boys remained in the club until approximately 2 or 3 o'clock in the morning. The beer was bought all at one time and I served the boys at the table. The beer was bought at the bar." Obtaining the statement was one thing, getting a signed affidavit was quite another. According to Perkins, Alexander "...stated very firmly to me that she would not sign any deposition or any other papers." Speaking off the record, when Perkins pressed for more specific times, Alexander estimated the men arrived around 12:15 a.m. and left at approximately 2:05. On the surface, the statement was a blockbuster, but Perkins realized there was a potential problem: Alexander wasn't certain she would be able to leave college to testify at the trial. Before leaving, Perkins wisely asked if anyone could confirm her story. Alexander thought bartender J.C. Hastings likely could, but he too had left the club and was now in New York City. Still, Alexander was their best witness yet. Obviously, the defense had to make sure she would be at the trial. Perkins also interviewed the club manager, "Warp" Schroeman, who said he saw Shepherd and Irvin come in at approximately 12:30 a.m., and confirmed that Alexander served them.

Things were looking up. The trial was still four months away and the defense already had a much stronger case than it did in 1949. But no one was celebrating. "Our case seemed to be in pretty decent shape, but no matter how much the facts might support him, a black man accused of rape by a white woman in the Deep South was always convicted, and no doubt this would also be the case in Lake County. Aware of the unlikelihood of a verdict of innocence, we hoped to get Shepherd and Irvin sentences of life imprisonment rather than execution. Even this much would be a major victory," Greenberg recalled.

As expected, on July 6 a Lake County grand jury reindicted Shepherd and Irvin. "It was one of the tightest, most complete cases I ever prosecuted," Jesse Hunter told reporters before blaming the NAACP for "causing trouble" in the first trial. This time, three of the 18 grand jurors were Negroes. Hunter told the press that a 500-name jury panel was selected from a list of 6,000 names, including "every Negro we could find in Lake County." And Hunter bragged that there might be even more Negroes on the panel when the retrial took place. "There will be plenty of Negroes on the trial jury. I wouldn't mind prosecuting the case before an all-Negro jury." It was vintage Jess. The ole' boy definitely had a flair for the vernacular.

In New York, Marshall realized it was time to get more involved, even though he already had a full calendar. Greenberg, Perkins and Akerman had fashioned a strong foundation for a defense, but Marshall wanted more ammunition. He wanted to find Lawrence Burtoft, who had joined the Army shortly after being interviewed by *St. Petersburg Times'* reporter Norman Bunin the previous year. Bunin's detailed notes convinced Marshall that Burtoft had to be located and subpoenaed: "On morning of July 16, about 7:15 a.m. he opened drive-in where he had slept. He saw Norma Padgett standing outside. He wasn't fully dressed, so ducked back inside. Came out again at 7:25. She said good morning calmly, asked him if anyone would be coming by who could give her a ride to Groveland. He said no, asked her if she wanted to come inside and wait. She did. Sat patiently, refused invitation to join him in morning coffee or take glass of water. At length she told him, without emotion, that she was worried about her husband, explaining that four Negroes had hit him on the head and dragged him into the bushes. She said they had taken her in their car and driven toward Center Hill (across county line). They took contents of her pocketbook. (She still had pocket book with her) When she begged to be released, they let her out of car about two miles from Center Hill and drove off toward Center Hill. (No mention of attack) In answer to question by Bartoft (sic) she said she would NOT be able to identify any of the Negroes. Could only say that one was very dark and one was 'high yellow.' She said she walked six miles back to Okahumpka. She didn't look disheveled. Had only slight scratch on knee and tiny rip in dress she said she got on barbed wire during walk." Bunin also noted, "Bartoft (sic) has seen Padgett dancing at B's place several times since July, without Norma." And, "Bartoft (sic) was subpoenaed by state after telling state's attorney this story, but was never called to testify." Yes, Burtoft had to be located. Marshall called a friend in the Pentagon, who found that Burtoft was stationed in North Carolina. But hope turned to dismay when the attorneys learned that his unit had been shipped overseas.

Bunin wasn't the only reporter feeding important leads to the defense. *New Leader* writer Terence McCarthy provided copies of statements from men he had interviewed at Club 436 around midnight on April 28, 1950. Willie Harris had told McCarthy that he had seen a "late model Mercury" with Lake County plates pulling away from "436 Club" around 2 a.m. on the night of the alleged attack. The statement was too vague to stand alone, but Perkins hoped that Harris might provide more specifics if he could locate him.

Marshall and Greenberg also contacted G.H. Binneveld, the Leesburg physician who had examined Norma after the attack, but had repeatedly refused to discuss his examination. Binneveld still wasn't willing to talk, but the tone of the brief "interview" convinced the defense attorneys that there was no proof of rape. Marshall was certain Binneveld's reluctance to talk confirmed that the medical examination was either inconclusive or contradicted the accusation of gang rape. If she had been raped, he would have confirmed it, wouldn't he? Obviously, the doctor was unwilling to stake his reputation -- and future income -- on providing testimony that would exonerate Negroes and expose a white woman as a liar. But would he come clean under subpoena? Marshall and Greenberg doubted he would give testimony favorable to the defendants.

The defense was also interested in the sheriff's failure to obtain a search warrant for the Irvin home, so Marshall dispatched Greenberg to Florida to accompany Perkins on a visit to Dellia and Cleve Irvin. The visit couldn't have been more productive. Not only did Mrs. Irvin reveal that Walter paid rent from his $30/week salary, she also showed the men her son's room, which had a padlock on the door. Technically, she had no right to give the deputy her tenant's personal belongings. Cleve told the lawyers, "My wife and I considered Walter's room as his room... Walter had the sole privilege of his room." Before leaving, Greenberg asked Cleve about the rumor that he had told his employer that his son Walter was guilty. Walter's father adamantly denied the charge, saying, "I never did tell Mr. Edge that my son was guilty. I have never talked to Mr. Edge about it." After obtaining clothes to take to Walter, Greenberg and Perkins set out to nail down two other loose ends. Greenberg wanted to take a look at James Shepherd's car, especially the tires. The attorneys also wanted to ask Clermont Negro John Dingle if the waitresses who worked the dance at the American Legion dance on July 15 were colored, and if so, if he knew their names.

Perkins was happy to have Greenberg by his side. Taking directions from afar from Akerman and Marshall was a bit tricky at times, since the two attorneys sometimes didn't agree. Shortly after Greenberg returned to New York, Akerman came to Florida to meet Perkins and Mike Thomas in Orlando to review their progress and make sure everything was in order for the arraignment. Akerman reported to Marshall that Perkins appeared ready and that Jess Hunter was determined to keep the trial in Lake County. Considering Hunter's past dealings, Akerman suggested that the Motion for Change of Venue be "prepared as carefully as possible" and filed at the last possible moment -- say, 10 days before the trial.

While Perkins immersed himself in the time-consuming task of locating defense witnesses, Marshall and Akerman focused on the so-called "physical evidence" the state presented at the first trial. Marshall decided to enlist the aid of a Miami detective he had worked with, Buck Owens to evaluate the casts of the footprints and tire tracks.

Perkins filed the Motion for Discovery on Aug. 23, the same day Judge Futch set the trial for Nov. 6. Perkins returned to Tavares at 10 a.m. the following day for the hearing on defense motions, but found an empty courtroom. At 10:15, Hunter finally arrived, presenting Perkins with the state's answer to the Motion for Discovery and explaining that the judge would be granting the defense permission to examine the state's tangible evidence. That evidence, particularly the items taken from Walter's room, continued to trouble Akerman. In a Sept. 3 letter to Marshall, he asked how Thurgood felt about the defense filing a motion to suppress evidence based on the search and seizure of Irvin's shoes. Akerman felt that a case could be made that the shoes were unlawfully obtained since Dellia Irvin had been intimidated by Deputy Yates, who did not have a search warrant to enter Walter's locked room, for which he paid rent. Akerman also suggested the NAACP interview Sam Doto, the night policeman who sold Shepherd gasoline on the night of the alleged crime, but had since moved to Pennsylvania. Finally, Akerman suggested he come to New York for a conference with Marshall and Bunin, the former *St. Petersburg Times* reporter, who had interviewed people who said they saw Irvin and Shepherd in Orange -- not Lake -- County after midnight on July 16.

When a month elapsed without a reply, Akerman sent another letter, in which he stated, "Inasmuch as the trial of the above case is now only one month off I think it advisable for us to consider certain matters that need immediate attention." Akerman wanted former Club Eaton bartender J.C. Hastings and Doto located and interviewed. More importantly, Akerman wanted to make sure Burtoft would appear and that Franklin Williams' deposition concerning his search for counsel be secured. Burtoft's statement was obviously crucial to the defense, and Williams' statement was the basis for articles II, III and IV of the Motion to Withdraw Plea of Not Guilty and Set Aside Arraignment.

Perkins was also waiting for answers. He had written to Marshall after forwarding the New York address of J.C. Hastings, and weeks later, still hadn't heard from back from the national office. Frustrated, Perkins wrote to Greenberg and asked *him* to interview Hastings.

Hunter had no clue the defense was having communication problems. The pace was much more relaxed in the prosecution camp, which had enjoyed a relatively quiet summer. Sure, there had been scattered reports of NAACP lawyers sniffing around Lake County, but no one had set foot in the clerk of the court's office. That changed on Oct. 16 when Perkins filed a bevy of motions. The first document, a 14-page Application For Removal of Cause, outlined previously cited instances of "prejudice and ill feeling," but the new motion ventured beyond previous motions. The latest motion included the following first-time charges:

- "Mob violence and lawlessness" necessitated the court order the defendants to be moved to another county for safe-keeping;

- Lake County officials had spread information that the Supreme Court had bowed to subversive influences in setting aside the conviction on a mere technicality;

- Prejudice and ill-feeling were so great that the court adopted and posted special rules before the trial;

And there was another surprise. According to the motion: "Prior to this case there existed between Willis V. McCall... and Alex Akerman Jr.... a friendly and cordial relationship. That shortly after the trial of your defendants it was necessary for their said attorney to contact the said Willis V. McCall by long-distance telephone. That before their said attorney could explain the nature of the business necessitating this call that said Willis V. McCall flew into a rage and used vile and abusive language toward your defendant's attorney, calling him, 'A God Damn Nigger Lover,' and warning him to stay out of Lake County, Florida."

The strongest language in the application was reserved for Hunter, who was accused of: telling reporters that the defendants had confessed; traveling to Washington to head off an investigation into McCall's men beating the defendants; increasing the indignation and hostility by constantly calling actions by the defendants, "an attack upon the fair name of Lake County, Florida;" and trying to impede NAACP fund-raising efforts. But the most serious charge was that Hunter had concealed the identity of Burtoft. According to the defense, "The said J.W. Hunter, as State Attorney, did have brought before him in his office one Lawrence Burtoft and upon questioning did learn... that she had told Burtoft that she had been raped but her acts and conduct led him to believe she had in no manner been harmed... Norma Padgett did state... that she would not be able to identify any of the four Negroes she stated had abducted her... the said J.W. Hunter did fail to call the said Lawrence Burtoft as a witness and did fail to advise your defendants or their counsel of the testimony that would be given by Burtoft..."

Perkins also filed a Motion to Suppress Evidence, charging Yates with "unreasonable search and seizure," when he entered the Irvin home on July 16, 1949, "without permission, search warrant, or other lawful authority," and demanded Dellia Irvin surrender her son's shoes and pants. The motion portrayed Mrs. Irvin as, "an ignorant woman not learned in matters of law," who was, "in a state of fear, anxiety and confusion."

McCall and Hunter were still fuming when the defense struck again two days later with a Motion for Change of Venue, which cited continued intimidation by county and state officials of the defendants, their families and race. The motion also charged McCall with trying to create the impression that the Supreme Court had bowed to "subversive influences" in granting a new trial, and stated that local newspapers made it impossible to receive a fair trial in Lake County.

While Hunter and his son Walton drafted answers to the charges, Akerman and Perkins continued to question why Marshall's staff still hadn't secured depositions of alibi witnesses Perkins had located. Akerman fired off another appeal to Marshall on Oct. 20. "I am quite disturbed in hearing nothing from you as to interviews of Hastings, Doto and Burtoft and their possible depositions. As there is only a little over two weeks before the trial I am afraid we may lose the benefit of valuable evidence. Since time is so short will you communicate direct with Attorney Perkins, sending me a copy of your letter, so he can take the necessary steps for the depositions," Akerman pleaded.

On Oct. 22, the LDF finally responded. After apologizing for being so late to answer (due to the heavy workload), Robert Carter explained that he had "finally managed" to get in touch with Hastings, the bartender on duty the night Shepherd and Irvin visited the Eatonville club. Hastings told Carter, "he would not recognize the men," but that Carol Alexander had served them, "…and that she told him, the next day, that the men had been in the place the night before." Carter's conclusion: "I don't believe that his deposition would be of any value to you." Carter also had bad news concerning Lawrence Burtoft: "… as you know he is now overseas. We had requested that he remain in the United States until the second trial, but this the Army refused, but said that in the event that we needed him when the trial came up we should make a request to the Army and they would act upon it. We wrote the Adjutant General advising him of the trial and importance of Burtoft's testimony, and asked that he be returned to the United States; and that in any event furnish us with his address so that we could contact him immediately." And there was more bad news: "With respect to Doto, we have checked and checked our files for his address in Pennsylvania which has been indicated was sent to us. We will continue to look for it…"

The response was unacceptable to Perkins, who had done a yeoman's job of finding one promising lead after another. "…I am very much disturbed about the case in that Lawrence Burtoft was to be one of our star witnesses… I sincerely hope you will contact Lawrence Burtoft because he is our life-line, and also Sam Doto… Time is of the essence, please use all forces to try to locate Burtoft and have him present for the trial." Perkins also expressed alarm that no one had made arrangements to follow up on Carol Alexander, the waitress who served Irvin and Shepherd. "…I deem it very necessary that your office should make arrangement for her to be present for the trial," he wrote. Perkins was peeved, but there wasn't much he could do. He could only continue to forge ahead and run down as many leads as time would permit. And there were plenty to chase.

Chapter 22 -- More Surprises

In the midst of last-minute preparations, Perkins received an urgent request to visit his clients. At the state prison, a concerned Walter Irvin told Perkins that the prison grapevine was reporting that Greenlee had turned stool pigeon and was going to testify against Sammie and Walter. When the rumor got back to Greenlee, Charles sent them a note, which Walter concealed until he could show it to Perkins. In pencil, Greenlee had scrawled, "Hello Sam & Walter; I receive a note from Walter but I think it silly. Look fellows I fell with you boys although I don't know weather you are guilty or not. So don't worry about me no one can push me up to hurt you boys in no way so stop worrying and beleave me. I went over to the office one day last week but it was nothing to it, just a free man work here trying to get me to change my story but that will never happen. And yesterday McCall and Ducon from Ganisville state Attorney and they went by and brought my mother and some other guy I did not no but the taril will be in Ganesville. And for God sake don't worry about getting hurt by Charles."

Perkins had a pretty strong hunch the rumor was linked to the actions of Sheriff Willis McCall. Greenlee confirmed as much when Perkins visited his cell. "I remember my mother came to see me. The sheriff or a deputy brought her. I remember her visit very vividly because they left us by ourselves in this room. I made it quite clear to her -- and everyone who was listening on the other side of the wall -- that if they thought I was dumb enough to talk about the case they were in for a surprise. I knew the walls had ears. They were in another room listening. Did they think my mother was going to come in and ask, 'Charles, did you do this? Did you do that?' and I was going to say anything? It was just common sense I was not going to say anything they wanted to hear," Greenlee recalled.

Perkins marveled that McCall would travel all the way to Raiford just to lean on Greenlee. He had heard numerous tales of the sheriff's cunning, but this was the first time he had seen evidence of McCall's trademark manipulation up close. Before returning to Orlando, Perkins reassured Irvin and Shepherd that Greenlee hadn't turned snitch.

The defense didn't have time to worry about tricks the prosecution might be cooking up. Marshall and his associates were trying to find out if Burtoft's unit would return to the States in time for him to appear at the trial, and if so, if Burtoft would be willing to testify. Finding the young private became the number one priority.

Finally, in mid-October, the defense got a break when it learned Burtoft hadn't shipped out after all, but was working in the supply department at Fort Jackson. Someone needed to fly to South Carolina right away. Professor S. Ralph Harlow, whom the Committee of 100 had sent to Lake County with Rev. Caxton Doggett to poll public sentiment toward the defendants, agreed to visit Burtoft. On the morning of Oct. 25, Harlow and Doggett dispatched a letter special delivery air mail to Fort Jackson to notify Burtoft that Harlow was coming to meeting with him. In the meantime, Doggett and Harlow would spend two days conducting interviews in and around Lake County. Spreading out across the county, it didn't take long for Committee of 100 canvas teams to glean valuable information. It seemed everyone had an opinion about the Groveland rape case. Even though two years had passed since the trial, most people interviewed still had strong feelings about the case. The detailed report proved to be an eye-opener. Below is a summary of interviews conducted in Lake County:

1) Mount Dora minister the Rev. Robert Blackburn -- "He affirmed with the judge in the case because he was a good judge. In reply to my suggestion that Pilate was also a good judge and that was one of the reasons we condemned him because he washed his hands and sent an innocent man to death and that this would make a good sermon topic for him, he did not seem interested. When we asked him whether he had read Judge Jackson's concurring opinion denouncing the trial he said he had not read it and when he was offered a copy, he did not want to take it. Undoubtedly he can sleep better if he does not know too much about this case...He wondered why 'there should be so much fuss over this little case.'...He is sure that the trial was fair and that the new trial will be fair, "because the people here are fair people." Harlow and Doggett left the interview depressed because, "that in our first interview we found that a spiritual leader of the community is so blind and so unwilling to see."

2) Mount Dora woman, 79-year-old Mrs. McDonald -- "Her comment was 'this community is fair to Negroes. They live there. We live here. They mind their business. We mind ours.' And the people in this neighborhood being fair, she is sure that they would have a fair trial."

3) Orange grove owner Jack Graves -- "When asked questions he informed us that he had traveled in over forty states and that there was no area in the entire United States where Negroes get such fair treatment as right there in that county. The trial was completely fair

and the boys were guilty. The next trial will also be fair… he just went on and on eulogizing the community and the fairness of the trial and that the Supreme Court was wrong."

4) George White, leading banker and member of Board of Control of the state schools of Mount Dora -- "Son of Methodist minister… He was most emphatic in regard to the guilt of the boys and the fairness of the trial. He complained that the boys had been dealt with far too lenient. 'If it had been my wife I would have led a mob there and killed them.'…He agreed that you could not find twelve white people who had not made up their minds that the Negroes were guilty."

5) J.G. Ray Jr., a Mount Dora contractor in his mid-30s with a wife and four children -- "Among the fairest of the white people with whom we talked…Very intelligent on the school board…it was quite evident that she and her husband are troubled about this case. He was turned down for jury duty in the case, although he was called, because when he was asked whether he had been influenced in the case he said, 'how can anyone in this section who has read the papers be free of some prejudice on the case?' Seated next to him was a man who was called next for jury duty and who was accepted and sat on this trial. This was the man who said to him 'What they ought to have done is take those n----- out, tie them to a stake and burn them.' This man and his wife concurred that it would be impossible to find twelve people in the area without preconceived ideas in the case. The wife said that no group of 'our friends who come to this house would say that the trial was unfair.'"

6) Paul and Mabel Norris Reese -- "Mrs. Rece (sic) attended the trial and wrote it up. People complained she had a pro-Negro attitude. Friends say she is pro-prosecution because she is a very close friend of the Prosecuting Attorney."

7) Elderly Tavares Methodist minister the Rev. J.W. Rogers and his wife -- "Mr. Hunter, prosecuting attorney was a member of his church… and had told them that he would be willing to try this case before an all-Negro jury and that he was sure of the guilt of the boys and that any fair-minded Negro would agree with him."

8) Attendant at gas station opposite courthouse in Tavares -- "He was rather dumb. Stated that it was a 'sad' case. Sad that it happened to a white girl. You can't expect to get any twelve jurors in this area who have not made up their minds. Folk here think they are guilty."

9) Mrs. William Burtoft, mother of Lawrence Burtoft -- "Mrs. Burtoft is certain that Mrs. 'A' lied on the stand and that the boys are not guilty. The mother thinks that her son has been intimidated by the sheriff and the prosecuting attorney. He refused to have his picture taken and was upset whenever his name was introduced."

10) Mrs. Herbert Whitehead, clerk in "leading attorney's office" -- "The trial was fair and that the next one will be also. In fact she added it is 'fairer than white boys would have received.'"

11) Attorney (Mr. Duncan) member of the state legislature -- "Again the same old story. The trial was fair. The next will be. I ought to add here that most of the people with whom we talked referred to the confessions that the boys had made."

12) Carl Lehman, former secretary of Christian Endeavor Society in the north -- "He was most emphatic that everything was fair and that everything will be fair in the next trial. Critical of the NAACP and he stated that the writers who came down there were liars, most especially those who represented the Negro press... Said they had been guilty of betraying the community with lies. Absolutely 100% certain that the boys are guilty. 'This court leaned over backward to see that the boys had a fair trial.'"

13) The Rev. Sparkman, retired Congregational minister -- "First person with whom we talked who has grave doubts about the whole affair. Doesn't believe that a Negro charged with rape against a white woman in that area would get a fair trial anywhere in the state. He is sure that Mrs. 'A' was not telling the truth on the stand. He went to some of the trial. Does not believe her story... Stated he cannot be publicly quoted by name, 'because I live here.' Again 'consciousness of kind' is the dominant force here."

14) C.D. Kinder, Negro school principal -- "Very intelligent. 'You will find it difficult to find a Negro anywhere who thinks the trial was fair or that any trial possibly could be.' He attended part of the trial. Stated that the general relationship between the colored and white community in that area is a friendly relationship. I got this from a number of Negroes from whom I talked as well as the white people. The conclusion is that this general feeling of good will exists only when the whites are sure that they are dominant and the Negroes keep their place."

15) Ignorant Negro worker by the roadside -- "Said that the trial was not fair. Said that soldiers came and he hid. Shows the fear among ignorant people."

16) Elderly couple, the Rev. and Mrs. Reed -- "They stated that they believe that the community was fair and that the trial must have been fair."

17) Three Negro bellboys and a Negro porter at the Hotel San Juan in Orlando -- "Very intelligent... Said they knew a lot about the case. Said that the trial was fantastic. Said that it was a frame-up. Said that all the Negroes feel that the trial was not fair and that no trial of these boys will be fair."

A second team of Committee of 100 volunteers headed by Professor Hornell Hart of the Duke University School of Religion and Rev. Paul Moore Jr., pastor of Grace Episcopal Church in Jersey City, uncovered even more startling information. Although the interviewees weren't named in the team's five-page report (perhaps because anonymity was promised) the information gleaned was astonishing. An interview with a "law enforcement officer recommended as one of the most outstanding in entire state of Florida by a mutual friend of one of the team members," was particularly revealing. According to the report, "He seemed a little uneasy that he should be questioned. He fixed the time of the trouble and (sic) the night of the alleged crime quickly, because one of two escaped convicts had been shot to death in Leesburg, and he said he fixed the time of arrival of Padgett -- husband of alleged victim at about 2:00 AM in Leesburg -- for there was a radio broadcast of the reported kidnapping that came in over his police car radio at about that time." The interviewers considered the statement "extremely important" since the prosecution "indicated that the kidnapping took place at a later time -- between 3:00 and 3:30 AM." The report of the interview continued, "Padgett, who appeared rather mussed up to Police Officer, left the Leesburg convict shooting scene with Deputy Sheriff Campbell -- now a police officer in Leesburg. Interviewee… was critical of Sheriff on ascertaining scene of crime and not much impressed with McCall's law enforcement efficiency."

A "leading veteran in Clermont" who "was familiar with the case" told interviewers that he "knew three of the Negroes involved. He also knew the Padgetts… Ernest Thomas' mother worked for him in home. She was a woman of ill repute in Clermont having run a house of ill-fame with a daughter as an inmate. The patriarch of Groveland area (L.D. Edge?) was openly hostile to team and mentioned that a good many people had been asked out of town for nosing into this case. He was suspicious of the lay members of the team and mentioned tar and feathers, but once he was convinced that we desired factual, grass-roots information, he told a connected, integrated story that would have done credit to a fiction writer." His story, after he got into it, started off with the startling angle that Thomas and Greenlee had arrived in Groveland "a couple of days" before the crime was committed. "He is firmly convinced of the guilt of the four boys and that the two boys who are being re-tried should be executed. He is very bitter over the criticism of Groveland -- pilloried for a crime that was not committed in Groveland. Bear in mind in perusing this accounting this is this man's story and it is recounted somewhat in detail because of some striking differences from testimony adduced at the first trial. In his story -- the four Negroes -- in Groveland for a couple of days before the crime -- had been carousing around and creating ruckuses around Groveland. Thomas' father is a white man -- known to the speaker and to the general community. Thomas a zoot-suited Negro that was a leader and a general trouble-maker in Groveland. His story put the four boys in the Mercury abduction car together in Clermont the night of the crime where they were seen and recognized by a filling station attendant under a good light. The attendant took special notice because he recognized the car as belonging to a Negro boy who worked with him in the filling station. He thought the car was stolen."

The sensational account continued, "The four boys -- with money running short and under the leadership of Thomas -- decided to rob Henry Singleton. Greenlee -- the stranger in town -- was to do the job. The other boys were known to Henry Singleton. When Greenlee knocked at the door, Singleton appeared with a gun because he thought there might be trouble -- since the four boys had been erecting trouble. Greenlee run when he saw Singleton's gun and while Singleton did not see the other three boys -- he heard them running away. Singleton reported this robbery attempt to Sheriff McCall and this brought officers to the Groveland area. The gas buying incident is supposed to have taken place subsequent to the hold-up attempt. The boys then drove around the loop -- to Okahumpka -- then turned back toward Groveland and it was then they saw the distressed automobile, stopped and offered aid. When their aid efforts were to no avail -- and on this well-traveled highway, utilized by many cars and trucks -- and they started to leave -- one of the Negroes said -- "That looks like a good piece of pussy. We ought to take her with us. Then the fight started and Padgett was assaulted and the girl kidnapped." The report continued, "This is still the patriarch's story. He was called at home in bed by his night watchman who had discovered Greenlee, armed with a pistol, drinking water at the Groveland filling station. Eventually, Greenlee was placed in the Groveland calaboose (?). The story-teller arose at 5:30 the next morning and a melon-grower (named Blonden?), seeing a light in this man's store, stopped and told him there was some sort of trouble toward Okahumpka -- that he had seen the sheriff's cars up there, so this man got into his car and went to the scene of the crime. Or at least to see the officers. On his return to Groveland he saw the Shepherd car parked in front of the Irwin (sic) house in the quarters and notified the officers. According to his statement the three boys -- who had dumped Greenlee -- were in bed together -- but when the law came in the room, they must not have searched it too close, for Ernest Thomas had been hiding behind the door -- or under the bed. They didn't get him. This man said that Irwin's (sic) father -- who works for him, as do two of the accused boy's brothers -- said Walter Irwin (sic) confessed to his father and that Walter's father told him. He closed telephones to press during the disturbances because the reporters were not telling the truth. He was in a business men's group organized, at that time, to protect the Groveland name. He expressed a bitter hatred for Alex Akerman of defense counsel. "He's worse than the niggers," he said. Norma Padgett's father works for him. He classified the raped girl as a good girl -- and deplored her experience. 'She's the one who was hurt.' He did not agree that outside people caused all the trouble. He acted as if he knew who did the burnings at first but then smoother (?) this over somewhat by saying this sort of action was to be expected when a white woman is raped. He said Shepherd's father had been in trouble with the white community for shooting cattle -- not for food, for meanness. This man went to school to with State's Attorney Jess Hunter. He also said he didn't want to talk much about the case "because he had been summoned." He is thoroughly convinced the boys are guilty and that they will get a fair trial and they will be executed."

Two women and a man previously unknown to the defense also offered surprising recollections. The first interviewee, a woman living near Okahumpka, said her husband saw Norma Padgett, "about 5:30 near their home which is not far from the Bertoft (sic) place at the Center Hill, Leesburg, Groveland road junction." Harry Moore also saw Padgett "sitting on the road near Center Hill about daylight." But the most startling recollections came from a Mrs. Twiss, who claimed to watch the girl through field glasses, as did her husband. According to Twiss, "she was not disheveled and she had her shoulder purse with her. She walked back and forth as if waiting for something -- then went to the Bertofts (sic) Place." The woman also confirmed that Burtoft took Padgett in his car toward Groveland. Then Twiss dropped a bombshell, saying, "Norma Padgett knew all three of the boys well -- all of them except Greenlee -- said they lived almost door to door. She also said Norma Padgett's reputation in the community was not good -- and that her sister had a bad reputation." The woman stopped short just of accusing Padgett of cavorting with Negroes. The canvassers thought the woman would be a "key witness."

Chapter 23 -- "It Was Them Or Me"

Charles Greenlee felt mixed emotions when he learned that Sammie and Walter were heading back to Tavares for a second trial. Now 18, Charles had been matured by prison labor and had long since resigned himself to doing his time, hopefully in anonymity. Still, on the morning of Nov. 6, he couldn't help wondering if the men he would be forever linked with were on their way to freedom. Sammie and Walter also wondered. They desperately wanted to believe the nightmare was finally about to end.

Sheriff Willis McCall and Deputy James Yates reached Raiford State Prison in the early evening of Tuesday, Nov. 6. In less than 18 hours, they would again deliver Walter and Sammie to the Lake County courthouse for a hearing on motions that could mean the difference between life and death. McCall was none too happy that the prisoners were getting another trial, let alone were still alive. One look at McCall and Yates told Sammie and Walter they'd better keep their thoughts of freedom to themselves. The high sheriff and his right-hand man were muttering threats as they led the prisoners to McCall's Oldsmobile. Shepherd and Irvin knew they were in for a long, tense ride.

After more than an hour of driving, the prisoners experienced an anxious moment when the sheriff turned off the main highway onto Highway 146, a country road that ran through the small citrus town of Weirsdale. As McCall pulled up to a Lake County patrol car parked alongside the road, Walter and Sammie tensed as Yates climbed out of the car. Was more brutality ahead? They watched closely as the lawmen talked in low tones. When the sheriff came back, he told the handcuffed prisoners to get out of the back seat and get in front. They knew enough to obey. Moments later, Yates got into his car, pulled ahead of McCall and sped away. As the taillights faded in the distance, McCall restarted his car and started down the twisting, unlit road.

After several miles, McCall began "shimmying" the wheels, then pulled over. Shepherd and Irvin exchanged nervous glances as the sheriff turned off the ignition and got out. After briefly inspecting the front tires, McCall climbed back in and set off. Only a few minutes passed until McCall again pulled over. He again checked the front tires, and then told the prisoners a tire had gone flat and that they would have to get out while he changed it. McCall then radioed Yates to get the attendant from the Umatilla Gulf service station to come out to fix the tire. Then all hell broke loose, the still of the winter night being shattered by five successive gunshots. Moments later, the sheriff was on his radio asking for help after emptying his gun into his handcuffed prisoners. The men had tried to escape, but McCall stopped them with a hail of bullets. McCall had dropped the prisoners less than two feet from the passenger door of the car.

Walter was terrified as he lay on the ground with life oozing out of him, but not too terrified to realize that his best friend wasn't moving. The sheriff had carried out his threats. So this is how the nightmare would end. Walter, who heard Sammie's terrifying last gasp, was barely clinging to life as blood filled his mouth. His excruciating pain was the result of a bullet in his chest that passed through a lung and just missed his left kidney, and another in his right shoulder. He didn't dare cry out. He wanted the sheriff to think he was dead.

Walter must have drifted off, because the next thing he knew Yates was standing over him with a pistol in his hand. Bang, flash and a searing pain in his neck. As Walter drifted in and out of consciousness, McCall's mind was racing. Shooting the prisoners had been easy. Now came the hard part. Time was of the essence. McCall needed as many "witnesses" as possible to support the story he would tell.

Fortunately for McCall, nearby Umatilla was crawling with friends and acquaintances that would support his story once they saw the rumpled shirt, bent glasses and cut on his head. Willis looked a sight by the time Yates returned with a contingent of McCall's friends and neighbors. The mayor and entire city council, along with attendees of a Umatilla Kiwanis Club meeting, a night policeman and town superintendent came to the aid of the distressed and ruffled sheriff. It was an amazing turnout for a weeknight in a small rural community that rolled up its sidewalks early each evening.

The sheriff told everyone he shot the prisoners in self-defense after one of them attacked him with the McCall's metal flashlight, breaking his glasses with a blow to the left side of his head. He hated like hell to have to shoot them, but it was him or them. After telling and retelling his story, McCall had the wherewithal to radio the Tavares jail and order the evening dispatcher to phone State Attorney Jesse Hunter, Judge Truman Futch and Judge W. Troy Hall, the acting coroner. McCall did not tell his dispatcher to call the prisoners' attorneys. And he didn't request an ambulance.

By the time the local press arrived in the person of *Eustis Lake Region News* Editor Marie Bolles, who was at her home in Umatilla when a friend delivered the news, approximately 30 people were milling about. "Mr. McCall came up to me and said, 'Marie, it's just one of those things. I hate it that it happened,'" Bolles recalled. McCall retold his story for the umpteenth time, this time taking his friends behind the car and opening the trunk to show them the flat tire service station attendant Spencer Rynearson had already changed. Some men instinctively punched the tire to prove to themselves it was indeed flat. McCall pointed out the nail embedded in the rubber.

Hunter and Hall rushed to the scene and the old prosecutor wasn't happy to find the defendants lying in the grass alongside the road, one with a bullet hole in his head. *Baltimore Afro-American* correspondent Stetson Kennedy arrived shortly after Hunter, just in time to hear Jess disgustedly tell McCall, "You have urinated in my whiskey." Kennedy wasn't sure what Hunter meant by the remark, but it was clear the state attorney wasn't pleased.

Nearby, Walter was growing weaker. He had survived the beatings and torture, and even a death sentence only to die on a dark rural road. McCall was receiving all sorts of attention, but no one appeared overly concerned about Irvin, except those who wondered aloud that somehow he was still breathing. Walter lost track of how many white men stood over him and Sammie. Poor Sammie. Finally, more than 30 minutes after the shooting, the jailer, Reuben Hatcher spoke up. "Then I mentioned something about an ambulance and they said, all right, go ahead and get the ambulance, so I picked up the microphone on Mr. Yates' car, and called headquarters station and told them to get an ambulance on out there." The ambulance still hadn't arrived when Dr. C.M. Tyre reached the scene. He promptly examined Irvin and found the prisoner "in extreme shock." Walter was somehow hanging on. Mercifully, Tyre gave him an injection to ease the pain. By the time the ambulance arrived it was after midnight and Walter's pulse was "imperceptible." The exceedingly long wait for transport was because the ambulance came from Dabney Funeral Home in Leesburg, more than 20 miles away. Waterman Hospital was just six miles from the scene of the shooting, but Waterman wouldn't transport Negroes.

Tyre followed the ambulance to the hospital, where Irvin was admitted at 1:15 a.m. in extreme shock. Walter was literally on death's doorstep, his right chest filled with blood and his pulse barely discernable. Tyre couldn't even get a blood pressure reading. The doctor immediately ordered Walter be given plasma and stimulants. He also made arrangements to pick up whole blood for a transfusion from Orlando and called for a specialist. Finally, a white man interested in saving Irvin's life instead of ending it. Orlando chest specialist and surgeon W. O. Fowler arrived well after 2 a.m. After examining the patient, who was still in critical condition, Fowler operated to drain blood from his lungs and remove a bullet.

While Irvin fought for his life, Hall was in conference with McCall and Hunter. The result: Hall decided to choose a coroner's jury then and there. From the three dozen people at the scene, Hall asked Bolles and McCall's friends Paul Bryan and John Nelson to serve. He also asked Methodist minister Frank Robinson Jr., L.T. Brennand and J.S. Allen. Hall told his appointees to be prepared to begin considering evidence in the morning.

At the San Juan Hotel in Orlando, attorney Jack Greenberg was totally unaware of the mayhem taking place on a rural Lake County road. Greenberg spent the eve before the start of the biggest trial of his life listening to boisterous Ku Klux Klansmen on the street outside his hotel room. The white-sheet brigade was very much aware that the Groveland defendants were about to be retried. The young attorney nervously pushed the nightstand against the door, as if that would keep the KKK from doing him harm. He then turned off the light, climbed into bed and hoped sleep would come. Thankfully, it eventually did.

Wednesday Nov. 7 began with a 7 a.m. wakeup call. As Greenberg pushed the nightstand away from the door to get the newspaper that had been shoved underneath, the *Orlando Sentinel Star* headlines leaped from the page: "Lake County Sheriff Shoots Two Negroes" and "Officer Kills Suspect in Attack Case" and "Pair Enroute to Hearing Try Escape." In disbelief, Greenberg read that McCall shot and killed Shepherd and seriously wounded Irvin during an escape attempt. Greenberg could hardly believe his eyes. There would be no trial today, perhaps ever.

At Fannie Bell's home, the terrible news nearly floored Henrietta (Irvin) Shepherd. "Someone woke James and myself up to say, 'James, your brother got killed last night. And Henrietta, your brother got shot and he's real bad off in the hospital.' That was something. That was something." Henrietta and her mother Dellia desperately wanted to go to the hospital, but the family didn't have a car and couldn't find anyone willing to take them.

Alex Akerman also began the day with the grim news, and soon found himself fielding reporters' questions. No, he "didn't know what has happened," and yes, he found it hard to believe that Irvin and Shepherd had tried to escape. "The last contact we had with the defendants was Tuesday at which time they appeared in good spirits and confident of vindication," said Akerman. The attorney quickly re-read the article. Akerman wondered what *had* really happened. Hopefully, Walter Irvin could tell him.

While Greenberg, Akerman and Perkins raced to the hospital, Irvin was feeling slightly stronger after having a blood clot removed and a bullet taken from his lung. He was now under the care of Dr. Rabun H. Williams, who also treated a gunshot wound made by the bullet that passed through his neck. The third bullet, which had entered the right side of the chest, remained lodged in his kidney. At the hospital, a grim scene greeted the lawyers. Walter was propped up in bed, awake, but drowsy from anesthesia. A tube ran out of his nose and his neck was heavily bandaged. Down the hallway, McCall was also sitting up in bed, having been admitted for "shock and a heart condition," although the sheriff's condition didn't prevent Deputy Yates from repeatedly popping into his boss' room for instructions.

McCall was still sheriff, and he wasn't about to let anyone see his prisoner, not even Akerman. The attorneys were most anxious to talk with their client, but the door to Irvin's room was blocked by Yates, who told them, "You might as well go away, because I ain't goin' to let you in." Moments later, Dr. Williams angrily brushed past the startled deputy, the attorneys in tow. At Walter's bedside, Akerman asked what had happened. "Well, we were going down the road…" Irvin began, but was interrupted by Yates, who had rushed into the room. "I have orders not to let anyone talk to this boy and I will have to go for further orders," Yates said as he moved between the attorneys and Irvin's bed. After ushering the attorneys outside the room, Yates rushed down the hall to confer with McCall, who told his deputy the attorneys could not interview Irvin without doctor's permission *and* a written order from Judge Futch. The news outraged Akerman and Greenberg. "I informed the deputy that the doctor had brought us in and that as provided by Section 901.24 of Florida statutes an attorney is always allowed to talk to his client, privately if he so desires. Whereupon the deputy stated that made no difference, that he had his orders direct from Willis McCall to whom he had just talked down the hall," Akerman recalled. Yates defiantly planted himself in front of the door of Walter's room.

The attorneys reluctantly retreated. Outside the hospital, an angry Akerman gave reporters an earful. "We had permission from the doctors to talk to him and we were in the presence of a nurse all the time and doctor part of the time," Akerman sputtered. "This action on the part of Willis McCall definitely established in my mind… that he is still in control of Irvin and all his activities, and it is my opinion that the only reasonable inference that can be drawn from McCall's activities is that as long as he can prevent it, he will not permit Irvin to tell his attorneys the facts leading up to the killing of Shepherd and the wounding of Irvin." After meeting with the press, Akerman called to get Futch's permission to interview Irvin, but the judge wasn't in. While waiting for the return call, the lawyers went for a walk around the hospital grounds, all the while being watched by Yates from a window. From there the attorneys went to the Western Union office. At 8:43, they sent a telegram to the governor, which said, in part: "Request you immediately investigate killing of Samuel Shepherd and mortal wounding of Walter Irvin by Sheriff Willis McCall last night allegedly killed while trying to escape… Request immediately investigation while facts fresh."

That morning, prosecutor Jesse Hunter phoned his friend, newspaper editor Mabel Norris-Reese. "Mabel, I don't believe those guys attacked the sheriff. I think it was all deliberate," Hunter said. Norris-Reese, who had backed the sheriff through thick and thin, was stunned. She wasn't the only one. *St. Petersburg Times* reporter John Gardner found plenty of shocked locals. He also found complacency. "The emotions of residents of the two central Florida towns (Eustis and Tavares) were typified by these street corner conversations: 'I hear you were going to be on the jury,' one man laughingly said to a companion. 'Yeah, we were going to really get a man, but he's already got,' the other grinned back. By contrast, Gardner spoke with "one gnarled oldster" who remarked, 'It ain't according to Hoyle. If that boy was wrong they should've proved it in court.'"

Ironically, the shooting wasn't even the lead story in the local newspaper, the *Leesburg Commercial*. The article, "Sheriff McCall Kills Negro in Escape Attempt" was dwarfed by the banner headline, "Leesburg Citizens Join In Surprise Ceremony Honoring J.W. Hunter at Courthouse." The story detailed a Tuesday morning party celebrating Hunter's 25 years of service attended by more than 250 dignitaries from across the state, including Florida Attorney General Richard Irvin. A glance at the guest list for the gala affair goes a long way toward explaining how Hunter and McCall were able to control things when the Groveland case broke more than two years earlier. Among the Lake County movers and shakers who feted Hunter were: newspaper reporters Norris-Reese and Ormund Powers; Mount Dora banker George White, who had testified to the county's racial harmony at a pretrial hearing in '49; L.D. Edge, prominent Groveland business leader who employed Cleve and Walter Irvin (and may have had a hand in directing McCall to the latter); physician Tyre; judges Futch and Hall; and, of course, McCall.

FBI agents Webb Burke (Miami) and Clyde Aderhold (Orlando) arrived at the hospital just before noon with orders to interview Irvin and conduct a thorough investigation. The agents managed to slip into Waterman without fanfare and quietly met with Irvin before a 2 p.m. rib resection. Walter was lucid enough to answer questions. The agents left undetected, but reporters soon learned of the bedside interview from members of the hospital staff who witnessed the conference. "Hospital attaches would not say what Irvin had told them, but they did reveal that he related 'an entirely different story' of the shooting," *Tampa Tribune* reporter Emmett Peter Jr. wrote. McCall, who couldn't believe Irvin had lived long enough to contradict him, bristled when he heard FBI agents were already poking their noses in his business. The sticky situation McCall found himself in was about to get stickier: by now, the hospital was crawling with local law officers, reporters, lawyers, federal agents, politicians, and county officials.

By early afternoon the story of the shooting was circulating nationwide, and with it condemnation. United Auto Workers President Walter Ruether was one of the first to sound off, saying, "This is not the first time a prisoner was shot because he was alleged to have tried to escape. We know that in state after state in America where Negroes come before the bars of justice there are two standards, one for Negroes and one for whites." Lester B. Granger, head of the National Urban League, ranted about Negroes being subjected to "punishment without crime" by racial segregation. Civil Right Congress (CRC) Executive Secretary William L. Patterson chimed in: "This murder was cold-blooded and premeditated. The Florida authorities had no intention of permitting these men a day in court." In a cable to the president of the United Nations, the CRC demanded U.N. intervention "to end the continuing policy of genocide... against the Negro people." Clarence Mitchell, administrative director of the Washington Bureau of the NAACP declared: "It is inconceivable that this could have occurred without some very careful planning on the part of law enforcement officers."

At Waterman Hospital, a steady stream of visitors waltzed into the sheriff's room o "official business," although members of the press were barred. Among the first to gain entrance was Judge Troy Hall, who found McCall sitting up in bed, wearing polka dot pajamas and a bandage over his left eye. His spectacles were missing the left lens. Behind locked door, the men drafted McCall's statement. It was a time-consuming process -- both knew that there could be no holes in the "official" version. Hall stressed that McCall must address questions already being asked -- questions about why McCall was alone with the prisoners and why he had taken a roundabout route to the county jail in Tavares. Finally, after several revisions, they had composed a declaration designed to answer every query a reporter or lawyer could raise. But McCall wouldn't be doing the talking, at least not yet. It would fall upon Hall to deal with reporters.

After meeting with the sheriff, Hall called an impromptu press conference for the eight reporters conducting vigils at the hospital. Hall said, "In making the trip to Raiford this time, the sheriff followed the pattern he had set in previous trips. He was accompanied on the unannounced mission by Deputy Sheriff Yates. They left Tavares separately, but joining together at Weirsdale en route. After obtaining the prisoners at Raiford they came back to Weirsdale together. There Deputy Yates picked up his own car and, according to plan, proceeded as a "lead car," followed by the sheriff in his car and the two prisoners. It is understood that all three men were in the front seat; that Irvin and Shepherd were handcuffed together; that en route to Umatilla the sheriff's car had a flat tire resulting from a nail puncture. Having radio communications with Deputy Yates' car, McCall called Yates to come to his assistance. Before Yates returned, the prisoner Irvin requested the sheriff to let him answer a call of nature. The sheriff, in granting the request, went around and opened the door on the passenger's side at which time prisoner Shepherd suddenly and unexpectedly lashed out with the sheriff's flashlight, striking the sheriff in the temple, and called to Irvin, to "get his gun." In the ensuing scuffle, the sheriff, who is a powerful physical specimen, gained control of his side arm, a .38 special, and shot his way free of his assailants. The prisoner Shepherd was killed. The prisoner Irvin was seriously wounded, but is improving and it is thought he may recover. The fearsome struggle was completed in a matter of seconds and before Deputy Yates returned. Upon Yates arrival, the sheriff instructed him to get help and a doctor for Irvin, who was still alive." Hall explained, that according to McCall, the shooting took place around 9:30 p.m., a "few miles west of Umatilla."

The response to the statement varied from unquestioning belief (by members of the local press) to expressed skepticism by scribes from newspapers outside McCall's domain. The skeptics found the wording of the "official" statement curious, particularly the line, "It is *understood* that all three men were in the front seat…" Why not just say, "All three men were in the front seat?" Hall told reporters that he knew McCall was telling the truth because he "saw a batch of the sheriff's hair in Irvin's hand when I got there." Hall also announced that a coroner's jury would investigate the circumstances surrounding Shepherd's death.

After finishing with Hall, the newshounds went in pursuit of others who were at the scene of the shooting. Jailer Reuben Hatcher, cornered by reporters when he came to visit McCall, confirmed the shooting occurred around 9:30, then grabbed a bit of the limelight by revealing that *he* was the person responsible for an ambulance being called. "I told him to hang on and we would get help to him." The reporters also tried to interview Deputy Yates, but attempts to question him were met with a scowl. Finally, the reporters also sought the prosecutor's views on the shooting. Surprisingly, Hunter was willing to talk. "Evidently Willis believed they both were dead, but I discovered Irvin was alive and sent for an ambulance." So now there were three heroes -- McCall, Hatcher and Hunter – who sent for an ambulance after realizing Irvin was still alive. The next edition of the *Orlando Sentinel* removed the name "Willis", amending Hunter's quote to, "*It was* believed they both were dead, but I discovered Irvin was alive and sent for an ambulance." Who was responsible for the revision? McCall?

Late that morning, McCall received Assistant State Attorney A.P. "Sam" Buie, county probation officer Fred Borg and Florida Peace Officers Association Chaplain the Rev. Lloyd King. Reporters, however, continued to be turned away by Yates and Dr. Rabun Williams, who seconded that McCall couldn't be questioned because the sheriff was suffering from shock and had been under treatment for a heart ailment for several years. In fact, the physician reported that the lawman had suffered *three* heart attacks in recent years. That was news to the reporters who had dealt with McCall for years. Reporters were also denied access to Irvin, whose condition was "still serious, but hopeful" after an early-morning operation to remove a blood clot. Williams added, "He was made good progress and it looks as though he will be all right."

The press wouldn't gain access to McCall until late in the day, when Dr. Williams finally acquiesced, although he warned writers that his patient was not up to answering questions. The sheriff had his family on hand when reporters were finally ushered in to see him. And "see" was the operative word. Wife, Doris, 18-year-old son, Malcolm, and 6-year-old son, Donnie were gathered around Willis' bed when the press quietly entered. It was a touching scene. When one reporter tentatively asked the sheriff how he felt, McCall drew Donnie close and replied, "Fair. I'm just happy to be here with my arm around this boy." Naturally, reporters wanted to hear from McCall's own mouth what happened on that lonely road just west of Umatilla, but McCall begged off. The sheriff said that Hall's explanation was, "substantially correct." He then told Don Rider of the *Orlando Morning Sentinel*, "I expect I'll get a lot of criticism for this, but I'd rather be criticized than dead." After a few photos were snapped, the reporters were ushered from the room.

In Washington, D.C., President Harry Truman was digesting a barbed telegram from NAACP Secretary Walter White. The missive warned that local authorities would try to "whitewash" the investigation of McCall's actions and urged the president to order an investigation "by every appropriate government agency." Attorney General J. Howard McGrath promptly announced that the Justice Department would investigate. White also cabled Florida Gov. Fuller Warren: "We understand you have ordered grand jury investigation of cold-blooded slaying of Samuel Shepherd and possibly fatal shooting of Walter Irvin by Sheriff McCall of Lake County. We commend you upon this prompt action and urge you to pursue it relentlessly to the end that justice may be served through the arrest, indictment and early trial of McCall on murder charges. Anything less will leave the State of Florida open to the charge of being a state in which the orderly process of law have broken down and been seized by criminal elements."

The shooting marked the second time Warren found himself under fire because of McCall and he didn't like it a bit. The governor wanted a face-to-face meeting with the sheriff, but he couldn't just march into the hospital where a media horde was waiting for the sheriff to explain why he needed six bullets to kill two manacled prisoners. Warren decided to arrange a private meeting away from the hospital, but first wanted to talk to Hunter, who had already conveyed his concerns during a phone conversation. Hunter agreed to meet the governor in Gainesville and ride with him the remaining hour to Palatka in northeast Lake County. It was the perfect place for a secret meeting. Set in a rural section of the county, Palatka was the last place anyone would expect to find the governor. But somehow reporters got wind of Warren's travel plans and were waiting for him. The governor tersely met queries with, "I cannot discuss the case at this time but I expect to be in a position to say something later." It was the classic "no comment," comment. Warren wasn't saying "boo" until he met with McCall. Warren had nothing to say to for publication, but he had said plenty to Hunter during the drive from Gainesville. Warren told the Hunter to tell McCall he should resign.

In Orlando, Paul Perkins was consoling Sammie Shepherd's parents and siblings when the press arrived. Perkins gave them something to write about when he revealed that he had just learned that while in prison, Sammie had undergone an operation to repair damage caused when McCall and his deputies beat him. Charlie Mae tearfully told the *Orlando Morning Sentinel*, "My boy complained of pains in his chest after the beating he got in 1949. I believe this operation he had was the result of those chest pains." Charlie Mae said she wasn't surprised her son had been shot down by the sheriff. Privately, Charlie Mae told Perkins she knew for a fact her son didn't attack the sheriff. Sammie was optimistic, not desperate. He would never jeopardize a chance for true freedom with a foolhardy escape plan. And, she could prove it, she told Perkins as he handed the surprised attorney an envelope postmarked Nov. 1, 1951 from Samuel Shepherd, prisoner No. 45539, Raiford, Florida. Inside was a two-page letter written in pencil:

"Dearest Mother; This will assure you that your recent letter has been received and read. It found Walter and me getting along okay. I'm very happy to hear that all are getting along fine. Mother, you're doing something I wouldn't do unless I just had to, that's pick beans. I don't see how you can do it. Mother, I got a letter from Henrietta, along with yours. All were fine. Also, Mr. Perkins, were up yesterday. He said he had seen some of you on Wed. He didn't get up on Friday, as he had planned, instead he was up on Tuesday. Love to all, including mother Fannie, the Moores and others. Mother, I had decided not to answer any more letters, but I thought it wise to answer your letter. Walter join in love to all, love to Irene and family. I hear she's planning to come home soon: what's the matter? Tell Fannie Lou, that. Mr. Perkins hasn't given me anything that Mrs. Clark sent to me. Maybe he didn't pick it up. Mother, about my watch. Sarah has it. I'm sure. You can get in touch with her through Mr. Sapp. I told James in a letter to see her and pick it up because I knew he had more convience than you have. Mother, what's Henry doing? And how is Emma doing in school? I'd love to see all of you, including the Old Man. "Smile," but especially you. Love to Mrs. Rice. Mother, you had better come on up. "Smile!" I might have something new to tell you about. Who knows? Ha, ha, ha. Mother, our hearing has been reset for the (7th) of Nov. instead of the (6th) and the trial will probably be set for the (13th). We don't know as yet. Hello, dad. How are you and that big truck doing? Fine, I hope. Hold everything down. I'll be with you against someday if "God," says so. You don't know how to use that truck. I can show you how it's done. "Smile." I must close now. Pray much. Love always, your son, Sammie. Mother, don't work too hard. You're not getting any younger. Love always. Mrs. C.M. Shepherd (answer) "Sammie."

Perkins was more convinced than ever that Sammie and Walter hadn't tried to escape. The letter was written by a man full of hope and love – a man who expected to be set free in a matter of weeks. Perkins left the grieving family members with a promise that the defense attorneys were committed to getting justice for Sammie and making certain Walter was protected from another attack.

Marshall arrived in the afternoon, being briefed about the sensational happenings during a drive from the Orlando airport to the Lake County hospital. There, Thurgood didn't have any better success gaining access to Irvin. After meeting with Perkins and Akerman, Marshall placed a call to Roy Wilkins in New York asking him to rally bureaus throughout the country. Marshall stressed that the outcry to the shooting needed to be loud and unrelenting.

The defense team still hadn't heard from Judge Futch, but he told reporters who tracked him down that the attorneys didn't need a court order to see their client. The only stipulation he had made was that Irvin, "not be disturbed any more than necessary because of his physical condition." Futch also said that the hearing scheduled for the previous day would be, "continued until further order of the court." Also, a special grand jury would be impaneled to look into the shooting Monday at 10 a.m.

By nightfall, members of the press were practically tripping over each other in their haste to file stories. It had become a very good news day after all, thanks to comments by Futch, Marshall and now McCall, who finally issued his own statement: "Since I and my office are involved in this matter, I have requested Judge Futch to appoint an elisor in my place for this particular case to handle and assist in any investigation to be made by the grand jury or any other investigative body." And there was more news from the courthouse: Hunter had announced that his son Walton would "handle all matters that might arise in my absence." Hunter didn't say where he was going, or why he would be away from his office during a grand jury investigation. He did, however, confirm that he would join Akerman in asking Gov. Warren to conduct a special investigation into the shootings.

Warren didn't waste any time in responding; in fact reporters were still lingering in the hospital hallways that night when the governor's top troubleshooter, Jefferson J. Elliott arrived to check on Irvin. When asked by a reporter if the governor had sent him, Elliott cryptically replied, "I'm here, and that's all I can say." Pressed to elaborate, Elliott said that the governor wanted a complete investigation, "letting the chips fall where they may."

Chapter 24 -- Walter's Version

When the defense attorneys returned that evening, they were accompanied by court reporter Alan H. Hamlin, who had been ordered to transcribe the interview so it could serve as an affidavit in the event Walter passed away, or was unable to testify at the upcoming trial. Unbeknownst to Marshall and his associates, it would be the third interview of the day for Irvin, who had endured a 45-minute question-and-answer session with the FBI and a visit from Dr. Tyre.

Tyre's visit was requested by nervous county commissioners, who asked the doctor to ascertain if Irvin's injuries were life-threatening. When Tyre arrived, he found that Yates was no longer standing guard, having yielded to a patrolman for the Eustis Police Department. Like Yates, the new man wasn't about to incur the sheriff's wrath by letting anyone see the prisoner, not even a doctor the commissioners sent. The sentry was taking orders from McCall, and only McCall, a stance that led to a heated argument when the doctor tried to enter. Trumbull dutifully reported the clash in the *Miami Herald*: "When he reached the room of Irvin he was stopped by Patrolman Dick Shirk of Eustis, who is also a deputy sheriff. The officer said, 'no pass from the court, no admission.' Angrily going to the telephone, he located Sheriff McCall," Trumbull wrote. The reporter excitedly crowded closer to the doctor as the physician's voice rose. "I'll give you just five minutes to straighten this thing out before I call the governor and ask him to suspend you, Willis, I mean it," Tyre shouted. After slamming down the receiver, the doctor pulled out a pocket watch and began pacing the hallway. Five minutes later, Tyre returned to the phone, asking the operator to connect him to the governor. But it was McCall, not Gov. Warren, who came on the line. Tyre exploded, hanging the phone back up after a short conversation.

Evidentially, the sheriff even controlled the switchboard operators. Soon Yates arrived and ushered the doctor into Irvin's room.

Tyre had finished his perfunctory examination (it appeared Irvin would pull through) and left just before an irritated and anxious Marshall triumphantly led a procession into Irvin's room. Thank God, Walter hadn't died while Thurgood was playing cat-and-mouse with McCall and the judge. Marshall and his associates wanted a private interview, but Elliott said it wouldn't be possible. Hamlin, Hunter, members of the press and a nurse crowded into the room with defense team members Perkins, Akerman, Greenberg and Marshall. Of course, Elliott was also on hand -- he wasn't about to let the attorneys out of his sight. Akerman began gently questioning Walter, who was extremely tired and having difficulty breathing. Irvin was a pitiful sight, looking small and weary tucked in the white sheets of the bed. "The Negro told his story despite the handicap of a feeding tube down his nose and into his throat, and after Akerman had assured him, 'no one is going to hurt you,'" Trumbull wrote. Walter's voice was low and raspy as he laboriously began recounting a horrifying tale of premeditated murder, not only by McCall, but by Yates. "Occasionally he paused in exhaustion, but after momentary rests he would continue in a low but firm voice," Trumbull wrote. Walter related that he and Shepherd were handcuffed together, sitting in the front seat of McCall's car as the sheriff followed the deputy onto a seldom-traveled clay road. And then the sheriff and Yates began talking on their radios.

Elliott: "What did the Sheriff say on the radio?"
Irvin: "I didn't get all that they was saying, didn't get everything."

Elliott: "Get some?"
Irvin: "Told him to go on ahead and check and so and so the Deputy Sheriff went on up a short ways in front of us, and he says, OK, and the Deputy Sheriff turned off to the right, I don't know where he went, I don't know where was he, and we turned off to the right and went on down the road a piece, and the Sheriff began to shimmy his wheels, and said, 'Something is wrong with my left front tire' and he pulled off to the side, and stopped, and pretty soon reached down and under the seat on the floorboard, and got his flashlight, it was a flashlight with a red band around the head of it, it had a red trim around it, don't know what you call that. He got the flashlight and got out of the car, on the right side he checked the tires, and on the left side he checked the tires, and then he got back in, and said couldn't find what was wrong, I don't think he went all the way around the car."

Irvin paused, then continued. "He got back in and taken off again, and drove on awhile, I will say a rough (sic) estimation of two more miles, and then he stopped again, and he stopped, and was trying to pull off to the side of the road, and he reached after the flashlight again, and got out and went around to the right side of the car, and kicked the right front wheel, and then he came on around to where Sammie was sitting on the right hand side of the car. I was sitting in the middle. Then he said, 'You SOBs get out and let me get a tire and fix my car' and I did not see any tires in back, but we had to obey, because he was the Sheriff, and so we went to get out, and Shepherd he taken his foot and put it out of the car, and was getting out, and I can't say just how quick it was, but he shot him, and it was

245

quick enough, and he turned, the Sheriff did, and he had a pistol and shot him right quick, and then right quick he shot me, shot me right here (indicating right upper chest) and he come on and when he shot me, he grabbed me somewhere by my clothes, and snatched me, he first shot Shepherd and that left Shepherd facing the face of the car, you know, the face of the car, then he shot me the time he reached and grabbed me, and snatched me, and Sammie too, he snatched both of us and that threw both of us on the ground, and then I did not say anything, I didn't say nothing, so after he snatched me, he shot me again, in the shoulder, and still I didn't say anything all that time, and I knew that I was not dead, and so I heard him say 'I got rid of them, killed the SOBs' but I still did not say anything. He ran around the car, and called the Deputy Sheriff on the radio, and I heard him say, 'Pull around here right quick, these SOBs tried to jump me and I did a good job,' and in about ten minutes the Deputy Sheriff was there. He came from towards Umatilla, and got out of his car, had pulled his car over to the side of the road, and that pulled the car over to where the Sheriff's car was parked, and the Sheriff's light were still burning. The Deputy Sheriff had a pistol, I don't know whether it was his pistol or the Sheriff's pistol, and Deputy he shined the light in my face, and he says to the Sheriff, 'That SOB is not dead' and then he said, 'Let's kill him.'"

You could hear a pin drop as Irvin paused, then resumed his story. "The deputy sheriff then pointed the pistol on me, and pulled the trigger, snapped the trigger, and the gun did not shoot, and so he took it back around to the car lights, and looked in it, and shined the light in it, and then something they said was about letting it stay cocked, and so he turned it on me again, and pulled it, and that time it fired, and went through here (pointing to his neck) and then I began to bleed and bleed, out of my nose." Irvin paused to take a deep breath. He was obviously tiring.

Akerman: "Is that Deputy Yates you say?"
Irvin: "Yes, sir. He shot me the third time, but I managed to pull through OK, cause I did not say anything, and did not let them know that I was not dead, and after all the people came, there was lots of people came there, and some of them predicted that I was not dead, I don't know whether they was all scared or what, anyway, there was so many different people around there and they was all talking so it did not mean much to me. I heard some remarks that 'he ought to have been dead long ago.'" After telling how Yates had fired the sixth and final shot, Irvin simply said, "I tried to keep them from knowing I wasn't dead."

Akerman: "I know you are tired, but there is just one or two questions. Had you tried to jump him? The Sheriff?"
Irvin: "No, sir."
Marshall: "Where was his gun, did he carry it on the right hand side next to you?"
Irvin: "No he carried it on his left."
Akerman: "Where was the flashlight?"
Irvin: "On the floor, under the seat, on the left hand side."
Q: "But both times he took the flashlight out of the car?"
Irvin: "Yes, sir, both times."

Marshall: "Did you ever try to escape that night?"
Irvin: "No, sir, never."
Q: "And you were in the front seat of the car?"
Irvin: "Yes. He put us both on the front seat."
Perkins: "Walter, did you have good hopes of coming out of this thing all right?"
Irvin: "Yes, sir, I sure did, for I sure did have high hopes of coming out all right, and why would I try to escape, didn't have no reason to."
Akerman: "How many times did the Sheriff shoot you?"
Irvin: "Two times."
Q: "How many times did Deputy Sheriff Yates shoot you?"
Irvin: "One time."
Q: "You were shot three times?"
Irvin: "Yes, sir."

Retelling the story had obviously sapped Irvin's already diminished strength. Perkins, who sat by Walter's side during his struggle to retell the horrifying events, reassured his friend as the room slowly emptied. Outside, Marshall was quick to share Irvin's version with the press, but was careful not to issue an ultimatum. The NAACP had been criticized for "outside interference" practically since the case came to its attention and Marshall didn't want to play into the Crackers' hands. Marshall decided to cast the NAACP as concerned observer, rather than judge, jury and executioner. Speaking from the steps of the hospital, Marshall told reporters, "We sincerely hope the good people of Lake County will insist that the action so obviously indicated by the sworn statement of Walter Lee Irvin will be taken immediately." A reporter than asked if Irvin's attorneys would swear out a warrant charging McCall with murder. "For the time being we will leave that to the people of Lake County," Marshall replied. Akerman added that he would ask the governor for "adequate" protection for Irvin. Marshall also demanded through Elliott that Gov. Warren replace McCall's deputies assigned to guard Irvin with state troopers. Finally, Marshall wanted Irvin removed from Lake County under guard of state troopers as soon as his condition improved enough that he could travel. The reporters hurried inside to see if Yates or McCall had any comment. Yates was tight-lipped when asked about Irvin's claim that Yates shot him in an effort to make sure he was dead. "It's a funny thing. No comment," was all the deputy would say.

That night, when the defense attorneys returned to Greenberg's hotel room, they found that the shooting remained the lead story in the final edition of Orlando newspaper. The main article reported that Hunter promised to ask the governor to make a "special investigation" and then quoted the grizzled prosecutor as saying, "This is the worst thing that ever happened in Lake County."

In scrutinizing the article, the defense attorneys noted that Hunter told the *Sentinel* he had been notified around 10 p.m., arrived 45 minutes later and found the prisoners still handcuffed together and lying on the ground. If true, that meant Irvin lay wounded at least an hour even though Waterman Hospital was just six miles away. As for Hunter's claim that "*Apparently* Willis thought they were both dead..." the lawyers saw Hunter's comment as a lame attempt to justify McCall's failure to act to save Irvin. After all, what sheriff wouldn't check a wounded man's pulse to determine if he was dead or alive? To Perkins the implication was clear: McCall knew Irvin wasn't dead; he was waiting for the prisoner to die. Hunter, who was reportedly "visibly upset by the shootings," was also asked why McCall was transporting the prisoners alone, to which he simply replied, "I don't know."

The next day, Nov. 8, Marshall asked the Justice Department to find McCall in contempt of court for killing Shepherd and wounding Irvin. In his letter, Marshall cited the case of U.S. v. Shipp. Stronger words followed. Marshall accused Florida of demonstrating "a determination to whitewash the whole affair," and charged that McCall had "control of the state's investigation into his conduct." Later, after huddling with Marshall and Greenberg, Akerman issued a statement saying the defense team hoped McCall would be indicted by a special grand jury which Futch had promised to call.

While Marshall and Akerman readily granted interviews, the governor's envoy, Elliott was noticeably quiet. His boss was also keeping mum. Warren would only say, "I have sent an investigator into Lake County to check all angles of the shooting." But plenty of people were talking. Irvin's sensational account was front-page news from Miami to Baltimore, and everywhere in between. The *New York Post* headlined its Nov. 8 story from Tavares, "Blood Lust of Sheriff and Aide Bared, Florida Anger Grows in Negro Killing." Jay Nelson Tuck wrote that, "Lake County 'law enforcement' officials were ducking, weaving and scattering for cover today as public indignation, both local and national, mounted over the killing of a manacled Negro prisoner and the critical wounding of another by the sheriff, Willis McCall."

Newspaper coverage resulted in the governor's office being bombarded with phone calls and telegrams calling for McCall's badge and a full and impartial investigation into the shooting. And the NAACP was determined to keep the heat on. In a letter to NAACP officers, Wilkins urged, "We must leave no stone unturned to see to it that the entire Nation learns the facts about this cold-blooded murder of a boy in shackles. We must bring every possible pressure to bear to the end that these legal lynchers are brought to justice. If we fail in this, our whole struggle for human rights will be in jeopardy." Wilkins then outlined a seven-step action plan to be implemented "IMMEDIATELY." Branches were directed to: arrange a "Groveland Memorial Protest Meeting;" send speakers to churches on Sunday, Nov. 11 to "tell the story;" invite people to join in the protest and contribute to the case; release a story giving facts of the case to local newspaper editors and radio stations along with date and place of protest meeting; send telegrams to President Harry Truman and attorney General J. Howard McGrath condemning the killing and "demanding removal of Sheriff McCall and his trial for murder;" canvas heads of "local organizations, ministers and business and professional men, labor leaders and other outstanding citizens of both races" to form an NAACP Groveland Citizens Committee to sponsor the protest meeting; call on the mayor, city council and other officials for comment and resolutions; and contact congressmen and senators to obtain statements to read at the meeting and for publicity.

Besieged by reporters, Judge Futch stressed that a grand jury hearing would have to wait until Irvin was able to participate and the coroner's jury had completed its duty. "It is uncertain because of Irvin's health whether the scheduled special grand jury will be impaneled next Monday, if I carry out my announcement, but I may not," Futch cryptically said. Of course, Futch said there would be little point in impaneling a jury if Irvin decline to testify. The judge also addressed McCall's offer to yield to an elisor from the day before. "The governor said he wouldn't recognize such a person," Futch told reporters.

The *Orlando Morning Sentinel* was all over the story, interviewing principals from both sides and devoting more than 100 column inches to the investigation into the shootings. The paper also published a small story based on the Rev. King's meeting with McCall. According to the minister, McCall was, "regretful of the shooting but feeling what he did was necessary." King then went on a tirade, saying, "What if this incident had happened in reverse -- that Sheriff McCall had been killed or nearly killed by the two Negroes? What would have been the public reactions? Again, I wonder what would be the attitude of the many national organizations demanding an investigation without whitewash if McCall had been killed. Would they have been as sympathetic over an officer of the law killed in the performance of his duty?" By now, the Baptist minister was in sermon mode. "It is high time sympathy be shown officers who must have difficult duties to do. Let us remember a sheriff of Marion County was killed recently by a prisoner he was bringing in. A constable of South Florida was also killed returning a prisoner to Florida," King concluded.

On Friday, McCall was quietly discharged. "I was ordered by the doctor to spend the night in the hospital for observation for a possible concussion. I did not think it necessary; however, I took the doctor's advice," the sheriff remarked. Released in the afternoon, McCall made a brief visit to his office, where he avoided waiting reporters. He then went home, where he was met by FBI agents. "They requested my gun, the clothes I was wearing at the time of the shooting and took samples of my hair," McCall said. When reporters called McCall's home in hopes the lawman was ready to talk, his wife said Willis was "attending to business" that had piled up during his two-day absence from his office.

Three Klansmen had also been attending to the business; the business of tracking down Akerman. A confidential informant would tell FBI agents: "…While riding around Eustis, Jackson went to Sheriff Willis McCall's house on two occasions, not finding him at home, Jackson then drove toward Tavares and on the way Eddie Jackson said to the informant, 'We are going to break you in right.' The informant said, 'Is that so?' Jackson said, 'Yes, we are going to kill Alex Akerman, he's up here defending these Negroes and getting a lot of that NAACP money. Jackson drove to the courthouse in Tavares and after parking the car in back of the courthouse, said to the informant, 'I'm going to see Sheriff McCall -- don't you say anything about it but he's a member. The informant heard the sheriff say, 'No, I'm covered and in the clear on this case and I don't want you to do it, it would only cause trouble.' The informant left the men's room and a few minutes later Jackson returned to the car, stating that he, Jackson, had met the sheriff in the corridor or lobby and had whispered to him to meet him in the men's room. Jackson said he then told the sheriff that he was up in Eustis with a couple of the boys to kill Alex Akerman."

The Klansmen drove from the courthouse back to the hospital in Eustis, reasoning that McCall may have nixed their murder plot, but he hadn't said anything against them putting a scare into Irvin's lawyer. The men staked out the hospital from a drug store across the street, but never saw Akerman's car. According to an FBI informant, Klansman "Eddie" Jackson said, "There is a Negro named Moore, a big SOB in the NAACP that lives in Mims, something has got to be done about him." Claude Waits replied, "We missed on this one (Akerman), let's go get him now." Thankfully, the impromptu plan to "get" Moore was abandoned because one of the men said he had to get back to Orlando.

That afternoon, McCall slipped out of his house to drive to St. Augustine, where he hoped to meet the governor, who was scheduled to give a speech at 8 p.m. McCall was looking for support, and was prepared to convince Warren that further race trouble would erupt unless the governor mimicked McCall's claim that the shootings were justified. McCall had left in secret, but again news of an impending meeting with the governor leaked out. Moments before Warren took the stage, a reporter asked about a possible conference with the embattled sheriff, to which the governor said he didn't know McCall was in town. Arriving too late to catch Warren, the sheriff followed him to Jacksonville, where the men met for about an hour late that evening in a hotel room.

Upon returning home, McCall met with Elliott behind locked door at the Tavares Inn. Neither man revealed what was discussed, but astute observers had a good idea of what happened. "After the conference the governor's representative, J.J. Elliott, sided with the defense of Sheriff McCall," the *Chicago Defender* reported.

McCall may have been in the clear with the governor, but FBI and Justice Dept. agents continued to crawl all over the shooting scene. Special Agent Webb Burke's G-men had even dug up a large area at the scene, sifting the sand in hopes of finding the only bullet unaccounted for: the one that passed through Irvin's neck. The missing bullet could tell a great deal. Finding the bullet near where the bodies had fallen would tend to support Irvin's claim that he was lying on the ground when shot a third time. If the bullet wasn't found, or was found several feet from the where Irvin fell, that would give credence to McCall's assertion that he shot the men while they struggled with him.

The Friday morning newspapers were filled with skepticism, and even condemnation, of Sheriff Willis McCall. Several reporters obviously believed the sheriff *had* committed murder, and were going to great lengths to circulate Irvin's account and print the reaction of his attorneys. Clearly, the defense lawyers and even other reporters were funneling tips to reporters friendly to the defendants. Stephen Trumbull of *The Miami Herald* noted that, "State Attorney Jesse W. Hunter, who according to apparently authoritative local reports, has no personal love for the sheriff, said he would make no statement until he had seen a transcript of the testimony of the surviving Negro." Apparently, Hunter's comment about McCall "peeing in my whiskey" was circulating among the press corps.

And Florida papers were finally challenging McCall's version of events for the first time since Norma Padgett cried "rape." The *New York Post's* Jay Nelson Tuck hit the nail on the head when he reported, "Innumerable contradictions in the stories of the officials concerned remained unresolved; innumerable curious questions remained unanswered. And for the first time in this hate-ridden area, the contradictions were being discussed, the questions were being asked, the indignation was being expressed by a substantial number of local white people. Many who believed that the prisoners were guilty of the crime charged and who believed that they had had a fair trial -- and no one outside of Lake County believed either -- were saying openly that their shooting constituted needless wanton killing and assault."

Chapter 25 -- More Questions Than Answers

Even before the coroner's jury convened, Jay Nelson Tuck predicted the outcome in a story headlined, "Stacked Inquest Mixes Whitewash For Florida Sheriff in Negro Killing." Tuck wrote, "The friends of Sheriff Willis V. McCall were jubilantly counting on his "complete vindication" today at a coroner's inquest into the death of Samuel Shepherd, shot and killed by McCall last Tuesday night. The whitewash was expected to be applied liberally in spite of the sworn statement of Walter Lee Irvin, 23, that McCall murdered Shepherd in cold blood and, with the help of Deputy Sheriff James L. Yates, tried to kill Irvin the same way." At the heart of Tuck's article: discrepancies concerning the sheriff department's radio log. According to Tuck, Hunter said he arrived at the scene of the shooting by 9:50 p.m., but the radio log showed Hunter, who lived more than 30 minutes away, had been called at 9:47. Tuck wrote, "That is why some observers are asking if a true log was kept at all and, if it was, was it destroyed and a falsified entry page substituted?"

As usual, accounts in local papers had a totally different tone. *Orlando Sentinel* reporter Ormund Powers speculated that filling station operator Spencer Rynearson of Umatilla would be a "key witness" at the inquest since he changed the flat tire on McCall's car shortly after the shooting. Evidently, the story that McCall had pulled over to let one of his prisoners answer the call of nature had been replaced by the "flat tire" story. According to the report, Rynearson said there was already a car full of people present when he arrived, McCall "seemed dazed" and it took the mechanic 15 minutes to change the tire. And yes, it did have a nail in it. Most significantly, Rynearson stated that when he asked the sheriff if the cut on his temple hurt, McCall told him his head hurt more where Shepherd had pulled out "a handful of hair." Rynearson said he saw hair in Shepherd's hand and along his shirt sleeve.

In Eustis, Dr. Williams was informed he would get his chance to tell what he knew when the coroner's jury began hearing testimony at 10 a.m. Saturday at Waterman Memorial Hospital. Williams appeared at the hospital an hour before the appointed time and asked to testify promptly, but two and a half hours later, he was still waiting. At 11:30, Judge W. Troy Hall told the doctor that his testimony wasn't wanted, and that he might as well leave. It was a curious directive, considering the jury was charged with determining how Samuel Shepherd died. If the doctor who had examined the body wasn't called, how interested could jurors be in learning the truth? Was a whitewashing in the works?

The coroner's jury had started its investigation by viewing Shepherd's body the night before. When jurors reconvened in Irvin's hospital room they were joined by Hall, McCall, Yates, Dr. Williams, Hunter; the governor's special investigator Jefferson J. Elliott; State Prison Inspector H.D. West, a court reporter; and a nurse. The press was also well represented. Notably absent: Perkins, who wasn't notified that the jury was going to interview his client, and Marshall and Akerman, who had flown to Washington for a meeting with Justice Department officials.

As the hearing began, Walter felt frightened and uncertain. After explaining the purpose of the inquest, Hall advised Irvin that this was his, "opportunity to make a statement concerning your observations, attending that shooting, of Samuel Shepherd, and what you can tell us at this time concerning that matter?" Irvin replied, "My lawyer is not here." Elliott, who hadn't come all the way from Tallahassee to have Irvin clam up, firmly informed Irvin that Akerman was unable to attend the hearing because he had been called to Washington. Hall tried again. "What can you tell us concerning the question I have just asked you?" Irvin did not answer. Hall tried a different tack: "Of course, Walter, you understand that you are not on trial this morning; this is a coroner's jury, seeking information concerning the death of Samuel Shepherd, and you are being given an opportunity as a witness to that death, to make any statement you desire to make here; and all we want you to do is to tell us the truth as you understand it, and can you make any statement at this time regarding that incident?" Reassured, Irvin slowly began.

Irvin said the intimidation began before the prisoners even climbed into the sheriff's Oldsmobile. "The Deputy Sheriff was with him, that's Deputy Yates, and they got us out of the prison, and when we got out to the main entrance of the prison, the north gate as we call it, that's the main entrance, well, there was a few threats made out there, but we didn't pay much attention to them," Irvin recalled. "...and so after that when Mr. McCall, the Sheriff, and this other deputy, Mr. Yates, got their pistols out... and then Mr. McCall said 'I am ready now for anything,' and that's the way we started out." It soon became apparent that Irvin's account of the ride from Weirsdale -- where Yates was dropped at his car -- to Umatilla would differ greatly from McCall's. While the sheriff claimed he had followed Yates at a distance, Irvin told a different story: "...and so Deputy Yates went on down the highway, and we went on and followed him down a pretty good ways, we were following him, and pretty soon he turned off the road, turned to the right, it was not a highway, it was a road, a road that turned off to the right, and so after that Sheriff kept straight ahead." At least one reporter noted an obvious contradiction with McCall's story: "If Yates' was serving as an advance lookout for troublemakers who might ambush the sheriff and his prisoners, why did Yates turn off onto a side road?"

After testifying that the sheriff stopped to check a "shimmying" of the tires, Irvin recalled, "he stayed out there quite a long time looking around, and then he came on back and got in the car, and so we taken off again, and this time he opened up with his siren, not real loud, but just a little bit," A signal to Yates? Hall didn't ask. Saying there was something wrong with the tire, McCall pulled over, took his flashlight from under the seat, got out and went around to the passenger side of the car. "...he came to the right hand front door of the car and said, 'You SOBs get out and let me get a tire to fix my car with,' and he had the flashlight in his hand and he snatched open the door and he unwhipped his pistol and shot. He shot both of us." As Irvin paused, Hall leaned forward and began plying Walter with questions.

Q: "Did he shoot you in the car?"
A: "Yes, he shot in the car, he shot us when Sammie was just getting his foot out of the door."
Q: "Who did he shoot first?"
A: "He shot Shepherd first."
Q: "Was Shepherd in or out of the car?"
A: "He was not exactly either in or either out, he shot him just as he was getting out, and Shepherd fell against the facing of the door, Shepherd did, and he shot him just as he was getting out of the car, and then he shot at me there in the car."
Q: "Were you still in the car when he shot you?"
A: "I was just getting out, but the bullet knocked me into the car, and then he snatched me out."

And Irvin continued to contradict the sheriff. After explaining that McCall shot him twice, Walter recalled, "...and then I heard him say, 'these SOBs tried to jump on me,' and I wondered what he meant by that, because we hadn't done that, and then he got on the radio right quick and called Deputy Yates, and said to him come immediately, these sons of bitches tried to jump on me, and I have done a damn good job of it' and then in about five or ten minutes Deputy Yates was there." Silence filled the hospital room. Irvin haltingly continued, "Well, so he called Deputy Yates, and Deputy Yates arrived there, and when he got there the Sheriff told him everything, and so then Deputy Yates came around the front of the car around to where we were on the ground by the side of the road, and the Sheriff must have met him around there at the front of the car, and I could hear them, I couldn't see them, I was not dead, and the Sheriff had his car lights shining, and they came around side of the car to where I was, and then the Deputy Sheriff looked at me and he said 'This nigger is not dead, we better kill this SOB' so I thought to myself, well, I guess they are going to kill me now, and then, I don't know whether it was his pistol or Sheriff McCall's pistol, but he took a pistol, and the pistol snapped, but it didn't go off, and so then he took the flashlight and shined it in the pistol and I heard them say something about keeping the gun cocked, or something like that, and then Sheriff Yates came back around and threw the pistol on me again, and pulled the trigger, and this time it fired, and it hit me right here in the neck (indicating by pointing neck), and I began to bleed out of my mouth and nose."

According to Irvin, McCall's next radio call was for someone to notify Hunter and Judge Futch. When pressed for specifics, Irvin admitted he didn't hear all of McCall's radio conversations. "...I was pretending to be dead, and I didn't want to have him know that I was listening to what he was saying because he might finish killing me." But Irvin clearly heard McCall and Yates talking after the deputy arrived. "The Deputy Sheriff told the Sheriff that I was not dead and he said 'Let's kill the son of bitch.'" If Walter had felt scared when the questioning began, he seemed to have recovered. He wasn't holding anything back. The deputy had tried to kill him and Walter didn't care if the man was in the room or not.

Q: "Who was the first one back there to you and Sammie and Sheriff McCall after you were shot?"
A: "Deputy Yates was the only one I can remember."
Q: "Can you remember that very clearly?"
A: "I sure can, he stood over me and shot me again."
Q: "If anyone else appeared before Deputy Sheriff Yates returned you would have seen them?"
A: "Yes, I certainly would have if they came to the side of the car where I was, I certainly would have seen them."

Hall wisely changed directions. Knowing the sheriff maintained he let the prisoners out of the car because they badgered him about needing to urinate, Hall sought clarification as his questioning of Irvin drew to a close.

Q: "Now, Walter, have you or Sammie at any time, or either one of you, made any request on the Sheriff to stop the car and let you urinate?"
A: "No, we had not."

Irvin, who had been answering questions for 40 minutes, was wearing down. Williams examined his patient and told Hall that testimony should be concluded for the day. In the hallway, Hall dismissed jurors for lunch. Following the meal at the Umatilla Hotel, the inquest moved to the crime scene, where McCall parked his car in the approximate position it occupied the night of the shooting. It wasn't McCall's first return to the scene. He had already watched the FBI dig up the ground in search of bullets. As the jurors, approximately 50 townspeople and nearly a dozen reporters watched, Hall began questioning Rynearson, the mechanic who had been called to change the flat tire. Rynearson told Hall that he was working on a house trailer behind his business when Yates came by to ask him, "to come out and fix a tire on the Sheriff's car." Rynearson quickly washed out his paint brush, threw a jack in the car, and sped to the sheriff's aid. He testified that Mayor Bryant Calhoun's convertible was already at the scene, and that McCall was talking to "two or three other men" besides Yates, "...and I heard Willis say that the colored boys tried to attack him, when he let them out to urinate…" Rynearson said he then changed the front left tire, which was flat. After putting the flat in the trunk, the mechanic returned home. The next witness, McCall, then identified the flat. Hall then drew the lawman's attention to a nail in the tire.

Q: "I will ask you to examine this nail here in the tire and ask you to state whether or not it appears to have been worn by contact with the pavement."
A: "Yes, it is worn, it looks as if it had been in the tire while the tire was being run; of course, it is a little rusty now."

If any juror thought it odd that Hall asked McCall to speculate what caused a nail to wear but hadn't posed the question to Rynearson (who changed hundreds of flats each year), they held their tongues. After each juror examined the front seat and front door of the car, Hall asked McCall to explain where he was standing when the shooting occurred. In demonstrating how he opened the door, McCall said, "Then he hit me right after I opened the door (indicating by position of body and by opening door), and I don't remember what happened exactly to the door, but I know it was closed afterwards, I think because I fell against it during the struggle, and I imagine that is why it fell shut again." The demonstration complete, the jury returned to the Umatilla Community Building, where the inquest reconvened at 2:42 p.m.

The first witness was Calhoun, 21-year resident of Umatilla and president of the Umatilla Fruit Company. Calhoun testified that council members were talking after their meeting when Yates came in around 9:30 p.m. and asked if the man who ran the filling station was around. After accompanying the deputy to Rynearson's, Calhoun returned to the meeting. A few minutes later, Yates came back, telling the mayor that, "the sheriff had some trouble with his prisoners, and had had to shoot them, and he told me that he thought the sheriff was hurt." Yates then suggested Calhoun and the other council members accompany him to the scene. "…he said he thought we had better get some help and get out there right away, because he didn't know how badly the sheriff was hurt." Calhoun told the jury that he and councilmen Sam Marks and Bill Latner were the first on the scene, and that Yates showed up, "about five minutes after we arrived." He then amended his estimation to, "somewhere between three and five minutes after we got there." According to Calhoun, Mr. Wolfe, City Engineer Joe F. Lee, James J. Hamrick and Johnny Williams appeared next, followed by Rynearson. Calhoun then launched into a surprisingly detailed account of the attack, an attack he hadn't witnessed. "Then Mr. McCall told us that one of these Negroes he identified as Shepherd attacked him, and hit him with a flashlight, and he said that Shepherd told the other Negro to grab his gun, and he said that he reached to get hold of his gun first, and he got it before the Negro did and began shooting, and said that Irvin had grabbed him in the hair of the head, and by the shirt, and then I noticed that there was some strands of hair in Irvin's hand, about the Negroes hand and in his hand and on his clothes, and it appeared to be hair different from the Negroes." None of the jury members found it odd that Calhoun noticed hair in Irvin's hand and on his clothes even though it was night and the prisoner was laying in grass alongside the road.

256

Marks not only echoed the mayor's in places, his story sounded downright rehearsed. Example: "The Sheriff would not let anybody touch the bodies of the prisoners, until after the States Attorney Hunter got there, and as soon as Mr. Hunter got there, they ordered the handcuffs off after he examined the prisoners, and I noticed some hair in the fingers in the right hand of this live Negro, I think his name is Irvin." No one seemed to catch that Marks said he saw hair in the right hand, which was handcuffed to Shepherd's left hand. A clump of hair had now been placed in three hands: Shepherd's right, and both of Irvin's hands, even though Walter couldn't have raised his right hand unless Sammie raised his left. Another comment that seemed a bit too pat: "...they came on the radio and said that they were not able to locate Dr. Williams, but that they were trying to get Dr. Tyre, which indicated that they had been asked to see about a doctor before we arrived." Of course, in a traditional court of law, the defense would have objected to such speculation.

Latner was next on the stand, and his recollection was *even more* detailed. He was not only the first witness to report that McCall told him, "one of these Negroes wanted to get out and answer nature's call," Latner also brought up the hair. "Well, I heard something mentioned about hair, it was not a Negro's hair that I saw in Irvin's hand, I am sure it was not Negro's hair that he had squeezed in his hand, and I also noticed that the flashlight was lying somewhere near his hand and Shepherd's hand." Latner did contradict Calhoun on one point, testifying that Rynearson passed him on the road. If true, Rynearson was the first on the scene, not two carloads of councilmen as Calhoun had said. Latner was also the only witness to say Hunter and Hall were among the earliest arrivals. "I was only there a few minutes, and then I came on back to the front of the car, and Mr. Hamrick, and you (Judge Hall), and Judge Hunter were there, and I got in my car with Mr. Hamrick, and I came on back to Umatilla."

After hearing from others who were at the scene, Hall called 15-year-old high school freshman John Anderson, who lived about a quarter of a mile from where the incident took place. Anderson told the jury he heard "either five or six" shots fired in rapid succession, but didn't hear any shots after that. Anderson's role was clear: to establish that McCall had fired *all* of the shots. Irvin had claimed the sheriff fired five shots, then Yates arrived a short time later and fired the sixth. The testimony surprised Trumbull, who had learned that FBI agents had canvassed the neighborhood without finding anyone who had heard the shooting.

Rigdon was the first witness to detail McCall's injuries. "Well, the left side of his head had a blood stream trickling down his face and his glasses were broken on that side, and I asked him if he had been hurt very much, and he said that his head hurt pretty much." Interestingly, even though others had arrived before Rigdon, the Umatilla cop was the first to mention McCall was bleeding and his glasses were broken. Dr. Douglas then provided a detailed description of McCall's injuries, which consisted of a swollen temporal region, laceration and dried blood on the left side of the sheriff's face. And Douglas was specific about an irritated spot of scalp about three or four inches in diameter where "some of the follicles had been relieved of hair." Douglas testified that the missing hair was on the left side of McCall's head, which means either the sheriff or the prisoners did some fancy

257

footwork if Shepherd struck McCall on the left side of his head with a flashlight and Irvin pulled out a clump of hair on the same side.

John S. Williams, who was coming out of the cafeteria across from the service station when Yates roared into town, was the next witness. Williams said Yates had been leading his vehicle and one driven by Calhoun, but that the deputy "had turned off somewhere," and wasn't at the scene when Williams and Calhoun arrived. Williams remembered Rynearson was first on the scene, contradicting Calhoun and agreeing with Latner.

Jailer Reuben Hatcher, who manned the Lake County Sheriff's Department radio the evening of Nov. 6, then testified to hearing McCall's first radio call to Yates at 9:40 p.m. "... so he said, that is Sheriff McCall said to Yates, 'turn back, I am having tire trouble,' so Yates said 'O.K.' and that is all I heard right then." A "very few minutes later," McCall was on the radio again, this time to KIB853, the sheriff's base radio at the courthouse. Hatcher's wife took the call. McCall told her to get in touch with Judge Hall and Hunter "as quick as you can and get them out here on the Umatilla-Weirsdale road as quick as you can." McCall didn't say what the trouble was, but Hatcher surmised, "It must be with the niggers." Hatcher took the elevator to the garage, got his car and picked up Hunter and then Hall, setting some sort of speed record if his testimony is to be believed.

Q: "When you were driving your car in transporting Mr. Hunter and myself out to the scene do you recall any questions or any conversation concerning time?"
A: "Someone asked me what time it was, and I think it was you, sitting in the back seat, and I said I don't know, but I have my watch with me, so I pulled the watch out of my pocket and handed it back to you in the back seat, because I was running too fast to look at it, and I told you to turn on the dome light and see what time it was, so you took the watch and looked at it, and I believe you said that it was ten minutes to ten, I am not sure..."

At the scene, Hatcher: parked the car; talked to McCall; walked over to the victims and shined a flashlight on them; felt for Shepherd's pulse; talked about calling an ambulance; walked over to Yates' car and called headquarters. Hatcher said the call to headquarters was made "about 10:05 p.m.," but his timeline simply doesn't add up. The drive from Tavares to Umatilla requires a good 20 minutes, without stopping to pick up two passengers. Even if he pulled his car out of the garage by 9:45 -- which is unlikely if the call came in at "9:42 or 9:43" -- it's inconceivable that he reached the scene and did everything he testified to by 10:05. Hatcher's testimony about the call for an ambulance was even more interesting. He testified that McCall had already called a doctor, but an ambulance hadn't been called even though Irvin was seriously wounded and presumed near death. The implication is clear: the doctor was called to examine the sheriff, not his prisoner.

Curiously, the governor's special investigator was called to discuss the radio log, even though J.J. Elliott wasn't even in Lake County the night of the shooting. Referring to a hand-copied page from the Sheriff's Department log book, Elliott reconstructed the chain of events:

Unstated time -- McCall to Yates: "Turn back, I am having tire trouble."

9:46 p.m. -- McCall to headquarters: "Send him two miles out on Umatilla-Weirsdale Road, having trouble."

9:46 p.m. -- Headquarters to McCall: County car 7 has been notified and is en route.

9:47 p.m. -- McCall to headquarters: Call Judge Hall and States Attorney Hunter.

10:00 p.m. -- McCall to headquarters: Call Dr. Tyre.

10:04 p.m. -- McCall to headquarters: Call Dr. Williams.

10:05 p.m. -- McCall to headquarters: Call Dabney (ambulance). Leesburg read message and Dabney is en route.

10:45 p.m. -- Headquarters to McCall: All parties notified.

Reporter Stetson Kennedy found it odd that the logbook itself wasn't presented, only a "copy from the original" made by Elliott. Hall didn't press McCall or Elliott to explain why the original wasn't introduced, and neither volunteered a reason. To Kennedy, it looked like McCall's buddies were stacking the deck in his favor. Hatcher confirmed the accuracy of his radio log, which revealed an ambulance was called just 19 minutes after the shooting. That revelation came as a surprise to Kennedy and other critics of McCall. Obviously, the log had been doctored to hide the truth: that more than an hour had passed before an ambulance was requested, despite Irvin being unconscious with an imperceptible pulse and "in extreme shock." Naturally, Hall asked Hatcher if he saw "any hair in the hand of the prisoner Irvin." Of course, Hatcher did. But the jailer contradicted previous witnesses, saying what appeared to be McCall's hair "was between the prisoner Irvin's fingers on his *left* hand." In fact, he said "left hand" twice.

Hall then called Yates, who testified that he drove ahead of McCall "to see that no road blocks or anything like that were in the way." He was at a red light in Umatilla when McCall radioed him about "tire trouble." Yates said he sought help at the Gulf service station, but "nobody was around," so he went to City Hall, where Calhoun directed him to Rynearson. After asking the mechanic to change the tire, Yates dropped Calhoun back at the City Hall. "I got in my car, and the radio was talking, and Willis was calling me again, and told me he had shot the Negroes, that they had jumped on him, and that he needed help and of course, my first impulse was to jump in my car and get right on out there, and he says to me on the radio bring help, and go and pick up Paul Bryan, on the way out here." Yates testified that his car was ahead of Calhoun and the others who left the council meeting to come to the sheriff's aid, but that they passed him when the deputy attempted to locate McCall's pal Paul Bryan. "...so I went on down the road ahead of them, and I turned in at the wrong house, I thought that Paul Bryan lived in the last house on the right hand side, and so I drove up to the house, the wrong one, and didn't see anybody there, or any lights on, so I had to back on out and switch around and go back to the first house, and I saw somebody and asked him which house Paul Bryan lived in, and he said where all the cars is, they are having a party there, so I drove over to their house where they were having a party, and I saw that everybody was there, and having a good time so I said to myself well, I just can't break up a party because I have already broken up a council meeting, so I went on back out to the road and went on back out to the scene of the shooting."

Yates' tale may have convinced the jury that he couldn't have shot Irvin because others reached the scene before he did, but skeptics found the story awfully flimsy. Neither Yates, nor McCall explained why Bryan was needed at the scene. And few believed Yates would disregard an order from the sheriff because he couldn't bear to break up a party because he had already broken up a council meeting (which Calhoun had testified was already finished, incidentally). As for turning into the wrong driveway, it's possible, but not plausible considering Yates knew Bryan. The "I turned into the wrong drive" explanation seemed made up to allow others to reach McCall before he did.

Yates also told jurors that he couldn't have shot Irvin because his gun was a .45 caliber. Of course, it was already a matter of record that the bullets recovered from the prisoner were fired by a .38. Moments later, perhaps for emphasis, Hall returned to the issue of Yates not being present when Irvin was shot. "At the time that you appeared on the scene there, after having notified the mayor, was that the first time that you had been there at that scene?" Of course, Yates answered in the affirmative. On that note, Yates stepped down.

Finally, the moment everyone had been waiting for: the sheriff was taking the stand. McCall testified that, "just after I crossed Ocklawaha River bridge, Shepherd informed me that he had a call to nature, and wanted to get out and I told him just to hold it until we got to Tavares to the courthouse that it would only be a few more minutes, so we came on to this curve in the road, where we were awhile ago (indicating the scene of shooting jurors viewed earlier that day) and so I made that curve, and come on around it but I noticed that the car did not straighten up easy the way it should, that was the first time I noticed it, I had noticed a little bit something wrong with the car, before that in the way it was steering, but it was not a severe pull until after I came around that curve making a left curve, and then the car would not straighten up correctly." McCall told the jury that he stuck his head out the window and, "I could hear the tire making a noise on the payment, like a flat tire does, and so I pulled over to the side of the road and stopped and stepped out there, and took my flashlight with me and shined my, with me, it is not a flashlight but is a light that I have attached to the cigarette outlet in the dashboard of the car, it is a pretty powerful light with a long cord on it, an extension cord. And so when I got out and I saw that the tire was over one half way down, and so I got back in the car and called Mr. Yates on the radio and told him that I had tire trouble and to get the boy at the Gulf service station there in Umatilla and get him to come out and fix it for me, and then about this time this boy Shepherd spoke up and said 'Sheriff if you don't let me get out of the car I am going to have to do it right here.'"

And then the testimony really became colorful.

Q: "Are you being polite because of the fact that there are ladies present, that is not his exact language is that correct?"
A: "Those are not his exact words, I am trying to be polite, I am phrasing it in polite language, but if it is necessary I will tell you what he said if necessary."
Q: "What you mean to say is that he said that he had a call to nature and that if you did not let him out of the car, he would find it necessary to do it where it was?"

A: "This is what he said 'I will piss in my britches if you don't let me out.'"

A few muffled laughs confirmed that McCall owned the jury. And he knew it. Hall asked him to continue.

A: "Well, I said 'all right, get out of the car and get it over with,' I think I said 'All right, damn it, get out and get it over with' and those were my exact words, and I opened the door, and they both got out of the car, and just as they stepped out of the car, and just as Shepherd was straightening up from getting off the seat, he hit at me with a flashlight and yelled to Irvin to 'get his gun' and hit me with the flashlight."
Q: "Was that your own flashlight?"
A: "Yes, that was my own flashlight, it always lays on the front seat of my car, anyone know me and knows my car know that there is always a flashlight lying on the front seat, I always carry it with me, and when he did that, it knocked me to my right knee, and against the car, and at that time one of the boys, I don't know which one grabbed me by the shirt and I don't know which one it was, and grabbed me by the hair of the head and had hold of my shirt and my hair, and then I grabbed for my gun and got to it before either one of them did and started shooting it."
Q: "How many times did you fire your gun?"
A: "I emptied the gun, it was full, there were six shells in it and I used every one of them. I just had to do it, it was either me or them and I beat them to my gun."

Having taken credit for all six bullets, McCall sought to reinforce that Yates wasn't first on the scene, saying, "Well, first there was a man who came by there in a car, and I stopped him and told him, and I told him that Yates was in town and probably was on his way back, and I told him to stop at Mr. Paul Bryan's and told him to get some people out there, and to get word to the night policeman, I wanted as many people to get out there as I could, and I thought the man that stopped and who I stopped at that time was Johnny, I thought it was Johnny Hobdy, but I'm not sure." McCall testified that Calhoun and "several people" reached the scene before Yates. After McCall was excused, the inquest adjourned.

It had been a disturbing day for Irvin's defenders. Not only had the sheriff's cronies parroted each other as if rehearsed, but the governor's "investigator" had been chummy with McCall throughout the proceedings. "Elliott, who was ostensibly assigned to conduct an impartial probe of the shooting and report his findings directly to the governor, openly fraternized with Sheriff McCall during the coroner's inquest," reported the Dec. 1 *Afro-American.*

The NAACP's Walter White drafted another appeal to Gov. Warren that afternoon. It was the strongest-worded telegram yet. "Revelation of what happened on night of November 6 as related by Walter Irvin is shocking beyond belief in this day and time," White wrote. "According to that statement Samuel Shepherd was cold-bloodedly murdered by Sheriff McCall and an equally wanton attempt was made to kill Irvin. We urge you to remove immediately McCall and his deputy Yates, to have them arrested for this killing and attempted murder and to appoint a special prosecutor for their trial. The nation and the

261

world looks to you to take every precaution to preserve Irvin's life and place him in the custody of law-abiding officers designated by your office."

The inquest reconvened back at the hospital at 6:10 p.m. for Tyre's testimony. The physician testified that he left the hospital at 10 p.m. on Nov. 6, and that minutes after reaching his Eustis home, his wife told him somebody who seemed "to be quite excited and upset" had just called. And then Tyre revealed what a great humanitarian the sheriff really was:

Q: "Did you have to send to Orlando for the whole blood for the transfusion?"
A: "Yes, we did"
Q: "Who made the trip for that?"
A: "I do not know, I requested that the whole blood be gotten, and I suggested that they get the road patrolman to do it, but the sheriff or one of the deputies sent for it, it was sent for by the sheriff."

Evidently, Hall wanted to ensure the point wasn't lost on the jury, for he pressed on.

Q: "Did you say that the Sheriff made the arrangements for obtaining the whole blood?"
A: "That's right. He or one of the members of his department went after the blood, that is my understanding."

And pressed on....

Q: "In other words, he volunteered to go and get the blood from the blood bank or have it gotten?"
A: "Yes, that is correct."

The questioning then turned to the bullet Tyre removed from Irvin.

Q: "Now, Doctor, can you state what caliber bullets those were?"
A: "Well, I can state what I think it was... I think it was a .38."

If the doctor's testimony was intended to prove that *only* McCall shot the prisoner, it was lacking. Tyre merely confirmed what both McCall and Irvin had already stated, that the sheriff shot Irvin twice. Tyre only examined one bullet, since the bullet lodged near the kidney wasn't removed. Also, Tyre never saw the bullet that passed through Irvin's neck. The bullets testimony was practically useless, not only because Tyre didn't examine two of the three bullets, but also because he was less than adamant that the removed bullet came from a .38. An independent ballistics expert should have examined the slug.

If Tyre was following a script, he either abandoned it or missed a cue on the next question. When asked if he had the "opportunity to observe whether or not the prisoner Walter Irvin had any hair in his hand?" The physician replied, "No, I did not observe that." Interesting that the one man who examined Irvin under bright hospital lights failed to see the hairs so many had seen in the dark. Hall immediately abandoned the subject.

Finally, it was time for the sheriff's final performance. And this time he brought props. McCall showed jurors his torn shirt and "badly battered" hat, then passed around the 3-cell Eveready flashlight he claimed Shepherd attacked him with. But the most dramatic piece of "evidence" was yet to come out of his briefcase. But then again, McCall always did have a flair for the dramatic.

Q: "Now, sheriff, do you have any other article of clothing that you had?"
A: "Yes, I do, here is the coat that I was wearing at the time, and if you will look at it, you will notice here on the sleeve are two pistol burns that look like powder burns from my pistol, which would indicate that I was shooting over my arms."
Q: "Now, sheriff, which sleeve of the coat are those powder burns on?"
A: "On the left hand sleeve."
Q: "Are they on the inside of the left coat sleeve?"
A: "Yes, sir, and I will say that Mr. Elliott just brought something out a moment ago, he told me that there could be a blast from the chamber of the gun as well as from the muzzle of the gun, and he said that would indicate the fact that the reason there are two distinct powder burn marks." Hall was setting the stage for Elliott's dramatic interpretation of what those powder burn marks meant, but the judge wasn't finished polishing McCall's image just yet.

Q: "Now, sheriff, did you come to the hospital here in Eustis after the shooting?"
A: "Yes, I did."
Q: "Was the prisoner Irvin brought to the hospital?"
A: "Yes, he was."
Q: "Have you provided careful guard and protection for the prisoner while he was here?"
A: "Yes, sir, continuously. I have posted deputy sheriffs at the entrance to this room for his protection twenty-four hours a day since he has been here."
Q: "Now, sheriff, did you or one of your deputies make a special trip to the blood bank in Orlando on Tuesday night in order to get whole blood from them for the treatment of the prisoner?"
A: "Yes, one of my deputies did. And I also signed a release for his operation, because no member of his family was here to do it, and so I signed a release for the doctors to operate."
Q: "Did the doctors require official permission from someone in authority before they began to operate?"
A: "Yes, that is true in all cases."
Q: "And you as Sheriff of Lake County granted the permission for that operation?"
A: "Yes, I did, and I would like to say this, that I have handled those prisoners during the first affair and have handled them at various intervals since then, and since the beginning of this affair, and we were using the same method that we always used, all along, and the fact is that I went there by myself and got them for the arraignment, and Mr. Yates carried them back to Raiford after the arraignment, and we used the same methods all along ever since." Hall had adroitly led McCall from sinner to saint. But the judge wanted to be sure jurors got the point that the sheriff was protector, not antagonist.

263

Q: "Approximately how many times have you transported these two prisoners to and from the state prison at Raiford to Tavares?"

A: "I would have to look at the books to tell you exactly about that, but they have been back and forth quite a good many times; of course, during the first trial more than they have since, but I can estimate that they were carried back and forth five or six times the other time. In fact, I kept those two boys in my basement in my home until I got permission to put them in Raiford the first time in order to protect them."

Q: "You did that to protect their lives, is that correct?"

A: "Yes, I did. If I was going to do something like they have said that I have done, I would have done it long ago. I just want to say that I am very thankful that I am still here instead of in my grave today."

The final testimony came from Elliott, who had unabashedly moved from observer to participant, a role some thought he was already playing behind the scenes. After qualifying himself as a firearms expert (official referee National Fire Arms Association and member Rifle Association of Southeastern United States of America), Elliott borrowed a gun and began his dramatic testimony. "All right, at this point I wish to say that I believe that this is the most important piece of evidence that we have before this jury, and I wish to show to the jury (taking up the coat belonging to Sheriff McCall and displaying the same to the jury); I want to show this coat to the jury and show to the jury that these two powder marks here, here is a square powder burn, it is a, and then there is another powder mark approximately three and a half or four inches away from the first one, and that would indicate that this was probably a three and a half or four inch pistol, because one of the marks is a blast from the cylinder of the gun, and the other is a blast from the muzzle of the gun." Holding up McCall's coat, he continued. "The blast from the muzzle of the gun results in a flowered effect of the powder burn, and the one from the cylinder is a more or less black squarish looking burn. Now, if that coat were on a man he would have to have his arm up like this (indicating by raising arm up to about level of forehead and looking under arm). It would be the same as if he were trying to fight somebody off or hold somebody off, and the location of these two powder marks indicates that he came very close to having his elbow blown off, which indicates to me some sort of struggle that was going on at the time of the shooting. He certainly was not target shooting. I feel that this is the best piece of evidence we have, because what we see here is that this smaller blackish burn on this coat shows this difference here, that the blast this squarish looking powder burn here indicates that it flashed out from the cylinder of the gun, and this burn over here would indicate that it came from the muzzle of the gun and flowered out. I felt as if I ought to give this information to the jury."

Elliott then demonstrated how, in his opinion, the left arm of the man wearing the coat would have "to be twisted up about in front of his face when the shot was fired." Members of the audience were still murmuring about the sensational testimony when McCall returned to the stand to reiterate that if he had wanted to murder the men he could have easily done so when they were first arrested. "If I was going to do it (shoot them), I'd have done it a long time ago," he said. "I hate that it had to happen," he added. In conclusion, McCall said, "I know that my gun did it all. I am thankful by God that I am here and not in heaven."

The inquest closed with the formalities of receiving the autopsy report on Samuel Shepherd into evidence, and statements by Hunter (stating he participated in the hearing at the direction of Judge Hall) and Hall (who said that Hunter and Elliott were given the opportunity to "further interrogate" each witness before said witnesses were excused). Reporter Stetson Kennedy marveled that there would be no appearance by Irvin's physician Dr. Rabun Williams, or testimony from Dr. George W. Engelhardt, who performed the autopsy on Shepherd. He also wondered why the 15-year-old boy had been called to testify about gunshots he heard, but other 'ear-witnesses' weren't. He had it on good authority that "teen-aged daughters were found who heard the shots, one of them fixing the time as early as 8:30." Why weren't they called?

Kennedy made a list of discrepancies and unanswered questions during the jury's 35-minute deliberation. Kennedy knew what their decision would be. They hadn't been out long enough. Sure enough, the foreman announced that, "Samuel Shepherd came to his death by gunshot wounds at the hand of Willis V. McCall. The said shooting was justifiable by reason that McCall was acting in line of duty and in defense of his own life." As Hall brought down his gavel on the proceedings, applause broke out. A few spectators cheered. Kennedy and Tuck looked at each other in disbelief. McCall had dodged another bullet.

Tuck would later write, "The inquest itself was an extraordinary proceeding. For 11 hours, with only a brief break for lunch, the proceeding rambled, ambled and wandered, doing everything except to consider the point -- and the only point -- that was before the jury: How did Shepherd meet his death? Ninety-five percent of the "evidence" introduced had no bearing whatever on the point. Three witnesses -- almost the only ones whose testimony might have been of any relevance -- were not even called." Besides doctors Engelhardt -- who performed the autopsy on Shepherd -- and Williams -- who attended to Irvin -- Tuck wondered why Leesburg fire chief R. L. Stevens wasn't called. After all, Stevens had heard McCall's radio dispatches on the night of the shooting. Tuck reasoned that "Stevens' account of what he heard on the radio would have had a bearing because Irvin's story opposed McCall's concerning what was said; the times of the various calls also have a direct bearing on the credibility of the witness."

Hunter had little to say when newspapermen came around, save for a puzzling statement. "I have attended each of the hearings today and have been subject to the orders of County Judge W.T. Hall and have taken part in this investigation as I have been directed to do by him," Hunter said. When asked to elaborate, Hunter declined. Obviously, he was washing his hands of the matter. Hall -- or was it McCall -- had orchestrated the inquiry and Hunter didn't want to have his name associated with it. When reporters questioned Hall about the puzzling comment, the judge shrugged and said he didn't understand the remark or Hunter's reason for making it. Another mystery.

Immediately after the inquest, Irvin was bundled into an ambulance to be returned to Raiford, this time accompanied by four state highway patrol units. Kennedy watched, and listened. "As Irvin was taken from the hospital, two veritable Crackers who had seemingly been standing as self-appointed guards all day in the alleyway were heard to mutter, "I wish to God I had a bomb." Gov. Warren didn't like acquiescing to the NAACP's demand that state troopers handle the transport, but he didn't have much choice. He couldn't afford another "accident" at the hands of Lake County officers. As McCall and Yates chatted with supporters in the lobby of the Fountain Inn, Kennedy picked up the coat McCall had left behind. He tried it on, twisting and turning his right arm in all sorts of contortions trying to recreate Elliott's explanation of the shooting. Try as he might, Kennedy couldn't see how the powder burns had been made during a struggle. Later, reviewing his notes, Kennedy pinpointed several other things that didn't sit right. First and foremost, how Umatilla's leading citizens had one after another given testimony supporting McCall's account of being attacked by the handcuffed prisoners. Their testimony smacked of coming straight from a script. For example:

▪ Spencer Rynearson, "heard Willis complaining of a bad laceration over his eye, and said that his head was hurting, and he mentioned the fact that his head was hurting him, and he looked dazed to me."
▪ Bryant Calhoun recalled, "I… walked up to him and asked him if he was hurt, and he said he didn't think so, he said that his head was hurting, and I noticed right then that he was bleeding from the left temple of his face and that his glasses were broken on that side, and I noticed that his shirt was torn and his hair was all messed up, and his clothes were all messed up and rumpled."

▪ Sam Marks, "...I asked the Sheriff if he was hurt badly, and he said that he had a pretty hard lick on his head and he was bleeding pretty badly."

▪ Bill Latner, "…and we proceeded out to the car where it was parked, Mr. McCall's car, and got out and went over and asked him how badly he was hurt, and he said not badly, that he had been hit on the head…" But later, Latner elaborated, "...and I noticed also that the sheriff's shirt was torn, I could not see any shirt under one side of his coat. It looked like it had been partly torn off, and I also noticed that blood was trickling down his face, and that his glasses were broken in one place."

▪ Harry T. Rigdon: "Well, the left side of his head had a blood stream trickling down his face and his glasses were broken on that side, and I asked him if he had been hurt very much, and he said that his head hurt pretty much…"

▪ John S. Williams: "…the sheriff's condition was not too good, because of the fact, I say that because I have known him twenty years, and he seemed to be in kind of a daze when I arrived there, and when I spoke to him he seemed to be in sort of a daze."

The most credible account of McCall's injuries was provided by 27-year-old Umatilla physician L.F. Douglas, who examined the sheriff at the scene and asked the sheriff to come to the doctor's office for a more thorough exam. "I found that his left temporal region was swollen, there was a laceration there, apparently caused by the bow of the glasses having been broken and having struck against his cheek, the glasses were broken, and the bow was bent." Douglas also confirmed someone had pulled hair out: "...I examined his head very closely, I examined his scalp, and he showed me where his hair had been mussed up, which I had noticed, and on the left hand frontal region, I noticed that there was a place about three or four inches in diameter, which was very red and irritated, where I noticed that some of the follicles had been relieved of hair, and I assumed that they had just been pulled out by force, because his scalp was all irritated and red." Of course, Hall never asked if the injuries could have been self-inflicted or introduced the possibility that Yates may have pulled McCall's hair out.

Kennedy was especially bothered that so many men testified to seeing strands of McCall's hair in Irvin's hand in the dark of night, with just car headlights and perhaps a few flashlights to illuminate the area. It was as if they had been specifically told to examine the prisoner's hand.

- Bryant: "... then I noticed that there was some strands of hair in Irvin's hand, about the Negroes hand and in his hand and on his jacket and it appeared to be hair different from the Negroes."

- Latner: "Well, I heard something mentioned about hair, it was not a Negroes hair that I saw in Irvin's hand, I am sure it was not Negroes hair that he had squeezed in his hand..."

- Rigdon: "...and one of them was still living, and he had a bunch of hair clutched in his hands, and on his jacket there was hair of the same kind, and he was lying on his right side."

- Williams: "...and I noticed that I later learned to be Irvin had some hair in his left hand, and on the front of his jacket, he had on a blue jacket, looked like a blue suede jacket..."

- Reuben Hatcher: "...it looked like his hair, it was between the prisoner Irvin's fingers on his left hand." Hatcher also testified he saw hair and "pistol burn" on Irvin's jacket.

- And finally, Yates: "...I helped Dr. Williams when he came up there, he tore up some prescription blanks that he carried with him, that he took out of his bag, and I held the papers, and he pulled some of the hairs out of the hand of the prisoner Irvin, and I put them in these prescription sheets, just like he picked them out of his hand, and I put them in that piece of paper, and wrapped them up, and gave them to you later on."

Kennedy marveled at what an observant lot the witnesses were. McCall obviously made a point of calling attention to the strands of hair. But was it part of his ambush plan to shoot the men, hit himself over the head, rumple his shirt and tear a clump of hair out to place in Irvin's hand? Or had Yates hit him and pulled out some hair? Too bad Kennedy didn't think to enlarge the photographs Bolles took of the prisoners lying next to McCall's automobile.

If he had, he would have seen that Irvin's fingers were slightly curled and there weren't any strands of hair between his fingers. The more Kennedy examined the testimony, the more questions he had. If, in fact, "there were 25 or 30 people standing around," why were so few called to testify? And that number was probably conservative, because McCall testified, "...in just a few minutes there was all kinds of cars coming, there must have been twenty or more cars." And we know at least two of the first cars on the scene carried three men.

McCall was basking in the glow of vindication. Kennedy watched in disgust as the sheriff rode up and down the streets in his car, "tipping his 15-gallon Stetson in acknowledgment of the plaudits of his admirers." As McCall drove past, a Negro leaned over to Kennedy and remarked, "I did so hope to see him busted to driving an orange truck."

Even though the inquest cleared McCall of wrongdoing, friends and foes alike were wondering: why McCall elected to drive a back road from Weirsdale to Umatilla, instead of the more direct, better lighted route to Tavares, Highway 441; and why he was transporting the prisoners alone. As to the latter, McCall would claim that he had transported the Groveland prisoners by himself many times. He would also make the incredible claim that he drove the back roads to avoid the possibility of an ambush. Neither explanation satisfied Akerman. Not then, not ever. "Well, it was kind of an alternate route, and it was not the most direct route," Akerman mused.

One would think both issues would have been raised at the coroner's inquest, but they weren't. And other testimony went unchallenged. For example:

- If the conversation McCall alleged he had with Shepherd regarding the "call to nature" took place, the sheriff was asking the impossible. Tavares wasn't a "few more minutes," it was more than a half hour from the Ocklawaha River bridge.

- Would McCall get out of his car on a dark night without his flashlight? Would he really leave it on the seat where Irvin could get it and hand it to Shepherd? Would he use the spotlight that plugged into the cigarette lighter instead of his flashlight to examine the tire? And what about fingerprints? If one of the prisoners had struck the sheriff with the flashlight, why wasn't it checked for fingerprints?

- If McCall made "several calls" on his radio as he testified, why are only a few recorded in the radio log submitted at the inquest?

- Who was this Johnny -- possibly Johnny Hobdy -- who allegedly happened upon the scene, and why didn't he stay? And why didn't he appear at the inquest?

- Was it really necessary to pump so many bullets into handcuffed men at practically point-blank range if their only weapon was a flashlight? The first bullet that entered Shepherd dropped the prisoner (who would have unwittingly pulled Irvin down with him), thus ending further threat of bodily harm to the lawman. The first shot into Irvin definitely ended the threat. Still, McCall kept firing.

- When did the shooting really take place? The radio log listed McCall's first call ("having tire trouble, turning back") at 9:40 p.m., but Jess Hunter told the Orlando Sentinel that he "reached the scene about 10 p.m., about 45 minutes after I was notified." Does that mean the shooting took place before 9:15 p.m.? If so, where was Deputy Yates between 9:15 and 9:30 p.m., when he called on the Umatilla City Council?

- How did Leesburg Police Department radio operator John W. Dean hear a call from the deputy's car (to contact Dr. Tyre at 10:05 p.m.), but R.L. Stevens, the LPD radio operator from 6-10 p.m., not hear any calls from McCall or Yates? Elliott's explanation that the sheriff's cars "were probably out of range," until 9:40 makes no sense because they were closer to Leesburg at 9:30 p.m. than they were at 10 p.m. when Dean picked up their transmissions.

Numerous questions lingered, but as far as Gov. Fuller Warren was concerned, he and McCall were in the clear. The governor based his conclusion on the Nov. 21 report Elliott filed. "After a very careful and exhaustive investigation I find that the Coroners Jury was well justified in its findings," Elliott wrote. "The F.B.I. have apparently decided to take the case to the U.S. Attorney for presentation to a U.S. Grand Jury, so that they will not be accused of "Whitewashing." They have no incriminating evidence."

That night, Hunter and Hall held a long closed-door session. Only Trumbull noticed, as the other reporters were either filing stories or returning to their homes. Not that Trumbull could score a scoop: Hunter and Hall refused to reveal what they had discussed. Trumbull could only guess, but he imagined it had something to do with Willis McCall.

Chapter 26 -- Moving Ahead

In Alexandria, VA, attorney Alex Akerman was fuming after receiving a four-page letter from the NAACP's Robert L. Carter. For Akerman, who two years earlier had taken the Groveland case when no other attorney would touch it with a 10-foot pole -- and for much less than he should have charged -- and who had stayed involved despite being recalled to Navy service, the letter was a slap in the face. In it, Carter questioned items on an invoice Akerman had submitted. The main bone of contention: that Akerman had exceeded the number of hours (50) he was authorized to spend preparing the case for retrial. Akerman didn't appreciate the criticism, especially since it came from Carter, who hadn't even set foot in Florida. As Akerman sat down to compose his reply, he was more than ready to remove himself from the case. All it had brought him was trouble. "I do know one thing, he said the Groveland case was the reason he was called up during the Korean War. He was so relieved because he knew his legal career in Florida was over. He was not upset, he was relieved... He always said he was not sorry leaving his law career in Florida," Akerman's daughter, Lucy said.

Akerman didn't mince words: "You have made many statements with which I could take issue but I will only mention a few of them... in taking this case it was on the basis of a pure business arrangement of being paid a reasonable amount for the time I would have to expend, not as a public service on one hand nor on the other to take into consideration the public disapproval and pain and anguish that a case of this type would cause me and my family. At the time I reluctantly agreed to defend the men at the first trial and set my fee for that trial at $2,500, it was with the full knowledge that the Association had tentatively agreed to pay Mr. Judge of Daytona Beach $4,500 for exactly the same work. In other words even though I knew that at that time you would have been willing to pay me at least $4,500 I did not ask it as I felt that $2,500 was reasonable. That has been my view throughout the case and the rate of pay to wit $7.50 per hour for preparation which I believe to be reasonable and you too must have believed it to be reasonable for that is the rate set forth in the budget and agreed to by you." Akerman then pointed out that he would have stayed within the 50-hour estimate if the NAACP hadn't asked him to attend conferences in New York and Washington. "I realize that you could feel that it does seem unfair for me to be paid $7.50 per hour merely to talk to you, Professor Harlow or Father Moore either in New York or Washington. On the other hand do you think it is quite fair to me to be paid either $50 a day for investigation or $100 for court appearances to go into Lake County with the attendant physical danger and disapproval by your closest friends? So you see Bob you must take the good with the bad on a case like this and only charge on the basis of the reasonable value of time expended whether it is for a nice quiet conference in your office with you and people of the type of Father Moore, Professor Harlow and Miss Caples or whether it is going into Lake County alone or with Paul Perkins and getting out of an automobile with Willis McCall, who has made personal threats against you, standing on the Court House steps with all the authority of the Sheriff's Office behind him and his gun strapped on him and you having to walk the 100 feet from the car to the Court House door directly towards him."

Akerman also set the record straight on the number of court appearances he had made. Carter claimed the attorney had made only seven, but Akerman answered that he had in fact made 14. "Now one or two other matters; your letter has a tendency to play down the part I have had in the case and to take all of the credit I have had for your office. Again let's look at the record; you remarked it had been your job to attempt to locate Mr. Burtoft, Alexander and Hastings. Miss Alexander was located by Paul Perkins under me. Her statement had already been obtained and her address well known. All your office did was to check with her. Burtoft was first discovered by Mr. Price of my office. We all knew that he was in the Army and many months ago you were charged with the responsibility of keeping in touch with him. When after constant appeals to you to know just where he was when he was badly needed you reported he was in Korea. Through Professor Harlow, for whom I give you full credit, and Mike Thomas, for whom you must give me full credit, it was discovered he was still at Ft. Jackson in South Carolina. As for Hastings, Perkins found him, you interviewed him, he was of no value. You state that the only intricate legal problem in the case is the Search and Seizure of Irwin's (sic) (you state Shepherd's) shoes and that Jack Greenberg is tracking down the law. This is probably true and Jack has done a swell job on this point but I cannot withhold this comment; I discovered this point, Greenberg is developing it. When I attempted to discuss it with you you frankly admitted you did not have enough knowledge of Criminal law and Evidence to comprehend it." Akerman had argued his position brilliantly. It was time for the summation. "So now Bob, where do we go from here? You do not like my fees and expenses. I do not like your inability to distinguish the forest from the trees so we both have told each other about it and I think it is a good idea and I have no ill feelings toward you and I believe you will take this letter in the same vein as you wanted me to take yours. But we still have Walter Lee Irwin (sic) and Willis McCall to consider. If we are to go ahead together we are going to work for only two things, the feeling (freeing?) of Irwin (sic) and the insistence on just punishment to Willis McCall. To accomplish this the former budget must be completely revised and subject to our ability to raise the necessary funds which I believe under proper handling are unlimited. Not one dime should be left unspent to accomplish these two ends. If I am to continue I shall expect without question a reasonable amount for every minute of my time regardless of whether enjoyable or not, to be paid. Naturally I realize that you must keep some limitation on the amount of funds expended but I feel that even if you spend four times more than you have ever spent on any case this would be small as this is by far the greatest case that either you or I will ever see in our lifetime. I would be more than glad to get out of the case altogether unless I felt that you, the Association and Irwin (sic) wanted me to continue just as bad now as you did on the night of August 22, 1949!"

Thurgood Marshall didn't appreciate the timing of Carter's letter. He and Greenberg couldn't afford to lose Akerman at such a critical juncture. If he withdrew from the case, young Paul Perkins would be the lone member of the defense team able to appear as counsel of record. Akerman, who was still a member of the Florida bar, was needed. Carter was instructed to straighten out the misunderstanding, and fast.

Meanwhile, the investigation into the shooting quietly continued. FBI agents Webb Burke and Clyde Aderhold had inspected the shooting scene and sifted the soil in search of bullets and had examined the bullet removed from Irvin's lung. Neither man would comment on what they had, or hadn't, found. Under pressure to reveal their findings, the FBI issued a statement that it would, "continue with its investigation of the case until it is satisfied," even though, "there was no more evidence to be turned up."

From the state capital, Gov. Fuller Warren instructed his troubleshooter J.J. Elliott to remain in Lake County for another day or two and see what he could learn. Stetson Kennedy, correspondent to *The Nation*, also stayed on, but for a different reason: he smelled a whitewash and wanted to play a hunch he had harbored since laying eyes on Elliott.

Unbeknownst to Elliott, Kennedy had joined the Ku Klux Klan in 1943 as an undercover agent for the Georgia Bureau of Investigation under the direction of Gov. Ellis Arnold. It was an unusual career choice to be sure, but Kennedy wasn't a typical Southerner. He had formed a loathing for the Klan in his youth when his family's long-time maid was raped and beaten by Klansmen in Jacksonville, Florida after she challenged a trolley driver who had given her the wrong change. As a self-proclaimed "Klan-buster," Kennedy had moved under a thick veil of secrecy: only two members of the Georgia Attorney General's staff were aware of his spying while he circulated through Atlanta's B. Gordon Klavern No. 5. "It would have been suicidal to have gone to the Atlanta Police Department. They wore their robes over their uniforms," said Kennedy. "The real threat to human rights in America today is not the bedsheet brigade, but the plainclothes 'Klux' in the halls of government and black-robe 'Klux' on the bench." During his time undercover, Kennedy frequently saw first-hand that the Klan had infiltrated high places: even governor's mansions. Kennedy had attended so many meetings and gone on so many "rides" that he had come to know a Klansman when he saw one. And Elliott looked like a Klansman.

Kennedy appeared to be just another well-wisher as he greeted Elliott two days after the inquest. "Although I was known to the rest of the press at the trial as something of a Klan-buster, the attaché knew only that I was a reporter, without knowing my name," Kennedy recalled. Elliott surely knew the name Stetson Kennedy, but he didn't know John S. Perkins, the name on the membership kard Kennedy had been issued by the Nathan Bedford Forrest Klavern No. 1. Kennedy/Perkins gained Elliott's confidence when he told the Florida investigator that he was a freelance writer doing a story for Southern Outlook, which was a widely-circulated mouthpiece for the Klan. Elliott took the bait, hook, line and sinker. After Kennedy displayed his KKK Kard, Elliott replied with the typical Klan greeting, "I see you know Mr. Ayack. I also know Mr. Akai." Every Klansman understood that A-Y-A-K was an acronym for "Are You A Klansman?" while A-K-A-I meant "A Klansman Am I." Kennedy then, "spoke certain other words to Elliott which are required under Klan law."

Satisfied the reporter was indeed a member of the Invisible Empire, and feeling expansive after McCall's vindication, Elliott was happy to share the moment with a brother Klansman. Kennedy recalled, "Leaning over confidentially, he said: 'I don't mind telling you, on the basis of that kard you just showed me, that when Irvin and Shepherd were first delivered to the state penitentiary at Raiford by Sheriff McCall, they had had the hell beaten out of them. When the Raiford officials stripped them for a routine induction physical, they found both prisoners covered with scars and wounds. To protect themselves, they promptly took photographs, sworn statements from Irvin and Shepherd, and filed reports. We had a devil of a time keeping them out of circulation. The statements the prisoners made didn't jibe with all the details, so I was sent over and told to get coherent statements from 'those nigger rapists.' Well, I got a statement, and there's no doubt about it -- they had beaten those boys before breakfast, after breakfast, and at all hours of the day and night. Of course, when you've been in the business as long as I have, you know you can't say 'please sir' to prisoners; you have to kick them around some. Irvin told me McCall used to kick him into and out of his cell." Perhaps the most sensational aspect of the conversation concerned why McCall would risk a political firestorm by shooting the prisoners: Elliott claimed the shooting assured McCall of being elected for at least three more terms. "McCall did not have a chance of getting re-elected before he shot the two colored men," claimed Elliott. Kennedy knew he had a helluva story. And he had a feeling it was about to get better. Elliott appeared to be on the verge of revealing his role in steering the coroner's inquest. And then Stephen Trumbull of *The Miami Herald* entered the room. Fortunately, Trumbull didn't call Kennedy by name. Stetson had to get out of there before Trumbull accidentally blew his cover. Kennedy quickly excused himself and made a beeline to his room, where he hastily gathered his toothbrush and razor. He had to get out of town, and quickly, before Elliott learned he had just been tricked into handing the story of the year to Klanbuster, Stetson Kennedy.

Anxious minutes passed. His secret obviously still safe, Kennedy hurried downstairs, told the desk clerk he was going out, but would return for his messages, then walked to the bus station and bought a ticket to Orlando. Informed that the next bus would leave Eustis in a half hour, Kennedy went to a nearby drugstore to pass the time. He spent the 27 minutes waiting, fully expecting Elliott or one of McCall's deputies to appear at any moment. During his wait for the bus, Kennedy did in fact see Elliott drive by, but the governor's man didn't stop.

In Orlando, before boarding the plane, Kennedy notified the FBI. He also placed a call to Thurgood Marshall in New York to recount the incredible conversation with Elliott. Kennedy must have been convincing, because Marshall promptly wired Gov. Warren to protest Elliott's conduct during the inquest. Wisely, Marshall stopped short of calling Elliott a Klansman. That allegation could wait for a private audience at the Justice Department. "In this case you sent your investigator J.J. Elliott to area to investigate. From his testimony at coroner's inquest it is obvious that he spent all of his time getting together defense for sheriff," the telegram said, in part. "Unless McCall is replaced and your representative J.J. Elliott is replaced and impartial persons are assigned the duty of presenting this case to grand jury State of Florida will stand indicted and convicted of racial injustice before eyes of the world."

The next day, NAACP West Coast Regional Director Franklin H. Williams read press accounts of the inquest into the shooting with a wary eye. When asked if he thought McCall shot the prisoners because he feared they might be cleared at the second trial, Williams said, "No, I think he was just going to get those niggers and shoot them. He decided he was going to execute them himself... He is a killer... This man is a, is a vicious killer." Sammie's family shared the feeling. "It was a dirty way of doing them. Trying to get them to get out and run and then shooting them down like a dog. You wouldn't do that to a dog," Sammie's sister, Fannie said.

The shooting was even a topic at a meeting of United Nations member nations in Paris, where Soviet Foreign Minister Andrei Vishinsky exclaimed, "This is what human rights means in the United States. This is the American way of life. I think some people should look after their own business, before sticking their noses into other people's business." The task of rebutting Vishinsky fell to Dr. Channing Tobias, the United States' Negro delegate to the UN. "We prefer to take our chances in a democracy," Tobias calmly stated. "If there had been such an incident in Mr. Vishinsky's country, there would have been no channel through which the incident could have been made public."

The NAACP was determined keep the heat turned up, and Marshall had plenty of fuel for the fire. Before leaving Florida, Thurgood had called a press conference in Orlando, where he proclaimed that the shooting controversy had done what the Negro press and NAACP had unsuccessfully tried to do: vindicate Irvin and condemn McCall. "Irvin's story was so convincing that all who heard it are certain that he and Shepherd were the victims of a deliberate cold-blooded plan to murder both of them before the retrial ordered by the Supreme Court," Marshall said. The *Afro-American* reported, "Even the local press is now convinced that the wanton slaying of Shepherd and the shooting of Irvin were the brutal, premeditated acts the NAACP attorney asserted."

The report Marshall presented to Walter White was so grave, the latter immediately wired NAACP branches to increase pressure on Florida authorities: "Thurgood Marshall back from Florida with shocking story not all of which in daily papers. Urge that your branch wire Governor Fuller D. Warren, Tallahassee, Fla. asking removal of Sheriff Willis McCall and Deputy James Yates and their arrest and prosecution for murder by special prosecutor to be appointed by governor. Also hold state responsible for safety of wounded Walter Irvin. Get others do same. Be sure reach as many churches as possible Sunday." White then directed Assistant Secretary Roy Wilkins to send telegrams to every influential organization he could think of, beginning with the UAW-AFL International. The telegrams encouraged each organization to follow the NAACP's lead in sending letters and wires to President Harry Truman, Attorney General McGrath and Gov. Warren.

Additional voices of protest came from the ministers who a week earlier had been sent to Florida by the Committee of 100 to conduct an "informal investigation" into the Groveland case. The Rev. Paul Moore told reporters, "There is very little doubt in my mind that it was murder." Dr. Ralph S. Harlow quickly seconded the assessment, saying, "There is no doubt at all in my mind either that it was murder. This case to me, is a stab in the back to our boys who are dying in Korea." The ministers also told the press that in Florida the public -- white and black -- were asking why the sheriff drove alone at night with the two condemned prisoners, and why McCall took a longer, less traveled route instead of the main highway. Their conclusion, which they reached *before* the shooting, was it would be impossible for the two defendants to receive a fair trial. The ministers also said there weren't 12 white jurors in Lake County who had not already made up their minds about the guilt of the defendants. According to the canvassers, those interviewed were divided into two camps: whites who said Irvin and Shepherd had received a fair trial; and Negroes who thought the original trial was a farce. The ministers said they were withholding the names of those they interviewed "for fear of the informants safety." The Nov. 10 newspaper article that carried the ministers' claims also announced that the NAACP had a signed statement from Shepherd's mother that said, "The two men had once been invited to try to escape in order to give the law enforcement officers opportunity to shoot them down."

On Sunday, Nov. 11 the Irvin family set out early for Raiford to see Walter, something they hadn't been able to do while he was hospitalized in Lake County. It was an emotional, but happy reunion. Walter was obviously in pain, but he figured the worst was behind him. He was going to live -- if his tormentors would let him.

Hindered by a persistent cough, Walter slowly began telling the story of his ride from Raiford to Tavares. "He (McCall) say a curse and said, 'I got a damn flat tire.' And (Walter) say he drove more and drove more, and then he said, 'you son of a bitches are going to have to get out and fix it,'" Henrietta Irvin recalled. "So Walter say, when he (McCall) did finally stop, say he got out of the car, kept the lights on. He walked in front of the car, came around to the side of Sam's door and he said, he was handcuffed to Sam here... So when he opened the door for Sam and Sam turned to get out of the car, Walter Lee say he shot him right in his forehead. Just like that. Said he shot him so fast, and he felt his weight moving till, he knew Sam was dead, but by that time he had shot him also. And I don't think

Walter Lee knew he shot him twice." Pain was etched on Walter's face as he relived the horrific moments. "Walter said he was blacking in and out. He said he remembers hearing him saying, 'come on back, I have killed the sons of bitches.' He said when Mr. Yates got back, he was shining his light on, he kicked Sam, and he shined the light on him and said this n----- is not dead. And he said he pulled out his gun and aimed right at his head, and it went right in his neck. And he said that time he was out. He went out. He said he tried to pretend that he was dead, so they wouldn't, you know, kill him. But he still was alive. He still was alive."

NAACP branches made sure Groveland was the topic of sermons in AME churches throughout the country that Sunday. The case had become a lightning rod, as evidenced by NAACP branches that had meandered along for years suddenly becoming active. The action of the already-vibrant Milwaukee branch was typical: a memorial and protest meeting on Nov. 11; telegrams to President Truman, Attorney General McGrath, Gov. Warren and other high-ranking officials; telegrams to 20 local social and civic organizations; petitions circulated and funds collected for the defense.

That evening, White exposed J.J. Elliott in a brutally frank telegram to Gov. Warren. White wrote, "Instead of removing McCall from duty at least temporarily after sworn testimony by Irvin to your representative you left him in complete charge of the case and of Irvin's safety. You also held a two hour conference with Sheriff McCall in a hotel in Jacksonville Thursday night. After this conference your representative J.J. Elliott testified in defense of McCall." White was through beating around the bush: he wanted Warren to know that the NAACP was fully aware a cover-up was underway. In closing, White wrote, "You still have an opportunity to demonstrate whether or not the State of Florida believes in fair play and justice. Unless McCall is replaced and impartial persons are assigned duty of presenting this case to grand jury State of Florida will stand indicted and convicted of racial injustice before eyes of the world and this with complete sanction and approval of the State of Florida. We still prefer to believe that Florida will not thus stand convicted. The answer is in your hands."

On Sunday, *New York Post* reporter Jay Nelson Tuck filed a story examining the possibility of a grand jury convening on Monday in Tavares to investigate the shooting. Even though Judge Futch had announced the session, Hunter had told Tuck he would ask the judge for a seven-day postponement. Tuck wrote, "It was believed that Futch was awaiting the final word from Gov. Warren, who is thought to have been in real control of the case from the beginning, though Warren has made no public statement and has not even answered requests for an interview."

Tuck also devoted several hundred words to the travesty that was the coroner's inquest, particularly, the so-called "evidence." Tuck wrote, "Much was made of testimony by several witnesses that Irvin held in his left hand, as he lay manacled to Shepherd's body beside a ditch on the lonely road, some hairs that appeared to have come from McCall's head. Much was made of McCall's introduction of a shirt he said was torn in the struggle. Most of all, much was made of McCall's jacket, which showed two powder burns on the inside of the left sleeve. Elliott, who qualified (sic) the coroner's satisfaction as a firearm's expert, said both burns had been made by one shot and they showed that McCall had his arm up as if to defend himself." Tuck couldn't believe the jury swallowed the explanations of how the shirt was torn, the hair was pulled and the powder burns occurred. "Nobody pointed out for the record that, whether Irvin was trying to escape or trying to save himself from cold-blooded murder he might have pulled McCall's hair in either case. Nobody pointed out that Irvin and Shepherd, whether trying to escape or whether just trying to stay alive, might have torn McCall's shirt, and, before the jury, none put on the coat and tried to examine the powder burns on a human arm. But I did it afterwards. And I could find no position in which I could hold my arm that would have made those powder burns possible without putting a bullet through my own arm," wrote Tuck, who thought it was obvious the powder burns were made *after* the incident.

Finally, Tuck made a convincing case that the shooting took place much earlier than the jury was lead to believe. He based his belief on statements made by dispatcher Reuben Hatcher, who testified that he received a call at 9:47 p.m. instructing him to bring Hall and Hunter to the scene of the shooting. Hatcher said he then phoned the two men, got his car out of the garage behind the courthouse, picked up Hunter at one end of town, then drove to the other end of town to get Hall. "It would be physically impossible to do all that in less than 30 minutes, and 45 would be more likely," Tuck surmised. Also, Hunter had previously stated that he arrived at the scene at 9:50. Tuck continued, "According to the log, the killing must have been done between 9:40 p.m., when McCall radioed Yates he was having tire trouble, and 9:45, when the sheriff radioed that something serious had happened. But if Hatcher, Hall and Hunter reached the scene at 9:50, the shooting must have occurred at least 30 minutes earlier, or before 9:20. If it took place at 9:20 there would have been ample time for Yates to have returned to the scene, fired the last shot into Irvin and then gone into Umatilla to pick up his witnesses and send a carload of them on ahead to the scene." Another sensational claim: "most of the Umatilla witnesses agreed that Yates first told them of serious trouble at about 9:30," but told a different story on the stand. Why? "He permitted all the witnesses to be in the room together and hear what had previously been testified, and possibly adjust their testimony to avoid conflict," Tuck concluded.

The Post also ran an editorial headlined, "In Florida's Jungle," which lamented the lack of press coverage the shooting received: "We think it is painful that, as of Friday, many leading U.S. newspapers had bestowed only fragmentary attention on the shootings. If Florida's officials can successfully whitewash this ruthless piece of lawlessness, all Americans will share a measure of the guilt. Some of Florida's leading dignitaries like to deplore 'out-of-state' intervention in their 'internal affairs.' But inhumanity and murder are never local incidents, whether they occur in Florida or Prague… The first obligation of establishing the facts belongs to the State of Florida. Having failed once in the proper application of law and justice, Florida must not falter this time. The rest of the country demands the most vigorous investigation and prosecution of such violence. If Florida cannot do the job satisfactorily, then the Department of Justice should step in. On a question where fundamental guaranties are so closely involved, the entire nation is vitally concerned." The magazine *The Crisis*, also ran a stinging editorial, which stated, "There is no civilized country on earth where a man could be killed in cold blood as Shepherd was by an officer sworn to uphold the law. Florida justice seems unable to function where the Groveland boys are concerned."

His brief, and mysterious, "vacation" over, Hunter returned to the business of getting Walter Irvin back in the electric chair. His first order of business: a reply to the defense motion to remove Hunter as prosecutor. The answer Hunter drafted was full of condemnation of the NAACP, which he charged had conducted, "one of the most scandalous, outrageous and untrue campaigns against the people of Lake County." Hunter claimed that, "The people of Lake County were pictured as barbarians, having a farcical trial at which jurors were said to have laughed about wanting to get on a 'lynch jury.' False statements about correspondents and attorneys being run out of the County all for the purpose of creating prejudice in the north against the people in Florida for the purpose of raising money… The reason why the NAACP could not employ white attorneys in this case was that no reputable attorney in Florida would join the NAACP and its lawyers in a campaign of slander and libel against the people of this state." Hunter also took the NAACP to task for calling on Negro churches to have mass meetings to discuss the Groveland case and raise money for the defense counsel. In conclusion, Hunter opposed dismissal because: 1) "there is no prejudice in this county against the defendants and they can be given a fair trial in Lake County;" 2) "the publicity which was given by newspapers in Florida two years ago went into every county in the State of Florida as well as Lake County;" 3) Lake County has complied with the U.S. Supreme Court decision that the jury be, "properly drawn as to the number of white and colored people in the jury box."

Judge Futch regained center stage on Monday, Nov. 12 when he called off the grand jury investigation into McCall's actions, telling the press there was "no need" for further investigation. According to Futch, "… If anyone questions the competency of the Sheriff or wants to charge him with misfeasance or malfeasance, that is an executive matter to be presented to the Governor of Florida and not a matter to be handled by the judicial department of the state… There is no need for a grand jury in Lake County, Florida, and none will be impaneled at this time." The Northern reporters gave Futch's announcement major play. One headline read: "What Florida Will Do About Slaying Of Negro: Nothing."

Naturally, the announcement caused a stir at the NAACP offices, where telegrams to Warren and McGrath were quickly composed. The telegram to the governor, read in part: "The good people of Florida have sacrificed all sense of justice and fair play on the altar of racial prejudice… It has been obvious from the time of the shooting that all of the officials of the county and state have used all their resources for the sole purpose of trying to bolster the unbelievable story of Willis McCall… The investigation of the alleged criminal conduct of McCall was conducted by Sheriff McCall. He kept all of the evidence such as his coat and flashlight in his possession… Who is there to speak for Shepherd and Irvin? How can anyone now complain of quote outside influence? It is up to you to act now." The McGrath wire read: "It is obvious that the State of Florida refuses to act. It is, therefore, up to the Federal government to see to it that a fair and impartial hearing is had to determine the guilt or innocence of Sheriff McCall."

Marshall also criticized McCall and Lake County's brand of justice in an exclusive interview with the *Chicago Defender's* Arnold deMille. "This is the worst case of injustice and whitewashing I have come across in my career. There is no question in my mind or in the minds of others who heard Walter Lee Irvin's statement that he and Samuel Shepherd were deliberately shot by Sheriff Willis B. (sic) McCall last Tuesday," Marshall exclaimed. "Shepherd was fatally wounded. But for a miracle, Irvin, too, would have been dead. Even at the time he talked, Irvin was still not completely out of danger. He had had one operation but still had another bullet left in him near his kidney which could not be removed at that time without killing him. The bullet hole in his neck reminded him with every breath and every word that he, too, could have been dead and might yet die. Any man in that condition is certainly not apt to lie. In listening to Irvin tell what happened you got the impression that he still wondered why the Lord had spared his life. Was it necessary to shoot two men, handcuffed together, three times in 'self defense?' Would not the body of the dead man have prevented Irvin, who was handcuffed to him, from running or doing anything else? Why did Sheriff McCall have only himself to guard two persons charged with capital offense on a road late at night? If Sheriff McCall was that brave, why would he have to shoot them six times? The last, and final questions, is: If Sheriff McCall was shooting to defend himself how could the bullets be so well placed that none of them went wild?" deMille wasn't the only reporter who gave Marshall ink. Thurgood had always been good copy, but few reporters had ever seen the lawyer this worked up. Marshall, who used to tell colleagues that he put his civil rights in his back pocket went he traveled the South, was pulling no punches on this one. "Irvin's story was so convincing that all who heard it are certain that he and Shepherd were the victims of a deliberate cold-blooded plan to murder both of them before the retrial ordered by the Supreme Court," Marshall told reporters.

Tuck gave credence to Marshall's claims in a Tuesday, Nov. 13 story in the *New York Post* headlined, "6 Wounds Indicate Prisoners Did Not Attack Florida Sheriff." According to Tuck, "Every one of the six bullet wounds in the bodies of Samuel Shepherd and Walter Lee Irvin gives powerful though silent evidence in favor of Irvin's charge that Sheriff Willis V. McCall murdered Shepherd and tried to murder Irvin in cold blood, an analysis by *The Post* showed today," Tuck wrote. Tuck's findings:

• Shepherd was killed by a shot to the head and the bullet "traveled inward, downward and forward," before exiting his head. If McCall's account was true, then Shepherd would have been between the sheriff and the car and the bullet "should have struck the car," but "there was no bullet mark on the car."

• If McCall was "struggling with a man who was trying to seize a revolver from your waist holster," Irvin would have been shot "in the head, shoulders or chest, probably from straight on." But Irvin was shot in the side of the chest, with the bullet traveling downward, which supported Irvin's claim that the prisoner was sitting on the front seat when McCall stood beside an open car door and shot him.

- "The second shot entered the left side of his chest, crossed his body and came to rest in his shoulder," which made perfect sense if Irvin was lying on his right side on Shepherd's body as witnesses testified.

- "The third shot struck him in the right side of the neck, went through and emerged from the left side. Not a single one of the shots that struck Irvin was fired from in front. All were fired from one side or the other. Moreover, had he been standing and struggling with McCall when the shot was fired into his neck, that bullet too would in all likelihood have struck the car."

Interestingly, no sources were quoted. Had one of the FBI agents talked? Was Marshall feeding Tuck? Or was the reporter playing amateur detective? No one knew. Regardless of the source, Tuck clearly felt the jury was negligent in failing to analyze the paths of the bullets. According to Tuck, "…not one scrap of this medical evidence was considered by the Coroner's Jury in the course of its "thorough job." The only medical evidence they were given was the brief testimony of a physician as to what he had observed at the scene while Williams was treating Irvin and a rapid reading of an autopsy report couched in complex medical language utterly unintelligible to the layman."

The barrage of media attention drew individuals and organizations intent on capitalizing on the misfortune of Shepherd and Irvin. The Groveland case was Marshall's all the way, but that didn't prevent the communists, who had elbowed their way into the infamous Scottsboro Case, from trying to use the shooting to grab some headlines. The National Committee of the Communist Party released a scathing statement demanding action by President Truman. The statement read in part, "The cold-blooded, brutal white supremacist lynching of one Negro youth and attempted lynching of another by Florida authorities this week was continuation of the Wall Street imperialists' policy of genocide against the Negro people of the United States -- a policy which has been exported overseas and taken a toll of three million Korean lives." The statement called for the following action by, "all labor unions, all fraternal organizations and church organizations, Negro and white, all organizations of individuals who want to stop fascism in America:"

- "First, that President Truman return at once from his vacation among the racist murderers in Florida and take charge of the punishment of Florida officials for the cold-blooded white supremacist killing of Samuel Shepherd and countless other Negroes."

- "Second, that Lake County and the State of Florida pay full indemnity to the families of the victims of this racist policy."

- "Third, that the District Attorney General of the State, and the FBI in that area be investigated to establish their complicity in these crimes."

Many of the reporters who covered the inquest had left Lake County and moved on to other stories, but Tuck continued to monitor the case. On Nov. 15, he reported that the FBI had found a spent bullet where Shepherd and Irvin were gunned down by McCall.

According to Tuck, "Such a bullet, if found in the sand on which the bodies lay, would be strong evidence to bear out Irvin's charge that McCall fired as Shepherd lay dead and Irvin lay wounded on the ground... The bullet and other evidence is now in FBI headquarters in Washington being tested and analyzed." On Nov. 16, Tuck broke another big story when he wrote that Futch was planning on granting the defense's change of venue request, and that the retrial of Walter Lee Irvin would be held in Gainesville, approximately 60 miles north of Tavares.

Tuck finally returned to New York after more than a week of filing hard-hitting stories from Lake County. McCall was glad to see him go. The Crackers may have initially rejoiced to learn the *Post* had sent Tuck instead of Ted Poston, but they soon realized the new reporter was as antagonistic as the former. Tuck's farewell: "'Good' Floridians Blind to Own Bias" was a parting shot worthy of Poston's award-winning coverage. It was a story no newspaper south of the Mason-Dixon line would have published. Tuck wrote, "Prejudiced? Don't call us prejudiced: we're not. We're kinder to Negroes than you Northerners are and we like them -- in their place. One of the decent citizens of Florida was talking. He was perfectly honest. He believes -- and with considerable justice -- that the Negro suffers in the North much the same discrimination that he does in the South, but in a subtler and more hypocritical form," Tuck wrote. "He couldn't see the snapper in those words, "in their place." He couldn't understand that, while the attitude he embodies might be all right for a Negro who wants charity, even at the price of servility, many if not all Negroes might prefer justice and independence. Such a Negro down here is called "uppity" or "biggity." To be uppity is perhaps the greatest crime a Negro can commit, short of assault upon a white person. They say Samuel Shepherd was uppity. His parents had done well enough so that he did not need servility to keep from starvation. That uppitiness may be what cost him his life... To this decent citizen -- and to almost every other citizen of this part of Florida -- the Supreme Court's action made no sense... They firmly believe that the Negro is inferior to the white man in intelligence, ability and morals. They regard him as a kind of grown-up child, to be accorded charity instead of rights, guidance instead of independence, paternalism instead of democracy. You can't shake these people with arguments, statistics, facts. They'll freely admit to you that, say, Ralph Bunche and Marian Anderson are among the greatest living Americans. They'll also freely admit that they would have neither in their homes... These are the good white people. It is hard to write at all about the "Cracker" -- some of whom believe the Negro is not even an inferior human being, but an animal, with no right at all but to work and not even that if it interferes with the work of the white man. You know the South's attitude on race before you come: you've been South before. You know what to expect in Lake County. Even so, it hits you like a slap in the face; hits you at every turn. The drinking fountains and toilets, each primly marked for white and colored. The fact that everyone refers, not to, say, Irvin, but, according to his taste, either to the Negro Irvin or the nigger Irvin. They tell you that the Negro's counsel Alex Akerman Jr., made a great mistake in their trial when he called Negro witnesses 'Mr.' it offended the jurors... They cannot see the sheer, filthy offensiveness of it when Sheriff McCall tells a public inquest that he opened his car window in the rain 'because the nigger smell got too strong.'"

While the *Post* went for the jugular, The *Orlando Morning Sentinel* continued to wear kid gloves. The paper reported that the bullet found in the sand had been fired by a .38 caliber pistol, before pointing out that Yates carried a .45 caliber revolver as his usual equipment. Of course, the conclusion that all six bullets had come from McCall's weapon was premature. FBI agents were still awaiting ballistics tests on McCall's gun, the recovered bullet and bullets removed from Shepherd and Irvin. Oddly, Yates' gun wasn't sent to Washington for comparison. Still, McCall and his supporters claimed vindication. "Physicians who examined Shepherd and Irvin said the bullet holes in the men were all apparently of the same size and in their opinion where made with a .38 caliber gun," the *Sentinel* reported. "J.J. Elliott, Gov. Warren's investigator, said that in his opinion all bullet holes in the two were made with the same gun or at least they appeared to be made with bullets of the same caliber. Elliott pointed out that a .45 slug would make a considerably larger wound than found in the two men."

Still, McCall was catching plenty of heat in the press, which only made the good ole' boys rally around their man. Just days after the shooting, McCall received a congratulatory telegram from the Florida Peace Officers Association, which read, "Proud of a fellow officer who with courage acted as a peace officer deserving our full comradeship." The *Afro-American* took exception to the commendation, saying, "This reminds me of the manner in which the Klan commonly sends letters of congratulations to quick-trigger policemen for killing colored persons 'in line of duty.'" Lawmen across the state had no doubt McCall had acted in self defense. "What happened on the road from Starke, that really happened. They were mean niggers," said Noel Griffin, who would become a Lake County deputy in 1956. After admitting he had never met Irvin or Shepherd, Griffin remarked, "You put two bucks together and you can't tell what they'll do... When a man is going back to jail they'll do funny things. And they'd been in jail before. And they don't want that. There's nothing worse than confinement."

Harry T. Moore, who sent a telegram urging suspension of McCall to Warren on Nov. 11, followed up with a detailed letter on Nov. 15. "...we are inclined to wonder if there was not some 'whitewashing' in an effort to clear the two officers. We even question the manner in which the investigation and inquest were held. According to Irvin's statement, McCall and Yates already had come within a fraction of an inch of killing him. Then why would these officers be permitted to enter Irvin's room -- probably with guns strapped to their sides -- while the Negro was giving testimony against them? Is it a wonder that Irvin had nerve enough to tell his side of the case under such conditions. We wish to renew the requests made in our recent telegram. Omitting the question as to whether or not McCall shot in self-defense, we think he ought to be suspended because of his carelessness in handling the prisoners. In the first place, was it wise and safe for one officer to be on a lonely road at night with two prisoners charged with a capital offense, when this one officer must drive the car and guard the prisoners? This, in our opinion, was carelessness in the 'nth' degree." In closing, Moore boldly laid the blame for shooting squarely at the feet of the governor. "It is quite plain to any close observer that Shepherd's life could have been spared, Irvin's suffering prevented, and the entire situation avoided if the proper precautions had been taken. In our letter to you on Aug. 4, 1949, we made this plea: 'We ask also that these

Negroes not be entrusted to the custody of Lake County officers again, but that they be permitted to leave Raiford only under a special guard appointed by you.'...If this request made to you in 1949 had been granted -- if State Patrolmen had been assigned to help escort these prisoners in all future transfers, this unfortunate incident of Nov. 6th could have been avoided."

On Nov. 17, Irvin's account of the shooting received widespread circulation in weekly Negro newspapers that had been caught short because the incident happened *after* the deadline for their Nov. 10 editions. The *Afro-American* summed up the atrocity in six-tier headline: "Prisoner Outwits Shooting Sheriff by Faking Death Groveland Case Youth" and a subhead that read, "With Bullets in Throat, Chest and Kidney, Lives to Tell How Trigger-Happy Officer Killed Shepherd, Wounded Him; Were Handcuffed."

Two days later, Hunter filed his answer to the defense's change of venue motion. The grizzled prosecutor pulled out all the stops in a five-page answer in which he denied, "each and every allegation," and derided the NAACP. "Certain designing persons took advantage of the flaring head-lines (sic) in reference to what had occurred in South Lake County to call the National Association for Advancement of Colored People into this case. Immediately a Negro attorney by the name of Franklin Williams, who is a radical hater of the south, announced in New York before he had made any investigation whatever, that the defendants were innocent... No witnesses were interviewed, although the names of the witnesses were placed on the indictment. No request was made for a copy of the indictment. Finally, after more than two weeks, no one having appeared for the defendants, the Honorable T.G. Futch appointed Harry Gaylord, a high-class, able and honorable attorney to represent them... These men were not satisfied with Mr. Gaylord's idea that this case should be tried on its merits because they were in the case for the sole purpose of creating race discord and capitalizing upon falsehoods to enable them to raise large sums of money in the north. The sums which were asked were so large that they could not legitimately be used in the defense of the defendants, especially in view of the fact that Lake County, under an insolvency affidavit, was paying all expenses except the attorneys' fees," Hunter wrote.

If only that were the case. When it became clear Irvin would live to be retried, fund-raising efforts were renewed. Marshall reminded NAACP supporters, "...It required great courage for white Attorney Alex Akerman of Orlando, Florida to risk his career in defending these boys; for Reverend Harlow and his associates to go into hate-ridden Lake County to investigate this frame-up; and for legal staff members of the N.A.A.C.P. to appear as associate counsel for the defense. But their courage needs the moral and financial backing of thousands of decent people if we are to bring Lake County under the operation of the American code of equal justice for all."

Marshall again urged the Attorney General's office to find McCall in contempt of the Supreme Court for slaying Shepherd. "This action of McCall involves not only the killing of Shepherd and serious wounding of Irvin but is a direct affront to justice in this country and was in defiance of the U.S. Supreme Court and the laws of this country," Marshall charged. Marshall told the *Chicago Defender*, "The question is this: Is a defendant in a state of criminal proceeding who has taken his case to the United States Supreme Court surrounded by special federal protection until the case if finally disposed of? Some experts in the Justice Department think such protection exists, that such a defendant is in a sense 'a ward' of the highest tribunal."

It was a long shot to be sure, but the scenario wasn't without precedent. Marshall found a case from the early 1920s (U.S. v. Shipp) where a state court defendant, who had asked the Supreme Court to review his case, was killed by a mob before he could be given a retrial. Marshall detected a parallel between the shooting and "Shipp," where a lawyer had released a prisoner to a mob, which lynched the man. "In that case the action was brought by the Attorney General of the United States and we believe this precedent authorizes you as Attorney General to take similar action in this case," Marshall wrote. "In the Shipp case, the act was not only against the sheriff, who violated a specific order to him concerning the prisoner, but also applied to the members of a mob which lynched the prisoner." In "Shipp," the U.S. Attorney General ruled that the murdered man was a ward of the Supreme Court. When mob members responsible for the murder were arrested, they were fined, then sent to jail for "contempt." The members of the mob were not covered by the order of the Supreme Court, but Justice Holmes stated, "It may be found that what created the mob and led to the crime was the unwillingness of its members to submit to the delay required for the trial of the appeal. From that to the intent to prevent that delay and the hearing of the appeal is a short step. If that step is taken the contempt is proved." Marshall told reporters that if a case against McCall was presented to a grand jury called by U.S. District Court and the sheriff was indicted and convicted for violation of the Civil Rights statute, the maximum penalty would be one year's imprisonment and a $1,000 fine.

Each day seemed to bring a new disclosure. Those keeping a close eye on the case could only wonder what would happen next. Few would have guessed the defense would receive a remarkable lead in the form of an anonymous typewritten letter delivered to Perkins' office in late November. The poorly composed letter corroborated Irvin's claim that he had been shot by Yates after he had been dropped by shots from McCall's gun. The letter read, "Sir if you are in need of a Witness that was (unintelligible) rite at that Sheriff when he Shot that Negro I will Put you on to a man that will testifi on any stand tha he and his budy Saw the hole thing this man is a organge pickir and come from up the country to pick fruit if you will make apointment to See him at Wintergarden his name is Will Wages and gets his mail at Wintergarden gen delivery. I am a friend to this negros dady I use to work his dad on the farm but I have lost site of the old man since all this has got up so I wish you would see Will Wages but as he is picking fruit you will have to write him to come to see you or make appointment so you can find at Wintergarden. Im doing this for the Negro as I use to no his dady and I no he was a good old Negro and I would like to help him if I can and he knows all you need to prove that he was shot after he fell by this other Sherif and his name is Will Wages Winter Garden Fla General delivery Please write him at once as he may leave."

Without delay, Perkins sent a letter via general delivery to Wages, asking the man to come to his West Jackson Street office in Orlando or to call his home. A reply, scrawled in barely intelligible longhand came just over a week later. "I had no car. An I am a roomer up stairs over Rexall Drugstor. I am hear from 7 at night til 6 in morning. Yours truly, W.E. Wages." Perkins went in search of Wages as soon as his schedule permitted. It was a futile trip: he couldn't find the mysterious man who could vindicate Walter Irvin.

Chapter 27 -- Stetson's Tale

Stetson Kennedy, who had chronicled Southern life in ground-breaking books *Palmetto County* and *Southern Exposure*, had no trouble convincing the editors at *The Nation* to let him second-guess Sheriff Willis McCall and the coroner's jury that cleared him in the murder of Samuel Shepherd.

Kennedy did so in the Nov. 21, 1951 article, "Ocala: Old Trials in New Bottles (Murder without Indictment)," which summarized the Groveland case from the beginning. Kennedy boldly wrote that, "When Irvin, Samuel Shepherd, and Charles Greenlee were arrested, the mob demanded that Sheriff Willis McCall surrender them for lynching. Instead, he deputized the mob and sent it on a manhunt for a fourth 'suspect,' Ernest Thomas." Kennedy then challenged Willie Padgett's identification of Irvin: "Mr. Padgett insisted that he had recognized Irvin upon the arrest at this home, and two policemen added that they had restrained Padgett from attacking Irvin at the time. Irvin, however, emphatically denied that any such identification or attempted attack took place. Padgett did admit that it was after witnessing Irvin's arrest that he 'identified' him from 'six or seven head of colored' at the jail." So where did Padgett identify Walter, at the Irvin home, or at the jail?

The ink was barely dry on article when editors at the *Afro-American* invited Kennedy to provide a first-person account of his investigation from Lake County, including the unwitting admission by the governor's envoy that he belonged to the Ku Klux Klan.

The *Afro-American* published Kennedy's riveting account, "Florida's Open Season on Prisoners," on Dec. 1. Kennedy wrote, "...the case seems to have no comparable precedent in all of America's history of Negroes who have been 'shot down in line of duty' by officers of the law." The inside story was gripping from the opening paragraph: "After a plane flight out of Florida and a midnight stopover at FBI Headquarters in Washington, I can now tell the world that an attaché to Gov. Fuller Warren's office has confided to me as a "brother Klansman" that law enforcement officials have long had and suppressed photographs and sworn statements attesting to the brutal beating of Samuel Shepherd and Walter Lee Irvin, while in the custody of the sheriff's office." In the second paragraph, Kennedy revealed that, "A Federal grand jury which was impaneled to probe rumors of such beatings back in 1949 was not given this conclusive and shocking evidence, and the prisoners have been too intimidated even to confide in their defense lawyers." Kennedy wondered what had become of the photos the FBI had taken of the prisoners, "which must have existed at least in triplicate." Kennedy also revealed that Sammie had told his mother of the brutal beatings, and that he had undergone an operation on as a result. Prison Superintendent L. Chapman promptly denied the allegation.

On page 2, under the headline "Evidence Freeing Shooting Sheriff Could Be Planted," Kennedy suggested that, "the whole thing could have been planned in advance, and the 'evidence' prepared before and after the event... Maybe he decided it was a case of kill or be killed -- literally for the prisoners or politically for him." As for the coroner's jury, Kennedy noted that "McCall was treated as a beloved guest of honor, and invited to interrupt at any point to 'clarify' whatever questions arose. Every witness heard and every piece of evidence received tended to vindicate the sheriff. On the other hand, not once did the judge or jury ask any questions which would even imply credence in any phase of Irvin's testimony. The most significant things about the inquest were the questions not asked and the witnesses not produced." Kennedy then pinpointed 10 "gaping holes into which a Federal grand jury might look for evidence that U.S. civil rights statures were violated..." Eight of the 10 "holes" had never appeared in print:

1. Testimony set the time of the shooting at approximately 9:30 p.m., but a woman and her two teenage daughters who said they heard the shots around 8:30 p.m. were not called.

2. Deputy Yates testified that he interrupted a meeting of the Umatilla City Council at 10 p.m. because McCall had radioed him to find a service station so he could get a flat tire repaired. However, the radio log showed McCall ordering Yates to "turn back" at 9:40. Was Yates at the shooting scene before the councilmen arrived as Irvin had claimed?

3. *Lake Region News* editor Marie Bowles said that the shooting victims were not handcuffed when she arrived, even though every other witness said the handcuffs stayed on until Hunter ordered them removed. When Kennedy asked Bowles about the discrepancy, she replied, "They positively were not handcuffed when I arrived, I don't care what the others say. But I guess I shouldn't discuss the case, since I am a member of the jury."

4. Leesburg Police officer John Dean testified he overheard radio calls McCall made after 10 p.m., but his boss, Chief Stevens, who was on duty until 10 p.m., wasn't called to testify about conversations he may have heard over the radio before Dean took over.

5. The jury accepted McCall's claim that the shooting took place around 9:30 p.m., but Irvin wasn't admitted to Waterman Memorial Hospital until 11:15 p.m. Kennedy knew -- he checked the hospital records. Waterman was six miles from the shooting scene, yet Irvin bled from three bullet wounds for an hour and 45 minutes.

6. McCall claimed one of the prisoners had struck him with his flashlight, but no questions were asked as to whether the light had been checked for fingerprints.

7. School children allegedly found unexploded .38 cartridges at the scene of the shooting before the area was searched by FBI agents. As for the cartridges the G-men found, no one asked whether the cartridges bore any marks of a firing pin, which would have been indicated by Irvin's claim that the gun had misfired twice before firing.

8. Much was made about the powder burns Jefferson J. Elliott found on McCall's coat, but the burns do not show in the photographs of the sheriff taken at the scene.

Kennedy was also intrigued by McCall's choice of words in summing up the shooting. "I know that my gun did it all," he had said. Kennedy noted that, "It may be purely coincidental, but it should be noted that McCall did not say he fired all of the shots."

In New York, Marshall focused on making the most of the shooting. The defense had no chance of getting the case moved out of Lake County before McCall gunned down his prisoners, but now Judge Futch would *have* to grant the request. With guidance from Marshall and Jack Greenberg, Orlando attorney Paul Perkins drafted a strongly-worded Motion for Change of Venue, which he filed the first week of December. In it, the defense charged McCall with the wanton and reckless murder of Shepherd, and Yates with attempted murder. The motion also stated that the coroner's jury had been quickly impaneled and that one member, before she even heard testimony, said McCall was completely justified in killing Shepherd. Perkins was referring to Marie Bolles, the photographer who was so conveniently summoned to capture the image of a disheveled McCall. In the amended motion, Perkins called the jury's verdict a "whitewashing" and said McCall's sworn testimony showed he was guilty of murdering Shepherd. Irvin's statement of Nov. 8 was attached as an exhibit. There was nothing subtle about the new motion.

Hunter promptly drafted replies to the defense motions. As expected, Hunter vehemently denied that he held any prejudice toward members of the Negro race, and went so far to say: "There is no prejudice in this county against the defendants and they can be given a fair trial in Lake County." Hunter claimed that Shepherd and Irvin tried to kill McCall and that the matter was thoroughly investigated by the coroner's jury. As for Bolles' comments, Hunter reasoned, "There was nothing improper in any member of said Coroner's Jury stating that McCall was justified in killing Samuel Shepherd before hearing the Coroner's testimony... the rule of evidence in a Coroner's inquest being entirely different from the rule of evidence covering petit juries, a fact which the attorneys for the defendant in this case seem not to know or have confused." After saying he had always protected the rights of Negroes, Hunter stated:

- "…the defendant's attorney and their employers are attempting to inject race hatred into this cause, which the State Attorney deplores."

- "That one Ted Poston, claiming to be a correspondent for certain newspaper in the North and a representative of the National Association for Advancement of Colored People, wrote certain libelous stories about the former trial of the defendants… and among other things, he charged that the prospective jurors, 'were begging for an opportunity to sit on the 'Lyncy jury' as he said they called themselves in the trial of this case; and further claimed to have been chased out of Tavares by a howling mob and run for a distance of thirty miles."

- "The matters and things set up in said motion… are false and known to be false by the attorneys who wrote this motion… they are not intended to settle any issue before this court but to be used in northern newspapers for the purpose of trying to create impression that the people of Lake County are unfair to colored people… this motion is a part of campaign of slander and libel against the people of Florida for the purpose of raising large sums of money to pay the salaries and expense of an army of persons using a criminal case as a means of raising money and creating race hatred and dissention in the South."

- "This court has no authority to disqualify or remove the state attorney of this circuit, said authority being vested on in the governor of the state."

- "As in everything else these attorneys (defense) have done in connection with this case, they have falsified this case or put construction on it that was not warranted by the facts themselves."

As for the charge that he had flown to Washington, D.C. to run interference for McCall, Hunter stated, "…he has not been in the City of Washington, D.C. in more than ten years and never in the Attorney General's office in his life." In addressing the change of venue motion, Hunter listed three reasons to keep the trial in Lake County. In addition to reiterating that there was no prejudice in Lake County, Hunter also claimed:

- "The so-called publicity which was given by the newspapers in Florida two years ago went into every county in the State as well as Lake County."

- "The Supreme Court of the U.S. has reversed this case for further trial on the ground that the jury was not properly drawn as to the number of white and colored people in the jury box. Lake County has fully complied with this decision of the U.S. Supreme Court."

Hunter's answer also included affidavits from long-time friends and associates, most who pulled out all the stops to portray Jess as a fair-minded humanitarian who lived to help his fellow man, particularly those with darker skin. The affidavit of Ocala attorney James

M. Smith Jr., who served as Hunter's assistant in the 5th Judicial Circuit office, 1935-'39, was typical. It said, in part: "J.W. Hunter has never exhibited any bias or prejudice against members of the colored race... J.W. Hunter has always taken a liberal, tolerant, fair and impartial attitude toward members of the colored race generally, and particularly in his dealings with those members of the colored race charged with crime."

Former Citrus County Sheriff Charles S. Dean cited a specific example of Hunter's impartiality: "... The Grand Jury found an indictment against a Negro for killing a white man... There was considerable feeling about the matter. At the close of the testimony Mr. Hunter called the affiant to one side and told him he did not believe the state had made a case against the man. I went with the State Attorney to the Judge who was Judge Stringer and Mr. Hunter quietly told him he intended to ask for a directed verdict and requested that I get the man out of the courthouse quietly and get him out of the county before the announcement was made. I left with the man and learned afterwards that after sufficient time was given, the State Attorney, J.W. Hunter, made motion publicly asking the jury to bring in a verdict of "not guilty". The Judge granted the motion and the jury returned in open court a verdict of "not guilty" and the court was adjourned..."
As for the motion to suppress evidence, Hunter simply noted that, "The question has already been adjudicated. Judge Futch has ruled on the evidence. It was sustained by the Florida Supreme Court and the U.S. court did not reverse this part of the evidence."

Just after sunup on Dec. 6, Walter Irvin was loaded into the back of a State Highway Patrol cruiser to return to Lake County for the 9:30 a.m. hearing on the defense motions. Walter had regained a measure of health in the 29 days since McCall and Yates pumped three bullets into his body, but his psyche was far from healthy. It was with fear and trepidation that he contemplated yet another return to Tavares, site of the nightmare that would not end.

Judge Futch heard testimony into the motions for change of venue, disqualification of Hunter and suppression of evidence in the same courtroom where the Groveland Three was found guilty two and half years earlier. Akerman began by asking Futch to allow Marshall and Greenberg to be admitted as counsel. Hunter immediately objected on the grounds that the attorneys, "both represent the National Association for the Advancement of Colored People, and Marshall has been responsible for the vicious, slanderous and libelous matter." The judge denied the motion, but said the NAACP attorneys could "remain inside the railing" of the courtroom. Even though Futch upheld Hunter's objection, the prosecutor asked to introduce evidence to support his objection. Amazingly, the judge allowed him to "re-open for the purpose of introducing that evidence." The defense attorneys could hardly believe their ears. Hunter might as well have been sitting on the judge's bench.

The prosecutor moved to introduce the Jan. 19, 1950 fundraising letter from the Committee of 100, the pamphlet carrying Ted Poston's article "The Story of Florida's Legal Lynching," a news article detailing fundraising efforts, and a photocopy of Marshall's Nov. 19, 1951 letter. Marshall couldn't sit idly by while Hunter abused legal protocol. He figured if Hunter could introduce evidence on a motion that had already been decided, then the judge had to allow him to speak. "I wish to make the point clear that as a lawyer I represent my clients, and them alone, and I am not responsible to anyone else at any time when I am representing a client, and the advertisement and strips which appear in these newspapers were put out by the Florida Committee of 100, and that committee has nothing whatsoever to do with my office... while I realize that money has been raised for use in this case, and it has been used in this case in the appeal to the United States Supreme Court, and for the purpose of that appeal and certain investigations, all those things have been done, and I am not responsible for them," Marshall told the court. Hunter responded that papers had been distributed to "stir up scandalous and libelous matter and material against the good people of Lake County, Florida," and that the "colored people of this very county... are known to be planning to hold a celebration just before this trial came out." Marshall was fuming as the judge quietly reiterated that he had already ruled on the motion.

Next, Akerman introduced the motion to disqualify Hunter, although the fiasco Futch had just allowed was a pretty good indicator that the prosecutor would be allowed to remain in the case. Akerman began by calling Mabel Norris-Reese, the editor of the weekly, 1,475-circulation newspaper the *Mount Dora Topic*. He planned to walk her through her articles of the past two years one at a time, but received a jolt when he asked if she had brought copies of news clippings specified in the subpoena. "The only thing I have are my file copies, and I do not want to relinquish them for any length of time, because of the fact that they are the only copies I have, and you have all of the copies of my newspaper stories about the former trial in the files of the former trial, and I do not at this time wish to give up my file copies because they are the only copies I have," the newspaperwoman answered. Akerman stopped in his tracks. Before Futch could respond, Hunter's co-counsel "Sam" Buie chimed in, "I don't think that newspapers should be compelled to exhaust their file copies." After examining the subpoena, Futch agreed. "I am not going to require the newspaper people to do the great amount of research work that would have to be done to determine which particular copies of the paper you wish to see, and if you want to specify the particular papers you want, that is one thing, but to request the newspaper people to go through their entire filing systems, since August 1949, to pick out each paper, about this case, is too much, and I am not going to require them to do so," Futch chastised Akerman.

Mind racing, Akerman quickly asked the judge to issue a subpoena to Norris-Reese for more than a dozen specific newspapers. Buie objected on the grounds she was being asked "to do a great deal of research." Futch sustained, telling Akerman that he was guilty of issuing, "blunderbuss subpoenas."

Hunter then suggested that Akerman call *Leesburg Commercial* Publisher Jack Grant, because the newspaperman had, "matters of a family nature that will call him at any minute." Akerman agreed, but Grant wouldn't be on the stand any longer than Norris-Reese. He didn't bring copies of his paper either, because "the only ones I have are the file copies at the office." Hunter was obviously toying with Akerman. Again, Akerman asked the court to issue a subpoena for specific issues. Again, Futch ruled against the defense. His back to the wall, Akerman decided to forgo the printed evidence as Grant was excused and Norris-Reese recalled. Akerman asked the witness if she remembered an article from "July or

August of 1949" which contained alleged confessions by Shepherd and Irvin. Norris-Reese said she didn't. Buie then objected that the line of questioning had, "no bearing whatsoever on this case." Futch sustained. Akerman, determined to come away with *something*, asked Norris-Reese if she and Hunter had engaged in a conversation shortly before Aug. 18, 1949 regarding alleged confessions that the defendants were planning on robbing Henry Singleton. Again, Buie objected. The judge advised Akerman to state the time and place of the conversation, but before he could comply, Norris-Reese offered that she couldn't answer the question without refreshing her memory. Akerman was only too glad to help, and when he handed her the Aug. 18, 1949 issue of *Topic*, Norris-Reese reluctantly agreed that Hunter had been interviewed for the article in question. Akerman asked if Hunter was the source for the statement, "Samuel Shepherd, age 22, one of the accused in this case, and Mr. Hunter obtained from him the first time a statement that the three, with a fourth Negro, who has since been shot, had started the wild night with plans to hold up Henry Singleton." Norris-Reese replied, "Well, I suppose I did, I must have or I couldn't have published it in that manner." Finally, a victory for the defense. But it would be short-lived. Mabel immediately vacillated, saying, "I cannot say definitely that I got it from him, it is not in quotations I do not believe, and of course, newspaper people use every roundabout way that they possibly can to obtain information, and I don't know whether or not it is a direct quotation, and I don't know just exactly where I did get it." Akerman doggedly tried to pin her down that Hunter was the source, but the editor squirmed away, saying, "Well, there are no quotation marks, are there?" Akerman had to admit that there were not. Realizing he was getting nowhere, Akerman then attempted to introduce the July 18th article into evidence. Buie quickly objected to the article as "immaterial and irrelevant." As usual, Futch agreed.

Akerman stubbornly moved on to a January 1950 article in which Hunter criticized the Committee of 100 for attempts to raise funds for the defense. Again, Norris-Reese didn't remember Hunter making the statement, but Akerman did get her to admit to writing an article based on letters and a telegram Hunter sent to Sen. Claude Pepper asking the legislator to repudiate, "scandalous and libelous articles in the *St. Petersburg Times*." Buie objected that the line of questioning was "far, far outside" of the motion. Again, Futch agreed. Akerman wasn't about to surrender. "I will be glad to argue the motion, your Honor, I have some law on it." Futch replied, "I don't care to hear any argument." Defeated, Akerman allowed Norris-Reese to step down.

Akerman held little hope of salvaging the hearing as he called Hunter to the stand. Hunter's memory was much better than Norris-Reese's, in fact, he boldly admitted to making statements about the Committee of 100 appealing for funds. "My statement was and still is that the people of this county were being scandalized and libeled," he began. He concluded his rambling retort by saying, "I am proud that I made the statement, and I am still proud that I made it." Akerman parried, "In that statement, did you use the word 'radicals?'" Again, Hunter didn't pull any punches. "Yes, I certainly did use the word 'radicals,' I don't know whether those were my exact words or not, but I certainly will say now that this whole thing has been in the hands of a bunch of radicals, and it is directed to the men who came here to create race hatred in this county, and I am not directing this against the

Defendant, I am directing it against that bunch of men who came here to try to create race trouble in this County, and that is my statement at this time."

Hunter also had crystal clear recall when queried about statements he made regarding Pepper. "There was a newspaper published in this state, supporting Claude Pepper, and what they did was publish the lying statement that Ted Poston made, and put it in the form of a pamphlet and were distributing it all over this state," Hunter recalled. "And they delivered it to the colored people all over Florida and in Lake County also, and therefore, I wired Claude Pepper, and asked him to stop the delivery of that paper, because I had been told that it was being distributed by his campaign headquarters, and I wired him and asked him to stop putting that out from his headquarters, and he wired me back and told me that he would not do it, he said that one hundred thousand colored people were registered in this state to vote, and that he did not want to hurt them, and so I told him all right, he could go from then on without me.

Hunter turned from bold to defiant when Akerman shifted questioning to Lawrence Burtoft, the young man who encountered Norma Padgett on the morning after her alleged abduction and rape. Akerman was still upset that the state had interviewed Burtoft before the 1949 trial, but had kept his existence a secret because Burtoft's testimony would support the defense claim that there was no rape.

Akerman: "Did you interview him as a prospective witness in this case?" Hunter: "Yes, I did, but I am not going to tell you what he told me, he is your witness and you can find out from him."

Akerman could barely believe his ears. "Now, Mr. Hunter, do you recall what he told you?" Hunter: "Yes, but I am not going to tell you what he told me, he is your own witness."

Akerman: "Will you please state what your information was that was given to you by Mr. Burtoft?" Hunter: "I will not, it will interfere with the trial of this case, and I am not going to disclose any information that he gave me."

An incredulous Akerman declared that Burtoft had told Hunter that the girl reported she wasn't harmed and couldn't identify her attackers. Further, it was the prosecutor's *duty* to present Burtoft's story to the jury. "That statement is entirely false. He made no such statement to me," thundered Hunter, who challenged Akerman to produce Burtoft, knowing full well that was impossible. "He's in the Army of the United States and outside the province of this court, he is in the armed forces of the United States, in North Carolina," Akerman testily replied. "Well, you will have to go further than that before you ever get him back here to make any such statement as that, because he never made the statement," Hunter exclaimed. Akerman held his tongue, he wasn't about to get into a shouting match with the old prosecutor. As Hunter returned to his seat, Futch announced he was ready to rule. Without fanfare, the judge granted the motion for change of venue. With Shepherd dead and Irvin calling it murder, Futch could hardly deny a change -- not with the NAACP screaming for the removal of McCall and Yates and a full investigation into the shooting.

Despite the change of venue ruling, Hunter was in a triumphant mood when he met with reporters on Dec. 13. Hunter claimed that he could finally close the book on the shooting because the FBI had concluded its investigation by confirming that all six bullets used in shooting Irvin and Samuel Shepherd had come from the same gun: McCall's .38-caliber Smith and Wesson Special revolver. Hunter said the FBI validated McCall's account of the shooting after digging up a bullet at the scene, the bullet that passed through Irvin's neck.

As so often happened in the Groveland case, Hunter's disclosure raised as many questions as it answered. First, the FBI report had *not* been released, nor the investigating agents produced. Hunter expected people to take his word for it. Second, Hunter's claim that all three bullets that entered Shepherd and were never removed contradicted the autopsy report, which indicated one bullet had exited his body. Hunter contended that "interpretation" was incorrect. Third, the fact that a bullet was found in the dirt near where the bodies laid supported Irvin's claim that he had been shot while lying prone. Whether the bullet was fired by McCall or Yates wasn't as important as the fact that whoever fired the bullet was attempting murder, since Irvin had already been shot twice and was lying handcuffed to a man who had already been shot three times. Whoever fired the shot was no longer defending himself.

Chapter 28 -- Brave Voice Silenced

On Dec. 14, the Justice Department announced it was giving "careful consideration" to Thurgood Marshall's demand that Sheriff Willis McCall be charged with obstructing the U.S. Supreme Court.

The next day, Judge Truman Futch returned to his pre-shooting form, announcing that Marshall and his right-hand man Jack Greenberg would be barred from defending Irvin. His reason: the NAACP "was stirring up trouble in the community." The judge then threw a sucker punch: the retrial would take place in Ocala in Marion County, the county adjacent to Lake. The close proximity to the site of the original trial -- Ocala was just 23 miles from the Lake County line -- was just one reason the change of venue was absurd. Marion was in the 5th Judicial District, which meant Futch would again preside. The LDF staff had expected the trial would be moved to a larger city like Jacksonville or Tampa, a locale more than a stone's throw from Lake. And Marshall and company were counting on a new judge.

With Negroes comprising 35 percent of a population of 16,000, Ocala appeared to have a more "enlightened" populace than Tavares. A closer examination would show that the city was hardly a model of peaceful white-black relations. The defense attorneys didn't know that on Friday, April 13, 1951 a 16-year-old Negro had killed popular Marion County Sheriff Edward Porter Jr., and the murder still weighed heavily on the minds of citizens. But Futch and Jess Hunter knew. If the trial couldn't be held in Lake County, Marion was probably the next best place to get a conviction. Marshall immediately announced that the

NAACP would embark on a "thorough investigation" to determine the racial climate of Marion County.

Five days later, Marshall rallied the troops with an "urgent" memorandum to NAACP branch officers. Marshall encouraged branches to "immediately" push for federal intervention into the shooting of Shepherd and Irvin, "urging that this matter be presented to a federal grand jury by a specially appointed Assistant Attorney General from Washington, and that this be followed by vigorous prosecution... As matters now stand, the determining factor as to whether or not there will be prosecution in this case depends upon the activities of our branches... If the federal government refuses to act in this case, not only will peace officers in the South be free to continue their wanton killing of Negro Americans, but this in and of it itself will continue to hamper our government in its international relations."

While the legal team pulled together the defense for the retrial, Florida's inglorious civil rights record became more tarnished. In Miami, Carver Village -- a housing development that recently opened to Negro tenants -- was rocked by a dynamite blast, not once, but twice. The Miami Hebrew School was also dynamited. The NAACP had accomplished so much, saved so many lives. But there was no way it could protect a single person from an explosion in the middle of the night.

Between the violence in Miami, the shootings of Irvin and Shepherd, and the recent indignity of being stripped of leadership of the Florida NAACP, Harry T. Moore more than ever viewed Christmas as a time for reflection. Money was tight, and now part of his income, though sporadic, had been taken away by the NAACP. "...he needed to be out doing something to make some money. Because he wasn't being adequately paid; that was my memory. I had concerns and sympathy -- he had a family to take care of -- and he had lost his job, hadn't he? This was his only source of income," attorney Horace Hill remarked. Still, it was a time to celebrate, not despair. Harry and Harriette Moore were preparing to observe their 25th wedding anniversary and Christmas with loved ones.

The Moore's school teacher daughter, Annie had already arrived, and her sister, Evangeline was on her way from Washington, D.C. when the Moores and Harry's mother retired for the evening on Christmas Eve. At 10:20 p.m. the still of the night was shattered when an explosion ripped through the house, destroying Harry and Harriette's bedroom. The Moore's son, Master Sergeant George Sims, who lived about 800 yards from his parents, was first to arrive. He and his brother Arnold rushed their father to the nearest hospital, in Sanford, 30 miles away. Moore died in his mother's arms en route.

Almost immediately, fingers began pointing McCall's way. After all, McCall's dislike of Moore, and the NAACP, was well documented. "Bomb in Florida kills Negro who led drive to try sheriff," screamed the headline in the Dec. 27, 1951 *New York Herald Tribune.* The subhead read, "N.A.A.C.P. Official Sought Prosecution of White Man Who Shot Prisoners; Wife Seriously Hurt." The press saw a connection. Many who had followed McCall's checkered career, did as well.

The same FBI agents who had spent most of November investigating the shooting of Shepherd and Irvin were quickly dispatched to Mims. They would soon be joined by more than 20 agents as the eyes of a nation watched to see if the perpetrators would be brought to justice, or if the dynamiting would be just another murder swept under the rug. Agents were instructed to work around the clock if necessary. Investigators began by scouring the homesite and adjacent area. Brevard County Sheriff H.T. Williams brought bloodhounds to track Moore's killers, and sure enough, the dogs picked up a scent. Unfortunately, they lost the trail about a half mile from Old Dixie Highway. And there were other dead ends. Agents found scant physical evidence, just a trail of footprints: size 7 to 9, left by a man with a long stride, some glass fragments and a heavy rubber washer that may have been used as part of the explosive device. FBI Director J. Edgar Hoover, who had Walter White and Thurgood Marshall breathing down his neck, wasn't pleased. Hoover directed agents to double their efforts.

White laid the murder of Moore squarely at the feet of Gov. Fuller Warren, whom he chided for consistently refusing "to take any steps to uphold law and order" in Florida. Privately, White felt that some of the state's highest elected officials were involved in the murder plot, a feeling he shared with Robert Saunders, who would eventually succeed Moore. The governor didn't appreciate the criticism, lambasting "carpetbaggers" and "hate mongers" who "come to Florida to try to stir up strife."

At the funeral service for Harry T. Moore at St. James Missionary Baptist Church in Mims, state investigators and Moore's brothers checked the church for explosives beforehand. The flowers that adorned the casket were shipped all way from Miami because local florists refused to deliver flowers to a Negro funeral. Even in death, Moore bore insults and threats of violence. The NAACP had made great progress, but injustice, hatred and violence were still commonplace.

As 1951 drew to a close, Paul Perkins was determined to ensure that Walter Irvin had the best possible defense. That's why he spent New Year's Eve driving to Jacksonville to meet with Carol Alexander's brother. The former waitress who had served Shepherd and Irvin on the night Norma Padgett claimed she was raped, was having second thoughts about testifying for the defense – or at least her sister was. "Naturally we should and will do anything possible to help – but this hinges on the question of her leaving school in the midst of her last semester in school," big sister wrote Perkins on Nov. 1. "I have been wondering just how did my sister recognize these particular boys, whether she did know them before, if she has seen them after the crime and can she make a positive identification under oath and under the pros. cross examination. For I'm sure that a lot of people were served that night – and just how would these two fellows stand out so." The letter alarmed Perkins, who convinced Alexander's brother to accompany him to Eatonville to help persuade Carol to appear. The ploy worked; between the pleas of Perkins and her brother's reasoning, Alexander reluctantly again agreed to take testify that she had served Shepherd and Irvin when they visited the club she worked at.

Harry T. Moore had bumped Walter Irvin off the front page, but a sensational claim that Shepherd and Irvin had discussed a plan to attack Sheriff Willis McCall during transport to Tavares catapulted the Groveland case back into the news on Jan. 4, 1952. Less than a week before his scheduled execution, death-row prisoner James Merlin Leiby, a convicted murderer, won a reprieve from the electric chair with the incredible tale that he overheard the Groveland defendants discussing plans to escape back in November. Leiby, who received the death sentence in 1949 for killing Baltimore pharmacist Leonard Applebaum and hiding his victim's body under a bridge, didn't explain why he waited two months to share such significant information.

Gov. Warren stayed the execution at the request of McCall, who wrote, "Even though Mr. Leiby has already made a signed statement which was turned over to the FBI, I believe that testimony from him in person would have great bearing in case the prejudiced groups in New York bring enough pressure to bear in Washington for the Justice Department to place this case before a federal grand jury. Anything you can do in this matter will be greatly appreciated."

At Raiford, news of Leiby's revelation came as a complete surprise to Assistant Prison Superintendent J.G. Godwin, who told reporters he didn't know Leiby had made the claim, didn't know the prisoner had been interviewed by the FBI, and "didn't know of any conversation Sheriff McCall could have had with him." Godwin and other prison officials wondered how Leiby could have overheard a conversation between the Groveland Two when Negro and white prisoners were segregated. The only place the two might have met, although unlikely, was on the "flat top" where condemned men awaiting execution were housed. The only other possibility: if the two had been held in adjacent solitary confinement cells, but that was even less likely. There was no record at Raiford that any of the three served time in solitary. So how did Leiby's story reach McCall? The sheriff wasn't saying.

For Marshall, the episode was more of an irritant than anything, just another of McCall's tricks to intimidate and harass Irvin and his defenders. McCall hadn't been able to coerce Greenlee into telling a lie on Walter and Sammie so he found a run-of-the-mill prisoner to cast aspersions on the Groveland boys. Nothing McCall or Hunter did surprised Marshall, who must have felt he had seen it all by the time 1952 rolled around. Violence, hatred, injustice and discrimination across the United States had marred 1951, and Florida again had a shameful record. Among the most notorious cases: Willie Vincent being beaten by three white men who fractured his skull by throwing him from a speeding car; a teenage shoeshine boy, Jimmy Woodard was shot five times, but recovered; and 26-year-old Melvin Womack, who was dragged from his bed by four masked white men, beaten, then shot to death. His body was found in an orange grove near Orlando. And, of course, there were the murders of Shepherd and Moore and the attempted murder of Irvin.

That hatred still flourished, was evident in the 1952 *Ebony* article, "South Weaves New Pattern of Violence," which read in part, "Today it is a handful of southern whites, a willful minority, who still believe in and practice violence to halt Negro demands for equal rights.

They operate as individuals rather than as mobs. Encouraged by lax police and bigoted politicians, they have flouted the law in their attempts to turn back the clock. With bombs, they have tried to stop admission of Negroes to lily-white universities, to halt a record number of Negro voters going to the polls, to stymie equal salaries for colored teachers and decent Federal housing for Negroes. In Florida alone, there have been a dozen bombings in recent months. The bomb pattern spread swiftly to other states." The heart-rending reality was that tireless campaigning by civil rights activists like Harry T. Moore hadn't ended terrorist acts against blacks, the attention had just made the bigots refine their methods to avoid detection. White terrorists had finally realized it was more difficult to trace a man who plants a bomb than a man who ties a noose, although the KKK never missed an opportunity to hold a lynching party.

The racists, stirred by increased talk of desegregation becoming law, were mobilizing throughout the South. A group calling itself the American Confederate Army for White Christians was launched at a secret meeting in Orlando in early 1952. In a mass mailing, the group proclaimed, "If necessary this organization will bear arms to uphold our Constitutional rights. If the Supreme Court ever outlaws racial segregation in the public schools, all members will take this as an invasion of our constitutional rights." When asked for clarification, KKK Grand Dragon Bill Hendrix revealed the group was compiling lists of members of the NAACP, Jewish B'nai B'rith fraternity and the Anti-Defamation League. Asked about the possibility of segregation being outlawed, Hendrix declared, "If law and order ever break down, we will hold them responsible!"

While the world waited for Moore's killer(s) to be brought to justice and for Irvin to be retried, readers of the *Afro-American* were asked to reflect on the top 10 stories of 1951. It wasn't a pretty list. To the editors who picked the stories, 1951 would be remembered for: two-day rioting in Cicero, Illinois; the bombing murder of Moore; the "Devil's Brew" incident in Atlanta where 38 died and more than 200 were hospitalized after drinking poison alcohol; the execution of the Martinsville Seven; Mack Ingram being sentenced to two years in prison on a rape charge for looking at a white girl from 75' away; and, of course, McCall shooting Irvin and Shepherd. *Afro-American* Assistant Managing Editor Art Carter called "the horrible slaying of Samuel Shepherd and the wounding of Walter Irvin" the top story of the year. Editor Cliff W. Mackay said McCall's ambush was tied for the third with the bombing slaying of Moore. McCall's shooting of the prisoners was fourth on the list of Philadelphia *Afro* Editor Samuel Hoskin. Surprisingly, only one *Afro* editor, Night Managing Editor Josephus Simpson, listed the Moore bombing as the top story of 1951.

Harriette Moore died just nine days after the bombing. She was 49. A week earlier, after mustering strength to view her husband's body at Burton's Funeral Home in Sanford, she had told a reporter, "I have nothing to live for now." She spent her final days in shock, but she stepped away from her grieving long enough to answer a barrage of questions from FBI agents. She couldn't shed any light on who would have committed such a horrific crime, but the interview did help investigators. When shown glass fragments and a heavy rubber washer found at the scene of the bombing, Harriette recognized the remains of a test tube and stopper, but stated without hesitation that she had never seen anything resembling a test tube around the house. She also mentioned Groveland when agents Clyde P. Aderhold and Robert F. Hartmann questioned her at Sanford Memorial Hospital on Dec. 26. "He never discussed his work with her but she knew that he had spent quite a bit of time working on the Groveland, Florida rape case," agents reported. "According to Mrs. Moore her husband had distributed pamphlets concerning this rape case until the United State Supreme Court reversed the decision of the state court in August, 1951. She said that since that time he had been writing articles for newspapers and magazines."

Frustration and anger grew with each day that passed without an arrest in connection with the bombing. On Jan. 5, the *Afro-American* summed up the feelings of the Negro community at large with an editorial headlined "Now Time For Action," which said in part: "The inescapable impression is formed that official Florida is not at all anxious to bring these hoodlums to justice. One begins to suspect that they fear to determine their identity lest it prove embarrassing to someone in high places."

Protests continued to arrive at the Florida statehouse, but the shockwaves extended far beyond the Sunshine State. The murder remained front-page news as far away as Asia and Africa and editorials appeared in newspapers as distant as France, Israel and the Philippines. Moore's murder was also being discussed at the White House, and even the United Nations. U.S. delegate Eleanor Roosevelt warned, "The harm it will do us among the people of world is untold." *Pravda* devoted a half-page article to the bombing, citing it as an example of capitalist evil. Feeling the heat, Warren announced that the State of Florida would offer a $2,000 reward in the fatal bombing. Meanwhile, Brevard County, state and federal investigators were working around the clock. But there were precious few leads to follow. Sheriff H.T. Williams and Coroner Vassar B. Carlton's initial investigation concluded the blast was caused by "nitroglycerine or some other chemical stronger than dynamite." FBI agents found little to support or debunk the theory.

Fed up with lip service from the governor, Walter White asked Attorney McGrath to receive, "at the earliest possible date" a representative delegation of religious, civic, labor and other groups from Florida and across the nation to discuss steps "which must be taken to end these outrages." White also contacted J. Edgar Hoover, who told the NAACP leader that he, "has never been so disturbed over a case." Hoover assured White that the agency wasn't turning a blind eye, the terrorists had just covered their tracks well. Agents had interviewed dozens of people who'd seen or talked to Moore during the last five months of his life, and wiretapped countless others.

Agents were even dispatched to interview Franklin H. Williams in San Francisco. Williams wondered what agents hoped to gain from questioning him, since he barely knew Moore and had moved to California well before the Christmas Eve murder. He soon found out. "I knew the FBI very well and the FBI came to me and this was after Harry T. Moore had been killed and they asked me to describe to the best of my ability the lead car of the three cars that we claimed had chased us. We did and he said, 'That fits perfectly the description of a car that was seen near Harry Moore's home on New Year's Eve (sic) when he was killed.'"

Williams wasn't surprised that a car spotted near Moore's home matched the description of a vehicle that chased Horace Hill's sedan after the Groveland rape trial. He also found it interesting that the FBI believed the "car chase" story that McCall and Hunter labeled a lie. In fact, there was no doubt in the agent's minds that the chase had occurred. "He said, 'We have witnesses that you were chased that night. We have people who saw you coming through Mount Dora and with these cars behind you,'" Williams recalled.

After interviewing virtually every black resident of Mims, and then turning the spotlight on the NAACP (after all, what would create more sympathy than the murder of one of its own?) the FBI took a good, hard look at KKK activity in central Florida, particularly the flourishing Orange County Klavern. Predictably, to a man Klansmen kept their mouths shut. Cooperating with the law carried the ultimate penalty. "You can't imagine the fear when (fellow FBI agent) Jim Shannon and I were working through Lake, Orange and Sumter counties," recalled FBI agent Frank Meech. "They knew our car, they knew where we were. You couldn't move without them knowing it. We talked to many people who said, 'Hell, no, I won't testify, I'd be dead tomorrow.'" Writer Stetson Kennedy wasn't surprised agents were getting nowhere. Kennedy told *Afro-American* reporter James L. Hicks that he had "asked the FBI in Washington not to send any Southern FBI agents to investigate the Florida incidents because he was convinced they would not do a real job."

Investigators kept saying no one was talking, but NAACP officials were experiencing success, albeit limited. After being told for the umpteenth time that no suspects had been identified, White angrily provided the FBI with names of three suspects who had publicly blamed Moore for working to add Negroes to the voting polls. In fact, White claimed that a Brevard County resident was responsible for planting the bomb. The sensational news that suspects had been identified first appeared in the Jan. 5, 1952 edition of the *Chicago Defender* under the headline, "Link KKK To Florida Bombing... State, FBI Acts; Name 3 Suspects." The article stated that FBI agents and state investigators had been given names of "three persons known to have threatened the widely known crusader." Actually, the FBI had already identified the three suspects through intense spying and phone taps, but agents were under orders not to divulge information that might scare off potential informants. The agency's prime suspect was Joseph Neville Cox, secretary of the Orlando chapter of the Ku Klux Klan, whom the FBI believed organized a handful of KKK "head-knockers" and arranged to purchase dynamite to place beneath the Moore's bedroom. But Cox would never be tried, he committed suicide the day after the FBI interview. The other two suspects would die of "natural causes" within a year of Moore's murder.

Agents even interviewed McCall after a tip that the Lake County sheriff had spoken at a KKK meeting in Astatula shortly after the bombing. McCall boldly admitted he attended the meeting, but not because he was a KKK member, only to tell Klan members that they were not obligated to talk to the FBI or even give their names. It was strange behavior for a lawman, to be sure.

"We lived a half block from the courthouse and I knew Sheriff McCall… We lived in a two-story house and my bedroom faced the street. One night in the early 1950s, I had already gone to bed, it must have been 11 or 11:30, when I heard a lot of noise coming from the street. When I got up and looked out the window I saw they were having a meeting of the Ku Klux Klan. While I was watching, Sheriff McCall rode right up in his sheriff's car and parked right in front of our house. When I first saw the car, I thought he was there to break things up. When he got out of the car he was wearing a white cape. That's how brazen he was back then." – Don Yates, June 12, 2003

The sheriff never admitted to being a card-carrying Klan member, but he proudly announced that he was a member of the National Association for the Advancement of White People. Agents Meech and Shannon questioned the sheriff extensively, but could find "nothing at all to feel he was involved in any way, except we knew he was in sympathy with the Klan." Even though he was far from forthcoming, McCall may have been the only lawman who talked. Meech recalled, "We'd go in and talk to someone in law enforcement and they'd say 'what the hell are you investigating that for? He was only a nigger.'" FBI agents had long ago realized that Florida was a state of police chiefs who looked the other way when the Klan moved. Worse yet, some top cops were high-ranking Klan officials.

Florida's racial problems remained front-page news as the Moore investigation meandered along. Gov. Warren begrudgingly began cooperating with the Feds, also adding another $6,000 to the reward offered for information leading to the conviction of the person who murdered the Moores. Horace Hill had no doubt a link existed between Groveland and Moore's murder. "I expected this kind of thing, reacting as they had done to the Groveland case. And there was a vendetta, that since the NAACP was behind all of this thing, they wanted to remove as much of this pressure as they could. He was the one who had invited the national NAACP into this case, and possibly if they could get him out of it that may quiet everything," Hill said.

Even though Florida was crawling with FBI agents and Justice Department officials, a feeling of fear existed that further violence against blacks could break out anywhere, any time. "… I installed lights all around my house to turn on at night," Hill said. "Amazing enough, a house was bombed about a block down from my house… Some said they were after me." Before the murder of Moore, Florida blacks had tread lightly when whitey was around. After Christmas Eve, 1951, blacks began worrying if the white man was hiding in the shadows. These were dangerous times, particularly for Perkins, now the only Florida attorney officially connected to the Groveland case.

Perkins was almost too busy to worry about his well being. McCall's shooting of Irvin and Shepherd had bought the defense some time, but Perkins had been so consumed with amending and filing motions that he hadn't had time to re-examine the alibi defense. On Jan. 9, he made time to write to Carol Alexander at Clark University to tell her that the trial would not be held Jan. 14, but would be in February and that he would inform her of the exact date "far in advance."

After considerable discussion with his staff, Marshall decided that the defense should seek another change of venue, even though the trial had been already been moved from Tavares to Ocala. And another strategy was germinating in Marshall's keen mind. The more he thought about commissioning a public opinion poll, the more he liked the idea. A professionally-conducted survey would definitely add bite to a motion for change of venue. Of course, the poll would have to be conducted in utmost secrecy. Otherwise, McCall was sure to interfere, and possibly intimidate those contacted. Greenberg told Perkins that, "The poll will be sufficiently well disguised so that its purpose will not be apparent to anyone who merely knows that such inquiries are being made." It was a bold strategy, one bound to be criticized by Hunter when he finally found out. Regardless of whether or not Judge Futch would admit the poll, it was worth a shot. For once the defense would have the element of surprise. "So that he does not claim surprise or waiver, I think that about a week before the hearing, we should notify him (Hunter) that we are raising this point," Greenberg wrote.

On Jan. 11, Akerman filed a motion to allow Marshall and Greenberg to enter the case. The motion claimed that Irvin was entitled to representation by an experienced attorney like Marshall, instead of Perkins, who had only been a member of the bar since 1950 and "had not acted as defense counsel in a capital case." For good measure, Perkins submitted a mirror motion. Perkins wrote: "That his chief defense counsel Alex Akerman Jr. is now on active duty with the United States Navy and because of such circumstance can only appear in the case at such times as will not interfere with his duties in the Navy and it is questionable as to whether or not the said Alex Akerman Jr. can appear at the trial to act as defense counsel for your defendant." Having Akerman say that Perkins lacked experience and Perkins say that Akerman's Navy obligations kept him from preparing was an unorthodox, but brilliant strategy. Irvin's signature of consent appeared on both documents.

Chapter 29 -- Once In A Lifetime Deal

Most Ocala citizens seemed unfazed by the impending retrial of the last of the Groveland boys, Walter Lee Irvin. "The residents of this city of 11,000 known for its cattle and its citrus and vegetable farms, evince no unusual interest in the case. *The Ocala Star-Banner* has not commented editorially on the trial but has run a few brief articles about it. Leading residents report that Ocala has been free of racial tension for years and point to the existence of well-run Negro schools and other community facilities," *New York Times* reporter Richard H. Parke noted.

Leading residents may not have felt racial tension, but it was a different story among Marion's Negroes. "They were all scared to death. They did not want to come out. We had some assistance in checking certain things, like what they knew about prospective jurors and things like that. Any number of them helped us on that, but generally speaking they were supportive, but did not want to be known," Akerman said.

As planned, the defense waited until the Feb. 11 trial was just nine days away to file the motion for change of venue. The strongly-worded document was easily the most acerbic attack yet, naming Judge Truman Futch, State Attorney Jess Hunter, Sheriff Willis McCall and the press as impediments to a fair and impartial trial. Clearly, the defense didn't think Ocala was an improvement over Tavares, 43 miles to the south.

Naturally, Hunter and McCall were enraged that the NAACP agitators had the nerve to seek a second change of venue. McCall had no doubt Marshall was behind latest motion, which repeated the claims already made to the Florida and U.S. Supreme Courts: that the prisoners had been beaten, adverse publicity made a fair trial impossible, prejudice and existed, McCall murdered Shepherd, and Hunter didn't conduct a fair and impartial prosecution. But the latest motion went farther, much farther. The new accusations:

- "There has been a deliberate attempt on the part of Willis V. McCall and J. W. Hunter to create the impression that the NAACP is a subversive and Communistic organization... this planned propaganda has been so successfully disseminated that should any juror have the courage to vote for an acquittal for your defendant, he would not only have to face the odium of his fellow citizens which such a vote would bring... but would stand charged before his neighbors with having bowed to subversive or Communistic influences."

- Hunter attempted to prevent contributions from being made for the defense of the Negroes by saying all expenses were being paid by Lake County.

- Due to the "whitewashing" by the coroner's jury that cleared McCall, "In the eyes of the people of Lake and Marion counties your defendant is branded as an attempted escapee, raising a strong influence of guilt in the minds of the people."

- "The prejudice and hostility against your defendant which is present in Lake County is present in almost the same degree in Marion County."

Hunter returned fire with a statement on Feb. 6, saying Marion was devoid of any prejudice and hostility "that would in any way deny the defendant a fair and impartial trial." In addition to his usual charge that the NAACP was, "trying to inject race and hatred into the situation," the prosecutor also waved the red flag, a favorite tactic of McCall's. "Their efforts to create race discord is following the Communist lines and causing the Communist Party to come into Florida and take advantage of this propaganda which they have put out. The NAACP, while they may or may not be subversive, are following closely the Communist line in attempting to create hatred and dissention between the races in Florida." Hunter also again took exception to the NAACP's fund-raising efforts, claiming that the, "enormous sum of $263,000" the organization raised was not to defend Irvin and others, but to inject racial hatred into the situation. Hunter didn't say where he got the $263,000 figure (Marshall would have given his left arm for that kind of money). McCall too criticized the NAACP, saying the motion to admit Marshall and Greenberg was an attempt, "to place themselves in a position where they may send out false and libelous matter to Northern newspapers against the officials of Lake County and the people of Florida -- and not to really defend Irvin."

With the trial less than a week away, the defense was still scrambling to finalize preparations. Irvin's lawyers still didn't know if former FBI man Herman Bennett would be able to examine casts of the footprints and tire tracks the state introduced at the '49 trial. Perkins had contacted Bennett in early November, but Bennett's workload had prevented him from flying to Orlando to examine the casts. And then another setback: Bennett became bedridden with a virus infection and told Perkins he wouldn't be able to be in Orlando until the first week of February. It was cutting it close to be sure, and no one knew if Bennett's

305

examination would lead to anything the defense could use. Other concerns involved alibi witnesses Carol Alexander (who had served Irvin and Shepherd beer at the Eatonville club on the night in question) and Daisy Lee Graham (who said she had shared a beer with the men at 2 a.m. on July 16). Perkins still hadn't heard from either woman, even though the NAACP had promised to send money for expenses.

On Monday, Feb. 10, Irvin formally petitioned Futch to allow Marshall and Greenberg to join the defense. Hunter was quick to object, saying that the attorneys were not members of the Florida bar, and thus had no right to practice in a Florida court. Futch found himself in a difficult position. To exclude Marshall and Greenberg would lend credence to cries that Irvin could not receive a fair trial and could be the basis for another reversal in a higher court. Despite Hunter's objections, Futch granted the motion. In the final analysis, the judge decided little harm could come from granting the request -- Irvin was headed for the chair regardless of who represented him. "I think he (Judge Futch) was contriving to bring in a conviction and have it affirmed," Greenberg recalled. "For instance, he first excluded us from the case, but we were delighted at that because it was another ground for reversal, but he thought about it overnight and he let us back in. It's not that he wanted us in you know, and he was leaning over backwards to make sure it wasn't reversed again." Obviously, the ruling was a huge victory for Irvin and his defenders. If anyone could work a jury, it was Marshall. "In a mass meeting he could bring an audience to its feet, clapping and stomping. In court, he was conversational and usually lectured as a professor might, although sometimes there were emotional riffs full of vivid imagery… Often, he preferred a tentative, brief advance to 'going for the gold' all at once. For Thurgood, this viewpoint was part of a more profound respect he had for judges. You never heard as many 'Yes, sirs' and 'May it please the courts' as when he argued a case," Greenberg said.

Marshall was off the sidelines and into the game, but it remained to be seen if Futch and Hunter would accord him the same respect they did his white peers. It didn't take Marshall long to realize that Marion County's Crackers weren't impressed by his status as an internationally-known attorney. A week prior, he was on the cover of *Collier's,* which proclaimed him the greatest civil liberties lawyer in the nation, but to most locals he was still just a nigger in a suit. The realization that Marion wasn't any more progressive than Lake was confirmed on the first day of trial, when Marshall lunched with Hunter and Ocala attorney Gus Musleh at Bennett's Drug Store across from the courthouse. Marshall's entrance was met with stares and disapproving looks by several customers. Clearly, segregation was still a way of life in Ocala.

McCall, however, was right at home. He may have been outside his jurisdiction, but he didn't leave his swagger and bluster in Lake County. Marshall had seen his ilk before, but Greenberg had only heard stories. He was about to view the sheriff's special brand of intimidation for himself. "He was a pretty sinister guy," Greenberg reflected. "I may have transformed him in my mind, but he was the stereotype of a southern sheriff -- big belly, big guy, gun on his hip. I never had any unpleasantness with him personally, but I was very aware he was a pretty terrible fellow." Perkins shared that view. The image of McCall glaring, with hand on his pistol, as he watched Perkins enter the courthouse burned an indelible image in the young attorney's mind. Greenberg understood why the veteran lawman left such a lasting impression on the young black attorney. "Perkins had to live down there -- you never knew what corner he'd (McCall) step around." Without doubt, Perkins had more at stake than Marshall and Greenberg. "When visiting LDF lawyers finished a controversial case, they got on a plane or train and went home. The local lawyers remained to take the heat from an enraged redneck population," Greenberg said. "Many faced efforts to disbar them. Judges, prosecutors, and clerks regularly humiliated them, requiring that their clients and their families sit in Jim Crow sections of courtrooms. Judges, clerks and white lawyers persisted in calling black lawyers by their first names, not out of friendship or familiarity, but to remind them and everyone else in the courtroom of their inferior status."

Hunter had lined up an impressive cast of community leaders to testify to Marion County's racial harmony. His star at the pre-trial hearing was Dr. L. R. Hampton, a dentist who had served the community since 1912 and was considered to be the richest colored man in the county. "The love and respect the white man has for the colored man and the confidence they have for each other is a beautiful thing to see. I believe that the colored man in Marion County (Ocala) has been treated fairer than in any other county in Florida," Hampton proudly proclaimed. Marshall, amazed that Hampton had used the word "love" in a statement about relations between white and black, asked what qualified Hampton as an expert on local race relations. The dentist replied that he felt he knew half the population well enough to discuss race relations. "The boy can have a fairer trial here than anywhere in the South," Hampton stated. Marshall wondered aloud how Hampton could make such a dogmatic claim. The dentist replied that he was familiar with conditions in other parts of the state from his contacts with patients "who come to me from all over Florida." An incredulous Marshall then asked whether Irvin could walk out of the courtroom unaccosted if freed, to which the dentist grudgingly admitted that, "some hothead might do something." Next, Marshall implied that the dentist had a vested interest in Marion County since he paid over $5,000 in taxes, then asked, "You want to stay here, don't you?" Hampton replied by shouting, "I am going to stay here." The remark drew laughter from members of the white audience. It was a command performance, and Hampton capped it by stopping to have a short conversation and a laugh with Hunter after leaving the stand.

Rev. M.L. Anderson, pastor of Mt. Moriah Baptist Church, characterized local whites as more liberal than anywhere else in the state. When Marshall pressed for an admission that Marion County had race problems like anywhere else, Anderson replied, "We have gotten to the place here where we can iron things out without too much trouble." Marshall felt disgust. But it would get worse. "Only county I would put up against Jerusalem in Christ's times," the preacher shouted before leaving the stand. A Negro in the balcony was heard to remark, "They killed Christ, too, didn't they?" And then there was Dr. Nathaniel H. Jones, a Negro physician who told the court that he believed race relations in Marion were "better than most places." Of the four Negroes presented by the state, only retired postal worker L.C. Rackard was less than emphatic, saying that he had not encountered enough prejudice "to mar feeling between the two groups." But Rackard was also willing to be led by Hunter,

---

testifying that, "I wouldn't say there isn't any prejudice in Marion County, but not enough to hurt." He too drew applause.

Marshall couldn't help feeling repulsed. And he wasn't alone. According to an article in the *Chicago Defender*, "Negro citizens in Ocala are furious over the statements of six Negroes who testified that there is no prejudice in Ocala and that Walter Irvin could get a fair and impartial trial." *Afro-American* reporter Buddy Lonesome wondered how "those Uncle Toms" who testified to Ocala's supposed racial harmony could sleep at night.

Marshall attempted to show that excessive pretrial publicity warranted a change of venue. But calling *Ocala Star-Banner* Editor R. N. Dosh to present articles concerning the case backfired on the defense when Dosh introduced a copy of the Negro paper the *Florida Sentinel* bearing the front-page banner headline, "Bishop Gregg Lauds Good Race Relations in Florida." Other whites mentioned the recent dedication of a public memorial to Negro veterans, examples of blacks winning lawsuits against whites and the lack of public demonstration when Sheriff Ed Porter was killed by a young Negro the previous year.

The good people of Ocala had spoken. Now Marshall wanted to hear from the segment of the populace that was too afraid, or too cynical to step into the courtroom. It was time to introduce the public opinion poll the defense had commissioned. Marshall was counting on Dr. Julian Woodard, executive of the Elmo Roper Institute, to prove that most Ocala residents had already formed an opinion as to Irvin's guilt.

The prosecution wasn't about to let Marshall and Greenberg establish a legal precedent by introducing a public opinion poll. "We object to anything in regard to this report with regard to any county except Marion County, because Marion County is the only county involved in any of the issues involved in this case," Hunter boomed. He then told Judge Futch that the poll constituted improper hearsay testimony and couldn't be considered evidence. After all, respondents weren't identified and therefore could not be questioned or cross-examined. Futch agreed, even though defense lawyers intimated that the poll might form the basis for an appeal to the highest court in the land if Irvin was convicted.

Akerman stubbornly argued that the report must be considered as a whole, since findings from other counties were included for the purpose of comparison. Futch paused to weigh the attorney's words. Introduction of a poll was new territory. He decided to defer his ruling until after testimony. To begin, Woodward explained that Jackson and Gadsden counties were selected for comparison purposes because they were far removed from Lake and Marion. Woodward explained that absolute figures in his report that by themselves might have little meaning took on significance when compared to results from Lake and Marion. Again, Hunter objected. Futch upheld, stating that the court would only recognize figures obtained from Marion residents. The court then recessed.

During the intermission, Akerman became alarmed when he overheard Hunter boasting about blocking the efforts to introduce the public opinion poll. When court reconvened, Akerman sought clarification. Before the judge could answer, Hunter quickly stated that

Woodward could testify concerning Marion, but that the Court had yet to rule on the admissibility of the report. Futch concurred, saying, "...my understanding was that he could submit the figures to Marion County, and I will rule later as to whether or not the report itself will be received in evidence." At the defense table, Irvin's benefactors shared a sinking feeling that the public opinion poll would never be admitted. As Woodward began explaining his report, Hunter objected that the document itself was the best evidence. But Woodward didn't want to just introduce the report into evidence, he wanted to explain how the survey was conducted. Hunter again objected on the grounds, "...this gentleman on this stand does not know of his own knowledge whether or not the answers were actually made to the questions." Obviously, Hunter had used the recess to regroup and come up with a plan to scuttle the poll. The judge agreed. Objection sustained. The Elmo Roper poll was dead in the water.

With the poll rendered useless, the motion for change of venue became nothing more than a piece of scrap paper. After hearing testimony from the state's 19 white and five Negro residents, Futch ruled against moving the trial, dismissing Woodard's poll and agreeing with Hunter that the study was "irrelevant." So much work, so much money down the drain.

Smarting from one defeat, Marshall and Akerman spent the remainder of the first day trying to block the clothing taken from Irvin's house from being entered as evidence. The defense called Irvin's mother Dellia, who testified she was terrified when Deputy Yates came to take the clothes Walter wore on the evening of July 15. Following Mrs. Irvin's testimony, the defense asked Futch to suppress the evidence since Yates obtained the clothes without a search warrant. Futch said he would take the motion under advisement and rule the next day.

Outside the courtroom, Marshall fumed. The public opinion poll had been the foundation of the change of venue motion. The only consolation: perhaps the Supreme Court would accept the poll when the defense appealed. And there would be an appeal if Walter was adjudged guilty.

Marshall's first day in court convinced him that Irvin's chances of acquittal with this judge, in this town, were slim. Ocala's racism wasn't as obvious as Lake County's, but the hatred was there, lurking just below the surface. The atmosphere didn't surprise Marshall, who had long since learned to watch his back and accept nothing at face value. Ocala was no exception to that rule. "And I went down for the trial, a white man met me in the hallway and it was real tense, state troopers and everything. And he showed me his credentials from the governor's staff, he was the governor's confidential adviser. He said, 'I'm here at the wish of the governor and everything I say is approved by the governor, and the first thing is that you look out.' He said, 'You'll see each guy that's got this kind of a pin on is a state trooper and well armed because they're trying to get you.' And I said, 'Who, Willis McCall?' And he said, 'No, the deputy is going to get you. And so go toward them, but not from them.' I said, 'Well, thank you, I appreciate that.'"

But the warning wasn't the primary reason J.J. Elliott took Marshall aside. The state had a deal to offer. According to Marshall, "He said, 'Second, the judge and the governor have been on the telephone and if Irvin will plead guilty, he'll give him a life sentence and he'll be sure he won't get the death penalty.' I said, 'Well, I can't decide that, Irvin will have to decide it.' 'Fine.' So I went to Irvin and I said, 'Look, your mother's here. I know, is there anybody else, a relative, somebody you can depend on?' He said he'd got an uncle. And I said, 'Well tell him to come with me.' So we went in the backroom and I told him the story and he said, well he said, 'You got the case reversed once,' and I said, 'Yeah, but eventually they can't find that... and odds are that they'll convict you. And Futch, the judge, I said he sure as hell will give you the death penalty, so it's up to you.' The moment of truth had arrived. Marshall fully expected Irvin to take the deal, and he was sure it was the only deal they would be offered. "He (Irvin) said, 'Well I guess I've got to make up my mind.' So he went over and talked to his mother and his uncle and the three of them came back and he said, 'Well I guess this is the only way out,' and I said, 'Well, it's up to you.' He said, 'Well, what do I have to do?' I said, 'Nothing, just stand up there and when they say 'are you guilty or not guilty,' you say: 'I'm guilty.' He said, 'What does that mean?' 'That you raped that woman.' He said, 'That I raped that whore? I didn't and I'm not going to say so.' So I know damn well that man was innocent. I know damn well he was innocent."

The episode also convinced Alex Akerman. "Jess Hunter, the state's attorney, had mellowed and had a somewhat change in attitude... At the start of the second trial, he came to us and said that if Irvin would plead guilty, he would recommend mercy, and that the judge had assured him that he would accept his recommendation. So we called a conference with Irvin and his family. At that time, he had already been sentenced to the electric chair, and we outlined the whole situation to him. We outlined the whole situation to him; we told him that the chances were very slim that it's going to be anything else in this trial, and that he could save his life by accepting the plea from the court. And he said to us, 'If I plead guilty, does that mean I'll have to say I did these things I'm charged with?' We said, 'Yes.' He said, 'Well, I'm not guilty and I won't do it.' And I couldn't help but think that here was a man seeing the electric chair staring him in the face and the chance to escape it, and that he must have been not guilty." It was an amazing decision, one Irvin made knowing full well his future would be determined by another all-white jury. He might have made a different choice if he had known the setbacks his lawyers were encountering.

On the eve of the trial, defense lawyers were forced to face the fact that alibi witnesses Carol Alexander and Daisy Lee Graham might not show up. Perkins had asked Alexander to arrive in Orlando on Saturday, Feb. 9, but the day had come and gone without a word from the waitress-turned-student. He hadn't heard from Graham either. And there was still a chance Burtoft wouldn't arrive in time to testify, even though the LDF had chartered a plane and arranged for Lawrence's father to fly up and accompany his son to Ocala. There were too many unknowns for Marshall's liking. Akerman wasn't happy either, but he figured the defense was still 10 times stronger than it had been two years earlier.

Judge Futch began the second day by denying the defense's Motion to Suppress Evidence. First, the change of venue shot down, and now the motion to suppress. It was August 1949 all over again.

The rest of the day was spent picking jurors from a panel of 94 white and six Negro men. Norma and her three-week-old son made a brief appearance, but didn't stay for the entire selection process. Irvin did, stoically watching as the attorneys questioned the good citizens of Marion County. The six percent chance of having color on the jury quickly evaporated as Assistant State Attorney A.P. (Sam) Buie used two of his 10 preemptory challenges to remove two Negro men in the first hour. He eliminated a third Negro in the second hour. The remaining minority members were excused after two announced they had already formed an opinion as and the other two revealed they were opposed to capital punishment. Almost 20 whites also offered that they had formed an opinion. If Futch recognized that the number of potential jurors who claimed to have already formed an opinion seemed to support Woodard's poll, he didn't admit it.

The defense didn't use a single preemptory challenge until the state tendered an all-white jury for acceptance. Akerman had learned from being handcuffed by Hunter when the Tavares jury was picked two years prior. Irvin's legal team promptly used seven of its 10 challenges, but still only felt good about one prospective juror: Charles H. Rogers, who claimed he hadn't heard of the case before Monday's change of venue hearing. By the time jury selection finally concluded just after 3 p.m., 53 prospective jurors had been questioned. Irvin's fate would be determined by seven farmers, two retired businessmen, a packing house employee, a merchant and a construction worker -- all white. The jury consisted of R.C. Reeves, grove foreman; John W. Markham, farmer; Charles W. Johnson, hardware store bookkeeper; F.L. Joyner, merchant; C. Hoyle Johnson, parts manager for construction company; Raymond E. Shafer, parts manager for motor company; Charles Scott, farmer; James B. Hunter, farmer; Clayton Clements, citrus concentrate worker; Thomas A. Jones, retired Western Union employee; Charles Atwell, merchant; and Charles S. Roebuck, electrician. To Akerman, this jury didn't look any better than the one at the original trial. He didn't expect a different verdict either.

Chapter 30 -- New Trial In Old Bottle

Unlike September 1949, this time the NAACP encouraged the Irvin family to attend the trial. Still, Dellia Irvin and her daughters, Henrietta and Louise were understandably apprehensive as they walked toward the Ocala courthouse. Granted, the atmosphere was less threatening than the air that pervaded the Tavares courthouse in '49, but the Irvin women still felt conspicuous and unwelcome. Henrietta was especially uncomfortable. She was seven months pregnant with her first child, a child fathered by Sammie Shepherd's older brother James. "I remember me and my sister and momma were standing on the steps in Ocala. And I said, 'I hope I don't see Walter Lee today, getting out of a police car.' And I no more said that when I looked up the street and here he come with about three or four state troopers behind him and three in front, and one holding on to him. And he was handcuffed like this in the front. And he came to the bottom of the steps. And at the Ocala jail you looked up the steps. And as he went to step up and he looked up and we saw the look on his face was a real beautiful smile when he looked up and saw us," Henrietta recalled.

Inside, nearly every seat on the main floor was filled with whites. The gallery above was packed with blacks. Scribes from around the country occupied press row. *The Associated Press, New York Post, Saturday Evening Post, Chicago Defender, New York Compass, Pittsburgh Courier* and *The Afro-American* were all represented, along with six Florida dailies.

The state again opened its case with Willie Padgett, who testified he and Norma were driving away from a square dance in July 1949 when his car stalled and he was trying to push it when a car carrying four colored men passed, then stopped and turned around. "Walter Irvin was the first man who got out of the car, on the right hand side of their car, and he walked over in front of their headlights, and asked me if we needed any help," Padgett testified.

Hunter: "And he is one of those colored men who assaulted you that night at that time?"
Padgett: "Yes, sir."
Hunter: "You are sure that is one of those men?"
Padgett: "I am positive."

Before moving on, Hunter had Padgett state that he had twice identified Irvin: first, at the Irvin home in Groveland that morning, and later out of a lineup of "six or seven head of colored people" at the state prison. Padgett then explained how he accepted the men's offer to help, and they were pushing the car when they suddenly ceased and looked at him "hostilely." Padgett said he became frightened, picked up a stick and struck two of the men as they advanced toward him. And then a third man came up from behind and hit him on the head. When he regained his senses, his wife was gone and he saw the Negroes' car speeding down the road. Willie recalled that he waited some time before another motorist helped him start his car and he then drove to Leesburg to report the crime. Willie said he and a deputy sheriff were searching for Norma when they met a car bearing his wife. According to Willie, his wife "was crying," was injured and "her clothes were torn and messed up." During cross examination, Akerman pointedly charged that Padgett had changed his testimony substantially from the trial in 1949 (where he said that he and Curtis Howard found Norma). Padgett weakly replied, "It has been almost three years." As Akerman pressed on, he discovered that Padgett's memory was full of holes. Especially when it came to what happened after the Negroes abducted his wife, leaving Willie stranded with a broken down car:

Akerman: "You remember whether or not you tried to push the car yourself?"
Padgett: "No, I don't remember."
Akerman: "About how long was it before this car came along that did push you off?"
Padgett: "I could not say."
Akerman: "It could have been as much as 30 minutes?"
Padgett: "Yes, it could."
Akerman: "Did any other cars pass by there after your wife disappeared?"
Padgett: "Yes, I believe there had been one or two."
Akerman: "I believe you said about three or four in the other trial, is that right?"
Padgett: "Well, I don't know."
Akerman: "Did you try to stop them?"
Padgett: "Yes, sir."

In conclusion, Akerman challenged Padgett about his identification of the car Shepherd and Irvin had been riding in.

Akerman: "Do you recall testifying in the former trial of this case in September of 1949, do you remember me asking you what color you thought the car was, and you answered that you thought that it was black, 'a black '46 Mercury?'
Padgett: Well, I said '46 or '48."
Akerman: "And you also said, 'I said it was black and later learned it was not.' Did you say that before?"
Padgett: "Yes, sir, I believe I did."

On redirect, Akerman hammered the discrepancy home.

Akerman: "What was the color of the automobile that you saw in front of the Irvin house in Groveland?"
Padgett: "Well, I learned later that it was a light green."
Akerman: "It is difficult to tell the difference between green and black at night, is it not?"
Padgett: "Yes, sir."
Akerman: "It was a dark colored car?"
Padgett: "Yes, sir."

The next witness, Padgett's wife, had better recall. Norma was now a mother of two, but still looked every bit the young innocent in print dress and red sweater. Young? Yes, she was only 19. Innocent? That was the image the state needed to convey. Speaking in a monotone, Norma told virtually the same story she had related at the Tavares trial, but added a few new details. When Hunter asked if her abductors had said anything to her as they drove away, Norma said, "Yes, they said, 'Don't holler or scream or they would shoot me." The courtroom was hushed as Hunter led Norma to the gang rape on a dark side road. Hunter had proved adept in handling his star witness, and now quietly, but firmly asked if she offered any resistance. It was a question that had to be asked, since Hunter knew the defense would surely broach the subject, and that Norma would reply, "no." By Hunter posing the question, the young woman would be able to explain why she didn't fight back:

Hunter: "Now, Norma, did you fight those Negroes in the car?"
Norma: "No, sir. I didn't."
Hunter: "Why didn't you fight them?"
Norma: "Because I was afraid to."
Hunter: "Did they threaten you?"
Norma: "Yes, sir."
Hunter: "In what way?"
Norma: "They said if I made any noise or screamed or hollered or tried to do anything, they would shoot me."

Hunter paused for a moment to let jurors dwell on the horror Norma had experienced. Now was the perfect time to repair Willie's botched description of the car. Norma testified that *she* carefully noted the condition of the car's interior, "Because so if I could get out of there alive I would be able to identify it." According to Norma, she was aided by a moonlit night, a light on the dashboard, a clock on the dashboard and the lighted speedometer. If Norma was to be believed, she had the presence of mind to note: three of the four windows were cracked; a piece of metal on the back floor, and lint on the back seat. Suddenly, it didn't seem so significant that Willie couldn't tell the difference between black, light green and blue. Of course, she also said that she had been taken to see the alleged car at Brooks' Garage the next day, which would explain how she was able to provide specific details.

According to Norma, after the men finished attacking her, they told her to get out if she didn't want to ride with them. She did and was walking down the road when the car suddenly stopped. Frightened, she ran into the woods, where she hid until daybreak, then resumed walking until a passing motorist gave her a lift. Norma's fluent, matter-of-fact testimony ended with her identifying Irvin as one of the men who raped her. For emphasis, Hunter asked Norma nine times, in nine different ways, if the rapist was in the courtroom. Nine times she replied, "Yes, sir." Irvin sat impassively as Norma repeatedly implicated him, although the *Ocala Star-Banner* reporter covering the trial was certain Irvin's "ordinarily medium-brown complexion" assumed "a ruddy red hue" when the young woman pointed to him and said Irvin was the second of four Negroes to attack her on the morning of July 16, 1949.

Greenberg was unimpressed by both the appearance and manner of the woman he had heard so much about. "It's easy to stereotype her. She was very young, obviously not very educated at all, very poorly educated farm housewife, so it's easy to make fun of her in a way. And I guess I did back then when I was younger and not as wise as I am now... So I sort of concede to her the fact she was a bit beyond her depth when she got into this thing, but I think she made a mistake and then she felt she had to stick with it. She was not an admirable woman, but she also wasn't someone to be put down."

Akerman knew better than to underestimate Norma. He realized he had his work cut out for him. This time Norma mentioned talking with Lawrence Burtoft at the restaurant in Okahumpka, and admitted she didn't tell the young man about what happened. The rest of her testimony went off without a hitch. "No, he didn't shake her," Greenberg recalled. "She stuck with her story. Some people tell lies very convincingly. Maybe they convince themselves they aren't lies. She might have believed these were the guys. She saw them by the light of the dashboard -- I can't see anything by the light of the dashboard."

Deputy James Yates also repeated the story he told at the first trial. He remembered searching for some time before finding a car fitting Padgett's description at the Irvin residence. After testifying that Willie said the car was "a dark 1946 Mercury sedan," Yates explained how they found it: "...we looked around in Groveland and looked around at all the cars around there, and then we went to Clermont and did not see him there and we got information there, I got a clue there as to who owned the car, and acting on that information we found out who owned the car and then we went from Clermont back to Groveland, and we saw this 1946 Mercury sedan sitting on the right hand side of the road..." The deputy said James Shepherd was behind the wheel, but that his brother Samuel and his friend Walter had driven the car the night before and were inside the house.

Next, Hunter walked Yates through his collection of evidence, beginning with Walter's clothes. Akerman immediately objected, "…by virtue of the fact that the same were obtained by unreasonable and unlawful search, and seizure…" Futch overruled. Akerman was back on his feet moments later during Yates' testimony of how he matched Irvin's shoes with footprints at the scene of the alleged crime. "We object to that question unless the proper predicate has been laid to qualify this witness as an expert on comparing tracks…" Again, he was overruled. Akerman raised the objection again minutes later. This time Futch agreed to remove the jury so Akerman and Hunter could establish whether or not Yates qualified as an expert. When asked how much experience he had in pouring footprint casts, Yates testified, "Well, about four years ago or better, and I have made a great many of them." But Akerman got the deputy to admit he had no formal training in the field and didn't protect the "integrity" of the tire tracks he made casts of. Incredibly, Yates also revealed that he made the casts of Irvin's footprints *after* he had obtained Walter's shoes. To Akerman, the brief question-and-answer session showed Yates was far from an expert, but Futch sided with the state that Yates' experience made the evidence "admissible and competent." The judge recalled the jury, then brought a close to the first day. Court would reconvene at 9:30 in the morning.

Hunter picked up where he left off when court resumed on Tuesday. Yates testified that he discovered a number of "plain" and "distinct" tracks in a dirt driveway off the main road from Okahumpka to Center Hill, where Norma said her abductors "turned in there and backed out again and gone on down road." Yates said the tracks were distinctive because, "…every tire on the car was slick… except the one on the right front side, there was no tread on the right front tire, but on the back right hand tire on the back of the car it appeared to be a new tread, and the track in the ground looked like a new tire track, and I think it was a tire that had been re-treaded." And Yates uncovered more evidence on an abandoned clay road.

Yates: "Well, we found an old handkerchief, a dirty old handkerchief that we found hanging on a bush there, and that is where it would be to the right hand side of the car, the way the car would be headed in there, and it was lying on some bushes, approximately 16 or 18 inches high."
Hunter: "Now, was there anything on that handkerchief, was there any substance on that handkerchief?"
Yates: "Yes, there was a piece of cotton or lint that was sticking on to the handkerchief."

Hunter then produced the handkerchief, which Yates said should have a "little piece of cotton" tied up inside. Of course, the cotton was there when the deputy dramatically untied the handkerchief, which Hunter passed among the jurors. Yates said he had found the same kind of cotton all over the back seat and floorboards of the car. Next, the pants the deputy had taken from Walter's room.

Hunter: "Now, Mr. Yates, are there any smears on the front of those pants?"
Yates: "Yes, sir, there are."

Hunter: "There are smears all down the side?"
Yates: "Yes, sir, there is."

Hunter passed the pants to the jury box without so much as a single word of explanation about the composition of the "smears."

During cross examination, Akerman left no stone unturned in attacking the state's second most important witness, second only to Norma. If Yates thought he was in for a repeat of the docile line of questioning he faced at the original trial, he was mistaken. The defense introduced a new line of attack, hammering Yates over the location of the alleged crime. Akerman asked that the jury be taken to the site of the alleged rape to see whether the spot was in Lake County or Sumter County (the latter was out of Yates' jurisdiction). Hunter objected, pointing out that it had already been determined that the site was in Lake. Futch agreed.

As for his investigative methods, Yates came under fire just as he had at the original trial. Akerman got Yates to admit that casts of the footprints were made *after* he had seized Irvin's shoes and that he hadn't taken photographs of the tire tracks. And Yates wasn't familiar with "recognized methods used by the Federal Bureau of Investigation." Hunter focused on repairing the damage during re-direct:

Hunter: "Now, Mr. Yates, did you ever hear of what he calls 'integrity' of those tracks, did you ever hear of that before?"
Yates: "No, sir, I never have, I don't know anything about it."
Hunter: "You were not looking for integrity of tracks were you?"
Yates: "No, sir."
Hunter: "You were looking for the tracks, were you not?"
Yates: "Yes, sir."

No doubt about it, Hunter knew what he was doing. The inference that those fancy big city lawyers had tried to trick Yates with high falutin' talk wasn't lost on the jurors. Hunter knew his people as well as he knew the law. Akerman went for broke on re-cross examination, asking Yates if Irvin had accused him and McCall of attempting to murder him. Hunter immediately objected, Futch sustained, and Yates left the witness box.

Curtis Howard, the filing station attendant, was next. Howard testified that Willie Padgett was, "bleeding down the side of his face," had shown up at "about 2:30 or 3 o'clock in the morning" and told him his wife had been kidnapped. The sheriff's department was called and before long Deputy Leroy Campbell and Padgett were searching for Norma. When Howard was relieved at 7 a.m., he headed toward Groveland to see if he could help. That's when he saw Norma, although he didn't know it at the time. "...I saw a young woman sitting or squatting in the grass by the side of the road, and when she saw my car, she ran about a hundred yards, and ran toward a dancing hall which is down there," Howard recalled. The witness said he didn't realize the woman was Norma until he saw a photo of her when he took Padgett home to get clean clothes. Howard and Padgett drove back to

Okahumpka, and sure enough, found Norma coming down the road in a car with a white man. "…and so we flagged them down, her husband had recognized her, and we met them in right in the middle of the road there, and she got out of that car and came over to her husband," Howard recalled. Akerman voiced an objection when Hunter asked if Norma, in Howard's presence, had made any statement about what happened to her. Akerman argued that Howard's answer would constitute hearsay, but the judge disagreed, paving the way for Howard to testify that Norma's legs were, "hurt and bleeding… her clothes were torn, and she was all messed up and dirty." He also noticed that "some of her underclothes were hanging down beneath her dress, and her dress was torn." According to Howard, Norma, "described to me what had happened from that time." Akerman declined to cross exam.

Night watchman Harry McDonald took the stand long enough to detail how he apprehended Greenlee. His testimony was straight out of September 1949 -- for a little while, that is. Akerman gave a start when Hunter asked, "Now, during that night at about 3:30 or 4:00 o'clock in the morning or somewhere in that period of time, did you arrest a man in Groveland?" McDonald, who had set the time at 3:15 in the original trial, answered, "Well, sometime between 3:15 and 5:30 in the morning, there was a young Negro boy who came to the service station…"

Akerman had just one question during cross examination. "You say you arrested him between 3:15 and 3:30 in the morning?" McDonald replied, "Well, it was between 3:15 and 3:30 that Saturday morning." The time clarified, Akerman allowed McDonald to step down. The defense lawyer wondered what other tricks Hunter had up his sleeve. In a different trial, with a different prosecutor, Akerman might have given the state the benefit of the doubt and considered McDonald's "5:30" answer an honest mistake. But this was Jesse Hunter, the man who had hidden Lawrence Burtoft in the first trial. The state rested just before noon after Hunter briefly questioned Luther Thomas (father of the late Ernest Thomas) and James Shepherd, Sammie's brother. Futch declared a recess until 1:30 p.m.

Akerman was reviewing his notes when he learned that Burtoft had arrived. Finally, the defense had caught a break. As Akerman watched jurors return to their seats, he noticed that Norma and her infant were absent, but Willie was very much in evidence, standing in the aisle. When court reconvened, Akerman called Burtoft, who had literally been rushed from the airport to the courthouse. Calling Burtoft was something of a gamble. The attorneys hadn't had time to prep their "star" witness, but based on the Rev. Doggett's meeting with the young private, they were confident he would tell the same story he had related to newspaper reporter Norman Bunin. Burtoft was the last man Hunter expected to see stride into the courtroom. Burtoft was a bundle of nerves, but knew he was morally obligated to testify. "They asked me why I came down to testify and I told them I'd just like to put it out of the way anyway. I didn't have enough sense not to testify," Burtoft recalled. He didn't have fear either. "Willis McCall told me I didn't have to come back or accept a subpoena because I was in the military. But I wanted to come back and I wanted to tell what I knew," Burtoft said. Akerman didn't waste time getting to heart of the state's case: Norma's credibility:

Akerman: "Now, when she was with you in your car, did she say to you that she had been abducted or kidnapped by four Negroes?"

Burtoft: "Yes, she did."

Akerman: "Did she make any statement to you as to her ability to identify those men?"

Burtoft: "She told me that she could not identify them, that one was light, and one was extremely dark and that's all she knew about them."

Akerman: "Did she make any complaint to you having been raped?"

Burtoft: "No, sir."

Akerman: "That is all."

On cross-examination, Hunter established that Burtoft lived and worked in Okahumpka, then took off the gloves.

Hunter: "Are you prejudiced against the State of Florida in this case?"

Burtoft: "No, sir, I am not, I am not prejudiced against anybody."

Hunter: "Are you not as a matter of fact in bad standing with the sheriff's office in Lake County, Florida?"

Burtoft: "No, sir, I am not."

Akerman: "May it please the Court, we object to this line of questioning, it is not proper. He can ask him if he has ever been convicted of any crime, but this line of questioning is improper."

Hunter: "I can ask him more than that."

Futch: "You cannot interrogate in that form."

Hunter: "Mr. Burtoft, I will ask you this question, 'Did you have any difficulty with the sheriff's office in Lake County about the operation of that dance hall, that causes you to have become prejudiced against the State of Florida?"

Akerman: "To which we interpose the same objection."

Futch: "The objection is overruled."

Burtoft: "No, I never did."

Hunter: "You never had any trouble whatsoever with the sheriff's office?"

Burtoft: "No, sir."

The question-and-answer session was sounding more like an interrogation than a cross examination. And Hunter was just getting warmed up.

Hunter: "Did you tell me the first time when I talked to you about this case that you had heard a woman pass by your place in an automobile screaming for help that night?"

Burtoft: "No, I didn't, I don't even know when they went by."

Hunter: "Didn't you tell me you heard a woman screaming for help going by your place?"

Burtoft: "No, sir, I did, I did not hear anything of the kind, and I don't know where you got any such information as that."

Hunter: "Didn't you offer your services to the state when this case was tried before?"

319

Burtoft: "No, I didn't, and I would not have had anything to do with it at all if you and a half a dozen other people hadn't come and bothered me and bothered me about it so many times, I was not going to say anything about it at all."

Hunter: "And because so many people bothered you about it as you say, you just got mad and decided to get even, is that right?'

Burtoft: "No, sir, I saw you a couple of times after that, and you subpoenaed me to come to your office, and I was going to help whoever I could help by telling the truth whether it was a colored person or a white person."

Hunter: "Now, as a matter of fact, Mr. Burtoft, did not I tell you that your testimony was not true and we were not going to use it in that first trial because the girl had told us that when she passed your place she was not saying a word, and I told you to get out, that we were not going to use any liars in the trial?"

Burtoft: "I don't remember."

Hunter: "You don't remember me telling you that?"

Burtoft: "No, I don't. You did not say that, you cannot fool me, I know what you said."

Akerman was proud of how well his witness was holding up under Hunter's attack. Akerman hoped the young private would continue hanging tough, because Hunter was growing angrier. The prosecutor then tried to establish that Burtoft had taken his story to Bunin, when in fact the newspaper reporter had come to him. Hunter's reasoning: "You were mad because somebody had talked to you about this case and you didn't like it, is that not right?" Burtoft couldn't figure out what the prosecutor was talking about. "No, sir, I have not been mad at anybody, and I am not mad yet," Burtoft replied. He soon would be.

Hunter: "Now, as a matter of fact, you have a great deal of animosity in this case, do you not?"

Burtoft: "No, sir, I do not. I am not against anybody."

Hunter: "As a matter of fact you are mad at the State of Florida and you are trying to get even, is that not right?"

Burtoft: "No, sir, it isn't."

Moments later, Hunter again tried to establish that Burtoft had a grudge against the State of Florida. The young private had no idea what Hunter was referring to.

Hunter: "You came on your own volition?"

Burtoft: "Well, I was helped by this subpoena."

Hunter: "As a matter of fact you are still trying to get even with the State of Florida, are you not?"

Burtoft: "No, sir, I am not, I am coming back to the State of Florida when I get out of the Army, I love the State of Florida, and I want to come back to it."

By now, Hunter was sweating. He had been cross-examining Burtoft for nearly 20 minutes. The prosecutor's tone turned sarcastic as he paced in front of the stand.

Hunter: "You say she was not hurt?"

Burtoft: "No, the only thing she said was that her feet hurt because she had been walking a long way."

Hunter: "You did not think anything about a girl being kept out in the woods all night long, you didn't think anything was wrong with that?"

Burtoft: "I did not know that she had been."

Hunter: "You did not take any interest in her condition at all, did you?"

Burtoft: "Well, from all I could see all she was doing was crying a little bit and sniffling once in a while."

Hunter: "And you took you own time about getting a car, did you not?"

Burtoft: "Well, I was not going to carry her on my back, the car was up at the house."

Hunter: "Then, you thought it was an ordinary thing for her to appear out there on the side of the road at daylight early in the morning, did that appear to be a normal everyday occurrence to you?"

Burtoft: "Well, I helped her, didn't I?"

At the defense table, Irvin's attorneys marveled at Burtoft's mettle and murmured about the liberties Hunter was taking. Akerman had been a whisker away from objecting several times, but the prosecutor seemed to pull back each time he arrived at the brink of impropriety. It may have been an error in judgment, but Akerman wasn't going to jump in unless Burtoft faltered.

Hunter: "Was there any reason why she would put any confidence in you?"

Burtoft: "I didn't ask, it was not my place to ask her, I just asked her if she thought she would recognize them, and she told me that she didn't think she could, she just told me the rest of her story voluntarily, and she just told me that she had been kidnapped by four Negroes, and I asked her if she thought she could identify them, and she said, 'no.'

Hunter: "You did not think that amounted to anything?"

Burtoft: "Well, I helped her."

Hunter: "Don't you think you would be helping her more if you told the truth for once in your life?"

Hunter had finally gone too far. Akerman objected, saying the question was improper and asking that it be struck from the record. Incredibly, Futch overruled. One can only imagine how swiftly Futch's gavel would have moved if the defense had employed such heavy-handed methods with a state witness. Encouraged, Hunter took another pock shot at the witness, asking, "Are you telling the truth in this case?" Burtoft testily answered, "Well, I felt that I should help the girl; I was not going to break my neck, I told you before, I have told you once before that I thought that she looked to be in a pretty calm condition for her husband to be lying down dead beside the road, and you told me when I told you that that she was not the type of girl to be showing her emotions, and she told me that her husband had been attacked and so I took her down towards there just as fast as I could and I don't know anything else I could do…" Finally convinced Burtoft wasn't going to buckle, Hunter turned the witness back to Akerman, who immediately excused him. The cross-examination had been exhausting. Hunter had used every trick in the book during a verbal assault that lasted almost 40 minutes. When asked about Hunter's performance, Greenberg lowered his eyes and said, "Hunter ridiculed him." And the judge allowed the verbal browbeating. All four members of the defense team were impressed by Burtoft, who refused to be intimidated by the lynch-mob mentality that prevailed inside the courtroom and the corridors of the courthouse. "They called me Nigger lover and all that," he recalled.

Walter Irvin, who followed Burtoft to the stand, couldn't help wondering what Hunter had in store for him. But first he had to get through Akerman's questioning. Irvin calmly related how he and Sammie Shepherd had gone to two night clubs in Eatonville in the early morning hours of July 16, drinking beer and playing the jukebox. Walter's testimony was short on detail, but he pulled it off without a hitch, even when Akerman asked about Walter's court martial. The defense knew it had to address the matter, because Hunter surely would.

Akerman: "Did you get in any trouble while you were in the Army?"
Irvin: "I had a court martial."
Akerman: "Did you get an honorable discharge from the Army?"
Irvin: "I didn't the first time, but I did the last time."
Akerman: "What was the dishonorable discharge for?"
Irvin: "For unlawful assembly in the company area."

Hunter started his cross examination by quizzing Irvin about the court martial. It took several questions, but Walter finally admitted "unlawful assembly" actually meant "disorderly conduct," and that he had been convicted and served a year in prison for the crime. The prosecutor was in control. But it wouldn't last. Walter denied knowing Ernest Thomas, denied that Henry Singleton had told him Thomas had tried to rob him, and denied knowing Greenlee. Undaunted, Hunter focused on establishing a timeline. Walter tried to be evasive, saying he did not have a "time piece," but Hunter finally pinned him down. Walter testified that he and Sammie: left Clermont "at about 11 o'clock;" arrived in Orlando about midnight; stayed at the first club "about an hour or an hour and a half;" and stayed "approximately an hour" at Club 436."According to Hunter, Walter's estimates meant that he "did not get back home until daylight." Wearing a look of confusion, Walter countered, "No, sir, it was earlier than that, it was early enough for me to get my rest and go to work the next morning." The prosecutor decided to move to the physical evidence. After Walter identified the shoes he wore that night, Hunter dramatically approached the stand with the pants.

Hunter: "Now, how did you get those smears on those pants, did you get those smears from the club?"
Irvin: "Well, when I pulled them off that night, there was no smears on them when I pulled them off."
Hunter: "You are positive of that?"
Irvin: "Yes, sir, I am."

The pants with the mysterious stain set aside, Hunter revisited the time element. Irvin testified that he arrived home, "somewhere between 2 and 2:30," but admitted he couldn't say for sure. Hunter, needing the time to be later, methodically reviewed Walter's testimony:

Hunter: "You testified you left Groveland -- Clermont about 11:00?
Irvin: "Yes, sir."
Hunter: "And you drove all the way to the Club Eaton which was 32 miles?"
Irvin: "Yes, sir."
Hunter: "How long did that take you?"
Irvin: "Approximately 40 minutes."
Hunter: "That would put you there about 12:00 midnight, would it not?"
Irvin: "Yes, sir."

No one seemed to notice that the prosecutor had just added 20 minutes to Irvin's estimates, 20 minutes Hunter needed to make his timeline work.

Hunter: "And you say you stayed there two and a half to three hours?"
Irvin: "No, sir, I didn't say that, I said an hour and a half."
Hunter: "That would be then from 12:00 until about 1:30 or 2:00?"
Irvin: "Well, we did not stay there until 2:00."

When Hunter asked if it was 2:45 when he left Orlando to return to Groveland, Walter replied, "Something like that." And then Hunter fattened the timeline again:

Hunter: "How long did it take you to drive back?"
Irvin: "About the same time as to drive over."
Hunter: "Then, it would be after 3:00 before you even started back?"
Irvin: "I don't know."
Hunter: "It would be just after 3:00?"
Irvin: "I guess so."
Hunter: "Just exactly the time that Greenlee was arrested, is that right?"

Akerman sprang to his feet. "We object to that question. This defendant was not there when Greenlee was arrested." Before Futch could rule, Irvin answered, "I could not say so, I don't know." Hunter had no more questions. He had done what he set out to do, put both Irvin and Greenlee in Lake County at 3 a.m. None of the jurors realized that Hunter had added 35 minutes to Irvin's time estimates: not only did he tack on 20 minutes to the trip from Clermont to Eatonville, he also added 15 minutes onto the return trip. It was an old trick, but still an effective one.

All in all, Irvin had handled Hunter's thrusts and parries masterfully. The defense was holding its own as Akerman prepared to wrap up his case with his final witness, Miami criminologist Herman V. Bennett, ex-FBI investigator, who had finally examined the plaster casts just days before.

Gary Corsair

Minutes into what would be a two-hour litany of investigative procedures and qualifications, it was clear that Bennett was far more qualified than Yates to testify about tire tracks and other "evidence." Even the most ignorant juror could see that Yates' opinions were just that, opinions. It was apparent Bennett was an expert. With 30 years of criminal investigating experience, Bennett clearly knew his subject. Hunter waited patiently for an opening to take Bennett down to size. Opportunity knocked soon enough, when the investigator began talking about examining the plaster casts before the trial:

Hunter: "Just a minute please, are you referring to any casts that are in evidence in this case?"
Bennett: "I am not in a position to answer that question."
Hunter: "May it please the Court, these casts are not in evidence in this case, we have not introduced them in evidence, and even though I would like to hear this tremendously important man, we seem to have a genius here before us, I would like to hear it, but I wish to point out to the Court that these casts are not in evidence."
Futch: "Are you objecting to testimony on these casts?"
Hunter: "Yes, sir, I am, unless the casts are in evidence."
Futch: "I think the object is good; it will be sustained."
Akerman: "May it please the Court, I want the jury excused from the room."

Futch complied, but the minute the jurors left the room, Hunter had a change of heart. Ever shrewd, always looking to exploit a weakness, Hunter suddenly realized he could use Bennett's stuffiness to his advantage. The prosecutor was pretty sure Bennett's penchant for using $10 words would backfire on the unsophisticated men sitting in the jury box. "Just a moment, I am going to withdraw my objection. I want to hear all of this learned testimony from this expert," Hunter said. The about-face puzzled Akerman, who wondered what Hunter had up his sleeve. He should have had an inkling when Hunter's assistant Sam Buie piped up, "Will you please let him indicate how long he has been doing that particular phase of this work? He is setting himself up to be an expert, and he has only given us a general background."

As Hunter and Buie had hoped, Bennett launched into an involved explanation. "Well, the subject of stains on clothing is a scientific question, and is something that can be microscopically and scientifically determined, that is to distinguish between stains, and of course in the field of scientific criminology you have to have a broad general knowledge of every department..." Hunter smiled to himself. The witness sounded just like a stuffy college professor. And he was still answering the question. "...there are several different methods in which stains are examined, and the principal and proper manner to examine them in the field of criminology is to examine them by microscope, and I wish to say here that I am not a chemist in order to determine exactly what a stain is in some cases, as to whether or not it is chemical, or blood, or what, it is often the task of a chemist, which I am not, but I do know enough about the general procedure of identifying stains to recognize when a particular stain or substance is blood or chemical of what, and I know enough to make a chemical analysis of such a stain." The former investigator may have known how

324

to identify stains, but he sure didn't know how to speak plain English. Hunter could tell by the lost look on the faces of the jurors.

To Hunter's delight, Bennett continued to use 100 words when 10 would do. One answer, to Buie's request that Bennett explain what fluorescent qualities existed in semen, lasted a full five minutes. After Bennett rambled on for several more minutes about solutions of ethylene blue, saffron, spermatozoa, ultra-violet ray lights, evaporation, test tubes and microscopes, he finally reached the point: if the pants had been sent to the FBI within three weeks, investigators could have determined if the stains were semen. Same thing with the lint on the handkerchief: after a long-winded explanation of what methods would have been used to compare the material with material taken from the back seat of the car, Bennett pointed out that FBI could have performed the tests. It was time to move on to the tire tracks. Bennett spent a full 10 minutes answering a single question about preserving the integrity of impressions left by tires. Again, the point of the rambling testimony was to establish that the FBI was capable of performing the evaluations he had just described. Bennett was boring jurors to the brink of tears. The expert had been in the witness chair for an hour, and he was just now beginning to discuss the footprint casts. After explaining that he had to reassemble the broken casts so he could photograph them, Hunter interrupted:

Hunter: "Are you an expert in that line of photography?"
Bennett: "Yes, sir, I have been doing it for 30 years."
Hunter: "You said you were not an expert in something, what was that?"
Bennett: "I said I was not an expert in chemistry."

Hunter's sarcasm-laced questions were playing well with spectators and jurors alike, many who had long ago tired of Bennett and his inflated opinion of himself. Akerman could only hope the witness still had the jury's attention as he prepared to head down the homestretch. It was time to play the trump card.

Bennett: "...as a result of my careful and thorough examination there is no doubt in my mind that the footprints were made by these shoes... There was one very illuminating fact in my examination, and before I state that, I would like to qualify one fact in the analysis of this kind of examination and would like to say this: when a person is walking, taking a step, as his foot comes in contact with the ground, the inside of the shoes is the first portion to actually come in contact with the ground, and the weight is shifted from the inside of the shoe back to the heel... as you step forward, the toe of the shoe is the last portion of the shoe to leave the ground as you step forward, and therefore, you leave an impression in the ground in direct proportion to the weight of your body, and the impression of the toe of the shoe and back of the heel will be clearly imprinted in the ground, and the principal wearing on any shoe is therefore on the ball of the foot, and the back of the heel, on the outside, and I found those identifying characteristics in these shoes, with one very significant exception, and this is this, in the left shoe I found a *convex* impression rather than a *concave* impressive, that was in the imprint in the ground, and it is my conclusion, that is a person were wearing a shoe and had his weight in that shoe, he would have left a concave impression in the ground, to make the impression, and it would have left a concave impression as the weight shifted from the front of the foot back to the heel, but it is my impression that that impression was made with a shoe with a shoe tree in it because if a shoe tree had been used, if, it could have been used in such a way that the maximum pressure was on the tip of the toe, and if a person had been walking in that shoe, there would have been a concave impression, and what I see from this case is a convex impression, and therefore in my opinion after carefully studying these shoes and casts, *there was no foot in the shoe at the time the impression was made."*

Bennett's testimony that the footprints had been faked should have rocked the courtroom. Unfortunately, he had taken such a roundabout route to his conclusion that he had lost most, if not every juror before he dropped the bombshell. Greenberg knew the faked shoeprints testimony was strong, but he wasn't sure the jurors caught the significance of Bennett's findings. Hunter wasn't taking any chances.

Hunter: Do you mean that every man that walks in his shoes leaves the same kind of impression, is that correct?"
Bennett: "Yes, unless he is deformed."
Hunter: "You mean that all footprints are alike?"
Bennett: "No, I mean that every person walks in the same way and will leave the same type of impression unless he is deformed."
Hunter: "Then you mean that everybody wears their shoes out the same way?"
Bennett: "That's right."
Hunter: "Then, how do you account for the fact that some people wear the soles or the heels out quicker than they do their heels, and vice versa?"
Bennett: "Well, he may have some injury, which has interfered with the operation of the leg muscles, so that he does not adhere to a normal walking procedure."
Hunter: "Then, your explanation of a normal walking procedure is that everybody hits the ground the same way and wears their shoes out in approximately the same way?"
Bennett: "That's right."
Hunter: "Do you know whether or not this defendant has hindrance to his normal walking operation procedure?"
Bennett: "My opinion is that there was no foot in that shoe when the impression was made."

Hunter wasn't getting anywhere. Buie leaned over and told his boss there were only two questions he needed to ask Bennett: who hired him, and for how much. Hunter nodded in agreement.

Hunter: "How much is your fee in a case of this kind?"
Bennett: "A hundred and fifty dollars a day, and fifty dollars a day expenses."
Hunter: "How many days?"
Bennett: "Well, for one day."
Hunter: "Is that all you're getting?"
Bennett: "No, sir, we will bill for additional time taken up during this trial."
Hunter: "Well, how much will your additional time fee be?"

Bennett: "At the same rate."

Hunter: For how many days?"

Bennett; "Approximately four or five days."

Hunter: "Then, as a matter of fact, you are getting from seven to eight hundred dollars to testify as an expert in this case about this stuff you have testified about?"

Bennett: "Yes, sir."

If jurors had been thinking about footprints made by shoes without feet in them, they weren't any longer. Hunter had stuck a pin in Bennett and deflated him. "Everybody laughed that he was getting so much money -- I guess to farmers that was a lot of money," Greenberg recalled. Hunter was finished with Bennett, as was Akerman. The defense rested after calling just three witnesses: Irvin, Burtoft and Bennett. It had been a strong presentation.

The state's rebuttal testimony consisted of Florida Highway Patrolmen Bill Norris and Claude Carroll, who both agreed that Willie identified Walter and tried to attack him at the Irvin home on the morning of July 16. According to Norris, Padgett said, "That is one of them." Carroll remembered Norma's husband saying, "I know that is one of them. I am going to get him if it's the last thing I ever do."

The state also tried to recall Walter to the stand. The obvious breech of courtroom protocol hit the defense attorneys like an electrical shock, but Akerman recovered in time to object that the defendant had already "had a vigorous, direct and cross examination, and he is not in good physical condition…" Before the judge could rule, Buie withdrew the motion with the promise/threat, "…we may recall him in the morning…" Futch brought the proceedings to a close on the recommendation of Hunter, who made sure the jury knew that he had "been ill as the Court well knows, and I am pretty tired…"

That night the defense team polished the closing arguments Akerman and Marshall would deliver. They also discussed the state's surprising attempt to put Irvin back on the stand, and how they could capitalize on it. The attorneys carefully worded a motion to have the case thrown out of court.

When court reconvened Thursday, Buie asked that the state be permitted to put Irvin back on the stand for additional cross-examination. Akerman immediately objected. Even though Futch sustained, Akerman asked the judge to excuse the jury. After the jurors filed out, Akerman asked Futch to declare a mistrial, "…because under the Constitution and the Laws of the State of Florida, a defendant is not required to take the stand in the case, and may it please the court, no comment can be made before the court or the jury as to the failure of the defendant to take the stand, and the state has twice in front of this jury requested that the defendant be recalled to the stand and forced to testify…" Futch denied the motion, as Akerman knew he would. But the motion was now a matter of record, and would be an important part of an appeal should Irvin again be convicted. Futch's actions didn't surprise *Afro-American* reporter Buddy Lonesome, who wrote, "With the exception of two slips he made, Judge Futch sustained the state. As fast as the defense counsel would leap up to object to some remarks made by Hunter or Buie, his assistant, The Judge would over-rule them -- sometimes even before the State offered any argument."

With the jury reseated, Hunter turned his attention to the footprint casts Bennett had called into question. Yates returned to tell jurors that then-deputy Leroy Campbell was present when the casts were made. Next, Campbell was called to confirm that he did indeed witness Yates collect the evidence. Campbell's testimony was significant -- Bennett may have been an expert, but the "outsider" was offering opinion, Campbell was an eyewitness that evidence *hadn't* been fabricated. The state subsequently introduced the tire casts and footprint casts into evidence. Broken or not, the casts made an impression.

Hunter's next order of business was discrediting Burtoft. Okahumpka resident Harold Wilson testified that Burtoft's reputation for truth and veracity was "not very good." Under cross examination, Akerman got Wilson to admit he hadn't seen Burtoft for "a year and a half." The next character assassin was long-time Okahumpka watermelon grower J.O. Gentry.

Hunter: "How long have you known him?"
Gentry: "Well, ever since the time he was 8 or 10 years old."
Hunter: "Do you know his reputation for truth and veracity pretty well?"
Gentry : "Yes, sir, I do."
Hunter: "Is it good or bad?"
Gentry: "Well, I guess it's like a lot of other people, there is always room for improvement."
Hunter: "Would you say his reputation is generally bad?"
Gentry: "Yes, sir."

In a surprise move, Hunter then called Sheriff Willis McCall. The defense lawyers quickly held a whispered conference. Hunter was in the middle of answering Hunter's third question when Akerman voiced an objection. Akerman argued that McCall couldn't be called since he had been present in the courtroom throughout the trial (subpoenaed witnesses were banned from the room until it was their turn to testify). Akerman insisted that since the sheriff hadn't been placed under rule, he shouldn't be allowed to testify. Futch had to agree. Even without McCall, the prosecutor was certain he had convinced the jury that Burtoft had been in trouble with the law. The jurors would believe what they wanted to believe, and Burtoft's word against the high sheriff's was a no-brainer. Hunter announced that the state rested.

Buie would handle the opening summation. His first priority: to counter Burtoft's claim that Norma wasn't upset and didn't mention being attacked. "...and she thought her husband was lying on the side of the road dead, and what difference does it make whether she did or she did not tell that man anything about what had gone on, and what do you think her condition, what do you think she had gone through, and how do you think she felt, after having been kept out all night long by four niggers, and carnally known and raped and ravished the way that poor girl was, and she thought her husband was lying by the road dead, and that's all in the world she was thinking about, and the minute she got to her husband the next morning, she told him exactly what happened, and that's all she needed to do," Buie ranted.

Hunter's assistant also painted Irvin as a cold-hearted, calculating criminal. "...there is a whole lot of difference between disorderly conduct and when you get *convicted* of disorderly conduct... when you get charged with unlawful assembly, that's something else entirely... usually you get some time in the stockade, and then you are dishonorably discharged, and that's what happened to Walter Irvin, and then he stayed in California for nearly a year, and then he came back to Groveland, and in less than two months after he came back to this state and Lake County, the evidence in this case shows that he raped this young white woman. Now, Gentlemen, what in the name of God possessed that man, what went on in this man's mind, what in the world went on in his mind?" A few minutes later, Buie returned to the theme: "...I feel sorry for him, I feel sorry for any man caught in this situation; I don't care whether he is white, blue, black, yellow or green; I feel sorry for any man who violently, forcefully, carnally knows any woman. There is something wrong about that, something terribly, terribly wrong, or there is something wrong in the mind of this man, or in his heart, something terribly wrong, but this man's record has shown conclusively that there is something wrong with him, either in his heart or in his mind, even beyond the sexual relation... there was trouble in his heart when he got out of the Army, and has stayed in his heart for two months after he got out, and two months after he got back home to Groveland, Florida, he got into this situation." According to Buie, the case boiled down to "...whether you believe her or the defendant. They are the only ones living who were present."

After Buie rambled for 45 minutes, Marshall took the floor. In a short, but dramatic presentation, Thurgood pondered the meaning of democracy rather than attack the state's case. He eloquently pointed out that "our Constitution is color-blind," and emphasized that Walter Lee Irvin did not act like a guilty man when officers arrested him. Marshall's approach was matter-of-fact, free of theatrics and emotional appeals. The *Dallas Times Herald* described the Marshall approach this way: "Instead of the righteous indignation of the firebrand, Atty. Marshall is affable, urbane and witty. And instead of Heaven-sent faith in his cause, he displays only a calm confidence in eventual victory."

Marshall's closing remarks were powerful and persuasive. "Everyone rebels against sex crimes when two races are involved; every good American has feelings about it. Cases like this are cases that try men's souls. But Supreme Court Justice Hall in 1896 described your responsibilities perfectly by stating that our constitution is color-blind. No one believes more in democratic principles of government than my people. Our government has decided that nobody, not even the state can take a man's life or imprison him except by trial. That's why you're here." Marshall then addressed the so-called evidence, pointing out that when it became obvious to Yates that the shoes Irvin was wearing on the morning of the 16th didn't match the prints made the night before, the lawman asked Irvin if he was wearing the same shoes. Irvin said, "no," the shoes he wore on Friday night were at home. "It seems a guilty man would not have said that," Marshall reasoned. In fact, there was nothing in

Irvin's actions that pointed to his guilt. He woke up, got dressed, had breakfast and was getting ready to walk to work with his father in Mr. Edge's groves. "The whole actions of Irvin that morning were opposite to those of a guilty man. He went through the normal course of business. I don't believe anyone who committed a crime of that type could be leading a normal life," Marshall said. Thurgood's calm, logical reasoning impressed jurors and spectators, alike.

After the noon break, Akerman took center stage. Curiously, he spent several minutes trying to cast doubt that the alleged crime took place in Lake County before getting down to the nitty-gritty. "We don't say that she was not raped or ravished in that place, but we do say that this defendant knows nothing about it... I feel that in this case where a man's life is involved, where evidence is available that should be brought in, then it should have been brought in to the case by the state. I understand that she was examined by a doctor, that she was taken to a medical doctor by the deputy sheriff, and I submit to you gentlemen that there should have been medical testimony in this case, and none was introduced to show whether or not this young lady was actually raped or ravished..." Akerman also had problems with the identifications Willie and his wife offered: "There was nothing in the world that she could have made such a positive identification by except the little dash light in the front of the car."

As for Willie, Akerman said, "Now, the color of the automobile is another thing, gentlemen, and I submit to you gentlemen that it is entirely possible that you can be mistaken, on a dark night, as to whether an automobile is a dark blue or black, or a dark green, but Mr. Willie Padgett told you that he thought it was a black car, and it might have been a dark blue car, but when they found that car the next morning, what did Willie Padgett say? Well, this is what he said, he says it was a light green car... and then we had James Shepherd on the stand and he told you that it was a dark blue Mercury that he owned... and I submit to you gentlemen that just as his memory was poor as to the identification of the color of the car, so his memory was poor as to the identification of the Negro men..." Akerman then tried to bolster Bennett, the expert witness Hunter had maligned and belittled. "...if we had purchased any testimony, I would have had him state that the plaster of Paris cast was not the print of a shoe which belonged to Walter Lee Irvin... if our witness Mr. Bennett had been lying on this stand, he would tell you that the footprint did not match the shoe of Walter Lee Irvin," Akerman reasoned.

By the time Hunter rose to deliver the state's final summation, he knew he'd be able to play it fast and loose without fear of reprisal from the bench. Sure enough, Hunter pulled out all the stops, calling Norma a "poor, Cracker girl" and describing Burtoft as a "biased individual." Hunter reasserted that Burtoft was lying about his conversation with Norma on July 16 and speculated that Norma withheld information about the rape because, "She's just a country woman who didn't know Burtoft and didn't want to tell that man she had been abused." He continued, "Did you ever see any greater bias in any man than in Burtoft's soul as he sat there? You going to believe Burtoft or that country girl?" Hunter then attacked the defense's so-called expert, "that man from Miami." Jurors were reminded that Bennett was being paid $200 a day by the NAACP. "He was paid $800 to sell you a bill of goods and he had to see it that way," Hunter told jurors.

Burtoft was the next target in Hunter's crosshairs. "Now, gentlemen, when you consider the testimony in this case, you have the testimony of this defendant, and his witnesses, and when you study the testimony you can consider the testimony of the man Burtoft who was on the stand here, and my friend criticized me for some of the questions I asked Mr. Burtoft, because I asked him if he did not have it in for the law enforcement agencies of Florida and Lake County, and by a technicality he stopped me from proving it…" Akerman, barely believing his good fortune, immediately bolted to his feet and asked Futch to remove the jury. After the jury departed, Akerman moved for a mistrial, "…because the statement made by the State's Attorney in his argument to the jury that I 'by a technicality' had kept evidence out of this case is an improper remark, and so highly prejudicial to the trial of this case, that a mistrial should be directed by this court." Futch didn't bat an eye, saying, "The motion is denied." Akerman then asked that the jury be instructed to disregard the statement that a technicality kept evidence out of the case. Again, Futch refused. The jury was recalled.

Hunter had gone to great lengths to portray Irvin as a hardened criminal, but he really bent over backward to depict Norma as the picture of innocence. "… she was an honest old Cracker girl, born and raised up in Lake County, Florida. She was a poor honest girl, and had never even probably been out of Lake County and had never been in any trouble in her life… I tell you gentlemen that there has never been any unlawful assembly in her life or anything like it, and you did not hear anything about her neighbors saying that they would not believe anything she said. And gentlemen, she never told you any scientific rot or theories; she was just an old common Florida country girl…" The implication was clear: Norma was one of them. Hunter was pulling at heartstrings. "Now, gentlemen, you have a right to sit on this jury for the protection of your women-folk, and I would like to tell you this example, on one historical occasion, there was a good woman, from a good family, on the eve of her wedding, and she was caught in the backyard and savagely raped, and she walked over to the edge of the cliff and hurled herself into eternity, rather than sacrifice that to which to her was dearer than life itself… That, gentlemen, was her chastity. Now, gentlemen, Norma Padgett, this simple little country girl, chose to live, and she has suffered the greatest tragedy that can befall any woman, and she will suffer for it the rest of her life, she has lived to tell the story, and don't you gentlemen forget that that thing, that horrible thing, will never be erased from her mind."

For insurance, Hunter, who was suffering from leukemia and set to retire Dec. 31, intimated he was arguing his final case. "I have been stricken with what may be a fatal disease, and have come to the realization that I may soon have to meet the Almighty. And I don't want to do so with any innocent man's blood on my soul, and gentlemen, I don't believe that I will ever do so, but I do want to leave this county in such condition, that you and your wives and your daughters and sisters and your sweethearts can walk and ride the streets of this county and this state in perfect safety, as you should do. I want to leave this county and this state in such a condition that no bunch of men can come in and snatch up your wife or your daughter and carry her out in the woods and rape her... Do you think that Norma Padgett will ever forget the terrible thing that happened to her and the terrible experience she had out there on that road that night? No, gentlemen, she never will." The tactic infuriated reporter Buddy Lonesome, who would write, "You should have heard that SOB-sister working on the prejudices of those crackers."

Marshall felt strongly that Hunter's comments constituted grounds for a mistrial. The judge's instructions to the jury provided further ammunition for an appeal to a higher court. The defense had asked Futch to instruct jurors to base their verdict on evidence not prejudice, but Futch had refused to include that wording in instructions to the jury. The defense had also requested that Futch instruct the jury to, "rigidly scrutinize" Norma Padgett's testimony since, "no other person was an immediate witness to the alleged act..." Again, Futch declined to use the suggested wording. The jury retired at exactly 2:30 p.m. after two-and-a-half days of testimony.

Marshall recalled the scene: "...while the jury was going on, I looked at the whole jury face to face -- all white, of course -- and everyone had a Shriner pin on him. Well, Judge [Truman] Futch and I had been off the record discussing Masonic business with my 33rd degree ring and he only had a 32nd degree ring. I told him he was in the wrong bunch. And I went up while the jury was out and I said, 'Judge Futch, I'm quite serious about this, I'm going to make 'em lose. Every one of those jurors has got a Shriners pin, did you notice that?' He said, 'Sure, I noticed it.' And I said, 'Did you also notice that the state's attorney -- three different times gave the Masonic distress signal to that jury?' He said, 'Yeah, as a matter of fact, it was four.' I said, 'Well, I'm going to make an objection.' 'I wouldn't do it.' And I said, 'Why not?' He said, 'There's nothing racial about that, he does it all the time whether you're white, black or green. He gives the distress signal all the time.'" Disgusted, Marshall went into the hallway to wait out the jury. "So a white man was there and he came up and he said, 'How long is the jury going to be out?' And I said, 'Damned if I know, I can't tell.' He said, 'I can tell.' I said, 'How?' He said, 'You see that man over there just lit up a cigar?' And I said, 'Yeah.' And he said, 'Watch it. When he's finished that cigar, the jury will come back.' I said, 'What the hell are you talking about?' He said, 'Several of those jurors obviously are cigar smokers and they're not going to waste that cigar. So after they'd decide the case, they're going to finish the cigar before they come in.' He stamped out his cigar. In comes the jury."

Akerman felt a dreadful sense of deja vu when the jurors filed back into the courtroom at 3:57. The all-white jury had deliberated just one hour and 23 minutes. They weren't out long enough. Irvin was heading back to Raiford and the electric chair unless the jury made a recommendation for mercy. Irvin, looking more like a college student than a criminal in a dark blue, double-breasted suit, white shirt and red tie, sat expressionless as jury foreman Thomas A. Jones solemnly read the verdict. Walter's sister, Henrietta had a sinking feeling. "After I heard the argument, or what was going on I told my momma to go outside with me because I felt like then that they were going to sentence him back, that they were going to sentence him back to the electric chair. So, by the time I got downstairs, I heard them bringing him downstairs, like two steps at a time. And a white woman was screaming and hollering, saying 'he's innocent, he's innocent, he's innocent.' And it happened so fast."

Guilty. The sentence: death in the electric chair. For the second time, there was no recommendation of mercy for Walter Lee Irvin. Marshall immediately made a motion for a mistrial on grounds that the state prejudiced the jury in its summation by inferring that defense withheld evidence from the state. Futch, of course, denied it.

Walter's mother wept as Marion County Sheriff Don McLeod, who got his job because a black boy killed his predecessor, escorted Walter to a panel truck that would take him to the state prison to be "electrocuted until he is dead." Walter's sobbing mother was waiting for Thurgood as he exited the courtroom. The attorney embraced the distraught woman, telling her, "Don't worry honey. With the faith of our people and the grace of God we'll be back." It was a bitter defeat for Marshall, one that would stay with him forever. "I felt that, Irvin's mother had me awake all night, every night. She had the most impressive face I've ever seen on a woman, real high cheekbones and a whole lot of red in that black, a whole lot of red, and lot of Indian. And she just had these piercing eyes and she told me not once, but four times, 'Don't you let my son die.' I'm going to be stuck with that for life."

Not surprisingly, the lily-white voice of Marion County, the *Ocala Star Banner,* heralded the verdict. Editor R.N. Dosh had chronicled the racial harmony during the pretrial hearing on the change of venue issue, and evidently saw nothing during the trial to change his opinion. In an editorial, the *Star-Banner* concluded, "...that the trial was conducted in an atmosphere of tranquility and that the people on the streets of Ocala seemed to be little concerned over what was going on in the courthouse... One of the Negro reporters for a northern newspaper, sent here to report the trial, is quoted as having stated that he and others were greatly impressed with the good race relations existing here. Other experienced newspaper men made similar comments... As one high court official was heard to remark, after conclusion of the trial, 'We have given him two fair trials and that is enough.'" The editorial writer must not have lunched at Bennett's Drug Store.

The verdict was front-page news throughout the country. The *Afro-American* trumpeted the decision with the bold headline PROOF OF INNOCENCE IGNORED AS FLORIDA JURORS DOOM IRVIN. The accompanying account by Lonesome reported, "In the face of concrete evidence which, in any other State would have proved him not guilty, Walter Irvin, 24-year-old veteran, was sentenced to death Thursday for his alleged participation in the attack of a young white matron."

Before returning to Orlando, Akerman promised reporters he would file a motion for a new trial on Monday. If denied, he was prepared to take his plea to a higher court. FBI agents Robert T. Nichwitz and Tobias E. Matthews were waiting for Akerman in the lobby of the San Juan Hotel. The agents explained that they were investigating the murder of Harry T. Moore. Akerman was adamant that even though Moore was a vocal critic of McCall during the Groveland controversy, Moore didn't assist in the defense in any way. Akerman told agents he believed Moore was killed because of his being a representative of the NAACP.

"He felt someone killed Moore, not for anything he said or did as an individual, but because he was a symbol of the effort of the Negroes in the State of Florida. He said he would not have been surprised if Sheriff McCall or someone connected with him killed Moore. He advised he had no proof or anything to substantiate this statement but that it was merely his opinion. He knew of no threats to Moore and was shocked to learn of Moore's death."

The Moore murder investigation was off the front page, but that didn't mean the file was closed. On Feb. 19, 1952, FBI agents Clyde P. Aderhold and Frank F. Meech traveled to Apopka to re-interview an informant who had previously told agents a Klansman named Earl Brooklyn had actually displayed floor plans of Moore's home at a KKK meeting. The informant told agents that Brooklyn, Tillman H. Belvin and Robert L. Judah discussed Moore and his home during a meeting in the fall of 1949. Agents reported that, "To the best of his recollection Brooklyn said in substance as follows: 'Listen, fellows, I've got a deal. Now this nigger Moore up at Mims is the head of the NAACP and he has played a very important part in trying to get the Lake County niggers cleared of that rape charge. He caused a lot of money to be sent down from New York to be used in defending the niggers. I have been over to Mims and have checked over the place carefully.' At this point the informant stated Brooklyn withdrew from his shirt pocket a piece of plain white paper which was crumpled and folded. Brooklyn unfolded the paper which was approximately 8" x 8" square and held the paper in his hands. Informant said he did not clearly see the drawing but to the best of his recollection there was the plan of a house drawn on the paper in pencil and he described it as being crudely drawn. Upon withdrawing this piece of paper and unfolding it Brooklyn said, 'I have here a plan of the house... I want to recase the place carefully and I am going to take some men over. Is there any of you men that want to go with me?'" Agents had also interviewed Belvin, who stated that he had heard from general conversation that some people from Miami might have come up "to do the Mims job." Agents finally had names to go with the despicable crime.

Chapter 31 -- Revelation

Reporter Buddy Lonesome's final word on the Ocala trial appeared on the front page of the Feb. 23, 1952, *Afro-American.* "As a result of my visit to this Southern outpost I am totally convinced that the lot of the colored man in the South will always be hard. No matter how good conditions may seem to be, one thing that the Southern 'cracker' will never tolerate is for the colored man to have his women. Because of that fear, he will always impose third-class conditions on his colored 'friends'... The murder of Sheriff Edward Porter by a 17-year-old colored lad is a strong case in point. By all accounts, (and I talked with several residents on this), Sheriff Porter was a fair, kindly peace officer. But when he was killed by young Orion Johnson -- there was not one colored person hurt, property damaged, or any other indication of mob reprisal. We all agree that's how it should be, but such sane action is hardly the norm for white residents of the Deep South, especially Florida. That's because no white woman was involved. But the infamous Groveland attack case, was an altogether different story. Five homes were destroyed, colored people were beaten, killed, and run out of town by mobs at point of guns and threat of the rope. The reason for this is clearly evident. State's Attorney Jess Hunter best expressed it when, even though he had heard the testimony many times before, he stood before the so-called attack victim in the tiny Ocala courtroom and asked in shocked tones: 'You mean he (pointing to Irvin) put his...' When the girl replied that Irvin had done such a thing to her, the faces of the men on the all-white jury bore the same incredulous expression. That's why this jury will find Irvin Guilty, and T.V. (sic) Futch, the whittling judge, will impose the death sentence on this 24-year-old youth who has gone through more hell than most combat hardened veterans."

In late March, Thurgood Marshall contacted Akerman and offered him $500 to take the case to the Florida Supreme Court. Akerman accepted, even though, "under ordinary circumstances I would not consider your offer of $500... However, I am well aware of the expenses incurred so far in this case and of the probable future expenses and realize the financial problem." Akerman reasoned he could devote time to the Groveland case when he traveled from Virginia to Florida to attend to "other matters." He figured he could represent Irvin as long as Paul Perkins continued to handle miscellaneous details and draft necessary briefs.

Marshall also directed Paul Perkins to draft and file the appeal, which cited numerous errors in the trial -- 22 to be exact -- and repeated the charge that Irvin's clothes were seized unlawfully. First and foremost, the petition charged: Hunter with making an "improper and prejudicial argument;" the court erred by overruling defense objections to testimony by Willie and Norma Padgett about an alleged conversation; and the court's refusal to permit the public opinion poll.

On May 6, Willis McCall was re-elected sheriff, his 6,577 votes almost doubling the combined totals of three challengers. Apparently, the negative publicity from the shooting of Shepherd and Irvin hadn't diminished his popularity. Perhaps it had increased it. The Florida press noticed: an editorial in the *Lakeland Ledger* said, "A great many Floridians have been of the opinion all along that McCall was guilty of dangerous carelessness in handling the two notorious prisoners. (The Negroes transferred from Raiford to Tavares to stand trial for rape.) But a majority of Lake Countians who voted Tuesday obviously did not regard it as inexcusable carelessness."

Perkins continued to be the NAACP's lone link to the remaining Groveland defendants, Irvin and Greenlee. And Marshall and Greenberg couldn't have asked for a better point man. Plus, Perkins was a bargain at $3.75 per hour. Marshall was now regularly sending work Perkins' way. Perkins could be counted on. But now that the battleground in the fight to save Irvin's life had shifted from Lake County to Tallahassee, where the appeal would be heard, Perkins wouldn't be able to help as often since the trip from Orlando to Tallahassee meant the loss of a whole day. An alternative needed to be found. Jacksonville attorney James H. Bunch as a likely candidate since he was well acquainted with Florida's Supreme Court justices. Perhaps Bunch could enter the case "as a friend of the court."

During a July 19, 1952 meeting in Washington, D.C. Marshall directed Bunch to travel to Tallahassee to test the waters. The reception from Assistant Attorney General Reeves Bowen was far from cordial. "We discussed and considered this matter at length but he emphatically refused my request. He said that it would just be another fight on his hands and much more work to do. He further said he would oppose my Petition to the Supreme Court to be permitted to file a brief and orally argue said cause as amices curiae," Bunch told Marshall. A meeting with Justice Roberts went better: he suggested that Bunch file a petition, but stressed that Bunch would be required to show good cause since he would likely be opposed by the attorney general.

In discussing the Tallahassee meetings with Marshall, Bunch expressed his concern that the appeal might not be strong enough. "I am of the opinion that we must, if possible, get more evidence into the record showing the facts in and about the deaths of the two defendants, and that since the deaths of these two defendants was brought about by the acts and doings of the Sheriff in his official capacity representing the State of Florida should not be permitted to bring about the deaths of two witnesses for the defendant, and then after depriving the defendant of his two witnesses, put him on trial for his life... I have a strong belief that if we can get the facts into the Record about the deaths of these two witnesses that we can save the life of Walter Lee Irvin." Bunch suggested Marshall rethink his strategy, telling Thurgood that it was premature to file a petition for Bunch to appear as a friend of the court. "It would be most unfortunate for us for my Petition to appear as amicus curiae to be denied by the Supreme Court and rather than taking that risk, it would be better for us to obtain the facts and then file a Petition in the Supreme Court to amend the Record as provided by Rule and then file another Petition to suppress the evidence introduced against the Defendant..." Marshall respectfully disagreed. He told Bunch to prepare the petition.

On Nov. 5, 1952, Bunch submitted his Petition of Amicus Curiae, which focused on the killing of Sammie Shepherd, saying "...the people of Florida would like to know whether the officers of the law can kill the witnesses of a Defendant charged with a capital offense, as herein set forth, and then put said Defendant on trial for his life, after they have put his witnesses in the cemetery -- that is not democracy -- the democratic way of life -- that is 'iron curtain' procedure..." As Bunch feared, his petition was denied. With that, Bunch bowed out of out the picture, telling Perkins, "There is not much more I can do herein. I regret exceedingly that my advice as to procedure in this case was taken so lightly. I certainly hope that Walter will be saved... I have done my best in this case for Walter and I certainly wish him success... I wish I could have done more for Walter."

Marshall, determined to get something for the money he paid for the opinion poll that Judge Truman Futch had rejected in Ocala, included the findings in the appeal. The numbers wouldn't be easy for the Florida justices to ignore: "If the report had been received into evidence and if testimony thereon had been admitted, defendant would have been able to show by this witness that a very substantial percentage of Marion County's population (43%) was certain of defendant's guilt (although an additional 20% thought him guilty but were not sure) and that an overwhelming percentage of Marion County's Negro population (84%) feared that if a member of the jury voted for acquittal, something might happen to him." The appeal then struck at the heart of the state's objection: that the validity of the poll was suspect because Dr. Woodward *didn't personally* interview the citizens questioned. "All the interviews were made by his authority and many times he actually overheard the interviews. At no time, could any one else, after receipt by him, touch the papers... This type of evidence, though in a form hardly as reliable as that submitted here, has long been admitted on motion for change of venue and has been admitted in other cases in which the issue has been the public state of mind," the appeal continued.

In keeping with previous appeals, the issue of extensive and adverse publicity was also raised. For added emphasis, the petitioners included the critical comments Sheriff Willis McCall made after the U.S. Supreme Court ordered a new trial in 1951. Mention was also made of the murder of Harry T. Moore. The defense was sticking to its contention that an impartial jury was an impossibility in Marion County because 53 jurors were called before a jury could be selected. And then there was the matter of moving the trial from Lake to Marion, where Sheriff Ed Porter had been murdered by a young black man: "Indeed the state conceded that the venue should be changed from Lake County and at the same time alleged that conditions prevalent in Lake were present elsewhere. We may ask, where would they be most present but in the county contiguous to Lake?" Irvin's attorneys also asked the Supreme Court to consider the following questions:

1) Did the court "abuse its discretion" by refusing to allow the public opinion poll into evidence?

2) "Did the court err in overruling defendant's motion to suppress certain evidence obtained by a search and seizure wherein defendant's ignorant, frightened mother gave same to a deputy sheriff after having taken same from defendant's private room upon demand of said officer?"

3) Did the court err in overruling the defendant's objection when Willie Padgett testified that his wife had been raped, and when Curtis Howard was allowed to testify that Norma had told him she had been raped?

4) Did Judge Futch err when he refused the defense's requested instruction which sought to inform the jury that "in a case where no other person was an immediate witness to the alleged act, the testimony of the prosecutor should be rigidly scrutinized?"

5) Did the court err in sustaining the state's objection when the defense asked Deputy James Yates if Walter Irvin had accused him and Sheriff Willis McCall of attempted murder?

6) "Is a fair trial accorded a defendant where the trial court permits the state attorney in his argument to the jury to refer to evidence that has been excluded by the trial court and to state that the matter could have been proven if the evidence had not been kept from the jury by a technicality on the part of defense counsel?"

7) Did the court err in overruling the defense objection when Deputy Yates offered his opinions regarding the tire tracks and footprints?

8) In his instructions to the jury, Judge Futch should have cautioned jurors against being influenced by public sentiment or prejudice. Instead, the judge refused to include the defense's proposed instruction.

The state filed its 42-page reply on Jan. 8. Attorney General Richard Ervin and Assistant State Attorney Reeves Bowen, who had argued against the original appeal back in 1950, contended:

- "The appellant did not produce a single witness who had any personal knowledge of the state of public opinion in Marion County… the state put on the testimony of both white and colored citizens which showed conclusively that there had been no excitement or prejudice in Marion County…"

- "…the purported report of the poll in Marion County was inadmissible because it was never shown that the persons who were interviewed gave the answers ascribed to them by the report… None of the interviewers were called as witnesses to establish the authenticity of the answers ascribed to the persons interviewed."

- Concerning the defense claim that Irvin's shoes and clothes were obtained by illegal search and seizure: "Yates testified without contradiction as follows: "Q. Was there any reason whatsoever why you could not have gone there and gotten the Judge to issue you a search warrant? A. Well, if he (referring to the appellant) had not told me where the clothes were and had not given them to me, then I would have gotten one."

- Regarding the defense claim that Dellia Irvin had no right to give her son's shoes and trousers to Yates because Walter Irvin paid rent: "…the trial judge had the right to disbelieve the mother's said testimony because: (a) She was an interested witness, being naturally and vitally interested in helping the appellant, her son, escape conviction for rape… (b) …she did not testify at the first trial that the appellant paid any board or rent or that he occupied a room by himself or that she and he considered that any particular room was his alone. Therefore, when the mother did testify to that effect something like two years later, the trial judge was entitled to believe that she had yielded to the temptation to fabricate a story that she thought might be helpful to her son's efforts to save himself from another conviction for rape and possible death penalty."

- Concerning Judge Futch's refusal to grant a mistrial when Hunter told jurors that he was prevented from asking Burtoft questions by a technicality raised by the defense: "If any error was committed in this regard, it was of a minor and inconsequential nature. The state attorney did no more than refer to that which the jury already knew…"

The Florida Supreme Court rendered its decision in Walter Irvin v. Florida on June 23, 1953 with Justices Thomas, Hobson, C.J. Roberts, Terrell, Sebring, Mathews and J.J. Drew reaffirming Futch on nearly every count. The court, in a detailed opinion by Justice Elwyn Thomas said, "…the testimony, taken as a whole, overwhelmingly supported the view that the appellant [Irvin] could be assured of all of the protection afforded by the law while he faced trial on the charge lodged against him." The defense had 90 days to make an appeal to the United States Supreme Court.

The justices also upheld Futch's refusal to consider the public opinion poll because Dr. Woodward did not actually conduct interviews, but merely tabulated results: "We cannot approve this method of determining the likelihood of a defendant's being unable to receive a fair trial in a given community and therefore cannot attribute any abuse of discretion to the rejection by the judge of the proposed testimony... Neither the witness, the one who had general supervision nor the one who served as field representative, pretended even to have made any interviews on which he could base an opinion as to facts which would support an application for change of venue. Any information he could give on the witness stand, would in our opinion, have amounted to hearsay based upon hearsay." And the justices echoed Hunter's sentiments that the competency of the Elmo Roper firm was suspect after the firm missed picking the winner of the 1948 presidential race. "We need say no more in this regard than quote the supervisor who said, in reply to questions about the survey conducted by his organization prior to the presidential election in 1948,'in that kind of a survey we were very badly wrong.'"

The justices' point-by-point rebuttal to the defense claims is summarized below:

To the defense claim that pretrial publicity made an impaneling a fair jury impossible--
"...the State introduced numerous witnesses, some of the Negro and some of the white race, from various walks of life, all of whom stated without reservation that the appellant could get a fair and impartial trial in Marion County... We think that the facility with which the jury was chosen emphasizes, in retrospect, the soundness of the judge's action. Only fifty-odd jurors were required from which to obtain a panel of twelve qualified to try the issue."

To the defense claim that Yates illegally acquired clothes from Irvin's home--
"The story of the deputy sheriff that upon asking for the articles the mother invited him in and that he accompanied her to the boy's room, was not contradicted... We believe that an interpretation of the incident as an unlawful search and seizure would be decidedly overdrawn."

To the defense claim that Willie Padgett's testimony that his wife told him she had been raped should have been stricken because he wasn't the first person she spoke with after the attack--
"...the objection was based on the fact that the husband was not the first, but the second... From the very nature of such an experience we think her reply to her husband, even in the other's presence, without telling the first man she saw, a virtual if not a total stranger, was entirely natural and that the admission of the testimony did not violate the spirit of the rule."

To the defense contention that it should have been allowed to ask Yates if Irvin had accused him and McCall of attempting to murder him--
"True, much latitude is allowed a cross-examiner of witnesses but the permissible scope of cross-examination is not so far-flung as to include a question of this type. While it was intended, ostensibly, to show hostility of the witness... if such procedure were approved, a

defendant could make an accusation, however idle, against a prospective adverse witness, then use his own charge, even if wholly unfounded, to his advantage."

To the charge that Judge Futch should have declared a mistrial because Hunter told jurors the defense had prevented him from proving Burtoft had a grudge against law enforcement agencies--

"We think this procedure was irregular; that the remark should not have been made, and having been, the court should have instructed the jury to disregard it. But we cannot ascribe to the error such importance as to justify a reversal... A trial of this magnitude and duration cannot be expected to be a pure procedural gem... If there has been any deviation from the proper path, the question immediately arises whether the digression was of such consequences as to have endangered fundamental rights. That is the reason for our 'harmless error' statute providing that, 'No judgment shall be reversed by any court of the State of Florida in any cause, civil or criminal, on the ground of improper admission or rejection of evidence or for error as to any matter of procedure unless in the opinion of the court after an examination of the entire case it shall appear that the error complained of has resulted in a miscarriage of justice'... When all the evidence in this voluminous record is considered independently, and then in connection with the remark of the state attorney, the irregularity which we have mentioned fades into insignificance."

But Justice Hobson thought Hunter's gaffe *was* significant. In a dissenting opinion, Hobson wrote, "...I believe that the trial judge committed error in refusing to instruct the jury to disregard the improper remark made to it by the state attorney. It is my view that the harmless error statute or rule should not apply in a first degree murder case where the verdict is one of guilty with recommendation of mercy."

On July 5, Paul Perkins mailed copies of Motion for Rehearing to the Florida Supreme Court and the Attorney General's office. The motion sought a new trial on six points:

1) Woodward should have been allowed to testify regarding the results of the Elmo Roper poll based on the Uniform Business Records as Evidence Act, Section 92.36 of the Florida Statutes. The statute covers reports presented to supervisors by subordinates in the regular course of business.

2) Regarding Yates taking Irvin's clothes and shoes: "The Court also apparently inadvertently overlooked the fact that Appellant's mother was ignorant of the law, uneducated, and in a situation in which any mother would be greatly frightened by a police office, no matter how polite.

3) Since Irvin contended that Yates attempted to murder him, appellant should have been allowed to cross-examine the deputy, which would have revealed he was hostile to Irvin. Also, appellant should have had "the opportunity to make reference to public documents... which establish that such charge is not without foundation."

4) Hunter's reference that the U.S. Supreme Court had ordered a new trial "by a technicality" held Irvin's attorneys up to ridicule and affected the "entire proceedings."

5) The Court inadvertently overlooked the fact that the "harmless error" rule in a capital case where no recommendation for mercy was made should not be applied where clear error exists, especially in a case where the issues were so many and often so difficult that it is impossible to know whether one little point may have swayed the jury... to convict or fail to recommend mercy.

6) Yates failed to describe the characteristics of Irvin's shoes, tires and tire tracks, but merely stated his conclusions and methods. The jury should have been allowed to form its own opinion.

On July 27, after the Supreme Court denied the petition for rehearing, Perkins argued for a stay of execution. The Florida justices ruled four days later, denying the petition and ordering that Irvin be executed. The Court automatically granted another 90-day stay to allow the defense reasonable time to appeal to the U.S. Supreme Court.

The fourth anniversary of the original trial of the Groveland boys came and went with Irvin still on death row. Walter had long ago given up on being freed; he just wanted to live as long and comfortably as he could. On Sept. 28, 1953, he entreated Perkins. "I know it's been a long time since I wrote you but I hope you will look over that fact for I am always praying that you are doing fine and enjoying good health. Mr. Perkins I want to know whether it's possible that you can get me back to a jail someplace, and this is my reason for wanting to get to a jail, so that I can receive and write mail from different ones and get some reading material and maybe a radio. Mr. Perkins, I trust that if it is possible I will appreciate it very much. Extend my regards to every one, and best wishes to you. Thanking you in advance. Sincerely yours, Walter L. Irvin."

Perkins definitely had Irvin on his mind, but finding a radio for Walter was the least of his concerns. Legal options exhausted, Perkins knew the only way to keep Walter alive would be to convince Gov. Dan T. McCarty, who had succeeded Fuller Warren, to grant clemency.

Chapter 32 -- Renewed Hope

Irvin's supporters were optimistic about appealing to Gov. Dan McCarty, a 41-year-old Democrat from Fort Pierce, who narrowly won the 1952 election and proved to be a no-nonsense administrator from the get-go. But McCarthy never got to consider Irvin's plight; he suffered a heart attack on Feb. 25, 1953 and died seven months later. Florida's Constitution stipulated the Senate President become acting governor, thus Charley Johns ended up in the State House.

On Jan. 18, the Supreme Court declined to review Irvin v. Florida. Walter would not get a third trial. Perkins immediately filed a Petition for Stay of Execution. Discouraged, but not surprised, the Legal Defense Fund attorneys began formulating plans to pressure the new governor, who was likely consumed with just one thing: finding a way to keep the coveted job that had miraculously fallen into his lap. The constitution stated that Johns would have to win a special election to stay in the governor's mansion.

With appeals to the Florida Supreme Court exhausted, the LDF implored NAACP branches to renew their cries for justice. Marshall also called on his friends in the press. *St. Petersburg Times* Tom Harris, who had been publicly criticized by McCall and Hunter for his paper's courageous stand in 1950, was happy to resume the push to save Irvin. On Feb. 15, 1954, the *Times* urged Johns and the parole board to exercise, "compassion and calm judgment" in changing Irvin's sentence to life imprisonment. "A great many persons who studied this case with great care, including two *Times'* reporters who worked on it for weeks, were never convinced of the guilt of the four defendants. There were unexplained discrepancies in evidence and other strange elements. In a calmer climate of opinion it seems certain that at least 'a reasonable doubt' as to guilt would have been in the minds of the jurors...With two of the accused dead and the other two in prison for life, even a vengeful 'justice' would seem served, " Harris wrote. The editorial concluded, "And because there is doubt, it is possible that sometime in the future it might turn out that the four were not guilty. It will then be too late for true justice if Walter Lee Irvin is electrocuted. Both compassion and calm judgment argue for his sentence to be changed to life imprisonment."

Johns didn't respond to the editorial. He had more pressing matters to worry about, specifically Florida's much-anticipated gubernatorial race, which was shaping up to be a three-way fight. Johns not only had to worry about Brailey Odem, but also a longshot named Leroy Collins, the 44-year-old son of a Tallahassee grocer who was elected to the state Senate in 1944.

When Collins challenged Johns to a televised debate in Miami, the governor saw a chance to scuttle one of the challengers. On May 13, thousands of Florida voters tuned in. Even more listened on the radio. The debate turned out to be an event anyone watching or listening would not soon forget. Time and time again, Johns brazenly continued talking after his time limit had expired, even after the moderator reminded him of the rule. Meanwhile, Collins was the model of decorum. As the contest neared its conclusion, Collins played his trump card. Collins' aide John Germany remembers: "...just before the debate one of the people in the studio came up and showed Roy a copy of an ad that was to be in the next day's *Miami Herald*. The ad proclaimed that Johns had been the winner of the debate. Roy carried through with his debate. And just before it ended Roy said, 'Governor Johns, I want to show you the ad that you have placed in tomorrow morning's *Miami Herald*.' With that he put the ad right in front of the television camera. Of course, Charley couldn't answer the question of how it got in there." It was a moment that could pay big dividends on election day.

On Aug. 10, the *Afro-American* implored readers to, "flood Governor Johns' desk at the State Capitol in Tallahassee with thousands of appeals for commutation of this unfortunate lad's sentence." The Northern press was doing its part to keep Irvin in the limelight. So was Perkins, but it wasn't easy.

Although he had proven himself time and time again, Perkins still had to go through Akerman and the LDF for direction. On more than one occasion, Perkins expressed a concern to Akerman, who forward it to Greenberg, who contacted Marshall. For Perkins, there was nothing expedient about working with the NAACP. At times weeks would pass before he received an answer to a simple question.

McCall, who had managed to stay out of the headlines in 1953, thundered back into the national spotlight in the spring of '54. Once again, protecting the white race propelled him back onto the front page. The source of McCall's ire: a fruit-picker named Allan Platt, who moved his wife and five children from Holly Hill, S.C. to Mount Dora that year. When parents called the sheriff after their children told them the new kids "looked like niggers," McCall showed up at the Platt residence to see for himself. As McCall lined the children up against the wall for photographs, Allan produced his marriage license and the childrens' birth certificates to prove they were not Negroes. McCall wasn't convinced.

Newspaper editor Mabel Norris-Reese also paid a visit to the Platts, but reached a completely different conclusion, which she courageously published. The *Topic* reported that the Platts were of Irish-Indian pedigree and were likely descendents of Sir Walter Raleigh's "lost colony" of Roanoke. Norris-Reese, who had already weathered having a cross burned on her lawn, 'KKK' painted on her office windows and her dog mysteriously poisoned, braced herself for the worst. She didn't have to wait long. Bryant Bowles, founder of the National Association for the Advancement of White People, took time out from his Florida lecture tour to stop by the *Topic* office, where he swore to "get even" with Norris-Reese.

The story made national headlines after the children were barred from Lake County schools. Things really heated up when 65 students signed a petition supporting the Platts being enrolled in school. Soon thereafter, someone drew a chalk line on the school sidewalk designating one side for "White People" and the other for "Nigger Lovers." A white boy who stood on the "Nigger Lover" side was pelted with rocks. *Time* magazine described the sheriff's confrontation with Allan Platt and his family this way: "The principal tried to be polite, but the sheriff was in no mood for the amenities. He pointed to Denzell Platt, 17, and declared: 'His features are Negro.' Then he pointed to (Laura Belle Platt), 13, and said: 'I don't like the shape of that one's nose.' After the lesson in anthropology, Roseborough surrendered. The Platts, he said, would have to stay out of school 'until the sheriff is satisfied.'" Naturally, the *Time* article irked McCall, and not just because it portrayed him as "beefy... dictatorial" and "bullying." His main complaint: that *Time* cast his nemesis Norris-Reese as a champion of the oppressed.

The *Orlando Sentinel's* Lake County correspondent Ormund Powers was more than happy to oblige when asked to set the record straight. Powers dutifully pointed out that *Time* gave the sheriff, "full credit for the Platt children's predicament," while ignoring the fact that both the Lake and Orange county school boards had officially classified the Platt children as Negroes and barred them from attending school. "McCall has been the whipping boy, however. Said he: 'I've had to take over the school board's job; I've had to take the brunt of this.'" Powers also addressed "reprisals" Norris-Reese told *Time* about: "a flaming cross on her lawn, the poisoning of her dog and the smearing of 'KKK' across her office windows." Powers reasoned, "This sounds as though the sheriff or his men personally committed these acts. They are neither so vicious nor so stupid."

After the landlady evicted his family after a visit from McCall, Allan Platt, frustrated and tired of being harassed, attempted to enroll his children in school in Orange County. When McCall found out he intervened and the school officials in Orange also barred the Platts. Finally, a private school in Mount Dora invited the Platts to enroll their children despite McCall's efforts to dissuade administrators.

The animosity that festered between the NAACP and Lake County's powerbrokers ensured that the two camps kept a wary eye on the other. McCall never missed a chance to criticize the NAACP, and Marshall returned the favor whenever the sheriff went too far. In October, a golden opportunity presented itself when Marshall learned that McCall had delivered a speech in Delaware denouncing school desegregation. The NAACP called for the sheriff's removal, to which Gov. Johns called McCall's remarks, "ill advised," but insisted the comments didn't affect his duties as sheriff. Johns' support of McCall told Marshall what he needed to know, that Florida's 32nd governor wasn't likely to commute Irvin's sentence. Sure enough, when Irvin's defenders petitioned the governor for clemency in November, Johns would not be swayed. With the election imminent, he had no interest in infuriating the sons of the South who still lived and breathed segregation. On Nov. 1, Johns set Irvin's execution for the week of Nov. 8.

When Walter awoke on Nov. 6, two days before execution day, he fully believed he had reached the end of the line. He longed to see his family one final time. He couldn't know that his family hadn't been notified. "I was working for a woman, doing housecleaning when I saw Walter's name in the headline of a newspaper that was folded on a table. I don't think she wanted me to see it. When I opened it up it said, 'Walter Irvin to die today.' When I saw that, my heart came up in my throat," Walter's sister, Henrietta said. "All I could think of was hurrying to get to my mother before she read it. I rushed over there, but it was too late. She was crying, she had already saw it."

Walter was saved when LDF attorneys obtained an 11th-hour conference with a U.S. Supreme Court justice, who granted another stay of execution. Marshall immediately directed Greenberg to draft a writ for consideration by the full bench of justices, who could either reaffirm Irvin's sentence or grant a hearing that would further stay his execution and could lead to another trial. The justices would consider the writ on Nov. 20.

With renewed hope, the Committee of 100 resumed efforts to get Irvin's sentence commuted. Moved by a letter from a fellow minister, Chairman Allan Knight Chalmers began drafting an appeal for funds to further the fight. According to Chalmers, the minister noted the sad irony that a November newspaper article announcing Irvin's scheduled execution also contained a story about a man fined $100 for raping a 14-year-old girl. "He, of course, is a white man. I will always believe that this (the Irvin case) is a miscarriage of justice. I know of nothing we can do now except to pray for Irvin," the minister wrote. Chalmers knew a thing or two about the power of prayer, and persistence. As head of the Scottsboro Defense Committee for more than a dozen years, he had been instrumental in securing release for most celebrated of the defendants.

On Dec. 1, 1954, the Committee of 100 mass-mailed letters and copies of a *St. Petersburg Times* editorial summarizing the flaws in the state's case against Irvin. "Walter Irvin is innocent of the alleged 'rape' of Norma Lee Padgett, for which he was convicted," Chalmers wrote. "I have convinced myself of this by personal investigation during the past five years in which I talked to State officials, members of the judiciary, ministers and members of the Negro and white population of Lake County, scene of the trial. This young man has three times refused an offer of a life sentence, on condition that he plead guilty." Chalmers outlined four ways concerned citizens could help the "desperate situation:"

writing letters to influential Floridians; refusing to get discouraged; keeping the letter so they could "quickly get a letter off about this case to some person in high authority" if need be; and they could send money. "Of course we need money. Particularly if the appeal for a third trial is granted Walter Irvin. The N.A.A.C.P. Legal Defense and Educational Fund has already met special legal costs amount to $47,732.46 in fighting for justice in this case. This is over and above the normal ongoing costs of the legal department whose work has so far saved Irvin's life. We cannot do what we have to without your undiscouraged and often repeated help." An envelope was enclosed so recipients could, "let us know what actions you have taken."

Chapter 33 -- Collins Stands Tall

New governor Leroy Collins had hardly settled into his office when letters concerning death row prisoner Walter Irvin began arriving. One of the first was from Sam Buie, who had assisted Jesse Hunter in prosecuting the Groveland defendants in 1949 and retrying Irvin in 1952. Buie, who had since succeeded Hunter as state attorney, was happy to continue his predecessor's campaign to see that the death sentence twice passed was carried out. "As you have probably noticed, or have been advised, the Supreme Court of the United States refused certiorari to this man (Walter Lee Irvin) and after the lapse of the usual time for presentation of petitions for rehearing, I hope and trust that you can issue the warrant of execution and get rid of this case once and for all. This is the last one of the old 'Groveland rape cases' defendants," Buie wrote.

Collins had plenty of things on his plate, but the U.S. Supreme Court's denial of the petition for certiorari for Irvin on Jan. 10 took away the option of the governor taking a long, leisurely look at the Groveland rape case. Walter was out of options, and was running out of time. His life literally depended on the NAACP convincing Florida's new governor to save him. Collins didn't know enough about the case to make an informed decision, but he knew enough to take a closer look when Jess Hunter, the man who had twice prosecuted Irvin encouraged the governor to spare Walter's life. Hunter, now seriously ill, questioned whether justice had been served. He was also convinced that Sheriff Willis McCall was out of control.

In a Jan. 15, 1955 letter, Hunter informed the governor about a gang of men who were breaking into Lake County homes and intimidating occupants while McCall turned a blind eye. "They follow the same plan. These two enter buildings and do the talking and the mob stands outside in the yard and mills around," the retired prosecutor wrote. Hunter claimed that the "raids" were being carried out by members of the Ku Klux Klan and the National Association for the Advancement of White People. Hunter concluded his letter with an appeal: "This matter is dangerous. There are certain people in this County whose lives are in danger from these people."

By the end of January, the telegrams and letters from Irvin supporters were piling up on the governor's desk. One of the earliest appeals arrived via air mail, special delivery on letterhead of The United Churches of Greater St. Petersburg. "We know that it is no easy responsibility that rests upon your heart as our Governor in making the final decision as to whether Walter Lee Irvin shall die. The character we know you possess will make this a hard decision for you and we ministers out of our compassion for all kinds and conditions of people (both good and bad) will sustain you with our prayers both before and after your decision," wrote Harold E. Buell and Ben F. Wyland, leaders of "the official co-operative agency of Protestantism for interdenominational service." An editorial from the *St. Pete Times* accompanied the letter.

Collins was well aware previous governors had denied clemency, but that didn't mean he had to. He had heard the rumors of a frame-up, and quietly asked two lawyers he trusted to pour through the "voluminous records" pertaining to the case. The lion's share of uncovering inconsistencies in the Groveland case fell on Tallahassee attorney Bill Harris, who immediately busied himself with picking apart transcripts from the trials, and subsequent briefs, writs, affidavits, etc., Collins also dispatched State Attorney William A. Hallowes to interview Charles Greenlee at Glades State Prison Farm in Belle Glade.

It had been more than two years since an official had questioned him about the case, but Greenlee stuck to the account he had always told. About the only new information gleaned during the two-hour discussion was that "both Irvin and Shepherd admitted many times that they had known Ernest A. Thomas for a long period of time prior to the date of the alleged rape." Of course, at the Tavares trial, Irvin testified that he didn't know Thomas. In conclusion, Greenlee, "stated again and again that he did not know Irvin and Shepherd and never saw either of them prior to being placed in the same cell with them in the Lake County Jail on the morning of July 16, 1949; that he did not know where either of them was on the night of July 15 or early morning of July 16, 1949 and, therefore, did not know whether or not either or both of them had raped Mrs. Padgett, as charged." In Hallowes' report to the governor, he noted that, "Greenlee, on being closely questioned, stated he knew Irvin was about to go to the electric chair, as he had been following his case and would like to help him, but, 'I don't know whether he's guilty or not. I won't say he did do it and I won't say he didn't -- I just don't know. I don't know where he was that night.'"

Meanwhile, Harris was becoming convinced there were numerous reasons for commuting the death sentence. From the get-go he encountered discrepancies, errors and distortions in the investigation of "the crime" and both the 1949 and 1952 trials. The realization that the Groveland case could well be a glaring miscarriage of justice weighed heavily upon the governor, but making such a sensational claim would surely bring swift and vocal criticism. Caution and secrecy were vital, and above all, the investigation had to be entirely independent. "Collins was a conscientious man. He went and got a lawyer," Greenberg recalled. "I think he kept that a secret to spare the guy any embarrassment."

McCall moved quickly when word reached him that Collins was considering commuting Irvin's sentence. He sent Collins the text of the Aug. 10, 1954 editorial in the Washington, D.C., *Afro-American* that encouraged readers to "flood Governor Johns' desk at the State Capitol in Tallahassee with thousands of appeals for commutation of this unfortunate lad's sentence." On the bottom of the page, McCall had scrawled, "I suppose you will be hearing from these people whose main objective is to make heroes out of all Negro criminals and criminals out of all law enforcement officers. They seem to think it is OK to rape our young women and murder such fine men as Sheriff Porter of Ocala. I see the committee of 100 is trying to raise another $50,000. They have written numerous letters in this campaign. Who are they paying all of this money to? I wish we knew." The note was typical McCall. It was as if the sheriff was saying, "Your predecessor didn't yield to a media-inspired barrage of appeals, and neither should you."

State Attorney Herbert Phillips also weighed in from Tampa. In a March 23 letter, Phillips offered to give Collins, "the facts as I got them, first hand, from witnesses called before a Federal Grand Jury at Ocala, when the NAACP sought to have Sheriff McCall indicted; and also the facts presented to me when McCall was forced to shoot Irvin and Sheperd (sic) in self defense after they had assaulted him." Phillips' reason for writing: "...since I am your personal friend and desire that the NAACP shall not prove itself more powerful than our courts... I see no reason why the leaders of the NAACP and those who follow their leadership should expect you and the other members of the Board to join them in setting aside the verdict of guilt of two juries, the judgment and sentence of the Circuit Judge, the two decisions of the Supreme Court of Florida, and the decision of the U.S. Supreme Court, upholding and affirming the death sentence imposed on Irvin." Five years after he dropped the ball on investigating McCall for misconduct, he had finally confirmed where his sympathies were.

Collins continued to be overwhelmed by the outpouring of support for Irvin, from unknown and prominent alike. The one-two publicity punch of the *St. Petersburg Times* editorial and the Committee of 100 letter was triggering an avalanche of letters. Even people with only rudimentary knowledge of the Groveland rape case were moved to advocate mercy. Case in point: Tallahassee resident Karl Dittmer who wrote, "I do not know much about the Irvin case nor have I had time to check on any statements, except that the editorial from the *St. Petersburg Times* is authentic." Still, Dittmer's sensibilities were aroused. "If only part of what is said in this letter or in the editorial is true, it gives me a 'creepy' feeling to be a citizen of the State of Florida and see this man executed without knowing whether the whole case has been carefully investigated by honest state officials."

Many who contacted the governor displayed an impressive knowledge of the subtleties of the case. For instance, attorney William W. Gay, speaking on behalf of the St. Petersburg Council on Human Relations, asked Collins to consider four factors:

- "Assuming a rape was committed, was Irvin properly identified? Instead of getting the finger prints from the car, Irvin is alleged to have pushed unto the road, the police matched castings of the tire and shoe prints at the scene of the alleged crime with the shoes and car of the defendant's. Since both the car and the shoes were in the custody of the Sheriff from the time of the defendant's apprehension, fabrication was possible."

- "No medical testimony was offered by the examining doctor. The omission was never explained."

- "The testimony covered in the elapsed time, as established at the trial, cast considerable doubts as to the occurrence."

- "The discrepancies in the stories of the husband and wife supply further doubt."

"I feel the high standards of proof required and the rigid tests for conviction, were not met," Gay wrote. "Two men linked to this crime are already dead -- two witnesses that reflect no credit to our State -- We refer to Thomas and Shepart (sic). A third, Greenlee, will spend his remaining years in prison. Is it justice or revenge that will be served by another corpse."

Warren H. Pierce, editor of *FLORIDA SPEAKS* and *Sunrise* magazine, also wrote. In a Feb. 22 letter, Pierce said, "The *St. Petersburg Times* -- I can say freely now that I am no longer associated with it -- did an extraordinarily fine piece of journalism on this case. Of the reporters who worked many days and weeks on it, two subsequently won important awards for their work on other stories and a third is now employed in a responsible position upon one of the nation's leading publications. The editors who directed the investigation and analyzed and dissected its results -- of whom I was one -- were drastically exacting in their demands for accuracy. In 25 years of working on a number of larger newspapers of the nation, I have never seen a more painstaking or skillful job of police reporting. Out of these weeks of work, I think the six or eight of us who participated unanimously would have strongly rendered this verdict: <u>Not proven</u>. I use that expression deliberately for I have legal training and all who worked on the case were experienced police reporters. We all know the difference between the moral certainty that one can get from interviewing persons in backwoods jook joints or country stores who don't know they're talking to reporters or investigators and getting the same persons to swear to the same story in court."

The Rev. Claxton Doggett, the Miami minister who assisted the defense in conducting a poll of Lake County residents prior to the retrial, also expressed his "earnest hope" that the governor would use his "influence to persuade the Pardon Board to save the life of Walter Lee Irvin." After stating that he had "studied this carefully for five years," Doggett explained why he felt a reasonable doubt: "Two things stand out in my mind about this case. First, no proof was offered in court that a crime had been committed, except the word of the woman. A doctor examined her but the doctor was not called to testify. Second, the State of Florida has received bad publicity all over the world and the execution of Irvin will be grist for the Communist mill." Another Methodist minister, Jack A. Davis of Winter Park, also claimed to have studied the case. He too believed considerable doubt existed. "If he had been tried farther away from Lake County (and the Orlando "Sentinel") than Ocala I believe he would have been cleared. I don't see how any Negro could get a fair chance in any dealings with Sheriff Willis McCall," wrote Davis.

Of all the letters that came across the governor's desk, the one written by Hunter made the deepest impression. Hunter wrote: "My recollection of the matter is about as follows: 1. "Mr. J.J. Elliot, a special agent of the Governor, and who assisted in the prosecution, made a proposition to counsel for the State and for the defendant to have Irvin plead guilty, which would carry life imprisonment instead of death. I considered the proposition with associates and we decided under the circumstances that it would be the best thing to do. Thurgood Marshall informed me that defense counsel would accept the proposition if it was approved by Irvin himself. After a long conference with Irvin, Marshall returned to us and stated that Irvin refused to accept the proposition, maintaining that he was not guilty of the crime and would go to the death chamber if it was necessary rather than to say that he was. His trial therefore proceeded and Irvin was convicted for rape without recommendation. 2. Before that time I had interviewed Irvin and he had taken the same position. On the morning after he was shot by Sheriff McCall and his chances for recovery were slim, I asked him to tell me confidentially, never to be used against him but for my own satisfaction alone, about the whole thing. He maintained then also that he was innocent." Collins was understandably impressed. Of course, the governor would need more than a gut feeling and Hunter's change of heart to take Irvin off death row.

In late June, McCall paid a visit to Collins, which the sheriff followed with a two-page letter. Concerning Hunter's about-face, McCall wrote: "In the opinion of many of Mr. Hunter's friends this act is a demonstration of senility and that he has been greatly influenced by a radical female editor who in the opinion of many citizens in this county has pink leaning in her editorials. It has been unfortunate, this woman with her ability in Journalism, has poisoned the minds of some people who took her articles for granted rather than dig into the truth and have allowed themselves to become doubtful of the true facts in the case," McCall wrote. He concluded by saying, "In my opinion and the opinion of many other citizens of this state, especially this section, it would be a gross miscarriage of Justice for Irwins (sic) sentence to be commuted to life imprisonment with possibility of later being pardoned. This would only be a victory for NAACP who has set out to destroy the authority of our courts, as it is an undisputable fact that they are the ones behind this movement. Should they accomplish this goal, it would mean one thing. That all a Negro criminal would need to do would be pick out some innocent helpless white woman as a target to satisfy his ravishing sexual desires, keep his mouth shut, proclian (sic) his innocence and let NAACP furnish the money and lawyers to beat the rap. Governor, at this time I have great confidence in you as a deep thinking man, I am praying that you will see fit to let the verdict of the Court stand and keep our great State safe for our fair womanhood. This obligation we owe to our children."

In the end, Collins based his decision on the findings of his investigators, primarily Harris' 16-page report, which meticulously exposed the flaws in the case. Harris had serious doubts about the Padgetts' identification of Irvin ("...this identification was made under the most difficult circumstances imaginable. Identification was of a stranger, a Negro; identification was made at night in the midst of a violent assault."), but that was just one of many areas he found lacking in the state's case. His findings:

Testimony and evidence-
"... that the only real basis for finding the defendant guilty of rape was the identification of the defendant by the alleged victim and her husband."

The defense-
"The best that can be said for the handling of the case by the Defense is that it was prepared in an extremely loose and unscientific manner. The prosecution, too, could have been handled in a more satisfactory manner."

Evidence-
"...there was no attempt whatever, either immediately after the crime or within such time as would be reasonable, to call into the case the available scientific crime analysis experts who could have nailed this case down and removed any reasonable doubt which might arise from the manner in which the case actually was prepared."

Footprint evidence-
"...the deputy sheriff testified that he saw the footprints that morning before they picked up Irvin. After they picked Irvin up, he viewed them again and took Irvin to the scene to compare his shoes with the prints. Finding that Irvin had on a different pair of shoes, they went back to his house, got another pair of shoes, then came out and compared the prints and finally, after all this, made plaster casts of the same. (This was approximately nine hours after the first viewing of the prints.)" Harris called the footprints, "the most flagrant example of the State's refusal to exercise its duty to convict the defendant by competent evidence."

Tire tracks evidence-
Yates waited hours to make casts of the tire tracks hours after he first had the opportunity to do so.

Irvin's trousers-
"...it appears that it would have been awfully simple for the smears on the trousers to have been turned over to a competent analyst for determination as to whether or not this substance was, in fact, semen. This could have been done at any time within three weeks after the smears got on the trousers." Instead, presentation of the trousers without explanation created "the obvious implication" that the smear was a semen stain, even though the composition of the smear could have been easily ascertained. "It is elementary that the presence of semen can be determined by standard scientific tests and that these

tests were available to the local law enforcement officials. But no such tests were made. Or, if such tests were made, this fact was never disclosed and the results were never introduced into evidence." Conclusion: the trousers should never have been allowed into evidence.

The pistol-
Harris dismissed the pistol as irrelevant, since it was established in court that the gun was in Greenlee's possession, and therefore could not have been used by Irvin in committing a crime 19 miles away.

Items unaccounted for-
"Another significant omission on the part of the State was that it was never shown that at any point in the record, whether they ever found Padgett's wallet or Mrs. Padgett's ring, compact or perfume, or in fact, if they ever looked for it. The State didn't even attempt to show that these items were in the possession of any of the defendants, let alone in the possession of Irvin."

Metal bar-
No testimony was offered to support Norma's claim that a metal bar was found in the car when officers confiscated the vehicle.

Lack of medical evidence-
"There was not even testimony of a doctor that Mrs. Padgett had, in fact, been raped."

License plates-
"Mrs. Padgett testified that the Negroes, after ravishing her, changed the license plate on the car. No attempt was made to show that there were two license plates in his possession, nor was there any showing that any effort had been made to find out whether the tag, in fact, had been changed recently on that car or not."

Lint-
Scientific analysis could have proved, or disproved whether the "lint" found in the car matched lint found near the crime scene. "Even though a scientific analysis of these pieces of 'lint' could have been made in order to make a true comparison, the State proceeded to rely on tenuous inference based on naked eye observations."

Willie Padgett's claim-
There was "no attempt to show that when picked up, any of the Negroes were marked in the slightest," in that Willie Padgett said he had "got in quite a few licks" with a two-foot long stick he defended himself.

Weak battery, weak headlights-
The Padgetts would have had great difficulty identifying Irvin since their car's headlights were dimmed by a battery so weak it wouldn't turn over the engine. "The fact that identification under these circumstances is most difficult is confirmed by Padgett's confused description of the automobile in which defendant allegedly rode. Although Padgett variously described

it as a 1946 or 1948 Mercury, Black, Blue, and light green, it was described by its owner as a 1942 dark blue Mercury."

Prisoners shot by McCall-
Harris devoted more than a page to what he called "collateral issue -- the shooting of Irvin and Shepherd by McCall." The governor's investigator zeroed in on Irvin's testimony that Deputy Yates' gun misfired, and that Yates checked the chamber and then fired a shot into Irvin's neck. "It is at that point that scientific investigation would have proven conclusively whether bullets from two different guns entered the body of Irvin." Harris dismissed the FBI investigation that cleared McCall. "I understand that the FBI did make some investigation in the case at this point, but I don't know anything of their conclusion." But Harris had a conclusion of his own. "Sheriff McCall in taking the two prisoners from Raiford in his car in the front seat along without any other officer with him was in its best light an act of gross and willful negligence, and in its possible interpretation an act of criminal negligence."

Collins made up his mind after Paul Perkins formally appealed for commutation before the Pardon Board on March 16. The governor knew full well that commuting Irvin's sentence would touch off a political firestorm, but it he was convinced it was the right thing to do. The other members of the pardon board weren't as sure.

The Governor commuted Walter Irvin's death sentence on Dec. 16, 1955, matter-of-factly telling reporters that the state failed to "walk that extra mile -- did not establish the guilt of Walter Lee Irvin in an absolute and conclusive manner." In announcing his decision, Collins attempted to head off the inevitable criticism that he was bowing to pressure from the NAACP. The governor's public stance had to address all accusations: that he bowed to the NAACP; the communists; and he commuted the sentence for political gain. As he mulled over in his mind and discussed potential responses with advisers, one strategy became clear: that he was directed by a higher source. For good measure -- or to convince the unbelievers -- he would also attack the case on scientific grounds.

In his official statement, Collins said, "Let me say that I was not misled in my action by any communist or fellow-traveler or by an association for the advancement of any racial group. As a matter of fact, I may say that pressure from these groups generally tends to confuse any matter in which they interfere. They do not help the man involved and they only complicate the administration of justice. I consider it needless to say that I am a bitter foe of all communists or persons of that persuasion. Not one of these persons influenced me in my decision." Collins involved the Creator in the second paragraph: "The laws of the State of Florida provide that Almighty God gave man the gift of life and charged each one of us with the duty of preserving life. It is a matter of conscience with each one of us to do all within our power to obey the direct mandate from God. So sacred is this duty, so widely do the people of Florida recognize our moral obligation in this respect that they have provided that the State may not take life except under very limited circumstances. Even this extreme penalty has been surrounded by many safeguards which we have provided through the entire legal process. We have rules regulating the investigation of crime, the arrest and interrogation of prisoners, we provide for an open trial before a jury, we request that twelve jurors arrive at the same verdict of guilty, we provide for the Supreme Court to review the record for possible errors in the law. In capital cases, before a man's life may be taken, so seriously do we the people of Florida consider this matter, we have added one safeguard. We have required that the Governor and his Cabinet review not only the law but all the facts in the case including how it was prosecuted and defended, how it was tried. If on all the case, the Governor and his Cabinet are satisfied that the man has had the full benefits of the law, its full protection, and if the Governor in his conscience before God is satisfied, then and only then should he sign the death warrant." Collins stressed that, "The evidence presented against Irvin was not the quality of evidence which in my opinion went the last mile in proving the State's case and which I think necessary in a capital case." With the table set, Collins methodically attacked the case point by point:

1. Both the victim and her husband testified that the four assailants pushed the stalled car. Push your hand against a car and see your fingerprints on it. Why didn't the law enforcement officers take these prints and make the necessary comparisons? This would have been strong evidence -- to convict if the men were the assailants and to free the man if they were not her assailants.

2. The victim testified that after the rape the assailants changed the plates on their car. There was no evidence at the trial to show if the plates on Irvin's car had been changed.

3. The doctor who examined the victim on the morning of the rape was available and should have been called as a witness for the prosecution. Such corroboration is standard in this type of case. Failure of the State to produce the doctor was very questionable procedure and left many issues unanswered.

4. There were numerous footprints at the scene of the abduction, where the men were pushing the stalled car, and at the scene of the rape, where the men got in and out of their car. No casts was (sic) was made of any of these prints until many hours after the officers had been at the scene. The shoes Irvin was wearing when arrested did not match the prints. Another pair of shoes was obtained in his home and brought out to the area. Only one cast was made of one footprint and it was made by an officer who admittedly had no training in this difficult work. An independent expert was produced by the defense at the trial who testified that the cast introduced by the state was made from the impression of an empty shoe. Casts of all footprints should have been made immediately on finding the prints, and preserved for evidence, and comparison with the shoes of the other defendants.

5. Certain stains appeared on Irvin's trousers. These were exhibited to the jury months after the event and the jury was permitted to infer that they were guilty stains. The F.B.I. crime laboratory was and is available to law enforcement officers, without cost to determine the exact nature of such stains. The trousers were not referred to the F.B.I. for such testing, as should have been done if proper police procedure was followed, and the jury should have had such a laboratory report. The state's failure to do this raises an inference that it was afraid of the results of such a test.

6. The victim and her husband were robbed of a wallet, a ring, a compact, some perfume and some money. The state failed to show if these articles were found in the possession of any of the defendants, and allows an inference that they were not so found.

7. The victim testified that the car in which she was raped had a metal bar on the floor of the rear section. It was not shown if there was (sic) such a bar in Irvin's car.

8. The victim's husband testified that he fought off the assailants with a stick and had got in quite a "few licks" on the defendants. It was not shown if the defendants were marked when arrested.

9. The opportunity to recognize the assailants was limited. The victim's husband admitted consuming a quantity of liquor, during the course of the evening. The only light he had to view one defendant's face was by his own weak headlights -- too weak to start the car -- the faces of the other assailants remained in the dark. When he first saw Greenlee he said, "that's not one of them." Later on, he identified Greenlee.

10. No one ever connected Greenlee with Irvin or Shepherd or saw them together before the crime. Greenlee was alone when he was arrested near this shed, for vagrancy at 3:15 a.m. No signs of an assault were visible on him. This arrest took place about nineteen miles from the scene of the rape and very close in time to the offense.

11. The law enforcement officers stated that the prisoners had confessed, and these alleged confessions were given wide publicity prior to the trial. The defense was prepared to show that these alleged confessions were beaten out of the prisoners, and would also exhibit the marks of the beatings. Needless to say -- the state did not attempt to introduce these alleged confessions.

12. Greenlee's case was different. Law enforcement officials have a recording of a statement allegedly made by Greenlee -- who in turn says that he made a statement at the point of a pistol.

In conclusion, Collins stated, "In view of the above circumstances it was my opinion that the state had failed in its duty to present the strongest and fullest case against the defendant Irvin. The state left too many loose ends, too many questions are unanswered; The conduct of some law enforcement officers was in the most favorable aspects, amateurish and unenlightened. The trial judge sat in both cases and refused to disqualify himself for the second trial; also he had made many errors prejudice (sic) to the defense during the defense trial (sic). Further, in his charge to the jury he should have told them that where the state fails to produce evidence which it had in its possession the jury could infer that the state did not produce the evidence because it would be prejudicial to the state's case (sic) such an elementary basic rule of Florida law was overlooked. In all respects my conscience told me that this was a bad case, badly handled, badly tried and now on this bad performance I was asked to take a man's life. My conscience would not let me do this. Accordingly, with others, I voted to commute the Irvin sentence to life imprisonment."

Collins desperately needed the other members of the pardon board to be as adamant as he had been. They weren't. State Secretary R. A. Gray and Attorney General Richard Ervin were most enthusiastic. Gray stated, "I will agree to commutation because I believe the governor has given this matter very, very thorough consideration. For reasons that he so well states, I agree to vote for commutation." While Gray and Ervin offered some semblance of support for Collins, albeit toothless, the other two members of the pardon board gave the impression their arms had been twisted. Comptroller Ray Green merely said, "I also agree to vote for it." According to an article in the *Orlando Sentinel*, Commander of Agriculture Nathan Mayo, "murmured something that was not audible but voted for clemency."

In Lake County, Judge Futch called Pardon Board members "docile and uninformed" and charged that they had "voted as the Governor requested and without having any opinion of their own."

Criticism also came from an unexpected source, Thurgood Marshall. After commending Collins for commuting the sentence, Marshall said, "... we are shocked to read the public statement of Governor Collins which follows the pattern of other southern officials in using the NAACP as the whipping boy for the repeated injustices against Negroes in the South. Governor Collins is completely in error in every statement concerning this organization. Under our rules we do not enter a case 'because of the bare fact that the defendant is a colored man.' We only enter cases where there is injustice solely because of race and color and where there is the possibility of establishing a precedent which will help insure due process of law for all without regard to race. Contrary to what Governor Collins has stated, this organization made a thorough and complete investigation of the circumstances surrounding the alleged crime before entering the case. One of the lawyers from this office along with two Florida lawyers, one of whom is white, made an on-the-spot investigation shortly after the alleged crime. They were seriously handicapped in their investigation by the complete breakdown of law enforcement machinery in the county involved, resulting in rioting and a posse killing. Despite all of this they were able to get the true facts in the case. We also used the services of several well-known private investigators, including one from Florida. As the result of this investigation, we were convinced and are still convinced that Walter Lee Irvin and the others charged with the crime are completely innocent... It is, of course, obvious that if the NAACP had not intervened in this case all three of those originally charged would have been long since dead and Governor Collins would not have had to request the Pardons Board to commute Irvin's sentence."

Marshall was in the minority; most Negroes who spoke up had only praise for the governor. Case in point: G.L. Porter, of the Florida State Teachers Association Inc., who wrote, "Had Mr. Marshall been close to the situation as we, who live in Florida, have been I think he might have reacted in an entirely different vein. What he said probably made good headline reading for northern newspapers, but it does not help us to move toward democracy down here, as we are trying to do. In view of all the circumstances here in Florida, the action of the Pardon Board should really be considered as a victory, and not as a defeat. It certainly would have been easier for the elected officials on the Pardon Board, who face the voters only a few short months from now, to have done nothing, or for the Governor to have signed the death warrant... What the pardon board did took political courage here in Florida. We do not have many forthright leaders who are willing to put further an effort to see that Negro citizens are given justice. It is natural that the Governor is going to be criticized for doing anything that appears to be helping any member of our group and I think we ought to be the last to make unjust criticism of a man who will go out of his way to see that justice is done... If anything would happen that should cause the governor to change from his present attitude toward us I know of no other state leader, at present, whom we could turn to. For the first time, to my knowledge, the Negro has a true friend in the Governor at Tallahassee."

To Collins' surprise, the heavy flow of letters and telegrams, -- both of praise and condemnation -- continued for months. By February, it was obvious that the issue would be a theme of the 1956 gubernatorial election. A number of vocal critics had stepped forward, but none was louder than Judge Truman G. Futch, who boldly proclaimed that Lake County would convene a grand jury to investigate the governor's actions. Incredibly, Futch revealed he would subpoena the governor to testify about his controversial decision. The fact that a county court would dare call the state's highest-ranking official on the carpet showed just how strong feelings remained about the Groveland case nearly six years after Norma Padgett cried "rape."

Collins was conspicuously absent when the grand jury convened on Feb. 27 in Tavares. The governor had already answered the grand jury in a statement: "There is nothing to investigate except Leroy Collins' judgment and conscience. Both are beyond the control or coercion of a grand jury. They are subject to review by God and the people of Florida. I assume full responsibility for the soundness of the decision of the Cabinet in commuting Walter Lee Irvin's death sentence to life imprisonment. I recommended this action and all other members of the Board assented... No responsibility can be any graver than that of deciding whether any human being shall live or die. Human life is jut as sacred whether it is clothed in a dark skin or a light one... The people of Florida have a right to expect their Governor to do what he conceives to be his duty, based upon his understanding and judgment. A Governor whose actions are influenced by vengeance, or by expediency, or by any other motive other than the right as he sees it, is not worthy of the high trust the people repose in him. Right or wrong, I, Leroy Collins, as Governor of Florida, have serious questions about the guilt of Walter Lee Irvin. His incarceration for the rest of his natural life based upon presently known facts and the decisions of our Courts is justified, but as Governor I cannot, and I will not, take his life. This is the course of duty as God has given me the intelligence to see it, and the strength to follow it."

Once State Attorney Sam Buie realized that the governor couldn't be forced to appear, Buie turned contrite. In a Feb. 27 letter, he wrote, "The Grand Jury has directed me to write you and extend an invitation to you to appear before the Grand Jury and discuss the matter voluntarily at your early convenience." A week later, Collins responded in a bitter letter in which he called the grand jury hearing a "so-called investigation," and pointed out that "a Grand Jury has no authority to review, modify, or rescind such an official act (commutation)." Collins continued, "It would be absurd if, after each meeting of the Board, the Governor and the other Cabinet members comprising the Board could be called upon to visit around over the State explaining reasons for action in individual cases to Grand Juries... If the Grand Jury wants to express its disagreement with our judgment, it has a perfect right to do so, but no possible good can come from any effort to continue a furor about it... it would only serve to harm our State by continuing to project this matter as a source of dissension and turmoil."

Publicly, Futch insisted that the grand jury was called to determine if the governor was guilty of an impropriety, but many Lake Countians saw through the ploy. "As former residents of Lake County and observers at the Irving (sic) trial we wish to deplore the cheap political slam at you by the so called petitioners of the Fifth Judicial Circuit. Unfortunately Lake County seems determined to keep itself in the spot light of adverse publicity on racial emotionalism. We feel that the commutation of Irving (sic) sentence was courageous and humane," wrote Mr. And Mrs. Paul J. Miller of Gainesville.

Instead of embarrassing Collins, the absurdity of a grand jury investigating the governor had the opposite affect. Praise for Collins' courageous act poured in from all over the Sunshine State. Pat Ford, a reporter at the *West Palm Beach Post-Times*, who claimed to be a close personal acquaintance with an attorney "who did a great deal of spade work for the defense," wrote, "After 18 years as a newspaperman I find your stand a convincing demonstration that all honor and decency have not disappeared from American public life... The ineptness of the original investigations handling has rankled in my memory to this day. Time might very well prove the whole thing nothing but a legalized lynching attempt."

Among the hundreds of letters Collins received, one from Clermont resident Harry Brown stood out. Brown, who referred to himself as, "an old time property owner citizen of Lake County," accused McCall of being behind the grand jury being called. Brown charged, "To me this is purely a political move on the part of, ---- Mr. Big McCall; This is the first year he had any real competition for sheriff's job; so he had to dig up these old dead bones to -- try -- to win votes. (Most certainly not on his own virtues or merits, for as a public officer; he certainly is very prejudiced)." A similar feeling was expressed in an anonymous letter from Leesburg: "I do not take sides in the case or in your decision but I agree with your right to do as your conscience dictates, and I truly believe that is what you did. The most any of us can do is what we feel God tells us is right... I do not like to write an unsigned letter, but with the situation as it is in Lake County, I prefer to remain just A Citizen." A number of letters were sent to editors of central Florida newspapers. For example, in the *Orlando Sentinel* of April 1956, "former Lake County resident" A.R. Saunders wrote, "Many of us that lived in Lake County, close to this scene and know a lot of the actual circumstances still doubt the guilt of Irvin."

Naturally, not every letter writer was as sympathetic. The bigots also had their say. John E. Heidenreich of Charlottesville, Virginia, said, "it would seem that now is the time for you to step down, and give the CHAIR to a worthy Floridian who will be the real protector of the right of the WHITE MAN to run his own affairs; who will remember, that, IT COULD HAVE BEEN A MEMBER OF YOUR FAMILY. The NAACP is very gleeful over your COMMUTATION of the death sentence of the RAPIST." One of the more interesting letters that crossed the governor's desk came from J.E. Peacock, who claimed to be a neighbor of McCall. "It gets under a Florida Cracker's skin to observe such frequent tactics as have been resorted to in efforts to break down the morale and efficiently (sic) of a man of Sheriff McCalls caliber. It seems that his County has been singled out from time to time for the ravages of Negroes upon white women and girls, and that because of his efficiency and untiring efforts, he has likewise been singled out as a target for those opposed to genuine law enforcement... Without doubt, more outside money was spent on behalf of the four Negroes who ravished a little white woman just over the line at Crows Bluff, than has ever been spent on a single case in Florida's criminal history. Yet, there was not a shadow of doubt as to their guilt. Yet, Sheriff McCall was tried and condemned by the press and "NAACP."

Collins' favorite letter was probably the one he received from prisoner #49309.C-59, Walter Lee Irvin, who wrote, "I want to extend my deepest appreciation to you for taking my case under careful consideration and because of your consideration my life were saved so, I want you to know that, as long as I live I must, and I will, with all sincere, look to you as my earthly god. Now that my health is failing, I do hope and pray that I will be able to go free someday because I feel, as I have, and I did for a lifetime, live a clean and law-abiding life, Sir!"

Eventually, Irvin faded from the public consciousness, but the Groveland case wouldn't go quietly. Nearly nine years after the purported crime, it was back in the news when the March 15, 1956 *Orlando Sentinel* carried the sensational bold-type headline, "Victim Opposed Chair" above Jim Hardee's byline and a Tallahassee dateline. "The victim in the 1949 Groveland rape case signed a petition in 1950 calling for abolishing of capital punishment in Florida, records of the Walter Lee Irvin case revealed yesterday," Hardee claimed. The reporter explained that on Aug. 2, 1950 both Norma and Willie Padgett signed a petition circulated by the Rev. Ben F. Wyland, president of the United Churches of St. Petersburg. The petition was sent to Collins on Sept. 21, 1950.

Norma may have wanted desperately to put the Groveland case behind her, but Lake County's politicos had other ideas. In the spring of 1956, Norma found herself dragged out of the shadows and back into the spotlight as a pawn in a political chess match between Gov. Collins and the man who sought to win back the statehouse, Fuller Warren. Collins, guest of honor at Lake County's Washington Birthday Celebration in Eustis, was preparing to ride in the parade when a pair of McCall's deputies escorted Norma to the governor's car. "You're the one who let out the nigger that raped me. How would you have felt if that had been your wife or daughter?" Norma shouted at the surprised governor. Collins recalled, "She said, 'Supposed I was your sister, would you have done that? Would you have commuted that sentence?' I said, 'I think I would have. I hope I would have. But that's irrelevant here. We're not here for the purpose of talking politics or making political issues. I'm down here to help the community. Be with the community.' McCall had set her up for that."

The Lake County press, which two years earlier took Collins to task for commuting Irvin's sentence, saw the episode for what it was: an orchestrated attempt to humiliate the governor. The *Eustis Lake Region News*, in an editorial headlined, "For Shame, Lake County," called the incident, "the evident product of a deliberate political reprisal." The editorial concluded: "Is all fair in politics? If so, then we have sunk to a new low in indecency. For shame, Lake County." An editorial in the *Tampa Morning Tribune* reached the same conclusion: "There's more than meets the eye in that rape-victim-confronts-Governor story issuing from Eustis... Twenty-four hours before this occurrence, the report was abroad in Lake County that political enemies of Collins were planning this very thing in an attempt to embarrass him. The confrontation, this report said, was supposed to take place at a Collins speech at a civic club dinner in Tavares Tuesday night. Instead, it was staged as the Governor was about to ride in a parade at Eustis the next morning." After noting that Padgett neither opposed the jury recommendation of mercy for Greenlee in 1949, nor the commutation of Irvin's sentence, the editorial concluded, "But now, during an election campaign, she is escorted by deputies of Sheriff McCall to "confront" the Governor on a public street in Eustis. We think any reader can add up these facts and arrive at the same answer. A rather depressing answer: Politics."

Collins' foes would continue to use the commutation of Irvin's sentence as a lightning rod throughout the campaign. The long-awaited opening of State Road 19 between Umatilla and Eustis provided the setting for a showdown between Collins supporters and those who wanted to see Warren return to Tallahassee. The April 22, 1956, *Orlando Sentinel* reported that, "Charges and countercharges flew thick and fast as a former governor, a candidate for governor, representatives of three other candidates, and two opponents for Lake County state senatorial posts, were heard. Both former Gov. Charley E. Johns and Circuit Judge T.G. Futch, rapped Gov. Collins' actions in commuting the death sentence of Walter Lee Irvin, convicted Negro rapist. Johns lauded Futch for calling the Lake County grand jury now probing why Collins recommended clemency in the case. Futch, who was stumping for Warren said, 'I wouldn't have accepted the invitation to speak if the governor hadn't tried to ridicule the courts of Lake County, Marion County and Florida... If that poor woman had walked up to his auto and said 'God bless you, Governor for saving the life of that poor Negro' it would have been on every television in Florida. Just because she asked him 'why' it was a dastardly crime." Collins' Lake County campaign manager P.B. Howell of Leesburg, was left to defend his boss. "After hearing him speak, you would think he is still in office," he said when asked about Warren's comments.

On May 4, the Lake County grand jury announced its findings: Collins and the State Pardon Board had the legal right to commute the death sentence of Irvin. The deduction came after 13 days of testimony from 23 witnesses. To save face, the grand jury hinted that it believed "some of the so-called new evidence upon which Collins may have based his clemency recommendation was misrepresented to him." The grand jury recommended that the Legislature make a full investigation of the Pardon Board's action. Also, that pardon boards notify local court authorities when an application for clemency would be heard.

Like a moth drawn to the light, McCall soon became embroiled in yet another controversy involving race. In October, the *Daily Commercial* reported that a 19-year-old Orlando girl, Marlene Taylor was being held at the Lake County jail on a morals charge stemming from a sexual liaison she had with two Negro airmen. As more details were made public over the next three weeks, it became apparent that McCall hadn't learned anything from the missteps he made during the Groveland rape controversy.

On Oct. 11, the Leesburg paper revealed that reporter Douglas Eller was denied permission to interview the girl when he called at the jail. The following day, an even more sensational report appeared: the girl had been arrested at McCall's personal cabin in the "Big Scrub," a forest in northern Lake County. The newspaper reported that a friend of the girl had tipped off McCall about the rendezvous between the girl and Maxie T. Deckard, 25, and Conley Gipson, 23. McCall and Taylor's friend arranged for the "date" to take place at McCall's cabin in the forest, where the waiting sheriff and his deputies burst into the cabin after the girl and one of the men got in bed. Before making the arrest, a deputy took photos of the naked couple, who both were bleeding from the forehead. The girl looked stunned, while the man had been rendered unconscious. Alarmingly, photos of the nude couple were soon being circulated throughout Lake County. In fact, the *Daily Commercial* owned two.

The sensational case, and McCall's refusal to allow reporters access to Taylor continued into November. The *Daily Commercial* finally took McCall to task in an editorial headlined "Some Questions That Must Be Answered." The editorial began, "The *Daily Commercial* is alarmed by what appears to be a breakdown of law and order at the top echelon in Lake County… During the raid, the Negro airman was pistol-whipped. The sheriff charged him with resisting arrest. However, the girl also received a bloody blow on the temple. How this happened is unexplained, *since she was not charged with resisting arrest*… The girl has been under lock and key in the county jail since that time. Sheriff McCall on five occasions has refused to allow newsmen and a newswoman to see her so that they could request an interview…"

In most parts of the state, McCall's latest controversy was overshadowed by the gubernatorial race. In the end, it wasn't much of a contest. Gov. Leroy Collins walked away with the Democratic nomination. Nineteen of 20 Florida daily newspapers that endorsed a candidate supported the incumbent. When the ballots were counted, Collins had 434,274 votes, which was 51.7 percent of the total vote and more than twice as many as the runner-up, Sumter Lowry. Warren finished a distant fourth. Fittingly, Collins was by and large the choice of Negro voters, as demonstrated in Jacksonville, where 19 precincts with almost exclusively Negro registration cast 9,920 votes for Collins, compared to 307 combined for this three opponents. In Miami, Collins bested his foes by 4-to-1 in nine Negro precincts.

Chapter 34 -- Sweet Freedom

Charles Greenlee, now 24, had been largely forgotten by the masses when he was captured after escaping from the Belle Glade State Prison Farm in 1957. According to the Associated Press, "(Constable A.E.) Richardson said Greenlee had been living a model life in Fort Pierce, had bought a car several weeks ago and was employed at the Indian River Refrigeration Terminal under the name Charles Lamont. A casual tip to the constable's office that Lamont was not his real name led to Greenlee's capture." According to a newspaper report, "The escaped convict admitted his identity after Richardson yanked up his pants leg and revealed a telltale scar on his left knee."

"I just got depressed one day so I went off. I got me a job, but then I had to have a way of getting back and forth from work. By the time I worked long enough and got me a few dollars I bought a car. I might as well have stayed at the work farm. I had about the same amount of freedom out working as I did in the work camp," Greenlee said. Surprised prison officials, who had entrusted Greenlee with operating a Caterpillar earth mover, didn't quite see things his way. The escape meant more time, but Greenlee was unfazed. "Yeah, they added more time. But what can you add to a life sentence?" The lure of freedom had been too strong to resist. Greenlee settled back into the prison routine and once again became a model prisoner.

The years passed, and a new decade began. Charles had all but given up on being released. And then the word came that he would be freed. "The man that really freed me, his name was Bully Crews. He was supposed to be one of the worst guards there but when I came up for parole, Bully Crews let me see what he wrote in my behalf. I don't think my daddy could have written a better recommendation," Greenlee recalled.

Greenlee, whose family had never stopped working for his release, was 27 years old when he was quietly paroled on July 26, 1960 after 10 years and 11 months in prison. His brother Roy, who had moved out of Florida, promised parole officials that his brother would have a job and place to live waiting for him when released.

Greenlee's family didn't even know Charles was getting out. The bus ticket the state gave him took Charles as far as Gainesville. From there he hitchhiked to the small town of Bronson, where his family had moved. Once there, he wasn't sure where to go. "My home was the first he came to," Charles' sister, Ethel Retha said. "I was sitting there watching TV. I had the door open and he came to the door and said, 'Can you tell me where Tom Greenlee lives?' I said, 'That's Charles!' We didn't even know he was getting out. I walked with him down to my momma's. She lived four doors down."

The Greenlee family reunion was joyous, but brief. Charles had no desire to spend even one more night in the state that had taken his innocence. Family friend, Leroy "Dude" Glover drove him back to Gainesville, where Charles caught a bus to a Northern state. "And he's been there ever since," said his sister Ethel Retha. "I had a brother who was in the Air Force here who offered to help me. I had a couple of options so I accepted that one. I got a job with the county and spent 17 years with them. Then they became my best customer," said Greenlee, who started his own heating and cooling company.

"All I had to do was work hard," Greenlee said. "Looking back at it, I'm satisfied it would have been easy not to get through it. I was able to get through it by applying my father's principles." Greenlee regularly returned to Florida to spend time with his father, especially after Tom Greenlee was paralyzed from the neck down after an automobile accident. "My mother took care of him like a baby for 28 years." Tom's injury and passing was devastating to his family, who drew strength from Charles' quiet determination and steely resolve. "He was self-motivated. And proud. And well educated. And he always loved his family," said his niece, Beatrice.

Greenlee and his co-defendants were no longer topics of conversation in Lake County when Willis McCall's department became involved in a case with striking similarities to the events of 1949. Just after midnight on March 11, 1960, deputies received a call that Charlotte Wass, a single, middle-aged white woman in Fruitland Park had been beaten and raped. The woman, who had crawled to her neighbor's house, told Deputy J.P. Spence her assailants were, "two Negro boys."

After sending the woman to the hospital with a Leesburg policeman, Spence called out the bloodhounds. The dogs brought by deputies Noel E. Griffin Jr. and Thomas "Bubbles" Ledford quickly discovered a scent that led to Leonard "L.C." Clarett's house. There, deputies arrested Clarett's grandson, Robert Shuler, a 20-year-old loader at a local citrus packing house, and his friend and boarder Levi Summers, a 20-year-old fruit packer.

At 8 a.m., at the direction of Sheriff Willis McCall, Deputy James Yates entered the case. At the Wass residence, Yates found "four different tracks at the house" and another track in a "sand rut" in the road west of the house. Deputies Spence and Lucius Clark made plaster of Paris prints of six tracks. Yates concluded that four suspects were involved, and returned to the house to see if he could find additional evidence. There Yates seized two handkerchiefs, one monogrammed and the other plain. Both were damp and bloodstained. Yates' next step mirrored his actions in the Groveland case. At Clarett's house, Yates "asked" to "look in the boys' rooms." In Summers' room, Yates says he found, "other handkerchiefs to match the one I found at the scene of the crime." He also found a bloodstained pair of shorts under Shuler's bed.

Fifth Judicial Circuit State Attorney Gordon Oldham Jr. assigned his assistant, John W. McCormick to interview the victim at Durham Young Hospital in Leesburg. He and court reporter Joan E. Tobey began questioning Wass at 1:30 p.m., a little more than 12 hours after she had been attacked. Wass gave a rambling account full of inconsistencies, including the claim that one of the men trying to break into her house, "must have been in his 40s or close to his 50s." She also said, "Whether he raped me or not, I don't know, because all I know he just kept strangling me, strangling me and strangling me." Wass sounded as if she wasn't sure what had happened. Finally, on Tobey's 14th page of testimony, Wass gave McCormick something he could work with: "I just begged him not to touch me and take his hands off me... Now, I believe then he raped me, I really do..." Wass still hadn't mentioned a name, or indicated she could identify her attackers. When the victim revealed that she had previously received a visit from two suspects, McCormick was heartened, until he asked if she, "recognized either one of those boys?" Wass replied, "No, not especially, but they could have been those boys... I am lying down, it could have been him, because I see now that these beds are high... That might have been him, because he was tall and had dark hair."

Yates was having better success. Summers admitted going with Shuler to rob Wass, but also implicated a friend, 23-year-old Jerry Chatman, an ex-con living in Leesburg and working at A.S. Herlong's packing house. Deputies Spence and Doug Sewell were sent to make the arrest. Shuler also admitted robbing Wass, but said his involvement ended there. He claimed Chatman hit and raped the woman. Under further questioning, Shuler said he and Summers wore old shoes for the robbery, then threw the shoes away afterward. At a clay pit south of Fruitland Park, deputies found a pair that matched one of the casts deputies had made of footprints at the scene of the crime. Two more shoes were found just south of the clay pit.

At Chatman's home, his wife gave deputies a pair of black boots, which they matched to another set of footprints. Spence and Griffin also found a pair of tan twill trousers, "that were bloody about the fly." At 8:30 p.m., Thompson began questioning Chatman. The third suspect told essentially the same story as Shuler. Incredibly, he also admitted to raping Wass.

NAACP state Secretary Robert Saunders sent Tampa attorney Francisco A. Rodriguez to investigate, and he ended up representing Shuler and Chatman. Summers, fully cooperating with the state and agreeing to testify against his partners in crime, was represented by Mount Dora attorney Roy Christopher. The trial lasted three days. As McCall anticipated, Shuler and Chatman testified that their confessions immediately after the crime were involuntary. But there would be no replay of Norma Padgett's dramatics. Charlotte Wass was adjudged incompetent. She would not take the stand. Shuler and Chatman were convicted of rape on March 21 and sentenced to the electric chair on July 7, 1960. Summers was convicted of being an accessory after the fact.

With Charles Greenlee finally free, Thurgood Marshall's staff turned its attention to the plight of Walter Irvin. Even though Irvin wasn't eligible for parole until 1965, Marshall directed Orlando attorney Paul Perkins to draft an application for conditional pardon. The application Perkins submitted on Oct. 7, 1960 restated that "substantial doubt" remained concerning the applicant's guilty and that Irvin had already paid dearly for. Perkins pointed out that:

- "There is still lodged in applicant a bullet from this shooting."

- "Prior to his imprisonment, applicant was a respected member of the community in which he lived and had no bad mark on his record other than for a minor infraction for military discipline while in the armed forces."

- "While in prison, applicant has maintained a consistently good record."

- "The conviction of applicant, his lengthy imprisonment, and his having been shot, all have punished him severely. No further imprisonment is needed either as punishment of applicant or as a deterrent to others."

For good measure, the application promised that Irvin would be "regularly employed in New York City" and would leave the State of Florida "immediately upon his release." A three-page summary of the case was attached to the application.

In early November, L.C. Clarett, the uncle of Fruitland Park rape case defendant Robert Shuler contacted Gov. Collins with startling news: Clarett possessed a letter from the victim in which she said Shuler did not participate in the rape. Clarett also charged that Oldham had bribed Summers with a steak dinner before taking his statement. Oldham disposed of Clarett's accusations in a three-page letter to the governor on Nov. 18, stressing that the defendants' statements had been voluntary. As for the most serious charge, that Shuler didn't rape Wass, Oldham pointed out that the official record showed that the victim was badly beaten with a gun, choked and kicked by the defendants Shuler and Chatman, and was unconscious a long period of time after the beating and assault. Oldham continued, "That as a result of said assault and badly mauling of the victim, she lost her mental capacity and was adjudged incompetent a short time before she was discharged from the hospital. She is currently under supervision in one of the State Hospitals for the mentally insane which resulted, in my opinion, from the attack and beating upon her the night in question." Oldham also reported that he personally met with Wass the day after the attack, finding her "completely incompetent."

The governor also received a letter from Charlotte's sister, Sally, and her husband Roland Kampmeier, who asked Collins to spare the lives of Shuler and Chatman. The Kampmeiers wrote that Charlotte, "…does not wish, nor do we, to see these young men pay the supreme penalty. We do not excuse their foul acts, which included breaking into her cottage and beating her, but we should like to see their sentences lightened. Our sister is also troubled by doubts whether one of the men was guilty as charged. That is Robert Shuler… she says she did not recognize him as one of her assailants." The Kampmeiers pointed out that Charlotte was still hospitalized and undergoing treatment and that, "any statements by her at present probably would not be taken to be competent. However, she hopes very much that you will extend executive clemency to those who harmed her, or are alleged to be those who did."

While the NAACP prepared to go to the wall for Shuler and Chatman, Irvin was feeling alone and forgotten at Raiford. Spending six years on death row and repeatedly being denied parole were taking a toll. He tried to be upbeat in his letters to his mother, but his health was worsening, a situation not helped by the manual labor he still had to perform. He longed to be transferred to a facility closer to home, or a work camp, as Greenlee had. Walter's family, still struggling financially, couldn't visit as often as he, or they, wished. As for the attorneys who had fought for him, they had faded from his life. He hadn't seen his first champion, Franklin Williams in 10 years. He'd even lost touch with Perkins, who had become a trusted friend, but had become bogged down by a growing law practice. And then, in August 1961, Walter's father Cleveland died. Walter asked to attend the funeral, but his request was immediately denied by the prison superintendent.

Dellia Irvin, feeling her son's despair through the pages of his letters, decided it was time to reintroduce herself to the now-famous Thurgood Marshall. "I know you are surprised to hear from me after so long a time, but I've never forgotten the year of 1949 when you and others stepped in to help with my son's case," Dellia wrote on Sept. 3, 1961. "If you don't remember me, I'm Walter L. Irvin's mother. I haven't forgotten you and Jack Greenberg. I often read about the good work you are doing up that part of the States. I must say, keep up the good work. You're a fighting man, fighting for Our rights. Mr. Marshall, I would like to know if you can tell me, 'Can my boy get a parole now? I mean, eligible for one?' He's been there since 1949 and sentenced to life for about 6 years. If so, how would I go about doing it? I haven't seen Mr. Perkins in 3 years. My son, he's still sick in there, and would like very much to get out. Would I have to get a lawyer? The Superintendent there at Raiford won't send him to a road camp like others, and he does very hard work. I would appreciate it very much if you would give me some advice on this Parole Business if you can. Thanking you in advance, keep up the good work" The letter was signed, "A Loving Mother, Mrs. Dellia Irvin." Mrs. Irvin also petitioned Jack Greenberg, who forwarded a copy of the letter to Paul Perkins, along with a one-sentence letter: "I wonder whether this time we can do something about the parole for Walter Irvin?"

While Perkins reviewed Irvin's file, Rodriguez was drafting appeals for Chatman, Summers and Shuler, whose prospects to beat the death chair were looking slim as 1962 began. And then a gift dropped out of the sky. "I was working at my office one morning when my secretary, Margie Johnson, told me that there was a White man who wished to speak with me… The man, Noel Griffin, was one of Sheriff McCall's deputies who decided that he could no longer stand by idly and see injustice continue. He confessed that Chatman and Shuler had been falsely accused and convicted on trumped up evidence," recalled Florida NAACP Field Secretary Robert Saunders.

Griffin had come forward after being fired on what he says was a trumped-up charge. "Willis and the Volusia County Sheriff set us up on a hog stealing charge after I told him I had enough evidence on one of his deputies. Willis got rid of me," said Griffin, who had joined the force in 1956. According to Griffin, the plaster casts of footprints allegedly made at the scene of the crime. "… were made by the deputies in Yates' yard."

Rodriguez immediately tried to stay the executions of his clients based on the new evidence, but his petition was denied. Still, hope remained: the FBI was looking into Griffin's allegations and the *Tampa Tribune*, which had chosen not to take a stand during the Groveland affair, began following the story. As for Griffin, he wisely began looking over his shoulder. "In later years when I got fired, a deputy named Ledford followed us around. It got to where people were calling my house and telling my wife, 'If he goes hunting today, he's not going to come back alive.' For three years I carried a gun strapped to the steering wheel," Griffin said.

Griffin's accusations were soon verified by FBI agents, who examined six plaster casts Yates made, as well as soil samples from the yard of the victim, and soil from the deputies' yards. Agents found that, "The soil from the casts is similar in physical characteristics and mineral composition to the soil from Clark's yard and is different from the soil from the victim's yard." The agents were also of the opinion that the shoes that made the footprints didn't have feet in them -- the same conclusion the defense expert Herman Bennett had made about Walter Irvin's alleged footprints 10 years prior at the trial in Ocala. "…the impressions represented by the cases K2 through K5, were very clear and flat as if shoes had been carefully placed in the soil. Usually the toe area is depressed or pushed back as the person shifts weight in a walking or running stride. This condition was not present in K2 through K5…" When the *Tribune* published the FBI's findings, Judge W. Troy Hall had no choice but to re-open the case. A 40-day stay of execution was granted Chatman and Shuler.

Ten years after Irvin was convicted on testimony that Walter's shoes matched footprints at the scene of Norma Padgett's alleged abduction, Yates was indicted for perjury for lying about the casts he made in the Wass investigation. Armed with proof that the state had manufactured evidence, Rodriguez submitted another appeal to the pardon board. Oldham and McCall promptly objected.

On Sept.11, 1963, McCall fired off a curt letter to agents Ted Tucker and Robert Anderson, who had requested a statement regarding possible civil rights violations in Florida v. Chatman and Shuler. McCall declined, following his post-Groveland script and pointing out that the accusations had been, "thoroughly reviewed… and in none of these investigations have they been able to find sufficient evidence to substantiate any of their accusations." McCall concluded his letter by writing, "You may rest assured that in my nineteen years as Sheriff I have never, nor will I ever, knowingly violate any one's (sic) civil rights." Like previous investigations into McCall's conduct, this one too would quietly fizzle and soon be forgotten. The sheriff had dodged another bullet.

The NAACP's efforts to win a new trial for Shuler and Chatman died on Feb. 19, 1964, when the Florida Supreme Court upheld the verdicts of the lower court. Retired Circuit Judge L.L. Parks concluded that a new trial was not justified because there was no evidence that the prosecution suppressed evidence or falsified evidence of footprints. The judge also found no evidence that rain had destroyed footprint evidence at the scene of the crime. Parks should have talked to FBI.

Walter Irvin had been imprisoned just shy of 15 years when he appealed to the District Court of Appeals in February. Inmate 49309 composed a two-page Motion to Vacate Sentence and sent it to the Marion County Circuit Court. After restating his innocence and claiming his constitutional rights had been violated at the retrial, he wrote: "Note: The petitioner declares that during his trial, his attorneys ask the court to present the doctor with the medical reports concerning the victim whom he was accused of (raping) and for three successive (sic) days no such evidence was ever produce (sic)… Also in 1957 the Supreme Court handed down the Mallory decision the court ruled he had been held too long (seven and a half hours) before arrangement. I Walter L. Irvin was held more than thirty days before going before a hearing."

On Feb. 26, 1964, Marion County Circuit Court Judge D.R. Smith denied Irvin's motion. In announcing his decision, Smith stated, "Defendant was represented by adequate counsel at the trial and at no time were his rights prejudiced through lack of counsel." Upon the advice of Perkins, Irvin decided to expand his motion and appeal to the State Court of Appeals. Irvin painstakingly hand printed a four-page appeal to Florida Attorney General Mr. Kyes on March 19, 1964. "The court erred in denying the defendant motion to vacate on the grounds the defendant was not properly represented by counsel at all stages of proceedings," Irvin wrote. He also told -- for the umpteenth time -- the horrific treatment he endured at the hands of lawmen intent on getting a confession: "…taken the woods and beaten… handcuffed to the steam pipe overhead and beaten again with rubber hose and blackjacks… taken way out in the woods and was handcuffed around a tree and were about to throw gasoline (sic) on us… taken to Sheriff McCall's house out in an orange grove and beaten again by McCall while still handcuff (sic)."

By the mid-1960s, McCall faced new challenges as the civil rights moment gained momentum throughout the South. But the ghosts of the past wouldn't die. From time to time, Groveland or the Fruitland Park rape case would rear their ugly heads. Case in point:

on May 22, 1966, McCall received a startling letter from Charlotte Wass, postmarked Austin, Minnesota. After thanking the sheriff for his kindness in transporting her to the hospital, "after 3 neighbor Negro lads attacked me," and mentioning that she regularly received letters from the Claretts and Shuler's Miami attorney, Wass delivered a lightning bolt. "Robert Shuler did not rape me and I wonder why he has been in condemned row of men. What penitentiary is he at and do you know what happened to the other two fellows?" Wass concluded by mentioning that Mrs. Clarett writes about how she needs Robert at home. McCall filed the letter. He had no intention of sharing it with Oldham, or anyone else.

Chapter 35 -- A Short Liberty

Walter Irvin was finally freed by Gov. Claude Kirk on Jan. 16, 1968, 18-and-a-half years after being convicted for a crime he swore he didn't commit. As a stipulation, Irvin was ordered to move as far south as possible. To the family that had nearly given up hope, Walter's release came as a shock. "No one knew Walter was going home. It was like we got a call today that Walter was being released tomorrow. His brothers Joe and Eddie and Louise and her husband E.T. went up to get him. They didn't even stop in Groveland, they drove straight to Miami to my house. He came to live with me," Walter's sister, Henrietta said.

Walter, now 40, moved in with Henrietta and soon landed a construction job. His sister hadn't realized the toll prison had taken on her brother. "The knots in the head and his teeth were practically all gone. I bought him teeth when he came to Miami and I bought him glasses. They really did a number on him," Henrietta recalled. Walter's mental state was nearly as bad as his physical condition. "He was angry. He was very angry," said Henrietta. Still, Walter led a law-abiding life, faithfully reporting to his parole officer on 14th Ave. With Henrietta's help, he gradually adjusted to a world that had changed dramatically while he rotted in prison. "Everything was so different. I had to show him how to put money in to ride the bus."

Former Gov. Leroy Collins, curious to see what course Walter would follow, continued to discreetly keep tabs on Irvin. Collins was pleased with the reports he received. "He had an excellent record, a fine person... I followed him the rest of his life. But he just made a marvelous record down there, working for this man, just very much pleased with him and believed in him and came to trust him tremendously."

Unfortunately, Irvin's hard-fought freedom vanished nearly as quickly as it had in 1949. In February 1969, Walter returned to Lake County to attend the funeral of his uncle, John Brown. Irvin spent the evening of Feb. 15 much as he spent the evening that led to his arrest 21 years earlier -- making the rounds of various nightspots, or "juking" as the younger men who accompanied him called it. Irvin's date was Emma Hobbs, but her brothers were along for the ride. The group stayed out all night, and Irvin slept in the car when the revelers stopped for breakfast. Later, Walter was carried to bed. When his friends tried to awaken him at 2 p.m. they realized he was dead. Dr. William Schutze said there was no indication of prior attacks and ruled out foul play. The autopsy showed little or no blood alcohol.

"We was going home after he got out of prison. We were going to Groveland when about 40 miles from Groveland all the lights in the car went out. I got out and looked at the lights but I couldn't find anything wrong. Then they came back on. When we got to Groveland we found out that he was dead. As near as I can figure, he died about the same time as the lights went out on the car." -- James Shepherd Jr., August 2002

Walter Lee Irvin was buried a week later without fanfare. He died without realizing how far the sacrifices he, Sammie Shepherd, Charles Greenlee (who many wrongly thought had long since died) and even Ernest Thomas had made -- would reach. Jack Greenberg, the Legal Defense Fund attorney who had participated in the second trial and subsequent appeals, called Groveland the "single most influential experience persuading me to launch the LDF capital punishment program in the late 1960s...."

The LDF eventually convinced the Supreme Court to rule that rape was not a death penalty offense. In Lake County, Sheriff Willis McCall read the news in disgust. The damn liberals had delivered another blow to law and order. McCall wondered where it would end. Not in his office, which still bore the look and feel of a time when the law didn't answer to anybody. Above the desk in his office hung a sign reading, "Never explain; your friends don't require it and your enemies don't believe you anyway." Other signs – reading "White Waiting Room" and "Colored Waiting Room" – came down in 1971, when the Nixon administration sued to integrate the Lake County Jail.

McCall continued to win re-election into the 1970s. He had weathered every conceivable storm and was still standing, some said taller than ever. He even survived Jesse Daniels, a mentally-deficient 18-year-old implicated for rape in 1957. Daniels, who was white, was hastily sent to the state mental hospital after "confessing," even though the victim had said her attacker was a Negro. Fortunately for Jesse, his distraught mother never stopped fighting to prove her son's innocence. She had no doubt where her son was on the night in question; as always he slept, teddy bear in arm, in his parents' room that night.

Jesse's mother succeeded in gaining his release in 1971. Shortly thereafter, she appeared with her son at a hearing in Orlando where a legislative committee was studying the case. In attendance was Margaret Hickman, the woman who had certified Jesse Daniels' confession 14 years prior. When introduced to Jesse, a shocked Hickman exclaimed, "Is *this* the real Jesse Daniels? But it was a Negro whose confession I took, and I watched him sign it!" It was later learned that McCall had jailed at least 23 Negroes and questioned as many as 30 following the rape in 1957. Those who followed the case through the years could only conclude that McCall had railroaded Daniels because it was "nicer" for a society matron to have been raped by a white man than a black.

Yes, McCall was still a feared man, even though his hair was turning to gray and his midriff to fat. He had used intimidation, violence and fear to maintain order in Lake County for 28 years, but his tactics finally caught up with him in 1972, when Gov. Reuben Askew suspended him on June 12 after a black male, Tommy Vickers died in his custody, apparently from being kicked repeatedly by the sheriff. McCall was furious by what he considered heavy-handed tactics by his least favorite governor since Leroy Collins. McCall's take on the born-again Askew: "He doesn't drink, he doesn't smoke, he doesn't cuss. What does he put on to make him smell like a man?"

Askew may not have fit McCall's definition of a man, but the governor was no shrinking violet. Askew called for a thorough investigation after the Lake County coroner ruled that acute peritonitis resulting from a blow to the abdomen was the cause of death. But no Lake County judge wanted anything to do with an indictment against the sheriff. After four Lake circuit judges declined to take the bench, Askew ordered the case to be tried in front of Florida Supreme Court Justice James Adkins.

After considering an affidavit supporting change of venue from former McCall deputy Noel Griffin, Adkins ordered the trial be moved to Orange County. In the affidavit, Griffin said, "Willis V. McCall has a reputation in Lake County for violence and retribution against those who oppose him in any manner. He exercises undue influence over the minds of the inhabitants of Lake County by virtue of that reputation. The citizens of Lake County are divided into two camps, the pro-McCalls and the anti-McCalls. I know of no one in the county who is unbiased in the matter. The pro-McCalls will vote not guilty regardless of evidence. The anti-McCalls will vote guilty no matter how slim the evidence might be, or more likely, will be so fearful of retaliation that they will exercise no independent will or judgment as jurors."

It took an entire day to choose a six-person jury. Eighty-two potential jurors were called, including five black men, before the jury box was finally filled. McCall seemed unfazed, occasionally nodding off to sleep as prosecution and defense attorneys haggled and eventually selected the four men and two women to decide the sheriff's fate.

The defense was confident McCall would be vindicated. And with good reason. Vickers, a truck driver from Miami who had suffered brain damage in a motorcycle accident, had a long and dubious history of violence. But he hadn't ended up in a Lake County jail for a violent crime; he was there because he failed to pay a $26 Florida Highway Patrol ticket for not having a current vehicle inspection sticker. Jailed on April 12, Vickers was allegedly kicked several times by McCall during a struggle on the morning of April 13. A week later, Vickers was taken to Waterman Memorial Hospital. Three days later, he was dead. A hospital official said the prisoner died from an infection of the abdomen likely caused by being struck in the stomach by a hard object.

Orange County State Attorney Robert Eagan accepted the role of prosecutor with zeal, subpoenaing 100 potential witnesses (only 20 would be called). Still, the sheriff was unconcerned. He had been in tight spots before and always came out smelling like a rose. While Eagan tried to put him behind bars, the 62-year-old McCall napped, did crossword puzzles and idly thumbed through the volumes of Florida criminal law. McCall was so indifferent that he slept during his attorney's argument for a directed verdict of acquittal because the state had "completely failed" to prove its case.

During the trial, defense co-counsel John Robertson portrayed Vickers as a violent, paranoid schizophrenic, telling jurors that Vickers had been released from a Miami jail just six days before being stopped in Lake County, and that while incarcerated he became violent on three occasions. The most serious incident resulted in an officer being sent to the hospital.

The defense was counting on white inmate trustees Jackie and Bobby Huffman and black prisoner Willis June to echo McCall's version of the scuffle. At the coroner's inquest, the men had testified that McCall only "popped" Vickers a couple of times while they held him down, but they sang a different tune at the trial. This time they said that they held Vickers on the floor while McCall kicked the prisoners repeatedly while shouting, 'This damn nigger ain't crazy! This damn nigger ain't crazy!" Their about-face was explained when Egan got the men to admit they had been threatened and told what to say at the coroner's inquest. "I'm a black man in Lake County. You want to know what I'm afraid of? I'm afraid of getting killed," stated June after being assured no harm would come to him if he told the truth. Shaken by the unexpected development, Robertson tried a new tack, telling jurors that Vickers' injuries occurred on April 12 (the night before McCall entered the cell) when two other prisoners, the Huffman brothers, beat Vickers twice.

McCall predictably downplayed his encounter with Vickers. "One morning he was causing such a commotion that it was demoralizing the entire prison population, as well as the whole sheriff department staff. I went up to the cell where Vickers was confined. I found that he had thrown his breakfast on the floor. I asked him to hand me his plate. He told me if I wanted it to come in and get it. I instructed the jailer to open the door and ordered the two trusties to clean up the mess. As they entered the cell, Vickers attacked one of them and they hit the floor with Vickers on the bottom. The second trusty went to help. In the meantime, Vickers was choking one of the trusties. I kicked his arm between the wrist and elbow and as I knocked the strange hold (sic) loose, my foot went down on his arm. I am sure it bruised his arm; I did not kick him in the abdomen as was later claimed." As usual, McCall painted himself with the brush of the persecuted, not the persecutor. "I just can't make myself in any way, shape, fashion or form believe that I did anything wrong. I did just what any normal person would have done."

Naturally, everyone wanted to see how the prosecution would cross-examine McCall. The point became moot when Eagan convinced Judge Adkins to allow the secret grand jury testimony of McCall to be read in full over. Adkins agreed over strenuous objections from the sheriff's attorneys. McCall's account of the incident: "I put my foot on his arm, and he flipped over like a tomcat and went on the floor on all fours, and I reached over and gave him some pops." Also, his trademark bravado: "I was going to take care of the situation one way or the other." Introducing testimony from the grand jury hearing was a shrewd move by Egan. This time, McCall's big mouth had put him in a tough spot, one he couldn't wiggle out of.

Testimony lasted two days, and indeed McCall had nothing to worry about: an all-white jury needed just 70 minutes to acquit him of second-degree murder and the lesser offenses of third-degree murder and manslaughter, even aggravated battery and aggravated assault.

Exonerated and convinced he still had a strong base of support; the lawman sought reelection for the seventh time. On Sept. 12 McCall won the primary, but two months later it was a different story. In the general election, McCall's 28-year reign came to an end when he suffered his first defeat. Guy Bliss was elected sheriff by a vote of 13,877-11,895. Finally, the good ole' boys who had long applauded McCall's aggressive tactics abandoned him.

Times had changed, and McCall's antics had brought too much unwanted attention upon Lake County. He had survived Groveland, Harry T. Moore, Communists, the NAACP, liberals, outside agitators and the press, but he couldn't survive Tommy Vickers. The majority of voters saw him as a dinosaur, a throwback to another era, a once-invincible "character" whose power base had gradually eroded along with his credibility. To the end, McCall remained convinced his undoing was caused by, "left-wing agitators" who inaccurately portrayed him as a racist, instead of a patriot. "I would hate to be remembered like some of them would like me to be remembered as an old sonofabitch," he told a reporter. In another interview, "Ole Willis" said, "I've been accused of everything but taking a bath and called everything but a child of God."

In McCall's eyes, "misunderstood" may have been the word he'd use to sum up his career. He would have preferred "lawandorder," a McCallism created by running three words together. "There have been many slanted stories published during my career as Sheriff, filled with innuendos, half truths and outright lies, by the liberal press," McCall said in 1988. "Because I did not agree with the manner they chose to take during the transition period during this difficult time, they branded me as a racist, criminal, or you name it. Being Chief Law Enforcement Officer in the capacity as Sheriff of Lake County, Florida, it fell my lot to enforce the laws as they were at the time," he continued. "I did so without fear or favor to anyone. I always believed if a law is bad or you happen not to like it, get it changed through the courts or legislative bodies, not with violence. We went through this treacherous and controversial time with minimal property damage and no bloodshed, as was occurring in other places. I met violent protestors head on and stopped them before they got started. By doing so I was branded a bigotist and all the other things aforementioned."

The Case That Wouldn't Die

In February 1990, *Daily Commercial* reporter Valerie Fields visited Groveland in search of old-timers willing to talk about Lake County's most famous case. The community had changed a great deal in the 40-plus years since the Groveland rape case. Citrus was no longer king: two freezes in the 1980s had taken care of that. Homer Williams, longtime resident who picked fruit during Groveland's heyday as a bustling citrus town, says the freezes that all but wiped out the citrus industry were the work of God. "God got tired of them messing over poor colored people. I know what it was." Few cooperated when Fields brought up the trouble of the summer of '49, and the few who did talk refused to give their names. Survivors of the racial unrest had waited long years for the truth to come out and knew now it was too late.

Willis McCall, now 83 and living on his sprawling Umatilla ranch, was still untouchable. McCall no longer wore the badge, but he would always be sheriff to the boys at Mason Jar Restaurant, where he went to swap stories when he tired of working around his ranch.

And then an era ended. McCall passed away on Thursday, April 28, 1994. For one final moment he was again the subject of headlines, homages and even criticism. The Umatilla church where the funeral service was held was standing room only. Once again, Groveland was the subject of headlines.

"I was Chief of Police in Orlando when Willis died. I was like 45 or 46 years old. Malcolm (McCall) called and said he wanted me to be a pall bearer. I hesitated. I was thinking how it would look to my black officers if I was pall bearer for this notorious sheriff who had a reputation as well as being a segregationist. Finally, Malcolm said, 'There's some damn things more important than your damn job. You're going to be a pall bearer. And I was, but I wore big sunglasses." -- Tom Hurlburt, July 2001

Even in death McCall was controversial. The *Daily Commercial* praised the legend for "his uncanny instincts and his absolute authoritarian stance," but also reminded readers that "the good old days were good only for the chosen elite." The editorial concluded, "McCall defended his actions to the last. And there are many who are still defending them. But it would be a mistake to let the death of this larger-than-life man to cast a rosy haze over the abuses that occurred during that period of America -- and Lake County -- history."

McCall had outlived all but one of the Groveland Boys. Charles Greenlee didn't celebrate when he heard the news. He had long since stopped hoping for McCall's death. Charles was at peace with himself. He had emerged victorious.

Appendix

Alex Akerman Jr. - After being discharged from the Navy in 1953, Akerman spent six months with the Civil Division of the Dept. of Justice, and then served as executive director of the Federal Trade Commission for five years. He then went into private practice in the Washington firm of Shipley, Akerman and Pickett, where he specialized in anti-trust law. Next, he was appointed a United States Magistrate in the eastern district of Virginia, a position he held until retiring in 1977 at age 69. Akerman died in April 1998. *"I think he did realize he made a personal sacrifice (when he agreed to represent the Groveland defendants), but he never regretted it,"* said Akerman's daughter Lucy Taft, Aug. 10, 2001

Fannie (Shepherd) Bell - Samuel Shepherd's sister passed away on August 14, 2002. She outlived her parents and all nine of her brothers and sisters. *"I hate going into Lake County because I just know there is going to be some ignoramus that will ask me about my family and that nasty business that went on... God made it all right for us. You have to have a little faith."* -- Fannie (Shepherd) Bell, March 2, 2001

Dr. G.H. Binneveld – The physician who examined Norma Padgett after the alleged rape died in 1990. His son says his father's medical files were destroyed in a natural gas explosion.

Norman Bunin – The former *St. Petersburg Times* copy editor/reporter is enjoying retirement in New England. He is an accomplished actor.

Lawrence Burtoft – Burtoft "pastored throughout Florida" before establishing a youth camp near Okahumpka.

Jefferson J. Elliott – Gov. Fuller Warren's special investigator died at the wheel of his car in Clearwater in 1957. *"He was a law enforcement officer for what he could do to help others, and a lot of times the northern news papers tried to make something out of what was happening in the South... But I can tell you about a time that he went and sat in the front of a black church thru a black funeral because they had "heard" that a bomb was planted inside."* – Elliott's daughter Violette, May 13, 2003

Jack Greenberg -- He remained with Thurgood Marshall for 12 years, then succeeded his mentor and continued waging civil rights battles in the courts for the next 23 years. By the time he retired in 1984, Greenberg had taken 40 cases before the United States Supreme Court, argued hundreds in lower courts, and put his signature on nearly all of the important civil rights legislation that came out of the 1950s and 60s. Today, Greenberg is a professor at Columbia Law School.

Charles Greenlee – Greenlee, who enjoys working and traveling, seldom visits Florida. He hasn't been in Lake County since 1949. *"I think I'm very fortunate. I tell my kids, I must be the luckiest man in the world."*

Tom Greenlee – Charles' father died in 1979 at age 94. He spent the final 28 years of his life bed-ridden after being paralyzed in an automobile accident.

Noel Griffin – McCall's former deputy served a term as Lake County sheriff in the 1970s before being defeated by George Knupp. Griffin lives on a sprawling farm near Eustis, Fla.

Horace Hill – Now in his 80s, Hill still takes an occasional case. His Daytona office is the same place it was when he assisted the NAACP in the Groveland case in 1949. Hill was involved in lawsuits to integrate Peabody Auditorium and world-famous Daytona Beach, site of a peaceful "swim-in" he participated in. In 1988, Hill was honored by the State of Florida for practicing law for 50 years. *"Groveland could happen again. It depends upon what we have learned and what we have seen that has transpired since this. We have made very limited strides in providing a fair and impartial trial for all segments of society."* – Horace Hill, Oct. 17, 2000

Tom Hurlburt, special deputy for Sheriff Willis V. McCall died Dec. 15, 1999. *"I think Dad would have told me in later years if he (Sheriff Willis V. McCall) had tried to kill them (Shepherd and Irvin). I can't believe that Willis would work that hard to keep them alive just to kill them later. He could be a tough SOB, but he wasn't nearly as tough as his reputation."* -- Tom Hurlburt, former Orlando police chief (1992-1995) and son of McCall special deputy Tom Hurlburt.

Henrietta Irvin – Walter's sister still lives in Miami, where she refuses to get old.

Stetson Kennedy – The former Klanbuster is now in his 80s. Most of his books are again available.

Thurgood Marshall – Became the first African-American United States Supreme Court justice in 1967. He died in January, 1993. He was 84.

Malcolm McCall -- Willis V. McCall's oldest son succeeded his father as sheriff in the 1970s and served one term. *"I really disagree with reopening old sores... Some people called him a segregationist, but that was the law at the time, but when the law changed, he changed... He did the best job he knew how to do at the time, he did about all that he could do... The criticism against him came from people that didn't know him. People who knew him knew he did the best he knew how."*

Willis V. McCall -- He would win seven elections and defeat 18 opponents during his illustrious career. He was also investigated for civil rights violations 38 times, but was never convicted of a crime. He died in 1994 at age 84.

Paul Perkins -- After building a reputation as an outstanding criminal defense attorney, in 1965 Perkins was appointed Orlando's first black city prosecutor. He resigned in 1969 to build his private practice, and later became a judge. In addition to playing a role in desegregating Orlando during the 1950s and '60s, Perkins was co-founder of the first savings and loan owned by blacks in the state, Washington Shores Federal Savings and Loan Association in Orlando. In 1973, Perkins helped bring charter government to Orange County. He died in July 1985, being survived by wife Jackie and sons Paul Jr. and Byron -- both attorneys.

Ted Poston -- African-American newspaper reporter who was nominated for a Pulitzer Prize for his series, "Horror in the Sunshine," which covered the Groveland trial. His coverage of the Groveland case was ranked as one of the top 100 works of Journalism in the United States in the 20th century by the New York University Journalism Faculty. Poston died in 1974.

Henry Shepherd – Sammie's father never returned to Bay Lake after his home was burned to the ground in the summer of 1949. He stayed in Orlando, dying of pneumonia at age 54. *"He worried a lot about that business over there. I think my dad worried himself to death."* – Fannie (Shepherd) Bell, March 3, 2001

James Shepherd – James moved from Groveland to nearby Clermont shortly after the trouble. His marriage to Walter Lee Irvin's sister Henrietta lasted nine years. James remarried in 1960. Sammie's older brother died in 1998. His first and second wife survive.

Franklin Williams – After serving as NAACP West Coast director, Williams was: assistant attorney general, state of California; African regional director, U.S. Peace Corps; U.S. representative to the United Nations; and U.S. ambassador to Ghana. *"It was, it was something out of Hollywood. It is hard to believe, it is hard now for me here at the University of Florida this afternoon if I talked to a group of black and white Floridians to have them accept that as recently as those years one man like Willis McCall could so dominate the lives of people in a county. Black and white alike as to an effect a tyrant who could take life, literally without fear of anybody touching him... I would not doubt, for example, if he knew I were here today speaking. I would not doubt that he would come and try to kill me. I do not want to cross him, all I have said about him will continue."* -- Franklin H. Williams, February 11, 1985

Bibliography

Daily Commercial, Jan. 6, 1949 -- Two New Lake Officials...
Mount Dora Topic, May 19, 1949 – 'Let's Overhaul Our Jury...
Mount Dora Topic, July 7, 1949 – Lake County Personalities...
The Miami Herald, July 17, 1949 – Young Husband Beaten...
Orlando Morning Sentinel, July 19, 1949 – Mob Violence Flares...
Orlando Evening Star, July 19, 1949 – Tense Quiet At Groveland
Orlando Sentinel, July 21, 1949 – Lake Jury Indicts Trio For Assault
South Lake Press, July 21, 1949 – Troops Patrol S. Lake County...
The Miami Herald, July 21, 1949 – No Groveland People In Mobs...
Mount Dora Topic, July 21, 1949 – Grand Jury Indicts Three...
Chicago Defender, July 23, 1949 – Florida Sheriff Stops Lynch Mob
Orlando Sentinel, July 23, 1949 – Liquor Ban Set In Lake County
Mount Dora Topic, July 28, 1949 – Parade Will Fete Cover Girl...
The Clermont and South Lake Press, July 28, 1949 – Negro...
Pittsburgh Courier, July 30, 1949 – Florida Refugees Fear Return...
Chicago Defender, July 30, 1949 – Jealousy Is Source Of Fla...
Pittsburgh Courier, Aug. 6, 1949 – 3 Prisoners Tied to Pipes...
Baltimore Afro-American, Aug. 6, 1949 – Posse 'Lynches' Fla...
Chicago Defender, Aug. 6, 1949 – NAACP To Defend...
Pittsburgh Courier, Aug. 13, 1949 – NAACP Arms to Aid Florida...
Mount Dora Topic, Aug. 18, 1949 – Surprise Witness...
Pittsburgh Courier, Aug. 20, 1949 – Fla. Trio Face Trial...
Chicago Defender, Aug. 20, 1949 – Set August 29 For Trial...
The Clermont News-Topic, Aug. 25, 1949 – Women Beg...
Mount Dora Topic, Aug. 25, 1949 – Weapons, Mob Gathering...
Mount Dora Topic, Sept. 1, 1949 – Lake County Personalities...
Orlando Sentinel, Sept. 1, 1949 – Lake Negroes Face Court...
Orlando Morning Sentinel, Sept. 1, 1949 – Lake Attack Trial...
Orlando Sentinel, Sept. 2, 1949 – Lake Attack Trial Gets Off...
Chicago Defender, Sept. 3, 1949 – Tension And Fear Scare...
Pittsburgh Courier, Sept. 3, 1949 – Witness Jailed As Trial Nears
Mount Dora Topic, Sept. 8, 1949 – 'Finis' Will Be Said Today...
Pittsburgh Courier, Sept. 10, 1949 – We're Innocent
Chicago Defender, Sept. 10, 1949 – 3 Railroaded For Rape...
Chicago Defender, Sept. 17, 1949 – Lawyers Heroes In Florida...
Pittsburgh Courier, Sept. 17, 1949 – Prepare Appeal for 'Florida 3'
The Afro-American, Sept. 24, 1949 – Does FBI Actually Ask...
Pittsburgh Courier, Sept. 24, 1949 – 'Justice' in Florida
The Nation, Sept. 24, 1949 – Florida's Legal Lynching
Editor & Publisher, Sept. 24, 1949 – N.Y. Negro Reporter Has...
Sunday Sentinel-Star, Feb. 26, 1950 – Tavares Trial Reporting...
St. Petersburg Times, April 7, 1950 – Did Groveland Negroes Get...

St. Petersburg Times, April 8, 1950 – Did State Get Right Men...
St. Petersburg Times, April 9, 1950 – Time Table, Based On State...
Ocala Star-Banner, April 15, 1951 – Sheriff's Murderer Has...
The Crisis, May 1951 – Another Chance for the Groveland Victims
Tampa Morning Tribune, July 7, 1951 – Lake County Again Indicts...
The Crisis, Nov. 1951 -- Florida Shooting
Orlando Sentinel, Nov. 7, 1951 – Hunter Honored By Lake Friends
Orlando Sentinel, Nov. 7, 1951 -- Honoring J.W. Hunter...
Orlando Morning Sentinel, Nov. 8, 1951 – Negro Shootings...
Tampa Morning Tribune, Nov. 8, 1951 – State And Federal Agents...
Daily Commercial, Nov. 8, 1951 – Leesburg Citizens Join In...
Jacksonville Times Union, Nov. 8, 1951 – Justice Dept. Orders...
Orlando Evening Star, Nov. 8, 1951 – Negro's Attorneys Say...
New York Post, Nov. 8, 1951 – Blood Lust of Sheriff and Aide...
St. Petersburg Times, Nov. 8, 1951 – Florida's Justice Is At Stake
Orlando Sentinel Star, Nov. 9, 1951 – A Deplorable Tragedy
The Miami Herald, Nov. 9, 1951 – Survivor Of Shooting Says...
New York Post, Nov. 9, 1951 – Irvin Swears: 'He Shot Sammy...
The Miami Herald, Nov. 11, 1951 – Coroner's Jury Frees Sheriff...
Orlando Morning Sentinel, Nov. 11, 1951 – One Man's Lake County
New York Herald Tribune, Nov. 11, 1951 -- In Florida's Jungle,
Orlando Sentinel, Nov. 13, 1951 – Lake Officials Ask Findings...
New York Post, Nov. 13, 1951 – 6 Wounds Indicate Prisoners...
Orlando Sentinel, Nov. 14, 1951 – FBI Finds .38 Slug At Lake...
Orlando Morning Sentinel, Nov. 15, 1951 – One Man's Lake County
Daily Commercial, Nov. 15, 1951 – Prosecuting Attorney Make...
Newsweek, Nov. 19, 1951 – Little Scottsboro
The Afro-American, Dec. 1, 1951 – Evidence Freeing Shooting...
The Crisis, Dec. 1951 – The Lake County Shooting; Walter Irvin's...
Orlando Morning Sentinel, Dec. 5, 1951 – Irvin Claims Sheriff...
The Baltimore Afro-American, Dec. 8, 1951 – Two Explosions In...
Pittsburgh Courier, Dec. 15, 1951 – Florida Bars 2 NAACP Lawyers
The Baltimore Afro-American, Dec. 15, 1951 – Bar Lawyer...
Orlando Morning Sentinel, Jan. 5, 1952 – Governor Enters Closing...
The Afro-American, Jan. 5, 1952 – Cicero and Fla. Violence Big...
Milwaukee Journal, Jan. 6, 1952 – Violence in the Garden of Eden
The Afro-American, Jan. 12, 1952 – Thurgood Marshall Will Make...
The Afro-American, Jan. 19, 1952 – AFRO Editor Pick Top News...
Orlando Sentinel, Feb. 3, 1952 – Irvin Seeks New Re-Trial, Site...
Orlando Evening Star, Feb. 7, 1952 – Fair Trial Promised In Marion
Orlando Morning Sentinel, Feb. 15, 1952 – Negro Convicted For...
The Afro-American, Feb. 16, 1952 – Fla. Governor's Aide In...
Chicago Defender, Feb. 16, 1952 – Irvin Ask For Marshall...
Pittsburgh Courier, Feb. 16, 1952 -- Second Groveland Trial Starts...
The (Baltimore) Afro-American, Feb. 23, 1952 –Irvin Again...

Chicago Defender, Feb. 23, 1952 – Irvin Gets Chair 2nd Time
Pittsburgh Courier, Mar. 1, 1952 – New Trial Sought For Irvin
Afro-American, March 1, 1952 – Irvin Seeks 3d Trial In Florida
Orlando Morning Sentinel, June 24, 1953 – Supreme Court…
Orlando Sentinel Florida Magazine, Dec. 6, 1953 – Hunter…
Orlando Sentinel, Jan. 19, 1954 – Irvin Gets Delay For U.S. Appeal
Orlando Morning Sentinel, Feb. 19, 1954 – Judge Futch Ordered…
Orlando Sentinel, Nov. 26, 1954 – Mystery Phone Calls Are…
Orlando Sentinel, Dec. 16, 1954 – One Man's Lake County
St. Petersburg Times, Dec. 16, 1955 – Sparing Irvin's Life…
The Lake Wales News, Feb. 23, 1956 – Collins and the Irvin Case
Tampa Morning Tribune, Feb. 24, 1956 – The Obvious Answer
Lake Region News, March 1, 1956 – For Shame, Lake County
Orlando Sentinel, March 15, 1956 – Victim Opposed Chair
Leesburg Commercial, March 15, 1956 – The Governor Declines
Orlando Sentinel, April 22, 1956 – Politicos Have Field Day…
Leesburg Commercial, April 22, 1956 – Futch Takes Stump…
Leesburg Commercial, Oct. 10, 1956 – Father In Tears…
Leesburg Commercial, Oct. 11, 1956 – Sheriff's Office Won't…
Leesburg Commercial, Oct. 12, 1956 – Arrest Took Place In…
Daily Commercial, Nov. 2, 1956 – Sheriff Bars Press From…
Times Union, June 28, 1958 – Bomb Slaying of NAACP Leader…
St. Petersburg Times, Feb. 7, 1969 – Groveland Rape Defendant Dies
Daily Commercial, Feb. 12, 1990 -- Many don't want to talk…
The Daily Commercial, April 29, 1994 – Legendary sheriff dies
St. Petersburg Times, Nov. 28, 1999 – A Southern sheriff's law…
The Winchester (Virginia) Star, Nov. 22, 2000
New York Times Book Review, June 10, 2001 – Letter to the editor…

Associated Negro Press Collection, Chicago, Illinois – Correspondence between Ramona Lowe and Claude Barnett, The Associated Negro Press (Dec. 4, 1938 – April 23, 1957); various press releases.

Florida State Archives --Transcript, State of Florida v. Walter Lee Irvin, 1952; Motion to Disqualify J.W. Hunter as State Attorney, Oct. 16, 1951; Coroners Inquest Transcript of Testimony, re: Inquest Into The Death of One Samuel Shepherd, Nov. 1951.

Lake County Records Dept. -- Transcript, jury selection, Aug. 1949; NAACP flier, The Story of Florida's Legal Lynching, Fall 1949; Letter Charlotte Wass to Sheriff Willis McCall, May 21, 1966;

Leroy Collins collection, Florida State Archives – Letter from Allen Platt to Collins, Jan. 3, 1955; Letter from A.P. "Sam" Buie to Collins, Jan. 12, 1955; Letter from Warren H. Pierce to Collins, Feb. 22, 1955; Letter from Norman A. Bunin to Collins, March 18, 1955; Telegram from C.A. Irvin to Collins, March 18, 1955; Letter from William W. Gay to

Collins, March 19, 1955; Letter from Herbert S. Phillips to Collins, March 23, 1955; Letter from William A. Hallowes to Collins, March 28, 1955; Letter from Caxton Doggett to Collins, March 28, 1955; Willis McCall and Collins (June 30, 1955, Oct. 10, 1955); Letter from McCall to Robert C. Adair, Oct. 11, 1955; Letter from Collins to John W. Davis, Dec. 19, 1955; Letter from L.A. Grayson to Collins, Dec. 30, 1955; Letter from Karl Dittmer to Collins, Feb. 7, 1956; Letter from Harry L. Brown to Collins, Feb. 16, 1956; Telegram from Mr. and Mrs. Paul J. Miller to Collins, Feb. 17, 1956; Letter from Floyd M. Irvin to Collins, Feb. 24, 1956; Letter from Collins to A.P. Buie, March 2, 1956; Letter from Walter Irvin to Collins, Aug. 8, 1956; Letter from J.E. Peacock to Collins, Nov. 5, 1956; Transcript, Tavares trial, Sept. 1949; Findings of Coroner's Inquest into death of Ernest Thomas, July 1949; Affidavit of Walter Irvin, Nov. 8, 1951; Statement by Gov. Leroy Collins, re: Calling of Grand Jury in Walter Lee Irvin Commutation Case, Feb. 16, 1956; Elmo Roper Agency study, Feb. 1952; Florida Supreme Court opinion, Walter Irvin v. State of Florida, June term 1953; Petition for Stay of Execution and Recall of Mandate, Walter Irvin v. State of Florida, July 31, 1953; Report, Review of the case of State v. Walter Irvin, from Bill Harris to Governor Collins

Harry T. Moore collection -- Letter from Moore to State Attorney J.W. Hunter, July 28, 1949; Letters from Moore to Gov. Fuller Warren (July 30, 1949, Nov. 11, 1951, Nov. 15, 1951, Dec. 2, 1951); Letter from Moore to Mabel Norris-Reese, Aug. 18, 1950; Memorandum from Franklin H. Williams to Gloster B. Current, re: Report of Florida Trip, Dec. 5, 1949; Letter from NAACP Director of Branches Gloster B. Current to Florida branch officers, Nov. 1, 1950; Letter from Lucille Black, NAACP Membership Secretary to Daniel E. Byrd, Nov. 21, 1950; Letter from NAACP Regional Coordinator Ruby Hurley to Gloster B. Current, Dec. 11, 1951.

Paul Perkins collection, courtesy Jackie Perkins -- Letter from The Committee of 100, Oct. 17, 1949; Letter from Horace E. Hill to Truman G. Futch, Nov. 26, 1949; Letter from J.W. Hunter to T.G. Futch, April 8, 1950; Letter from John Dingle to Thurgood Marshall, May 1951; Correspondence between Alex Akerman Jr. and Thurgood Marshall (Oct. 6, 1951, March 30, 1952); Correspondence between Robert L. Carter and Perkins (Oct. 22, 1951, Oct. 25, 1951, Nov. 10, 1951, Oct. 31, 1952); Letter from Perkins to Carol Alexander, Oct. 29, 1951; Letter from Samuel Shepherd to Charlie Mae Shepherd, Nov. 1, 1951; Letter from A.S. Alexander to Perkins, Nov. 1, 1951; Letter from Perkins to Will Wages, Nov. 27, 1951; Anonymous letter to Perkins re: Irvin shooting, Nov. 1951; Telegram from Thurgood Marshall to Gov. Fuller Warren, Nov. 30, 1951; Letter from W.E. Wages to Perkins, Dec. 5, 1951; Correspondence between Jack Greenberg and Alex Akerman Jr., Jan. 10, 1952, April 13, 1952; Correspondence between Perkins and Alex Akerman Jr. (June 14, 1951, July 3, 1951, Sept. 11, 1951, Jan. 16, 1952, March 26, 1952); Correspondence between Perkins and Herman V. Bennett (Nov. 3, 1951, Jan. 16, 1952, Jan. 17, 1952, Jan. 27, 1952); Correspondence between Perkins and Jack Greenberg (Jan. 18, 1952, Jan. 25, 1952, Jan. 28, 1952, Feb. 21, 1952, Dec. 14, 1953, Oct. 4, 1961); Letter from James H. Bunch to Thurgood Marshall; Letter from Walter Lee Irvin to Perkins, Sept. 28, 1953; Letter from Allan Knight Chalmers, The Committee of 100; Letter J.W. Hunter to State Board of Pardons, March 14, 1955; Letter from Lula L. Mullikin to Perkins, Oct. 28, 1960; Correspondence between

Perkins and Dr. Allan Knight Chalmers (Nov. 3, 1960, Nov. 9, 1960); Letter from Dellia Irvin to Thurgood Marshall, Sept. 3, 1961; Statement of Henry Shepherd, July 29, 1949; Statement of Charles Greenlee to Horace Hill, July 31, 1949; Statement of Samuel Shepherd to Horace Hill, July 31, 1949; Summary of Medical Report on Charles Greenlee, Walter Irving (sic) and Samuel Shepherd by Nelson W.V. Spaulding, M.D. & Jean C. Downing, D.D.S., Aug. 7, 1949; Statement of Charles Greenlee, Sept. 9, 1949; Transcript of Walter Irvin interview by J.J. Elliott, State Prison, Raiford, Nov. 17, 1949; Transcript, hearing to investigate claims by Ted Poston, Dec. 29, 1949; Application for Pardon, Walter Lee Irvin, Oct. 17, 1960; Transcript of Testimony on Motion of Defendants to Withdraw Pleas of Not Guilty and to Set Aside Arraignment, Jan. 20, 1950; Transcript of testimony and proceedings, hearings on motion for change of venue, disqualification of states attorney, and suppression of certain evidence, Dec. 6, 1951; Brief of Appellee, Walter Irvin v. State of Florida, filed in Supreme Court of the State of Florida, Jan. 8, 1953; Motion to Vacate Sentence, Walter Lee Irvin, Feb. 7, 1964; Affidavit, Franklin H. Williams, Nov. 7, 1951; Affidavit of Charles Peterson, undated; A Draft of Opinions and Conclusions On a Survey of General Opinion in Lake County, Hart, Moore, Thomas Team, Oct. 24-27, 1951.

Fuller Warren collection, University of South Florida -- Telegram from Harry T. Moore to Warren, Nov. 7, 1951; Telegram from NAACP Executive Secretary Walter White to Warren, Nov. 9, 1951; Letter from Alex Akerman Jr. to Warren, Nov. 10, 1951; Telegram from Thurgood Marshall and Alex Akerman Jr. to Warren, Nov. 11, 1951; Telegram from Thurgood Marshall to Warren, Nov. 13, 1951; Letter from J.J. Elliott to Warren, Nov. 21, 1951.

Author's collection -- Emails from Robert Saunders to author (April 3, 2001 & Aug. 17, 2001); Letter from Fannie (Shepherd) Bell to author Sept. 10, 2001; Letter to author from Emory S. Akerman Jr., Dec. 31, 2002; Email from Jack Greenberg to author, May 21, 2003; NAACP brochure Groveland U.S.A., summer 1949; Lake County Sheriff Dept. booking record, Jesse Daniels, Dec. 23, 1957; Notes of Jan. 5, 1950 interview of Norma Padgett by Norman Bunin (Courtesy Norman Bunin); Certificate of Death and autopsy report, Walter Lee Irvin, March 7, 1969 (Courtesy Henrietta Irvin).

Interviews

Alex Akerman Jr. (by David Colburn, University of Florida Oral History Project, May 3, 1984 transcript); Irene Akerman (Aug. 10, 2001 by author); Fannie (Shepherd) Bell (March 2, 2001 by author); Geoff Binneveld (by author); Norman Bunin (March 5, 2001 and Sept. 10, 2001 by author); Lawrence Burtoft (Jan. 27, 2000 and July 8, 2000 by author); Jack Greenberg (May 5, 2000 by author); Charles Greenlee (Dec. 20, 2000 and Jan. 5, 2001 by author); Noel E. Griffin (Aug. 20, 2001, Sept. 10, 2001, Sept. 23, 2001 by author); Johnny Griffin (by Robert Thompson); Horace Hill (Aug. 6, 1992 transcript and by author, Oct. 17, 2000); Tom Hurlburt (July 11, 2001 by author); Henrietta Irvin (March 24, 2001, Aug. 19, 2001, Aug. 25, 2001 and March 7, 2003 by author); Ethel Retha (Greenlee) Jackson (Jan. 9, 2003 by author); Malcolm McCall (Nov. 28, 2000 by author); Jackie Perkins (June 15, 2000 & July 13, 2000 by author); Paul Perkins Jr. (June 15, 2000 by author); Joseph E. Price Jr. (May 20, 1993 transcript); Lucy Taft (Aug. 10, 2001 by author); Franklin Williams (by David Colburn and Steve Lawson, University of Florida Oral History Project, Feb. 11, 1985)

Other sources

Robert and Helen Saunders Collection, University of South Florida; Herbert S. Phillips Papers, University of South Florida; *Crusaders in the Courts* by Jack Greenberg; NAACP Milwaukee Branch manuscript collection; FBI file 44-2772 Groveland; FBI Harry T. Moore file; FBI file, Thurgood Marshall; Manuscript Division, Library of Congress; FBI Report, re: Jerry Chatman and Robert Shuler, suspects; Charlotte Wass, victim rape, Nov. 7, 1962; Southern Reporter, 2d Series, pgs. 880-885, Shepherd et al. v STATE;

About The Author

Gary Corsair won 15 awards during a distinguished newspaper career that featured stints as a reporter, editor and publisher. Newspapers he headed won 24 state and regional awards for excellence. He began his writing career in 1976 as a sportswriter for *The Kokomo Tribune*. In 1992, Corsair launched a newspaper devoted to covering local sports. He then moved to Florida, where he served as editor of *The Zephyrhills News, Tri-County Sun* and *The Villages Daily Sun*. In The Villages, Corsair also won awards for TV reporting, and served as an anchor and news director. Corsair, wife Gwen and children Stuart, Cassie, Caleb and Garrett live in Florida, not far from Groveland. For more information visit: www.grovelandfour.com

Printed in the United States
19449LVS00001B/278

9 781414 072432